Staying Off the Beaten Track was foun
ago by Elizabeth Gundrey. As it grew
coverage – the first edition contained
hundred entries, this one about 600
brother, Walter Gundrey, became
involved and is now taking the m
running the book. Elizabeth remains actively
involved as a consultant.

Staying Off the Beaten Track is regularly the best-
seller among Britain's b & b guides. It is a book for
all seasons.

VOUCHERS WORTH £18

(by courtesy of the houses concerned)

This voucher is worth £6 at any establishment marked with a **V** sign in the lists on pages **xi–xix** and **xxi–xxii**, provided it is presented **ON ARRIVAL** and not later. It is valid throughout **1997**, and may be used if a room is booked for **3** or more consecutive nights. Only one voucher usable per room.

This voucher is worth £6 at any establishment marked with a **V** sign in the lists on pages **xi–xix** and **xxi–xxii**, provided it is presented **ON ARRIVAL** and not later. It is valid throughout **1997**, and may be used if a room is booked for **3** or more consecutive nights. Only one voucher usable per room.

This voucher is worth £6 at any establishment marked with a **V** sign in the lists on pages **xi–xix** and **xxi–xxii**, provided it is presented **ON ARRIVAL** and not later. It is valid throughout **1997**, and may be used if a room is booked for **3** or more consecutive nights. Only one voucher usable per room.

OFFER OF NEXT EDITION

Using an out-of-date edition can lead to costly disappointments. A new edition appears every November, updated, with fresh entries added, some deleted and all revised, and with vouchers worth £18 valid for the next year. Make sure you are not using an out-of-date edition by sending a stamped self-addressed envelope to Explore Britain, Alston, Cumbria, CA9 3SL, for an order form on which you can apply for the 1998 edition even before it reaches the shops. No need for a letter: just put SOTBT 1998 on top left corner of the envelope you send.

AND SCOTLAND TOO

There is also an edition of *Staying Off the Beaten Track* for Scotland, from the Borders to the Highlands. Full particulars will be on the order form, which will also give details of money-saving offers to mail-order purchasers.

ENGLAND & WALES 1997

STAYING OFF THE BEATEN TRACK

ELIZABETH GUNDREY
and WALTER GUNDREY

*A personal selection of moderately priced
guest-houses, small hotels, farms and country houses*

16th EDITION
1997

Edited by Jacqueline Krendel

ARROW

TO ANDREW, WITH LOVE

Published by Arrow Books Limited in 1996

1 3 5 7 9 10 8 6 4 2

First published in Great Britain 1982   Eleventh edition 1991
by Hamlyn Paperbacks   Twelfth edition 1992
Arrow edition (Sixth edition) first published 1986   Thirteenth edition 1993
Seventh edition 1987   Fourteenth edition 1994
Eighth edition 1988   Fifteenth edition 1995
Ninth edition 1989   Sixteenth edition 1996
Tenth edition 1990

Arrow Books Limited
20 Vauxhall Bridge Road, London, SW1V 2SA

Random House Australia (Pty) Limited
20 Alfred Street, Milsons Point, Sydney,
New South Wales 2061, Australia

Random House New Zealand Limited
18 Poland Road, Glenfield
Auckland 10, New Zealand

Random House South Africa (Pty) Limited
PO Box 337, Bergvlei, South Africa

Random House UK Limited Reg. No. 954009

Designed by Bob Vickers
Maps by Rodney Paull

Printed and bound in Great Britain by
The Guernsey Press Co. Limited, Guernsey, C.I.

Front cover picture: **Melbury Mill**, Dorset
Back cover pictures (from left to right): **Vauld Farmhouse**, Herefordshire;
Ennys Farm, Cornwall; **Crasken**, Cornwall; **Walnut Tree Farmhouse**, Kent;
Cherry Court, Berkshire; **Dairy Farm**, Northamptonshire

A CIP catalogue record for this book is available from the British Library

ISBN 0-09-936031-4

The author and publishers would like to thank all those owners who allowed us to use their drawings. Additional line drawings by Rhona Garvin and others.

Although every care has been taken to ensure that all the information in this book is correct and up to date, neither the author nor the publishers can accept responsibility for details which may have changed since the book went to press.

Acknowledgments

We acknowledge with much appreciation the assistance of the rest of the SOTBT team (Jan Bowmer, Jennifer Christie, Andrew Cockburn, Pat Gundrey, Jonathan May, Kate McCarney and Nancy Webber) as well as of all the proprietors of houses.

Elizabeth and Walter Gundrey

CONTENTS

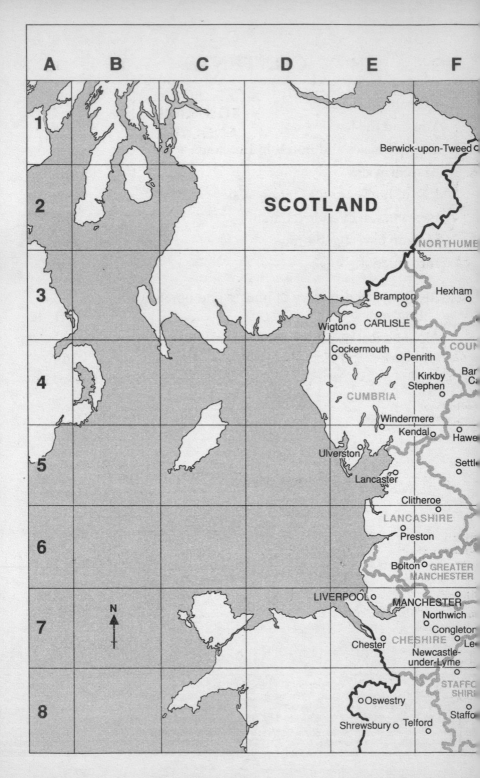

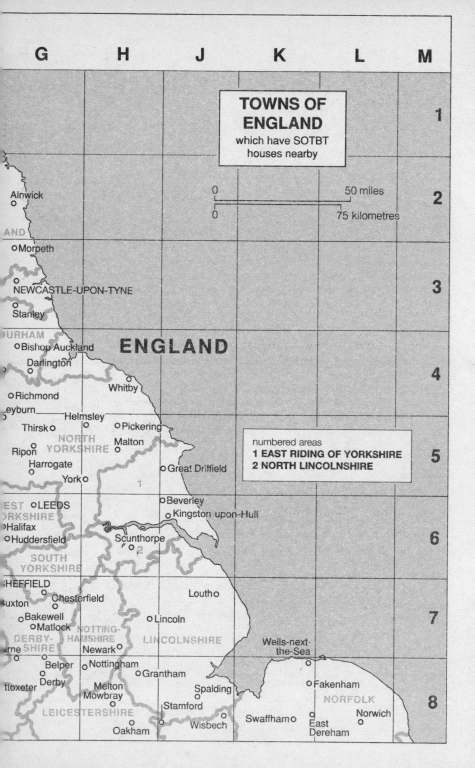

TOWNS OF ENGLAND
which have SOTBT houses nearby

0   50 miles

0   75 kilometres

ENGLAND

numbered areas
1 EAST RIDING OF YORKSHIRE
2 NORTH LINCOLNSHIRE

Alnwick

AND

Morpeth

NEWCASTLE-UPON-TYNE

Stanley

URHAM

Bishop Auckland

Darlington

Whitby

Richmond

eyburn

Helmsley

Thirsk

Pickering

NORTH YORKSHIRE

Malton

Ripon

Harrogate

Great Driffield

York

EST

LEEDS

ORKSHIRE

Beverley

Halifax

Kingston upon-Hull

Huddersfield

Scunthorpe

SOUTH YORKSHIRE

HEFFIELD

Louth

Chesterfield

uxton

Bakewell

Lincoln

Matlock

NOTTING-HAMSHIRE

LINCOLNSHIRE

DERBY-SHIRE

rne

Newark

Wells-next-the-Sea

Belper

Nottingham

Derby

Grantham

lloxeter

Fakenham

Melton Mowbray

Spalding

NORFOLK

Stamford

LEICESTERSHIRE

Swaffham

Norwich

Oakham

Wisbech

East Dereham

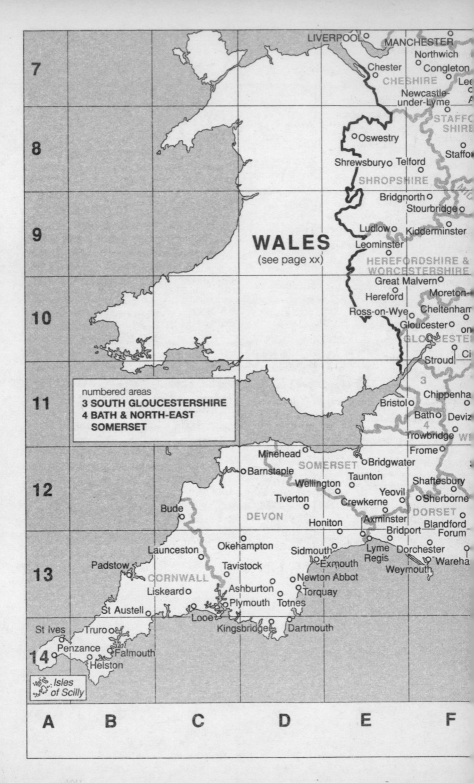

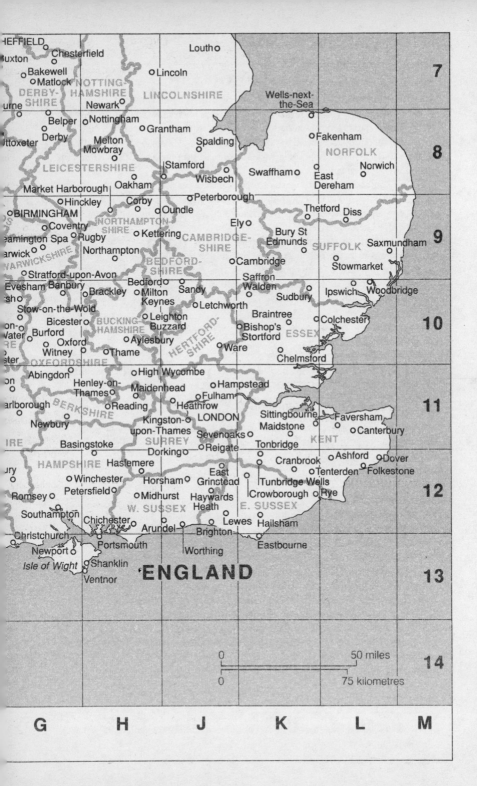

YOU AND THE LAW

Once your booking has been confirmed – orally or in writing – a contract exists between you and the proprietor. He is legally bound to provide accommodation as booked; and you are legally bound to pay for this accommodation. If unable to take up the booking – even because of sickness – you still remain liable for a very substantial proportion of the charges (in addition to losing your deposit).

If you have to cancel, let the proprietor know as soon as possible; then he may be able to re-let the accommodation (in which case you would be liable to pay only a re-letting cost or forfeit your deposit). Phone if you are going to arrive late.

(**A note to overseas readers.** It may be an acceptable practice elsewhere to make bookings at several houses for the same date, choosing only later which one to patronize; but this way of doing things is not the British practice and you are legally liable to compensate any proprietors whom you let down in this way.)

NOTE: The houses in this book have been personally visited by the authors or on their behalf. **At any of them (London excepted) you may stay for as little as £12.50–£20 (for bed-and-breakfast)** although at about a quarter of them the best rooms cost more. Prices may rise in high season. Owners, and prices, can change overnight; so check before you book. At many places, you can dine without staying: see entries under **'Dinner'**.

COMPLAINTS: If anything was not of reasonable standard (e.g. chilly bedroom or badly cooked food) you are entitled to claim a reduction on your bill, but *only if* you had previously told the proprietor and given him or her a chance to put matters right. In a recent court case involving a restaurant meal, it was ruled that, because a customer had not made a specific complaint at the time, he had no right subsequently to withhold payment (he had cancelled his cheque). The moral is obvious: if dissatisfied, you are expected to say so at once and not later. We regularly inspect; and also will forward complaints to proprietors. Write to: Walter Gundrey (SOTBT), % Arrow Books, 20 Vauxhall Bridge Road, London SW1V 2SA.

Readers' comments quoted in the book are from letters sent to us: they are not supplied via the proprietors.

LIST OF HOUSES & HOTELS

Most of the hotels, houses and farms in England appear in the main part of this book in alphabetical order. However, for convenience in locating them, they are all grouped in the following list according to counties and certain geographical areas, including – where there are houses in this book – the new unitary authorities which came into effect on 1st April 1996. On the left is the nearest town (sometimes distant), with its map reference (see pages vi–ix), followed by the house or hotel and its nearest village.

Establishments marked with a V will accept the discount vouchers from page ii. Other discounts to readers are described in the text.

ENGLAND

Nearest town	Map ref. (see p. vi-ix)		Page
BEDFORDSHIRE			
Bedford	**J.10**		
Church Farm, Roxton		V	118
Firs Farm, Stagsden West End		V	96
The Grange, Ravensden		V	118
Orchard Cottage, Wrestlingworth			289
Leighton Buzzard	**H.10**		
Gower Cottage, Totternhoe		V	239
(Old Vicarage, see Buckinghamshire)			239
Sandy	**J.10**		
Highfield Farm		V	141
BERKSHIRE			
Maidenhead	**H.11**		
Beehive Manor, Cox Green		V	20
Woodpecker Cottage, Warren Row		V	365
Newbury	**G.11**		
Chamberhouse Mill, Thatcham		V	211
Marshgate Cottage Hotel, Hungerford			194
Nalderhill House, Wickham Heath		V	211
St Mary's House, Kintbury		V	285
Reading	**H.11**		
Cherry Court, Burghfield Common			54
BUCKINGHAMSHIRE			
Aylesbury	**H.10**		
Foxhill, Kingsey		V	104
Old Vicarage, Wingrave		V	242
Poletrees Farm, Brill		V	104
(Brackley, Northamptonshire)	**H.10**		
Mill Farmhouse, Westbury		V	200
(Henley-on-Thames, Oxfordshire)	**H.11**		
Little Parmoor, Frieth			181
High Wycombe	**H.11**		
White House, Widmer End			354

Nearest town	Map ref. (see p. vi-ix)		Page
Whites' Farmhouse, Radnage			354
Whitewebbs, Chalfont St Peter			355
(Leighton Buzzard, Bedfordshire)	**H.10**		
Old Vicarage, Mentmore		V	239
Milton Keynes	**H.10**		
Richmond Lodge, Mursley		V	242
CAMBRIDGESHIRE			
Cambridge	**J.9**		
Glebe House, Longstowe		V	108
Old Rectory, Swaffham Bulbeck		V	108
Springfield, Linton			300
(Yardleys, see Essex)			300
Ely	**K.9**		
Old Egremont House		V	220
Spinney Abbey, Wicken			220
Peterborough	**J.9**		
(Castle Farm, see Northamptonshire)			47
Wisbech	**J.8**		
Bramley Cottage			32
CHESHIRE			
(Buxton, Derbyshire)	**G.7**		
Hardingland Farmhouse, Macclesfield Forest		V	130
Chester	**E.7**		
Castle House		V	48
Mitchell's			48
(The Mount, see Flintshire, Wales)			391
Newton Hall, Tattenhall		V	213
Roughlow Farmhouse, Willington			279
Tilston Lodge, Tilston			213
Congleton	**F.7**		
Canal Centre, Hassall Green		V	45
Northwich	**F.7**		
Barratwich, Cuddington			15

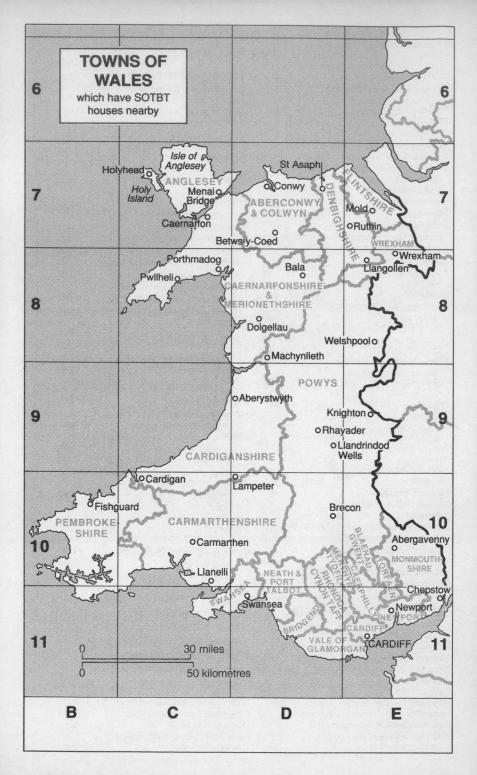

TOWNS OF WALES
which have SOTBT houses nearby

6   6

Isle of Anglesey

Holyhead

Holy Island

ANGLESEY

St Asaph

Menai Bridge
Conwy

ABERCONWY & COLWYN

FLINTSHIRE

DENBIGHSHIRE

Mold

Ruthin

7   7

Caernarfon

Betws-y-Coed

WREXHAM

Wrexham

Porthmadog

Pwllheli

Bala

Llangollen

CAERNARFONSHIRE & MERIONETHSHIRE

8   8

Dolgellau

Welshpool

Machynlleth

POWYS

Aberystwyth

Knighton

9   9

Rhayader

Llandrindod Wells

CARDIGANSHIRE

Cardigan

Lampeter

Fishguard

Brecon

PEMBROKESHIRE

CARMARTHENSHIRE

Abergavenny

10   10

Carmarthen

MONMOUTHSHIRE

Llanelli

NEATH & PORT TALBOT

BLAENAU GWENT

TORFAEN

Chepstow

SWANSEA

RHONDDA CYNON TAFF

MERTHYR TYDFIL

CAERPHILLY

NEWPORT

Newport

Swansea

BRIDGEND

CARDIFF

11   11

VALE OF GLAMORGAN

CARDIFF

0   30 miles

0   50 kilometres

B   C   D   E

WALES

The hotels, houses and farms in Wales are grouped in the following list according to their new administrative areas, which came into effect on 1st April 1996.

EXPLANATION OF CODE LETTERS

(These appear, where applicable, in alphabetical order after the names of houses)

C Suitable for families with children. Sometimes a minimum age is stipulated, in which case this is indicated by a numeral; thus **C**(5) means children over 5 years old are accepted. In most cases, houses that accept children offer reduced rates and special meals. Do not expect young children to be lodged free, as babies are. (Readers wanting total quiet may wish to avoid houses coded **C**.)

D Dogs permitted. A charge is rarely made, but it is often a stipulation that you must ask before bringing one; the dog may have to sleep in your car, or be banned from public rooms.

M Suitable for those with mobility problems. Needs vary: whenever we have used the code letter **M**, this indicates that not only is there a ground-floor bedroom and bathroom, but these, and doorways, have sufficient width for a wheelchair, and steps are few.

PT Accessible by public transport. Houses indicated by the code **PT** have a railway station or coach stop within a reasonable distance, from which you can walk or take a taxi (quite a number of hosts will even pick you up, free, in their own car).

S Indicates those houses which charge single people no more, or only 10% more, than half the price of a double room (except, possibly, at peak periods).

X Visitors are accepted at Christmas, though Christmas meals are not necessarily provided. Some hotels and farms offer special Christmas holidays; but, unless otherwise indicated (by the code letter **X** at top of entry), those in this book will then be closed.

HOW TO HAVE A GOOD TIME

As the readership of this book grows so does the diversity of readers' tastes. The detailed descriptions are meant to help each one pick out the places that suit him or her best; but there are still readers who write to complain about bar or carpark noise at inns (so why pick an inn rather than a house without a bar?), and the presence of dogs (why go to a house with the code letter **D**, meaning dogs accepted, or to a farm where dogs are almost certainly kept?). Light sleepers should avoid rooms overlooking, for instance, a market square: not all houses in this book are rural.

Some people have very particular requirements; and it is up to them to discuss these when telephoning to book. Many hosts in this book are more flexible than big hotels, and all are eager to help if they can. The sort of things to bear in mind are: a bad back, needing a very *firm mattress*; special *dietary* requirements, and *allergies* to feather pillows or animals; a strong preference for *separate tables* rather than a shared dining-table – or vice versa; *fewer courses* than on the fixed menu; *twin beds* rather than double beds – or vice versa; freedom to *smoke* – or freedom from it; a particular wish for *electric blanket*, *hot water-bottle*, etc. or a dislike of *duvets;* the need to arrive, depart or eat at *extra-early* or *extra-late* hours; an intention to pay by *credit card* (this should not be taken for granted, particularly at small guest-houses).

The code letters that appear after the name of each house will help you identify houses suitable for children, dogs, people with mobility problems, users of public transport, etc.: for full explanation, see inside front cover or page xxii. Please also use the 'how to book' checklist on page xxiv when telephoning.

It's best to stay at least 2–3 days: you cannot possibly appreciate an area if you only stay overnight (prices per night are often less, too, if you stay on). The vouchers on page ii are usable for 3-night stays. At some houses, 1-night bookings may be refused.

When to go? Seaside resorts or other places suitable for children will be at their busiest (and dearest) in July–August and during half-term holidays (especially, in late May, which is also a bank holiday period). Houses which do *not* take children tend to have vacancies in July and August – even in the popular Cotswolds, for instance. Other peak periods are, of course, Easter, Christmas, New Year and the bank holiday in late August. There are local peaks, too (the Gold Cup races at Cheltenham or the regatta at Henley, for instance, are apt to fill hotels for miles around), and local troughs (Brighton, a conference centre, is least busy in high summer). In holiday areas, travel on any day other than a summer Saturday if you can. Make travel reservations well in advance. And if you don't have a car, with one phone call (0891 970910) to the Tram, Bus and Coach Hot Line, you can get an itinerary for any route you might need, complete with times and even reservations if required.

One final tip on ensuring that you get all that you hope for: at the end of each season, throw away this year's copy of the book and get next year's edition before it sells out in the bookshops later in the year (you can soon recoup its cost by using the fresh set of accommodation vouchers it contains). Here's why this is so important. A reader wrote as follows: 'The house was dirty; room smelt damp; toilet-seat wobbly and stained; under-pillows had no cases; grubby carpets . . . (etc.)'. The house had changed hands years ago, and been dropped from this book as a consequence; but the reader was using an out-of-date edition. Prices change, so do telephone numbers and much else. Change of owner or inflated prices are the two most common reasons why houses are dropped; a third is that we find somewhere better – or of better value – nearby.

TELEPHONING TO BOOK: A CHECKLIST

Book well ahead: many of these houses have few rooms. Further, at some houses, rooms (even if similarly priced) vary in size or amenities: early applicants get the cheapest and/or best ones. Mention that you are a reader of this book: sometimes there are discounts on offer exclusively for readers. Telephoning is preferable to writing to enquire about vacancies, and, in many cases, the best time is early evening.

1. Ask for the owner by the *name* given in this edition. (If there has been a change, standards and prices may differ.)
2. Specify *your precise needs* (such as en suite bathroom, if available), see previous page. (Do not turn up with children, dogs or disabilities if you have not checked that these are accepted or provided for.) Elderly people may wish to ensure that their room is not above the first floor.
3. Check *prices* – these, too, can change (particularly after spring). Ask whether there are any bargain breaks. Are credit cards accepted?
4. Ask what *deposit* to send (or quote a credit card number). Overseas visitors may be asked to pay up to 50 per cent.
5. State your intended *time of arrival*, what meals are wanted and at what times. (If you should then be late, telephone a warning – otherwise your room may be let to someone else. It is inconsiderate to arrive late for home-cooked meals prepared especially for you.) Most proprietors expect visitors to arrive about 5pm. In country lanes, finding your way after dark can be difficult.
6. Ask for precise instructions for *locating the house:* many are remote. Better still, ask for a brochure with map to be posted to you. Check where to park.
7. Few proprietors expect visitors to stay out of the house in the daytime; but if you want to stay in, check this when booking.

At houses where dinner is not served, a light supper can often be obtained (if ordered in advance), ranging from sandwiches to family 'pot luck'. (Packed lunches too.)

PRICES

This book came into being to provide a guide to good accommodation at prices suited to people of moderate means. That remains its policy.

In the current edition are houses at which it is possible to stay, at the time of publication, for as little as £12.50–£20 for b & b – that is, per person sharing a double room. (However, for the best rooms in the house, or later in the year, you may well be asked for more. **Check when booking.**)

The prices are as quoted to us when the book was in preparation during 1996. But sometimes unexpected costs force proprietors to increase their prices subsequently: becoming liable for VAT or business rates, for instance.

You can see from the text data when price rises occur. For instance, in the Isle of Wight few proprietors raise prices until summer (if then), while in the Lake District and Yorkshire Dales many put them up in spring.

Inclusive terms for dinner, bed-and-breakfast (particularly for a week) can be much lower than those quoted here for these items taken separately. Most houses in this book have bargain breaks or other discounts on offer, some exclusive to readers. A 'bargain break' is usually a 2- or 3-day booking including dinners, at a discount; usually at low season only.

INTRODUCTION

ARE YOU A TOURIST?

Perish the thought! (A visitor, traveller, holidaymaker, yes; but never that nasty parasite, a tourist.)

But you are, you know: everyone who stays away from home, except on business, is a tourist. (One of those whose petrol fumes pollute the roads, whose parked car is a blot on the landscape, whose demands for en suite bathrooms and central heating deplete resources.)

No, we aren't *really* trying to make you feel guilty! Exploring Britain, and getting to know how one's fellows live, is all to the good; and in this book, pointedly called *Staying Off the Beaten Track*, we encourage the British (and others) to get to know one another and their own country better by travelling round it. Not just by pounding along motorways to Bath, York, Stratford-upon-Avon and so forth but by discovering unfrequented spots and *lingering* there (oh, do bring back again the relaxing, stress-free, stay-put holiday!).

Of course there is an upside even to fast motorways: with their help, one can so quickly get from home to a little-known beauty-spot that the short-break holiday is increasingly feasible and popular. Many people now prefer five short breaks to one long holiday a year; and research among GPs has produced the interesting statistic that 83 per cent of patients regularly taking such breaks have fewer stress-related ailments.

The philosophy of *Staying Off the Beaten Track* is, for the most part, to encourage unhurried travel on byroads (by car or even – yes – bus) to small villages and small b & b houses, where the occasional arrival of a few guests has little impact on the environment. This way of travel is for discriminating people who appreciate an authentic experience of country life and do not want commercial 'entertainments', 'sights' and 'attractions' all round the clock. Their presence provides some local employment and gives a small boost to local economies.

Sixteen years' experience of producing this book annually has shown that the average reader wants to find in its pages ideas for unexplored places suitable for a few days' break outside high summer (how wise: records show that the green and temperate months of April – June are not too crowded but usually less rainy than July – September): spots in which quietly to clear the mind, invigorate the spirit and restore the body – at minimal cost.

We are sometimes asked our favourite, least spoiled areas for such breaks. If you want to get away from cities, industry, major roads and railways, then head for the Pennines (Derbyshire up to Northumberland), or Shropshire and Herefordshire with Wales beyond, or *north* Devon. Though the north-west is famous for the Lake District, it's the scenic north-*east* that is more peaceful; while East Anglia's villages beat those of the Cotswolds for picturesque tranquillity.

In general, the North is underrated – both its scenery and the variety of local activities. These embrace Celtic festivals and pudding races, caving courses and re-enactments of mediaeval battles, folk dancing and unique lakeland sports, experts to guide you on forest cycle-rides, archaeology trails or seabird-watching, falconry and regattas, steam rallies and sheepdog contests.

Walking has never been better, with footpaths now so numerous and well marked. Among various booklets etc. to help you, we recommend 'Britain for

Walkers' (free from the British Tourist Authority, Thames Tower, London W6 9EL (tel: 0181-846 9000); 'Greenways' – disused railtracks, towpaths, etc. (£4.95 from Sustrans, Freepost BS7739, Bristol BS1 4BR); 'Waterway Walks', 70 miles along the canal linking Bath to Reading – another long one links Birmingham to London (£1 from Kennet & Avon Canal Trust, The Wharf, Couch Lane, Devizes, Wiltshire SN10 1EB); and the latest long-distance way-marked footpath, over 200 miles from Buckinghamshire to the Peak District (Countryside Commission, Cumberland House, Broad Street, Birmingham BJ5 1TD). You don't have to go all the way! Nor is distance the object if you go on guided wildlife walks – spotting anything from bats to moths, owls to wildfowl (one good source for information is the Wildfowl and Wetlands Trust, Slimbridge, Gloucestershire GL2 7BT; tel: 01453 890333). Family rambles and other walks: Ramblers' Association, 1 Wandsworth Road, London SW8 2XX (tel: 0171-582 0878).

Not that mass tourism, so vital to Britain's economy, is all bad. It has led to the creation of some truly worthwhile new sights of interest – like the various Sea Life Centres (Scarborough and Blackpool have fine examples) or the imaginative Eureka! museum for children at Halifax in Yorkshire, and the Anything to Declare? exhibition in Liverpool – even the immensely popular Chocolate World at Bourneville in the Midlands. These can well stand an influx of visitors because they were created specifically for them.

For those wanting closer involvement in country life, there are courses in such pursuits as deerstalking (not killing), clay-pigeon shooting, four-wheel driving, trout fishing and so on – or more sedentary pursuits such as tracing one's own genealogy in county record offices. Then there are gardens: every county has guides – we were particularly struck by the wealth of historic private gardens open in south Somerset, for example (for leaflet, tel: 01935 71279).

To add to appreciation of the countryside we recommend:

'Out in the Country', 'National Parks', 'Heritage Coasts' and lists of Country Parks and Areas of Outstanding Natural Beauty: all free leaflets, from the Countryside Commission, Crescent Place, Cheltenham, Gloucestershire GL50 3RA (tel: 01242 521381).

National Nature Reserves (there are 120) and Sites of Special Scientific Interest (over 3000) can be visited; for details apply to English Nature, Northminster House, Peterborough PE1 1VA (tel: 01733 340345). Nearly 2000 other nature reserves are run by the Royal Society for Nature Conservation (membership details from them at The Green, Nettleham, Lincolnshire LN2 2NB; tel: 01522 544400). The Royal Society for the Protection of Birds has another 120 reserves: membership details, RSPB, Sandy, Bedfordshire SG19 2DL (tel: 01767 680551).

All agricultural shows are detailed in *Showman's Directory*, £5 from Lance Publications, Brook House, Mint Street, Godalming, Surrey GU7 1HE. Vineyards to visit (250) are in a free guide from the English Vineyards Association, 38 West Park, London SE9 4RH (tel: 0181-857 0452); and cheese-makers who welcome visitors are in one from the Farmhouse Cheese Bureau, Box 457, Wells, Somerset BA5 1UX (tel: 01749 77953). The Tourist Information Centre in any place you visit will have details of other such possibilities.

For the literary-minded, there is the new *Reader's Guide to Writers' Britain*, by Sally Varlow (Prion Books), covering the country from Daphne du Maurier's Cornwall to J.M. Barrie's Scotland.

ALPHABETICAL DIRECTORY OF HOUSES AND HOTELS IN
ENGLAND

Prices are per person sharing a double room, at the beginning of the year. You may be quoted more later or for single occupancy.

Prices and other facts quoted at the head of each entry are as supplied by the proprietors.

Where certain county names were replaced on 1st April 1996, these have been given in brackets in the first line of main entry addresses.

Paradise House (see page 251)

ABBEY HOUSE

Monk Soham, Suffolk, IP13 7EN   Tel: 01728 685225
West of Saxmundham. Nearest main road: A1120 from Stowmarket to
Yoxford.

3 Bedrooms. £18–£23 (less for 6 nights).
All have own bath/toilet. Tea/coffee facilities.
Views of garden, country. Washing machine
on request.
1 Sitting-room. With open fire, central
heating, TV.
Large garden
Closed from November to February.

'Fish, fish, do your duty!' the rector who lived here in the late 19th century used to admonish the inhabitants of his ponds (still there), which had originally provided Friday food for monks at the abbey (long vanished). This and other anecdotes of his life at Abbey House are in a book by his son which Sue Bagnall shows her visitors. It was he who planted the huge oaks, beeches and limes in the grounds. The architect was Teulon, a high-Victorian gothicist.

Sue and her husband have made the old rectory comfortable and have furnished it with antiques, keeping the atmosphere informal. Among fine old features they have restored is a magnificent cast-iron fireplace in the dining-room. Colours are soft (pale buff or shell pink, for instance).

Guests are welcome to look at the livestock which includes Jersey cows (calves sometimes), sheep, chickens, ducks and peafowl. In the large garden, there is croquet and a swimming-pool.

The Norfolk Broads are within reach; historic Norwich; bird reserves along the coast; old-fashioned seaside towns like Southwold; Lowestoft with its sands and its busy fishing port. At nearby Snape Maltings, there are annual concerts, part of the Aldeburgh music festival.

Other sights include Somerleyton and Helmingham halls, Framlingham and Orford castles, Bressingham Steam Museum (with gardens), the Otter Trust, wildlife or farm parks, Saxtead windmill, rural crafts, vineyards and inns.

Readers' comments: Delightful. Excellent. Would be happy to make a return visit. The very best we have ever stayed in. House, food and hospitality outstanding. House and location beautiful, cooking superb, and the friendliest hostess we've met. Had a wonderful time.

1997 has been designated Britain's 'Year of Opera and Musical Theatre'; and it is the East of England which has received the top accolade for its programme of events then (the runners-up were Devon & Cornwall and, in Yorkshire, Leeds). So music-lovers need to book early there!

ALDENHAM WEIR

C D M PT

Muckley Cross, Shropshire, WV16 4RR   Tel: 01746 714352
North-west of Bridgnorth. Off A458 from Bridgnorth to Shrewsbury.

6 Bedrooms. £19. All have own shower/toilet. Tea/coffee facilities. TV. Views of garden, country. No smoking. Washing machine on request.
Light suppers if ordered. No smoking.
2 Sitting-rooms. With central heating, TV. No smoking.
Large garden
Closed from December to February.

This lovely woodland location by the winding Mor brook, set well back from the road, enchanted the Coldicotts so much that a few years ago they built themselves and their children a very attractive, architect-designed house here. Once there had been a watermill – hence the weir and the old mill-race which are features of the beautiful site. Stephen did much of the work himself, to the highest standards; and Jennifer has furnished the house with equal care – using a lot of polished pine and rose-patterned fabrics in pink or blue. Older visitors may appreciate the two ground-floor bedrooms with French doors opening onto the garden, where there are rustic seats by the waterside from which to watch for kingfishers and woodpeckers. Alternatively, one can sit or even breakfast in the hexagonal conservatory, furnished with bamboo armchairs. As well as bedrooms, the upper floor of the house has a sitting-area for guests, containing television and tourist information, and a family suite with sitting-room. Children enjoy petting the donkeys (from a sanctuary) in the paddock.

The nearby market town of Bridgnorth is unusual – part is high up (here are half-timbered houses and the remains of a castle) and the rest so far below that a steep cliff-railway links the two. You can see traces of cave dwellings in the cliff.

Readers' comments: Very good indeed. Fantastic place, fantastic welcome.

At Aston Eyre is a little Norman church with some exceptional stone carving. Next to it is **CHURCH HOUSE** which was originally a wheelwright's cottage with a workshop. Now Margaret Cosh's home, it has some quarry-tiled floors, low beams and a brick inglenook in the sitting-room. Up a narrow staircase is a neat, cottage-style bedroom; another is on the ground floor and has French doors opening onto a terrace, garden with summer-house and Margaret's small-holding. The breakfast-room, too, has French doors with a view of

the beautiful Shropshire countryside. Light suppers or three-course dinners (by arrangement). Closed from November to March. £18. [Tel: 01746 714248; postcode: WV16 6XD]

3

ALFOXTON COTTAGE

Holford, Somerset, TA5 1SG   Tel: 01278 741418

West of Bridgwater. Nearest main road: A39 from Bridgwater to Minehead (and M5, junction 23).

3 Bedrooms. £16–£18 (less for 4 nights). Prices go up in June. Views of garden, country. No smoking. Washing machine on request.

Dinner. £16 for 4 courses and coffee, at 7pm. Non-residents not admitted. Wine available. No smoking.

1 Sitting-room. With open fire, central heating, record-player. Piano. No smoking.

Small garden

Closed from December to February.

All round the cottage are the Quantock Hills and pretty hamlets, an Area of Outstanding Natural Beauty. Nearby Alfoxton House (now a hotel) was tenanted by Wordsworth and his sister, and they used to walk along here to visit Coleridge (his cottage, now NT, is open).

The cottage is truly remote, up in the Quantock Hills with their views across the Bristol Channel to Wales. You may believe you are never coming to it as you follow twists and turns up the small wooded lane to the top of the hill.

This little house is now the home of Richard and Angela Delderfield. Rooms are small and low but pleasantly furnished – for instance, bamboo or velvet bedheads and a grandfather clock and flounced armchairs by the log fire in the sitting-room, from which a door leads to the garden, woods, a trickling stream, donkeys and chickens.

Angela's cooking is one of the main attractions of staying here. She sometimes serves as a starter prawns in a creamy sauce containing whisky, or perhaps lettuce soup. Chicken breasts will be cooked with coriander seeds and lemon juice. Into her salads may go unusual ingredients such as spinach, sunflower seeds or hot crisp bacon with slivers of avocado. She makes flans of rhubarb and lemon or orange and almonds.

Readers' comments: A wonderful establishment. A lovely home in a beautiful area. Very hospitable, food and service excellent. Friendly and genuine people. Truly gifted cook. Delightful hostess. Very enjoyable stay. Very friendly. Delightful.

At the foot of the hill is **QUANTOCK HOUSE**, Holford, a 17th-century cottage of stone and thatch; beams and huge inglenook inside, and outside a flowery garden. Most guests dine at the Hood, a mile away. The samplers, embroidered cushions and patchwork spreads in the en suite bedrooms (one on the ground floor) are all Pam Laidler's work. £18–£20.

Readers' comments: 'Soaking up the atmosphere' is a holiday on its own! Mouth-watering food. Cannot praise too highly: I could have stayed for ever. Incomparable food. Excellent cook; made very welcome. Excellent accommodation, gracious and attentive hostess. [Tel: 01278 741439; postcode: TA5 1RY]

THE ARCHWAY
C(10) **PT S X**

College Road, Windermere, Cumbria, LA23 1BY   Tel: 015394 45613

Nearest main road: A591 from Kendal to Ambleside.

5 Bedrooms. £18–£20 (less for 3 nights). Bargain breaks. Most have own bath/shower/toilet. Tea/coffee facilities. TV. Views of garden, country. No smoking.
Dinner. £12.50 for 2 courses and coffee, at 6.45pm (not Sundays). 3 courses in winter. Non-residents not admitted. Vegetarian or special diets if ordered. Wine available. No smoking. **Light suppers** if ordered.
1 Sitting-room. With open fire, central heating. No smoking.
Small garden

The Windermere–Ambleside axis is the heart of the Lake District, for which many first-time visitors head. The Archway is in a side road close to the centre of Windermere (and conveniently near the railway station). It is in a Victorian terrace typical of those in Lake District towns, built of the green slate much used for houses hereabouts, and stands above road level behind a sloping garden.

A big semicircular arch divides the sitting-cum-dining-room, which has stripped wood chairs and tables at one end and, at the other, cretonne-covered settees and chairs around a handsome fireplace. Walls are painted dusty pink; there are books everywhere; and on the walls here and throughout the house are prints, posters, Victorian engravings and other pictures, all chosen with a discriminating eye – not surprisingly, since Tony Greenhalgh has a degree in the history of art.

Anthony and Aurea, who share the cooking, are enthusiasts for food and wine. Breakfast could include home-made muesli, yogurt, granola, muffins and crumpets; and American pancakes or, more conventionally, kippers, Cumberland sausage or black pudding. A winter dinner might be cream of watercress soup or vegetable terrine; roast lamb with home-made rowanberry jelly; and such a pudding as frangipani tart or bread-and-butter pudding – sweets are a speciality.

Readers staying three nights receive free elderflower wine and fudge at dinner.

Readers' comments: Pleasant atmosphere. Good food. They really know how to make guests happy. Attention to detail is perfect. Where else could you get such comfort, good food, good company? Truly excellent. A fabulous time. Hospitality and atmosphere excellent.

ARCHWAY HOUSE

Kirklington, Nottinghamshire, NG22 8NX   Tel: 01636 812070

C(5) **D S**

West of Newark. Nearest main road: A617 from Newark to Mansfield (and M1, junction 27).

3 Bedrooms. £16.50–£18.50 (less for 2 nights). All have own bath/shower/toilet. Tea/coffee facilities. TV. Views of garden, country. No smoking. Washing machine on request.
Dinner (by arrangement). £12.50 for 3 courses and coffee, at 7.30–8pm. Non-residents not admitted. Vegetarian or special diets if ordered. **Light suppers** if ordered.
2 Sitting-rooms. With open fire, central heating,TV, record-player.
Large garden

Early this century, the wealthy owner of a coalmine built himself this spacious mansion, its big bay windows overlooking croquet or tennis lawns, with chestnut trees now grown to a great height. As the grounds are bounded by a haha, there is an uninterrupted view of the surrounding fields and parklands. Snowdrops and wood anemones abound early in the year.

Erica Henson has furnished the rooms appropriately with antiques, Victorian watercolours and portraits, big sofas, and mahogany and silver in the dining-room where a cherry carpet complements walls of billiard-table green. Trained at the celebrated Tante Marie cookery school, she serves such meals as mackerel pâté, boeuf bourguignonne, and lemon meringue pie.

Another of her skills is furniture decoration (ragging, dragging and other painted effects), examples of which are to be seen around the house. She has used her artistic skills to good effect in bedrooms that have, for instance, garlanded quilts, beribboned curtains or pintucked spreads. There are a snooker table for guests' use and practice golf greens: Colin, a retired headmaster, is a keen golfer and can introduce visitors to a wide choice of inexpensive courses in the area.

Kirklington is only three miles from Southwell with its famous 13th-century minster (and racecourse); Sherwood Forest is not much further.

Nearby Newark is a town well worth exploring. The dramatic ruins of a 12th-century castle destroyed during the Civil War are reflected in the waters of the broad River Trent (boat trips available). There's a vast cobbled market place with grandiose town hall, colonnade and mediaeval inns – one with carved angels. More angels (painted and gilded) in the lofty church, too, which has stained glass and monuments. There are byways to explore, a museum of quaint mementoes from the town's turbulent past, the house where Prince Rupert stayed after defeat at Marston Moor, and much else.

In the vicinity, black-and-white villages can be discovered and such church treasures as the 14th-century Easter sepulchre at Hawton. Laxton is celebrated for having retained to this day the strip-farming system which prevailed in the Middle Ages: fields are divided into strips, and each farmer is allotted a number of these. Newstead Abbey (1170) was Byron's home (he is buried at Hucknall) and still contains possessions of his; there are lakes in its extensive grounds. By contrast, D. H. Lawrence's childhood home at Eastwood is a miner's cottage – also open to the public.

Winsley Hill, Limpley Stoke, Wiltshire, BA3 6EX   Tel: 01225 722547
South of Bath. Nearest main road: A36 from Bath to Warminster.

2 Bedrooms. £18 (less for 4 nights or continental breakfast). Price goes up from May to September. Tea/coffee facilities. Views of garden, country, river. Washing machine on request.
Dinner. £12 for 3 courses with aperitif and coffee, at 7.30pm. Non-residents not admitted. **Light suppers.**
1 Sitting-room. With open fire, central heating, piano.
Large garden

A typical English country house, built of honey-coloured Bath stone, the Challens' secluded home stands on the banks of the River Avon: walks along it or the nearby canal and fishing are among the attractions of this very scenic area.

Ursula has furnished the sitting-room with tangerine armchairs, oriental rugs and antiques that show up well against walls painted peach, on which hang many paintings by Peter who, after serving as a major in the Gurkhas, turned to a completely different career as an artist. Through the bay window is a serene view of the well-kept lawn and landscaped grounds, with tennis and croquet.

Other rooms are equally pleasing, with attractive wallpapers and leafy views. The Challens offer visitors pre-dinner drinks (no extra charge). Typical of the kind of meal Ursula serves: avocado pâté; chicken in a honey-and-mustard sauce with vegetables from the garden; a brûlée of brown sugar, cream and yogurt over raspberries. Alternatively, visitors can go out to the excellent Nightingales restaurant in the village or to the Hop Pole inn.

At Bradford-on-Avon steep roads converge to the mediaeval bridge with domed chapel-turned-lockup on it. It takes time to discover all Bradford's handsome houses, Saxon church, vast tithe barn and old inns. A few miles away is Bath, and northward, such other lovely spots as Corsham, Lacock (mediaeval abbey and museum of photographic history) and the Chippenham–Calne area.

Readers' comments: Wonderful people, very friendly. Elegant; lovely meals. The Challens make one feel like their house-guests. Excellent accommodation and food. A place of peace and comfort.

A two-bedroom suite occupies the ground floor in beautifully converted **BRIDGE COTTAGE**, Ashley Road, Bathford. There is a little dining-room for light suppers; a particularly pretty bathroom, with flowery fitments; and a spacious, fitted bedroom in Laura Ashley style with windows at each end. Across the courtyard is another, equally attractive suite, with its own patio garden. Tubs of begonias and petunias fill every corner: Ros Bright is a very

keen gardener. £18–£20. [Tel: 01225 852399; postcode: BA1 7TT]

AYRMER HOUSE

Ringmore, Devon, TQ7 4HL   Tel: 01548 810391
West of Kingsbridge. Nearest main road: A379 from Kingsbridge to
Plymouth.

4 Bedrooms. £16–£18. Some have own bath/shower/toilet. Tea/coffee facilities. TV. Views of garden, country, sea. Balcony. No smoking. Washing machine on request.
Dinner. £11 for 3 courses and coffee, at 7pm. Less for 2 courses. Vegetarian or special diets if ordered. No smoking. **Light suppers.**
2 Sitting-rooms. With open fire, central heating, TV, record-player. No smoking.
Garden

The superb view down a broad valley to the sea (where the Eddystone light-house flashes at night) is what brings many visitors here: big picture-windows, a terrace and a wide verandah outside three of the bedrooms make the most of it. This is National Trust land, threaded by a stream and path to the secluded beach and to the long coastal walk which can take you to Salcombe or to Plymouth.

Jim and Ella Dodds, who keep sheep on this land, have a most unusual farm-house – completely modern and with such natural features as walls of timber or stone, polished slate for floors or hearth, and an open-tread staircase to one bed-room suite with its own sitting-room. William Morris fabrics contrast with white walls in most rooms.

Except in high summer, Ella offers such meals as salmon, a choice of pud-dings (pavlova, tarts and chocolate pudding for example) and cheeses. Bread is home-baked.

Readers' comments: Delightful house and view. Charmingly decorated. Warmly welcomed, home-from-home atmosphere, excellent service, most restful. Excellent meals.

At attractive little Kingston, **TORR HOUSE** – built in 1800 – has been furnished by Joyce Kies with antiques that complement such period details as shuttered windows and shapely arches. Up a graceful staircase with a verandah are rooms with pretty bed-drapes and basins; they have garden or farmyard views. (Meals by arrangement.) The house is in an area of narrow ferny lanes and sunlit panoramas, sandy beaches and beautiful estuaries. Plymouth is not far away and Norman

will fetch you from its station. £15. [Tel: 01548 810723; postcode: TQ7 4PT]

BANK COTTAGE

Bryher, Isles of Scilly, TR23 0PR   Tel: 01720 22612

rear view

5 Bedrooms. £19.50–£23.50. Prices go up from June. Some have own shower/toilet. Tea/coffee facilities. Views of garden, country, sea.
Dinner. £14.50 for 4 courses and coffee, at 7pm. Non-residents not admitted. Vegetarian or special diets if ordered. Wine available. No smoking. **Light snacks available.**
1 Sitting-room. With central heating, TV. Bar.
Small garden
Closed from November to February.

Visitors here have a superb sandy beach (right outside) virtually all to themselves; beyond it is one of England's most beautiful seascapes, dotted with 22 islets.

Mac Mace works as a diver: sometimes diving for lobsters and crabs or for archaeological finds, including Spanish doubloons, on the many nearby wrecks; sometimes for sea urchins, the decorative shells of which are exported by the thousand. He and his wife Tracy take a few guests in their cottage (built at least 300 years ago, but with later additions). The attractive rooms have low ceilings and thick walls to keep winter's gales at bay. Bedrooms are cheerful and bright. One en suite bedroom has its own balcony with sea view.

Many visitors are content just to sit all day in the colourful garden (facing south-west) to enjoy the view of the bay, sheltered by the pink-flowered escallonia hedges; or they can use a small boat and go out fishing. The sunsets are outstanding. A gate opens onto the beach, but although the climate is warm here, the sea is not. The garden is at its most colourful in early summer (fuchsias, flowering cherries, tulips and arum lilies abound); the islets are best in late spring, when they are smothered in pink sea-thrift.

Vegetables and loganberries are home-grown, rolls home-baked, eggs from the Maces' hens. A typical meal cooked by Tracy may start with fish or fish pâté, followed by a roast or casserole. Tracy particularly enjoys making puddings like banana mousse or sherry trifle and her vegetarian meals are imaginative. Sometimes meals are served outdoors, using the granite barbecue.

Visitors arriving by boat from St Mary's are met and their baggage taken up for them by tractor or Land-Rover.

Readers' comments: Wished we could stay for ever! Felt completely at home; happy and relaxed atmosphere. Comfortable room, excellent food. Simply delighted, a marvellous time. Nothing is too much trouble. Excellent food and accommodation, good hosts. Now a regular and much-loved destination.

*View from
Bank Cottage*

BANK VILLA

C(5) D

Masham, North Yorkshire, HG4 4DB   Tel: 01765 689605
North-west of Ripon. Nearest main road: A6108 from Ripon to Leyburn.

7 Bedrooms. £18 (less for 4 nights). Price goes up from April. Some have own shower. Views of garden, country. No smoking
Dinner. £15 for 3 courses, at 7.30pm. Non-residents not admitted. Vegetarian or special diets if ordered. Wine available.
2 Sitting-rooms. With central heating, TV.
Large garden
Closed from mid-November to mid-February.

Good food is the principal attraction at Bank Villa, where Phillip Gill (former administrator of York's arts festival) is an inspired cook.

The villa is a late Georgian stone house set back from the busy road, with a steep terraced garden behind it (where there is a sunny summer-house in which to sit). Here are grown fruit and vegetables for the kitchen.

Dinner is served in a pleasant room – pretty Old Colonial china and rush mats on the antique tables contrast with the William Morris Chrysanthemum wallpaper. Phillip cooks, and his partner Anton van der Horst serves, such delicious menus as home-made ravioli, duck confit, and ginger and kirsch meringue glacé.

Bedrooms, too, are attractive, many with floral wallpapers and pine furniture, and some with a glimpse of the River Ure at the foot of the hill. There are plenty of books around, and one of the sitting-rooms is for guests who like reading.

Masham, a little market town, has a church with interesting features; and, in mid-July, a traction-engine and steam fair. The town stands at the foot of Wensleydale, in an area of great historic as well as very varied scenic interest: within a few miles are two abbeys, three castles, one cathedral and a stately home. There are scenic roads, markets, the sight of racehorses exercising, waterfalls, a beautifully restored Georgian theatre (at Richmond) and fine gardens.

Bedale, which has had a market since the 13th century, is a town of pleasing buildings. Don't miss Fountains, finest of all the Yorkshire abbeys.

If you visit Ripon, you can hardly miss the big inscription over the market square: 'Except ye Lord keep ye cittie, ye Wakeman waketh in vain'. And if you are there at 9pm, you will see and hear the wakeman (i.e. watchman) blowing his buffalo horn and wearing a frock coat, a cocked hat, white gloves and a silver badge on his arm. The office dates back to Alfred the Great, who gave the city its first charter and a horn in AD 886. The wakeman was there to keep an all-night watch for Viking raiders, and he had to blow the horn to let the citizens know that he was on duty. The nocturnal patrol ceased centuries ago, but the horn-blowing continues. The wakeman's house, built in 1250, is now the city's tourist information centre. Below the cathedral is a Saxon crypt, all that remains of Ripon's first Christian church, which was destroyed by those same raiders, and in it is a fine monument to a wakeman of the past.

Readers' comments: A great start to our stages to Scotland: we'll be back. Food as good as in the priciest restaurants. Energetic, cheerful and efficient. Comfortable and welcoming. Excellent food and pleasant proprietors.

BARK HOUSE HOTEL   **D**
Oakfordbridge, Devon, EX16 9HZ   Tel: 01398 351236
North of Tiverton. On A396 from Exeter to Minehead.

6 Bedrooms. £19–£28 (less for 7 nights). Some have own bath/shower/toilet. TV. Views of garden, country, river. Washing machine on request.
Dinner. £14.50 for 4 courses (with some choices) and coffee, at 8pm. Less for fewer courses. Non-residents not admitted. Vegetarian or special diets if ordered. Wine available. **Light suppers** if ordered.
1 Sitting-room. With open fire, central heating.
Large garden
Closed from December to February.

In a wooded valley through which runs the River Exe is a stone building of unusual origin. It was once used as a tannery, the oak bark for which was brought from Exmoor Forest. Today, it has been handsomely converted; and Pauline and Douglas West provide visitors with complete comfort. Books, good pictures, thick Berber carpets, antiques, pot-plants and the flicker of a cheerful log fire set the scene.

In the dining-room brown and pink tablecloths contrast with white walls; around the tables are either pews or Windsor chairs. Every bedroom is different. No. 1 has a bow window with window-seat from which to enjoy the tranquil view; no. 4, art nouveau nymphs on the ceiling – however did *they* get there! No. 6 is a huge family room with its own ancient arched door to a rock garden with pool, and leaded casements. The garden is outstanding. (Parking is on the opposite side of the often busy road.)

Dinner may begin with smoked salmon mousse or fish chowder or eggs en cocotte. With a daube of beef will be served potato galette and other vegetables. The fresh peach Melba has an orange-and-raspberry sauce.

Readers' comments: Beautiful setting; excellent cooking; friendly and cheerful hosts. Have stayed four times. Charming hotel and surroundings. Very comfortable. A delight in all respects. A wonderful find. Marvellous food. Welcoming. Lovely big room. We ended up good friends. Friendly and cheerful hosts. Food memorable. Wished we could have stayed longer. Highly recommended. Most comfortable, friendly hosts, excellent cuisine.

Northward in Somerset, 15th-century **OLD MANOR** at Lower Marsh, Dunster, stands on marshes that lead to the sea. There is a chapel over the front porch: its barrel-vaulted roof has carved bosses.

Gillian Hill's bedrooms differ, the most striking being the huge rooms with the wood pegging of the cruck-beamed roof open to view. Breakfasts here are exceptional, with home-grown fruits. (Light snacks only.) £19.50–£24.

Reader's comment: A most enjoyable two weeks. [Tel: 01643 821216; postcode: TA24 6PJ]

11

BARN COTTAGE

Church Road, Leigh, Surrey, RH2 8RF   Tel: 01306 611347
South-west of Reigate. Nearest main road: A25 from Reigate to Dorking (and M25, junction 8).

2 Bedrooms. £18 (less for 3 nights). Price goes up from June. Tea/coffee facilities. TV on request. Views of garden, country. Washing machine on request.
Dinner. £12 for 4 courses (with some choices) and coffee, at times to suit guests. Non-residents not admitted. Vegetarian or special diets if ordered. **Light suppers** if ordered.
1 Sitting-room. With open fire, central heating, TV. Piano in dining-room.
Large garden

Visitors to Barn Cottage are welcomed in grand style – a large Union flag will be flying at the entrance gate. Pat Comer will also fly the Stars and Stripes when American visitors come to stay.

The barn dates back to the 17th century and was converted in the 1930s. Original beams are much in evidence, as are mahogany antiques and pieces of Copenhagen china, the latter collected over the years by Pat. Her tapestries cover chairs in the sitting- and dining-rooms; and a talent for painting is displayed in her watercolours for children, on sale at the cottage.

Bedrooms are comfortable, with wildflower bedcovers and curtains.

Lattice-paned windows look out onto immaculate lawns, lovingly tended by the Comers. One can sit on the patio and enjoy the beautiful view of a garden and fish pond. There are swings and a sandpit to keep children amused, a swimming-pool and a hard tennis court. Pat took part several times in Junior Wimbledon and won the Girls' Doubles in 1948. Mike too has been involved in sport – he played cricket for Devon.

Evening meals, served with home-grown vegetables, are available by arrangement, and, in summer, cream teas are served on the lawn.

The village of Leigh, voted best-kept village in Surrey on more than one occasion, has an ancient church, built originally in the 1300s and then rebuilt during the 15th century. This stands directly opposite Barn Cottage. Further along the quiet road is the old Plough inn (meals also available here).

Walton Heath Golf Club, where both the Ryder Cup and the European Open have been played, is within easy reach and Pat, a member for over 50 years, will be more than happy to introduce guests to the club and take part with them in a round of golf.

All is peace and tranquillity here and yet it is only 15 minutes' drive to the M25, Gatwick Airport or Redhill Station, where regular trains can take you into the centre of London within half an hour. The Comers will drive visitors to and from the airport or station; and cars can be left at Barn Cottage for a small daily charge.

Book well ahead: many of these houses have few rooms. Do not expect dinner if you have not booked it or if you arrive late.

BARN HOUSE   C
The Street, Rodmell, East Sussex, BN7 3HE   Tel: 01273 477865
South of Lewes. Nearest main road: A27 from Lewes to Brighton.

7 Bedrooms. £15–£18 (less for 7 nights or continental breakfast). Prices go up from May. Bargain breaks. All have own bath/shower/toilet. Tea/coffee facilities. TV. Views of garden, country. No smoking.
Light suppers if ordered.
1 Sitting-room
Large garden

In the 'twenties a 17th-century flint barn was completely transformed into this modern house, at which the Queen Mother used to be a regular visitor – not the only royal connection, for Elizabeth I once owned a house in the picturesque village. Rodmell's most famous resident was, however, Virginia Woolf who lived at Monks House – now a National Trust property – until in 1941 she drowned herself in the river. (In her house you can see furniture painted by her sister Vanessa Bell and by Duncan Grant whose own home, Charleston, is also open to the public.) Dirk Bogarde, who grew up near here, has described Virginia marching about the watermeadows, wispy hair knotted under floppy hat, singing to herself and picking wildflowers. All around are views of water-meadows and of the high Downs beyond – good walking and birdwatching country.

In April 1920 Virginia wrote to Vanessa: 'Here we are with the bells ringing for church – daffodils out – apple-trees in blossom – cows mooing – cocks crowing – thrushes chirping' (all just as it is today).

Bernadette Fraser has furnished Barn House well – some rooms have fabrics designed by Duncan Grant, and one has a four-poster. On many walls are flowery decorations which she has stencilled herself, and there are antiques, paintings and tapestries in the rooms. Bernadette will provide sandwich suppers; for a full dinner, it is necessary to go into Lewes or Brighton, where there are many restaurants, or to the local pub.

In the centre of Lewes itself is the **FELIX GALLERY**, in Sun Street. The little gallery is devoted entirely to cats – craft-made or antique, western or oriental, metal, china or wood. On the floor above are simple but pleasant bedrooms, well-equipped. The White-heads do not serve dinners but have no objection to food being brought in; however, many visitors eat at the White Hart's carvery. The small house, which dates from William IV's reign, is at the site of a Roman fort, long built over. £18.

Reader's comment: Fresh, clean and charming, and everything a traveller could possibly need is supplied. [Tel: 01273 472668; postcode: BN7 2QB]

BARNFIELD FARM CDS
near Charing, Kent, TN27 0BN   Tel: 01233 712421
North-west of Ashford. Nearest main road: A20 from Maidstone to Ashford (and M20, junctions 8/9).

4–5 Bedrooms. £18–£20 (less for 3 nights). Tea/coffee facilities. Views of garden, country, river. No smoking. Washing machine on request.
Dinner. £12.50 for 3 courses and coffee, at 7pm. Non-residents not admitted. Vegetarian or special diets if ordered. Wine available. No smoking. **Light suppers** if ordered.
2 Sitting-rooms. With central heating, TV, record-player. No smoking.
Large garden with tennis court.

This historic farmhouse was built about the time of the Battle of Agincourt (1415). One steps into a large hall, where the oak framework of the house is exposed to view (draped with hop bines) and a cask holding shepherds' crooks stands in one corner – for outside are sheep pastures, with arable fields beyond. The main sitting-room has an exceptionally large inglenook. Along one beam hangs a set of handbells, on which Christmas is rung in every year. The dining-room has an especially fine door made from a church chest. There is another comfortably furnished sitting/dining-room for guests' use, with plenty of books.

The bedrooms are fresh and unpretentious, and some overlook the River Stour.

Some of the furnishings were made by Martin Pym's grandmother, and at every turn of the wandering corridors there is something interesting to see.

Phillada serves such meals as egg mayonnaise, casseroled lamb cutlets, and chocolate mousse – loading a hot-tray on the sideboard for second helpings. Guests may be offered a glass of Martin's heady, home-brewed cider.

Readers' comments: Enjoyed our stay very much; a warm welcome. Unobtrusive but charming hostess. Delightful house and garden. Excellent meal. Nicely secluded position. A house full of treasures and perfectly beautiful. Delightful.

In a valley east of Charing is **DEAN COURT FARM,** Westwell, a 200-acre sheep farm close to the Pilgrims' Way. The house's name is listed in Domesday Book, but the present building is 200 years old, with some early 20th-century additions – for example, the garden room, which has comfortable cane furniture and views over Eastwell Park, which the farm borders. Tony Lister, a chartered surveyor, and his wife Susan encourage an informal family atmosphere. They both have a good eye for pictures, which cover the walls. Accommodation is simple, with good-sized rooms. One has pink-striped walls, another exposed beams covered with rosettes from

family successes in three-day eventing. There is a good walk around the farm perimeter and interesting wildlife. Susan provides evening meals by arrangement. Canterbury, Folkestone and Dover are all within easy reach. £16–£18. [Tel: 01223 712924; postcode: TN25 4NH]

BARRATWICH C(3) S X
Cuddington Lane, Cuddington, Cheshire, CW8 2SZ Tel: 01606 882412
South-west of Northwich. Nearest main road: A49 from Whitchurch to
Warrington.

3 **Bedrooms.** £16. Tea/coffee facilities.
TV. Views of garden, country. No smoking.
Washing machine on request.
Light suppers if ordered.
1 **Sitting-room.** With open fire, central
heating, piano.
Large garden

Just beyond the Delamere Forest is Cuddington village and this Victorian cottage
with a large garden from which to enjoy the fine views of open countryside. These
include a valley trout lake that, like many other Cheshire meres (old marl
diggings), attracts unusual birds – and birdwatchers.

Visitors enter a white and celadon hall with galleried staircase leading to fresh,
cottagey bedrooms – one with white boarded wall, another with stencilled decoration. There is a pink sitting-room opening onto a prettily tiled conservatory, many
antiques, and a wall with five generations of family photos.

Mary Riley prides herself on her good breakfasts, with fresh fruit and farm
eggs. While she will usually provide a light supper, the nearest pub which serves
food is only a mile away, and there are more restaurants in Northwich.

Among more famous sights close by are picturesque Great Budworth – familiar to Hinge and Bracket fans; the unusual salt museum at Northwich; and the
mansions of Arley Hall and Marbury Park. Chester is 12 miles away.

The riverside salt town of Nantwich is well worth a visit: black-and-white
houses throng quaint streets such as Welsh Row, there are carved figures on the
old almshouses, and in the mediaeval church is an exceptional stone-vaulted roof
with carvings. The Cheshire Cat inn dates from 1500. More carvings and stained
glass are in the church at Malpas, where half-timbered houses overhang steep
streets; it is near No Man's Heath which has a view over miles of rhododendrons
to a mock-Gothic castle. The ruins of a real, hilltop castle (Beeston) are best
viewed from the rose-filled churchyard of Tarporley.

To explore Delamere Forest go on foot, but for a good car tour you could
drive to Little Budworth (old buildings and a millstream); Georgian Tarporley,
with a network of back lanes; the historic city of Chester; Ellesmere Port, which
has a splendid collection of historic canal boats by a series of locks; and ancient
Frodsham. Or go to Bunbury where alabaster monuments are a feature of the
church; Beeston where timber-framed houses cluster round the castle; and Brown
Knowl from which you can go up Bickerton Hill to get stunning views across
Wales.

Readers' comments: A warm welcome. Warmth and hospitality; setting peaceful.
Delightful. Charming; hosts most helpful and friendly. How welcome I was
made.

BARTON OLD VICARAGE   C D PT
Tirril, Cumbria, CA10 2LR   Tel: 017684 86307
South-west of Penrith. Nearest main road: A6 from Penrith to Shap
(and M6, junction 40).

3 **Bedrooms.** £17–£19.50 (less for 3 nights). Prices go up from May. TV (in one). Views of garden, country. No smoking. Washing machine on request.
Dinner. £14 for 4 courses and coffee, at 6–8pm. Less for 2 courses. Non-residents not admitted. Vegetarian or special diets if ordered. Wine available. No smoking. **Light suppers.**
2 **Sitting-rooms.** With open fire, central heating, TV, piano, record-player.
Large garden
Closed from December to February.

A mediaeval church and a Victorian vicarage make a familiar pair in the English countryside, reminders that rural populations, church congregations and clerical households all used to be much larger than they are today. Here, both isolated church and vicarage lie almost buried in trees, some of the finest being in the wooded part of the Walkers' big garden. The rooms too are big, with the heavy pitch-pine joinery of the period. Folding doors lead from the sitting-room, with its view of Helvellyn, to the music room – which lives up to its name, as it contains a Bechstein grand and music stands. Geyve Walker (a solicitor who is active in local affairs) is the pianist, the children play stringed instruments, and friends or guests sometimes join in as well. There is also a large collection of classical records and the bookshelves are well filled too.

Scottish Sherie Walker is not only a linguist but a trained cook. Seated round a circular dining-table, guests might eat watercress soup or fish mousse, followed by pork en croûte; or (as foreign visitors in particular sometimes request) a Cumbrian meal of soup, smoked sausage, hotpot, and a plate pie.

Bedrooms are large, with fine views towards the mountains of the Lake District. Ullswater, the most beautiful of the larger lakes, is only a short drive away. Bicycles on loan, or routes for walkers suggested.

Readers' comments: We received a warm welcome, comfort, an excellent dinner. The house stands in a lovely situation and is well furnished. Very impressed, relaxed and welcoming atmosphere. Excellent.

The Eden Valley is scattered with pleasant villages, their houses built of red sandstone. **HILL TOP** overlooks the centre of Morland. It is furnished with antique and reproduction pieces in keeping with the 18th-century house; one bedroom has the use of a capacious cast-iron bath. £17.50.

The house is owned by May Smith, who continues to provide food of the high standard for which **Link House**, Bassenthwaite Lake (in this book since 1989) became particularly well known. [Tel: 01931 714561; postcode: CA10 3AX]

16

BATES GREEN
Arlington, Polegate, East Sussex, BN26 6SH   Tel: 01323 482039
North-west of Eastbourne. Nearest main road: A22 from Eastbourne to East Grinstead.

3 Bedrooms. £19–£26 (less for 4 nights or continental breakfast). Prices go up from April. All have own bath/shower/toilet. Tea/coffee facilities. TV. Views of garden, country. No smoking. Washing machine on request.
Dinner (in winter only). £14 for 3 courses (with choice of puddings) and coffee, at 7.30pm. Non-residents not admitted. Vegetarian or special diets if ordered. No smoking. **Light suppers** if ordered (all year).
1 Sitting-room. With log fire, central heating. No smoking.
Large garden

Goliath poppies mingling with tiny blue borage: that is the kind of unexpected juxtaposition of colour and scale which delights Carolyn McCutchan and makes her lovely garden so memorable. It is open to the public annually under the National Gardens Scheme, but visitors staying at the house can enjoy its colours all the year round. There are stone paths and steps beside a lily-pond bordered by rocks and shrubs, a herbaceous circle around a lawn with sundial, unusual plants everywhere, a tennis court, and beyond all this a large pond frequented by ducks and a big bluebell wood which is a carpet of colour every May. The McCutchans have laid out woodland walks.

The house itself is tile-hung in traditional Sussex style. It began life in the 18th century as a gamekeeper's cottage on the Michelham Priory estate, but has since been much enlarged. The sitting-room is beamed and panelled, with flowery cretonne armchairs around the log fire. The dining-room has leaded casements opening onto the garden. From the brick-floored hall, stairs rise to the pretty bedrooms (apricot or rosy bedspreads with matching curtains) and bathrooms. Dinner might consist of leak and cheese soufflé, fillet of lamb, and Sussex pond pudding.

Readers' comments: Lovely house and garden, sumptuous bedrooms, lovely food. Best we have been to. Beautiful house, excellent food, wonderful hosts.

Breakfast in the conservatory at Bere Marsh House (see page 21)

17

BEECH VILLAS

1–3 Borough Lane, Saffron Walden, Essex, CB11 4AF   Tel: 01799 516891

C D M PT S X

Nearest main road: A1053 from Saffron Walden to Braintree
(and M11, junction 9).

3 Bedrooms. £16–£17 (less for 3 nights). Some have own shower/toilet. TV. Views of garden. No smoking. Washing machine on request.
Dinner (if ordered). £9.50 for 3 courses and coffee, at 6.30–7.30pm. Less for 2 courses. Non-residents not admitted. Vegetarian or special diets if ordered. No smoking. **Light suppers** if ordered.
1 Sitting-room. With open fire, central heating, TV, piano, record-player. No smoking.
Small garden

This pair of pretty villas was built in 1820: their glass-roofed verandahs with iron columns are very typical of the period. Inside is a little sitting-room with pink velvet chairs (and occasionally a glimpse of trombone, horn or other instruments: the Butlers are a musical family). The bedrooms are pleasantly furnished with – for instance – stripped pine and ice-blue walls, blue bedspread of fringed brocade from Portugal, blue-and-white china and pretty Spice Island curtains. A pine-and-white children's room has plentiful toys and books. There is also a cellar games room with darts and snooker.

Marilyn will produce such simple meals as home-made soup, lasagne and fruit salad (she has a wide range of vegetarian dishes); or you can eat well at the Eight Bells; or very well at the Saffron Hotel. Marilyn trained in aromatherapy, and you can book a session during your stay if you want a relaxing experience.

Readers' comments: Made to feel so welcome and relaxed. Very friendly and knowledgeable. Haphazard family home – we felt like part of the family.

Two miles into the countryside outside Saffron Walden are **GUNTER'S COTTAGES**, Thaxted Road, originally built in 1840 as homes for farm-workers' families, now combined and modernized. The special attraction of staying at No 1 is (surprise!) a heated, indoor swimming-pool built onto the back. This is directly accessible from the guests' self-contained suite of bedroom and bathroom. There is a spacious dining-room where Pat Goddard will serve sandwiches if you do not want to go into the town for a meal. An interesting feature of Gunter's is the pargeting: decorative exterior plasterwork, usually found only on the historic houses of Essex

and Suffolk but here a modern artist-craftsman has created some outstanding work – particularly the owl and the huntsman on, of all things, garage walls. No smoking. £16–£17.50.
Reader's comment: Welcoming and helpful. [Tel: 01799 522091; postcode: CB10 2UT]

THE BEEHIVE   C(6) **D S X**
Church Lane, Osmington, Dorset, DT3 6EL   Tel: 01305 834095
North-east of Weymouth. Nearest main road: A353 from Weymouth towards
Wareham.

3 Bedrooms. £16–£18 (less for 3 nights or continental breakfast). Prices may go up at Easter. Bargain breaks. Some have own shower/toilet. Tea/coffee facilities. Views of garden, country. No smoking. Washing machine on request.
Dinner. £9.50 for 3 courses and coffee, at 7.45pm (not in summer or on Sundays). Non-residents not admitted. Vegetarian or special diets if ordered. No smoking. **Light suppers** by arrangement.
1 Sitting-room. With open fire, central heating. TV. No smoking.
Small garden
Closed in January.

Mary Kempe's father was Lord of the Manor at Osmington; and this little thatched stone cottage was the holiday home of her childhood. While the manorial lands passed into other hands, she was pursuing an academic career at the universities of Nairobi and London: the former accounts for the presence of African crafts in the old cottage, which is now her permanent home.

It is tucked away – in a pocket-handkerchief garden – down a lane leading to countryside of great beauty, with lovely walks; fine coast is only a mile away.

The friendly sitting-room is a place of books and watercolours, lead-paned windows and comfortable sofas or chairs. Breakfast is served in the big, cork-floored kitchen warmed by a stove (you can buy jars of Mary's home-made jams). She produces, in the winter, imaginative dinners with many dishes based on traditional local recipes and produce – for instance, Martlemas (or Michaelmas) beef, which is marinaded in wine and vinegar then rubbed with spices before being baked. Before this might come Dorset pâté or a soup; and after it blueberry pie or buttered oranges. Or you eat well at the nearby Smugglers' Inn.

Readers' comments: Superb; delightful haven of peace; a marvellous hostess. One of the best meals we have ever sampled. A lovely welcome. Breakfast was excellent. A wonderful person. So comfy; Mary so full of helpful info.

By the seashore is **THE CREEK** at Ringstead. A rambling house, built in the 1920s and later extended, it is the home of Michael and Freda Fisher, retired headmaster and headmistress. Portraits of their ancestors line the walls of this elegantly furnished house, which has quite stunning views across open sea. In summer you can swim in the heated pool, or walk through the garden and down onto the beach for a dip, or take a coastal walk as far as Swanage. Bedrooms are small and neat; one has attractive flower studies on its walls. Freda was a professional cook, so expect interesting dinner

menus (by arrangement). (The Creek is reached by a toll road but guests do not pay.) £17.50 (b & b).
Readers' comments: Delightful. A natural hostess. Will return again. Friendly and interesting people. Cooking most excellent. [Tel: 01305 852251; postcode: DT2 8NG]

19

BEEHIVE MANOR

C(12) **PT**

Cox Green Lane, Maidenhead, Berkshire, SL6 3ET   Tel: 01628 20980
South of Maidenhead. Nearest main road: A4 from Maidenhead to Reading
(and M4, junction 9).

3 Bedrooms. £19–£28.50. All have own bath/shower/toilet. Views of garden. No smoking.
Light suppers by arrangement.
1 Sitting-room. With open fire, central heating, TV. No smoking.
Small garden

An exceptional mediaeval building – from the strange, carved heads at the front door to the beautiful stone roses around the fireplace of the long sitting-room, from linenfold panelling to stained-glass panels (dated 1560) of ships and coats-of-arms. Low ceilings have chamfered beams, lattice-paned windows open onto a garden where paths wind among camellias, ceanothus, wisteria and a multitude of other flowers.

More linenfold woodwork and a fireplace of carved stone are in the dining-room (where breakfasts are served at a great refectory table); while upstairs every bedroom door has a different wrought-iron latch. One has 'ropework' ceiling-beams; another, pine panelling. All have been attractively furnished (with, for instance, fabric and wall-frieze of yellow peonies). Bathrooms are marble-floored.

The Manor is run by sisters Barbara Barbour and Sue Lemin, who not only are a mine of information about the many sights in the vicinity but may also take visitors to Heathrow Airport (15 minutes away) or the railway (which runs between London and Bath).

Cox Green is very close to Windsor (with castle, and Legoland theme and amusement park for families), Eton, the lovely Savill Gardens, Runnymede (the Kennedy memorial), Hampton Court, Stratfield Saye, the Shire Horse Centre, Bekonscot miniature village, several world-famous racecourses and an excellent theatre-restaurant in the watermill at Sonning.

Terrace at Street Farmhouse (see page 309)

BERE MARSH HOUSE

Shillingstone, Dorset, DT11 0QY   Tel: 01258 861133
North of Blandford Forum. Nearest main road: A350 from Blandford Forum
to Shaftesbury.

2 Bedrooms. £16–£18 (less for 3 nights
mid-week). Prices go up from April. Tea/
coffee facilities. Views of garden, country,
river. Washing machine on request.
Dinner. £12–£17 for 4 courses (with
choices) and coffee, from 7.30pm (not
Sundays and Mondays). Less for 2 courses.
Vegetarian or special diets if ordered. Wine
available. **Light suppers** if ordered.
2 Sitting-rooms. With open fires, central
heating, piano, record-player (TV available).
Bar. Conservatory.
Large garden
Closed in January.

It is the food which brings most visitors here, for in the restaurant James and
Felicity Roe serve gourmet meals. In the past, Felicity used to cook directors'
lunches in London and then worked at the celebrated Peacock Vane hotel on the
Isle of Wight during its heyday.

There's a conservatory (with grapevine) where meals are usually served, and
armchairs surrounding a log stove in the hall of the 18th-century house. In the
garden are a tennis court, summer-house overlooking a rock garden in a dell and
a big vegetable garden. Beyond are far views over good walking country.

As to the meals, the Roes operate a sensible system. Although their repertoire
is very considerable, they let the first party to book dinner choose the menu for
that night, for all comers: that way, they can provide dishes from freshly bought
and cooked ingredients and (there being no waste) at a very reasonable price. So
it pays to make your reservation and study their list of dishes well in advance.
Most dishes are such classics as mushrooms à la grecque, boeuf Stroganoff and
crème brûlée.

There are plenty of good drives around here. For instance, one might go via
Sturminster Newton and Mere (which has a 16th-century inn that was a Royalist
stronghold during the Civil War) to visit the world-famous landscaped gardens
and lake of Stourhead and the 18th-century mansion itself (full of art treasures).
Alternatively, via Shaftesbury (described elsewhere) one could drive to Tollard
Royal on a road of hairpin bends that is an outstanding scenic route with superb
views when you get to the top. Along the way, lynchets can be seen – narrow
terraces constructed on the steep hillsides to make cultivation possible. This is
part of Cranborne Chase, for a thousand years a royal hunting forest: at Tollard
Royal the hunting-lodge of King John has been carefully preserved (the village
church is also worth a visit, particularly for its effigy of a knight in armour; and
also Larmer Grounds park when it is open – there are oriental temples and a
wooden theatre).

Other places of interest in the vicinity include the 15th-century manor house
at Purse Caundle and Sherborne for its golden abbey and two castles.

Readers' comments: Food even better than expected, good and interesting wine
list.

BERRY HALL

Great Walsingham, Norfolk, NR22 6DZ   Tel: 01328 820267
North of Fakenham. Nearest main road: A149 from Sheringham to Wells-next-the-Sea.

5 Bedrooms. £17.50. Some have own bath/shower/toilet. Tea/coffee facilities. TV. Views of garden, country. No smoking.
Dinner. £10 for 3 courses and coffee, at 6.45pm. Non-residents not admitted. Vegetarian or special diets if ordered. No smoking.
1 Sitting-room. With open fire, central heating, TV. No smoking.
Large garden

This is a fine Tudor house in big grounds named after the merchant who built it in 1532. Once Rupert Brooke's family lived here. Now it is the home of Doris Wilson and Joan Sheaf. Many rooms, all very big, have fine panelling; in the hall are a flagstone floor and impressive oak ceiling; Portuguese Delft tiles decorate the dining-room. There is a great balustraded staircase and unusual antiques. Swans glide in the moat; and a peacock parades amongst the rosebeds. For dinner Doris cooks such dishes as watercress soup, lamb noisettes in sherry sauce, and meringues with strawberries.

Readers' comments: Most attractive, comfortable and spacious. Food cooked to perfection. Charming and characterful. Lovely home; spacious room.

Over the **OLD BAKEHOUSE** (33–35 High Street, Little Walsingham), a restaurant renowned for good food, are excellent bedrooms, double-glazed to reduce street noise.

From 1550 until recent times, part of this house was a bakery and the old ovens are still to be seen. Above an ancient cellar bar is a large, lofty dining-room – in the 18th century it was a corn exchange. There is a great brick fireplace at one end, and huge iron-hinged door. Chris and Helen Padley serve such delectable table d'hôte meals as fresh peaches baked with cheese and herbs; banana-stuffed chicken with a mild curry-and-almond sauce; and ice-cream coffee-cake; there is a wider à la carte choice too. £17.50 –£20 (b & b).

Readers' comments: Gourmet food; friendly and efficient. Loving attention to detail; food superb. Food wonderful. Comfortable rooms, friendly and accommodating hosts. Food first class. Took real pains to make us welcome. [Tel: 01328 820454; postcode: NR22 6BZ]

BICKFORD GRANGE   C D S

Bickford, Penkridge, Staffordshire, ST19 5QJ   Tel: 01785 840257
South of Stafford. Nearest main road: A449 from Stafford to Wolverhampton
(and M6, junction 12).

5 **Bedrooms.** £18 (less for 4 nights).
Some have own bath/shower/toilet. Tea/coffee
facilities. Views of garden, country. No
smoking.
Dinner. £10 for 3 courses and coffee, at
times by arrangement. Non-residents not
admitted. Vegetarian or special diets if
ordered. **Light suppers** if ordered.
1 **Sitting-room.** With open fire, central
heating, TV, piano, record-player.
Large garden

Once a farm (hence the huge bell to call fieldworkers in to dinner), this Georgian
house, which was built in 1800, still has a stone-flagged hall but its architectural
features are grander, from a prettily plastered ceiling to the balustraded terrace
overlooking its lawns: glass doors open onto this from the handsome blue sitting-
room. The long dining-room, with mahogany and silver, has views of the fields.
On the second floor is a suite of two double rooms that would be ideal for a
family. Even the single bedroom here is spacious. Outside is a heated swimming-
pool.

Gail Bryant enjoys cooking homely meals.

Lovely countryside surrounds the Grange, and there is much of interest to see
– not only in this county but over the Shropshire border towards Telford and
Ironbridge. Weston Park is one of many stately homes (full of art treasures and
set in a Capability Brown deer park, at its best in azalea time – it was immortal-
ized by P.G. Wodehouse as 'Blandings Castle'); others include Boscobel (Charles
II's refuge) and Shugborough Hall. More places of interest include: Stuart
Crystal, Wedgwood and other potteries, an aerospace museum, many gardens,
ruined abbeys and castles, a working watermill and outside Stafford the continuing excavation of its Norman castle site (20 acres), with an interpretative trail for
visitors.

Readers' comments: Really superb. Beautifully furnished. Beautiful setting, room
spacious and comfortable, food very good, most helpful.

Bedroom at Old Hall (see page 224)

BICKLEIGH COTTAGE HOTEL   C(12) PT S
Bickleigh, Devon, EX16 8RJ   Tel: 01884 855230
South of Tiverton. On A396 from Exeter to Tiverton (near M5, junction 27).

9 Bedrooms. £19.50–£23.50 (less for 7 nights). Most have own bath/shower/toilet. Tea/coffee facilities. Views of garden, country, river.
Dinner. £10.50 for 3 courses and coffee, at 7pm. Non-residents not admitted. Vegetarian dishes if ordered. Wine available. No smoking.
2 Sitting-rooms. With central heating, TV. **Bar.**
Large garden
Closed from November to March.

Built about 1640 and later extended, this very picturesque thatched cottage has been run as a small hotel by the same family for over 60 years. It stands on a busy road by the River Exe, with a foaming weir a few yards downstream: everyone's ideal of a typically Devonian beauty-spot.

The rooms downstairs are full of antiques such as old chests and carved oak chairs, as well as a collection of blue glass and other interesting trifles including articles of Honiton lace made by Mrs Cochrane, which are for sale. The bedrooms are more simply furnished, though one has a four-poster bed. For total quiet, ask for a river-facing room (there are several). Outside is a pretty riverside garden with a fish-pond and a glasshouse containing a collection of cacti and succulents.

Meals are of plain home cooking, a typical menu being smoked mackerel, roast lamb, and pineapple meringue.

A good day's outing via Tiverton (which has a castle) would be along the Exe Valley (visiting opulent Knightshayes Court, lavishly designed by William Burges in 1869 amid beautiful gardens) to Dulverton – old woodlands giving way to open moors as you travel towards Exmoor. In Dulverton are mediaeval lanes and an ancient bridge, tempting shops, a weaver's workshop and Exmoor's interpretation centre. There are good walks in Eggesford Forest on the way to the steep village of Lapford, in the church of which are outstanding Tudor woodcarvings. Crediton's stately church once had cathedral status (built of red sandstone, it has stained-glass windows depicting the life of its patron St Boniface). In the vicinity are other stately homes, such as Fursdon (Fursdons have lived in it from the 13th century to the present day) and Bickleigh Castle which, among other unusual exhibits, has espionage gadgets invented by the original of 'Q' in the James Bond novels. Bickleigh's watermill houses a craft centre. At South Molton (northward) you can see an exhibition of cider-making, and the Quince Honey Farm with bees busily at work. You can also take a trip on horse-drawn canal barges.

Coldharbour Mill, Uffculme, is the permanent home of the New World Tapestry, at 264 feet by 4 feet the biggest embroidery in the world. Mrs Cochrane was one of 200 volunteers who worked on it between 1976 and its first public showing in 1994.

Readers' comments: Delightful. A favourite place. Beautiful position, good meals. Delightful cottage and scenery. Lovely setting, lots of history and charm. Very friendly. Excellent, lovely spot.

BLACKWELL GRANGE

C(10) **M S**

Blackwell, Warwickshire, CV36 4PF   Tel: 01608 682357
South of Stratford-upon-Avon. Nearest main road: A3400 from Stratford
towards Oxford (and M40, junctions 11/12).

3 Bedrooms. £18–£25 **to readers of this
book** (less for 5 nights). Prices go up from
May. All have own bath/toilet. Tea/coffee
facilities. Views of garden, country. No
smoking. Washing machine on request.
Dinner. £15.50 for 3 courses (with choices)
and coffee, at times to suit guests. Less
for 2 courses. Non-residents not admitted.
Vegetarian or special diets if ordered. No
smoking. **Light suppers** if ordered.
1 Sitting-room. With open fire, central
heating, TV.
Large garden

Stone-flagged floors and deep-set windows with chamfered mullions give this
Cotswold house great character – but the Vernon-Millers had a tremendous
task to give it modern comfort too. Liz has decorated the rooms with style –
beribboned curtains in a shell-pink bedroom, for instance; fabric patterned with
peonies and lilac; comfortable armchairs; very nice bathrooms. An en suite,
ground-floor bedroom, overlooking the garden, has been specifically designed for
disabled guests.

Many of the walls are decorated with old sporting prints, and an inglenook
fireplace is the setting for a collection of country bygones and Victorian kitchen
tools. Dinner, by candlelight, could consist of such dishes as home-made pâté,
game, damson ice cream (served with a platter of meringues), and cheeses. Self-
catering guests may eat in the house.

Outside is a thatched barn, usually crammed full of hay for the thoroughbred
horses and pedigree sheep, and among the staddlestones (rick-stones) of the
garden strut the miniature Wyandottes which provide breakfast eggs.

Stratford-upon-Avon and Warwick are a few miles away; and the famous
villages (Broadway, Chipping Campden, etc.) and gardens of the Cotswolds.

Readers' comments: Outstanding accommodation and warmth of hospitality. Most
charming hostess. Kind and attentive.

Bedroom at Northleigh House (see page 216)

BOLEBROKE WATERMILL   C(7)
Edenbridge Road, Hartfield, East Sussex, TN7 4JP   Tel: 01892 770425
South-east of East Grinstead. Nearest main road: A264 from East Grinstead
to Tunbridge Wells.

5 **Bedrooms.** £18–£35 (less 10% for 3
nights to readers of this book only).
Prices go up from April. All have own
bath/shower/toilet. Tea/coffee facilities. TV.
Views of millpond, country, garden. No
smoking. Washing machine on request.
Light suppers if ordered. Vegetarian or
special diets. No smoking.
2 **Sitting-rooms.** With central heating. No
smoking.
Large grounds
Closed from December to February.

Remember Pooh-sticks?. The river that carried Pooh's sticks away is near the
millstream that powered the wheel of this ancient mill, first recorded in
Domesday Book. More recently, it appeared in the film, 'Carrington'.

Visitors here have the choice of staying in either the white weatherboarded
watermill or the Elizabethan miller's barn. With just two bedrooms and a large
sitting-room in each building, guests are assured of seclusion in rustic surroundings. If you stay in the mill, however, you will need to be nimble, for when David
Cooper restored it he was careful to retain every original feature that he could –
steep and narrow stairs to each bedroom, bathrooms tucked into what were once
the big corn-bins, for instance. In the large sitting-room there are still millstones,
the grain-hopper and overhead gear-wheels to be seen from the comfort of large
armchairs or the bed that folds down from a wall. The bedrooms above are white
and airy, with skylights; dried flowers hang from the rafters. For meals, guests
descend through a hatch into the adjoining house.

For the less agile (and not too tall), the barn has a very pretty ground-floor
bedroom and an upstairs 'hayloft' room with a four-poster.

In the evening, a light supper may include toasted or club sandwiches (vegetarian if required), home-made cake, fruit and Sussex cheeses.

Readers' comments: Food beautifully cooked and served. Friendliest welcome,
service excellent. Beautiful room.

The addresses of houses are geographically correct but postal
addresses sometimes differ (for correspondence, the only essential
element is the postcode).

Information about the nearest town and 'A' road helps you to
locate the whereabouts of any village on a map; but before setting
off it is necessary to get precise instructions from your host as
many houses are very much 'off the beaten track'.

BOSWEDDEN HOUSE HOTEL   C D S
Cape Cornwall, St Just, Cornwall, TR19 7NJ   Tel: 01736 788733
West of Penzance. Nearest main road: A3071 from Penzance to St Just.

8 Bedrooms. £18 (less for 7 nights). All have own toilet; most have own shower. Views of garden, country, sea (or, from one, carpark).
Light suppers. Wine available.
1 Sitting-room. With open fire, central heating, TV. Piano. **Bar.**
Large garden
Closed from December to February.

Once the mansion of an 18th-century mine-owner, this house is kept immaculate by Mary Stokes and Sheila Bond, from the bedrooms (some overlooking the distant sea) to the sitting-room and dining-room, both with big windows to make the most of the sunny views. There is double-glazing as well as a log fire for winter comfort. An indoor swimming-pool is available at certain hours.

This far part of Cornwall is so different from the rest of England that it feels like another country (it has much in common with Brittany): wild, ancient, beautiful and mysterious. Land's End is only a few miles away, also the cliffside Minack Theatre, coastal beauty-spots between fishing villages like Mousehole and such sandy coves as Lamorna on the south side of the peninsula.

Northward one passes Botallack and an area peppered with disused tin mines ('Poldark' country). Gurnard's Head, Morvah and Sennen Cove are all interesting places – particularly the last, with its silvery sands and view back to Cape Cornwall.

Along the lanes are high banks gay with pink campion and herb Robert, celandines, violets or wild garlic flowers – even the occasional palm tree to contrast with tiny streams among ferns and homely cottage-gardens. That is Cornwall's prettier face, but it can be wild and dramatic too, with barren granite rocks looming over bleak moors, or Atlantic gales whipping the sea into a boiling cauldron and contorting gorse permanently into witch-like shapes: between this coast and America there is nothing but 3000 miles of pounding ocean.

For prehistoric remains go inland. For walks with magnificent views, follow stretches of the coastal footpath that goes all round Cornwall (or take buses all the way round).

Readers' comments: Very high standard. Nothing too much trouble. Perfect hotel and surroundings. Excellent accommodation. Like being with friends at home.

BOUCHERS FARMHOUSE

Bentham, Gloucestershire, GL51 5TZ   Tel: 01452 862373
South-west of Cheltenham. Nearest main road: A46 from Cheltenham to
Stroud (and M5, junction 11).

2 Bedrooms. £13.50. Price goes up
from April. Views of garden, country. No
smoking.
1 Sitting-room. With open fire, central
heating. TV. No smoking.
Large garden

Previously a farm, Bouchers is still surrounded by hayfields just beyond the
garden, where rock doves fly across the lawns to a graceful weeping willow. A
sundial on one wall declares the date of the house, 1661, and of the old cider-
house which is now Bruce's workshop.

Inside all is immaculate and very comfortable, and you will get a warm
welcome from Anne Daniels as you step through the front door straight into the
big U-shaped living-room. Here velvet armchairs are grouped round the hearth
where an open fire crackles in winter, and a grandfather clock ticks the time away.
Round the other side of the U is the dining-room, for breakfast only (visitors eat
other meals at local inns or at one of the many restaurants in Cheltenham).

Bentham, on the edge of the Cotswolds, is close to the route south to Bath.
Gloucester with its cathedral, historic Cirencester (don't miss the Roman
museum), Tewkesbury and the Forest of Dean are all within easy reach, as are
Prinknash Abbey and the Wye Valley. Also in the area are Slimbridge Wildfowl
Trust, Westonbirt Arboretum and Badminton House (a Palladian mansion,
where the Queen is often seen at the spring horse trials).

Cheltenham's Regency houses date from its heyday as a fashionable spa. The
town needs repeated visits to see everything. Racegoers throng here at Gold Cup
time; others come for various arts festivals.

Readers' comments: Service excellent – the sort for which you would expect to pay
double the price. Will go there again. Very satisfied. Excellent value. Wonderful
hosts, fantastic setting. Did everything possible for us.

South of Cheltenham lies the hamlet of
Cowley and 19th-century **MANOR
BARN**, cleverly converted into a home
by Linda and Andrew Roff. Bedrooms,
in white and pink with pine doors and
some brass bedsteads, are light and
airy. The sitting-room, with open fire,
and dining-room are on a split level,
with a charming gallery above to watch
the sun setting in the valley below.
Light suppers only. (No smoking.)

£16.50–£19. [Tel: 01242 870229;
postcode: GL53 9NN]

BOWER LODGE
C(6) D PT S

Well Lane, Repton, Derbyshire, DE65 6DR   Tel: 01283 702245
South-west of Derby. Nearest main road: A38 from Derby to Burton-upon-Trent (and M1, junction 24).

6 Bedrooms. £18–£30. Some have own bath/shower/toilet. Tea/coffee facilities. TV. Views of garden, country. Washing machine on request.
Dinner. £15 for 4 courses and coffee, when required. Non-residents not admitted. Vegetarian or special diets if ordered. Wine available. **Light suppers** if ordered.
1 Sitting-room. With open fire, central heating, TV.
Large garden

Mercian kings made Repton their capital over a thousand years ago and, by the River Trent, they built an abbey, in the handsome crypt of which (open to view) they were buried. Despite Viking and Cromwellian depredations, the ancient church is well worth a detour. All down the High Street are scores of historic stone buildings, many now used by Repton's public school; and at the end is this lane of large houses in wooded grounds (one by Lutyens).

Rooms here are spacious and handsome, elegantly furnished by Elizabeth Plant. In one pretty sitting-room with Corinthian pillars she has used chinoiserie fabrics and festoon blinds, with old china and good paintings around; in another, leafy fabrics contrast with coffee-coloured walls, French doors opening onto a terrace. The dining-room has pretty china and placemats (the separate breakfast-room can be used by any visitors who prefer to eat on their own). Here Elizabeth – who does outside catering too – serves such meals as melon, coq-au-vin, brandy ice cream with fruit sauce, and cheese (vegetables come from the garden). Sunday lunch is available.

Bedrooms (some on the second floor) are well furnished and, in some cases, have views of fine trees and the lily-pond.

The area abounds with stately homes; there are lovely reservoirs and canals for boat trips, and good walks. For overseas visitors, two airports are conveniently near.

William the Conqueror gave land near Ashbourne to the Shirley family, who still own much of it (they forfeited the rest as a result of siding with Cromwell in the Civil War). It includes the pretty village of Shirley and **SHIRLEY HALL** in Derby Lane where the Fosters now farm. In a richly panelled Tudor sitting-room, the family's elaborate coat-of-arms has survived the centuries. Some bedrooms (two are en suite) have huge mahogany furniture, exposed timbers and board doors, and views of the sweeping lawns, beyond which lies a pond with tench and carp. Sylvia does light suppers only. The house is close to Edmaston Manor, built by Lutyens, with a notable garden to visit. £16–£19. [Tel: 01335 360346; postcode: DE6 3AS]

BRADFORD OLD WINDMILL

4 Masons Lane, Bradford-on-Avon, Wiltshire, BA15 1QN
Tel: 01225 866842
East of Bath. Nearest main road: A363 from Bath to Trowbridge (and M4, junction 17).

4 **Bedrooms.** £18 **(one room for readers of this book only)**–£35. Less for 3 nights. Prices go up from April. Most have own bath/shower/toilet. Tea/coffee facilities. TV. Views of garden, country. No smoking. Washing machine on request.
Dinner. £19 for 3 vegetarian courses and coffee, at 8pm (on Monday, Thursday and Saturday only). Non-residents not admitted. Special diets if ordered. No smoking. **Light suppers** if ordered.
1 **Sitting-room.** With central heating. No smoking.
Small garden
Closed from December to February.

The Napoleonic wars brought prosperity to this area (where cloth for uniforms was woven) but with peace came depression. As a result, the baker who in 1807 had built a windmill here went broke. In 1817 the mill ceased to function, and its sails and machinery were removed. Today its stump is simply a very unusual stone house, perched on a hillside within picturesque Bradford-on-Avon. From it there is a view full of interest, overlooking a higgledy-piggledy array of old roofs.

It is now in the imaginative care of Peter and Priscilla Roberts, a much-travelled couple (engineer and teacher) who have brought back finds from the Far East, New Zealand, Tahiti and Australia which now decorate the rooms – as do pictures and mementoes of their other enthusiasms, from canal boats to whales.

Every room has its own character and shape: some are circular. In the sitting-room, William Morris sofas and furniture of stripped pine face a log fire and there are maps on the walls. One bedroom (with the best roofscape view of all, through a pair of deep-set pointed windows) has a circular bed with a spread patterned with wildflowers and butterflies. In another, there are windmill pictures, arrangements of dried flowers and tea things laid out on top of an old barrel. Draped Tahitian fabrics contrast with pieces of driftwood, and there is even a water-bed covered with a patchwork bedspread.

Their cooking, too, is eclectic (even breakfasts are imaginative with such options as hash browns, muffins or croissants, and home-made yogurts). Meals range from wholesome 'soup trays' (with cheese and apple juice too) to an occasional Thai meal which may include eggs in a spicy coconut sauce; fresh green or purple broccoli stir-fried in sesame oil and spiced with ginger; bananas baked in citrus juices and honey, garnished with toasted almonds. Less exotic dinners are normally available too, but all evening meals must be booked in advance.

There is a tiny, Victorian-style garden around the foot of the mill stump and from it one gets a good view of Bradford's notable buildings – a panorama that includes a colossal 14th-century tithe barn, river bridge with one-cell prison actually on it, and an 18th-century cloth mill.

Readers' comments: Everything you could want. Very friendly, I thoroughly enjoyed my visit.

BRADLE FARM
Church Knowle, Dorset, BH20 5NU   Tel: 01929 480712
South of Wareham. Nearest main road: A351 from Wareham to Swanage.

3 Bedrooms. £18–£19 (less for 7 nights). Bargain breaks. All have own bath/shower/toilet. TV. Views of country. Washing machine on request.
Light suppers if ordered.
1 Sitting-room. With open fire, central heating, TV, record-player.
Large garden

From this handsome Victorian house of local Purbeck stone there are beautiful views – across the duckpond – of the so-called Isle of Purbeck and of the gaunt ruins of Corfe Castle looming over all. Window-seats at the shuttered casements help you to make the most of these, with unlimited help-yourself tea and home-made cake in hand. Upstairs, low corridors lead to bedrooms (one is particularly spacious) with similar views.

Holes have lived here for generations, with what is now 1400 acres of their mixed farm (cows, sheep, corn) stretching right down to the sea and up to high Swyre Head. The long coastal footpath goes through their land: you can watch milking and lambing or help feed the chickens . . . or just laze by the log fire.

Although Gillian sometimes provides guests with snack suppers, she has an arrangement with the thatched New Inn to give her visitors a discount on their good Dorset meals – it has a skittle alley too.

The coast is only 1½ miles from the house, with beautiful walks there and inland too. Sandy beaches alternate with shingle and rock pools. There are varied museums as well as interesting sights in Poole, on Brownsea Island and at Lulworth Cove, with the resort of Bournemouth only a half-hour drive away.

Readers' comments: Superb. Welcoming hospitality.

Just outside Church Knowle (at Bucknowle) is **BUCKNOWLE HOUSE,** an imposing Victorian dwelling of Purbeck 'marble'. A black-and-white tiled hallway leads one up a broad staircase, with intricately carved balustrade and galleried landing, to spacious bedrooms decorated in bold colours. One double, in bottle green and blue with modern tartan curtains, has a lovely view of Corfe Castle. Another, in pale terracotta, has an attractive carved bedhead. Dinner (by arrangement) is served in the elegant blue-and-gold dining-room, walls hung with old prints, and, at one end, a grand overmantel mirror. Afterwards guests can relax by the fire in the sit-

ting-room, where family portraits and mirrored wall-sconces decorate the walls. Sara Harvey (Prue Leith trained) and her husband Richard (a Master of Wine) can provide French-based cooking to a high standard. There is a tennis court sometimes available to guests. £20–£25. [Tel: 01929 480352; postcode: BH20 5PQ]

BRAMLEY COTTAGE   C(5) M PT S
Sutton Road, Wisbech, Cambridgeshire, PE13 5DU   Tel: 01945 463132
North of Wisbech. On the A1101 from Wisbech towards Boston.

rear view

2 Bedrooms. £15 (less for 3 nights or continental breakfast). Bargain breaks. Both have own bath/shower/toilet. Tea/coffee facilities. TV. Views of garden, country. No smoking. Washing machine on request. **Light suppers** if ordered.
Garden

In Fenland, willows fringe roads, wildflowers throng verges, clear blue skies shed a unique light over vast fields of grain or vegetables that sweep to the horizon. Many of the fields have sunk below road level since Dutch engineers in the 17th century drained the watery fens to dry out into some of England's most fertile land. Produce was (and is) brought into Wisbech, making it a prosperous little town with fine Georgian houses flanking each side of the River Nene.

Just outside it, on the main road into Lincolnshire, stands little Bramley Cottage (and Bramley apples do still grow in its garden). Small rooms, homely in style as befits a Victorian farm cottage (one is on the ground floor), are kept immaculate by Audrey O'Donnell – a very caring hostess, who also runs an antique shop in Wisbech. The big attraction of staying here is the colourful garden, created from an overgrown jungle, which is beautifully laid out around a pool with cascade. It provides fresh salads for the light suppers occasionally available, and an attractive view from the conservatory sitting-room. There's a barbecue in the garden, and the long Nene Way footpath is close by.

Wisbech is worth a lingering visit for its historic buildings, which include handsome Peckover House (NT) and, facing it across the river, the birthplace museum of Octavia Hill – not only co-founder of the National Trust but pioneer of the first movement to replace city slums with good housing. There is a superb rose festival every June.

It is also ideally placed to visit Norfolk (mediaeval King's Lynn, the heritage coastline, Sandringham, glorious churches and many fine mansions), Lincoln for the cathedral, Spalding for tulip-fields and the spring flower parade, and Cambridgeshire (Cambridge University, stately homes, Wicken Fen – preserved by the NT to show how the wetlands were before drainage ended the rich wildlife habitats).

This is a great area for painting and photography (because of the light); and for gardeners, likely to return home laden with lavender bushes, African violets and much else grown here.

Houses which accept the discount vouchers on page ii are marked with a V on the lists at the beginning of this book, see pages xi–xix and pages xxi–xxii.

BRATTLE HOUSE
C(12)

Watermill Bridges, Tenterden, Kent, TN30 6UL Tel: 01580 763565

Nearest main road: A28 from Ashford to Hastings.

side view

3 Bedrooms. £18.75–£28 (less for 4 nights). All have own shower/toilet. Tea/coffee facilities. Views of garden, country. No smoking. Washing machine on request.
Dinner. £17 for 4 courses and coffee, at 7.30pm. Less for 2 courses. Non-residents not admitted. Vegetarian or special diets if ordered. No smoking. **Light suppers** if ordered.
1 Sitting-room. With central heating. No smoking.
Large garden

Reputedly this was once the home of Horatia, illegitimate but much-loved daughter of Nelson and Lady Hamilton, who was only five when Nelson died. Now it is surrounded by 11 acres of garden, meadow and woodland.

The tile-hung house (parts of which date back to the 17th century) has great dignity – white marble fireplace from the 18th century; wide, panelled doors with handsome brass fittings; bay windows with leaded casements. The Rawlinsons are a painter and calligrapher, and their work hangs on the walls. They have furnished the rooms in suitable style with, for instance, a pale thick carpet contrasting with a dusky pink wallcovering in the dining-room, and many pot-plants everywhere.

Bedrooms are equally handsome. There are two very large rooms at the front with window-seats, brick hearths and draped bedheads. From these, one can enjoy a view of the church where Horatia's husband was vicar, and of the steam train which occasionally puffs by: a scene at its most lovely when the sun goes down. Another is all roses and cream, with a little black iron grate, sloping floors, and an old brick chimney thrusting up through its bathroom.

Breakfast and tea are served in a conservatory off the sitting-room, which is in the oldest part of the house.

Although the Rawlinsons are themselves vegetarian, Maureen cooks such evening meals as sweet-sour cucumber, lamb with apricots and almonds, and chocolate roulade. They usually dine with their guests.

Readers' comments: Excellent service. Tasty and imaginative food. Elegant, gracious house in beautiful countryside. Delightful couple. Enjoyed every minute. So nicely furnished. Dinner up to Michelin-star standard. Absolutely beautiful. No amenity they do not extend. Food gourmet. Outstanding accommodation and service.

To help those en route to the continent, via tunnel or ferry, Kent County Council has produced an excellent booklet with map, called *Off the Motorway,* which will tempt you to tack on a day or so (going or coming) to explore any of 139 attractive places to visit in this beautiful and historic county.

BROADSTONE BARN

BROADSTONE BARN C(12) **D S**
Lower Walditch Lane, Walditch, Dorset, DT6 4LA   Tel: 01308 427430
East of Bridport. Nearest main road: A35 from Bridport to Dorchester.

3 Bedrooms. £18.50–£20. Some have own bath/shower/toilet. Tea/coffee facilities. Views of garden. No smoking. Washing machine on request.
1 Sitting-room. With log stove, central heating, TV.
Closed in January and February.

A fine old barn of golden stone was most handsomely converted, with its original character carefully retained, to make this beautiful house. Rugged stone walls and slate floors contrast with a splendid open-tread spiral staircase with a rope handrail. Val and Guy Barnes have grouped bamboo sofas round the stove in a big room with glass doors on both sides. In the dining-room, a particularly impressive pine table and fiddleback chairs stand under old rafters still exposed to view and a new gallery where there are wicker armchairs. Adjoining this gallery are attractive bedrooms (one has windows on three sides); one of the bathrooms is particularly elegant, its tiles patterned with cornstalks. Outdoors is an area chequered with cobbles and paving around a raised, circular lily-pool; a lawn with seats; and a vegetable garden frequented by badgers.

At breakfast, not only marmalade and bread are home-made but yogurt too; and black pudding is among the choices on offer. There is unlimited tea and coffee available in the sitting-room at all times.

Dorset is a wonderful county for walkers, particularly along the nearby coast, while those who want to explore it on wheels can hire mountain bicycles at the house.

The great iron waterwheel at **MILL FARM**, Powerstock, ceased to turn long ago but the wandering stream still goes by the old farmhouse in its secluded valley, so sheltered that palms grow there. It can be reached by a dramatic drive over Eggardon Hill (the 'Egdon Heath' of Hardy and Holst) and along lanes where celandines and bluebells throng the banks. The sea is only five miles away. This is a truly traditional farm: board ceilings, tiled floors, dresser with blue-and-white china, coal fire and the slow tick of a grandfather clock – with the landowner's ducal coat-of-arms on one wall. There are cows, chickens and ducks around; and for dinner Elaine

Marsh serves a proper farm meal – soup, a roast, fruit salad, and cheeses. £17.50 (b & b).
Readers' comments: A lovely farm. Pretty and spotless bedrooms. Warm welcome, delicious breakfast, hope to go back. [Tel: 01308 485213; postcode: DT6 3SL]

For explanation of code letters (C, D, M, PT, S, X) see inside front cover.

BROOKFIELD FARM HOTEL   C D M X
Winterpit Lane, Plummers Plain, West Sussex, RH13 6LU
Tel: 01403 891568

South-east of Horsham. Nearest main road: A281 from Horsham to Brighton (and M23, junction 11).

rear view

25 Bedrooms. £20–£26. All have own bath or shower and toilet. Tea/coffee facilities. TV. Views of garden, country, lake. Washing machine on request.
Dinner. A la carte, at 6.30–9pm. Vegetarian or special diets if ordered. Wine available. **Bar snacks.**
1 Sitting-room. With open fire, central heating, TV, video, record-player. **Bar.**
Large garden

Over the years, John Christian has added to and improved his farmhouse extensively, creating a busy, small hotel (his sons farm the surrounding land). Apart from the well-equipped bedrooms, some small and two on the ground floor, and the comfortable sitting-room with its open fire and array of brass and copper, there are now several dining areas, a bar opening out to the garden, a billiards room, a sauna and small gym, fishing and a big play area at one side for children – who can also enjoy paddle-boats on the lake and riding the donkeys. There is a seven-hole golf course and golf-driving range, and a minibus for escorted tours.

Manager Carol and her chefs set high standards of home-style cooking – one might enjoy a filling soup with home-cured ham in it, a really good steak pie, or a beautifully presented and copious prawn cocktail.

Travellers using Gatwick appreciate the convenience (and economy) of parking their car at Brookfield while away; and, no matter how early or late their flight, the Brookfield minibus takes them to or from the airport. Honeymooners like the four-poster suite with Jacuzzi.

Readers' comments: Cheerful surroundings, friendly hospitality.

An elegant Victorian house, **WEST-LANDS** on Brighton Road at Monk's Gate, Horsham, has been very well furnished by Kathleen Ticktum, with much emphasis on light colours and complete comfort. There is a very lovely flower garden with terrace and lily-pool (floodlit at night). A good choice for anyone who values peace, though the main road can be busy. Only light snacks provided: there are nearby inns for meals. No smoking. Parking (and taxi-service) for visitors flying from Gatwick. £20–£22.

Readers' comments: Immaculate. Friendly. Most outstanding accommodation. Warm hospitality. The perfect b & b – a bit special. [Tel: 01403 891383; postcode: RH13 6JD]

35

BROOKLAND

Peacock Lane, Middle Tysoe, Warwickshire, CV35 0SG Tel: 01295 680202
South-east of Stratford-upon-Avon. Nearest main road: A422 from
Stratford-upon-Avon to Banbury.

3 Bedrooms. £17 (less for 3 nights).
Tea/coffee facilities. Views of garden,
country. No smoking. Washing machine on
request.
Dinner (if ordered in advance). £11.50 for
3 courses and coffee, at 6.30pm. Non-
residents not admitted. Vegetarian or
special diets if ordered. No smoking. **Light
suppers** if ordered.
1 Sitting-room. With open fire, central
heating, TV, record-player.
Small garden
Closed in January.

The first battle of the Civil War was fought nearby at Edgehill (in 1642, not long
before this cottage was built), a dramatically sharp ridge on the border of
Oxfordshire and a fine car drive today. Charles I narrowly missed a defeat that
could have prevented his army from moving on to London and all the long
struggles which followed until he was beheaded in 1649. It is difficult to imagine
such violent deeds while enjoying this tranquil spot today.

When one visits Brookland, one's first impression is of flowers everywhere,
butterflies thronging the tall yellow spires of verbascum, stone troughs brimming
with colourful blooms. There is a little sun-lounge where one can sit under a vine
to enjoy the morning sunshine, while inside grandfather clocks tick peacefully.
The old stone cottage still retains many of its original features, such as the tinder-
box cupboard built into an inglenook fireplace; and Topsy Trought has furnished
the dining-room with carved, cane chairs in William-and-Mary style.

Topsy makes wedding- and birthday-cakes for local families, but it is Tim who
does the elaborate and colourful decorations of sugar fruit and vegetables. Topsy
says her most popular meal is a peach-and-pineapple starter, gamekeeper's
casserole, and loganberry mousse. A homely and hospitable atmosphere.

As to sightseeing, most visitors head first – of course – for Stratford-upon-
Avon, but Warwick and its castle, Leamington Spa and Coventry are all near.
Tysoe is named after the same Saxon god whose name was given to Tuesday.

Readers' comments: Outstanding. Most beautiful and interesting. Lovely hosts.
Fresh, attractive. Charming hosts. First class. Lovely enjoyable stay.

Bloxham village (Oxfordshire) is a web
of steep and twisting lanes, greens, a
stream, thatch, flowers, old pumps and
richly golden stone walls. **THE
KNOLL**, perched above Little Bridge
Road, is an 18th-century guest-house
in a pretty walled garden, and near
the Oxfordshire cycleway. One room is
particularly pretty, with its mulberry
Laura Ashley decor; and there is a single room. Wendy Woodward serves

only light snacks, but two inns are near.
£17.50–£20. [Tel: 01295 720843;
postcode: OX15 4PU]

36

BROOKSIDE

CDSX

Lustleigh, Bovey Tracey, Devon, TQ13 9TJ   Tel: 01647 277310

North-west of Newton Abbot. Nearest main road: A382 from Bovey Tracey to Moretonhampstead.

rear view

3 Bedrooms. £18 (less for 4 nights). Tea/coffee facilities. Views of garden, country, river. No smoking. Washing machine on request.
Light suppers if ordered.
1 Sitting-room. With central heating, woodstove, TV. No smoking.
Garden

A show village of the Dartmoor National Park, Lustleigh is sometimes crowded with sightseers – but even then Brookside, well tucked away, is peaceful. It looks across its garden to the village cricket field: the visitors' TV room upstairs has a balcony from which one can watch matches being played.

The landscaped garden is raised up on what was once a railway embankment. Round it winds the River Wrey, and one can sit above its waters on the little bridge across which trains once puffed their way. As a backdrop to all this are the high moors where the famous Dartmoor ponies roam free.

One enters Judy Halsey's old house through a combined sitting/breakfast-room, which has a great granite hearth (with woodstove) at one end. A twisting stair rises to bedrooms furnished in simple cottage style. The house was originally a thatched cottage belonging to a 15th-century farm, now the Cleave Inn, which serves good dinners.

This is an excellent area for birdwatching. Mountain bicycles, guided walks and maps are available.

Lustleigh has an ancient history: there are prehistoric remains, King Alfred bequeathed it to his youngest son and its church is in part 13th-century.

Readers' comments: Excellent hospitality, tranquil surroundings. Beautiful views, excellent food.

Also in the Dartmoor National Park is an exceptionally pretty, 450-year-old cottage of white walls and thatch: **CORBYNS BRIMLEY**, Higher Brimley, near Bovey Tracey. It has been attractively furnished by Hazel White in a style that is in keeping with its age. Snack suppers, or visitors may eat at the Toby Jug, Bickington; the Rock Inn, Haytor Vale; or at the Rumbling Tum. £18–£20.
Readers' comments: Superb views, splendid accommodation, caring

proprietors; shall return again and again. [Tel: 01626 833332; postcode: TQ13 9JT]

BROWNHILL HOUSE

Ruyton XI Towns, Shropshire, SY4 1LR   Tel: 01939 260626

South-east of Oswestry. Nearest main road: A5 from Shrewsbury to Oswestry.

CPTSX

3 Bedrooms. £17–£18 (**less to readers of this book** and for 3 nights). Prices go up from April. All have own bath/shower/toilet. Views of garden, country, river. Clothes-washing on request.
Dinner. £10 for 4 courses and coffee, at 6.30pm. Less for 2 courses. Vegetarian or special diets if ordered. **Light suppers** if ordered.
1 Sitting-room. With open fire, central heating, TV, record-player.
Large garden

It is the garden which brings most visitors here. Although when they moved in Roger and Yoland Brown had not the slightest interest in gardening, within a few years the potential of the large, steep site had converted them into enthusiasts and then experts – despite the fact that thin soil and a north-facing aspect were anything but propitious. Brambles, nettles and the remains of a scrapyard had to be cleared, and the slope terraced.

Undaunted by all this, they created an outstanding garden – or, rather, a series of gardens. By the use of steps, paths, walls and banks they have provided a variety of experiences for the visitor – here a paved walk, there wild woodland, 500 different shrubs, 20 kinds of fruit or nut, a vegetable garden with glasshouses. They visit great gardens here and abroad, coming home with new ideas: a Roman garden with pond and gazebo; a Thai miniature garden; a laburnum walk inspired by one at Bodnant; parterres, walks, follies, rock gardens, statuary and a bog garden, all contributing different scenes which unfold as one wanders around. At the foot is the River Perry (free fishing available). Plants are on sale for charity.

As to the house itself, the bedrooms are comfortable but basic; redecorated annually. The beamed sitting-room has a huge stone fireplace. Meals are served in the large farmhouse-style kitchen, and may comprise such things as soup made from the garden's vegetables or salade niçoise, stuffed pork with a crisp crumb coating, and a compote of garden fruit. Breakfasts are exceptional. Fruit juice will be freshly squeezed (from the Browns' own berries or peaches, for example), bread is baked in the village and jams are home-made by Yoland. Pancakes, omelettes and home-made fishcakes are also available.

The curious name of the village has a simple explanation – 11 small settlements were amalgamated in about 1155. Yoland has written a lively book about the history of Ruyton XI Towns, which you can buy. She starts 200 million years ago when the red sandstone was laid down which now gives distinctive character to houses in this area. Here, Normans built a castle, watermills and church; by the 14th century Ruyton had a weekly market (and a court) – no longer, alas; it became involved in the border wars with Wales, 15th century, and the Civil War, 17th century; Conan Doyle worked here as a doctor in 1878.

Readers' comments: Most generous hosts, excellent hospitality. Very warm welcome and a really delicious meal. Wished we could have stayed longer.

BUCKNELL HOUSE

C(12) **D PT**

Bucknell, Shropshire, SY7 0AD   Tel: 01547 530248
West of Ludlow. Nearest main road: A4113 from Ludlow to Knighton.

3 Bedrooms. £17.50–£18.50 (less for 3 nights). Prices go up from April. Bargain breaks. Tea/coffee facilities. TV. Views of garden, country.
Light suppers by arrangement.
1 Sitting-room. With central heating, TV, piano.
Large garden
Closed in December and January.

In the early 18th century, the clergy lived well: this huge and handsome house, honeysuckle and wisteria clambering up its walls, was a vicarage then. The vicar would have approved of the equally handsome way in which Brenda Davies has furnished it – the dining-room with Sheraton chairs and fine wallpaper; the sitting-room with big velvet armchairs, curtains of pale green silk, a large gilt mirror over the Adam fireplace, cream brocade wallpaper and alcoves of china; flowers everywhere. Bedrooms are just as good, with lovely country views towards Wales. All are spacious; one has antique furniture, pretty floral fabrics and wicker armchairs. There are family touches everywhere. Breakfasts here are substantial (the honey is home-produced, marmalade home-made).

The grounds (garden and watermeadows) are secluded, looking across the valley of the River Teme to Wales. There are rosebeds, daffodil drive, shrubbery, croquet lawn, a hard tennis court, shooting, and fishing in the river. The Davieses also keep ducks and geese, horses and hens. The surrounding woodlands and hills are full of wildlife.

Visitors come to this part of the country to enjoy the peace, the birdwatching opportunities and the many good walks there are in the vicinity – across grouse moors and the nearby Welsh and Shropshire hills, along the Elan Valley, and the old coaching road to Devil's Bridge and Aberystwyth, where you may also spot the now-rare red kite. Mediaeval Ludlow – beautifully preserved – is near, and one can follow the 'Black-and-White Trail' of Herefordshire's old villages. Other popular attractions are Powis Castle and the Ironbridge Gorge Museum. Both Brenda and Peter Davies were born in the area (see **Monaughty Poeth**) and their enthusiasm for the countryside around here is infectious. They are happy to advise on the best places to head for and there is a wealth of tourist literature in the house to browse through or buy. Some guests who stayed here were even taken by Peter on a midnight ride to see rabbits by moonlight!

Readers' comments: Wonderfully comfortable bed, breakfast an ample repast, some of the most beautiful countryside in England. Such excellence and outstanding amenities; marvellous people. Pleasant welcome. Warmth and comfort. Delightful couple; nothing was too much trouble. Looked after us splendidly. Could not have been more welcoming. Delightful garden; splendid breakfasts.

When writing to the authors, if you want a reply please enclose a stamped addressed envelope.

39

BUCKYETTE

Littlehempston, Devon, TQ9 6ND   Tel: 01803 762638

North of Totnes. Nearest main road: A381 from Newton Abbot to Totnes.

6 Bedrooms. £17.50. Price goes up from June. All have own bath/shower/toilet. Tea/coffee facilities. Views of garden, country.
Light suppers if ordered.
1 Sitting-room. With open fire, TV, piano.
Garden
Closed from November to February.

The curious name of this house appears in the Domesday Book and is believed to be a Saxon word meaning 'head of spring': the spring is still there, and in use. The present building, made from stone quarried on the farm, dates from 1871. It is on a commanding site with far views, and is furnished with Edwardian pieces suited to the scale of the lofty rooms. In the sitting-room is a log fire for chilly days, and for sunny ones tall French doors open onto a wisteria-hung verandah. The peppermint-pink dining-room has particularly handsome tables, which Roger Miller himself made from timber from the estate, and pictures of theatrical costumes. Bedrooms are not elegant but comfortable. Everything about the house is solid, comfortable, unpretentious, and very English. Children are particularly welcome. There are four good pubs for meals, two of them within a mile.

Littlehempston is well placed for a family holiday because the safe sands of Torbay are so near – as are Paignton's zoo, miniature gardens, a scenic steam railway and river trips. There are plenty of inns, theatres and concerts including those at Dartington's celebrated arts and crafts centres. Totnes, a centre for complementary medicine, has its castle and streets of ancient buildings.

Readers' comments: Amazingly good welcome. Beautifully served food. Very charming lady – I will go again.

Inglenook fireplace in sitting-room at Sampsons Farm Restaurant (see page 286)

BULMER FARM

C(12) **D M PT S X**

Holmbury St Mary, Surrey, RH5 6LG Tel: 01306 730210
South-west of Dorking. Nearest main road: A25 from Dorking to Guildford
(and M25, junction 9).

8 Bedrooms. £18–£20. Some have own
shower/toilet and TV. All have tea/coffee
facilities. Views of garden, country, lake.
Washing machine on request.
1 Sitting-room. With open fire, TV,
record-player.
Large garden

In the folds of Surrey's high North Downs (most of which are so scenic that they
are in National Trust protection) a number of very picturesque villages lie hidden,
and Holmbury is one. Near the centre stands Bulmer Farm, built about 1680.
One steps straight into a large dining-room with gleaming furniture, and through
this to an attractive sitting-room – a room of pink walls and old beams, chairs
covered in cretonne patterned with pink poppies, logs crackling in front of the
cherubs and harps of an old iron fireback in the inglenook. It opens onto the large
garden (with croquet).

Upstairs are pleasant, spacious bedrooms with cottage-style furnishings. Five
additional and very comfortable rooms (with en suite showers) have been created
in outbuildings for guests staying two nights or more.

Outdoors, David Hill will show you the lake he created a few years ago, now a
haven for herons, kingfishers, Canada geese, snipe and other wildfowl: it won a
conservation award.

B & b only, but the area is full of inns offering good meals, such as the Royal
Oak (300 yards away), the Parrot at Forest Green and the Stephen Langton at
Friday Street.

Some tourists find this a good area in which to stay while visiting London –
train day-tickets cost very little, and the journey takes three-quarters of an hour
(from Dorking).

The surrounding area of woodland and hills is one of the finest beauty-spots near
the capital, truly rural, and dotted with footpaths to follow, historic churches and villages with craft shops, trout farms, antiques and the like. Dorking and Guildford
(the latter with castle ruins, river trips and a good theatre) are each well worth a
day's visit. The Royal Horticultural Society's gardens at Wisley are near, too; so are
Leith Hill (walks), Clandon Park and Polesden Lacey (stately homes), and
Hatchlands (NT house with an interesting collection of old musical instruments).
Several fine gardens open to view. Beautiful Shere has monthly antique fairs.

You can go via pleasant lanes to reach Farnham, a largely 18th-century town
at the foot of a mound with castle: the local museum has William Cobbett
memorabilia, while another (at nearby Tilford) has an open-air display of old
agricultural machinery. Birdworld is an exceptionally good park with exotic birds.

Readers' comments: One's every wish is catered for. So warm and friendly. Made
so welcome, made to feel like one of the family. Picturesque, restful. Ultra quiet.
Friendly, helpful owners. Good food. A great time. Very good accommodation
and lovely area. Area wonderful, excellent place to stay to visit London.

BULMER TYE HOUSE   C D S PT X
Bulmer Tye, Essex, CO10 7ED   Tel: 01787 269315
South-west of Sudbury. Nearest main road: A131 from Halstead to Sudbury.

4 Bedrooms. £17.50. Some have own bath/toilet. Views of garden. No smoking. Washing machine on request.
Dinner (only if pre-booked). £10 for 2 or 3 courses and coffee (time by arrangement). Non-residents not admitted. Vegetarian or special diets if ordered. No smoking. **Light suppers** if ordered.
3 Sitting-rooms. With open fires, central heating, TV, piano, record-player. No smoking.
Large garden

One of Gainsborough's most famous paintings is of the Andrews family whom he knew when he lived in Suffolk. It was one of their sons, a parson, who in the 18th century 'modernized' this house, most of which dates back to the reign of Elizabeth I, by putting in huge sash windows and so forth.

Today its old timbers resonate to the sound of music (played by family or guests), for Peter Owen is a maker of very fine clavichords – and much of the interesting furniture seen in the rooms. A hexagonal table with a complex pattern of end-grain triangles is his; so is a throne-like chair of elm, its joints secured with wood pegs only; and also a dolls' house – which is in fact a scale replica of Bulmer Tye House itself.

His wife is an authority on antiques, about which she writes articles and books (under the name of Noël Riley); so not surprisingly there are some unusual period pieces in the house. Instead of using furnishing fabrics with a traditional look, the Owens have contrasted the antiques with strong modern patterns – a Bauhaus design for curtains in one room, an Aztec-style pattern in another, in colours such as tangerine and blue. A Chinese sunshade, inverted, makes an unusual ceiling lightshade. There is a large Bechstein in one of the sitting-rooms and log fires in all three. In one bedroom, with a handsome bed, 19th-century Persian curtains and a Laura Ashley pattern co-exist happily.

The quarry-tiled kitchen is decorated in brilliant primary colours and on one wall screen-printed Spanish tiles give a trompe l'oeil effect. Here guests eat with the family round a huge pine table and are apt to get drawn into family life, including anything from duets to political debates. Garden produce often goes into the making of soups and of fruit puddings; wine, lemonade and elderflower cordial are all home-made and Peter bakes the bread. Some of the dishes guests enjoy most are beef-and-lentil flan, Roman cobbler (pork and mushrooms with a topping of semolina and cheese), fish pie and, for vegetarians in particular, a cheesy bread-and-butter pudding served with stir-fried vegetables. For breakfast, you will be offered home-made muesli, bread and marmalade, as well as free-range eggs (no fry-ups).

The large garden is notable for its fine trees (some are 200 years old) which include copper beeches, walnuts, cedars and yews, as well as a number of unusual plants. There is a grass tennis court.

Readers' comments: Characterful house, beautiful garden, very informal and friendly. Very interesting house, superb garden.

42.

BURLEIGH FARM

Bladon Road, Cassington, Oxfordshire, OX8 1EA Tel: 01865 881352
North-west of Oxford. Nearest main road: A4095 from Chesterton to Witney.

3 **Bedrooms.** £18–£20 (less for 2 nights). Prices may go up in May. Two have own bath/shower/toilet. Tea/coffee facilities. TV. Views of garden, country. No smoking.
Light suppers if ordered.
1 **Sitting-room.** With open fire, central heating, TV, piano. No smoking.
Large garden

In the 18th century, the farming scene was drastically changed by the Enclosure Acts. Not only were villagers no longer allowed to cultivate wide open spaces under the traditional 'strip' system, but there was constant encroachment on their common pastures by the local lord's multiplying flocks of sheep – 'growth industry' of the time. Hedges were planted to enclose fields, and farmhouses were built in remote spots among them, into which villagers moved as tenants of the lord. They then paid rent to farm his fields, each field being as large as one team of oxen could plough in a day.

Burleigh was one such 'enclosure farm' on the great Blenheim estate. It is still owned by the Duke of Marlborough, and farmed by the Cooks, who keep a herd of pedigree Friesian cows.

The stone house combines historic character (stone floors, log fires) with modern comfort. From some bedrooms there are distant glimpses of Oxford's spires and from others of Blenheim Palace, a romantic prospect when the setting sun glints on the far windows. Visitors are welcome to look round the farm and to follow footpaths through its fields to Bladon church, where Churchill is buried. Another footpath, to Wychwood Forest, was Charles I's escape route when he and his men fled unnoticed while the Roundheads kept watch round Oxford. Little Cassington itself is even more historic – Bronze and Iron Age relics have recently been found, and the church is Norman. Its name means 'cress town': there is still cress in the stream which flows into the Thames.

Readers' comments: Very efficient and well furnished. Warm welcome. Most friendly, welcoming, and extremely helpful and knowledgeable about local amenities.

At 17th-century **OLD FARMHOUSE** on Station Hill, Long Hanborough, Vanessa Maundrell serves meals (vegetables come from the garden) in a stone-flagged dining-room with a dresser full of blue Spode china. One of the sitting-rooms has her collection of some 40 pot-lids over the inglenook. Beams, rugged stone walls and deep-set windows with far views are complemented by flowery fabrics, Victorian bedspreads and family treasures. Outside is a pretty cottage-garden with old iron pump among the foxgloves. £18–£19.50.

Readers' comments: Made very welcome. Most comfortable room, excellent breakfast. [Tel: 01993 882097; post-code: OX8 8JZ]

43

BUTTONS GREEN FARM

Cockfield, Suffolk, IP30 0JF   Tel: 01284 828229
South of Bury St Edmunds. Nearest main road: A1141 from Lavenham towards Bury St Edmunds.

3 Bedrooms. £18 (less for 2 nights). Tea/coffee facilities. Views of garden, country. Washing machine on request.
Dinner (by arrangement). £10 for 3 courses and coffee, from 6.30pm. Vegetarian or special diets if ordered. **Light suppers** if ordered.
1 Sitting-room. With open fire, TV.
Large garden
Closed from November to mid-March.

Behind a big duck-pond and masses of roses stands an apricot-coloured house built around 1400, the centre of an 80-acre farm of grain and beet fields. It has mullioned windows and a Tudor fireplace upstairs.

In Margaret Slater's sitting-room, with large sash windows on two sides, a pale carpet and silky wallpaper make a light background to the antiques and velvet armchairs grouped round a big log stove. The dining-room, too, has a log-burning stove in the brick inglenook, and leather-seated chairs are drawn up at a big oak table. Here is where Margaret serves meals with home-grown or home-made produce, her own chutneys and marmalade. Among her most popular starters are egg mayonnaise and home-made pâté. A chicken or other roast may follow and then, for instance, chocolate soufflé or raspberries and cream.

Twisting stairs lead to big beamed bedrooms with sloping floors, which Mrs Slater has furnished with flowery fabrics, pot-plants and good furniture.

The farm is only a few minutes from Lavenham, one of the county's show villages – very beautiful (but, in summer, often very crowded), with a guildhall owned by the National Trust and a spectacular church.

Readers' comments: Lovely house. Charming hosts. Good home cooking. Just perfect. Delightful, friendly, comfortable. Very good value. Good meals. Very nice people. Excellent all round. Simple but good cooking. Very friendly: excellent atmosphere.

Just the other side of Lavenham is Brent Eleigh and Jean Gage's **STREET FARM**, its apricot walls half-timbered, its garden well-groomed. Inside are beamed ceilings and fine furnishings – big velvet armchairs, and Hepplewhite-style chairs in the dining-room, for instance – and a comfortable sitting-room with a log fire. Bedrooms are spacious and immaculate, with good private bathrooms. There are pleasant country and river views. Closed from December to February. £19–£20.
Readers' comments: Very friendly.

Comfortable. Beautifully maintained, very quiet. Best b & b we've had. Everything to make one feel welcome. Beautiful surroundings. [Tel: 01787 247271; postcode: CO10 9NU]

44

CANAL CENTRE   **C D M P T S X**
Hassall Green, Cheshire, CW11 4YB   Tel: 01270 762266
South-west of Congleton. Nearest main road: A534 from Congleton to Crewe
(and M6, junction 17).

6 Bedrooms. £16–£18 (less for continental breakfast). Bargain breaks. Some have own bath/shower/toilet. Tea/coffee facilities. TV. Views of country, canal. Washing machine on request.
Dinner. £11 for 3 courses (with choices) and coffee, from 7pm. Less for 2 courses. Vegetarian or special diets if ordered. Wine available.
1 Sitting-room. With open fire, central heating, TV.
Small garden

The Trent & Mersey Canal (1777) was one of the earliest canals, designed by James Brindley as part of a network uniting the Mersey estuary to the west with the great River Trent in the east. There is an immense flight of 30 locks, known as 'Heartbreak Hill', through which the canal barges were lifted from the plains of Cheshire high up to the vicinity of Stoke-on-Trent; halfway lies pretty little Hassall Green and a complex of 18th-century buildings which once served the boatmen.

Today the former stables and bakery are a shop catering for holiday boats calling in at the marina (it also sells traditionally painted canalware); and adjoining it Ray and Sue Paine have created very attractive bedrooms for visitors, using Laura Ashley fabrics and thick carpets (the ground-floor bedroom is particularly spacious and elegant). Picture-windows in some rooms make the most of canal views beyond a lawn with sunshades where people take tea in summer (in winter, there is a log stove ablaze in the sitting-room).

Evening meals are available in the tea-room; or in an à la carte restaurant by a lock, where one might perhaps select salmon terrine, chicken and sultanas in a creamy sauce of honey and lemon, and a gâteau – all freshly prepared.

All this is within a low hum of the motorway (making the Canal Centre a convenient stopover en route to or from Scotland, for instance), and midway between two outstandingly scenic areas – the Peak District and North Wales. Nearby there are a nature trail and towpath walks (or you can take a narrow-boat trip along the canal), spectacularly sited Beeston Castle which was started in 1225, Stapeley Water Gardens – the world's most outstanding water-gardening centre (glass pavilions, fountains, etc.), Jodrell Bank (planetarium and hands-on experience of astronomy) and Cheshire Farm (try 20 flavours of ice cream, or enjoy a farmhouse cream tea) as well as NT properties and the chance of china bargains in the Potteries. The village is close to Sandbach with its celebrated Saxon remains, Elizabethan market and ox-roast in May, historic half-timbered houses and award-winning floral displays. Every April there is a parade of historic transport which combines with a national town criers' contest and an arts festival.

Prices are per person in a double room at the beginning of the year.

CARNWETHERS

C(7) **D M PT**

Green Lane, Pelistry Bay, St Mary's, Isles of Scilly, TR21 0NX
Tel: 01720 422415

9 Bedrooms. £34–£49 **including dinner** (less for 7 nights). Prices go up in May. Bargain breaks. All have own bath/shower/toilet. Tea/coffee facilities. TV. Views of garden, country, sea.
Dinner. 4 courses (with choices) and coffee, at 6.30pm. Non-residents not admitted. Wine available. No smoking.
2 Sitting-rooms. With open fire, central heating, TV. **Bar.** No smoking.
Large garden
Closed from October to April.

rear view

St Mary's, the principal island in the Scillies, is only three miles long. Even its centre of action, Hugh Town, can hardly be called busy by mainland standards (though it does receive tides of day-visitors during high summer), and so it is easy to find any number of unfrequented coves or beaches close by. Pelistry Bay is one of these – sheltered from wind, calm and unspoilt. Around it are pines and ferns, coastal footpaths and nature trails.

Carnwethers is more than an ordinary guest-house (and a very good one, at that). Its owner is Roy Graham, well known in the island and beyond as an underwater explorer and photographer, and a marine archaeologist – with 30 years in the Navy before he came here. Even non-experts appreciate his library of books on maritime subjects (wrecks, shipping, fish, wildlife, boats) and his immense knowledge of Scillonian history and ecology. His illustrated lectures in St Mary's twice a week should not be missed. He has assembled a number of videos about the islands which he shows to visitors, and can advise on boating or diving.

As to the house itself, this was once a farmhouse, but has been modernized. It is still surrounded by fields. Every room is as neat as a new pin. There is a bar and lengthy list of good-value wines, a heated 30-foot swimming-pool within sight of the sea itself but sheltered by granite walls and flowering shrubs, sauna, games room (for table tennis or pool) and croquet lawn.

Meal times fit in with the times of the buses that take visitors into Hugh Town for slide shows which are usually packed out, concerts and the pubs.

Local produce is much used by the chef for meals: fish (obviously), new potatoes, free-range eggs, home-grown vegetables and home-made marmalade, for example. A typical meal might comprise soup or fruit juice, roast turkey, and roly-poly pudding or fudge cake. Breakfasts include options like haddock and kippers. In the sitting-room, there are pictures of ships and seascapes. Bedrooms are agreeably decorated – one with four-poster; some spacious ones, with armchairs, open onto the very lovely garden.

Diving, boating and fishing can be arranged.

Readers' comments: Happy, friendly atmosphere. Could not ask for more. Nothing is too much trouble. Complete satisfaction.

How to get there: Ferry or helicopter from Penzance; airplane from several west country airports (connecting with flights from Heathrow, etc.).

Essential to book well ahead.

CASTLE FARM   C M X
Fotheringhay, Northamptonshire, PE8 5HZ   Tel: 01832 226200
South-west of Peterborough. Nearest main road: A605 from Peterborough to Oundle.

breaks. All have own bath/shower/toilet. Tea/coffee facilities. TV. Views of garden, country, river. No smoking. Washing machine on request.
Dinner. £10 for 2 courses and coffee, at 7.30pm or by arrangement (not Sundays). Non-residents not admitted. Vegetarian or special diets if ordered. **Light suppers** if ordered.
1 Sitting-room. With open fire, central heating, TV.
Large garden

6 Bedrooms. £17.50–£24 (less for 5 nights). Prices may go up in June. Bargain

In the castle that was once here, Richard III was born. Later, Mary Queen of Scots was, after many similar imprisonments, confined here at the end of her life. After her execution, her heart was secretly buried in the mound on which the castle stood: part of the land belonging to Castle Farm today. The thistles that grow here are called Queen Mary's Tears.

At the Victorian farm, one steps straight into Stephanie Gould's huge quarry-tiled kitchen where a pine staircase rises to spacious bedrooms that are spick-and-span, all with good views (one of them looks onto the farmyard in one direction and to the ancient church in the other). There are very good bath- or shower-rooms, and much stripped pine. The big, comfortable sitting-room, too, has a view to enjoy – of the swift River Nene beyond the lawn, and a picturesque bridge. The Goulds have converted outbuildings to make more bedrooms.

Stephanie produces traditional meals of two courses (such as lamb navarin with three or four vegetables including, for instance, home-grown asparagus, followed by sticky pear-gingerbread) or one can eat well at the nearby Falcon Inn.

Fotheringhay church is particularly fine, and contains interesting tombs. To the south is Oundle, famous for its public school (a delightful little town within a loop of the river, on which you can go boating).

Readers' comments: Very relaxed. Good breakfast. Lovely view. Beautifully furnished. Excellent room. Friendly young hostess. Could not have been more hospitable. Rooms excellent and very up-market. Excellent facilities.

Just west of Oundle is the hamlet of Stoke Doyle and a quintessential English inn, the **SHUCKBURGH ARMS.** But to its unspoiled 17th-century character, Paul Kirkby has added the comfort of cherry velvet chesterfields and panelled walls in the bar, where logs blaze in a stone inglenook. Food (in bar or restaurant) is excellent, there are real ales to sample, and the mulberry-and-white en suite bedrooms are not only of the

highest standard but well segregated from the inn by a garden. £20. [Tel: 01832 272339; postcode: PE8 5TG]

47

CASTLE HOUSE   **C D PT S X**

23 Castle Street, Chester, Cheshire, CH1 2DS   Tel: 01244 350354

Nearest main road: A483 from Wrexham to Chester (and M56, junction 16).

5 Bedrooms. £20 to readers of this book only. Sunday half-price if part of 3-night booking, October to March. Some have own bath/shower/toilet. Tea/coffee facilities. TV. Washing machine on request.
1 Sitting-room. With open fire, central heating.
Small garden

Right in the middle of the city but in a quiet by-road, this interesting house has a breakfast-room which dates from 1540 behind an 18th-century frontage and stair-case. The arms of Elizabeth I (with English lion and Welsh dragon) are over the fireplace. It is both the Marls' own home and a guest-house with modern bed-rooms that are exceptionally well furnished and equipped. Bed-and-breakfast only, for Chester has so many good restaurants; but visitors are welcome to use the kitchen. Newspapers and local phone calls are free. Coyle Marl, a local businessman, is an enthusiast for Chester and loves to tell visitors about its lesser-known charms.

The city is, of course, of outstanding interest – second only to Bath and York in what there is to see. It is surrounded by ancient walls of red sandstone, just outside which is a large Roman amphitheatre. The most unusual feature, however, is the Rows: here, steps from street level lead up to balustraded galleries overhanging the pavements, serving a second level of small shops above the ones below. Chester's cathedral of red stone dates back to the 14th century and the city's zoo is outstanding.

Readers' comments: Welcoming. Breakfasts absolutely first class. Excellent room and hospitality. Delightful hosts. So welcoming and friendly. Delightful, pretty room. Breakfast a delight. First class. Exceptionally good host. Liked it immensely. Very atmospheric, nice people. Comfortable room, helpful hosts.

MITCHELL'S (28 Hough Green) is on the road out of Chester which leads to Mold, in Wales: a handsome house of 1856 with large windows and fine, high-ceilinged rooms which Helen Mitchell has furnished in period: but-toned velvet chairs, old clocks, even a Victorian baby-chair and sewing-machine. Some rooms have a leafy outlook and there is a lily-pool cascade that is lit up at night. There is parking space (an asset in Chester), with buses to the centre passing outside. One bed-

room (en suite) is on the ground floor. £19–£20. [Tel: 01244 679004; post-code: CH4 8LQ]

CATHEDRAL GATE HOTEL   C D PT X
36 Burgate, Canterbury, Kent, CT1 2HA   Tel: 01227 464381
(M2, junction 7, is near.)

24 Bedrooms. £20–£35. Full breakfast extra from March. Prices go up from April. Bargain breaks. Some have own bath/shower/toilet. Tea/coffee facilities. TV. Telephone. Views of cathedral (some). Washing machine on request.
Dinner. About £13 for 3 courses, at 7–9pm. Less for fewer courses. Non-residents not admitted. Vegetarian or special diets if ordered. Wine available. No smoking. **Light suppers.**
2 Sitting-rooms. With central heating. Bar.

The cathedral has a great, sculpted, mediaeval gateway. Tucked beside it is a row of shops and restaurants, above part of which is this upstairs guest-house (which has direct access to the cathedral precincts), not luxurious but characterful.

Even in Saxon times there was some kind of hospice here; and when the martyrdom of Thomas Becket in 1170 began to bring pilgrims to Canterbury in their thousands, it was in these beamy rooms that many of them stayed.

The bedrooms are reached via a maze of narrow corridors and creaking stairways which twist this way and that. All are quiet (for Burgate is now semi-pedestrianized); and some at the top have superlative views across the cathedral precincts to the great tower and south transept – floodlit at night (during summer).

When the small hotel was taken over by Caroline Jubber and her husband, they greatly improved most bedrooms – some of them reached via a rooftop walkway – while retaining ancient beams, leaded casements and bow windows. There are now two sitting-rooms, which include a bar, and one splendid 'mediaeval' bathroom where modern tiles contrast with dark beams. Breakfast (continental in summer, unless you pay extra) is brought to you in the small dining-room or in your bedroom. An evening meal is available, or there are many good restaurants close by. Bedrooms are well equipped and comfortable. One has a four-poster. Some look across old roofs and red chimney-pots where pigeons perch. The hotel's locked carpark (for which there is a charge) is several minutes' walk away.

It is, of course, the cathedral which brings most visitors to Canterbury: one of Britain's finest and most colourful, with many historical associations. It is the site of Becket's martyrdom (commemorated in some of the finest stained glass in the world) and houses the splendid tomb of the Black Prince, and much more.

The ancient walled city still has many surviving mediaeval and Tudor buildings, the beautiful River Stour, old churches and inns, Roman remains, two theatres, and lovely shops in its small lanes. The Heritage Museum is well worth a visit to see some of the city's most important treasures.

This is a useful place to stay before or after a ferry-crossing to the continent – or as a base from which to explore the historic south Kent coast, the Cinque Ports, Dover Castle and Dover's famous Roman 'Painted House', the Minster Abbey at Ramsgate, or the Kent countryside.

Readers' comments: Incredible situation. Very nice people. Location superb. Delicious breakfasts. We can't wait to return.

CAUSA GRANGE
C(12) S

Rosley, Caldbeck, Cumbria, CA7 8DD   Tel: 016973 45358

South-east of Wigton. Nearest main road: A595 from Carlisle to Cockermouth (and M6, junction 41).

2 **Bedrooms.** £18–£24 (less for 3 nights). Both have own bath/shower/toilet. Tea/coffee facilities. Views of garden, country. No smoking. Washing machine on request.
Dinner. £12 for 4 courses (with choices) and coffee, at 7pm. Non-residents not admitted. Vegetarian or special diets if ordered. No smoking. **Light suppers** if ordered.
2 **Sitting-rooms.** With open fire, central heating, TV. No smoking.
Large garden

Once a farmhouse, Causa Grange was built in 1856 as one of the first works of what is now the giant contracting firm of John Laing. It has luckily escaped subsequent interference, so marble fireplaces, tiled floors, pine joinery, and so on are still intact, and the painted and gilded cornice in the sitting-room has never been defaced with whitewash. (A second sitting-room is available to those who want to avoid television.) Ann Falck has decorated and furnished the house in keeping while adding such amenities as an extra-large cast-iron bath and bidet to serve one of the bedrooms, which are particularly well equipped. Colours are harmonious, with discreet use of paint and paper on dadoes and ceilings.

One of Ann's dinners (available, like packed lunches, by arrangement) might comprise smoked salmon pâté, braised beef, apple-and-blackberry crumble, cheese, and fruit.

Outside the well-tended garden (Ken Falck's enthusiasm) is beautiful countryside, with the Lake District, the Scottish border, and the west Cumbrian coast not far beyond.

At Whelpo ('Wolf's lair'), outside Caldbeck, **SWALEDALE WATCH** is a dairy and sheep farm, named after the breed of sheep kept here. There are rooms in the modern farmhouse and also two in a converted byre which share a sitting-room and a kitchenette. Guests eat in a big dining-room in the house, which is set in fine scenery and good walking country just inside the Lake District National Park. Cookery enthusiast Nan Savage serves, for instance, Highland prawns, chicken baked with honey, and chocolate roll; bread is home-baked, and vegetarian menus are possible. Caldbeck is one of the Lake District's prettiest villages,

with an old inn (handy for lunch), a churchyard where lie John Peel and the real-life heroine of Melvyn Bragg's *Maid of Buttermere*, and a restored watermill for craft shops and a good vegetarian restaurant. £17–£19. [Tel: 016974 78409; postcode: CA7 8HQ]

CEDAR LODGE   C PT
13 Lambridge, Bath, (Avon), Bath & North-East Somerset, BA1 6BJ
Tel: 01225 423468
On A4 from Bath to Chippenham.

3 Bedrooms. £20–£29.50 (less for 3 nights or continental breakfast). Prices go up from April. Bargain breaks. All have own bath/shower/toilet. TV. Views of garden. No smoking.
Dinner (by arrangement). From £15 for 3 courses (with choices) and coffee, at 6–8pm. Non-residents not admitted. Vegetarian or special diets if ordered. **Light suppers** if ordered.
1 Sitting-room. With open fire, central heating, TV. No smoking.
Garden

The 18th-century merchant who first owned this fine house celebrated peace when the American War of Independence ended by installing a window etched and painted with the American eagle bearing an olive branch. This is on a curved landing of the elegant staircase, one of many striking features in the house. At back and front are walled gardens, the latter with ample trees (as well as frog pools) to screen the verandahed house from the road into Bath: bus stop outside.

Derek and Hungarian-born Maria Beckett have furnished the house with 18th- and 19th-century antiques, an abundance of pictures and books, needle-point cushions, mementoes such as a collection of coronation mugs, bowls of dried flowers, and an alcove full of dolls and toys for visiting children. There is a small conservatory in which to take coffee and petits fours after one of Maria's cordon bleu dinners.

Upstairs are bedrooms with bay windows and handsomely panelled doors of stripped pine. One has a pine half-tester bed with lace drapery; another, bedheads of buttoned pink velvet; the third, a very wide four-poster and quilted spread.

When no dinner is available, the Becketts will drive guests to a restaurant they recommend. Cars can be left in secure parking (important in Bath).

Readers' comments: The home was warm with friendship, hosts more than gracious, very restful.

The **OLD BOAT HOUSE**, Forester Road, is a rare survival: an un-spoilt Victorian boating-station with distinctive black-and-white verandah overlooking a quiet, willow-fringed reach of the River Avon, and with an open-topped launch available in season to take you (free) into the centre of Bath – unless you prefer to punt or row yourself. Four generations of Hardicks have built, repaired and hired out wooden skiffs and other craft here: you can still see these being clinker-built in the traditional way.

Some bedrooms face the rambling garden and trees; the best has windows

on two sides and a verandah overlooking riverbank and geese (as does the sitting-room). No smoking. Separate from the house is a riverside restaurant, also with verandah. £20–£25 (b & b). [Tel: 01225 466407; postcode: BA2 6QE]

CERNE RIVER COTTAGE

C PT

8 The Folly, Cerne Abbas, Dorset, DT2 7JR   Tel: 01300 341355
North of Dorchester. Nearest main road: A352 from Dorchester to Sherborne.

2 Bedrooms. £18. Price goes up from April. Both have own bath/shower/toilet. Tea/coffee facilities. Views of village, garden, country, river. No smoking. Washing machine on request.
Dinner (by arrangement). £7.50 for 2 courses and coffee, at 7pm. Non-residents not admitted. Vegetarian or special diets if ordered. No smoking. **Light suppers** if ordered.
1 Sitting-room. With central heating, TV. No smoking.
Small garden

A good view of the Cerne Abbas giant, an enormous pagan chalk-cut figure, is afforded from the twin room of this pretty 18th-century cottage. At one time a tannery and then a school, it is now the home of Ginny Williams-Ellis, her husband Nick, a landscape gardener, and their children. Not surprisingly, their garden (where guests can have breakfast in summer) is particularly pleasant, with the River Cerne meandering through it.

They have worked hard to restore their home. In the dining-room guests can enjoy home-made apple juice with their breakfast and jam made from the many fruit trees in the garden. Eggs are free-range and milk is organic. Dinner might be a roast or lasagne, followed by apple crumble or a pavlova. Bedrooms are simply furnished in pastel shades; the double has a good brass bedstead and view of the garden.

Cerne Abbas grew up around a now ruined 10th-century Benedictine abbey, and a useful 'town trail' guides you through the village. St Mary's Church is well worth a visit. Its fine east window has 15th-century glass thought to have come from the abbey.

Readers' comments: Thoroughly recommended. Made very comfortable.

Also in Cerne Abbas is **SOUND O'WATER,** in Duck Street, a former inn which Jean and Doug Simmonds have modernized to provide a comfortable guest-house. Some rooms are in an annexe opening onto a pretty garden that wanders down to the winding River Cerne. Light suppers offered, but all Cerne's inns do good food. Cerne is a lovely village and with the famous giant on its hillside. £17–£18.50.
Reader's comment: Very comfortable

and friendly. [Tel: 01300 341435; postcode: DT2 7LA]

Some proprietors stipulate a minimum stay of two nights at weekends or peak seasons; or they will accept one-nighters only at short notice (that is, only if no lengthier booking has yet been made).

CHASE LODGE

C D M PT X

Park Road, Hampton Wick, Surrey, KT1 4AS   Tel: 0181-943 1862
North of Kingston-upon-Thames. Nearest main road: A308 from Staines to
Surbiton (the M25, M3 and M4 are also near).

10 Bedrooms. £15–£31 (less for 3 nights).
Prices go up from April. All have own
bath/shower/toilet. Tea/coffee facilities. TV.
No smoking (in one).
Dinner. £14 for 3 courses (from the à la
carte menu **to readers showing a copy of
the current edition of this book**) and
coffee, from 8–10pm. Less for 2 courses.
Vegetarian or special diets if ordered. Wine
available. No smoking. **Light suppers** if
ordered. Summer barbecues.
2 Sitting-rooms. With open fire, central
heating. TV, video. **Bar.**
Small garden

Not only can you park your car here for a small daily charge and be taken to and
from Heathrow Airport, but it is also a very handy place at which to stay in order
to explore the 'royal' stretch of the Thames Valley (monarchs chose nearby
Richmond, Hampton Court, Kew and Windsor for their palaces). Park Road is
in a quiet conservation area, a street of pretty little Victorian villas with cottage-
gardens, yet only a minute or two from a railway station, buses and the shops of
Kingston.

Chase Lodge has been redecorated with interesting pieces of Victorian furniture and decorative trifles in its sitting-room and elsewhere. There are African
violets and other pot-plants in some rooms. One has a tented scarlet-and-green
ceiling and a mural of a crusader castle in its bathroom. Another, a four-poster
with lace. All have very good en suite showers or bathrooms.

For dinner, Nigel Stafford-Haworth, formerly chef at a 5-star hotel, prepares
varied menus. (Supper trays and Sunday lunch available, too.) As all bedrooms
have phones, breakfast can be ordered in bed.

At the back is a tiny, sun-trapping patio with a few seats among the flowers.

Denise pays great attention to detail and takes immense trouble. Not many far
more costly hotels provide room-service free, and baby-sitting can also be
arranged. A self-catering house, well equipped and with maid service, is available
half a mile away.

There is an enormous amount to see and do in the neighbourhood: walks
among the deer and chestnut trees of Bushey Park or along the towpaths,
Hampton Court – with *son-et-lumière* shows at night – and its gardens (with
maze), horseracing at Kempton and Sandhurst, tennis at Wimbledon, rugby at
Twickenham, and any number of regattas and festivals in summer. Richmond
deserves at least a day to itself, to explore the byways and curio shops off the
green, the stunning river view from the top of the hill, and the 3000 acres of
Richmond Park. There are also Georgian or earlier mansions in fine grounds
(Ham House, Orleans House, Marble Hill, Syon Park, Chiswick House,
Hogarth's house and Osterley Park).

Readers' comments: Superb hosts. Very comfortable. Without fault. Best b & b ever!
Friendly and attentive. Great attention given. Delightfully furnished and all
the facilities expected. Unusual and attractive dining-room. Delicious dinner.
Comfortable and pleasant.

CHERRY COURT

C(7) PT S X

Hollybush Lane, Burghfield Common, Berkshire, RG7 3JS
Tel: 01734 832404

South-west of Reading. Nearest main road: A4 from Reading to Newbury (and M4, junction 12).

3 Bedrooms. £19–£22.50. All have own bath/shower/toilet. Tea/coffee facilities. TV. Views of garden. No smoking. Washing machine on request.
Dinner. £15 for 4 courses and coffee, at 7.30pm. Vegetarian or special diets if ordered. Wine available. No smoking. **Light suppers** if ordered.
2 Sitting-rooms. With open fire, central heating, TV, record-player.
Large garden

Typical of its county and its period (turn-of-the-century), this is a spacious, solid and dignified house. Rooms are well carpeted and furnished, mostly in pinks and greens. A log fire crackles on chilly days, and for sunny ones there is a heated swimming-pool in the grounds. A sunken garden is full of roses – when not eaten by deer. Fruit and eggs are home-produced.

Jacqueline Levey serves such meals as pâté, salmon hollandaise, and fresh fruit salad, after which one can relax in a small sun-room with a grapevine overhead.

Heathrow is a half-hour taxi ride, and you can park your car at Cherry Court while you are abroad.

Visitors come to this area for the open-air theatre of Bradfield College, for the trout lakes, to ride, or for the many golf courses in the county. To the west lies picturesque Hungerford, famous for it scores of antique shops (many open even on Sundays). Nearby are the windswept heights of the Berkshire Downs where racehorses train, and you can walk along the prehistoric Ridgeway Path. The sites of Iron Age forts or burial mounds dot the area. The Kennet Valley is in complete contrast – fertile meadows with birch and oak woods beyond, a great area for birdwatchers. In and around both Lambourn and Newbury are historic buildings, stately homes and pretty villages.

Readers' comments: Remarkably hospitable and friendly. Very pretty. Ideally located. The nicest people – exceptional. Lovely house, first rate.

Meals under the vine at Little Parmoor (see page 181)

CHURCH HOUSE

C(12) **X**

Grittleton, Wiltshire, SN14 6AP   Tel: 01249 782562
North-west of Chippenham. Nearest main road: M4 (junctions 17/18).

4 Bedrooms. £19.50–£27.50 (less for 3 nights). All have own bath/shower/toilet. Tea/coffee facilities. TV. Views of garden, country.
Dinner. £15.50 for 4 courses (with wine) and coffee, at 8pm. Vegetarian or special diets sometimes.
2 Sitting-rooms. With log fire, central heating, piano.
Large garden

This little-known but very beautiful village lies just off the M4 midway between London and Wales: a cluster of elegant houses, a great Tudor-style mansion, and church, all built from golden Cotswold limestone.

Church House began life in 1740 as a huge rectory, which it took six servants to run. Around it are lawns with immense copper beeches (floodlit at night), an orchard, fields of sheep and a covered swimming-pool, well heated in summer (84°), as well as a walled vegetable and fruit garden which provides organic produce for the kitchen, where Anna Moore produces imaginative meals if these are ordered in advance. A typical menu might comprise quail-egg salad; chicken breasts in honey, lime and mustard; tarte tatin, British cheeses, fruit, and wine (included in the price).

Anna and her family treat all visitors as house-guests and she often escorts overseas visitors on sightseeing tours. Some she takes to the Royal Shakespeare Theatre (Stratford is 1½ hours away), with a champagne picnic supper on the banks of the Avon afterwards. The Moores are a musical family, and occasionally arrange music evenings – there is one huge room with a grand piano used for this purpose. Watching polo can be arranged. There is a croquet lawn and a sun-bed.

The house has handsome and finely proportioned rooms. In the yellow sitting-room (which has an immense bay window overlooking the garden) are antique furniture, interesting paintings and a large log stove. The dining-room is equally handsome: raspberry walls, an Adam fireplace of inlaid marble and, on the long mahogany table, silver candelabra and Victorian Spode Copeland china. The most impressive architectural feature is the graceful staircase that curves its way up to the second floor, where the guest-rooms are furnished with antiques; some have their bathroom facilities behind screens.

There is an immense amount to see and do in the neighbourhood. Close by is Badminton (celebrated for the annual horse trials, attended by the royal family); Bath is only 12 miles away (you can Park & Ride from Lansdown, 15 minutes away); and the many historic (and prehistoric) sites of Wiltshire, such as Avebury, are all around. Both the west country and the Cotswolds are accessible from Grittleton. Malmesbury Abbey, Castle Combe and Westonbirt Arboretum are favourite sights.

Readers' comments: Anna Moore is an excellent cook. Bedrooms spacious and most comfortable. Peaceful. Lovely beds, charming house. Happy memories.

CLAY LANE HEAD FARMHOUSE   C PT
Cabus, Garstang, Lancashire, PR3 1WL   Tel: 01995 603132
North of Preston. On A6 from Preston to Lancaster (and near M6, junctions 32/33).

3 Bedrooms. £15–£18 (less for 5 nights). Two have their own bath/shower/toilet. Tea/coffee facilities. Views of garden, country.
Light suppers (not Wednesdays).
1 Sitting-room. With open fire, TV, piano, record-player.
Small garden
Closed from November to March.

Though hardly off the beaten track – it stands on the A6 – Clay Lane Head Farmhouse could easily be missed as one sped by, on the way to or from Scotland or the Lake District. It would be a good place to break a long journey, though it deserves more than a brief overnight visit, for both house and surroundings have much to offer visitors who like an easy-going atmosphere.

The stone house, which is more characterful than it appears to be from the outside, is basically 16th century, and some of the internal walls are of plastered reeds. It is a rambling, beamy old place, full of family antiques and Victoriana, with a book-lined sitting-room to sprawl in (it has a log fire); and it has not been modernized. The rooms face away from the main road. Although this is no longer a working dairy-farm, there are cattle, goats and sheep.

Joan Higginson, a pharmacist, is willing to provide soup and sandwiches by arrangement.

Start by visiting the Garstang Discovery Centre before you investigate the hinterland – notably the Trough of Bowland, which is like a miniature Lake District without the lakes. The steep, heather-covered hills here are excellent for walking and picnicking, and there are picturesque stone villages and mansions to visit. One such is Browsholme Hall, a little-altered Jacobean house still in the possession of the family which provided the hereditary Bowbearer of Bowland. Historic towns such as Lancaster and Clitheroe are not far, and the Lake District and the resorts of the Lancashire coast are within an easy day trip. Other popular outings include Lancaster Castle, Cockersand Abbey, Sunderland Point, Beacon Fell country park and Brock Bottom nature trail.

Because the M6 motorway is near, it is easy to get to Lancashire's great cities which, although no great pleasure in themselves, do house a number of places of considerable interest – such as the restored Albert Dock and an outpost of London's Tate Gallery at Liverpool, and the outstanding Museum of Science and Granada Studios in Manchester. Blackpool, with its famous tower and miles of sands, is near: a recent attraction there is a huge, tropical, indoor swimming-pool. In this direction, too, are Fleetwood (port and fishmarket) and the pleasant resort of Lytham St Anne's.

Readers' comments: Very enjoyable. Attentive service. Concerned for our every comfort, spotless rooms. Interesting place. Very satisfactory. Friendly and bright. Very comfortable.

CLAYBATCH FARMHOUSE   S
Blatchbridge, Somerset, BA11 5EF   Tel: 01373 461193
South of Frome. Nearest main road: A361 from Frome to Shepton Mallet.

rear view

2 Bedrooms. £18 (less for continental breakfast). Price goes up from April. Both have own bath/shower/toilet. Tea/coffee facilities. Views of garden, country. No smoking. Washing machine on request.
Dinner (by arrangement). £14 for 3 courses, and coffee, at 7.30pm. Non-residents not admitted. Special diets if ordered. No smoking. **Light suppers** sometimes.
1 Sitting-room. With open fire, central heating, piano. No smoking.
Large garden
Closed from mid-December to mid-January.

Jacqueline George, a professional cook, has another outstanding talent: a flair for combining beautiful colours. Her early 18th-century home is a perfect setting for both her skills.

The big sitting-room is memorable. Duck-egg blue walls and the mellow patina of walnut furniture contrast with the brilliance of apricot chairs grouped round a stone fireplace – their colour echoed in Warners' pheasant and peony fabric on the sofas. Big casement doors open onto a sloping lawn, flowerbeds and watergarden. The dining-room has Chippendale-style chairs (Prince of Wales feathers decorate their backs) with tapestry seats made by her aunt; and on the Etruscan red walls hang oil paintings. Here Jackie serves such dinners (on your night of arrival only) as smoked trout pâté; pork fillet with juniper berries and garden vegetables; crème brûlée with raspberries; and cheeses (pre-dinner drinks are included). On other nights, guests can eat well in Frome, or at local pubs.

Bedrooms, too, are charming with little rosebuds on one bedspread, Chinese pavilions on another, for example.

Claybatch used to be part of the Longleat estate. The great Elizabethan mansion of Longleat is one of England's stateliest homes, full of art treasures and famous for its free-ranging lions in part of the grounds landscaped by Capability Brown. Stourhead, too, is near: a Palladian mansion with fine gardens.

Somerset is a county of great beauty, its landscape punctuated by impressive church towers from the resplendent Perpendicular period of mediaeval architecture, big stone barns and little stone villages, with Bath itself just over the county boundary to the north; Wells and Salisbury are close. Geology is what accounts for its great variety, with buildings made of stone that ranges from lilac to gold (for every quarry is different), and a landscape of hills and levels contrasting with one another. Monks drained marshes (still crisscrossed with their ancient ditches) between hills of great beauty but quite dissimilar from one another – the Mendips, the Quantocks and Exmoor. Where streams carved their way through rock there are gorges and caves.

Readers' comments: Made most welcome, delicious meals, beautiful home. Such a welcoming house and relaxing atmosphere, food plentiful and delicious.

CLEAVERS LYNG
D PT X

Church Road, Herstmonceux, East Sussex, BN27 1QJ   Tel: 01323 833131
East of Hailsham. Nearest main road: A271 from Horsebridge towards Bexhill.

7 Bedrooms. £20–£25 (less for 7 nights). Bargain breaks. All have own bath/shower/toilet. Tea/coffee facilities. TV (some). Views (some) of garden, country. Balcony (some). **Dinner.** £12.50 for 3 courses (with choices) and coffee, at 7pm. Vegetarian or special diets if ordered. Wine available. No smoking. **Light suppers** if ordered.
2 Sitting-rooms. With open fire (in one), central heating, TV. No smoking (in one).
Large garden

The unusual name means a woodcutter's (cleaver's) hill by a marsh (lyng). Many centuries ago this was a yeoman's house, and its tile-hung exterior is typical of Sussex.

The bedrooms in this small hotel are prettily furnished, and some have views of the garden and its apple-trees, with the far distant hills beyond.

Sally Simpson serves such dinners (or Sunday lunches) as seafood cocktail, steak pie, and orange mousse.

Herstmonceux village is the centre of Sussex trug-making (trugs are traditional garden baskets made from slats of willow), one of many pretty Downland villages around here. Many craftsmen work here and wrought iron is a local speciality. Popular sights include Michelham Priory, Batemans (Kipling's last home), Battle Abbey, Pevensey Castle and picturesque Alfriston. The coast is near, with such resorts as Hastings and Eastbourne.

The garden of pretty, lattice-paned **ASHLANDS COTTAGE** adjoins the estate of Batemans. Beyond its herbaceous beds and neat brick paths is a far view across the scenery that inspired 'Pook's Song' and you can glimpse Pook's Hill from the garden.

Trained as a singer, Nesta Harmer made her home here after many years spent in Bermuda; the pretty mahogany beds in one room came from there. Both rooms have wide views and a light, airy feel.

Beyond the garden is a wood in which Nesta has cleared a glade and planted woodland flowers. The inns and restaurants of Burwash are two minutes' walk away. £17–£18.
Readers' comments: Beautifully furnished, magnificent views. Home-from-home service, restful and delightfully furnished. Superb views, very comfortable. Very personal and gracious attention. View from our bedroom truly magnificent. Very generous and helpful. [Tel: 01435 882207; postcode: TN19 7HS]

CLIFF HOUSE

Devonport Hill, Kingsand, Cornwall, PL10 1NJ Tel: 01752 823110
South-west of Plymouth. Nearest main road: A374 from Plymouth towards
Looe.

3 Bedrooms. £16–£20 (less for 3 nights). Prices may go up from Easter. All have own bath/shower/toilet. Tea/coffee facilities. Views of garden, country, sea. No smoking. Washing machine on request.
Dinner. £20 for aperitif, 4 courses, coffee and wine, at times to suit guests. Less for 4 courses alone or 2 courses. Vegetarian or special diets if ordered. No smoking. **Light suppers** if ordered.
2 Sitting-rooms. With open fire, central heating, TV, CD-player, video. Balcony. No smoking. Piano.
Small garden

Just across the Devon/Cornwall border lies a neck of land that is almost an island and which most tourists pass by. But if one leaves the main road to follow a woodland route along the winding banks of the River Lynher (frequented by swans), one comes to a little world of billowing green hills and high-banked lanes that plunge up and down until, right at the tip, one reaches the Mount Edgcumbe estate and the point at which ferries (car or pedestrian) arrive from Plymouth as they have done since time immemorial. This is the Rame peninsula, an Area of Outstanding Natural Beauty; and here, in a fishing village of coloured or red sandstone cottages, small shops and bistros, is 17th-century Cliff House – perched high above the sea and within a few yards of the south Cornwall coastal path.

From its hexagonal bay windows or the verandah, one can watch naval ships passing in and out of Plymouth Sound or, in the opposite direction, children playing on the sands of Cawsand Bay. To make the most of these views, the sitting-room (with sofas and log stove, the television end curtained off) is on the first floor. Some guests enjoy playing the Blüthner boudoir grand piano. On the walls of the house are paintings by local artists that are for sale. Some bedrooms, too, enjoy the fine views – the largest having armchairs in the bay window. There is one with a cupboard full of books for children. Some visitors have found parking awkward.

Ann Heasman is not only a fount of information about the locality but an enthusiastic wholefood cook – of such meals as lentil pâté with spiced fruit salad, carbonnade of beef or local venison, and chocolate roulade or rhubarb fool – and she bakes her own bread.

The house is on the edge of the Mount Edgcumbe country park, at its heart a much restored Tudor mansion and fine gardens, both landscaped and formal. As well as developing the gardens, successive generations created such adornments as an orangery, shell fountain, conservatories, a fern dell, pavilions and memorials. There are also fortifications, Tudor and Napoleonic, to guard the sea approaches.

The peninsula is so full of interest that it would take an age to explore it all.

Readers' comments: Delightful owner, made us so at home. All standards excellent, breakfast marvellous. Didn't want to leave. Delightful: look forward to another stay. Wonderful location. Lovely, friendly welcome, dinners delicious, beautiful landscape, would go again time after time. Wonderful six days. Made us feel instantly at home; house so friendly, comfortable and stylish; cooking absolutely superb. Enjoyed every moment.

CLOW BECK HOUSE

C D M

Monk End, Croft-on-Tees, North Yorkshire, DL2 2SW   Tel: 01325 721075
South of Darlington. Nearest main road: A167 from Northallerton to Darlington.

5 Bedrooms. £19–£22.50. All have own bath/shower//toilet. Tea/coffee facilities. TV. Views of garden, country. Washing machine on request.
1 Sitting-room. With open fire, central heating, TV, record-player.
Large garden

Heather Armstrong being a teacher of beauty therapy, it is not surprising that the rooms in Clow Beck House have been decorated and furnished with some flamboyance! The big sitting-room is in shades of the royal blue of the Chinese carpet, with white details such as Adam-style panels on walls and alcoves by the fireplace. Chandeliers hang over the armchairs and settee, which have carved wooden frames and blue velvet upholstery, and the swagged curtains are also in blue.

There is another chandelier in the marble-floored hall with its big gilt mirror. Up the oak staircase, one bedroom, in pink, has a tented fabric ceiling and a satin bedhead. The en suite double bedroom, in blue, has a canopied bed and Victorian mahogany furniture, and the twin room is in shades of yellow. More bedrooms (two with dressing-rooms) are in a separate converted stable block.

Even the large and luxurious bathroom has been equipped in style – dark blue carpet, fawn dado, and shell-shaped washbasin. In the dining-room, the oak furniture is from one of the craftsmen for whom Yorkshire is well known.

Though hardly typical, this is indeed a farmhouse, and from it David Armstrong runs a mixed holding which – though the house is less than 10 years old – has been in his family for generations. Unlike most farmers, he is a keen gardener and puts a lot of time into the big open garden in front of the house.

'Lewis Carroll' spent his early life in Croft, where his father was rector.

Only a few miles from the A1, **MOULTON MANOR** in the village of that name is a tall Elizabethan house where James I once stayed and which has been little altered since the 1670s. It was then that two great oak staircases were added (with a rare contemporary dog-gate); one leads to the guest-rooms under the roof, which overlook the orchard and large garden. Another 17th-century addition is the big carved-stone fireplace in the sitting-room. Gourmets walk to the Black Bull in the village to dine. Good but cheaper pub meals are a short drive away (as is the birthplace of George Baltimore); Sara Vaux will take you to them. £16–£17. [Tel: 01325 377228; postcode: DL10 6QG]

COACH HOUSE   **C D M P T S X**
Belton-by-Grantham, Lincolnshire, NG32 2LS   Tel: 01476 573636
North of Grantham. Nearest main road: A607 from Grantham to Lincoln.

4 Bedrooms. £17–£19 (less for 4 nights). All have own bath/shower/toilet. Tea/coffee facilities. TV. Views of garden, country. No smoking. Washing machine on request.
Dinner (if ordered). £12 for 4 courses and coffee, at about 7pm. Wine available. No smoking. **Light suppers.**
1 Sitting-room. With central heating, TV, video. No smoking.
Large garden
Closed in January.

Along the High Dyke nearby, the Romans built a road which was still in use, centuries later, as a stagecoach route. For an overnight stop on the long haul from Cambridge to York the coaches paused here at an inn, next door to which the buildings of Ancaster stone that are now the Nortons' home were stables surrounding a coach yard. All very different today, with tubs of petunias where the coaches used to clatter in and out. And very peaceful, even though the busy A1 is only five minutes away.

Bernard Norton has created such attractive features as a second, sun-trapping courtyard with a fountain in the centre of a circle of blue-brick paving: an attractive view to enjoy while dining. The guests' sitting-room has French windows which open onto the garden. There are ground-floor bedrooms (one with court-yard view, one with none) and others upstairs – be prepared for rafters and steps – which have roof-lights. Sue has made ruffled pelmets and, on one bed, a prettily draped corona, using silky pink or rose-patterned fabrics.

For dinner she may offer you minestrone, lemon chicken, and strawberries.

All around the conservation village is National Trust land to provide good walks, a plethora of golf courses including one with 45(!) holes and, just up the road, the exceptionally fine mansion of Belton House: in its collection of coaches are some that used to do the Cambridge–York run. There is a particularly good garden centre nearby.

Belton is in an attractively wooded part of the county, well placed to visit the splendid Vale of Belvoir in one direction and historic Lincoln in the other.

Readers' comments: Delightfully situated, very attractively furnished. Meals cooked to perfection. Very friendly and helpful. A lovely stay, food good.

Near Skillington is 18th-century **SPROXTON LODGE**, popular with walkers because the long Viking Way borders its fields. This is a homely, working farm – with silver ploughing-trophies won by Ted on display to prove it! He still has his very first tractor of 40 years ago, now almost a museum piece. Unpretentious comfort (and an enormous, carpeted bathroom) are what hospitable Eileen Whatton pro-

vides here, with dinners or snacks by arrangement. £15 (b & b). [Tel: 01476 860307; postcode: NG33 5HJ]

COACH HOUSE AT CROOKHAM   C D M S
Cornhill-on-Tweed, Northumberland, TD12 4TD   Tel: 01890 820293 or
01890 820284
South-west of Berwick-upon-Tweed. On A697 from Wooler to Coldstream.

11 Bedrooms. £19–£34 (less for 7 nights). Most have own bath/shower/toilet. Tea/coffee facilities. TV. Views of garden, country. Washing machine on request.
Dinner. £15.50 for 4 courses (with some choices) and coffee, at 7.30pm. Non-residents not admitted. Vegetarian or special diets if ordered. Wine available. No smoking.
2 Sitting-rooms. With open fire, central heating, TV, record-player.
Large garden
Closed from mid-November to mid-March.

This is almost on the border of Scotland, and very close to the site of Flodden Field, where in 1513 Henry VIII's armies slaughtered the King of Scotland and 10,000 of his followers: the very last mediaeval battle with knights wearing armour, and swords or arrows the principal weapons. Each August there is a tremendously emotive spectacle commemorating it.

The Coach House is a group of several old farm buildings forming a square around a courtyard which traps the sun. What was the coach house itself is now a highly individual sitting-room, with lofty beamed ceiling and great arched windows where there used to be doors for the carriages. One looks onto an orchard where rare brown Soay sheep graze. Colours are light and cheerful, and there is a log fire in an enormous brick fireplace.

An old dower house has panelled doors of stripped pine, pointed 'gothick' windows, rare chestnut beams, an old Victorian kitchen-range, two immensely high attic bedrooms and a dining-room (one of two).

In the main part, some of the ground-floor bedrooms look onto paddocks. All are light and airy, with interesting paintings and a file of leaflets on the many local places worth visiting. They have fridges which guests find useful for a variety of purposes (baby's feeds, dog's meat, insulin or soft drinks).

The owner, Lynne Anderson, used to travel a great deal when she was a singer and so has a lot of practical ideas about what travellers need – disabled travellers in particular. She had doorways made wide, and steps eliminated.

Porridge is properly made from pinhead oatmeal, and breakfast includes bacon from an Edinburgh smokery, sausages from a local butcher, and free-range eggs. Dinner has a choice of six starters; a roast or casserole; puddings like lemon meringue pie or one of 15 home-made ice creams; cheese and coffee. Organic produce is used increasingly. (There is also a small gift shop where you can buy food products prepared in the Coach House kitchens, as well as local specialities.)

Readers' comments: Warm and friendly owner; professional efficiency. A great success! Wonderful. So much room, the very best breakfast, and Lynne is exceptionally good at making guests at ease with one another. Outstanding. Charm, friendliness, service; cannot be too highly praised, meals difficult to better at any price. Everything a guest might want.

COACHMAN'S COTTAGE
Hanlith, Malham, North Yorkshire, BD23 4BP   Tel: 01729 830538
East of Settle. Nearest main road: A65 from Skipton to Settle.

C(8) S

3 Bedrooms. £18–£19 (less for 3 nights). All have own bath/shower/toilet. Tea/coffee facilities. TV. Views of garden (most). No smoking. Washing machine on request.
1 Sitting-room. With open fire, central heating. TV, record-player. No smoking.
Small garden

Up a narrow road leading to only a few farms and a private mansion is this 17th-century cottage, which has been extended into its adjoining barn to create a rambling home where every bedroom has its own character.

There is a private sitting-room, with tea things, for the use of one bedroom (or two if a family is staying). Otherwise, guests can chat (in front of a log fire in cool weather) with the hospitable Monica and Glyn Jenkins. Monica runs the local history society, so she is knowledgeable about the area. The cottage being on the Pennine Way and both the Jenkinses being keen walkers, fellow enthusiasts are well catered for, with masses of books and leaflets and the Jenkinses' own recommendations for walks.

This is an area of fine scenery, most notably around Malham. Picturesque Settle, with it many antique shops and lively market every week, is at one end of the spectacular railway line to Carlisle.

A few hundred yards down the road, the inn next to Kirkby Malham's mediaeval church is the nearest place for dinner, but within a short radius are many other excellent pub restaurants, including the nationally known Angel at Hetton.

A peaceful place hidden at the end of its own road, **WENNINGBER FARM**, near Hellifield, used to be a drover's cottage. It is surrounded by fields where Texel sheep and suckler cows (Blonde d'Aquitaine) are kept, overlooked by trim, cream-painted bedrooms. Downstairs, a green-and-gold suite faces a stone fireplace with polished iron pots and kettles around it. Behind, Windsor chairs surround the oak breakfast-table. Though snack suppers can be arranged with Barbara Phillip, most guests make use of the

area's variety of good restaurants. £17.50–£19. [Tel: 01729 850856; postcode: BD23 4JR]

Book well ahead: many of these houses have few rooms. Do not expect dinner if you have not booked it or if you arrive late.

63

St Agnes, Isles of Scilly, TR22 0PL   Tel: 01720 422373

3 Bedrooms. £18 (less for continental breakfast **and less to readers of this book between Easter and Spring Bank Holiday**). All have own bath/shower/toilet. All have tea/coffee facilities. Views of sea. Laundry done (within reason) for week-long visitors. No smoking.
Dinner. £11 for 4 courses and coffee, at 7pm. Less for fewer courses. Non-residents not admitted. Vegetarian or special diets if ordered. No smoking.
1 Sitting-room. With open fire. No smoking.
Garden
Closed from November to Easter.

There are very few coastguards living in the many coastguard cottages still left around the shores of England: electronic surveillance has taken over from the man with the spyglass. Needless to say, such cottages were always well sited for sea views, on coasts where high seas and jagged rocks make spectacular scenery but are hazards for ships, and where coves and inlets were an attraction to smugglers.

One such group of cottages stands on a high point of St Agnes, a little island so unspoilt that there are no cars and no hotel – only a small shop with a good selection of drinks and books. It is a paradise for those who want nothing more than sunshine early or late in the year, wildflowers, walks, birdwatching and peace.

Wendy Hick provides accommodation for guests in two adjacent cottages. She has furnished the rooms simply but attractively, with interesting objects around. The sitting-room has a William Morris suite and views out to the sea, polished board floors, many books on the shelves and an open fire for chilly evenings. The pieces of iron-studded furniture are from Curaçao, where her late father-in-law was a mining engineer. The collection of old bottles (from inkwells to flasks that contained sheep-cures) are mostly local finds.

The food is all of a very good, homely style: bread is home-baked, soups home-made, clotted cream is from a friendly neighbourhood cow, fish (of course) straight out of the sea, and new potatoes from the fields around.

Visitors reach St Agnes via St Mary's, from which boats take them in 15 minutes to the little quay at St Agnes. (Wendy will supply all the times etc. for getting to Scilly by rail and boat or helicopter.) Luggage is conveyed for them up the steep track that leads to the few cottages; past the Turk's Head inn (for a really succulent Cornish pasty, pause here!) and past Rose Cottage and Covean which serve Cornish cream teas and light lunches. Whatever track you follow, there is a superlative view at every turn. This is a great place for birdwatchers, particularly in autumn when rare migrants arrive. But even at other times it is a pleasure to watch the red-legged oystercatchers, for instance, scuttling like busy mice among the rock pools on the shore.

Readers' comments: Excellent in every respect. Good food, lovely scenery, such nice people. Warmly welcomed, well looked after, delicious food, excellent value; beautiful and peaceful place. Superb food and hospitality.

COLDRED COURT FARM

C M PT

Church Road, Coldred, Kent, CT15 5AQ   Tel: 01304 830816

North-west of Dover. Nearest main road: A2 from Dover to Canterbury.

3 Bedrooms. £18–£22.50 (less for 2 nights). Some prices go up from April. Bargain breaks. All have own bath/shower/toilet. Tea/coffee facilities. TV. Views of garden, country. No smoking. Washing machine on request.

Dinner. £12.50 for 3 courses and coffee, at 7–8pm. Less for 2 courses. Non-residents not admitted. Vegetarian or special diets if ordered. No smoking.

Light suppers if ordered.

2 Sitting-rooms. With open fire (in one), central heating, TV, piano, record-player.

Large garden

Not only does Truda Kelly make all the ice cream, preserves and bread (new-baked by 7am!) but she and her mother have filled the house with crochet bed-spreads, embroidered or patchwork curtains, dried flowers and other decorative touches. Their scented candles, herbal lotions and local honey are on sale.

In this 16th-century house, windows have leaded panes and there are inglenooks, stone-paved floors and board doors. In the cellar are TV and pool rooms; a ground-floor bedroom is in what was once a dairy.

Meat, herbs and eggs come from the farm, through which the North Downs Way passes.

Many visitors use this as an overnight stop en route for France by the ferries. Others stay longer to explore this corner of the 'Garden of England' and to visit Canterbury with its cathedral and Dover with its castle on the famous white cliffs.

Readers' comments: Delightful; warm, family atmosphere, food good. Very good. Most kind and friendly.

After many years in the RAF, John Drover, and his wife Rosemary became hoteliers in Dover before they both retired to **DRAYCOTT** in Green Lane, Temple Ewell, a small village just outside the port. The Drovers have decorated this Victorian house with Laura Ashley prints and borders in keeping with the period – creams, maroons and blues, original picture-rails and fireplaces. There is a small study area where guests may sit and read and also a sitting-room with television, both shared with the proprietors, as is the bathroom. One daughter is a paper conservator and has produced a beautifully leather-bound visitors' book for the house. Simple home cooking is provided, by

arrangement, with fresh ingredients and home-made puddings. Guests may also relax in good weather in the pretty (but vertiginous!) terraced garden at the rear of the house. No smoking. Closed in winter. £17. [Tel: 01304 823060; postcode: CT16 3AR]

65

COLLEGE HOUSE
Chapel Street, Broadwell, Gloucestershire, GL56 0TW Tel: 01451 832351
North of Stow-on-the-Wold. Nearest main road: A429 from Stow to Moreton-in-Marsh.

3 Bedrooms. £20 (**to readers of this book only**)–£29. Less for 5 nights. All have own bath/shower/toilet. Tea/coffee facilities. TV. Views of garden, country. No smoking. Washing machine on request.
Dinner. £16.50 for 3 courses and coffee, at 7.30pm. Non-residents not admitted. Vegetarian or special diets if ordered. No smoking. **Light suppers** if ordered.
1 Sitting-room. With open fire, central heating.
Small garden

Broadwell is a charming and unspoilt little village, once the home of the Knights Templar, with lovely Cotswold stone houses of which 17th-century College House is a fine example.

Stylishly furnished by Sybil and Robert Gisby, bedrooms (including the least expensive) are spacious and comfortable, all with big double beds and large bathrooms too. One in lemon and white has an unusual Victorian 'slipper' bathtub, another an elegant sleigh-bed.

Sybil is a former restaurateur and produces imaginative menus. You might start with Stilton and mushroom crêpes, to be followed by lamb and rosemary casserole in winter, or pesto salmon and salad in summer, with a fresh fruit meringue to finish. There is a stone-flagged and shuttered sitting-room to relax in. Plenty of colourful guidebooks to help you plan the next day of your holiday. You may sleep safely in this house, secure in the knowledge that Cotswold stone lions guard the perimeters, warding off any evil spirits!

Reader's comment: Very comfortable.

A couple of miles east lies Adlestrop, a small village yet at one time with its own railway station celebrated in an Edward Thomas poem. The old station sign now marks your arrival in the village. In Main Street is **HONEY-BROOK COTTAGE,** a new house of local stone which Margaret and Bob Warrick designed and built themselves, with evident skill. There are two bedrooms, both en suite; the smaller double in peach and blue also has its own excellent walk-in shower-room downstairs. Visitors can relax in a small conservatory, off the sitting-room, in summer. Breakfast includes home-baked rolls and honey from the Warricks' own hives. Dinner is sometimes available, or transport can be

arranged to the nearby Fox for good food. No smoking. Closed in winter. £18.50–£20.
Readers' comments: Breakfast was wonderful. Every consideration. Most accommodating hosts. Very good value. Made us most welcome. Hospitable and helpful. [Tel: 01608 658884; postcode: GL56 0YN]

COOMBE FARMHOUSE

C(5) M S

Widegates, Cornwall, PL13 1QN Tel: 01503 240223
North-east of Looe. On B3253 from Looe to Widegates.

10 Bedrooms. £20 (less for 2 nights if dinner is taken). Price goes up from Easter. Bargain breaks. All have own shower/toilet. Tea/coffee facilities. TV. Views of garden, country, sea. No smoking. Washing machine on request.
Dinner. £14 for 4 courses and coffee, usually about 7pm. Non-residents not admitted. Vegetarian or special diets if ordered. Wine available. No smoking.
1 Sitting-room. With open fire, central heating, TV, video films. Bar. No smoking.
Large garden
Closed from November to February.

At this spacious and comfortable guest-house, built on a marvellous site with a distant sea view, Alex and Sally Low provide many extras such as a swimming-pool, croquet and a stone-walled games room for snooker and table tennis. Antiques, paintings and interesting objects fill the house.

From a glassed-in verandah are views of terraced lawns where peacocks roam, and of a pond (one of several) frequented by coots. Elsewhere, ponies graze, there are rhododendron woods and camellias grow wild. One bedroom opens onto this garden; others upstairs have armchairs from which to enjoy the view. Visitors can picnic in the garden.

A typical dinner may comprise something like home-made soup, roast duck, a fruit sponge with Cornish clotted cream, and cheeses (including local yarg). Visitors help themselves to drinks, writing down in a book what they have had.

Readers' comments: Excellent! Friendliness and warmth. A wonderful experience. Place superb, hospitality gracious. A haven of peace. Excellent food.

The **OLD RECTORY**, high up in Duloe Road, St Keyne, is an early 19th-century building with very handsome architectural features, and fine furniture in keeping with this.

In the sitting-room (with glass doors to the garden) are capacious velvet sofas and, through an arch, a green and red bar. Two bedrooms have lacy, modern four-posters; one bedroom is on the ground floor.

Pat and John Minifie either offer snacks or such dishes as soup, a roast or locally caught fish (with garden vegetables), and meringues or bread-and-butter pudding. £20–£25 (b & b).
Readers' comments: Excellent cooking with quality ingredients; warm and welcoming. Charming atmosphere of true repose and Victorian elegance. Food exceptional. Very good; nice people. Very well furnished; food beautifully cooked. Quite exceptional. [Tel: 01579 342617; postcode: PL14 4RL]

COTTAGE CREST   C PT

Castle Hill, Woodgreen, Hampshire, SP6 2AX   Tel: 01725 512009
South of Salisbury. Nearest main road: A336 from Ringwood to Salisbury.

3 Bedrooms. £19–£20 (less for 3 nights). All have own shower/toilet. Tea/coffee facilities. TV. Views of garden, country, river. No smoking. Washing machine on request.
Light suppers if ordered.
Large garden

Bedrooms here are some of the most beautiful and well-equipped in this book. A great brass bed with pink-and-white lacy linen is in one; it is in an L-shaped room with windows on two sides from which to enjoy superb views of sunsets over the River Avon in the valley below. There is no guests' sitting-room, but there is a garden suite with private sitting-room facing this view.

One can sit on a paved terrace with a little pool, or take a zigzag path down to a lower garden, or walk straight into the New Forest.

Romsey and Broadlands are very near; Beaulieu, Salisbury and Winchester, too.

Readers' comments: Delightful, made so welcome, very comfortable. Most charming and friendly. Very warm welcome. Made most comfortable. Garden suite beautifully furnished, and with fresh flowers. Charming hostess, friendly and interesting too.

Old Romsey Road, Cadnam, no longer leads anywhere (its days ended when a nearby motorway replaced it). Little, white **WALNUT COTTAGE** stands in a pretty garden (with an old well) which traps the sun. One bedroom opens onto this.

All the rooms have been attractively furnished by Charlotte and Eric Osgood, who did much of the work themselves. There are two sitting-rooms, one with windows on all three sides. For meals other than breakfast, Charlotte recommends the White Hart inn nearby. £18.50–£20.

Readers' comments: Beautifully located, most helpful people. Delightful couple, charming rooms, comfortable; superb breakfasts. Very impressed by their care and attention. Faultless accommodation and welcome. Splendid. Brilliant hosts. Really enjoyed our stay. Lovely, and most comfortable. Very kind hosts. Made most welcome; situation ideal. [Tel: 01703 812275; postcode: SO40 2NP]

For explanation of code letters (C, D, M, PT, S, X) see inside front cover.

68

COVE HOUSE (No. 2)   **C D PT**
Ashton Keynes, Wiltshire, SN6 6NS   Tel: 01285 861221
South of Cirencester. Nearest main road: A419 from Swindon to Cirencester
(and M4, junctions 15/16).

3 Bedrooms. £19–£25 (less for 7 nights, or for 3 nights until March). Discounts for repeat bookings. Two have own bath or shower and toilet. Tea/coffee facilities. TV (in one). Views of garden.
Dinner. £16.50 for 3 courses and coffee, at 7.30pm (not Sundays). Less for 2 courses. Vegetarian or special diets if ordered. **Light suppers** if ordered.
2 Sitting-rooms. With open fire, central heating, TV.
Large garden

The narrow trickle running through this little village is in fact the infant Thames; you can walk right to its source from here. All around is a chain of large pools (originally gravel-diggings) now known as the Cotswold Water Park, which more or less encloses Ashton Keynes as if it were an island: birdwatchers come here to view the waterfowl.

Here Peter and Elizabeth Hartland live in one half of a 17th-century manor house (with later alterations) surrounded by a particularly lovely and secluded garden which has a succession of lawns and a paved carriage yard with barbecue beside its lily-pool. One of its previous owners was Puritan John Richmond, who had a part in founding Taunton, Massachusetts.

Indoors is a large, friendly sitting-room; a dining-room that has antiques and huge heirloom paintings; and Elizabeth's lovely flower arrangements everywhere. In the small library is an alcove lined with a large-scale, illuminated map of the area. Here Peter keeps a collection of packs for visitors, each full of carefully compiled information about various day outings and his own 'good food guide' to local eating-places. Yet another sitting-room, upstairs, is for TV and viewing a video of local sights.

Bedrooms have individuality – one green-and-white sprigged; another very flowery; a third (turquoise, with brass bedheads) has an unusual domed ceiling. Flowers are usually present.

Elizabeth uses garden produce for meals, at which the Hartlands dine with their guests. You might start with gazpacho or home-made pâté, perhaps; to be followed by a roast or salmon mayonnaise and then perhaps fruit sorbet or rhubarb-and-orange pudding.

Ashton Keynes is on the edge of the Cotswolds. Among other sightseeing possibilities the following are within an easy drive: Cheltenham, Oxford, Burford, Avebury, Bath, Stratford-upon-Avon, Marlborough, Blenheim, Cirencester, Malmesbury, Bibury village – also the gardens of Hidcote, Barnsley House and Kiftsgate. Ashton Keynes has fruit and trout farms nearby. Antique shops are numerous.

Readers' comments: Stayed several times. Excellent in all respects. Beautiful house, relaxed and friendly hosts. They could not have been kinder or more welcoming. The best breakfast I've ever had. Superb. Really lovely home and grounds, very helpful. Friendly; enjoyed our stay.

COWLEIGH PARK FARMHOUSE   C(7) D PT
Cowleigh Road, Great Malvern, Worcestershire, WR13 5HJ
Tel: 01684 566750
Nearest main road: A449 from Worcester to Ross-on-Wye (and the junction of
the M5 with M50).

3 **Bedrooms.** £18–£20 (less for 7 nights).
Prices go up from April. All have own
bath/shower/toilet. Tea/coffee facilities. TV.
Views of garden, country. No smoking.
Washing machine on request.
Dinner. £13.50 for 3 courses and coffee,
at 7pm (Monday–Friday only). Less for
2 courses. Non-residents not admitted.
Vegetarian or special diets if ordered. No
smoking. **Light suppers** if ordered.
1 **Sitting-room.** With open fire, central
heating, piano.
Large garden

The half-timbered house is 350 years old, and some of its beams are even older
(taken from a 13th-century moated manor house which once stood in the field
behind it). Approaching it from the high Malvern Hills, one passes along lanes
of larches and crags, shadows alternating with sunshine, the distant landscape
vanishing into a soft haze. On driving up to the door, there is a tranquil scene –
snowy alyssum spreading over old stone walls, an ancient cider-press on the brick
terrace. (The Worcestershire Way starts here.)

Beyond the slate-flagged hall, Sue Stringer has furnished the low-beamed
rooms attractively – comfortable antique chairs are placed around a large
inglenook in the main sitting-room, in one corner of which stands a Broadwood
grand piano. In the dining-room there is a yew refectory table with 18th-century
rush-seated chairs, near the window so that guests can enjoy the view of the
garden. Bedrooms have deep-pile carpets, stripped pine, board-and-latch doors,
and soft colours. One has a particularly pretty view, of lily-pool and rock garden.

Sue's dinners are imaginative – starting with, for instance, Stilton-and-
apple soup or salade niçoise; possibly with goulash to follow, and blackcurrant
gâteau.

The house has its own piped Malvern water.

Readers' comments: Warm, hospitable and friendly. Wished we could have stayed
longer. Very relaxing and comfortable home. Pretty rooms. Charming home.
Made very welcome. Food excellent and plentiful. Really nice welcome. Very
comfortable. Delicious breakfasts. Rate this very high.

**You stand a better chance of finding the right accommodation at
the right price in the right area if you are using an up-to-date
edition of this book, which is revised every year. Obtain an order
form for the next edition (published in November) by sending a
stamped addressed envelope, with 'SOTBT 1998' in the top left-
hand corner, to Explore Britain, Alston, Cumbria, CA9 3SL. You
will also receive a money-saving offer for 'Staying Off the Beaten
Track in Scotland' too.**

CRACROP FARM   S

Kirkcambeck, Cumbria, CA8 2BW Tel: 016977 48245
North of Brampton. Nearest main road: A6071 from Brampton to Longtown.

3 Bedrooms. £20. All have own shower/
toilet. Tea/coffee facilities. TV. Views of
garden, country. No smoking.
Light suppers by arrangement.
1 Sitting-room. With central heating, TV,
record-player. No smoking.
Large garden

Agriculture and forestry still predominate in the Border hills, truly unspoiled
countryside. The rolling western marches are less bleak than those to the
north-east, being well watered by streams and small rivers, and having plenty of
woodland, rich in wildlife.

Typically for the area, Cracrop is principally a stock farm, where the friendly
Stobarts are pleased if visitors take an interest in the work. Semi-finalists in a local
conservation competition, they have produced an excellent farm trail leaflet which
gives an insight into the holding and its interesting past, and also leaflets for walks
of a few miles from the house. Sturdier walkers have plenty of routes to follow, too.

If walking is not exertion enough, in the Victorian house are an exercise bike
and a rowing-machine (and a snooker table), and to recuperate in, a sauna (for an
extra charge) and a spa bath. Then you can relax in the garden to the sound of
the ornamental stream.

Bedrooms are sizeable, two giving views of the northern Pennines and the
Lake District hills, the other of the farmyard. Each has its own character, with
colour-co-ordinated furnishings. The downstairs rooms are comfortably furnished
in conventional style.

There is a choice of pubs for dinner, including the Abbey Bridge Inn by the
river at Lanercost, where the picturesque priory is partly ruined and partly in use
as church and village hall.

Though so out of the way, Cracrop is a good centre for outings long or short:
to see the notable Saxon cross at Bewcastle a few miles away; Hadrian's Wall and
Naworth Castle; or Kielder Water and the Border Forest Park which are a little
further.

Reader's comment: Superior accommodation.

The addresses of houses are geographically correct but postal
addresses sometimes differ (for correspondence, the only essential
element is the postcode).
   Information about the nearest town and 'A' road helps you to
locate the whereabouts of any village on a map; but before setting
off it is necessary to get precise instructions from your host as
many houses are very much 'off the beaten track'.

CRANDON HOUSE

Avon Dassett, Warwickshire, CV33 0AA   Tel: 01295 770652
South-east of Leamington Spa. Nearest main road: A423 from Banbury to
Coventry (and M40, junctions 11/12).

3 Bedrooms. £18–£20.50 (less for 7 nights).
All have own bath/shower/toilet. Tea/coffee
facilities. TV. Views of garden, country. No
smoking. Washing machine on request.
Dinner (by arrangement). From £13.50 for
3 courses (with some choices) and coffee, at
7pm. Vegetarian or special diets if ordered.
No smoking. **Light suppers** if ordered.
2 Sitting-rooms. With woodstove, central
heating, TV.
Large garden

A 'hostess of the year' award was once won by Deborah Lea – the most unassuming of people – who with her brother runs this guest-house on a smallholding
where a few rare British white cattle, sheep and poultry roam free. One can sit in
the glass sun-room to watch the geese and ducks enjoying life, with a view of hills
beyond. There is a separate television room with log stove, and a terrace outside;
in another direction, the small disused quarry (now overgrown) from which
Crandon stone was hewn is a picturesque feature. Everything about the house,
built in the 1950s, is solidly comfortable. The pink or blue bedrooms (with en
suite bathrooms) have nice pieces of furniture (a walnut suite, for instance, and a
shellback brocade chair) and large windows.

Deborah uses much home produce in the 'old-fashioned food' which her
guests love. A typical menu: garlic mushrooms, roast lamb, and chocolate mousse
– quality and presentation are outstanding. Breakfast options include porridge,
kippers and smoked haddock.

Readers' comments: We felt extremely welcome, no detail was overlooked.
Splendid hosts, house immaculate. Meals superb.

The village of Warmington,   near
Warwick Castle, Stratford and the
M40, is so tucked away that few
tourists find it. Around a sloping green
with duck-pond are ranged rows of
cottages built from local stone, and
POND COTTAGE is one of these. Vi
Viljoen has furnished its rooms with
great elegance – gleaming antique
furniture and silver contrast with the
rugged stones of the sitting-room
walls. One pretty bedroom is all blue –
from the silk bedspread to the birds-
and-flowers wallpaper. Vi serves such
meals as home-made soup, chicken
with almond sauce, a tart of her own

fruit or home-made ice cream. £17.50
(b & b).
Readers' comments: Delicious food,
extremely good value. Like staying
with a friend, every need anticipated.
[Tel: 01295 690682; postcode: OX17
1BU]

CRASKEN
C(14) D PT S

Falmouth Road, Helston, Cornwall, TR13 0PF   Tel: 01326 572670
Off A394 from Helston to Falmouth.

3 Bedrooms. £17.50–£20.50 (less for 2 nights; **less to readers of this book staying 5 or more nights**). Prices go up in July and August. Views of garden, country. Washing machine on request.
Dinner. £16.50 for 3 courses and coffee, at 7–9pm. Less for fewer courses. Non-residents not admitted. Vegetarian or special diets if ordered. **Light suppers** if ordered.
1 Sitting-room. With open fire, central heating, TV.
Large garden

Down a very long drive is a rare survival – a 17th-century farmhouse built court-yard-style, rather French, with its granary and old carpentry-shop adjoining it. The ancient midden (for dung), a 'listed' structure, is now a pretty, low-walled garden. And in the grounds a prehistoric site has been discovered – the name 'Crasken' is Celtic for 'settlement'. The granite walls of the house are two feet thick, a handsome background to tubs of flowers outside and arrangements of dried flowers within. The rooms are full of 'unconsidered trifles', from rag dolls to an array of willow-pattern plates, nosegays of wildflowers to log-cabin patchwork, Victorian crochet and jugs, rag rugs, pots of begonias. Additional rooms in out-buildings have their own baths, etc.

Jenny Ingram serves such good home-made meals (if ordered in advance) as crab and broccoli au gratin, chicken in lemon sauce, and meringues with gooseberry cream – the eating of which can be accompanied by a continuing soap-opera just outside the window, the never-ending domestic strife of a family of white ducks and one black intruder. Elsewhere you will find goats and donkeys as well as, in spring, a wonderful variety of wildflowers. In addition to some unusual plants, such as Himalayan honeysuckle, the garden has a grapevine.

Readers' comments: Best I have visited. Peaceful, picturesque and very welcoming. Uniquely decorated, secluded and peaceful. Most friendly, kind and thoughtful. Splendid place, not pretentious.

Near the centre of the lovely Lizard peninsula is **ROSEVEAR BRIDGE COTTAGE,** west of Mawgan, on a little tributary of the River Helford. A white house with neat brown shutters, it began life as a cowman's cottage centuries ago. Everything, including the sloping garden, is trim, the windows are low and deep-set, and an open-tread staircase rises through the sitting-room to immaculate bedrooms, varying in size. Hazel Howard uses garden produce for such homely meals as chicken pie and trifle. Closed in winter. £15.50–£16 (b & b).

Readers' comments: Absolutely loved it. Extremely friendly and helpful. [Tel: 01326 221672; postcode: TR12 6AZ]

73

THE CRAVEN

CMSX

Fernham Road, Uffington, Oxfordshire, SN7 7RD   Tel: 01367 820449
South-west of Oxford. Nearest main road: A420 from Oxford to Swindon
(and M4, junction 14).

7 Bedrooms. £14–£26 (less for 7 nights). Prices go up from May. Some have own bath/shower/toilet. Views of garden, country, river. No smoking. Washing machine on request.
Dinner. £13.50 for 3 courses (with choices) and coffee, at 7pm. Non-residents not admitted. Vegetarian or special diets if ordered. Wine available. No smoking preferred. **Light suppers** if ordered.
2 Sitting-rooms. With open fire, central heating, TV, video, record-player. No smoking preferred. Piano.
Large garden

Three hundred years ago, this cream-walled and thatched house was a hostelry – later described in *Tom Brown's Schooldays*.

One of the best bedrooms is on the ground floor – its four-poster hung with cabbage-rose chintz, its pillows in embroidered Victorian pillowslips; in the pretty bathroom is an antique weighing-machine. Upstairs, where passages and steps turn this way and that, are other beamed rooms, equally attractive – for example, a white iron half-tester bed is draped with white voile and covered with a white lace spread, in a room with blue sprigged wallpaper. The single rooms are as attractive as the double ones, and the bathrooms too.

The beamed sitting-room, with a log fire in its inglenook, has among other antiques a particularly splendid grandfather clock made in Lincolnshire.

Carol Wadsworth serves dinners at a big pine table in her huge L-shaped kitchen with scarlet walls and a dresser of blue-and-white china – or occasionally in the brick-paved courtyard among tubs of plants. A typical dinner: watercress soup, chicken in cheese sauce, and chocolate rum gâteau. Sunday lunches too.

Readers' comments: Charming place and proprietor. Friendly. Special and enjoyable. Nothing too much trouble, house most attractive, dinner delicious.

A long drive leads through pheasant woods to 300-year-old **ASHEN COPSE** (at Coleshill). It is built of stone and brick; and around lie the 600 acres of the Hoddinotts' farm.

This is an ideal house to bring children for a country holiday as there is a particularly good family room separate from the rest. By the staircase to the other room are row upon row of colourful rosettes won at pony shows by the Hoddinotts' daughter every year since she was eight. From this bedroom you can look beyond the small swimming-pool (unheated) to the famous Uffington White Horse and the prehistoric Ridgeway.

From Ashen Copse there is a

footpath all the way to Great Coxwell Barn, built by monks in the 13th century. No smoking. Light suppers if ordered. £18–£20 (b & b).
Readers' comments: Attractive house, pleasant welcome and attention. A tremendously positive experience. [Tel: 01367 240175; postcode: SN6 7PU]

CRESSBROOK HALL   C D M

Cressbrook, Derbyshire, SK17 8SY   Tel: 0500 121248 (free)
East of Buxton. Nearest main road: A6 from Buxton to Bakewell.

3 Bedrooms (plus 5 in cottages).
£17.50–£30.50 (less for 3 nights). Prices go
up from April. Some have own bath/shower/
toilet. Tea/coffee facilities. TV. Views of
garden, country, river. No smoking
preferred. Washing machine on request.
Dinner. £16.50 for 3 courses (with choices)
and coffee, at 7pm. Non-residents not
admitted. Vegetarian or special diets if
ordered. Wine available. No smoking
preferred. **Light suppers** if ordered.
1 Sitting-room. With open fire, central
heating, TV, piano, record-player. No
smoking preferred.
Large garden

A spectacular mansion in a spectacular setting, looking over a deep limestone
gorge at the end of which is the old watermill that, in the early days of the cotton
industry, brought its owner the wealth with which to build himself this palatial
home in 1835. The gorge is almost alpine, the extensive gardens were laid out by
an assistant to Paxton (of Chatsworth and Crystal Palace fame), and the rooms
are of exceptional splendour. Great windows overlook a balustraded terrace.

Some bedrooms are on two floors of the main house: one has a remarkable
domed ceiling and a bay window from which to enjoy the superb view, right down
to the old mill and the village that was uniformly designed in keeping with the Hall
itself. Others are in lodges mostly for self-catering (with optional meals in the Hall).

Beryl Bailey and her husband redecorated all the plaster ceilings in good colour
combinations. They added a conservatory with small fountain, where meals are
sometimes served instead of in the big dining-room. A typical dinner: melon,
boeuf bourguignonne, and mille-feuilles (breakfasts are equally ample).

The Baileys have provided a beauty therapy room, sunbed, sauna, fitness
equipment and games room for visitors to use (fee for the first three) as well as a
children's play area away from the house, football/cricket ground, and a laundry.

Readers' comments: Idyllic situation. Welcomed with warmth and sincerity.
Strongly recommended.

As one of England's golf champions
(1972), Mary Everard used to travel
the world but eventually chose the
remote hamlet of Rowland (just north
of Bakewell) in which to settle down.
Here, at 18th-century **HOLLY COT-
TAGE**, she welcomes guests to her
elegant sitting-room, a raspberry-and-
white dining-room furnished with old
maple chairs from America, and pretty
bedrooms with white board doors.
Dinner or supper available by arrangement. No smoking. £18–£19.

Readers' comments: Excellent in every
way. Lovely house, warm welcome,
good food and wonderful setting. [Tel:
01629 640624; postcode: DE45 1NR]

CRIB FARM
C(7) S

Long Causeway, Luddenden Foot, West Yorkshire, HX2 6JJ
Tel: 01422 883285 (Messages: 01422 886230)
West of Halifax. Nearest main road: A58 from Rochdale to Halifax
(and M62, junction 24).

4 Bedrooms. £15–£18 (less for 3 nights).
Some have own shower/toilet. TV. Views of
garden, country. No smoking.
Dinner (not in winter). £8.50 for 3 courses
(with some choices) and coffee, at 6.30pm.
Vegetarian or special diets if ordered. Wine
available. **Light suppers.**
1 Sitting-room. With open fire, central
heating, piano. Bar.
Large garden
Closed in November and December.

A necessary break to change horses on the long cross-Pennine journey from
Lancashire to Yorkshire brought this 17th-century moorland house into being, for
originally it was a coaching inn. Centuries later it became – and still is – a dairy-
farm, though its role as a haven for travellers continues too, even though they now
arrive by car, by train (to Halifax) or even by air (to Leeds). The Hitchen family
have been here since 1815 and a framed auction notice on the wall proves it.

The old house has a warm and hospitable atmosphere, with rooms decorated
in light and cheerful colours. Comfortable and unpretentious, it was first
recommended because of Pauline's cooking. A typical menu: melon or home-
made asparagus soup, home-reared turkey with garden vegetables, a choice of
puddings from strawberries and cream to apple pie, or cheeses.

Luddenden Foot, which lies below the farm, once had a railway station, where
Branwell Brontë worked as a clerk, and the village will be familiar also to viewers
of Thora Hird's 'In Loving Memory'. From the farm there are sweeping views to
the wild uplands of Midgley Moor, but down below Branwell found his station
dank and depressing – 'hacked out of a great black rock-face', as Lynne Reid
Banks describes it in *Dark Quartet*. He, the rich son of a local mill-owner, and Irish
labourers together drank themselves silly at local inns; and it was at Luddenden
that he first took drugs too, stealing money from the station till to pay for them.

Readers' comments: A welcoming farming family. Very comfortable and easy. A
very happy week.

Terraced houses used to be built one
on top of another to fit the steep slopes
of Hebden Bridge. A pair of these have
been united to form **PROSPECT
END** (8 Prospect Terrace, Savile
Road), where the guest-rooms are
approached through the garden, while
the kitchen/breakfast-room above them
is at street level and the sitting-room
windows look onto treetops. The two
en suite bedrooms, in pale pink, are
neat and well equipped. Ann Anthon
can provide dinners, but most guests
go to the many restaurants in the town,

which has become something of a
cultural centre for the south Pennines
and has some interesting shops. £16.
[Tel: 01422 843586; postcode: HX7
6NA]

CROFT HOUSE

Newton Reigny, Cumbria, CA11 0AY   Tel: 01768 865435
North-west of Penrith. Nearest main road: A6 from Penrith to Carlisle (and M6, junction 41).

rear view

3 Bedrooms. £18–£20 (less for 3 nights). Bargain breaks. Some have own bath/shower/toilet. Tea/coffee facilities. TV. Views of garden, country. No smoking. Washing machine on request.
Light suppers sometimes.
1 Sitting-room. With open fire, central heating, TV, record-player. No smoking.
Large garden
Closed from mid-December to mid-January.

In an unpretentious Cumbrian village, Croft House is an elegantly proportioned house built in 1755, now the home of Gina and Richard Farncombe. Gina, who went to art school only as a mature student and now works as an illustrator, has her paintings and drawings all over the house, and one wall of the entrance hall is covered with her mural of local scenery, with Saddleback (Blencathra) in the background. (Smiling at it is a Victorian portrait of one of Richard's ancestors, who had an adventurous life for a lady of her period.)

All the rooms are of the scale one would expect in a Georgian house, and they are decorated to advantage in plain colours. In the sitting-room, settees face each other across an oriental rug in front of an open fireplace with glazed bookcases on each side.

No evening meal is served because the village inn offers excellent food, though a light supper can often be produced. Like breakfast, this may be served in a conservatory at the back, under a grapevine which may be as old as the house. Beyond the lawn is a nature reserve and pond where badgers and unusual birds may be seen. On the horizon are the peaks of the Lake District – Saddleback and Skiddaw.

Up the staircase – lined with more of Gina's striking paintings – the bedrooms have plain coloured walls, carved pine bedsteads, some antique furniture, and William Morris fabrics. They include a family suite with bunk room and bathroom. There is an additional bedroom in a converted barn (usually for self-catering), which has a woodstove as well as its own bathroom. Or some people like to sleep in a comfortable gypsy caravan in the grounds (the Farncombes used to have several of these, which they used for conducted treks into the Lake District). Guests have free membership of a local country club, with swimming-pool, tennis courts, etc.

The village takes its name from one of William the Conqueror's barons. His seat, in the next village, is not open to the public, but you can peer into the private dungeon he maintained. A few miles away, Hutton-in-the-Forest, often open during the summer, is a Jacobean mansion with fine gardens and woods. Ullswater is close, but this peaceful and little-known area has great attractions of its own.

Readers' comments: Delighted. Everything was right.

CROSSWAYS FARM   **C D PT S**

Raikes Lane, Abinger, Surrey, RH5 6P7.   Tel: 01306 730173
South-west of Dorking. Nearest main road: A25 from Guildford to Dorking
(and M25, junction 9).

3 **Bedrooms.** £17–£19 (less for 5 nights).
Prices go up from Easter. Some have own
bath/toilet. Tea/coffee facilities. Views of
garden, country. No smoking. Washing
machine on request.
Light suppers.
1 **Sitting-room.** With open fire, central
heating, TV, piano, record-player.
Small garden
**Closed from mid-December to mid-
January.**

Meredith's *Diana of the Crossways* (one of those books most people have heard of
and few have read) took its title from this historic building of unusual architectural interest, which featured in a film about the 17th-century diarist John Evelyn.

One steps through the arched door in a high wall to find a small, enclosed
garden with a flagged path leading to the wide front door of the house. In its
façade decorative brickwork combines with local sandstone, and Dutch-style
arches curve over the small-paned windows. There is an immense chimney-stack
towering above – 30 feet in circumference. But the most striking feature of all
is the great oak staircase inside, its two flights leading up to large, beamed bedrooms, simply but comfortably furnished (there is a suite consisting of a double
and a twin room with bathroom); the balusters and newels are handsomely
carved.

The house has had many owners since it was built about 1620. For the last 30
years, the Hughes family have farmed here, producing beef and corn. By arrangement, Sheila Hughes serves homely farmhouse meals (like Irish stew, fish pie,
roast chicken etc.), or you can eat well at, for instance, nearby Wootton Hatch.
Breakfast options include, if ordered in advance, such extras as fishcakes or
kidneys. There is a croquet lawn.

Readers' comments: Warm welcome. Comfortable.

A mile or so westward is one of
Surrey's beauty-spots, picturesque
Shere with old cottages around a
stream. Here is **CHERRY TREES**, in
Gomshall Lane, a traditional 'twenties
brick and tile-hung house in a garden
of winding flowerbeds and colourful
shrubs (with seats in leafy nooks from
which to enjoy hill views). One of
the bedrooms is on the ground floor,
in former stables overlooking the
pretty garden. There is also a swimming-pool. Breakfast is served in a
cream-walled room with oak dresser
and leaded casements; for dinner,
Olwen Warren recommends the White

Horse inn a few yards away. No
sitting-room for guests. No smoking.
Closed in winter. £18–£19.
Reader's comment: Excellent location
and perfect treatment. [Tel: 01483
202288; postcode: GU5 9HE]

78

CWM CRAIG FARM   C S X
Bolston Road, Little Dewchurch, Herefordshire, HR2 6PS
Tel: 01432 840250
North-west of Ross-on-Wye. Nearest main road: A49 from Ross to Hereford
(and M50, junction 4).

3 Bedrooms. £15–£17 (less for 2 nights).
One has own shower/toilet. Tea/coffee
facilities. Views of garden, country.
Light suppers if ordered.
1 Sitting-room. With open fire, central
heating, TV.
Large garden

The 18th-century farm near the River Wye would be a good choice for a family.
Children can watch very tame, hand-reared calves being fed, and use the games
room which has a snooker table and dartboard. A good family room (with
figured walnut suite and shapely bevelled mirrors) has books, television and
games; also a particularly good bath- and shower-room. There is a second dining-
room (with kitchen) reserved for those who want to bring in their own food; and a
utility room.

All rooms are high and light, kept in immaculate condition by Gladys
Lee, with far views through their large sash windows. Fine architectural details
including marble fireplaces, arches and panelled doors are complemented by pink
velvet wing chairs or others in William Morris covers.

In the attractive garden, an old stone cider-press is now planted with colourful
busy Lizzies.

Readers' comments: Beautiful and quiet house, tastefully furnished, comfortable
beds: quite wonderful. Lovely friendly people. Amazing attention to detail – three
kinds of marmalade, and even the shower is computerized! Quite entranced: I
defy anyone to better it.

Picturesque Hoarwithy, on the River
Wye, has not only an exceptional
Italianate church, with much use of
marble, porphyry and other exotic
materials, but also a good guest-house
in an 18th-century building called the
OLD MILL. The mill-race flows
through the garden, clematis and roses
grow up the front of the cream-painted
house. Beyond a tiled and stone-walled

hall is a beamed sitting-room with
woodstove and a dining-room of
scarlet-clothed tables (a typical meal:
melon-and-prawn cocktail, chicken
casserole, chocolate roulade). Carol
Probert has furnished the bedrooms in
cottage style. £16–£18.

Readers' comments: Hospitable and
helpful. Excellent accommodation.
Made to feel very much at home,
food excellent. Friendly welcome,
picturesque building, pleasant outlook,
dinners imaginative. A lovely room;
friendly hospitality. [Tel: 01432
840602; postcode: HR2 6QH]

DAIRY FARM   C D M S
St Andrews Lane, Cranford, Northamptonshire, NN14 4AQ
Tel: 01536 330273
East of Kettering. Nearest main road: A14 from Kettering towards Cambridge.

country. No smoking. Washing machine on request.
Dinner. £12 for 3 courses (with choices) and coffee, at 7pm. Less for 2 courses. Non-residents not admitted. Vegetarian or special diets if ordered. No smoking. **Light suppers** if ordered.
1 Sitting-room. With open fire, central heating, TV, record-player. No smoking.

3 Bedrooms. £19–£25 (less for 14 nights). Some have own bath/shower/toilet. Tea/coffee facilities. TV. Views of garden,

Garden
Closed from mid-December to mid-January.

This is not in fact a dairy-farm but arable and sheep. Its name derives from the old dairy around which the manor house was built, in 1610. It is a fine building with mullioned lattice windows in limestone walls and a thatched roof. Its noble chimney-stacks, finials on the gables, dormer windows and dignified porch give it great character. In the grounds stands a circular stone dovecote (mediaeval) with unique rotating ladder inside, used for collecting the birds and eggs from the 400 pigeonholes that line it.

Audrey and John Clarke have hung old family portraits in the sitting-room, and furnished the house with things like oak chests and ladderback chairs that are in keeping with it. Some bedrooms, one with four-poster, overlook church and mansion nearby.

Meals consist of straightforward home cooking – soups, roasts, fruit pies – using fruit and vegetables from the garden. Mrs Clarke also does a cordon bleu menu, which costs a little more and has to be ordered ahead.

Visitors enjoy croquet, and walks (by a willow-fringed stream, across-country, or simply to the Woolpack Inn). This is good cycling country, too. Sightseeing possibilities include Burghley House, Boughton House, Rockingham Castle, the mediaeval stone town of Stamford, Althorp, Lamport and Kirby Halls, Peterborough Cathedral, Cambridge, Fotheringhay, Uppingham and Oundle. And at Kettering, Wicksteed Park is an ideal place to take children. Oundle is as attractive as many old Cotswold towns, for the local stone is the same, but much less frequented by tourists. The buildings of its famous public school are like an Oxford college. One can take boat trips on the River Nene, and visit watermills and a country park just on the outskirts, or the gardens at Coton Manor. For the equestrian-minded, there are the Burghley horse trials in September.

The farm is close to the borders of both Cambridgeshire and Bedfordshire which means that it is also easy to visit such places of interest as Elton Hall, Hinchingbrooke House (a much altered Norman nunnery) and 18th-century Island Hall; or Bromham watermill on the banks of the Ouse, Stevington windmill, Stagsden bird gardens and all the Bunyan sights in and around Bedford (which has the exceptional Cecil Higgins art gallery too). Grafham Water is a big, naturalized reservoir. Huntingdon has a Cromwell museum.

Readers' comments: Very special, will return. Delicious food; peaceful; attentive hosts. Very kind, food plentiful, peaceful. Delightful house and setting. Good, friendly reception. Good food, relaxed atmosphere.

DAMSELLS LODGE   C D M PT S

The Park, Painswick, Gloucestershire, GL6 6SR   Tel: 01452 813777
North of Stroud. Nearest main road: A46 from Stroud to Cheltenham
(and M5, junction 13).

3 Bedrooms. £19.50–£21.50 (less for 3 nights or continental breakfast). Bargain breaks. One has own shower/toilet. Tea/coffee facilities. TV. Views of garden, country. Washing machine on request. **Light suppers.**
1 Sitting-room. With log stove, central heating, TV, piano.
Small garden

This very comfortable house was originally the lodge to the nearby mansion. It is in a peaceful rural lane and has truly spectacular views from every window across a small garden of lawns, stone terrace and flowering shrubs. Only breakfast and snack suppers are provided – guests eat dinner at the nearby Royal William or in one of Painswick's restaurants: the Royal Oak or Country Elephant, for instance.

Judy Cooke is a welcoming hostess who soon makes friends with her visitors. She has made the Lodge immaculate and very comfortable. The huge sitting-room has windows on three sides, and a big log stove. Everywhere there are thick carpets and good furniture (even the bathroom is pretty luxurious). Perhaps the best bedroom is one separate from the house: it is in a one-floor garden cottage, with huge sliding windows through which to step straight onto the lawn or to view the distant hills while still in bed, and ideal for anyone who finds stairs difficult.

Painswick church is famous for its 99 enormous yews, centuries old, clipped into arches or other neat shapes, and for its fine peal of twelve bells. In an ancient ceremony every September, children dance and sing round the church. The village has many antique shops. To the north lies the cathedral city of Gloucester (it houses the outstanding National Waterways Museum, among many other sights), and to the south the wooded Cotswold Hills, with particularly spectacular views from Minchinhampton and Rodborough commons (National Trust land).

The steep ups and downs of this hilly area mean there are many scenic car rides – for instance, in the direction of Prinknash Abbey (part mediaeval, part modern – with a viewing gallery above the monks' pottery and a collection of exotic birds) from which there are views to the River Severn – or go to the observation point high above the beech woods of Cooper's Hill, topped by a may-pole. Further on is Crickley Hill (with three trails to choose from – geological, archaeological or ecological – and more superb views). You could return via Birdlip and Sheepscombe; or take the Ermine Way (a Roman road, straight as a spear) to Cirencester, perhaps returning via Sapperton, sited on a steep ridge which overlooks the 'Golden Valley' of the River Frome – truly golden in the autumn, when the beech woods turn colour. The church at Sapperton has splendid carvings.

Readers' comments: Excellent accommodation; the place and the owners delightful. Immaculate; lovely setting, gorgeous view; helpful. Friendly. Always lovely. Absolutely marvellous. Delightful hosts. Wonderful, homely place. Perfect setting. First-class accommodation. Helpful, and very warm welcome. Impeccably kept house, quiet. Friendly welcome. Great place to stay.

DEEPLEIGH

CPTX

Langley Marsh, Somerset, TA4 2UU   Tel: 01984 623379
North-west of Taunton. Nearest main road: B3227 from Taunton to
Wiveliscombe (and M5, junction 25).

3 Bedrooms. £18–£19.50. All have own shower/toilet. Tea/coffee facilities. TV. Views of garden, country. No smoking. Washing machine on request.
Light suppers if ordered.
2   Sitting-rooms. With wood-burning stove, central heating, TV.
Large garden

Through high banks of red earth smothered with honeysuckle and foxgloves, one makes one's way into a little frequented yet very lovely part of Somerset to find this mediaeval house perched on a hillside. Its cream walls make a perfect backdrop to tubs of flowers; and from the chairs on its paved terrace are fine views.

Susan and Derek Clarke have furnished the hotel most attractively. In one room, a pretty blue-and-white bordered wallpaper matches frilled curtains with blue ribbons; in the beamed sitting-room (which has a wall of oak planks at one end and an inglenook at the other) there are a number of comfortable sofas, colourwashed walls, and oriental carpets to match. Each bedroom is different – Laura Ashley paper in one, silky Chinese-style fabrics in another, a lacy coverlet in a third.

Many paths converge here, from what were once quarries (now picturesquely overgrown). Previously, Deepleigh was a cider-house frequented by the thirsty quarrymen. The room where the cider-press once stood now boasts its original fireplace, salvaged from the lumber room. Light suppers only, but guests can dine very well at the Three Horseshoes in the village, two minutes' walk away, or at a variety of excellent local pubs.

Sitting-room at Deepleigh

DEERFELL
C

Blackdown Park, Fernden Lane, Haslemere, Surrey, GU27 3LA
Tel: 01428 653409
South of Haslemere. Nearest main road: A286 from Haslemere to Midhurst.

2 Bedrooms. £18 (less for 3 nights). Both have own bath/shower/toilet. Tea/coffee facilities. TV. Views of garden. No smoking. Washing machine on request.
Dinner. £8.50 for 2 courses (with choices) and coffee, from 6.30pm (not Sundays). Non-residents not admitted. Vegetarian or special diets if ordered. No smoking. **Light suppers** if ordered.
1 Sitting-room. With open fire, central heating, record-player. No smoking. Piano.
Large garden
Closed from mid-December to mid-January.

The Black Down, a Stone Age stronghold 8000 years ago, rises to nearly 1000 feet. The ferny lane that winds up it, beech trees arching overhead, gives way to sandy heathland where, in Tudor times, iron nodules were grubbed up to be forged into guns, pots and the decorative firebacks that are to be seen in old houses for miles around. To provide power for their forges, the ironworkers dammed streams – hence the chain of 'furnace ponds' which one passes on the way up.

One of the wealthiest ironmasters built himself in 1607 a mansion that is still here, just over the Sussex border. (Deerfell was originally its coach house, erected three centuries later.) Cromwell occupied it during the Civil War, and Tennyson was a frequent visitor; you can see the home he built and where he died, at the National Trust carpark on the other side of the Down.

As to Deerfell, its conversion from coach house to home was well done, retaining such features as stone-mullioned windows and latched board doors, but with such modern additions as a glass sun-room and a fireplace of green marble. Elizabeth Carmichael has furnished it with antiques, old rugs and colour schemes which are predominantly soft brown and cream. Bedrooms are comfortable and spacious. Meals (which are usually served in the handsome dining-room with grandfather clock, piano and an ancestral portrait of William IV's physician) are well cooked, ample and unpretentious – for instance, moussaka and treacle tart or chocolate cheesecake. Breakfast sometimes includes wild mushrooms.

London is only 45 minutes away by train from Haslemere.

Readers' comments: Very comfortable and pleasant stay. Lovely home. Felt relaxed and rested. Everything very much to our liking. Total peace and quiet. Warm and friendly.

Facts (prices, etc.) at the top of entries are supplied by the proprietors themselves. While every effort is made to ensure that these are correct at the time of going to press, they may alter thereafter: please check when you book.

DELF VIEW HOUSE   **PT S**
Church Street, Eyam, Derbyshire, S30 1QW   Tel: 01433 631533
North of Bakewell. Nearest main road: A623 from Chapel-en-le-Frith towards
Chesterfield.

2 Bedrooms. £18–£26. Prices go up from
April. Bargain breaks. One has own shower.
Tea/coffee facilities. TV. Views of garden,
country. No smoking. Washing machine on
request.
Light suppers if ordered.
1 Sitting-room. With open fire, central
heating, piano. No smoking.
Large garden

In 1665, infection from the Great Plague travelled from London to Eyam in a roll
of cloth. Heroically, the villagers cut themselves off lest they should infect others
in the county. They held their church services outdoors in a hollow called the
Delf, above which was this gritstone house (much enlarged in 1830). Every
August a commemorative service is held in the Delf for the 259 (out of 350) who
died.

Today, Delf View is one of the most elegant houses in this book, lovingly
restored by architect David Lewis and his wife. They have furnished it with such
outstanding antiques as silver-legged beds from France painted with romantic
pastoral scenes, a Sheraton four-poster elegantly draped, an inlaid fortepiano of
1820, a ship made by Napoleonic prisoners-of-war, and an alabaster Wren fireplace salvaged from London. Sometimes candles are lit in the crystal chandelier
of the blue sitting-room. There are a sunken bath in a brown-and-gold bathroom,
embroidered towels, Augustus John drawings . . . and to complement all this you
may be offered at breakfast a soufflé omelette or apples poached in Calvados, as
well as local bacon and so forth. Breakfast is served in a stone-flagged dining-
room in which a bust of Florence Nightingale looks out through a prettily draped
window to a flowery courtyard. Outside is a garden with a croquet lawn which
overlooks the Delf.

Reader's comment: Very pleasing room and excellent breakfast.

Sitting-room at Laurel Farm (see page 175)

84

DEMESNES MILL

C(5) PT S

Barnard Castle, County Durham, DL12 8PE   Tel: 01833 637929
Nearest main road: A66 from Scotch Corner towards Brough.

4 Bedrooms. £17.50–£20 (less for 3 nights). Two have own bath/shower/toilet. Tea/coffee facilities. TV. Views of garden, country, river. Balcony. No smoking. Washing machine on request.
1 Sitting-room. With open fire, central heating, TV, record-player. No smoking.
Small garden
Closed from December to February.

After 25 years in Canada, Joan and Bob Young returned to their native county and fell for a near-derelict mill on the River Tees. Years of hard and patient work have transformed it.

Where four pairs of millstones once ground flour is now a long sitting-room furnished in antique style. Windows overlook the rushing river immediately below and a new conservatory at one end gives a splendid downriver view of a natural weir, where herons, dippers and kingfishers are often seen. Under the beamed ceiling supported by cast iron columns, some of the mill mechanism survives, including one of the millstones. Off the sitting-room is the breakfast-area where Joan's visitors help themselves from an extensive buffet with fresh baked bread.

Below, at water level, are the gears through which the stones were driven and the waterwheel, which Bob is still working on. Made of cast iron, the works were installed around 1824, when the mill, which had occupied the site since the 15th century, was brought up to date.

The big bedrooms upstairs, which overlook the weir, are decorated elaborately and have bathrooms equipped to high Canadian standards. The single room is more generous than many such.

The mill once served all the farms on the enormous Raby estates (whose centre – Raby Castle – is one of the highlights of this interesting area). It is approached across the Demesnes, a big public open space almost in the centre of Barnard Castle, where numerous eating-places are within walking distance for dinner.

Piercebridge is a carefully conserved village accessible from Scotch Corner on the A1. **HOLME HOUSE** is just outside it, over the North Yorkshire border by a matter of yards. Down a metalled farm road, it is a spacious Georgian house furnished with antiques and with many sporting prints and watercolours around. Guests breakfast at a long, stripped-pine farmhouse table (light suppers if ordered). Anne Graham's family are animal-lovers, and there is a variety of livestock at the adjoining farm, which is

managed by her husband. The two bedrooms have splendid views of open countryside, and there are interesting Roman remains nearby. £16.50. [Tel: 01325 374280; postcode: DL2 3SY]

85

DORNDEN   **C D**

Church Lane, Old Sodbury, (Avon), South Gloucestershire, BS17 6NB
Tel: 01454 313325
North-east of Bristol. Nearest main road: A432 from Bristol to Old Sodbury
(and M4, junction 18).

9 Bedrooms. £20–£25 (less for 2 nights at weekends or 4 mid-week). Prices go up from Easter. Bargain breaks. Some have own bath/shower/toilet. TV. Views of garden, country. Washing machine on request.
Dinner. £9.50 for 3 courses (with choices of sweet) and coffee, at 6.45pm. Non-residents not admitted. Vegetarian or special diets if ordered.
1 Sitting-room. With central heating, piano.
Large garden
Closed from mid-September to mid-October.

An immaculate garden surrounds the big guest-house – flowerbeds and box-hedges in trim and neat array, with a large vegetable and fruit garden to supply the kitchen. From its lawns and grass tennis court, set high up, there are splendid views.

This is the place for a quiet stay, well placed for exploring the scenic counties of Somerset, Wiltshire and Gloucestershire around it. All the rooms are sedate and comfortable in a style appropriate to what it was: in mid-Victorian days, a vicarage and with features of the period still retained – from the beautifully polished tiles of the hall to the terrace onto which the sitting-room opens.

Daphne Paz serves traditional favourites at dinner – such as roasts, steak-and-kidney pie, or trout with almonds, followed by a choice of, say, sticky toffee pudding, pies or crumbles, and fresh soft fruit from the garden in summer, and then cheeses: very moderately priced.

Old Sodbury is conveniently placed near a motorway yet is a quiet retreat at the south end of the Cotswolds. In its immediate vicinity are 17th-century Dyrham Park (which the NT regards as one of its most spectacular properties – its tapestries and its gardens are outstanding) and Westonbirt Arboretum.

Quickly reached from, for instance, London, it is also well placed as a centre from which to go sightseeing. Bath and Bristol are near, and Wales only a short hop across the Severn estuary; while, using the M5, one can quickly arrive in Somerset, Devon and the rest of the west country. But there is no need to go far.

Close by is Castle Combe – a most picturesque village, nestling in a valley around which wooded hills climb high (it's a place of mellow stone houses, a turreted church with lovely fan-vaulting, canopied market cross, and a twisting brook that flows under its ancient bridge). Other lovely villages include Biddestone and Badminton in particular. Two things contributed to the beauty of north-west Wiltshire: the fact that wealth (from wool weaving) was amassed during a period of fine architectural style, and the availability of lovely gold or creamy stone with which to build. Rivers watered fertile pastures and carved out valleys where woodlands flourish.

Readers' comments: Strongly recommended. Cooking of high standard. Excellent value. Very friendly. Always excellent, delightful hosts. Friendly attitude, always ready for a laugh.

DOWER HOUSE   **C(8) PT S**
Bradford Peverell, Dorset, DT2 9SF   Tel: 01305 266125
North-west of Dorchester. Nearest main road: A37 from Dorchester to Yeovil.

3 Bedrooms. £16.50 (less for 4 nights). Price goes up from April. All have own bath/toilet. Tea/coffee facilities. Views of garden, country. No smoking. Washing machine on request.
Light suppers sometimes.
1 Sitting-room. With open fire, central heating, TV, piano. No smoking.
Large garden
Closed from December to February.

One steps straight into the dining-hall of this 1830s house, with oriental rugs on a floor of polished boards, Chippendale-style chairs and interesting heirloom paintings. From the coral-walled sitting-room, bookshelves surrounding its log fire, is a pretty village view framed by the shutters of the sash windows.

Upstairs, past more books and a doll's house on the landing, are attractive bedrooms with sprigged wallpaper, pine or flower-painted bedsteads, and real cotton or linen sheets and old spreads which Kips Eaton regularly tracks down in Dorchester market. Old-fashioned bathrooms are another pleasure in keeping with the style of the house – as are the large walled garden (providing fruit and vegetables), the home-made cakes at teatime, and Michael's home-baked bread at breakfast. Jam, too, is home-made and honey comes from the Eatons' hives.

When Kips provides a light supper it is likely to comprise something like fennel and prawn pasta followed by raspberries with meringues and cream. Full dinners may be available.

Readers' comments: Very pleasant. Particularly welcoming and a beautiful home. Wonderful: we felt welcome and at home. Whimsical collections. Warm, happy, gracious hosts. Very friendly. Breakfasts generous and delicious.

Thatched roof, latched doors, low beams and flagged floors are as you would expect in 1586, the year when **OLD MANOR COTTAGE** at Winterborne Steepleton was built. In the thick walls, little leaded casements are stone-mullioned; and floors slope with age. Charmian Goodenough-Bayly has furnished the rooms in simple cottage style, white walls complemented by pine furniture. Her husband made model ships when in the Navy: these, his collection of shells, and his mementoes of years in the Middle East give the house individuality. Outside, a brilliant japonica is a feature of the flint-walled garden. Charmian's dinners (which

include a glass of wine) comprise such courses as kipper pâté, roast chicken, and treacle tart. £15–£20 (b & b).
Readers' comments. Very nicely furnished. Friendly and interesting hosts. [Tel: 01305 889512; postcode: DT2 9LZ]

EASTCOTT MANOR　　　　　　　　　　　　　　　C D S
Eastcott, Wiltshire, SN10 4PL　　Tel: 01380 813313
South of Devizes. Nearest main road: A360 from Devizes to Salisbury.

4 Bedrooms. £18–£21 (less for 3 nights; and **15% reduction to readers of this book for 3 nights, December to February**). All have own bath/shower/toilet. Tea/coffee facilities. TV (in two). Views of garden, country. No smoking preferred. Washing machine on request.
Dinner (if ordered in advance). £15 for 4 courses, wine and coffee, at 7.30pm. Less for 2 courses. Non-residents not admitted.
Light suppers if ordered.
1 Sitting-room. With open fire.
Large garden

As early as 1150 there was a house on this spot. The present building has parts dating back to the 16th century, but every century since has added its contribution. Furnishings vary. Most are fine antiques – the refectory table in the dining-room (its walls hung with ancestral portraits) is 400 years old, for instance; and one alcove houses Crown Derby and other porcelain. Up the oak staircase with barley-sugar balusters are attractive bedrooms; the largest has peach-and-white panelled walls with big sash windows at each end and rural views. There is now a conservatory.

In outbuildings or paddocks are always some of the Firths' horses: they have trained many well-known 'trials' horses. Janet's other great interest is cookery, for which she has a number of diplomas. A typical meal, served on a generous help-yourself basis: fish soufflé, lamb provençal, caramelized fruit and cheeses (vegetables and fruit are home-produced). Jam and cordials for sale.

Readers' comments: Lovely house. Friendly and helpful. Delicious food. Very much enjoyed. Kind and welcoming. Delicious supper.

Westward lies West Ashton, the former vicarage of which is **WELAM HOUSE**, in Bratton Road. It was built from Bath stone in 1840 in the 'goth-ick' style so fashionable then – hence the pointed windows, arched fireplaces and stained glass in the hall (with the crest of Lord Long, a great local landowner at the time). There is exceptionally decorative plasterwork, particularly in the sitting-room added in 1865, which has pomegranates on the ceiling and massive Jacobean-style pendants. Outside is a lawn with lily-pool, bowling green and putting; alter-natively, there is the shady canopy of a weeping cherry under which to recline

in a deckchair on a sunny day. Elizabeth Cronan serves only light suppers. Closed in winter. £16.
Readers' comments: Very comfortable. Excellent value. Lovely, peaceful house. [Tel: 01225 755908; postcode: BA14 6AZ]

EASTON HOUSE   **C**
Chidham Lane, Chidham, West Sussex, PO18 8TF   Tel: 01243 572514
West of Chichester. Nearest main road: A259 from Chichester towards
Portsmouth.

2 Bedrooms. £18–£20 (less for 3 nights or
continental breakfast). Bargain breaks. One
has own bath/toilet. Tea/coffee facilities.
Views of garden, country, sea. No smoking.
Washing machine on request.
1 Sitting-room. With log stove, central
heating, TV, video, piano, record-player.
Small garden
Closed from mid-December to mid-January.

Every corner of this Tudor house has been filled by Mary Hartley with unusual
antiques and trifles. A modern white-and-red poppy wallpaper contrasts with old
beams, oriental rugs with stone-flagged floor, scarlet folkweave curtains with
antique furniture. All around is a fine collection of mirrors (Spanish, art deco,
rococo – every conceivable kind) and pictures of cats; Mary is musical, and guests
are welcome to play on the Bechstein or join in chamber music sessions. It's a free-
and-easy atmosphere, a house full of character and cats. Bathrooms are pretty.

Although only breakfast is served (one can dine well in Chichester, particularly at the Droveway, at the Old House at Home in Chidham, or in nearby
Emsworth), visitors are welcome to linger in the comfortable lime-green sitting-
room with its log stove (where tea is served on arrival); or in the garden, under
the shade of magnolia and walnut trees.

Peaceful Chidham looks across an inlet to ancient Bosham, one of the most
picturesque sailing villages on the winding shores of Chichester's lovely natural
harbour (with boat trips): very popular and crowded in summer. Chichester itself
is near. It has a mediaeval cathedral, Georgian houses and a theatre.

Wherever you drive or walk there is fine scenery; and plenty of interesting
sights within a few miles – such as the Weald and Downland Open-Air Museum
(acres of ancient buildings reconstructed), the huge Roman palace of Fishbourne,
a brass-rubbing centre in Chichester, crafts complex in Bosham and fine gardens
at West Dean. Around Chidham harbour are lovely walks.

Readers' comments: Peaceful house with great character, very reasonably priced. A
marvellous place. Mrs Hartley anticipates her guests' every need. Excellent. Most
comfortable, helpful and friendly.

Opposite the church is the **OLD
RECTORY,** built in 1830 and now
well furnished by Peter and Anna
Blencowe in traditional country-house
style (most rooms have en suite bathrooms). The large garden has a swimming-pool (unheated) and the elegant
sitting-room a grand piano. Bed-and-
breakfast only. £18–£24.
Reader's comment: Wonderful garden
and furniture. [Tel: 01243 572088;
postcode: PO18 8TA]

EDEN HOUSE C D PT S
120 Eastgate, Pickering, North Yorkshire, YO18 7DW Tel: 01751 472289
On A170 from Thirsk to Scarborough.

3 Bedrooms. £16–£18 (less for 3 nights). Bargain breaks. Some have own bath/toilet. Tea/coffee facilities. TV. Views of garden. Washing machine on request.
Dinner. £10.75 for 4 courses (with choices) and coffee, at 6.30pm. Non-residents not admitted. Vegetarian or special diets if ordered. Wine available. No smoking.
1 Sitting-room. With open fire, central heating.
Small garden
Closed in January.

With years of experience as international hoteliers behind them, Adrian and German-born Gaby Smith are food and wine enthusiasts who bake their own bread, make their own sausages and preserves, smoke their own fish, and grow their own vegetables. Visitors who can decide by 3pm have a choice of four to six fish and meat dishes for their first and main courses and might settle on pork-and-apple terrine, and fish-and-shellfish pie with dill, followed by a choice of puddings.

The house is a pair of 250-year-old cottages in a terrace in the lively town of Pickering, which is at one end of the North Yorkshire Moors steam railway and has a castle and a folk museum. Though it is on the main road, noise from traffic, which is light at night, has never proved a problem. In any case, two of the bedrooms are at the back. They overlook the long garden, where the Smiths have made a pond and installed a barbecue; there is private carparking at the far end, which is an asset in Pickering.

Bedrooms are bright and neat, and very thoughtfully equipped, even down to shoe-polishing kits and dressing-gowns for those who have forgotten to bring their own. Downstairs, the dining-room and cosy little sitting-room are furnished with country antiques and cretonne-covered chairs.

Readers' comments: Everything immaculate and cosy, delicious evening meal, wish we could have spent longer.

The best approach to 18th-century **BRAMWOOD** (19 Hallgarth, Pickering) is from the back, through an old archway built for coaches. Beyond what was once the stable yard there is now a pretty and secluded garden. All the bedrooms are immaculate, some of them spacious.
Readers' comments: Lovely rooms. Comfortable bedroom. [Tel: 01751 474066; postcode: YO18 7AW]
Note: As this edition went to press, we learned that the house had changed

rear view

hands. The new owners are Georgina and Steve Hackett, but we have no information about prices, meals, etc.

EDGCOTT HOUSE

C D PT S X

Porlock Road, Exford, Somerset, TA24 7QG   Tel: 01643 831495

South-west of Minehead. Nearest main road: A396 from Tiverton to Dunster.

4 Bedrooms. £18–£22 (**less for 3 nights to readers of this book only,** or 7 nights). Prices go up from Easter. One has own bath/shower/toilet. Views of garden, country. Washing machine on request.
Dinner. £11 for 4 courses (with choices) and coffee, at 7.30pm. Non-residents not admitted. Vegetarian or special diets if ordered. **Light suppers** if ordered.
1 Sitting-room. With open fire, central heating, TV, piano.
Large garden

Trompe l'oeil murals, in 'Strawberry Hill gothick' style, cover the walls of the long dining/sitting-room. They were painted in the 1940s by George Oakes, who became a director of the distinguished interior decorating firm of Colefax & Fowler. The tall bay windows of this room open onto a tiled terrace from which there is a fine hill view beyond the old, rambling garden where yellow Welsh poppies grow in profusion, and wisteria clambers over the pink walls of the house. In the long entrance hall (red quarry-tiled floor contrasting with whitewashed stone walls) are Persian rugs and unusual clocks. Bedrooms are homely; throughout there is a mix of antique and merely old furniture, with more trompe l'oeil alcoves or doors.

Gillian Lamble's style of cooking is traditionally English and she serves such meals as mackerel pâté, roast lamb, lemon meringue pie, and cheeses.

Readers' comments: Mrs Lamble is kindness itself. A house of character. She went out of her way to be helpful. Food excellent. Will definitely return. A lovely house. A favourite. One of the best. Absolute find; food excellent.

Outside nearby Luckwell Bridge, in a lovely position, is an 18th-century farm with apricot walls: **CUTTHORNE,** where Ann Durbin produces candlelit dinners with much home produce (meat and game). Bedrooms in the house are excellently furnished (all have bathrooms), and one has a carved and tapestry-hung four-poster. In the sitting- and dining-rooms are antique rugs, log fires and brass-rubbings.

There is a courtyard where chickens roam, and a pond with exotic species of ducks and geese. Trout fishing and shooting available. No smoking. £17.50–£23.50. (Two immaculate cottages have their own kitchens and dining facilities for either b & b or self-catering: guests can dine in the main house.)

Readers' comments: Excellent food, kind hosts, quiet setting. Attractive rooms, comprehensively equipped. The Durbins were most helpful. Good food, well presented. [Tel: 01643 831255; postcode: TA24 7EW]

EDGEHILL HOTEL   **C D PT**
2 High Street, Hadleigh, Suffolk, IP7 5AP   Tel: 01473 822458
West of Ipswich. Nearest main road: A1071 from Ipswich towards Sudbury.

12 Bedrooms. £20–£35 (less for 3 nights and mid-week). Bargain breaks. All have own bath/shower/toilet. Tea/coffee facilities. TV. Views of garden, country. No smoking. Washing machine on request.
Dinner. £15 for 4 courses (with choices) and coffee, at 7pm (not Sundays). Less for 2 courses. Vegetarian or special diets if ordered. Wine available. No smoking. **Light suppers** if ordered.
1 Sitting-room. With central heating.
Large garden

Hadleigh, once a rich wool town, went through bad times but is now prospering again. As a result, its very lengthy High Street is full of shops enjoying a new life as wine bars, antique shops and so forth. It is a street of colourful façades, pargeting (decorative plasterwork), overhanging bay windows, carved wood details, ornamental porches and fanlights over the doors. Behind lie river meadows.

One of the High Street's many fine historic buildings to have been rejuvenated is a Tudor house with Georgian façade which is now this private hotel. Rodney Rolfe, formerly the manager of a motor dealer's, took over Edgehill Hotel in 1976 and began to convert it. The well-proportioned rooms have been furnished with style, and attractive wallpapers chosen for each one. In all the spacious bedrooms there are thick-pile carpets and good furniture. The sitting-room has glass doors opening onto the walled garden where an annexe has some bedrooms.

Angela Rolfe, previously a teacher, and her mother do all the cooking and use home-grown raspberries, strawberries, vegetables and other produce from the kitchen garden. She serves soup, roasts, organic vegetables and desserts such as raspberry pavlova, ginger meringues, rhubarb and ginger fool (not on Sunday; and ordering ahead is always necessary). She is not only a good cook, but also makes and sells crafts.

This is a good base from which to explore the very pretty countryside and villages nearby, and such well-known beauty-spots as mediaeval Lavenham, Dedham, Woodbridge on the Deben estuary, Kersey and Long Melford.

In addition, Suffolk has a tremendous variety of interest for garden-lovers. For instance, there are in the vicinity of Hadleigh and Ipswich a council-house garden shown on 'Gardener's World' (at Charsfield), colourful woodland gardens at Little Blakenham with a number of rarities, the seed-trial fields of Thompson and Morgan and formal riverside gardens around Letheringsett's watermill.

Wind- and watermills are a particular feature of the Suffolk countryside. Some notable ones are Bardwell windmill where you can buy stoneground flour (occasionally, the mill is operated by steam); Buttrums 6-storey windmill at Woodbridge – where there is also the famous watermill operated by the movement of the tides; the marsh drainage mill at Herringfleet on the edge of the Broads; and a superb 18th-century windmill at Saxtead.

Readers' comments: Absolutely excellent. High standard.

92

ENFORD HOUSE

Enford, Wiltshire, SN9 6DJ   Tel: 01980 670414
South-east of Devizes. Nearest main road: A345 from Marlborough to Salisbury.

C D PT S

3 Bedrooms. £15–£17 (less for 3 nights). Tea/coffee facilities. Views of garden. Washing machine on request.
Dinner (when available). £14 for 5 courses (with choices) and coffee, at 7–8pm (must be ordered by lunchtime). Less for 3 courses. **Light suppers** if ordered.
1 Sitting-room. With open fire, central heating, TV.
Garden

Stonehenge is only a few miles away and, in fact, Enford (being on Salisbury Plain) is surrounded by prehistoric remains of many kinds.

The 18th-century house (once a rectory) and its garden are enclosed by thatch-topped walls – a feature one finds in those parts of Wiltshire where, stone being non-existent, a mix of earth and dung with horsehair or else chalk blocks were used to build walls (which then needed protection from rain). The house has pointed 'gothick' windows on one side, doors to the garden on another. Antiques furnish the panelled sitting-room, which has a crackling fire on chilly nights. Bedrooms are simple, fresh and conventionally furnished.

Sarah Campbell serves, on pretty Watteau china, soups that she makes from garden vegetables, roasts, puddings such as gooseberry fool or lemon soufflé, then cheeses. The Campbells tell their guests a great deal about the area – not just its historic sights for they are knowledgeable about its wildlife (Salisbury Plain has a tremendous variety of wildflowers as well as larks and lapwings), where to go for the finest views from the surrounding downs and the best walks.

Readers' comments: Everything quite delightful. A charming hostess and excellent food. Very comfortable. Pleasant and relaxed time.

Southwards, in the scenic Woodford Valley, at Lower Woodford, are **MANOR FARM COTTAGES** where a party of visitors could have their own cottage – thatched and mediaeval or flint-walled and Victorian; gathering together with others in one of these for breakfast, prepared by manager Heather Yelland. For other meals, the Wheatsheaf Inn close by has an excellent menu. The cottages are simply but pleasantly furnished, well carpeted, and with restful rosy colour schemes. All have gardens, sitting-rooms, washing machines. (Fly-fishing can be arranged.) Closed

from October to April. £17.50–£19.50.
Reader's comment: Excellent in all respects. [Tel: 01722 782393; postcode: SP4 6NQ]

FAIRFIELD HOUSE   C D M PT
44 High Street, Corsham, Wiltshire, SN13 0HF   Tel: 01249 712992
South-west of Chippenham. Nearest main road: A4 from Bath to Chippenham
(and M4, junction 17).

3 Bedrooms. £16–£17 (less for 5 nights).
All have tea/coffee facilities. TV. Washing
machine on request.
Small garden

Within a peacock's cry of Corsham Court (a palatial Elizabethan mansion with a famous collection of paintings and other treasures) is a quiet and picturesque street, a backwater despite its name – which, in the 17th century, was lined with the cottages and workrooms of Flemish weavers. Fairfield House was lucky to survive an explosion of gunpowder stored next door during the building of Brunel's Box Hill railway tunnel in 1836–41, when every spare bed in Corsham was occupied by railway navvies.

At Fairfield House, one steps straight into a low, white breakfast-room with jade paintwork and curtains, beyond which lie two bedrooms and bathroom, with more upstairs. Christine Reid has furnished all of these with exceptional grace – using either silky cream duvets or pretty patchwork (made by her mother) on the beds, wallpapers patterned with small roses or with Chinese-style pheasants. White-shuttered windows are set in deep embrasures; fresh or dried flower arrangements are everywhere. This is altogether an exceptionally attractive house. Breakfast only; for dinner, visitors go to the Jaipur, Methuen Arms or other restaurants in the little High Street.

Readers' comments: Delightful; great food; very welcoming. Excellent.

Converted stables, weatherboarded and pantiled, provide the accommodation in **THE COTTAGE**, Westbrook, near Bromham, a quiet hamlet once the home of Thomas Moore, the Irish poet.

Inside, the roof beams are still visible. The bedrooms (on ground floor) have been furnished in keeping with the style of the building and Gloria Steed has added such decorative touches as patchwork cushions and pincushions which she made herself. Through the bedroom windows one can sometimes see deer and rabbits, with a distant landscape created by Capability Brown. At breakfast there will be local produce, home-made muesli and compotes of fruit. One can dine very well at the Lysley Arms. £18.

Readers' comments: Full of charm and character. We couldn't have asked for more. [Tel: 01380 850255; postcode: SN15 2EE]

FAIRSEAT HOUSE   **C D PT X**

Station Road, Newick, East Sussex, BN8 4PJ   Tel: 01825 722263
East of Haywards Heath. On A272 from Haywards Heath to Uckfield.

3 Bedrooms. £18 **to readers of this book**–£30 (less for 4 nights). All have own bath/shower/toilet. Tea/coffee facilities. Views of garden, country. No smoking. Washing machine on request.
Dinner. £22.50 for 4 courses, wine and coffee, at any convenient time. Less for 2 courses. Vegetarian or special diets if ordered. Wine available. **Light suppers** if ordered.
1 Sitting-room. With open fire, central heating, TV. Library with piano, cassette recorder. Also a quiet sitting/writing-area.
Large garden

Readers who previously enjoyed Roy and Carol Pontifex's hospitality at Old Cudwells will be glad to know they are still doing b & b at their new home, which is only three miles away. It is a big, yellow stucco Edwardian house – large and light – with a striking two-storey, arched window. It stands in its own spacious grounds, which have a covered and heated swimming-pool available for most of the year. The library's big French windows open onto the garden, which faces south, and occasionally dinner is served on the terrace.

As before, visitors will enjoy Carol's decorative touches, the buttoned velvet chesterfields, Persian rugs, fiddleback chairs and a number of particularly interesting 18th-century portraits: one ancestor was Robert Chambers (of dictionary fame) and a painting of his daughter, Lady Priestley, hangs on a wall. Carol wove some floor rugs herself, on an old outsize loom from Scandinavia. Everywhere handsome Edwardian fittings – from fireplaces to lamps – have been retained or installed.

Up the wide staircase are attractive bedrooms and good bathrooms – one has a Victorian rolltopped bath, another has a hip-bath with overhead shower.

Carol and Roy have always enjoyed meeting people, and entertaining: so those visitors who order a full dinner are treated to such meals as salmon mousse, fillet of beef, a savoury which might be mushrooms on toast, and lemon pie (wine included). Alternatively, they can have fewer courses or even a light supper such as quiche and salad, and this too would be served by candlelight. Breakfast eggs are as fresh as ever, for when the Pontifexes moved their Buff Orpingtons came too. Also in the grounds is a flock of Gotland sheep.

London is only 45 minutes away by train; Gatwick Airport the same, by car. In the area there is plenty to enjoy (in addition, the south coast is soon reached): Ashdown Forest, the beauty-spot of Ditchling Beacon, the 'Jack and Jill' pair of windmills, pretty villages like Lindfield, the Bluebell Line steam train, and such sights as Standen House, Chartwell (Churchill's Tudor house), Batemans (Kipling's) and the castles of Bodiam, Hever and Lewes. Brighton, with the Prince Regent's oriental Pavilion is near; Eastbourne and Tunbridge Wells too. Then there are all the great gardens for which Sussex is famous: Wakehurst, Sheffield Park, Borde Hill, Nymans, Leonardslee and Heaselands. Newick itself is celebrated for the bonfire and firework display held on its green every Guy Fawkes night – the 'guys' now usually include unpopular politicians or even local busybodies!

FIRS FARM   C D X

Stagsden West End, Bedfordshire, MK43 8TB   Tel: 01234 822344
West of Bedford. Nearest main road: A422 from Milton Keynes towards
Bedford (and M1, junction 14).

3 Bedrooms. £15–£17.50. One has own shower/toilet. Tea/ coffee facilities. Views of garden, country. No smoking. Washing machine on request.
Light suppers if ordered. No smoking.
1 Sitting-room. With open fire, central heating, TV.
Large garden

Until 1922, this arable farm and all of Stagsden was Crown property, which is why the village inn (renowned for its food) is called the Royal George. The Hutcheons have farmed here for generations.

There's a homely sitting-room with log fire; and Pam's bedrooms are roomy – some overlook the swimming-pool and lawn (where chickens roam), others the farm buildings.

The university at Cranfield is close, and there are air shows there and at Shuttleworth. Southward you can motor the 35-mile 'Mid-Beds Scenic Route' which goes through some of the county's most scenic moorlands and heaths, over streams and hills, and with a score of interesting sights at which to stop – such as Woburn Abbey and safari park. Picturesque villages like Aspley Guise and Millbrook abound, so do mediaeval inns. It is worth getting the leaflet that details this route (as well as others about walks, numerous nature reserves, etc.) from any Tourist Information Centre in the area.

Northward too, the scenery is lovely (some of it in the care of the National Trust), particularly in late spring when the wildflowers and pink chestnuts are in bloom and fields of yellow rape add a brilliant touch. Wide open spaces alternate with wooded hills, there are thatched cottages, old mills and winding streams – many of them tributaries of the very beautiful Great Ouse. Stately homes include Luton Hoo and Hinwick; gardens – Wrest Park and Old Warden's Swiss Garden; museums – the world-famous Cecil Higgins art gallery, Luton Museum (local lace among its exhibits) and Stockwood Park (other local crafts). There are half a dozen bird or wildlife centres, and (at Leighton Buzzard) a restored steam railway. The county has its own airport at Luton.

THANK YOU . . . to those who send details of their own finds, for possible future inclusion in the book. Do not be disappointed if your candidate does not appear in the very next edition. We never publish recommendations from unknown members of the public without verification, and it takes time to get round each part of England and Wales in turn. Please, however, do not send details of houses already featured in many other guides, nor any that are more expensive than those in this book (see page xxiv).

FISHPONDS FARM   C D

Brook, Kent, TN25 5PP   Tel: 01233 812398
East of Ashford. Nearest main road: A20 from Ashford to Folkestone (and M20, junction 10).

2 Bedrooms. £16. Both have own bath/ shower/toilet. Tea/coffee facilities. TV. Views of garden, country.
Large garden

Trust the map that Di Owen sends her guests when they book and, down winding country lanes, some three miles from Wye, you will eventually reach Fishponds Farm: a 19th-century tile-hung and whitewashed building, originally two labourers' cottages. Standing in the Wye Downs Nature Reserve, the house has a large garden with banks down to a small spring-fed lake with waterfall – in previous times a sheep-dip. The grounds are home to a variety of wildlife including deer, foxes and badgers, and in the downstairs toilet you will find a constantly growing list (compiled by John, a much-travelled retired diplomat) of the numerous different birds seen here. Two large bedrooms are prettily furnished, each with its bath- or shower-room: the twin in pink with quilted bedspreads, the double with dark pine bed and prints of 18th-century Jamaican scenes. Breakfast is taken in a beamed dining-room decorated with African artefacts reflecting the Owens' time spent in that continent. Plenty of maps for walking and tourist information available.

There is no formality at 15th-century **RIPPLE FARM**, Crundale, where the Baurs grow organic produce. They are an artistic family: Chagall posters are pinned on the walls. Hop bines or bunches of dried flowers hang from ceilings, floors are of polished boards, and there is much use of stripped pine. In each of the bedrooms there is a platform (plus ladder) for children's beds above their parents'. The bathroom is on the ground floor, along with the sitting/dining-room for guests. This is a simple room with shuttered windows, pyjama-stripe wallpaper and log stove. Outside are an 18th-century

rear view

barn, now a games room, and the remains of three oast houses – hop kilns. (Maggie does light suppers only.) £17–£17.50. [Tel: 01227 730748; messages: 01227 730762; postcode: CT4 7EB]

To help those en route to the continent, via tunnel or ferry, Kent County Council has produced an excellent booklet with map, called *Off the Motorway*, which will tempt you to tack on a day or so (going or coming) to explore any of 139 attractive places to visit in this beautiful and historic county.

FITZ MANOR

Fitz, Bomere Heath, Shropshire, SY4 3AS Tel: 01743 850295
North-west of Shrewsbury. Nearest main road: A5 from Shrewsbury to
Llangollen.

3 Bedrooms. £16–£25 (less for 7 nights).
Tea/coffee facilities. Views of garden,
country. Washing machine on request.
Dinner. £12.50 for 4 courses and coffee, at
times to suit guests. Less for 2 courses.
Non-residents not admitted. Vegetarian or
special diets if ordered. **Light suppers** if
ordered.
2 Sitting-rooms. With open fire, central
heating, TV, record-player.
Large garden

This outstanding manor house was built about 1450 in traditional Shropshire
style – black timbers and white walls. It is at the heart of a large arable farm.

The interior is one of the most impressive in this book. A vast, blue dining-
room with parquet floor and Persian carpet overlooks rosebeds, pergolas and yew
hedges. It is furnished with antiques, paintings by John Piper and a collection of
Crown Derby. In the oak-panelled sitting-room there are damask and pink velvet
armchairs around the log fire (or guests can use the glass sun-room). Between
these two rooms are the arched hall and a winding oak staircase; one door here is
carved with strapwork and vines, on the tiled floor are Persian rugs and oak chests.

Bedrooms differ in size. For instance, adjoining one huge room with armchairs
from which to enjoy views of the Severn Valley and Welsh hills is a white cottage-
style bedroom – a useful combination for a family (and there is a playroom).

Dawn Baly's candlelit dinners often start with home-made pâté; casseroled
pheasant sometimes appears as the main course, with home-grown vegetables;
pudding may be chocolate mousse; and then there are cheeses.

The garden is still much as it was when laid out in Tudor times, although now
there is a heated swimming-pool and croquet lawn. Guests are encouraged to use
the land – for barbecues, picnics, swimming or fishing in the river.

Readers' comments: Lovely place – quite magical. Dinner was extremely well
cooked, abundant and well presented. No attention to detail spared.

Leaton's **OLD VICARAGE** was built
in 1859 for an archdeacon: hence the
many pointed or trefoil-arched windows, the arcading in the sitting-room,
handsome floor-tiles and doors of
ecclesiastical design. One very big bedroom has a bay window and another
an oriel from which to enjoy views of
the garden. One Victorian bathroom is
particularly attractive. Joan Mansell-
Jones serves snack suppers or dinners
such as watercress soup, baked gammon, and apple and hazelnut galette;
much is home-grown or home-made.
£15–£16 (b & b).

Readers' comments: Beautiful house and
garden, kind friendly welcome, delicious dinner. We were really spoilt.
[Tel: 01939 290989; postcode: SY4
3AP]

FLEARDON FARM
Lezant, Cornwall, PL15 9NW   Tel: 01579 370364 (Messages: 01579 370760)
South of Launceston. On A388 from Launceston to Plymouth.

2 Bedrooms. £18–£20 (less for 3 nights or continental breakfast). Both have own bath/shower/toilet. Tea/coffee facilities. TV. Views of garden, country. No smoking. Washing machine on request.
Light suppers if ordered. No smoking.
1 Sitting-room. With open fire, TV. No smoking.
Large garden

Tolkien devotees should head for Lezant because here, in the newly modernized barns of Fleardon Farm, is an art gallery displaying the work of Roger Garland, creator of those brilliant and intricate covers to the Hobbit books.

The farmhouse itself belongs to his parents and here Doreen Garland welcomes bed-and-breakfast guests (for dinner, they usually go to the Springer Spaniel inn, or the White Hart in Launceston). The 250-year-old house has a surprising interior after one enters through a conventional porch (filled with geraniums), for there is a big open-plan kitchen/dining-area with mahogany staircase to the floor above. The large sitting-room with windows on three sides has a log stove, sofas and a profusion of pot-plants. A handsome feature is the polished hardwood floors throughout. The bedrooms have pleasant views (and excellent bathrooms): one overlooks the cobbled courtyard, another a waterfall and stream.

The grounds are full of interest: in addition to a lawn with flowerbeds and shrubs, there is a decorative folly with weathervane and a lake frequented by Canada geese.

Close by are many National Trust gardens and such NT houses as Cotehele and Lanhydrock. Lydford Gorge is a popular riverside walk of three miles. Golfing enthusiasts head for the champions' golf course at St Mellion. Launceston, ancient capital of Cornwall, has a castle and historic jail. Bodmin Moor and Dartmoor are both about 12 miles away, and the coast is about 20 miles.

Readers' comments: Welcomed warmly, gardens beautiful, a place we would return to. Lovely place, pleasant and friendly hostess.

To find the right accommodation in the right area at the right price, use an up-to-date edition of this book – revised every year. For an order form for the next edition (published in November), send a stamped addressed envelope with 'SOTBT 1998' in the top left-hand corner, to Explore Britain, Alston, Cumbria, CA9 3SL. You will receive a money-saving offer for 'Staying Off the Beaten Track in Scotland' too.

FOLDGATE FARM   **C S**
near Bootle Village, Cumbria, LA19 5TN   Tel: 01229 718660
North-west of Ulverston. Nearest main road: A595 from Whitehaven towards
Millom.

3 Bedrooms. £14–£15. Views of country,
sea, river. No smoking. Washing machine
on request.
Dinner. £9 for 4 courses and coffee,
at 6pm (or later by arrangement). Non-
residents not admitted. Vegetarian or
special diets if ordered. No smoking. **Light
suppers** if ordered.
1 Sitting-room. With open fire, central
heating, TV. No smoking.
Small garden
Closed in December.

A real Cumbrian farm near Millom, and well outside the main tourist areas, it
covers 170 acres on which are kept Swaledale and Herdwick sheep as well as
some cattle. The approach to the farm is through a cobbled yard, with a great
stone byre and stables at one side, Muscovy ducks perching on a dry-stone wall,
and sundry old iron pots and kettles filled with stonecrop, London pride or
primroses. A stream slips quietly by. Pat, the sheepdog, comes bounding out to
greet visitors.

The rooms have old furniture, some of which appeared on the 'Antiques Road
Show'. Guests sometimes eat with the family, by a dresser where mugs hang, the
clothes airer suspended overhead and a grandfather clock ticking in one corner.
There are bacon-hooks in the ceiling, horn-handled shepherds' crooks stacked in
the hall, and a bright coal fire in the evenings. Mary Hogg does most of the talking as she serves guests a proper farmhouse meal, and her husband is glad to tell
visitors about his sheep and all the local goings-on – guests are welcome to watch
the life of the farm, and to join in at haymaking time in July or August.

You'll get real country fare here: Cumberland sausage, 'tatie pot', plum pudding with rum sauce, farm duckling, Herdwick lamb or mutton, rum butter on
bread, currant cake with tea on arrival and at bedtime, and jams made from local
bilberries, pears, or marrow and ginger. There are free-range eggs for breakfast.
This is a thoroughly unpretentious, homely and friendly place to stay.

As to the countryside around, there are the moors of Corney Fell close by and
roads winding up and down, with sea views. A renowned maker of Cumberland
sausage and ham is only a mile away.

Up the coast from Corney is Ravenglass, a port from Roman times but long
since silted up. It is the terminus of a narrow-gauge railway, built to transport
iron ore but now a very popular tourist ride. Take it to Boot for a drink at the pub
and a look round the craft gallery and the cornmill (not working), then return to
the mill at Muncaster (which is working during the summer). At Muncaster
Castle, they breed and release owls, which you can see. Transport enthusiasts will
want to visit the railway museum at Ravenglass and the motor museum at Holker
Hall. At Sellafield, the visitor centre of the nuclear industry has become a popular
tourist attraction.

Readers' comments: Excellent food, good company. Good food. Lovely welcome.
A great success. Never a dull moment! Food, atmosphere and welcome couldn't
be faulted. Delighted with our welcome, the food and all the local attractions.

FOREST FARMHOUSE
C D PT S

Mount Road, Marsden, West Yorkshire, HD7 6NN   Tel: 01484 842687

South-west of Huddersfield. Nearest main road: A62 from Oldham to Huddersfield.

3 Bedrooms. £15 (less for 2 nights). Tea/coffee facilities. Views of country. Washing machine on request.
Dinner. £7 for 3 courses (with choices) and coffee, at 7pm. Vegetarian or special diets if ordered. **Light suppers** if ordered.
1 Sitting-room. With central heating, TV, organ, record-player.

The Industrial Revolution concentrated the textile industries into the mechanized mills which are still to be seen all over Yorkshire and Lancashire. Until then, spinning and weaving were done in people's homes, whole families working together and often combining weaving with farming. Forest Farmhouse was just such a dual-purpose home.

Standing at 1000 feet, the house is now surrounded by a golf course (which visitors can often use) and moorland, much of it owned by the National Trust, at the top of the Peak District National Park. There was never a forest: the word is used in its sense of a hunting-ground and, at least according to the deeds of the house, the royal family still has the right to use it. This is a typical farmhouse of its kind, built of dark gritstone at least 200 years ago, with mullioned windows and stone-slated roof. Inside, the beamed wooden ceilings are low and the guests' sitting-room has a big stone fireplace. Seamus, the enormous and friendly Irish wolfhound, sometimes ambles about. Bedrooms, some with exposed masonry, have pine fittings.

Genial Ted and May Fussey run the place with walkers in mind (the open moors and the nearness of the Pennine Way attract them here). May provides, for example, home-made soup or grilled grapefruit, pork steak in breadcrumbs with fresh vegetables, and chocolate pudding with white sauce. All bread is home-made: 'If I can't make it, I won't buy it!', she says.

Climbing, angling and hang-gliding are some of the pastimes available nearby. The area is also of interest for its industrial and social history. The Luddites used to plan their campaigns in an inn that stood up the road from Forest Farmhouse. Many of the mills they attempted to sabotage are still working, producing yarn or worsted, and there are plans to open a nearby one to visitors. The country's longest canal tunnel starts near Marsden and is being restored. There are museums, exhibitions, canal-boat trips, and walks both waymarked and guided, to help to bring the past to life. Marsden, which has its own theatre company, is where much of the television series 'The Last of the Summer Wine' was filmed. Holmfirth, where the series is based, is only a few miles away.

Houses which accept the discount vouchers on page ii are marked with a V on the lists at the beginning of this book, see pages xi–xix and pages xxi–xxii.

FORTH HOUSE   **C D M PT X**
44 High Street, Warwick, CV34 4AX   Tel: 01926 401512
(M40, junction 15, is near.)

2 **Bedrooms.** £18 (less for 3 nights or
continental breakfast). Price goes up from
April. Bargain breaks. Both have own bath/
shower/toilet.   Tea/coffee facilities.   TV.
Refrigerator. Views of garden. No smoking.
Washing machine on request.
Light suppers if ordered.
2 **Sitting-rooms.** With open fire, central
heating, TV. No smoking.
Small garden

Past the antique and craft shops of the busy High Street is a terrace of trim
Georgian houses; overhead looms Warwick Castle. Not exactly 'off the beaten
track'. But behind no. 44 lies a secret place: a long garden stretching far back.
Stone steps and paths flank the lawn, rosebeds and pool; an ancient wisteria
clambers high. Here is found an entire garden-suite for visitors: virtually a flat
with its own kitchen, and all on the ground floor. It is not only spacious but very
pretty – roses and ribbons on the bathroom curtains, the bath's sides made of
pine.

There's another bedroom at the back of the house, on the first floor. This has
a pine table and rush chairs for meals (if you want to take these in privacy), and a
sofa. Elsewhere are marble fireplaces, ruffled curtains in big bay windows.

An extra bonus for many guests is often the sight of Labrador pups at play –
Elizabeth Draisey breeds them as guide dogs for the blind.

Stratford-upon-Avon and Oxford are easily reached.

Readers' comments: Prettiest, best equipped room we've had; large and quiet.
Highly recommended.

West of Warwick and not far from
Stratford is Claverdon, and Doreen
Bromilow's home, **WOODSIDE** in
Langley Road, with its own wildlife
reserve. Hillside woods, untouched
since mediaeval times, have rare old
trees and traces of ancient farming
techniques. Furnished with antiques,
Woodside has a good bedroom on
the ground floor and a pretty family
room. In the dining-room, you eat

such meals as soup, a roast, and apple
pie. There is a Bernese mountain
dog. £18–£25.

Readers' comments: Very comfortable,
food very well prepared. [Tel: 01926
842446; postcode: CV35 8PJ]

Prices are per person in a double room at the beginning of the year.

FORTITUDE COTTAGE

51 Broad Street, Old Portsmouth, Hampshire, PO1 2JD   Tel: 01705 823748

Nearest main road: A3 from London to Portsmouth.

3 Bedrooms. £19–£22 **to readers of this book.** Prices go up at Easter. All have own bath/shower/toilet. Tea/coffee facilities. TV. Some have sea views. No smoking.

Carol Harbeck's little cottage – one room piled on top of another – backs onto her mother's (also a guest-house), with a flowery little courtyard and fountain between the two: its appearance has won it awards. It is named for the Fortitude Inn, once next door; itself named for HMS *Fortitude*, a ship-of-war which ended as a prison hulk – overlooked by the big bay window of Carol's first-floor sitting-room. This is Portsmouth's most historic area. From here, Richard the Lionheart embarked for the Crusades, Henry V for Agincourt, and the first settlers for Australia. It's a place of ramparts and bastions, quaint buildings and byways, much coming-and-going of ships and little boats. The waterbus leaves from the quay just outside.

All the rooms in the cottage are prettily furnished. One can dine well at The Seagull or the Still & West. Handy as a stopover for people using Portsmouth's port, Fortitude Cottage deserves a longer stay, for Portsmouth (and its adjoining Victorian resort, Southsea) have so much to offer: HMS *Victory*, the *Mary Rose*, HMS *Warrior*, the Royal Navy's museum and that of the Marines, cathedral and historic garrison church, Henry VIII's Southsea Castle, the D-Day museum, Hayling Island and the wild places of Chichester Harbour, clifftop Victorian forts, Roman/Norman Portchester Castle, and Dickens's birthplace.

Readers' comments: Excellent accommodation, spotless. Absolutely excellent, high standard. Delightfully unusual. What a find! Particularly enjoyable. Such an interesting old house, very comfortable.

Near the city is Denmead and in Hambledon Road you will find **FOREST GATE**, the graceful 18th-century house of Torfrida Cox and her husband, with a large garden. It is on the 70-mile Wayfarers' Walk. This is an informal home furnished with antiques. Meals (which have to be ordered in advance) include such dishes as Armenian lamb pilaff or moussaka, mousses or lemon meringue pie. Each bedroom has a bath or shower. £18–£20.

Readers' comments: Like staying with friends. Bedroom comfortable, dining-room elegant. [Tel: 01705 255901; postcode: PO7 6EX]

FOXHILL
Kingsey, Aylesbury, Buckinghamshire, HP17 8LZ   Tel: 01844 291650
South-west of Aylesbury. On A4129 from Princes Risborough to Thame
(and near M40, junctions 7/8).

3 Bedrooms. £18–£21. Some have own shower. Tea/coffee facilities. TV. Views of garden, country. No smoking.
Light suppers if ordered.
2 Sitting-rooms. With central heating, TV. No smoking.
Large garden
Closed in December and January.

The instant impression is delightful: sparkling white house beyond green lawns where Muscovy ducks waddle with their young towards a pool crossed by an arching stone bridge. The gnarled remains of an immense 500-year-old elm tree stand beside the drive. At the back of the house is a garden with heated swimming-pool, against a distant view of the Chiltern Hills.

The interior is just as attractive. The house having been the home of architect Nick Hooper and his family for many years, it is not surprising that its modernization was done with imagination and with care to respect its 17th-century origins. In the hall, floored with polished red quarry-tiles, a wrought-iron staircase leads up to bedrooms with beamed ceilings, attractive wallpapers and rugs, and restful colour schemes. Board doors have the original iron latches. The breakfast-room (which also serves as a sitting-room) has brown gingham tablecloths and rush-seated chairs. Here Mary-Joyce – a warm, gentle hostess – usually serves only breakfast, recommending for other meals restaurants in the ancient market town of Thame, only a few minutes away.

Thame is a lively place in autumn when the mile-long market place at its heart is filled with stalls for the annual fair, and is a mecca for gourmets.

Readers' comments: Wonderfully kind hosts, lovely home, top of our list! Beautiful house, meticulously kept; charming, friendly and helpful. The Hoopers and their home are charming. A good welcome and nice house.

There is clematis round the porch of **POLETREES FARM** (Ludgershall Road, Brill), baskets brimming with begonias and lobelias hang on the walls, and all around are roses, apple-trees and views of fields. Inside, stone walls, oak beams and an inglenook with a rare window beside it have survived five centuries.

Anita Cooper has furnished her ancient home well and has collections of old railway keys and of earthenware boots. Dinner may comprise such dishes as home-made soup, roast pork, chocolate mousse, and cheese with fruit. (No smoking.) £19 (b & b) **to readers of this book.**

Readers' comments: Fantastic weekend! Very friendly; felt totally at home. Comfortable, and lovely breakfasts. Would recommend Poletrees time and time again. [Tel: 01844 238276; post-code: HP18 9TZ]

FOXLEIGH HOUSE　　　　　　　　　　　　　　　C(10) **D PT S**
Foxleigh Drive, Wem, Shropshire, SY4 5BP　Tel: 01939 233528
North of Shrewsbury. Nearest main road: A49 from Shrewsbury to
Whitchurch.

2 **Bedrooms.** £18.50 (less for 3 nights or
continental breakfast). Bargain breaks.
Both have own bath/shower/toilet. Tea/
coffee facilities. TV. Views of garden.
Washing machine on request.
Dinner. £11 for 4 courses (with choices)
and coffee, at 7pm. Less for 3 courses. No
smoking. **Light suppers** if ordered.
1 **Sitting-room.** With open fire, central
heating, record-player. No smoking.
Small garden

Well tucked away in this little market town is handsome Foxleigh House, the
most memorable feature of which is the fine sitting-room. Its cocoa walls, coffee
ceiling and Chinese carpet are an excellent setting for antiques that include inlaid
tables and a series of Hogarth prints. Bay windows open onto the croquet lawn
and its towering Wellingtonia.

In the dining-room, Barbara Barnes serves such meals as avocado, roast lamb,
trifle, and local cheeses.

The bedrooms have 'thirties suites of figured maple, and the hall a gallery of
ancestral portraits.

Wem still has many historic buildings, including the 17th-century Lowe Hall
where the infamous Judge Jeffreys lived. From here you can visit the 'Shropshire
Lake District', seven meres frequented by wildfowl, near another old market town
– Ellesmere. This is close to Oswestry, a picturesque town with a ruined castle,
and the straggling village of Ruyton XI Towns (also with castle), built of red
sandstone. Hilly Hodnet, full of black-and-white houses had a rector who wrote
famous hymns, including 'From Greenland's Icy Mountains', and there is a 60-
acre garden with pools at Hodnet Hall. Beyond lies Market Drayton, birthplace of
Clive of India: its ancient market among the many half-timbered houses has been
taking place on Wednesdays for 700 years.

And Shrewsbury itself is near. Almost islanded within a loop of the River
Severn, it is a treasury of superb black-and-white buildings with several fine
churches (one is round), gardens (Darwin, born here, is commemorated in a
statue) and museums. It deserves repeated visits to explore twisting lanes (with
such curious names as Dogpole, Shoplatch or Coffeehouse Passage), the castle,
the main square with flower-baskets hung around an open-pillared market hall,
and all the exceptionally decorative black-and-white houses.

The house of Clive of India is open as one of Shrewsbury's many museums,
and between the town walls and the river are the Quarry Gardens (Percy Thrower
designed these). Ellis Peters's novels are set in the area.

Readers' comments: Very welcoming, homely. Super stay. Welcome and friendliness in abundance, bedrooms exceedingly comfortable. Well appointed, food
superb. Very good, nice couple. Lovely welcome, delicious dinner, house fascinating. Accommodation and food very good. Very welcoming; well thought out
menus; peaceful and comfortable surroundings. Most welcoming and helpful,
evening meal excellent. A very pleasant experience. Can't praise too warmly.
Made us feel so cared for.

FRITH FARM HOUSE

Otterden, Kent, ME13 0DD   Tel: 01795 890701

C(10) **X**

South-west of Faversham. Nearest main road: A20 from Maidstone to Charing (and M2, junction 6).

3 Bedrooms. £18–£23.50 (less for 3 nights). **5% reduction for readers of this book.** All have own shower/toilet. Tea/coffee facilities. TV. Views of garden, country. No smoking. Washing machine on request.

Dinner. £17.50 for 4 courses and coffee, from 7pm. Less for 2 courses. Non-residents not admitted. Vegetarian or special diets if ordered. No smoking. **Light suppers** if ordered.

1 Sitting-room. With open fire, central heating, record-player. No smoking.

Large garden

Once, there were cherry orchards as far as the eye could see: now Frith has only six acres. (From their fruit – 'If I can grab it before the birds do!' – Susan Chesterfield makes sorbets for her gourmet dinners.)

They say money doesn't grow on trees. Not true, for those cherry trees financed the building in 1820 of this very fine house where a fountain plays outside the pillared front door. Maroon damask wallpapers and sofas are in keeping with its style. The bedrooms are beautifully decorated and very well equipped (one has a four-poster).

In a very lovely dining-room, fiddleback chairs and a collection of antique plates contrast with a bold geometrical Kazak print (Liberty's) used for the curtains, and with the white dishes of German bone china on which Susan serves such meals as avocado with taramosalata, sorbet, lamb steaks with capers, meringues glacés, and cheeses.

In the polygonal conservatory Susan provides not only breakfast but dinner parties for local people.

The house is so high up on the North Downs (an Area of Outstanding Natural Beauty) that its views across orchards and woods extend – in the case of one of the pretty bedrooms – as far as the Isle of Sheppey, which is a distant twinkle of bright lights after darkness falls. The Downs can be explored at the pace of bygone days in a landau or on horseback: details on request.

Canterbury is, of course, the magnet which draws most visitors here but there is a great deal more to east Kent than this. For a scenic drive, go across the North Downs to the valley of the River Stour, the Tudor village of Chilham (with castle and grounds) and Battle of Britain museum at Manston Airfield, and then to Hastingleigh.

Readers' comments: Extremely helpful, beautiful home, delicious dinner.

Houses with short entries are just as good as ones with longer descriptions; and they include some of the most popular houses in the book. They may, however, have fewer rooms, a shorter season, higher prices or fewer amenities (such as meals).

GADBROOK OLD FARM
C D PT S

Wellhouse Lane, Betchworth, Surrey, RH3 7HH Tel: 01737 842183
West of Reigate. Nearest main road: A25 from Reigate to Dorking (and M25, junction 8).

2 Bedrooms. £17.50 (less for 3 nights). Tea/coffee facilities. TV. Views of garden, country. No smoking. Washing machine on request.
Dinner. £10 for 3 courses and coffee, from 6.30pm. Less for 2 courses. Non-residents not admitted. Vegetarian or special diets if ordered. No smoking. **Light suppers** if ordered.
1 Sitting-room. With open fire, central heating, TV. No smoking.
Large garden

If you look into the pond at the front of this lovely 15th-century farmhouse, you will see an old christening stone, and in the garden, near a fallen yew tree, is an old water pump.

Gadbrook Old Farm, nestling deep in the Surrey countryside, is the home of Derek Bibby and his New Zealand-born wife, Jeanette. Although not a working farm, Gadbrook is not short of visitors of the feathered kind: ducks and hens wander about and the occasional pheasant comes to call.

Inside, oak beams are a feature of every room. In the low-ceilinged sitting-room, filled with antiques amassed over four decades, cretonne sofas are grouped round a large inglenook fireplace. A cubbyhole in the inglenook was once used for storing salt, a precious commodity in times past. Guests eat at a large oak dining-table, seated on Jacobean chairs.

The bedrooms, with their whitewashed walls and pale green carpets, have fine views. The Edwardian beds in the twin room are particularly handsome.

Derek's watercolour landscapes are displayed throughout the house. Having formerly worked in the toy industry (he invented the Cindy doll), he now spends much of his time painting, undertaking some commissions.

Jeanette, who for several years cooked lunches at a private school, will serve such dinners as asparagus and salmon mousse, chicken with apricot and ginger, and chocolate roulade.

The coming of the railway in 1847 made this picturesque area more accessible to London. These days, regular trains from nearby Reigate or Redhill will whisk you into London within 45 minutes. The M25 is a short drive away and the Bibbys are happy to drive guests to Gatwick Airport, also nearby.

The addresses of houses are geographically correct but postal addresses sometimes differ (for correspondence, the only essential element is the postcode).

Information about the nearest town and 'A' road helps you to locate the whereabouts of any village on a map; but before setting off it is necessary to get precise instructions from your host as many houses are very much 'off the beaten track'.

GLEBE HOUSE C
Park Lane, Longstowe, Cambridgeshire, CB3 7UJ Tel: 01954 719509
West of Cambridge. Nearest main road: A1198 from Huntingdon to Royston
(and M11, junction 12).

2 Bedrooms. £18.50–£19 (less for 7 nights). Both have own bath/shower/toilet. Tea/coffee facilities. TV. Views of garden, country. No smoking. Washing machine on request.
Dinner. £15.50 for 3 courses and coffee, at 5–8pm. Less for 2 courses. Vegetarian or special diets if ordered. No smoking. **Light suppers** if ordered.
Small garden

Scalloped white bargeboards round the roof are like a demure lace collar on the pink walls of this secluded 16th-century house. A former owner added architectural finds, such as the bas-relief of a ram which decorates one gable. In summer, poppies, clematis and peonies contribute colourful touches; and moorhens nest below the briar roses surrounding the garden pond. Over the old lych gate honeysuckle climbs. The house was (as 'glebe' indicates) church property.

Charlotte Murray has decorated all the rooms attractively, using soft pinks and greens in the bedrooms (one is a family room) and deep mulberry for the dining-room where she serves either simple meals or dinners cooked to professional standard – for Charlotte, after training at the Cordon Bleu Cookery School in London, used to cook for City directors' dining-rooms. She chooses dishes to suit her guests' tastes, one popular menu being carrot-and-coriander soup, pork tenderloin stuffed with mushrooms, and almond applecake. When children stay, she can do a separate and early meal with simpler food.

Charlotte bakes bread daily. Another of her skills is making dried-flower arrangements, and she offers produce and crafts for sale.

Readers' comments: Absolutely lovely. Beautiful house, warm and comfortable. Terrific supper. Friendly, helpful. Lovely food, helpful hostess. Very comfortable, warm and tasteful. Lovely supper. Nice hostess. Delightful bedroom. Very friendly. Memorable cordon bleu cooking. Cosy, well kept and lovingly decorated.

On the other side of Cambridge is Swaffham Bulbeck and the **OLD RECTORY** which was built in 1818 for the Rev. Leonard Jenyns, a distinguished naturalist who was offered but declined a place on the *Beagle* expedition, recommending instead his pupil Charles Darwin – who was a frequent visitor to the rectory.

Jenny Few-Mackay frequents salerooms to seek out all the Victoriana which furnishes the house in the style of Jenyns's time: one room has a handsome brass bed from which, through big windows, to enjoy the view of fields. There is a garden and swimming-pool; plus billiards in a converted barn. The best place for dinner is the Hole in the Wall at Little Wilbraham (or the Red Lion in Swaffham Prior). £18–£23.50. [Tel: 01223 811986; postcode: CB5 0LX]

GOODMANS HOUSE   C D M S X

Furley, Devon, EX13 7TU   Tel: 01404 881690
North-west of Axminster. Nearest-main road: A30 from Honiton to Chard
(and M5, junction 25).

6 Bedrooms. £17–£22 (less for 2 nights).
**To readers of this book only: less £12
per double room for 3 mid-week nights
half board, February to April except
Easter week.** Prices go up from June.
Bargain breaks. All have own bath/toilet.
Tea/coffee facilities. TV. Views of garden,
country. No smoking.
Dinner. £17 for aperitif, 3 courses (with
choices) and coffee, at 7pm. Vegetarian or
special diets if ordered. No smoking. **Light
suppers** sometimes.
1 Sitting-room. With central heating. No
smoking.
Large garden
**Closed in December and January,
except Christmas and New Year.**

This is the model of what a small country-house hotel should be. Robert and Pat
Spencer sold their previous, larger hotel to pursue the ideal of 'smaller is better'
and give every guest personal attention.

The house (mostly 18th-century, some parts much older) had been steadily
crumbling away for the last 80 years. Much of the renovation was done by the
Spencers, after which it was completely transformed with well-chosen furnishings to
create an ambience that is elegant without being formal. Complimentary aperitifs
are served in the Georgian garden room, before a candlelit dinner in a long, arched
dining-room with inglenooks at each end. The bedrooms are some of the most
attractive in this book, with handsome bathrooms.

Alternatively, some families (and smokers) prefer to have accommodation in
garden cottages – sometimes let on a wholly self-catering basis but also used for
those who want to take meals in and enjoy the amenities of the main house. Even
though these have their own kitchens and living-rooms, they cost less per head
than bedrooms in the house. Dinner can, if you prefer, be brought to your cottage.

Pat qualified with a first-class pass at her catering college, and every meal she
produces is a memorable experience, using their own produce (which includes
sheep and poultry) and also local, organically reared meat – as Bob used to be a
butcher, he buys expertly. Occasionally there are barbecues beside one of the
three lily- and fish-pools in the grounds. A typical menu: seafood and mango
platter, pork with apricot and orange stuffing (imaginatively prepared vegetables),
hazelnut meringues with raspberries.

A palm and a jacaranda testify to the mildness of the climate here. In autumn,
the fiery and varied colours of foliage are a delight. There are orchards and ponds.

Readers' comments: Comfortable rooms, wonderful food. Service most friendly,
surroundings elegant. Excellent accommodation and wonderful food, extremely
thoughtful people. Breathtaking scenery, very caring hosts, delicious food. A
super place, standards as high as ever. I can't think of anywhere nicer to spend a
few days. Excellent. A unique and very special place. Cottage most comfortable.
Made so welcome and had delicious food. Cannot speak too highly of it.

GORSELANDS FARMHOUSE   **C D M X**
Boddington Lane, near Long Hanborough, Oxfordshire, OX8 6PU
Tel: 01993 881895
North-east of Witney. Nearest main road: A4095 from Woodstock to Witney.

5 Bedrooms. £17.50–£21 (**less for 4 nights to readers of this book** or continental breakfast). Prices go up from August. Bargain breaks. Most have own bath/shower/toilet. Tea/coffee facilities. TV. Views of garden, country. No smoking.
Dinner. £12.95 for 3 courses (with choices) and coffee, from 7–9pm. Less for 2 courses. Non-residents not admitted. Vegetarian or special diets if ordered. Wine available. No smoking. **Light suppers** if ordered.
1 Sitting-room. With open fire, central heating, TV, piano. No smoking.
Large garden
Closed from mid-March to mid-April.

Within a short stroll of North Leigh's Roman villa (it had 60 rooms, and is famous for the intricate mosaic floor and well-preserved central heating system) is this comfortable home of Cotswold stone, the oldest part originally a barn. Today it is run as an 'auberge' by Barbara Newcombe-Jones. Beyond the stone-flagged hall is a sitting-room with log fire, a games room with full-size billiard table, and a conservatory where Barbara's staff serve such meals as melon with Parma ham, coq au vin, chocolate mousse, and French cheeses.

Bedrooms, simply furnished but comfortable, are spacious and in the bathroom of one is an oval bathtub. Well-behaved children are welcome; and Barbara can arrange for a baby-sitter. There is a tennis court.

Gorselands is close to both Oxford and historic Woodstock; spectacular Blenheim Palace (in baroque style, set in grounds landscaped by Capability Brown and now with a huge new maze, as well as boats on its lake); the Cotswold Wildlife Park where exotic animals roam in the gardens and park of an old manor house; Churchill's grave at Bladon (Blenheim, his birthplace, has a Churchill exhibition); and Cogges Farm Museum where life on a Victorian farm is recreated.

Oxford itself – its colleges, churches and museums – needs no description, but there is always something new to be seen for those who stay several days. In 'The Oxford Story' you ride (literally) back through 800 years of history; Curioxity is a 'hands-on' science gallery. A recent addition (at Magdalen College) is a version of Leonardo's 'Last Supper', even better – some say – than the one in Milan.

The blacksmith from the Blenheim estate once lived in 18th-century **MAYFIELD COTTAGE** (at West End in the pretty village of Combe), the home of Rosemary and Stan Fox. They discovered a little inglenook hidden in a wall, a feature of which is the salt ledge – to keep that precious commodity dry in times when homes were incurably damp. Breakfasts are served at one end of this room, chinoiserie sofas furnish the other. Doorways are low and ceilings

beamed. Closed in winter. £17–£19. [Tel: 01993 898298; postcode: OX8 8NP]

GRAFTON VILLA FARM   C M PT S

Grafton, Herefordshire, HR2 8ED   Tel: 01432 268689

South of Hereford. On A49 from Hereford to Ross-on-Wye.

3 Bedrooms. £18–£19 (less for continental breakfast). All have own bath/shower/toilet. Tea/coffee facilities. TV. Views of garden, country. No smoking. Washing machine on request.

Dinner (by arrangement only). £14 for 4 courses (with choices) and coffee, at 7pm. Non-residents not admitted. Vegetarian or special diets if ordered. No smoking. **Light suppers** if ordered.

1 Sitting-room. With open fire, central heating, TV.

Large garden

Closed in December and January.

The 18th-century farmhouse, set well back from the road, is furnished with antiques and well-chosen fabrics. Each bedroom is named after the woodland of which it has a view (Aconbury, Dinedor, Haywood), for the panoramic scenery in every direction is one of the attractions of staying here. The pretty family room also overlooks the farmyard with its free-ranging chickens and ducks – sometimes foals too. Bath- and shower-rooms are good; the little sitting-room snug, its velvet chairs grouped around the fire. The sunny dining-room looks onto patio and garden from which come vegetables for the table.

When she is able to serve dinner (by arrangement only), Jennie Layton's portions are generous. Meals often feature cider soup, chicken breasts in tarragon sauce, and a hazelnut meringue gâteau with which she serves hot apricot sauce. Her vegetables are imaginatively prepared: carrots may be cooked in orange juice, beetroots appear in Stilton sauce, courgettes with tomatoes and basil. As well as conventional breakfast choices, she may offer you fruit compote, poached haddock and croissants.

The house is close to the cathedral city of Hereford and within a few miles there are other historic towns such as Ledbury, Ross-on-Wye and Hay-on-Wye ('book city') as well as picturesque villages like Weobley, Eardisland and Pembridge. Such beauty-spots as Symonds Yat, the Black Mountains, the Malvern Hills and the River Wye are all close, too.

Cider-press in garden
at Grafton Villa Farm

THE GRANARY

M S

Main Street, Clanfield, Oxfordshire, OX18 2SH   Tel: 01367 810266
South-west of Witney. Nearest main road: A4095 from Witney to Faringdon.

3 Bedrooms. £16–£18 (**less for 7 nights to readers of this book** or continental breakfast). Prices go up from June. Bargain breaks. Some have own bath/toilet. Tea/coffee facilities. Views of garden, country, river. No smoking. Washing machine on request.
1 Sitting-room. With central heating, TV. No smoking.
Small garden

A willow-fringed stream runs alongside the village road as it pursues its course to the Thames. On the other side are an 18th-century cottage, Victorian shop and old granary that have been turned into a guest-house. There is a beamed dining-room, and guests have their own sitting-room. The best and quietest bedroom is on the ground floor (with its own bathroom); the others are above. Throughout, Rosina Payne's house is spotless, airy and decorated in light and pretty colours. (B & b only; good bar meals are available at the Clanfield Tavern.)

This part of the Cotswolds is full of interest. One drives through a landscape threaded with streams, among fields where cows or sheep doze in the sun. In late spring, Queen Anne's lace billows along every verge, and apple-blossom dances in sugar-pink against bright blue skies. The lanes lead one to such famous sights as Bourton-on-the-Water, Stow-on-the-Wold, Bibury watermill, Burford (and its wildlife park), Witney's farm museum or old Minster Lovell Hall. Further afield are Cirencester, Cheltenham, Oxford and Woodstock (with Blenheim Palace). But there is no need to go far for interesting things to do. Just along the road is Radcot and the oldest bridge over the Thames, from which (in summer) narrow-boat trips set out for 18th-century Lechlade. And William Morris's Kelmscott Manor is close.

Readers' comments: Warm and friendly. Accommodation excellent, breakfast delicious. We couldn't praise enough.

At **MORAR FARM**, Weald Street, in nearby Bampton, Janet and Terry Rouse take exceptional care of their guests – whether it is by involving them in their many activities (Morris-dancing, bell-ringing, spinning wool) or by their close attention to detail (two fresh towels provided daily, unlimited fruit juice at breakfast, filling vacuum flasks free of charge, etc.). Their home is a modern stone house, comfortable and trim, which stands in an attractive garden. During winter, Janet may serve a meal comprising home-made soup, beef with Yorkshire pudding and six vegetables, Bakewell

pudding and fruit to follow. No smoking. £19–£20 (b & b).
Readers' comments: Excellent! Janet is a delight. Sunday bell-ringing was a highlight of our trip. [Tel: 01993 850162; postcode: OX18 2HL]]

GRANCHEN

Church Road, Bitton, (Avon), South Gloucestershire, BS15 6LJ
Tel: 0117 9322423
North-west of Bath. Nearest main road: A431 from Bristol to Bath
(and M4, junction 18).

3 Bedrooms. £15–£17 (less for 3 nights or continental breakfast). Bargain breaks. Views of garden, country. No smoking. Washing machine on request.
Dinner. £10 for 4 courses and coffee, at times to suit guests (not Thursdays). Non-residents not admitted. No smoking. **Light suppers** if ordered.
1 Sitting-room. With open fire, central heating, TV, piano. No smoking.
Small garden
Closed from December to February.

Where once the Romans had a camp, the Normans built a manor house – now called the Grange – with a vast, separate kitchen (and a big, stone pigeon-house to supply the table). Granchen is that kitchen: it was altered by John Wood, the celebrated 18th-century architect of Bath, who gave it the distinctive round windows and triple arches which make its façade unique. (He lived at the Grange while working on nearby Bath.) The ruined pigeon-house can be seen in the lovely walled garden, in the shadow of the church's great, crocketted tower (adorned with the heads of Edward III and his queen, in whose time it was built), among the gargoyles of which kestrels sometimes nest.

The stone-flagged sitting-room is dominated by an enormous arched, stone inglenook – it looks big enough to spit-roast an ox. Liberty curtains in glowing colours contrast with almond-green walls, Valerie Atkins's patchwork cushions match the russet tones of the oriental rugs, and to one side of the hearth are her elegant appliqué pictures of farm gates and hedgerows (she trained at art school and some of her creations are on sale at Granchen). On Thursday evenings, a local madrigal group gathers round her Bechstein to practise with her.

Valerie's other accomplishments include cooking. Using garden produce, she prepares such meals as chicken-and-lentil soup, baked gammon with cauliflower cheese, and redcurrant fool. Meals are served in a coral dining-room (with unusual, carved stickback chairs from Canada) which looks through a pilastered archway into her kitchen.

Everywhere there are interesting touches – wildflower wallpaper in a bathroom, a dresser with blue-and-white china and, in the garden, clematis scrambling through the boughs of a rare apple-tree which bears red-fleshed fruit.

Readers' comments: Perfect. Lovely house, made very welcome. Charming atmosphere. Beautiful house. A lovely time.

> **Some proprietors stipulate a minimum stay of two nights at weekends or peak seasons; or they will accept one-nighters only at short notice (that is, only if no lengthier booking has yet been made).**

THE GRANGE

Alverstone, Isle of Wight, PO36 0EZ   Tel: 01983 403729
North of Shanklin. Nearest main road: A3055 from Ryde to Ventnor.

C PT S

7 Bedrooms. £18.50–£20.50 (less for 4 nights). Prices go up from June. All have own bath/shower/toilet. Tea/coffee facilities. Views of country. No smoking.
Dinner. £13.50 for 4 courses (with choices) and coffee, at 6.30–7.30pm. Less for 2 courses. Non-residents not admitted. Vegetarian or special diets if ordered. No smoking. **Light suppers** if ordered.
1 Sitting-room. With open fire, central heating, TV, piano. No smoking.
Garden
Closed in December and January.

This immaculate guest-house, with light and modern rooms, was once the hunting-lodge of Lord Alverstone – MP for the island and Lord Chief Justice at the turn of the century. He built the whole village (around an old mill recorded in Domesday Book), the first in England to have water piped to each house because he banned strong drink in his village, which is why there is still no inn.

Geraldine Watling provides very good meals (she is a qualified cook) and husband David, who formerly worked in the space industry, is most helpful with books and maps for walkers: the island is threaded with scenic footpaths.

Meals usually comprise a soup such as carrot and barley, a roast or a dish such as boeuf bourguignonne, and then a traditional pudding (like steamed apple and syrup pudding) with the option of a light alternative such as lemon chiffon.

Readers' comments: Relaxed and happy atmosphere. Imaginative cooking. Warm and welcoming. Excellent accommodation, wonderful food. Very comfortable. Good rooms. Extremely welcoming. Very good home cooking. Absolutely spotless, beautifully decorated. A real family welcome. Made us feel so welcome.

In Shanklin itself is **CAVENDISH HOUSE**, Eastmount Road, with particularly pretty rooms, Laura Ashley fabrics and well-chosen colours complementing antiques. Lesley Peters has emphasized the architectural features of the Victorian house by, for instance, painting the plasterwork vine of one ceiling blue, and filling an old tiled fireplace with pot-plants. Each bedroom has a table and chairs for breakfast as there is no dining-room. For other meals, guests go into Shanklin. A nearby cliff-lift takes you down to the sands, or you can walk through the famous scenic chine

(a steep ravine). Buses go to all parts of the island. Outstanding sights are Osborne House and Carisbrooke Castle. £15.50–£17.50.
Readers' comments: A real pleasure. Lovely house. [Tel: 01983 862460; postcode: PO37 6DN]

THE GRANGE   **C M PT X**
New Road, Burton Lazars, Leicestershire, LE14 2UU   Tel: 01664 60775
South-east of Melton Mowbray. Nearest main road: A606 from Melton
Mowbray to Oakham.

3 Bedrooms. £18.50 **to readers of this book.** Price goes up in April **but with £1 discount to readers of this book.** All have own bath/shower/toilet. Tea/coffee facilities. TV. Views of garden, country. Balcony (one). No smoking. Washing machine on request.
Dinner. £15 for 4 courses and coffee, from 7pm. Less for 3 courses. Vegetarian or special diets if ordered. Wine available.
Light suppers if ordered.
2 Sitting-rooms. With open fire, central heating, TV. No smoking in one.
Large garden

Until recently this was the home of the McAlpine family – a creeper-covered country mansion in 18th-century style with such features as leaded window-panes, arches, prettily plastered ceiling and barley-sugar banisters on the oak staircase.

Pam Holden has decorated the rooms with imagination, and hung the walls with good paintings. In one aquamarine sitting-room are shell-pink armchairs; in another, snug and with an open fire, is Chinese-style wallpaper. There is one rosy ground-floor bedroom with a large bathroom; a yellow bedroom upstairs has its own balcony. The four-poster room has a particularly good bathroom (and every guest is provided with an outsize bath-sheet). There is a small kitchen for guests' use.

Landscaped grounds include a sunken garden, orchard and paved terrace with chairs from which to enjoy the view across terraced lawns to the Vale of Stapleford, tea- or coffee-cup in hand.

Pam, a trained cook, enjoys preparing such dinners as melon with straw-berries, chicken tarragon, pecan pie and cheeses.

As to the strange name of the village, in the Middle Ages it was a leper (lazar) colony, established here because of the reputedly healing properties of the local spring water.

Melton Mowbray, of pork-pie, Stilton cheese, and fox-hunting fame, has had a market from Saxon times and this is still carried on in the big market square. Its church is the finest in the county. In the great mansion of Stapleford Park are treasures that include a collection of 400 Staffordshire statuettes; other stately homes are Burghley (on a hilltop with fine views), the mediaeval Bede House at Lyddington; and, of course, great Belvoir Castle which dominates the Vale of Belvoir below it. Rutland Water is near. There are magnificent tombs in Bottesford's church and an exceptional carved arch in Tickencote's. Wing has a rare mediaeval maze; Waltham-on-the-Wolds, a smock windmill; Uppingham, the 16th-century courts and quadrangles of its famous school; Oakham, a market square still with stocks and butter-cross. All around are undulating hills (wolds), with small woods among sheep pastures threaded by a maze of lanes and cottages of pinkish stone which have slate or thatched roofs.

THE GRANGE C(12) **X**

Torrington Lane, East Barkwith, Lincolnshire, LN3 5RY Tel: 01673 858670

North-east of Lincoln. Nearest main road: A157 from Wragby to Louth.

2 Bedrooms. £18–£20. Both have own bath/shower/toilet. Tea/coffee facilities. TV. Views of garden, country. No smoking. Washing machine on request.
Dinner (by arrangement). £12.50 for 3–4 courses (with choices), sherry and coffee, at 7pm. Vegetarian or special diets if ordered. No smoking. **Light suppers** if ordered.
1 Sitting-room. With open fire, central heating. No smoking.
Large garden
Closed in December.

Set in acres of farmland (mainly arable) which adjoin a conservation area, this late-Georgian house is on a working farm. Until recently, it was the home of Anne and Richard Stamp (see below). Now son Jonathan has inherited the farm business.

Built in 1820, the house has sash windows deep-set in shuttered embrasures. The hall has a stained-glass door, black-and-white floor tiles, and a graceful staircase leading up to attractive bedrooms.

Outside is a conservatory full of flowery pot-plants and a lawn with topiary, swing-settee, croquet and tennis. Children, too, will enjoy the large garden (the Stamps have two young ones of their own).

Sarah Stamp (a trained home economist and accomplished cook) serves for dinner, for example, watercress and salmon roulade; chicken in white wine and tarragon sauce; chocolate brownie gâteau.

The Grange has won three conservation awards, and has a private trout lake (where guests can fish or relax with a picnic and enjoy the solitude), as well as direct access to nature trails. It is also ideally situated for visiting Lincoln and the Wolds.

Down the lane, but still part of Grange Farm, is **BODKIN LODGE**, which Anne and Richard Stamp have furnished with great care, adding much character to this stylish home. From the entrance hall, doors open onto a light, airy sitting-room with floor-to-ceiling windows and far-reaching views. Paintings and ornate mirrors hang on the walls, and French windows lead onto a terrace, where breakfast may be served in the summer.

Bedrooms are en suite: one has direct access to a sun-deck with a grapevine.

Anne (who occasionally writes short stories for women's magazines) serves meals such as smoked haddock and chive creams; lamb with apricot stuffing; and almond and pear flan. (No smoking.) £18–£22.50 (b & b).

Readers' comments: The standard of food, presentation, etc. could not have been bettered. Welcomed as friends; excellent food. Wonderful ambience, perfect hosts. [Tel: 01673 858249; postcode: LN3 5RY]

THE GRANGE

CDS

Northwold, Norfolk, IP26 5NF   Tel: 01366 728240
North-west of Thetford. Nearest main road: A134 from Thetford to King's Lynn.

3 Bedrooms. £17–£22 (less for 5 nights). Some have own bath/shower/toilet. Tea/coffee facilities. TV. Views of garden. Washing machine on request.
Dinner. £12.50 for 4 courses and coffee, at 7.30pm. Less for 2 courses. Non-residents not admitted. Vegetarian or special diets if ordered. No smoking. **Light suppers** if ordered.
1 Sitting-room. With open fire, central heating, TV, record-player. No smoking.
Large garden

Behind Northwold's church, its 18th-century rector not only built himself a very fine house but laid out a 12-acre garden with rare trees to which has been added a heated swimming-pool.

In the dining-room, there is a plan of the original house. The coral walls in here match chinoiserie curtains patterned with pheasants, and there is a fireplace handsomely carved. Pretty Villeroy & Boch china complements such meals as mushroom pots, salmon parcels with watercress sauce, almond meringue with apricot coulis, and cheeses.

Not only is Sue Whittley an accomplished cook but, with a colleague, she runs weekend cookery courses – demonstrations plus practical work. And she is an expert needlewoman, hence all the attractive cushions in every room. Her husband's excellent watercolours (of local scenery and wildlife) fill the walls, and many are for sale.

A galleried staircase leads to bedrooms furnished with, for instance, William Morris fabrics and lace bedspreads. Some of the deep-set, shuttered sash windows overlook the flint and stone tower of the 13th-century church.

Readers' comments: Superb grounds, exceptionally nice hostess, very good food.

Much hard work went into adapting early Victorian **CORFIELD HOUSE**, Sporle, and creating a particularly pretty garden. Inside, Linda Hickey has used delicately patterned wallpapers, much pine and rattan furniture, soft blues and pinks. There is a ground-floor room with bathroom that would suit any disabled person.

A typical dinner might comprise crab and avocado salad, boeuf bourguignonne, raspberry clafouti (a type of pancake) and some unusual cheeses. Martin runs the Tourist Information Centre at nearby Swaffham and both he and Linda are mines of information about the area. £18.50–£20.

Readers' comments: Strongly recommended. Excellent value. Superb breakfast. First class. Outstanding dinners. Helpful and considerate hosts. The loveliest house we have stayed in, food superb, delightful people. [Tel: 01760 723636; postcode: PE32 2EA]

117

THE GRANGE (No.1)   **C**(5) **D S X**
Sunderland Hill, Ravensden, Bedfordshire, MK44 2SH   Tel: 01234 771771
North of Bedford. Nearest main road: A428 from Bedford towards St Neots
(and M1, junction 14).

rear view

3 Bedrooms. £18 (less for 3 nights or continental breakfast). Some have own bath/shower/toilet. Tea/coffee facilities. TV. Views of garden, country. No smoking. Washing machine on request.
Dinner. £14 for 3 courses (with choices), sherry and coffee, from 6pm. Less for 2 courses. Vegetarian or special diets if ordered. No smoking. **Light suppers** if ordered.
2 Sitting-rooms. With log stoves, central heating, TV, video, cassette-player.
Large garden

This large manor house has been divided into three dwellings, of which No. 1 is the handsome home of Patricia Roberts, with views downhill of terraced lawns and great cedars, flowering shrubs and a copper beech. Patricia has furnished the rooms in keeping with the architectural style, with chandeliers in each room. Good paintings (some by her daughter) hang on silky coral walls; silver, big velvet armchairs and Chippendale furniture are in one room; another has damask curtains and a Victorian sofa. Even the bathrooms are carpeted and have flowery wallpaper. The snug little dining-room is in fact a book-lined alcove behind a blue satin curtain (sometimes another is brought into use when there are two families being accommodated).

Dinner is very attractively presented. Salmon and pheasant often appear on the menu but guests can have whatever they like if it is ordered in advance. (Sunday lunch also available.)

Patricia has much information to share about sightseeing in Bedfordshire, and it is still possible to identify places which inspired passages in Bunyan's *The Pilgrim's Progress*.

Readers' comments: Nothing too much trouble. Food delicious. Charming hostess. Wished we could have stayed longer. Dinners imaginatively prepared. Elegantly furnished, and every comfort. Kind welcome, we felt at home. Excellent.

It is a surprise to find such a peaceful village (a thatched church as well as thatched cottages) as Roxton only a mile from the busy Great North Road, the A1, and in its High Street **CHURCH FARM** – part 17th- and part 18th-century. One bedroom has a royal coat-of-arms carved in the wall, dating from Stuart times.

A beautiful breakfast-room has a Chippendale-style table and a sideboard with its original brass rails. Bedrooms are in a guest wing. There is a pleasant sitting-room with a log fire and paintings on the walls. For dinner,

Janet Must recommends restaurants in either St Neots or Bedford, but visitors are welcome to bring their own snack suppers in. £16–£18. [Tel: 01234 870234; postcode: MK44 3EB]

118

GRASSFIELDS
CDS

Wath Road, Pateley Bridge, North Yorkshire, HG3 5HL   Tel: 01423 711412
North of Harrogate. Nearest main road: A59 from Harrogate to Skipton.

9 Bedrooms. £20 **(to readers of this book only)**–£22.50. Less for 3 nights. Prices go up from Easter. Bargain breaks. All have own bath/shower/toilet. Tea/coffee facilities. TV. Views of garden, country. Washing machine on request.
Dinner. £12 for 3 courses and coffee, at 7pm. Non-residents not admitted. Vegetarian or special diets if ordered. Wine available. **Light suppers** if ordered.
2 Sitting-rooms. With open fire, central heating, TV. Bar.
Large garden
Closed in December and January.

This country house is set back from the road, in its own gardens: it is a handsome Georgian building surrounded by lawns and trees. Most rooms are spacious and comfortably furnished. Barbara Garforth studies her visitors' interests and provides helpful information on local areas of interest, including many local walks. There is a tranquil and informal atmosphere.

Meals are prepared from local vegetables and produce wherever possible, including free-range eggs and Nidderdale lamb. A typical menu: pear and cream cheese salad, local beef, apple and mincemeat tart – all in generous quantities. There is a wide selection of wines.

Pateley Bridge is an interesting small town (in an Area of Outstanding Natural Beauty) with a number of good shops, set on a junction of several roads, which makes it a fine centre from which to go sightseeing. Grassfields is in the heart of Nidderdale, where there are crags, glens, lakes and How Stean gorge.

Lovely Nidderdale, being outside the National Park area, is less frequented than some other dales. It has some very old reservoirs created by damming the River Nidd, now well naturalized and full of ducks, geese, herons and other birds (200 species have been recorded, including some rare migrants). The effect is reminiscent of the Lake District. How Stean is a romantic gorge with a stream cascading into a rocky cleft 70 feet deep (good home-made cakes at the modest café nearby). From the churchyard at Middlemoor, high up at the head of the dale, there are spectacular views down the length of it.

From here one can easily motor to a number of Yorkshire's spectacular abbeys – Bolton, Jervaulx, and Byland. Also Harewood Hall, Newby Hall and garden, and half a dozen castles; as well as the strange natural formations of Brimham Rocks.

Readers' comments: Stayed twice: excellent. Most comfortable and quiet. Most helpful. Very fine food. Well furnished. Good food and plenty of it. Thoroughly enjoyed our stay, and every mouthful. Wonderful. Very friendly atmosphere. Very comfortable, good food, delightful atmosphere, splendid location. Very comfortable stay.

When writing to the authors, if you want a reply please enclose a stamped addressed envelope.

119

GREEN LANE HOUSE   C D PT X

Green Lane, Hinton Charterhouse, (Avon), Bath & North-East Somerset, BA3 6BL   Tel: 01225 723631

South of Bath. Nearest main road: A36 from Bath to Warminster.

4 Bedrooms. £18–£21.50 (less for 3 nights). Some have own shower/toilet. Tea/coffee facilities. Views of garden. Washing machine on request.
Light suppers if ordered.
1 Sitting-room. With open fire, central heating, TV.
Small garden

The hilly village of stone houses with colourful gardens gets its name from the Carthusian ('charter house') monks who in the 13th century had a priory here, its remains still to be seen though not open to the public. The house (originally three cottages) dates from 1725 and descendants of the family who inhabited it then still live in the village.

Today it belongs to Christopher Davies and his wife Juliet who previously spent nearly 30 years in hotel management overseas.

The restored house has such features as an old fireplace in one room and a massive stone inglenook in another, board doors and round-arched, wood-shuttered windows: these contrast with more modern furnishings and colour schemes – huge, white cutwork ginger-jars as bedroom lamps, lyre-back dining-chairs, bamboo-patterned tiles in a very pretty bathroom, comfortable Parker Knoll chairs in the bedrooms. The Davieses have added mementoes from their years overseas, including alabaster from Oman, papyrus paintings from Egypt, curiously shaped palm fruits from the Seychelles and an ostrich egg from Tanzania. There is a walled cottage-garden.

Two inns in the village serve meals, or snack suppers can be arranged.

Readers' comments: Service very friendly and helpful, accommodation excellent.

Bedroom at Welam House (see page 88)

GREENEND COTTAGE   C D PT
Colthouse, Hawkshead, Cumbria, LA22 0JS   Tel: 01539 436346
East of Windermere. Nearest main road: A593 from Ambleside towards
Broughton-in-Furness.

2 Bedrooms. £16 (less for 3 nights or continental breakfast). One has own bath/toilet. Both have tea/coffee facilities. Views of garden, country. No smoking. Washing machine on request.
Light suppers if ordered.
1 Sitting-room. With woodstove, central heating, TV. No smoking.
Large garden
Closed from mid-December to mid-January.

This typical-looking Lake District cottage, white-walled and slate-roofed, is of such interest internally that the National Trust, which owns it, has compiled a dossier recording every detail – young Isabel Gordon will show you a copy. Built in 1648, the cottage is full of contemporary oak woodwork: panelling, partitions, joinery, cupboards, and floors which have the dark patina of three and a half centuries of use.

In the beamed sitting-room, where Isabel serves breakfast, settees face a woodstove. If the story is true, it is in this room that Wordsworth wrote *The Prelude* – he certainly lived here for a time. The window by the breakfast-table looks out onto a garden with a large yew tree, and a quiet lane beyond. Bedrooms, pleasant and characterful, are reached by an impressive old staircase.

Hawkshead – within walking distance of Colthouse, a quiet hamlet – is the place for evening meals. The village is mostly owned (and strictly conserved) by the National Trust, which was founded in this part of the world, and motor traffic is excluded. It is one of the Lake District's most popular tourist destinations, not least because of the school that Wordsworth attended while lodging at Greenend Cottage (it was the late Brian Redhead's favourite Cumbrian building). There are good pubs, and shops for such things as crafts and outdoor clothing.

Readers' comments: Very quiet; a very friendly and caring person.

Buried in dense woodland on the unspoilt side of Windermere, **SILVER-HOLME,** near Graythwaite, south of Hawkshead, is a mansion built in the early years of Victoria's reign. It has very large rooms with high windows, all of which look eastward across the waters of the lake. From them you may watch deer grazing – even from one of the private bathrooms! Each bedroom has an impressive mahogany bedstead from the period of the house. In the Venetian-red dining-room, its walls hung with engravings, George Walker might serve, for example, prawn cock-

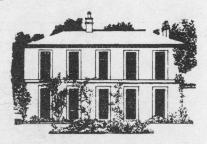

tail, lamb cutlets, and peach flan. £20 (b & b) **to readers of this book.** [Tel: 015395 31332; postcode: LA12 8AZ]

GREENHAM HALL

Greenham, Somerset, TA21 0JJ   Tel: 01823 672603

West of Wellington. Nearest main road: A38 from Wellington towards Exeter
(and M5, junctions 26/27).

6 **Bedrooms.** £17.50–£20 (less for 3
nights). Bargain breaks. Some have own
shower/toilet. Views of garden, country.
Washing machine on request.
Light suppers if ordered.
2 **Sitting-rooms.** With open fire, central
heating, TV, piano.
Large garden

This great castellated pile with buttresses topped by barley-sugar finials stands
on a commanding hilltop site. It was built at the height of the Gothic Revival
period, but fell on hard times – in some of its splendid, high-ceilinged rooms, hay
and even tractors were stored. Then the Ayre family came here and restored the
mansion including the west wing (to left of picture) where extra bedrooms are
available.

Rooms have impressive floor-to-ceiling windows, arched and stone-mullioned;
solidly made, panelled doors; and ogee arches. From the huge galleried hall (with
log stove, concert piano and the biggest dresser you are likely to see – carved and
inlaid), a staircase with 'gothick' banisters and stained-glass windows rises to the
bedrooms. The very large family room is especially impressive, with carved bedheads and a bay window-seat from which to enjoy the sight of terrace, lawn and
stately trees.

Reader's comment: Very comfortable and pleasant.

Dining-room at Cedar Lodge (see page 51)

GREYS

Margaret Roding, Essex, CM6 1QR Tel: 01245 231509
North-west of Chelmsford. Nearest main road: A1060 from Bishop's Stortford to Chelmsford.

3 Bedrooms. £18–£19 (less for 3 nights mid-week). Prices may go up in April. Tea/coffee available. Views of garden, country. No smoking.
Light suppers by arrangement.
1 Sitting-room. With central heating, TV. No smoking.
Large garden

Once a pair of farmworkers' cottages, Greys became the Matthews' home when they moved out of their large farmhouse to let their son take over management of the farm. They painted the exterior apricot – in typical East Anglian style – and furnished the rooms simply (a mixture of Habitat and antiques) and with light, clear colours. The beamed breakfast-room has pine furniture and rhododendron patterned curtains; from the sitting-room, a glass door opens onto the large garden.

'It's lovely when guests book in for one night and then stay for several,' says Joyce. This often happens because so many people think Essex consists of Dagenham's motorworks, Southend's trippers and little else – then, when they come here, find a revelation.

The eight Roding villages include some of England's prettiest, in an area of winding streams and lanes, flowery inns, colourwashed houses with pargeted walls (decorative plasterwork) under thatched roofs. Many visitors arrive at Harwich or at Stansted Airport, then base themselves here to visit London (45 minutes by train from Epping), Cambridge, Roman Colchester and the rest of East Anglia. But there is much to enjoy close by, including picturesque Thaxted (which has music festivals and a church of cathedral-like splendour), old Dunmow, which still has the four-yearly award of the Dunmow Flitch to happily married couples – the next ceremony, complete with bewigged judge, will be in 2000, Greensted (unique Saxon church made of wood), and the attractive towns of Saffron Walden and Bishop's Stortford.

These are only a beginning. Go to Waltham Abbey for the enormous church where King Harold was buried after defeat by William the Conqueror. To Maldon to see great, russet-sailed sailing-barges along the picturesque waterfront. To Mersea for the oysterage. To Clacton for the pleasures of an old-fashioned seaside resort. At Mountfichet Castle you might find a wildflower festival in full swing or a herbal weekend; in one of many fine manor gardens, a typical country fête; on village greens, Morris dancers; windmills in full sail; great shire horses on show at Toppesfield; displays of sheep-shearing; exhibitions by the many local craftsmen and artists; guided walks. The area also has the Imperial War Museum's collection of historic aircraft, etc. (at Duxford), two wildlife parks and numerous National Trust properties within easy reach. Saffron Walden has a museum internationally renowned for its 'worlds of man' gallery, particularly the Aborigine exhibits.

Every night you could dine at a different, excellent local inn.

Reader's comment: Warmth and good food.

GROVE HOUSE

C(8) S

Hamsterley Forest, County Durham, DL13 3NL Tel: 01388 488203
West of Bishop Auckland. Nearest main road: A68 from Darlington to
Corbridge.

3 Bedrooms. £18 (less for 7 nights). Price goes up from March. All have own bath/shower/toilet. Tea/coffee facilities. Views of garden, country. No smoking. Washing machine on request.
Dinner. £14 for 5 courses and coffee, at 7.30pm. Vegetarian or special diets if ordered. Wine available. No smoking. **Light suppers** if ordered.
2 Sitting-rooms. With open fire, central heating, TV. No smoking.
Large garden

Hamsterley Forest is a 5000-acre Forestry Commission holding in the hills of County Durham. Much of it consists of commercial conifers, but down one side lie 1000 acres of old mixed woodland, which the Forestry Commission manages for recreational purposes, with drives, waymarked walks, two rivers, a visitor centre and so on. A few houses are buried in this beautiful forest, among them Grove House, once an aristocrat's shooting-box; another is the home of David Bellamy.

Grove House is now the home of businessman Russell Close, his wife Helene and their three children. It is a peaceful place, surrounded by its own big gardens and reached only by a forest road (private but metalled). The windows of the prettily furnished guest-rooms look across the lawn into the forest, where you may see woodpeckers at work. Birdsong is the loudest sound you will hear.

The downstairs rooms have a touch of aristocratic grandeur, with the addition of some unusual fittings brought from Germany by Helene's grand-parents, from whom she inherited them (notice the art deco doorhandles). Settees and armchairs in the enormous sitting-room are covered in William Morris fabrics.

Helene prepares all the food from fresh ingredients. Meals usually consist of a first course such as a fish gratin; home-made soup; followed by a main course which is often game from the forest; and then a cold sweet such as meringues with ice cream and hot chocolate sauce. She discusses guests' preferences beforehand.

Visitors using the self-catering cottage can take meals in the house.

Bicycle hire and pony trekking are available, but should you tire of walking, driving, cycling or simply sitting in the forest, there is a huge expanse of deserted heather moorland a few miles away. The other attractions of this little-known county include High Force waterfall, Raby Castle, the magnificent Bowes Museum (château-style), Beamish open-air museum and of course Durham Cathedral.

Readers' comments: Delicious, imaginative food. Fairytale house in beautiful set-ting. Good value. Greeted as old friends. A wonderful 'find'; it was perfect. Idyllic. Exceptionally varied menus, beautifully cooked. Excellent. Marvellous situation, food and welcome. Absolutely charming. A trip to paradise! Of a very high standard in every way. One of the nicest dinners.

GROVE HOUSE   S

Levisham Station, North Yorkshire, YO18 7NN   Tel: 01751 472351
North of Pickering. Nearest main road: A169 from Pickering to Whitby.

3 Bedrooms. £18–£20 (less for 7 nights). Some have own bath/toilet. Tea/coffee facilities. Views of garden, country. No smoking. Washing on request.
Dinner. £12 for 5 courses (with choices) and coffee, at 7pm. Non-residents not admitted. Wine available. No smoking.
1 Sitting-room. With open fire, central heating, TV, piano. No smoking.
Large garden
Closed from November to Easter.

Levisham is a remote moorland village reached by a narrow, twisting and steep road, but Levisham Station is remoter still, at the end of another mile and a half of spectacularly scenic road. So why was a station built in the middle of moors and forests?

When the railway was being laid out, the then lord of the manor gave permission for it to run through his land on condition that there was a station for him to use just outside the gates of his house. Now the manor house (largely rebuilt in the 1820s but fundamentally much older) is a guest-house, run by Neville and June Carter. Views from the windows are impressive, of wooded hills and moors, and also of the North Yorks Moors Railway. Many guests like to watch the steam trains run on this, one of the country's best-known preserved lines.

A typical dinner (with bronze cutlery and crystal glasses): cream of sweet pepper soup, plaice stuffed with salmon, and a choice between gooseberry cake and Grand Marnier ice cream.

Picturesque Kirkbymoorside and Pickering are to the south (with York a little further); northward are bays and beaches.

Goathland, also on the North Yorks Moors Railway, is one of the largest and prettiest of the National Park villages, where sheep crop the grass right up to the front gates of the stone houses and the television series 'Heartbeat' was filmed. When the railway came in the last century, shipowners and the like built houses here and commuted to work in Whitby. Now many of their villas are hotels, one such – on The Common – being **THE FAIRHAVEN**, owned by Clare and Keith Laflin. As well as a large and comfortable lounge, there is a bar and snooker room. Bedrooms all have excellent views of the village and the moors. In the dining-room, where

the wallpaper goes with a large yucca plant, you might be served prawn fritters or soup, escalope of turkey, and a pudding or ice cream or cheese.
Readers' comments: Excellent country hotel. Their standards are of the highest. £19–£23. [Tel: 01947 896361; postcode: YO22 5AN]

GUITING GUEST-HOUSE   **C D PT S**
Post Office Lane, Guiting Power, Gloucestershire, GL54 5TZ
Tel: 01451 850470
West of Stow-on-the-Wold. Nearest main road: A436 from Andoversford
towards Stow-on-the-Wold.

3 Bedrooms. £18–£22.50 (less for 4 nights or continental breakfast). All have own shower/toilet. Tea/coffee facilities. TV. Views of garden, country. No smoking. Washing machine on request.
Dinner. £15 for 4 courses (with choices) and coffee, at 7pm. Non-residents not admitted. Vegetarian or special diets if ordered. No smoking. **Light suppers** if ordered.
2 Sitting-rooms. With open fire, central heating, TV, record-player.
Small garden

This is a quintessential Cotswold village with stone cross on a green, mossy roofs, roses and wisteria clambering up mellow, sun-soaked walls – much of it just the same as four centuries ago. The name refers to the River Windrush which flows by ('gyting' is Saxon for a rushing brook) and to a 13th-century magnate, le Poer, who owned the village at the time when wool-weaving was beginning to prosper.

The village once had five inns – of which this house, then known as the Bell, was one – thronged with beer-drinkers during the Whitsuntide Fair. It still has its celebratory occasions but of a quite different kind: an annual music festival every July. And there are still hill sheep with particularly fine, white fleece – though preserved as a rare breed now, at the nearby farm park (see below).

Changes to the 450-year-old guest-house have been done with sensitivity. New pine doors have wood latches; the dining-room floor is made of solid elm planks from Wychwood Forest; logs blaze in a stone fireplace with ogee arch; and in the snug sitting-room are flagstones with oriental rugs (elsewhere in the house are rag rugs which Yvonne Sylvester made herself). Yvonne has filled a bay window with begonias and shelves with china that she collects; her meals are served on wildflower-patterned china. Bedrooms are pleasantly decorated, with such touches as beribboned cushions or an old cane-backed rocking-chair, and four-posters. Through the stone-mullioned window of one is a view of another cottage made colourful by hanging flower-baskets.

As to dinner, Yvonne will cook whatever you want, but a favourite menu is trout from a nearby fish farm, chicken in lime and ginger sauce, strawberry baskets with cream, and cheeses.

The Cotswold Farm Park just north of the village is home to the Rare Breeds Survival Trust which exists to preserve historic breeds of farm animals that might otherwise die out, and here you can spend a day among, for instance, little Soay sheep first domesticated by Stone Age man and piglets of a prehistoric strain.

Readers' comments: Extremely welcoming, nothing was too much trouble. Went out of their way to look after us. Charming house; spotless and tastefully decorated. Outstanding in every way. Marvellous hosts. Made us so welcome. Beautiful house. One of the happiest breaks I've had. Nothing too much trouble. Charming, faultless, relaxing, ideal. Very relaxed atmosphere. Our favourite, will definitely return. Marvellous cook, tasteful rooms.

GUY WELLS
C(10) **D S**

Eastgate (road), Whaplode, Lincolnshire, PE12 6TZ   Tel: 01406 422239
East of Spalding. Nearest main road: A151 from Spalding to King's Lynn.

3 Bedrooms. £17–£20. Bargain breaks. Prices go up from April. One has own shower/toilet. Tea/coffee facilities. TV (by request). Views of garden, country. No smoking.
Dinner. £10 for 2 courses and coffee, at 7pm. Vegetarian or special diets if ordered. No smoking. **Light suppers** if ordered.
1 Sitting-room. With log stove, central heating, TV. No smoking.
Large garden

Springs in the land around this Queen Anne house are what gave it its name. It is in a lovely and secluded position, surrounded by a traditional garden, trees, and beyond that the Fens. The Thompsons have daffodil and tulip fields as well as glasshouses where they cultivate spring flowers and lilies. Tour them with Richard, and buy flowers or bulbs to take home.

The interior of the house is full of imaginative touches – like the addition of an alcove with domed top and scallop-edged shelves to one side of the brick hearth where a log stove stands. Raspberry velvet tub chairs contrast with homely stripped-pine doors. And there is no sound louder than a slow-ticking clock.

Hall and staircase are pretty (with sprigged wallpaper, an old cedar chest, prints and bouquets of flowerheads dried by Anne) leading to the bedrooms – one of which is huge, with en suite shower-room, a bedspread with tucks and pink ribbons, and windows on two sides. Another has a half-tester bed with antique bedhead. Needlepoint weekends are run occasionally by local expert Ann Ellis.

Visitors who choose Guy Wells do so in order to explore the superb churches of the county, to enjoy its birdlife or the spring flowers, for the easy cycling (it's a level area) or just for the peace. And for Anne's wholefood cooking (using their own vegetables, honey and eggs). For light suppers she makes all her own pâtés, soups, quiches or ratatouille. A two-course dinner may consist of a traditional roast or casserole and puddings like raspberry pavlova, cheesecake or (a delectable speciality) a crème brûlée in which yogurt combines with cream as a topping to brandied grapes.

From Whaplode, one can easily explore most of Lincolnshire and much of Cambridgeshire, too – Peterborough, in particular, is worth a day for its cathedral, river trips, local museums and shopping centre. Also easily accessible are King's Lynn, and royal Sandringham House which is now open to the public during the summer. Go to Boston for its great church and the Guildhall (museum, and the cells where the Pilgrim Fathers were imprisoned). The Georgian town of Wisbech has Octavia Hill's birthplace (museum) and Peckover House (NT) by the river.

Readers' comments: Lovely people. Enjoyed the cooking so much. Delightful lady, friendly, excellent cook, very pleasant house. Lovely place, superb food, nice lady. Very warm welcome, happy atmosphere, glorious food. Interesting part of the country, have visited twice. Welcoming couple, pleasant place. Great hospitality, food good, accommodation excellent.

THE HALL C(5) **D M PT S**

Great Hucklow, Derbyshire, SK17 8RG   Tel: 01298 871175
North-east of Buxton. Nearest main road: A623 from Chapel-en-le-Frith
towards Chesterfield.

4 Bedrooms. £18–£24 (less for 4 nights).
Prices go up from May. Some have own
bath/shower/toilet. Tea/coffee facilities. Views
of garden, country.
Dinner. £14.50 for 3 courses and coffee, at
7pm. Less for 2 courses. Vegetarian or
special diets if ordered. **Light suppers.**
1 Sitting-room. With woodstove. No
smoking.
Large garden
Closed in December and January.

This, like many Derbyshire villages, is famous for summer 'well-dressings': huge
mosaics of flower-petals depicting religious themes.

Rows of small, mullioned windows give the 17th-century Hall particular
charm, and in the former kitchen (now a dining-room) the original fireplace,
which would have housed a great spit, has been exposed. Walls three feet thick,
which keep the house warm in winter and cool in summer, have here been painted cream. John Whatley has restored an unusual, very narrow, cellar-to-attic
window which lights the staircase. In one of the very big family rooms there is
a huge cockerel he carved, as well as stools and bedside tables made by him.
The bath- and shower-rooms contain his decorative mirrors. A twin room in the
converted barn, with its own sitting-area and warm-hued pitch-pine floor, has a
carved headboard of his own making.

Guests greatly enjoy the large garden.

Angela is a discriminating cook, using fresh garden produce, local game, and
imaginative recipes. A typical dinner might comprise: her own pâté; chicken pie
accompanied by ratatouille and boulangère potatoes; then unusual water-ices.

Readers' comments: More than satisfied. Dinner one of the most superb meals I
have ever had, quite perfect. Most friendly welcome. Most enjoyable. Very
comfortable. Excellent food. In a beautiful setting. Charming people. We
couldn't have been better fed and looked after if we had been staying at the Ritz.
Beautiful house being lovingly restored.

**THANK YOU . . . to those who send details of their own finds, for
possible future inclusion in the book. Do not be disappointed if
your candidate does not appear in the very next edition. We never
publish recommendations from unknown members of the public
without verification, and it takes time to get round each part of
England and Wales in turn. Please, however, do not send details of
houses already featured in many other guides, nor any that are
more expensive than those in this book (see page xxiv).**

HALL FARM HOUSE   C S

Gonalston, Nottinghamshire, NG14 7JA   Tel: 01159 663112
North-east of Nottingham. Nearest main road: A612 from Nottingham to
Southwell.

3 Bedrooms. £20–£25 (less for 3 nights or continental breakfast). Bargain breaks. Some have own bath/shower/toilet. Tea/coffee facilities. Views of garden. No smoking. Washing machine on request.
Dinner (by arrangement). £15 for 4 courses (with choices), drinks and coffee, at 7.30–8.45pm. Less for 2 courses. Non-residents normally not admitted. Vegetarian or special diets if ordered. Wine available.
Light suppers for children.
2 Sitting-rooms. With open fires, central heating, TV, piano, cassette-player.
Large garden

To the attractions of the house itself, which was built early in the 18th century, are added the varied pleasures of a pretty garden which include rosebeds, a large heated swimming-pool, tennis court, fish-pond and vegetable garden from which come fruit and other produce for the dinner-table. Stables have been converted to provide a games room (with table tennis).

Rosemary Smith's visitors eat either in the beamed and quarry-tiled dining-room (its French doors open onto the garden) or in the big kitchen. She uses a lot of Prue Leith and Delia Smith recipes. (A typical dinner: tomato vinaigrette, chicken Florida with rice and salad, applecake with clotted cream, and cheeses – wine included.)

The sitting-rooms, also beamed and with oak floors, have antiques and, in one, mallard-patterned sofas around the brick fireplace. A feature of the attractive bedrooms are spreads Rosemary bought at the auction of a Sherwood Forest mansion, Thoresby Hall.

Visitors come for a variety of reasons – to enjoy the National Watersports Centre, to browse through the many antique shops, follow riverside walks, or visit innumerable stately homes, such historic towns as Southwell and Newark, and the Robin Hood exhibition in Sherwood Forest. Nottingham itself is full of interest: the castle (now a fine museum – the jewellery department is especially enjoyable) is perched on a 130-foot crag of stone riddled with tunnels and caves, the lace museum is outstanding, there are some very ancient inns, and an 18th-century quarter is well worth exploring on foot. There are trips on the River Trent, a splendid natural history museum (in Elizabethan Wollaton Hall, surrounded by a deer park), two theatres and a concert hall. And, in Brewhouse Yard, a recreation of bygone life in a group of old cottages. Other museums are devoted to canal history, the Salvation Army (Booth's birthplace), costume and, at Eastwood, D. H. Lawrence (his birthplace). At the pretty village of Papplewick is an outstandingly ornate Victorian pumping-station. Southwell Minster and Byron's Newstead Abbey are not far.

Houses which accept the discount vouchers on page ii are marked
with a V on the lists at the beginning of this book, see pages xi–xix
and pages xxi–xxii.

HARDINGLAND FARMHOUSE
Macclesfield Forest, Cheshire, SK11 0ND   Tel: 01625 425759
West of Buxton. Nearest main road: A537 from Macclesfield towards Buxton.

3 Bedrooms. £18–£22. Bargain breaks. All have own bath/shower/toilet. Tea/coffee facilities. Views of garden, country. Washing machine on request.
Dinner. £13 for 3 courses and coffee, at 7pm (not Sundays). Vegetarian or special diets if ordered.
1 Sitting-room. With open fire, central heating, TV.
Large garden
Closed from December to February.

It is exceptional to find at one house outstanding surroundings, food and furnishings: Hardingland is just such a place.

The secluded house is perched high up on the fringe of the Peak District National Park, on a hillside with stupendous panoramic views below. Anne Read's reputation is so high that she has cooked for such demanding clients as the Manchester Stock Exchange. And her 18th-century house has been furnished with style.

Anne used to be a professional caterer, winning an award at Buxton's Salon Culinaire in 1989. She uses a great many of John Tovey's Miller Howe recipes when she prepares for her visitors such meals as tarragon apples with Boursin cheese; lamb cutlets in ginger and orange sauce; an array of imaginative vegetables like French beans with almonds, caramelized carrots, herbed potatoes and orange and sunflower-seed salad; chocolate pots. The Reads' own smallholding provides beef and lamb; venison comes from forest deer.

The large sitting-room has comfortable sofas covered in a William Morris satin. Between the deep-set windows watercolours hang on the walls. The beamed dining-room is furnished in Regency style, and one of the bedrooms has an attractive apricot and pale turquoise colour scheme. Bathrooms are excellent.

Outside, wide stone steps beside a lily-pool lead to a paved garden and lawn sheltered by a stone-walled herbaceous bed. The garden is high above a deep valley across which are hills and the pine plantations of Macclesfield Forest.

Readers' comments: Food excellent. Went to so much trouble. Whole atmosphere very good, will go again. Beautifully furnished.

You stand a better chance of finding the right accommodation at the right price in the right area if you are using an up-to-date edition of this book, which is revised every year. Obtain an order form for the next edition (published in November) by sending a stamped addressed envelope, with 'SOTBT 1998' in the top left-hand corner, to Explore Britain, Alston, Cumbria, CA9 3SL. You will also receive a money-saving offer for 'Staying Off the Beaten Track in Scotland' too.

HARESCOMBE LODGE
Watergate, Cornwall, PL13 2NE   Tel: 01503 263158
North-west of Looe. Nearest main road: A387 from Looe to Polperro.

3 Bedrooms. £18–£20 (less for 3 nights). All have own bath/shower/toilet. Tea/coffee facilities. Views of garden, country, river. Washing machine on request.
Dinner. £10 for 3 courses and coffee, at 7pm. Non-residents not admitted. Vegetarian or special diets if ordered. **Light suppers** if ordered.
1 Sitting-room. With open fire, central heating, CD-player.
Garden

Of all the idyllic settings in this book, Harescombe Lodge's situation at the bottom of a winding, wooded, one-track road (with stream trumbling through its garden just feet from the windows on its way to join the West Looe River) must be one of those closest to perfect. The house, built in 1760 and once the shooting-lodge of the Trelawne estate, is cosily furnished with some fine antiques, including an enchanting Victorian high chair. The two cottagey bedrooms upstairs have excellent bathrooms, and a third room in adjoining Fig Tree Cottage (its namesake is right beside the door) is just as attractive, with the added attraction of privacy if required.

As befits a former Metropolitan Police officer, Barry Wynn has put together a comprehensive file of information, though the subjects are local attractions rather than felons; he is happy to discuss visitors' plans with them and advise on suitable days out.

True to its traditions, Harescombe Lodge still offers the best of hospitality; Jane's soup (accompanied by home-made rolls) might be followed by local lamb roasted in hay, or steak-and-kidney pie, with bread-and-butter pudding or fresh fruit salad to finish.

Pretty Looe is a half-hour walk along the river path; all the attractions of the south Cornish coast are within easy reach.

Readers' comments: Food exceptional; wonderful welcome; made to feel completely at home. First class; very comfortable. The house has real charm; beautifully furnished; evening meals really superb.

Across the river above East Looe, the imaginative conversion of Anne McQueen's **PENVITH BARNS** at St Martin unearthed an underground tunnel whose original purpose is still obscure; Anne has gathered a file of historical notes for her own and her guests' interest. What is known is that parts of the barn are 500 years old (you enter the kitchen under an original beam), and a millwheel found in the tunnel now forms the hearth of the back-to-back sitting- and dining-room fires. Bedrooms are immaculate, with

roomy showers; dinner might comprise home-made soup, fresh local trout, and Bakewell tart. £13–£20 (b & b).
Readers' comments: Highly recommended; extremely good meal. [Tel: 01503 240772; postcode: PL13 1NZ]

131

THE HAVEN   C D M PT S
Hardwicke, Herefordshire, HR3 5TA   Tel: 01497 831254
West of Hereford. Nearest main road: A438 from Hereford to Brecon.

6 Bedrooms. £20 **to readers of this book**–£26 (less for 4 nights). Prices may go up from Easter. Some have own bath/shower/toilet. Tea/coffee facilities. TV. Views of garden, country. No smoking. Washing machine on request.
Dinner. £13 for 4 courses (with choices) and coffee, at 7.30pm. Non-residents not admitted. Vegetarian or special diets if ordered. Wine available. No smoking. **Light suppers** if ordered.
2 Sitting-rooms. With open fire, central heating, piano. No smoking in one. Bar.
Large garden
Closed in December and January.

Kilvert, a frequent visitor to this house when it was a vicarage and its garden much used for charity fêtes, wrote in his now famous diary that paintings done by the vicar's wife were auctioned – but her flowers and birds still adorn one door.

There is a ground-floor bedroom (with bathroom) equipped to suit disabled people – even a wheelchair for use under the shower – and with a view of the unheated swimming-pool in the garden. Janet Robinson has stencilled the walls with a waterlily pattern to match the Liberty fabrics used in the furnishings.

In every room her flair for decoration is evident. One bathroom (raspberry and gold, with sunken bath, bidet and two basins) is not so much a bathroom as an event.

Meals are unusually imaginative: scrambled eggs with rosemary and sesame toast might be followed by chicken with pink grapefruit, and then red fruit mallows.

The Robinsons sometimes run special activity weekends on such subjects as Kilvert's diary, book-collecting (Hay-on-Wye is near) or 'hidden treasures'.

Self-catering accommodation above the old stables and coach house is occasionally used by b & b guests.

Readers' comments: Exceptional, have booked to go again. Kind and genuine hospitality. Very comfortable; food lovely. Very thoughtful, cooking outstanding. First-class room, food excellent. Friendly and stimulating company.

Just over the Welsh border, at Llanigon, is a dairy-farm with a big H-shaped house built in the year of the Spanish Armada: **TYNLLYNE** – 'house by the lake'. Low beams, three-foot-thick stone (or oak plank) walls and the turned balusters of the wide oak stair all date from that period. One bedroom has a high brass bed with broderie anglaise and a big carpeted bathroom. Outside is a terrace (with barbecue), an immaculate lawn, and a stream-and-woodland nature trail. For dinner, Lynda Price might serve (on local Black Mountain pottery) melon with port, venison, and chocolate

mousse – always with many choices. No smoking. Closed in winter. £19–£20 (b & b).
Readers' comments: The best food I have tasted; beautiful bathroom. [Tel: 01497 847342; postcode: HR3 5QF]

132

HEATH HOUSE   C X
Scords Lane, Toys Hill, Kent, TN16 1QE   Tel: 01732 750631
South-west of Sevenoaks. Nearest main road: A25 from Sevenoaks to Reigate
(and M25, junction 6).

2 Bedrooms. £16.50–£18.50 (less for 4
nights). TV. Views of garden, country. No
smoking. Washing machine on request.
Light suppers if ordered.
Large garden

Octavia Hill, co-founder of the National Trust, lived near here (at Crockham
Hill) – gardening, mapping the innumerable footpaths needing preservation, and
ultimately presenting to the Trust the top of Toys Hill, which commands a
superb view over the Weald of Kent. She followed this gift with Ide Hill 'for the
people of England for ever . . . a breezy hill, wide view, woodland glades, tiny
spring, all yours and mine and every citizen's for all time to come'. And so it all
remains today, together with hundreds more lovely acres in the area that are now
in the Trust's possession. At her death in 1912, the government offered a
Westminster Abbey funeral, but she is buried at her beloved Crockham.

It is over the scenery which she preserved that Heath House looks out, and
from close by is one of the footpaths to Ide Hill which she mapped – a very pretty
walk.

Two hundred years ago, it was just a cottage for workers at Scords Farm but it
has been extended by Mike Murkin's own hard work to make the lovely home it
is today. The original walls were built of Sevenoaks greenstone quarried in the
garden and, there being no more of this, Mike bought part of a demolished house
made from it so that the new wing should be indistinguishable from the old, with
clematis and honeysuckle climbing up both. Bedrooms have fresh, pale colour
schemes. The sunny breakfast-room opens onto a paved terrace, a lawn with
seats, and a view across a pond towards Ashdown Forest. Patricia is willing to
provide snack suppers for guests.

At Bough Beech, on the road to
Tonbridge, is 15th-century **JESSOPS**,
home of artist Frank Stark, whose
landscapes line the walls. Every room
has unusual antiques and other interesting finds from afar. There are beams
and lattice windows, pot-plants and
bouquets of dried flowers, a buttoned
leather sofa and grand piano. Two of
the rooms have private showers, etc.
Outside are a flowery garden and the
Starks' pets: geese, ducks and dogs.
Judith's excellent breakfasts include
varied home-made breads, croissants

and her own marmalade. (Snack
suppers by arrangement.) No smoking.
£17.50–£19.50. [Tel: 01892 870428;
postcode: TN8 7AU]

HEAVERS

C D

Chapel Street, Ryarsh, West Malling, Kent, ME19 5JU   Tel: 01732 842074
West of Maidstone. Nearest main road: A228 from Tonbridge to Rochester
(and M20, junction 4).

2 Bedrooms. £15–£18 (less for 7 nights or continental breakfast). Prices go up in July and August. Bargain breaks. Tea/coffee facilities. Views of garden, country. No smoking. Washing machine on request.
Dinner (must be ordered in advance). £13 for 4 courses and coffee, at 7.30pm. Less for 2 courses. Vegetarian or special diets if ordered. No smoking. **Light suppers** if ordered.
1 Sitting-room. With open fire, central heating, TV, video, piano, record-player. No smoking.
Large garden

Perched on a hilltop, this red brick farmhouse with dormer windows in the roof and clematis around the porch is at the heart of a smallholding. Until a few decades ago, the old house was occupied by generations of the same farming family which built it in the 17th century.

The little sitting-room has very comfortable armchairs grouped around the brick hearth (stacked with logs), which still has the old bread oven alongside. It's a cosy room, with ticking clocks, a collection of china pigs and good books.

Jean Edwards enjoys cooking a wide repertoire of dishes (whenever she travels in France, she always returns with new recipes). She bakes her own bread; honey, eggs and lamb are home-produced.

Beamed bedrooms are small but prettily furnished. The Edwards have collected stuffed birds and maps for the walls, and pot-plants for every window-sill. Through the windows are views of the Downs or of the garden which, even in winter, is colourful. There's an old pump in it, a brick patio, and a children's swing.

Readers' comments: Very good indeed. As charming as could be; convivial hosts; mouth-watering and plentiful food. Charming house, food delicious. Well informed, witty and helpful hosts. Gourmet dinners.

'Stella Henden, postmistress/telephonist, lived here over 50 years . . . loved by all who knew her'. So runs the rather touching inscription on a plaque at the **OLD POST HOUSE**, Fairseat, an 18th-century cottage, its walls hung with climbing clematis Montana. It is the home of Nevill Acheson-Gray, a solicitor and part-time antique dealer, and his wife Elizabeth. Breakfast as well as evening meals, to be ordered in advance, are taken in a light and airy double-aspect dining-room. (A typical meal: avocado, salmon mousse, and chocolate roulade.) Windows are hung with tapestry curtains and splendid antique tie-backs. Small bedrooms are decorated in cottage style. Guests may sit in the hallway-cum-sitting-room or on the small patio overlooking the pond. No smoking. £16.50.

Readers' comments: Made very welcome. Excellent cooking. [Tel: 01732 822444; postcode: TN15 7LU]

134

HERMITAGE MANOR

Canon Pyon, Herefordshire, HR4 8NR   Tel: 01432 760317
North-west of Hereford. Nearest main road: A4110 from Hereford to
Knighton.

3 **Bedrooms.** £18–£25 (less for
continental breakfast). All have own
bath/shower/toilet. Tea/coffee facilities. TV.
Views of garden, country. No smoking.
Light suppers on arrival only.
3 **Sitting-rooms.** With open fire, central
heating, TV, piano. No smoking.
Large garden
Closed from December to February.

An *escalier d'honneur* sweeps grandly up to the front door which opens into a room
of baronial splendour, its ceiling decorated with Tudor roses and strapwork,
motifs which are repeated on the oak-panelled walls. Through stone-mullioned
bay windows are some of the finest views from any house in this book. There is
also a very lovely music room (damask walls and velvet chairs are in soft blue; the
limewood fireplace has carved garlands).

The bedrooms, and their bathrooms, are of the highest standard and very
large. No. 6 has a view of a hillside spring flowing through stepped pools of pinkish limestone (from a quarry in the area) which Shirley Hickling created when she
was converting this exceptional house. She and her partner Bert Morgan serve
bed-and-breakfast only – but there are good inns nearby, and Hereford is only 10
minutes away. (Croquet and boules in the garden.)

Walking and watching the deer or birds bring visitors to this scenic area – the
Wye Valley (with Symonds Yat viewpoint), Malvern Hills, Welsh border, Offa's
Dyke path, Brecon Beacons and Black Mountains are all accessible.

Readers' comments: Magnificent view, magnificent bedrooms. So outstanding that
we stayed several times this year and last. So pleased by house and view we stayed
longer. Fantastic, delightful host and hostess. Enjoyed our stay very much. The
equal of 4-star hotels. Probably the best b & b.

Judy Seaborne's very good home cooking is the main attraction of **STONE
HOUSE FARM**, Tillington. The setting is very peaceful, with fine views,
and children in particular enjoy spring
visits when there are lambs, calves and
foals to be seen. A typical meal: home-
made soup, a roast (the farm's own
meat), fruit pie – served from Royal
Worcester dishes, in a dining-room
with log stove. (Sunday lunch is also
available by arrangement.) Made of
solid stone, the house is well away
from any road, and has fine greenery
beyond its small orchard. There is an
old pump in the front garden. £16.50.

Readers' comments: Well fed and
received with great friendliness. Food
of high quality and ample. Most
welcoming; excellent cook. A real
farmhouse experience. [Tel: 01432
760631; postcode: HR4 8LP]

HERON LODGE   D P T S X
Edgworth, Lancashire, BL7 0DS Tel: 01204 852262
North of Bolton. Nearest main road: A676 from Bolton to Ramsbottom.

3 Bedrooms. £17.50 (less for 3 nights or continental breakfast). Price goes up from Easter. Bargain breaks. All have own bath/shower/toilet. Tea/coffee facilities. Views of garden, country. No smoking. Washing machine on request.
Light suppers if ordered. No smoking.
1 Sitting-room. With central heating, TV, cassette-player. No smoking.
Large garden

If your image of the industrial north-west is all clogs, shawls and dark satanic mills, moorside villages like Edgworth should serve as a reminder that in this part of England you are never far from spectacularly beautiful countryside.

There had been a building on this site for as long as anyone could remember when the Miltons bought the single-storey property in the late 1980s and set about converting it into an immaculate, traditionally styled family house. Building work on the dining-room (which incorporates a massive old beam from a derelict barn) was suspended in the summer of 1995 to allow a pair of swallows to raise two broods in the rafters; bats flit around at dusk and kingfishers have been spotted on Bradshaw Brook (a tributary of Manchester's Irwell) as well as the herons which gave the house its name. Local stone has been used in the construction, much of it salvaged from the demolition of the big house nearby, once the home of the Warburtons of bread-making fame.

Bedrooms have generous floral curtains, and lacy covers on Victorian brass bedsteads (one king-size) in two of them. Edwardian-style fittings in the excellent shower-rooms enhance the period atmosphere. Another bedroom at the back of the house (possibly preferred by sleepers-in, since the road through the village, while normally quiet, does carry some commuter traffic to Bolton and Blackburn) is a very pretty L-shaped twin with patchwork quilts and pine and has an attractive adjoining bathroom.

Guests tend to converge on the comfortable quarry-tiled kitchen, especially on baking days; for Roland Milton, who has lived in the village all his life, is renowned for his boiled fruit cake as well as for the rhubarb pies he makes to share with friends. Light suppers only, but there is a variety of good, reasonably priced eating-places within easy reach.

Samuel Crompton, inventor of the spinning-mule, lived at Hall i' th' Wood a few miles away on this side of Bolton; mediaeval Turton Tower is very close. Steam enthusiasts find their way to the East Lancashire Steam Railway visitor centre at Ramsbottom. Both walkers and drivers will find Roland a knowledgeable and enthusiastic guide to all the area's many attractions.

Facts (prices, etc.) at the top of entries are supplied by the proprietors themselves. While every effort is made to ensure that these are correct at the time of going to press, they may alter thereafter: please check when you book.

HIDEAWAY   D M S
Red Lion Yard, Wells-next-the-Sea, Norfolk, NR23 1AX
Tel: 01328 710524
Nearest main road: A149 from Cromer to Hunstanton.

3 Bedrooms. £15–£19 (less for 7 nights). Bargain breaks. All have own bath/shower/toilet. Tea/coffee facilities. TV. Views of garden. Washing machine on request.
Dinner. £8.50 for 3 courses (with choices), at 6.30–7pm. Vegetarian or special diets if ordered. Wine available. **Light suppers** if ordered.
1 Sitting-room. With central heating, TV. Bar.
Small garden
Closed from mid-December to mid-January.

Aptly named, these converted stables are – although only 200 yards from the lively harbour – so tucked away that they take some finding! Beyond a secluded courtyard garden (the nicest of the bedrooms is actually in this), a door opens into a small sitting-area with help-yourself bar and tea-making facilities. Beyond this lie further bedrooms, compact in size and neat rather than characterful in style – all with en suite bathrooms and on the ground floor. You can use the sauna or spa bath for no extra charge.

From the tables in the dining-room is a view through sliding glass doors of a little paved patio, flint-walled. And, a considerable asset in the town centre, Hideaway has its own parking space for cars.

Ex-teacher Madeline Higgs and her two helpers run the guest-house on very well-organized lines. There is a surprising range of choices for dinner (five starters, eleven main courses, six puddings): you are asked to select what you want at breakfast-time, so everything is freshly prepared. A typical choice might be a mousse of Stilton, avocado and prawns; lamb in red wine; lemon pudding.

There are special rates for the over-60s outside high season.

This part of Norfolk is not only beautiful but exceptionally well provided with things to do or see – come rain, come shine. Within a very few miles of Wells are four stately homes, seven ancient castles or abbeys, five outstanding gardens, five steam railways, a dozen museums covering all manner of subjects from lace to toys and lifeboats to seashells, five wind- or watermills, three animal-life centres, various crafts, and a dozen nature reserves of differing kinds: 19,000 acres of the north Norfolk coast are conserved as being of international importance. Not to mention the long-distance coastal footpath (you don't have to go the whole way!), the attractive little inns, spectacular churches (within which elaborate carving is usually one of their great glories), an undulating landscape, countless mediaeval and 18th-century houses, markets, delicious seafood and country produce cooked to a high standard, and wide blue skies of unusual clarity.

Readers' comments: Can't fault it in any way. We have returned many times. Most hospitable. A perfect cook, delicious meals. Winter weekends are very, very good value.

HIGH POPLARS   C D S X
Hinton, Blythburgh, Suffolk, IP17 3RJ Tel: 01502 478528
North-east of Saxmundham. Nearest main road: A12 from Ipswich to
Lowestoft.

3 Bedrooms. £20–£22 (less for 7 nights).
Prices go up from June to September. One
has own bath/shower/toilet. No smoking.
Washing machine on request.
Dinner. £16 for 3 courses, wine and coffee,
at 8pm. Less for 2 courses. Vegetarian or
special diets if ordered. No smoking. **Light
suppers** if ordered.
1 Sitting-room. With open fire, central
heating, TV.
Small garden

For four centuries, right up to 1976, the same family, Blois, farmed here: there
are memorials to them in Blythburgh church. The latest of the Blois still live
nearby, at Cockfield Hall.

Now the half-timbered house is Mary Montague's home. She has furnished it
with unusual antiques such as a Spanish dresser, a collector's cabinet from the
18th century, country dining-chairs and sofas upholstered in an art nouveau
Liberty fabric. On the dining-room floor are heavy tiles of Spanish clay; and
up winding stairs are big bedrooms (one of which has exposed joists separating
two single beds) with, for instance, pink patchwork spreads and cushions, and
particularly good bathrooms.

Mary, who dines with her guests, might prepare such meals as mushrooms in
garlic or Cromer crabs to start with; roast beef, or sole stuffed with mushrooms
and prawns; then Belvoir pudding (a steamed lemon pudding with meringue and
apple surrounding it) or crème caramel; wine is included.

Hinton is in P. D. James country, an area where wildlife still flourishes – barn
owls nest in the lane, you may hear nightingales, and there are masses of wildflowers. Mary's own pond is frequented by herons, kingfishers and ducks.

The hamlet lies a little way inland from Suffolk's 'heritage coast', now
carefully conserved as an Area of Outstanding Natural Beauty: stretching from
the fishing port and sandy resort of Lowestoft in the north, via the old-
fashioned seaside towns of Southwold (a flowery place, with a series of
village greens) and Aldeburgh, to the big Victorian resort of Felixstowe in
the south. The sea constantly erodes this coast (go to nearby Dunwich to
see this most dramatically – the whole of the mediaeval port has been lost to
the tides). At Blythburgh is a great church with huge clerestory through which
you can see the sky, rearing up above a sandy heath of dunes.

Readers' comments: One of the best. Charming and helpful. Delightful. Delicious
dinner. Very warm and friendly. Lovely place. Made everyone feel welcome.

1997 has been designated Britain's 'Year of Opera and Musical Theatre';
and it is the East of England which has received the top accolade for its
programme of events then (the runners-up were Devon & Cornwall and,
in Yorkshire, Leeds). So music-lovers need to book early there!

HIGH WINSLEY COTTAGE   X

Burnt Yates, North Yorkshire, HG3 3EP   Tel: 01423 770662
North-west of Harrogate. Nearest main road: A61 from Harrogate to Ripon.

5 Bedrooms. £18.50–£21.50 (less for 7 nights). Prices go up from Easter. Bargain breaks. All have own bath/shower/toilet. Tea/coffee facilities. Views of garden, country. No smoking.
Dinner. £12.50 for 3 courses and coffee, at 7pm. Non-residents not admitted. Vegetarian or special diets if ordered. Wine available.
2 Sitting-rooms. With open fire, central heating, TV. No smoking in one.
Large garden
Closed in January and February.

Weird shapes loom above the moors – a 50-acre outcrop of stone which wind and rain have carved into surreal forms: Brimham Rocks.

Off the road leading to these is a one-time farm cottage now much extended, which has been modernized with care by Clive and Gill King. From the parquet-floored dining-room one steps down to a sitting-room where rosy sofas face a log fire and sliding glass doors open onto a terrace with views to the far hills. Lawn, flowers, orchard and bantams add to the charm.

Colour schemes have been well chosen, here and upstairs. A blue-and-white bedroom has a matching bathroom; Laura Ashley briar-roses predominate in another, furnished with antiques; a large room has windows on two sides and comfortable armchairs from which to enjoy the views.

Gill was once one of 'Miss Gray's young ladies' at the Bay Tree, Burford: those readers who knew the cooking standards there will rightly guess that High Winsley Cottage, too, can be depended upon for good and imaginative food. Gill also lived, and cooked, in Paris for a while.

She puts as much care into making the simplest dishes as into a dinner such as lemons with a stuffing of smoked fish, pork in a spiced orange sauce, and apple jalousie. Her own or local produce is used; bread is home-baked.

Burnt Yates is not only in the middle of a very scenic area (Nidderdale is among the loveliest yet least frequented of the Yorkshire Dales, and popular Wharfedale is not far away) but is also close to several traditional spa towns – Ilkley is particularly pretty in spring when the cherry-blossom is out on the trees that line its shopping streets, and the riverside gardens are coming into flower. The town has excellent restaurants, tea-rooms and bakers; a grocer specializing in cheeses and ham on the bone for picnics; plenty of bookshops, antique and craft shops; and historical interest, from ancient Saxon monuments to Tudor and 18th-century buildings. The invaluable local guide (free from the Tourist Information Centre in the library) gives maps for walks, short and long; tells you where to watch fell-racing, hang-gliding or international tennis.

Readers' comments: Excellent in every respect. Hospitality and food superlative. Excellent, considerate hosts. Room delightful. Like being entertained by friends. Very beautiful and cosy rooms, very friendly and charming host and hostess. The best cooking we ever had in the UK. A haven of peace, delightfully furnished rooms. A lovely stay, food good. Nothing but praise. First-rate b & b. Accommodation and food excellent. Very professional and welcoming.

HIGHFIELD

Ivington Road, Leominster, Herefordshire, HR6 8QD   Tel: 01568 613216
Nearest main road: A44 from Worcester to Leominster.

3 Bedrooms. £17.50–£19 (less for 2 nights). Prices go up in April. Bargain breaks. All have own bath/shower/toilet. Tea/coffee facilities. Views of garden, country. No smoking. Washing machine on request.
Dinner. From £12 for 3 courses and coffee, at 7–7.30pm or when requested. Less for 2 courses. Vegetarian or special diets if ordered. Wine available. No smoking. **Light suppers** if ordered.
2 Sitting-rooms. With open fire, central heating, TV, record-player. No smoking in one.
Large garden

Twin sisters Catherine and Marguerite Fothergill so loved cooking and entertaining that they gave up London careers to come here and make a full-time occupation of these pursuits. They learnt cooking from Robert Carrier and Prue Leith.

The big comfortable house, built in Edwardian times, stands among fields just outside the old market town of Leominster. The sisters have furnished it handsomely – Chippendale-style chairs in the dining-room, for instance, scalloped pink tablemats and napkins (with flowers and candles to match), Eternal Beau china, William Morris armchairs. Outside are sunny rosebeds and, on a paved terrace, white cast-iron chairs from which to enjoy the scene, drink in hand.

Not only are dinners very special but breakfasts too can be memorable – with such options as home-made brioches, fishcakes, kedgeree, home-cooked ham.

For other meals, residents can take the house menu or (after their first night) can choose a gourmet one which might include Marsala chicken-liver puffs; cider-baked gammon with orange sauce; profiteroles or pear pie with brandy cream to finish.

Readers' comments: Nothing was too much trouble. Cooking, service and friendliness made my stay seem like a house party. Excellent food and attention. Ideal. Everything perfect.

At **CHURCH HOUSE,** Lyonshall, Kington, you may be tempted to order a unique creation: a pin-tucked blouse, lace- or ribbon-trimmed in Edwardian style, each specially designed for its recipient by Eileen Dilley. The 18th-century house, too, is filled with her needlework and Edwardiana. In her Victorian-style dining-room, Eileen serves such dinners as home-made pâté, chicken in mustard sauce, and apple meringue. There is much emphasis on local produce and recipes.

Outside are donkeys in a paddock, many trees in the garden, and fine views beyond the haha. (No smoking.) £15–£18.
Readers' comments: Excellent quality.

Highly recommended. I have been four times in one year. Superior to lots of hotels. Superb meals. Delighted with the reception received. Peaceful surroundings. Warmly welcomed, room pretty, breakfast a delight. [Tel: 01544 340350; postcode: HR5 3HR]

HIGHFIELD FARM   C D M

Sandy, Bedfordshire, SG19 2AQ   Tel: 01767 682332
North of Sandy. Nearest main road: A1 from Biggleswade to Peterborough.

6 Bedrooms. £17.50. Price goes up from April. Most have own bath/shower/toilet. Tea/coffee facilities. TV (some). Views of garden, country. No smoking. Washing machine on request.
1 Sitting-room. With open fire, central heating, TV. No smoking.
Small garden

Set well back from the A1, Highfield Farm is surrounded by fields of peas or wheat. Two single cottages a century ago, the house is now enlarged and painted sparkling white outside, with a trim lawn and colourful flowerbeds. The interior is equally immaculate, the six bedrooms (two on the ground floor in former stables) having such features as bedheads matching the yew furniture hand-made locally. The L-shaped sitting-room has soft colours and comfortable armchairs. Margaret Codd provides breakfasts only.

This is an area with many NT properties: Cardinal Wolsey's imposing dove-cote and stables at Willington, the palatial mansions (and gardens) of Ascott and Waddesdon, Bernard Shaw's house, Pitstone windmill, even a NT inn (the mediaeval King's Head at Aylesbury). There are Bunyan sights in and around Bedford (and in the town is a notable art gallery, the delightful Cecil Higgins Museum by the swan-frequented river). You can walk the Greensand Ridge path or wander in Maulden Wood, and look at Shuttleworth's historic aircraft collection or the 140 kinds of bird in the RSPB's headquarters reserve, which has beautiful gardens too. Wrest Park has impressive watergardens around a mansion. The De Grey mausoleum, too, is worth seeking out for the fine monuments inside; near it is Flitwick nature reserve, a rare type of moorland with lakes.

Bedroom at Upper Green Farm (see page 330)

HILL FARMHOUSE   **C D**
Bury Road, Hitcham, Suffolk, IP7 7PT   Tel: 01449 740 651
North-west of Ipswich. Nearest main road: A1141 from Hadleigh towards Bury
St Edmunds.

3 Bedrooms. £17 (less for 5 nights). Price goes up from March. All have own bath/toilet. Tea/coffee facilities. TV. Views of garden, country.
Dinner. £10.50 for 3 courses (with choices) and coffee, at times to suit guests (not Tuesdays and Thursdays). Non-residents not admitted. Vegetarian or special diets if ordered. No smoking. **Light suppers** on Tuesdays and Thursdays.
3 Sitting-rooms. One with open fire, central heating.
Large garden
Closed from November to February.

Part Tudor, part early Victorian, this handsome house provides a choice between the spacious, traditional bedroom at the front of the house (with cornfield views); or the snug low-beamed ones at the back, with little oak-mullioned windows and rugs on brick floors. The brick oven and hearth of Tudor times are now a decorative feature which Pippa McLardy fills with arrangements of dried flowers.

One enters the main house through a hall of powder-blue and white, with cherry-carpeted staircase. Pale pink sitting- and dining-rooms have mahogany antiques, a carved pine fireplace and views of countryside or garden (there are duck-ponds, a freestanding swimming-pool, croquet and badminton). Pippa is an imaginative cook: for dinner one might choose between fennel Mornay or stuffed vineleaves; pork normande or Scotch salmon; raspberry-and-cream choux or lemon sorbet. Eggs and vegetables are often home-produced.

Hitcham is centrally placed within a triangle of historic towns (Bury St Edmunds, Sudbury – Gainsborough's birthplace – and Ipswich) and surrounded by very lovely countryside, ideal for walking as well as touring. The great mediaeval 'wool' churches of the area are justly famous.

This unspoilt region is a patchwork of farmland and fens, low hills and a varying shoreline (much favoured by birdwatchers), secretive valleys and wild heaths.

On the main road through Hitcham is **MILL HOUSE** where black swans grace the large pond. There is no sitting-room, but guests often linger in the sunny conservatory (where breakfast is served in summer), which overlooks the large landscaped garden and tennis court. Judith White provides dinner or a light supper by arrangement, or there is good food at the White Horse down the road. £13–£14.

[Tel: 01449 740 315; postcode: IP7 7LN]

For explanation of code letters (C, D, M, PT, S, X) see inside front cover.

HILLBROOK HOUSE   **C D M PT X**

North Elham, near Canterbury, Kent, CT4 6UX   Tel: 01303 840220
North-west of Folkestone. Nearest main road: A260 from Folkestone to
Aylesham (and M20, junction 12).

3 Bedrooms. £17–£20 (less for 5 nights
or continental breakfast). Bargain breaks.
Some have own bath/shower/toilet. Tea/
coffee facilities. TV. Views of garden,
country. No smoking. Washing machine on
request.
Dinner. £10 for 2 courses and coffee,
at 7.30pm. Non-residents not admitted.
Vegetarian or special diets if ordered. No
smoking. **Light suppers** if ordered.
1 Sitting-room. With open fire, central
heating, TV. No smoking.
Large garden

Families with young children are especially welcome at this large detached
Victorian house just east of the Elham Valley. It is the home of Charlotte and
Jeremy Sisk, she a BSc in home economics and former restaurateur, he an estate
agent with an interest in a wine business. The house was almost a shell when they
bought it, but they have worked hard to restore it, putting in old stripped-pine
doors (where there were empty doorways) and a rather splendid Victorian
fireplace and oak surround in the ground-floor family room, which has peach
rag-rolled walls, marbled cupboard tops and a very pretty bath/shower-room with
gleaming white and blue tiles laid in diamond pattern.

One bedroom upstairs has celadon candlewick bedspreads with green-and-
white flowered and striped wallpaper, the other has ruched red-and-white holly-
hock-patterned blinds. The shared bathroom has a pretty scrolled pelmet and
blind.

Breakfast is served in a dining-room with peach and blue fleur-de-lys
patterned walls and Edwardian-style curtains, at a solid table of Mavolas wood,
an African mahogany hewn from one tree trunk, and brought back from Kenya,
where Charlotte spent her early years. Evening meals are also eaten here, and, as
you might expect, Charlotte is an accomplished cook with a wide repertoire; her
recipes include Folkestone fish pie, Indonesian-style chicken with spices and
coconut, and many French-based dishes. Alternatively, there are two pubs in
Elham which the Sisks recommend, one with traditional food, the other more
adventurous. The house lies mid-point on the recently opened Elham Valley Way
and there is ample opportunity for exploring the countryside around here. Dover
and Folkestone are within easy reach.

To help those en route to the continent, via tunnel or ferry, Kent County
Council has produced an excellent booklet with map, called *Off the
Motorway,* which will tempt you to tack on a day or so (going or coming)
to explore any of 139 attractive places to visit in this beautiful and historic
county.

HOATH HOUSE   C

Penshurst Road, Chiddingstone Hoath, Kent, TN8 7DB   Tel: 01342 850362
North-west of Tunbridge Wells. Nearest main road: A264 from Tunbridge
Wells to East Grinstead.

2 Bedrooms. £19.50 (less for 2 nights).
Tea/coffee facilities. TV. Views of garden,
country. No smoking. Washing machine on
request.
Dinner. £15 for 3 courses and coffee, from
7.45pm. Less for 2 courses. Non-residents
not admitted. No smoking. **Light suppers**
if ordered.
1 Sitting-room. With open fire, central
heating, piano. No smoking.
Large garden
Closed from December to February.

Chiddingstone Castle, near the very pretty Tudor village of that name, was for
four centuries the seat of the Streatfeild family. The senior branch of the remaining Streatfeilds now live in Hoath House – a building of exceptional mediaeval
interest which, starting as a simple hall house, has had wings and other additions
built on through the centuries. The result is rambling and characterful.

One enters through a high hall, originally the mediaeval hall house. On a
Breton sideboard in the oak-panelled dining-room are carved lively scenes of
cider-making and other country pursuits. The massive, chamfered beams of the
sitting-room, its lattice-paned windows and the plastered walls where the hand-
prints of the Tudor builders can still be seen, are impressive.

To reach the bedrooms one passes through passages with 18th-century ancestral portraits, despatch-boxes, writing-cases still containing letters from Queen
Alexandra, huge chests and a great Grenadier Guards drum: all family heirlooms.
The rooms vary – a vast family bedroom has a sofa in the bay window. There is
an enormous bathroom in 'thirties style. For your own snack suppers, one room
has refrigerator and table.

Jane Streatfeild provides dinners that are straightforward in style: home-made
soup or pâté; devilled chicken, chops or a joint; fruit fool or pie; and she uses as
much fruit and vegetables as are in season in the garden.

Readers' comments: Our favourite. Exceptionally friendly and helpful. Fascinating
house. Excellent. Helpful and welcoming. Wonderful, interesting house. Like
stepping back into the first Elizabethan age. Stunning views. Could not have been
kinder. Charming, very interesting. Quite an experience to stay here.

**The addresses of houses are geographically correct but postal
addresses sometimes differ (for correspondence, the only essential
element is the postcode).**

**Information about the nearest town and 'A' road helps you to
locate the whereabouts of any village on a map; but before setting
off it is necessary to get precise instructions from your host as
many houses are very much 'off the beaten track'.**

HOE HILL   C(5) **S X**

Swinhope, Binbrook, Lincolnshire, LN3 6HX   Tel: 01472 398206
North-west of Louth. Nearest main road: A16 from Louth to Grimsby (and
M180, junction 5).

4 Bedrooms. £17–£25 (less for 3 nights).
Prices may go up from April. One has own
bath/shower/toilet. Tea/coffee facilities. Views
of garden, country. No smoking. Washing
machine on request.
Dinner (by arrangement). £12 for 3 courses
(with choices), a sherry and coffee, at
7–7.30pm. Less for 2 courses. Vegetarian or
special diets if ordered. No smoking. **Light
suppers** if ordered.
1 Sitting-room. With open fire, central
heating, TV.
Large garden
Closed in January.

'You're lucky to be going there!' said the garage proprietor from whom I asked
the way. So good is Erica Curd's cooking that she often gives demonstrations to
groups of six in her impressive kitchen with its U-shaped counter.

One enters the white house, built in 1780, through a porch filled with
geraniums. Off a poppy-papered hall is the large and attractive sitting-room, its
light pink and clear blue scheme picking up the colours from a Raoul Dufy
print of Nice. Antiques and a marble fireplace contrast with modern furniture
of bamboo. Glass doors open onto a terrace and croquet lawn shaded by a big
chestnut tree. One particularly attractive bedroom overlooks the walled garden
and has an extra-large bed (which can be made into twin beds if required) and a
spacious en suite bathroom with a spa bath.

As to the meals which have won Erica so much local renown, you might
be offered a choice of cheese-stuffed mushrooms or watercress soup with home-
baked rolls before, for instance, roast duck (or fish straight from Grimsby, or
local game perhaps). The choice of puddings might be a home-made sorbet
accompanying melon and crème de menthe or a traditional favourite such as
bread-and-butter pudding. With the coffee come chocolates. Breakfasts, too, are
impressive, with such options as Lincolnshire sausages, kippers, kidneys in bacon,
kedgeree and occasionally Arbroath smokies.

For those who like to seek out lovely but little frequented parts of England,
the Wolds - where Swinhope lies - will come as a pleasant surprise. The northern
Wolds rise high and have extensive views, but the southern part is 'Tennyson
country' (he used to play skittles in the White Hart at Tetford). To either side of
the Wolds are attractive old market towns: 18th-century Louth (which not only
has a fine market hall but a 16th-century church with the tallest spire in England),
and Market Rasen, originally a Roman settlement. Somersby has Tennyson's
birthplace and the garden that inspired him to write 'Come into the garden,
Maud'. The area is one of woods and streams.

Readers' comments: Absolutely first-rate, the best I have found. Meals excellent,
greeting warm and sincere. We have made this a regular venue for family
get-togethers. Excellent room. Outstandingly friendly welcome. High quality
food. Couldn't praise too highly, perfect hosts, nothing lacking, super value.
Excellent cook; made very welcome.

HOLE MILL

Branscombe, Devon, EX12 3BX   Tel: 01297 680314
East of Sidmouth. Nearest main road: A3052 from Lyme Regis to Sidmouth.

3 Bedrooms. £16–£18 (less for 3 nights). Prices go up from April. Views of garden, country, stream. No smoking. Washing machine on request.
Light suppers if ordered, or guests can use kitchen.
1 Sitting-room. With open fire, central heating, TV. Piano. No smoking.
Large garden

A scenic lane winds up then very sharply down – one hears rushing water and clucking hens before the former cornmill comes into sight below. Its origins date back hundreds of years, and there are stories of a murder, smugglers and other dark deeds – but today all is peace.

Within the thick and crooked stone walls are beamy rooms reached by steps up or down, which Rod and Amanda Hart have furnished in antique style, with a collection of clocks (they aren't allowed to chime upstairs!), Victorian bric-a-brac, and a cage with young Adrian's family of enchanting, bushy-tailed Chinchillas. In one bedroom is a particularly high iron bedstead from which you can watch the bubbling stream and the comings and goings of deer.

If you want more than a snack supper, the village has a choice of pubs and restaurants; a lift can usually be arranged. The Harts are infinitely flexible, even willing to serve breakfast at any hour: 2.20pm is the record!

Branscombe is close to a delightful stretch of coast where sandy beaches alternate with shingle and rock pools. The South-West Coastal Path passes this way.

Readers' comments: Most welcoming, house done up beautifully, peaceful. Goose eggs for breakfast!

On the edge of Branscombe village lies **COXES BARTON**, originally a large 16th-century barn. Sally-Ann Horman, a keen carriage-driver (guests are welcome to take a ride) and interior designer from Adelaide, has imaginatively refurbished the rooms to the highest standards. Visitors can relax in the Hormans' large sitting-room in front of a wood-burning stove or in the mellow pine farmhouse kitchen. Here breakfast is served (or in your room if preferred). Bedrooms are spacious and have en suite bathrooms. One double room has its own entrance leading onto a patio; another (twin) overlooks

the garden (an extra bed or cot can be provided). Everywhere are original pen drawings by Douglas Horman, and attractive watercolours.

Light suppers use fresh local or home-grown produce, or you can dine at the Mason's Arms in Branscombe village. £17–£18. [Tel: 01297 680536; postcode: EX12 3BJ]

HOLEBROOK FARM　　　　　　　　　　　　　　　　　C M X
Lydlinch, Sturminster Newton, Dorset, DT10 2JB　Tel: 01258 817348
South-west of Shaftesbury. Nearest main road: A357 from Sturminster
Newton to Stalbridge.

6 Bedrooms. £18–£23 (less for 3 nights). Some have own shower/toilet. Tea/coffee facilities. TV. Balcony (one). Views of garden, country. Washing machine on request.
Dinner (by arrangement). £13.50 for 3 courses and coffee, at 7pm. Wine available.
1 Sitting-room. With open fire, central heating, TV.
Small garden

A long track brings one into the yard behind this large farm; on one side are stables handsomely converted into bedrooms and on the other, a new wing where there are more bedrooms. You are likely to enter via the big old kitchen, with its original flagged floor and stone ovens carefully preserved – it is here that Charles Wingate-Saul serves dinner. (The main course may be anything from lasagne to pheasant; puddings include chocolate roulade or treacle tart; and there are always prize-winning local cheeses too.) Those booking self-catering accommodation may dine in the house if they wish.

From a gracious sitting-room (apricot walls, damask chairs, log fire) deep-set, pine-shuttered windows overlook the lawn at the front of the house beyond which are apple-trees and a kitchen garden. The house is full of interesting objects acquired abroad; and in a huge attic bathroom is a varied collection of hats (to which visitors have contributed).

The stable rooms include some that are enormous, each with sitting-room and bathroom. Stripped pine has been used a lot, and old horse-stalls retained as room-dividers. Small concealed kitchens are useful for visitors who want to prepare any meals themselves, and there are plenty of armchairs. There are also a games room with pool table, a swimming-pool and clay-pigeon shooting. There is a low-season programme of 'activity' weekends.

Readers' comments: Made so welcome and had a lot of fun. Relaxed and helpful. Excellent accommodation, helpfully equipped. Meal delicious and outdoor pool a boon. Very good value. Had a wonderful stay. Like part of the family. Very happy and comfortable place, friendly atmosphere. Food excellent.

STRAWBERRY COTTAGE at Packers Hill, Holwell, is partly 16th, partly 18th century, built of thatch, stone and brick, with cottagey furnishings of high standard. There is a comfortable TV room which is well supplied with tourist literature; one bedroom has an en suite shower. The cottage is situated in quiet countryside near Sherborne. (As well as excellent breakfasts, Vivienne Powell provides light suppers if ordered.) £16.50–£17.50.
Readers' comments: What a find! I want

to go back! [Tel: 01963 23629; postcode: DT9 5LN]

HOLLY TREE   C(10) **M S**
East Witton, North Yorkshire, DL8 4LS   Tel: 01969 622383
South-east of Leyburn. Nearest main road: A6108 from Masham to Leyburn.

4 Bedrooms. £20–£25 (less for 7 nights). All have own bath/shower/toilet. Views of garden, country. No smoking. Washing machine on request.
Dinner. £12 for 5 courses (with choices) and coffee, at 7.30pm. Non-residents not admitted. Vegetarian or special diets if ordered. Wine available. No smoking. **Light suppers** if ordered.
2 Sitting-rooms. With open fire, central heating, TV. No smoking.
Small garden
Closed from November to February.

This is one of Wensleydale's more peaceful villages, a pretty group of cottages around a green, where sometimes strings of racehorses trot by on their way to exercising on the moors. All around is some of England's most magnificent scenery – the Yorkshire Dales – and towns which are honeypots for antique collectors. In the 12th century, part of the house provided stabling for the horses of monks travelling between the great Cistercian abbeys which are a feature of this area. A curiously shaped breakfast-room, with built-in settle and window-seat, was the 'snug' when the house used to be an inn.

Beyond the sitting-room, which has a crackling fire and huge grandfather clock, are two small garden-rooms with glass doors opening onto terrace and lawn with seats from which to enjoy the far view. The formal dining-room has scarlet walls and curtains contrasting with white shutters, blue alcoves filled with flowers, and antique furniture. Everywhere there are steps and odd angles.

Bedrooms are particularly pretty. One, for instance, has a brass bed with white and apricot draperies; in its bathroom (blue wallpaper, pale blue curtains) are two basins and a bidet. Another has a rose-swagged frieze, pink-and-white beds, and a green chaise longue skilfully upholstered by Andrea Robson herself. There is also a garden bedroom with its own shower, basin, toilet and foyer.

Andrea Robson's greatest skill is cookery (she won the Gas Boards' 'Cook of the Year' award in 1981). Typically, one of her dinners (preceded by free sherry) might comprise salmon mousse and then her own recipe for chicken breast en croûte (it has a mushroom stuffing and a coat of pâté and ham, inside a flaky-pastry crust). The pudding might then be pears – stuffed with walnuts and cherries, coated with chocolate and brandy, and served with cream.

Andrea's family has roots in the area going back to the early 1500s: an 18th-century ancestor was the Bard of Coverdale.

The nearest small town is Middleham: 18th-century houses cluster around the market place and there's a ruined castle. Well worth a visit are Wensley's riverside church, Ushaw bridge, Jervaulx Abbey and an inn (at Carlton, in Coverdale) with a Saxon burial-mound in its yard. Horse-riding can be arranged.

Readers' comments: Food truly excellent. A lovely home. Very warm welcome. Wonderful food and accommodation. Very comfortable, superb cuisine, delightful house. Cannot be faulted. Everything was just perfect. Freshly decorated and very comfortable. Fun to be with! Charming house, incredible food. Exceptionally comfortable, food superb. Some of the best value and comfort in the UK.

HOLMFIELD

41 Kendal Green, Kendal, Cumbria, LA9 5PP   Tel: 01539 720790
Nearest main road: A591 from Kendal to Windermere.

3 Bedrooms. £18–£20 (less for 4 nights or mid-week). One has own shower/toilet. Tea/coffee facilities. TV. Views of garden, country. No smoking. Washing machine on request.
2 Sitting-rooms. With open fire, central heating, TV, record-player. No smoking.
Large garden

When the woollen cloth for which Kendal was once famous was still made in the town, Kendal Green was a tenterfield, where the fabric was stretched out to dry. It was donated to the public in the last century, and now this grassy expanse stands surrounded by trees as a peaceful open space on the edge of the town. In a little cul-de-sac at one end is this house, built in the reign of Edward VII and showing the influence of the progressive architecture of the time.

Inside, the rooms are light and airy, and Eileen Kettle has appropriately decorated and furnished them in harmonizing pastel colours. Though the house is close to the town centre, the views from this elevated spot are wide, from Kendal Castle's ruins on the other side of the town to the hills of the Lake District (the boundary of the National Park is close). In the foreground is a large and well tended garden, with a croquet lawn, swimming-pool and summer-house.

The garden is overlooked by a big sitting/dining-room with a characteristically Edwardian inglenook at one end. Here guests help themselves to a big choice of fresh and stewed fruit and breakfast cereals while Eileen cooks – she has become particularly adept at providing for people with special requirements, such as coeliacs. The table is laid with her own silverware, for she is an amateur (but trained) silversmith. Guests often buy her work.

Barry Bond laboured long and hard to restore this typical Lake District dwelling, **BATEMAN FOLD COTTAGE**, to which he has added a bedroom extension in keeping, with windows on three sides. The second, small bedroom (with bunks) is just across a passage, reached through an old oak door which shows the depredations of long-dead pigs!

French windows lead into the multi-level garden, where there are a billiard-table lawn, seats and a barbecue, as well as white doves and a tame peacock.

Byways from the remote hamlet near Crook where this cottage stands take one, by a short drive or a long walk (both pleasant), to a choice of four pubs for good evening meals. £16–£18.

Readers' comments: Interesting, relaxing and even amazing. [Tel: 015395 68668 (evenings); postcode: LA8 8LN]

149

HOLMHEAD   C PT

Greenhead, Northumberland, CA6 7HY Tel: 016977 47402
East of Brampton. Nearest main road: A69 from Carlisle to Hexham.

4 Bedrooms. £19–£23 **to readers of this book only** (less for 2 nights). Prices go up from Easter. Bargain breaks. All have own shower/toilet. Tea/coffee facilities. Views of garden, country, river. No smoking. Washing machine on request.
Dinner. £17 for 5 courses and coffee, at 7.30pm. Non-residents not admitted. Vegetarian or special diets if ordered. Wine available. No smoking. **Light snacks.**
2 Sitting-rooms. With central heating, TV, video, record-player. Bar. No smoking.
Large garden

Beside a salmon river, just where the walkers' Pennine Way crosses the Roman wall, this remote house has the ruins of Thirlwall Castle looming overhead (Edward I once stayed there). Just outside are the remains of a Roman turret, somewhere under the lawn or sunken garden, awaiting excavation; and some Roman stones were re-used when the house was built. All this, with the distant moors, is within view through the windows of the guests' large and comfortable sitting-room upstairs – copiously equipped with games, toys and facilities to make unlimited hot drinks. Pauline Staff used to be a tour guide, and so is immensely helpful with advice on sightseeing. She occasionally gives visitors talks with slides, or may even show them around. In winter, guided walks and discounts on tickets to museums are available. Pauline's husband is descended from Guy Fawkes.

There is now a bridge over the river which used almost to isolate the house; farm gates may need to be opened (and shut again) as one crosses the fields.

Although some of the bedrooms are small, there are all kinds of unexpected 'extras' in this out-of-the-way house: a foot-massager for weary walkers; pure spring water; table tennis; snooker; snacks at any hour; and the company of Rex, a Hungarian visla hound. Pauline likes to cook local dishes and has even experimented with Roman recipes cooked in the area around AD 300 (one favourite is honey-roast ham in pastry). She makes all the preserves, chutneys, cakes, bread and scones. A typical dinner might comprise: melon with kiwi fruit; trout in hollandaise sauce; almond meringue with wild raspberries in whipped cream (eaten at a big candle-lit table). Out of season, a ground-floor self-catering flat (suitable for those with mobility problems) is available for b & b, and groups can be accommodated over Christmas.

Breakfast choices include haggis, black pudding, kedgeree, muffins, crumpets and occasionally a Scandinavian buffet.

This is a splendid area for walks (with or without a National Park guide). The Northumberland National Park starts here; there are associations with Walter Scott and Catherine Cookson. Some of the most popular sights include the Roman Army Museum, Naworth Castle and Talkin Tarn. But it is, of course, Hadrian's Wall that is the biggest attraction of all.

Readers' comments: Good. Incredible setting, wonderful dinner, extremely helpful. Friendly; meals excellent. Excellent accommodation; highlight was the food. Delightful place, superb meals. Situation beautiful, food excellent. Mealtime a joy. Food excellent; kindness and hospitality terrific. Hospitable, comfortable, excellent food. Food memorably good. Comfortable; very knowledgeable hostess.

HOME FARM   **C D PT S X**
Church Lane, Old Dalby, Leicestershire, LE14 3LB   Tel: 01664 822622
North-west of Melton Mowbray. Nearest main road: A46 from Leicester to
Newark-on-Trent.

5 Bedrooms. £20 (less for 5 nights). All
have own bath/shower/toilet. Tea/coffee
facilities. TV (some). Views of garden,
country. No smoking. Washing machine on
request.
Light suppers if ordered.
1 Sitting-room. With open fire, central
heating, TV, piano. No smoking.
Small garden

Set in an idyllic garden and facing the church, this 18th-century house (extended
in 1835) has great charm and an atmosphere of peace. Clematis and quinces grow
up its walls, and lawns extend beyond espaliered apples and herbaceous beds. (It
is no longer a farm.) Two single bedrooms are in a barn.

Indoors, every room has old furniture, pot-plants and white walls. Country-
style dining-chairs surround the long table where breakfast is served, a fire
crackling on chilly mornings. Val Anderson's collection of 'twenties and
'thirties photographs of local hunting personalities hangs here (including one
of the then Prince of Wales, who first met Mrs Simpson at nearby
Burrough Court).

Normally, Val serves only breakfast as the award-winning Crown Inn nearby is
popular for other meals: 'the best food in the Vale of Belvoir', Val says. Home-
grown fruit is served at breakfast.

Guests at Home Farm find plenty to do in the area, visiting Belton and
Burghley Houses, Belvoir Castle, Newstead Abbey (Byron's house), Wollaton
Hall, Whatton Gardens and the Donington Motor Museum. Calke Abbey, with a
famous state bed, has fine grounds laid out in 1772. The National Watersports
Centre, Vale of Belvoir, Trent Bridge and Rutland Water are other attractions.

Old Dalby, which lies deep in hunting country (between the Quorn and
Belvoir hunts), is rich in history. Its parish church has a collection of marble
tombs (of the local Noel family) from the Tudor period. In 1687 the Duke of
Buckingham sold the village to the notorious Judge Jefferies (the 'Hanging
Judge'), who died two years later in the Tower of London, and in 1793 the village
was purchased by the Hon. Mrs Bowater, a patron of the arts. A member of her
circle brought the young Beethoven's music to England, and it may have been
heard first at Old Dalby Hall.

Leicester is of some historical interest, with a mediaeval guildhall and much
altered cathedral; it has about a dozen museums, some with a technological
emphasis – there is even one devoted to the history of gas! – and botanical
gardens run by the university.

Readers' comments: Finest breakfasts, charming and delightful hostess. Excellent in
every respect. Lovely little place, a return visit here for sure. As good as ever.
Recommend the welcome, the breakfasts and the pub. The home, the area, and
most importantly the proprietors are delightful. Friendly and helpful owners,
beautiful house and garden. Always made most welcome. Very comfortable room,
outstandingly good breakfasts.

151

HOOK GREEN POTTERY   C D PT S
Clay Hill Road, Hook Green, Lamberhurst, Kent, TN3 8LR
Tel: 01892 890504
East of Tunbridge Wells. Nearest main road: A21 from Tonbridge to Hastings
(and M25, junction 5).

3 Bedrooms. £16–£20 (less for 4 nights).
Tea/coffee available. Views of garden,
country. Non-smokers preferred. Washing
machine on request.
Dinner (if ordered). £10–£12 for 3 courses
and coffee, from 7pm. Non-residents not
admitted. Vegetarian or special diets if
ordered. **Light suppers** if ordered.
1 Sitting-room. With open fire, central
heating. No smoking.
Large garden

After 20 years as a London art director, Don Morgan trained as a potter at
Dartington in Devon for two years and then returned to this house – tile-hung in
typical Kent style – as both home and studio. You can buy his wares here.

Outside are geese and a croquet lawn; jasmine, fuchsias and climbing
geraniums. The dining-room has a large table at the window and a log stove on
the great hearth of nooks and crannies. Via the kitchen is Don's brick-floored
showroom. In the cosy sitting-room, its walls decorated with a bold William
Morris wallpaper, there are plenty of books. Upstairs is an old four-poster,
broderie anglaise draping the top, in a room with French flowery blue wallpaper
and an old Victorian fireplace complete with trivet. There's a view of the local
inn, a picturesque half-timbered building. Sometimes the Morgans let one of their
sons' bedrooms to teenage guests.

For dinner (served on Don's pottery), Ruth produces such meals as a help-
yourself chicken casserole or moussaka with garlic bread; blackcurrant crumble or
home-grown raspberries and cream, then cheeses.

Readers' comments: Thoroughly enjoyed our visit and dinners. The most delicious
food. Somewhere we would definitely recommend and return to.

On a wooded hillside close to
Tunbridge Wells is a hidden hamlet,
well called Modest Corner. Here is
NUMBER TEN, home of Dutch-born
picture-framer Anneke Leemhuis.
The ground-floor bedrooms are simple, furnished with pine and Laura
Ashley wallpapers and fabrics; the
bathroom is good. Meals (such as
lamb with ratatouille, followed by
trifle) are eaten in Anneke's kitchen.
Visitors can explore the many footpaths in the surrounding countryside.
Only five minutes from a station with
fast trains to London. £18–£20.

Readers' comments: Homely atmosphere, wonderful walks. Unequalled
hospitality and helpfulness. I have
stayed four times and am continually
impressed. [Tel: 01892 522450; postcode: TN4 0LS]

HOPE BOWDLER HALL

Hope Bowdler, Church Stretton, Shropshire, SY6 7DD   Tel: 01694 722041
North of Ludlow. Nearest main road: A49 from Shrewsbury to Ludlow.

2 Bedrooms. £18. Tea/coffee facilities.
Views of garden, country. No smoking.
Washing machine on request.
Light suppers if ordered. No smoking.
1 Sitting-room. With open fire, central
heating, TV. No smoking.
Large garden
Closed from December to February.

The ancient, stone manor house was 'Georgianized' in the 18th century – hence the handsome sash windows and graceful staircase, though older features such as stone-flagged floors still remain.

Rosaleen Inglis has decorated the sitting-room in apricot, furnished the dining-room with a fine mahogany table and damask wallpaper, and for one of the bathrooms found tiles with Shropshire views.

The big engraving of officers at the Siege of Lucknow (1857–8) and the impressive ceremonial sword were possessions of John's great-grandfather who commanded the garrison during the siege of Lucknow, one of the major events in the Indian Mutiny. (The then Mrs Inglis had to live for months, with the other wives, in rat-infested cellars: some kept prussic acid at hand in case the mutineers succeeded in taking Lucknow.) Among his other ancestors was the first Bishop of Nova Scotia.

Outside is a large garden with pool frequented by mallard ducks, a hard tennis court and bluebell wood.

Hope Bowdler is ideally placed for walkers, lying between those famous Shropshire hills, the Long Mynd and Wenlock Edge. Shrewsbury and Ludlow are both near – also Stokesay Castle, the Acton Scott farm museum, Ironbridge (with the Coalport china museum), and the outstanding gardens of Hodnet Hall, Burford House (Tenbury) and great Powis Castle.

The legendary Celtic leader Caractacus fought his final battle against the Romans in these hills: his fortress was on a hilltop near here, one of the many pre-historic or Roman sites in the area. Now more peaceful activities prevail: rambling in the beautiful Carding Mill Valley, for instance; golfing on one of the country's highest courses; gliding; sampling Church Stretton's many restaurants and antique shops; or birdwatching.

Readers' comments: Accommodation charming, proprietress most hospitable. Enjoyed an excellent week. We second your observation.

Houses with short entries are just as good as ones with longer descriptions; and they include some of the most popular houses in the book. They may, however, have fewer rooms, a shorter season, higher prices or fewer amenities (such as meals).

HORSLEYGATE HALL

C(5) S

Horsleygate Lane, Holmesfield, Derbyshire, S18 5WD   Tel: 0114 2890333
North-west of Chesterfield. Nearest main road: A621 from Baslow to
Sheffield.

3 Bedrooms. £18–£20.50 (less for 4
nights). Prices go up from April. Some have
own bath/shower/toilet. Tea/coffee facilities.
Views of garden, country. No smoking.
Washing machine on request.
Light suppers if ordered.
1 Sitting-room. With open fire, central
heating, TV. No smoking.
Large garden

Garden enthusiasts, in particular, will enjoy staying here to see the transformation
wrought by Margaret Ford on a sloping site which was an overgrown wilderness
when she took over. The house too (part early Victorian, part Georgian) had
hardly been touched for generations: in some ways an advantage, for its original
features were intact and have now been carefully restored – even to the stone-
slabbed floors.

The Fords painted the panelling in the sitting-room apricot and grey, with
fabrics to match. What was once the children's schoolroom (where they found a
large bottle of ink still lingering, and one of the desks) is now a breakfast-room –
where, incidentally, you may be lucky enough to have garden raspberries offered.
Here and elsewhere are Margaret's various 'flea market' finds which add to the
character of the house.

There are spacious bedrooms, some with armchairs from which to enjoy the
superb Peak District scenery (you would not guess that the centre of Sheffield is
only 20 minutes away). Stripped pine doors, beribboned curtains and baths set in
alcoves are features of the house.

Margaret serves only snack suppers because she is too busy to cook: busy, that
is, with her consuming passion – the garden. She started as a complete novice,
but within a few years created a fascinating terraced garden of stone walls, hidden
patios, woodland paths, rock garden descending to a lily-pool, herbaceous beds
and brimming stone troughs: one pleasure after another reveals itself as you
wander round.

If you want more than just the hill scenery, there are stately homes to visit
(Chatsworth, Hardwick and Haddon Hall), the market town of Bakewell, and
Sheffield for its many and varied attractions: excellent art gallery, cathedral,
industrial heritage museum with steel craftsmen (the 'little mesters') at work, an
industrial hamlet (bellows and waterwheel still active), and one of the prisons of
Mary Queen of Scots.

Readers' comments: Very impressed. Picturesque and quiet location, with good
views. Friendly and helpful. Enjoyed our stay tremendously.

**Houses which accept the discount vouchers on page ii are marked
with a V on the lists at the beginning of this book, see pages xi–xix
and pages xxi–xxii.**

HOWARDS GORHUISH

Northlew, Devon, EX20 3BT   Tel: 01837 53301

North-west of Okehampton. Nearest main road: A30 from Okehampton to Launceston.

4 Bedrooms. £15–£18. Some have own bath/shower/toilet. Tea/coffee facilities. TV (in one). Views of garden, country. No smoking. Washing machine on request.
Dinner. £10 for 3 courses and coffee, at 7pm (not Sundays, Tuesdays or Thursdays). Non-residents not admitted. Vegetarian or special diets if ordered. No smoking. **Light suppers** if ordered.
1 Sitting-room. With open fire, central heating, TV, video. No smoking.
Large garden

Not long ago, this 'long-house' was still being used as its 16th-century builders intended: cattle at one end, living quarters in the centre, and storage at the other.

Rugged stone walls, inglenook, low doorways and many steps are a reminder of its past. The contrasting decor, of oriental furnishings (which the Richards brought back from Hong Kong) and English antiques, marries surprisingly well with this background. All around the remote, pink-walled house are acres of garden and orchard and beyond these spectacular views of Dartmoor's tors. And in an outbuilding is an excellent games room for children – adults too – with table tennis, sofas, and books.

On four evenings a week, Heather serves dinner – with such imaginative dishes as prawn-and-lobster bisque, lemon chicken, a brandy sponge into which also go chocolate and cream, and cheeses.

She is an accomplished quilter: every room has examples of her work and such sparkling colour schemes as peppermint and white or coral and white. A particularly good bathroom has pretty tiles complementing the pine fitments.

There is stabling and grazing for three visitors' horses.

Readers' comments: Superb. A very charming couple, delightfully attentive. Wonderful location, fine accommodation.

The boat house at Tarn House Farm (see page 160)

HULLERBANK   C(12) PT
Talkin, Cumbria, CA8 1LB   Tel: 016977 46668
South of Brampton. Nearest main road: A69 from Carlisle to Brampton
(and M6, junction 43).

3 Bedrooms. £18 (less for 7 nights). Price goes up from April. Bargain breaks. All have own bath/shower/toilet. Tea/coffee facilities. Views of garden, country. No smoking.
Dinner. £12 for 3 courses (with choices) and coffee, at 7pm. Vegetarian or special diets if ordered. Wine available. No smoking. **Light suppers** if ordered.
1 Sitting-room. With open fire, central heating, TV. No smoking.
Small garden

Little Talkin village is in an interesting part of the country, surrounded by fells that are popular with walkers and near a country park and tarn with various watersports. Hadrian's Wall is also quite near: the most interesting parts at this end of it are the Banks Burn stretch and the fort at Birdoswald. The Scottish border country and the Lake District are easily reached too, and the beautiful Eden Valley lies to the south. Brampton is an old market town: Alston and the city of Carlisle are not far. Talkin used to be a stopping-place for monks making their way to Lanercost Priory: part of this is in ruins, but the lovely nave is still used as a church and what was the guests' solar is a village hall.

For railway enthusiasts, nearby are vestiges of the track of a railway which predates the steam age, where Stephenson's *Rocket* ended its working life, and the station where printed tickets were invented by a stationmaster who tired of filling in each ticket by hand.

Hullerbank is in a secluded spot only half a mile from the village, and offers farmhouse accommodation at its most comfortable. Though this is only a 14-acre smallholding, Brian and Sheila Stobbart are local farming people. The sheep they raise provide the chops and joints which guests greatly appreciate. Lamb (or other straightforward farmhouse dishes, all entirely home-made) might be preceded by soup, or grapefruit or prawn-and-mushroom parcels, and followed by apple pie, for example, to which the orchard and garden have contributed.

Readers' comments: Comfortable facilities, friendly hosts, a lovely part of the country. We are definitely planning a return visit. Very friendly. I can definitely recommend Hullerbank. Very comfortable and spotlessly clean. Delightful house, every comfort. Dinners and breakfasts exceptionally good. Hosts extremely considerate, excellent accommodation, first-class food.

> **Some proprietors stipulate a minimum stay of two nights at weekends or peak seasons; or they will accept one-nighters only at short notice (that is, only if no lengthier booking has yet been made).**

HUNTHOUSE FARM

Frith Common, Worcestershire, WR15 8JY   Tel: 01299 832277
West of Kidderminster. Nearest main road: A456 from Tenbury Wells to
Kidderminster.

C(8) D

3 Bedrooms. £17.50–£18. All have own
bath/shower/toilet. Tea/coffee facilities. Views
of garden, country. No smoking.
1 Sitting-room. With open fire, central
heating, TV, record-player.
Large garden
Closed in December and January.

In this part of England, very fine, old timbered houses are a characteristic sight –
evidence of agricultural wealth in centuries past. This 16th-century house is
typical: inside, antiques complement the oak beams and big fireplaces (in front of
which Jane Keel will offer you tea and home-made cake when you arrive); and
outside is rural peace with fine views on all sides – the Clee Hills in one direction,
the Teme Valley in the other. There are horses and sheep on the farm lands.
Bedrooms are trim and freshly decorated, the dining-room spacious. It's said that
Elizabeth I once stayed here on her way to Wales.

There are innumerable good walks in this hilly northern part of
Worcestershire, particularly in Wyre Forest, and plenty of 'sights' to visit – such
as Witley Court (with its exceptional baroque church), the Elgar Museum (his
house is at Lower Brockhampton), the gardens of Burford House and several
National Trust properties. In addition to exploring the historic towns of the area
(Ludlow, Bewdley and Worcester), shop for bargains in glass at the Stuart and
Brierley factories, for china at Royal Worcester, and carpets in Kidderminster.

In whichever direction you go, your drive will usually be traffic-free and scenic
whatever the season.

Readers' comments: Splendid establishment, breakfasts superb, stunning views.

Bedroom at Beechenhill Farm (see page 303)

HURDON FARM   C M
Hurdon, Cornwall, PL15 9LS   Tel: 01566 772955
South of Launceston. Nearest main road: A30 from Launceston to Bodmin.

6 Bedrooms. £15.50–£18.50 (less for 4 nights). Prices go up from May. Some have own bath/toilet. Tea/coffee facilities. Views of garden, country. No smoking.
Dinner. £10.50 for 4 courses and coffee, at 6.30pm (not Sundays). Non-residents not admitted. Vegetarian or special diets if ordered. No smoking. **Light suppers** if ordered.
1 Sitting-room. With open fire, central heating, TV. No smoking.
Large garden
Closed from November to mid-April.

The 18th-century stone house is in a picturesque area, not far from Dartmoor and Bodmin Moor (both the north and south coasts are within reach, too). It has large sash windows with the original panelled shutters and built-in dressers in the dining-room. The sitting-room has large and comfortable chairs and a great log stove. The most interesting room is, however, the big kitchen-scullery where an old slate sink and pump stand alongside the modern washing machine, and in the granite fireplace is an array of old jacks, trivets, and a built-in Dutch oven.

Upstairs, all is spick-and-span with fresh paintwork and light, bright colour schemes in the bedrooms. There is also a family suite (made pretty by an old-fashioned rosebud wallpaper) on the ground floor, where the dairy used to be.

Meals, often prepared by Margaret Smith's daughter Nicola, are above average 'farmhouse fare', with imaginative starters, in particular. Her soups are accompanied by home-made rolls; lamb or coq au vin by such vegetables as courgettes au gratin, cabbage cooked with onion and bacon, potatoes dauphinoise (with milk and cheese) or creamed turnips; her puddings include raspberry pavlovas, chocolate rouleaux and home-made ice creams – always followed by cheeses. She uses the farm's own produce and clotted cream.

Visitors can join in farming activities. Some even rise at 6am to give J.R. his bottle; *this* J.R., too, is a black sheep but the bottle contains milk not whisky!

From Launceston you can visit the majestic and romantic north Cornish coast, or head inland to wild Bodmin Moor to discover hidden, unspoilt villages. The coast has stark cliffs, waterfalls and wide sands; the moor, high tors that can be reached only on foot or horseback. Don't miss the elaborately carved church (St Mary's) in Launceston itself, an old-world market town. The area is full of Arthurian legends; and Daphne du Maurier's Jamaica Inn is on the moor. An otter park, a steam railway, Lydford Gorge and Launceston Castle add to the interest of the region.

Cotehele and Lanhydrock are two very impressive National Trust houses in the vicinity, and most visitors also enjoy Morwellham Quay, Dobwalls theme park near Liskeard, and the National Shire Horse Centre at Yealmpton.

Readers' comments: Charming lady. Recommended for value, friendliness and atmosphere. Fantastic, very good value. Lovely room. Superb atmosphere. Idyllic – we were spoilt! Excellent meals, very comfortable, very reasonable. Enjoyable and relaxing. We return year after year. Well above average farm cooking. Food of the highest standard. Everything immaculate. Superb food.

HUXTABLE FARM   C M
West Buckland, Devon, EX32 0SR   Tel: 01598 760254
East of Barnstaple. Nearest main road: A361 from South Molton to Barnstaple.

6 Bedrooms. £20–£23 (less for 3 nights outside high season). Prices go up from Easter. All have own bath/shower/toilet. Tea/coffee facilities. TV. Views of garden, country. Washing machine on request.
Dinner. £13 for 4 courses (with choices) and coffee, at 7.30pm. Vegetarian or special diets if ordered. No smoking. **Light suppers** if ordered.
1 Sitting-room. With open fire, central heating, TV.
Small garden, farmland and woodland.

Oak beams and screen panelling, bricks for open fireplaces and bread-ovens, flagstones for the floors – all are still to be seen in this house, built in 1520.

The main room of Huxtable Farm was originally a hall-house before being converted into a long-house (that is to say, rooms at one end, cattle byre at the other, all in one long row), and around it were added outbuildings that include a barn and roundhouse (now providing extra accommodation). Today it is the very comfortable home of Antony and Jackie Payne who farm the land and manage the accommodation. It is also the home of Antony's parents, Freddie and Barbara, a doctor and a teacher, both much-travelled – which accounts for the presence of such touches as carved window-frets from the Yemen.

On the farm are sheep (in April, lambs), goats, chickens, and a kitchen garden with vegetables, fruit and herbs. Children are encouraged to feed the animals, pick wild strawberries from the banks of a private lane, and get up early to spot deer which stray in from the adjoining woods. There is a stream to paddle in, a tennis court – and a particularly well-equipped fitness room and sauna. From here, visitors can join the 'Tarka Country Trail' which passes by the farm.

The Paynes really do welcome even the smallest children, not just tolerate them; and provide not only cot and high chair but even a baby alarm and night-light in the big family room; and kitchen high-teas and breakfasts specially for children. There are also ride-on toys, sandpit, Wendy-house and swings.

Bedrooms in the farmhouse, up stairs which some may find tricky, are cottagey in style (those in the barn have a light, airy look: peach and white, with bamboo furniture; bathrooms are as beautiful as the bedrooms).

Jackie uses produce from Exmoor and Dartmoor, as well as from the Paynes' own extensive garden. A typical 4-course candlelit dinner starts with, perhaps, a choice of artichoke soup or liver pâté; then there might be roast lamb and vegetables (both from the farm) with an interesting sauce; followed by the choice of a creamy dessert, possibly using whortleberries picked on the moors, or a hot fruit pudding with clotted cream – you help yourself from a sidetable – and Devon cheeses. With coffee there is home-made fudge. Bread is home-baked, and with your meal comes a glass of Freddie's home-made wine.

Readers' comments: Excellent. Very good evening meals. Wished we could stay longer. Lovely setting. Delightful hostess. Very relaxed atmosphere. Excellent treatment, wonderful surroundings. Enjoyed our stay; excellent meals, relaxed atmosphere. Accommodation excellent, food superb, atmosphere very congenial.

ING HILL LODGE D X

Mallerstang Dale, Cumbria, CA17 4JT   Tel: 017683 71153
South of Kirkby Stephen. Nearest main road: A685 from Tebay to Brough.

4 Bedrooms. £20–£25 (less for 7 nights). Bargain breaks. All have own shower/toilet. Tea/coffee facilities. TV. Views of garden, country, river. No smoking. Washing machine on request.
Dinners. £12.50 for 3 courses and coffee, at 7pm. Non-residents not admitted. Vegetarian dishes if ordered. Wine available. No smoking. **Light suppers.**
1 Sitting-room. With open fire, central heating, record-player.
Large garden

Mallerstang must be the Cumbrian valley least known to tourists. Yet it is rich in associations, real or legendary: King Arthur, Dick Turpin, the Romans and the Vikings, Thomas à Becket, Michael Faraday. Along one side of the valley runs the famous Settle to Carlisle railway, and on the fells above, the last wild boar in England is reputed to have been killed.

Ing Hill – built probably as a hunting-lodge in 1820 – stands above the valley floor, and the views are splendid, especially from the bedrooms. The latter have neatly co-ordinated fabrics and ingenious bedheads-cum-backrests designed by Tony Sawyer. A retired surveyor, he has done all the design and conversion.

Sheelagh Sawyer provides menus to suit the appetites of the walkers who stay here: typically, mushroom soup, steak pie, and blackberry crumble with cream.

As a change from exploring the upper reaches of the River Eden, which rises at the valley head, visit Kirkby Stephen for its antique shops and interesting mediaeval church approached through a curious classical colonnade.

Readers' comments: Warm welcome, excellent hospitality, beautiful surroundings. Standard of a top hotel. Food plain but delicious. Thrilled by standard of accommodation. Marvellous hospitality. Delightful furnishings and location. Food excellent, accommodation outstanding. Made us so very welcome.

A few miles over the fells is **TARN HOUSE FARM,** near Ravenstonedale, where Michael Metcalfe-Gibson, who was in banking until he took over this family property a decade ago, keeps sheep and dairy cows. Sally offers such dinners as sardine terrine, pork chops provençale, and chocolate brandy pudding (with some choices), using as much local and farm produce as she can. (Sunday lunch and packed lunches too.) She serves dinner in a room where there are still stone shelves (it was once a dairy): much of the stone and woodwork of the 17th-century house is unchanged. There is a prettily

furnished twin bedroom and a plainer double room with a good view of the tarn (small lake). £14–£15.
Readers' comments: Very strongly recommended. Truly warm welcome, very homely. Excellent cooking. Lovely walks on the fells and around the tarn. [Tel: 015396 23646; postcode: CA17 4LJ]

IOLANTHE

86 Wildwood Road, Hampstead, London, NW11 6UJ   Tel: 0181-455 1417

(M1, junction 1, is near.)

2 Bedrooms. £20. Tea/coffee facilities. TV. Views of garden, heath. No smoking. **Light suppers** if ordered. **Small garden**

For country quiet while in London, this is the place to be. The Hampstead Garden Suburb was founded by the philanthropist Henrietta Barnett in 1907 when, appalled at the housing conditions of London's poor, she determined that as the Underground spread northward a new all-classes community should be built there – green and leafy, with cottages and manor houses in 16th- and 17th-century styles.

At its centre is St Jude's, a great Lutyens church, low-eaved without and frescoed within. Alas for Dame Henrietta's idealism: today only the well-to-do can buy even the smallest cottage.

Situated right by Hampstead Heath, Iolanthe is a Lutyens-style house. Here, Rosy Gill provides breakfast and snack suppers either in visitors' rooms or downstairs – overlooking or even on the terrace of the garden. (No sitting-room, but there is also a first-floor terrace which guests are welcome to use.) Bedrooms are light and airy, with cottage-style furnishings and fresh white walls.

Central London is 20 minutes away by Underground.

Readers' comments: Excellent; very good value.

Drawing-room at Beehive Manor (see page 20)

IRELANDS FARM   **D S**

Irelands Lane, near Henley-in-Arden, Warwickshire, B95 5SA
Tel: 01564 792476
South-east of Birmingham. Nearest main road: A3400 from Birmingham to
Stratford-upon-Avon.

3 Bedrooms. £17.50 (less for 3 nights).
All have own bath/shower/toilet. Tea/coffee
facilities. TV. Views of garden, country. No
smoking. Washing machine on request.
Light suppers if ordered.
1 Sitting-room. With central heating, TV,
record-player. No smoking.
Large garden

In the middle of Shakespeare's Forest of Arden was built ancient Lapworth Hall,
later re-named after the family who extended it. A copy of the first Ireland's will
(1559) hangs in the house; in it he wrote 'I bequeath my soul to almighty God, to
the parishioners a cow, to my wife all the corne, six pieces of pewter, two potts
and two pannes . . . the salt meat in the rouffe . . . ' and so on. Stone-flagged
floors have survived the centuries, but much of the present house was built in
1820.

All around are the Shaws' fields (arable or pasture) and downhill lies
the Tapster Brook: the whole area is one of undulating hills with small hidden
valleys and a history that goes back to Saxon, Roman and even prehistoric times.
Boats on the Birmingham–Stratford canal add touches of bright colour to the
scene.

In the house, stairs twist up and down to bedrooms that are light, roomy and
comfortable. One has a sofa and a pretty little Victorian fireplace. There are
pleasant, farmhouse-style furnishings (much oak in the dining-room). Although
picturesque Henley has a dozen eating-places as well as many antique and craft
shops, notable church, etc., Pamela will prepare snacks for anybody who does not
want to dine out – exhausted, perhaps, by a day at the National Exhibition Centre
(only 15 minutes away); or in Birmingham, Warwick or Stratford-upon-Avon; or
spent walking the nearby Heart of England Way which links the Pennines to the
Cotswolds.

**THANK YOU . . . to those who send details of their own finds, for
possible future inclusion in the book. Do not be disappointed if
your candidate does not appear in the very next edition. We never
publish recommendations from unknown members of the public
without verification, and it takes time to get round each part of
England and Wales in turn. Please, however, do not send details of
houses already featured in many other guides, nor any that are
more expensive than those in this book (see page xxiv).**

JINLYE   **M X**

Castle Hill, All Stretton, Shropshire, SY6 6JP   Tel: 01694 723243
South of Shrewsbury. Nearest main road: A49 from Shrewsbury to Ludlow.

3 Bedrooms. £20–£28 (less for 7 nights or continental breakfast). Bargain breaks. All have own shower/toilet. Tea/coffee facilities. Views of garden, country. No smoking. Washing machine on request.
Dinner. £15 for 3 courses and coffee, at 7pm. Non-residents not admitted. Vegetarian or special diets if ordered. No smoking.
2 Sitting-rooms. With open fire, central heating, TV, piano. No smoking in one.
Large garden

This area calls itself 'the Shropshire Highlands': it is the country of A. E. Housman, Mary Webb and Brother Cadfael. One of its most towering heights is the primaeval ridge called Long Mynd and on these windy and magnificent moors you can see for miles. It is here, 1400 feet high and surrounded by 6000 acres of National Trust land, that Jan Tory has her guest-house, built in traditional style with stones from an old demolished building. Around it is a spectacular land-scaped garden.

The big, front sitting-room with woodblock floor and velvet chairs has a deceptively old look: its beams came from an ancient barn, its windows are lattice-paned, the walls are of exposed stone. This room opens onto a sheltered terrace. Pretty bedrooms have superb views.

A second sitting-room at the back has blue chinoiserie sofas around the fire-place, and in the dining-room are sideboards of carved oak. Here visitors enjoy specialities like lamb cooked in white wine with Parma ham, or chicken (a half-bird each) with port and mushroom sauce. You help yourself from an array of puddings. Cheeses follow, and then liqueurs with your coffee.

As to the strange name, *lye* is an Old English word for a clearing in a wood.

Readers' comments: Very comfortable. Stunning garden. Large amounts of good food. Beautiful house and garden, abundance of good food. Splendid spot, very peaceful, excellent meals.

In the foothills of the Long Mynd, **RECTORY FARM** stands near the village green of Woolstaston. It is a fine half-timbered house surrounded by big clipped yews that may be 400 years old. Inside is panelling elaborately carved with pomegranates and roses. Three sitting-rooms open into one another, and all the en suite bedrooms are spacious, immaculate and with fine views – particularly one from which you can see the Wrekin beyond the lawns, rosebeds and lead nymphs of the garden. There is a long oak table in the dining-room used for breakfast;

Jeanette Davies serves no other meals, so visitors go to the restaurants of Church Stretton. £20.
Reader's comment: A delightful home. [Tel: 01694 751306; postcode: SY6 6NN]

KARSLAKE HOUSE HOTEL   C(10) **D M**
Halse Lane, Winsford, Somerset, TA24 7JE   Tel: 01643 851242
South of Minehead. Nearest main road: A396 from Minehead to Exeter.

7 Bedrooms. £19.75–£22.50 (less for 3 nights). **5% off to readers carrying this book.** Prices go up from April. Bargain breaks. Most have own bath/shower/toilet. Tea/coffee facilities. TV. Views of garden, country. No smoking. Washing machine on request.
Dinner. £15.50 for 4 courses (with choices) and coffee, at 7.30pm. Vegetarian or special diets if ordered. Wine available. No smoking.
1 Sitting-room. With wood-burning stove. No smoking. **Bar.** No smoking.
Garden
Closed from December to February.

This one-time malthouse (parts of it date from the 15th century) is now run very professionally by Maureen and Nigel Messett. June is an ideal time to visit, when high Exmoor, unlike some places, has few visitors.

Beyond the large, light dining-room is a small bar; and, for residents, a sitting-room with original inglenook fireplace. Narrow, scarlet-carpeted passages twist and turn. Upstairs are pretty bedrooms and attractive bathrooms. There is one ground-floor bedroom (with bath).

There are always choices on the four-course menu: one might choose crêpes filled with asparagus in béchamel sauce, Somerset pork in cider and cream with fried apple rings and garden vegetables, and strawberry shortcake or special bread-and-butter pudding. Meat is local; vegetables and fruit are home-grown whenever possible.

Winsford, an ancient village (and birthplace of Ernest Bevin), has eight bridges over the several streams which converge here, thatched cottages, an art gallery in an 18th-century chapel, and the Royal Oak inn (12th century) which provided material for Blackmore's book *Lorna Doone*. It is a good centre from which to explore Exmoor: quite near are the viewpoint of Dunkery Beacon and the Caractacus Stone, a 5th-century memorial to a nephew of Caradoc, one of the defenders of Britain against the Romans.

Towards the Devon border is 'Lorna Doone country' (Oare church, in lovely woods, was the scene of her wedding); and also Dunster Castle with its working watermill. The area is ideal for walkers of every grade.

Readers' comments: Friendliest of hosts. Good service, with a personal touch.

Facts (prices, etc.) at the top of entries are supplied by the proprietors themselves. While every effort is made to ensure that these are correct at the time of going to press, they may alter thereafter: please check when you book.

164

KELLEYTHORPE FARM   C D PT S
Great Driffield, (Humberside), East Riding of Yorkshire, YO25 9DW
Tel: 01377 252297
On A163 from Market Weighton to Great Driffield.

3 Bedrooms. £17–£18 (less for 2 nights). Some have own shower/toilet. Tea/coffee facilities. Views of garden, country, lake. Washing machine on request.
Dinner. £10 for 3 courses (with choices) and coffee, at 7pm. Vegetarian or special diets if ordered. **Light suppers** if ordered.
1 Sitting-room. With open fire, central heating, TV.
Large garden

This big 18th-century farmhouse, partly rebuilt after wartime bombing, has been in the Hopper family since the early 1800s. It takes its name from 'kell', the Anglo-Saxon word for spring, many of which rise in the small lake just at the back of the house. The bay window of the large sitting/dining-room overlooks the lake (as does one bedroom), and there is a terrace with chairs from which guests can watch the ducks and – with luck – kingfishers. This is the source of the River Hull, which gives the downstream city its name. There are lakeside and woodland walks on the 200-acre farm.

In spite of the size of the house, with its wide staircase hung with oil paintings, this is not a formal place, and family antiques – old furniture, pewter and silver – are scattered around almost casually.

Dinner here might consist of smoked trout or asparagus; pork fillet en croûte (much of which would have been produced on this or the family's other farm); and a fruit pudding. It must be ordered in advance.

Walking is popular in this part of the world, which is on the edge of the Wolds. Other attractions are the coastal scenery, historic York and Beverley, and such mansions as Burton Agnes (Elizabethan) and Sledmere (Georgian). Factories for pottery (at Hornsea) and rock – the peppermint kind – (at Carnaby) actively encourage visitors.

Off the road to Beverley is the hamlet of Arram and century-old **CROW TREE FARMHOUSE**. In this quiet spot, hospitable Margaret Hart's two bedrooms (one a single) have – like the downstairs rooms and the conservatory – pleasant views of the croquet lawn, the smallholding, and the adjoining fields. The Harts keep a goat, a cow, horses and a few sheep, and the neighbouring farmer likes talking to visitors. Lamb and vegetables are largely home-produced: a summer menu might include marinated beef, fish pie, and chocolate fondue. There is a self-contained flat too. £15–£18 (b & b). [Tel: 01964 550167; postcode: HU17 7NR]

KIMBERLEY HOME FARM   C S
Wymondham, Norfolk, NR18 0RW   Tel: 01953 603137
South-west of Norwich. Nearest main road: A11 from Norwich to Thetford.

4 Bedrooms. £18–£22.50. Some have own bath/shower/toilet. Tea/coffee facilities. Views of garden, country. Washing machine on request.
Dinner. £12.50 for 3 courses and coffee, at guests' convenience. **Light suppers** if ordered.
1 Sitting-room. With open fire, central heating, TV.
Large garden
Closed from December to March.

This is a beautifully furnished farmhouse with stables at the front and a large garden at the back, onto which the glass doors of the large sitting-room open. There is a pond with ducks, and a hard tennis court. Apart from the hundreds of acres of crops, the main activity at Kimberley is training and racing horses.

The bedrooms are particularly pretty, the bathroom excellent, and the dining-room has a long Regency table. Jenny Bloom is not only a superb cook but a generous one, leaving pheasants or joints of meat on a hot-tray from which guests may help themselves, and she is apt to whisk away a half-demolished chicken merely in order to replace it with a fresh one. Starters are imaginative (avocado mousse, for instance), and puddings delicious.

You can have the exclusive use of rooms if you wish, or get more involved with the family and the farm. There is a very good attic family-suite.

Norwich is one of the most beautiful of mediaeval cities, complete with castle and cathedral, full of craft and antique shops in cobbled byways. The county has a great many stately homes and even statelier churches, wonderful landscapes and seascapes, and, of course, the Broads. The Sainsbury Art Centre outside Norwich is exceptional. The coast, King's Lynn and Cambridge are about an hour away.

This is an excellent spot from which to explore in all directions. Bressingham Hall has fine gardens and steam engines. Beyond Diss (market on Fridays) are the very colourful villages of Burston and Shelfanger. East Dereham has an unusual town sign (two legendary does), an interesting church, an archaeological museum in cottages with decorative plasterwork. Go to the Norfolk Wildlife Park to see bears and otters, to Harleston for spring blossom or summer roses and the River Waveney. Further afield, in Suffolk, there are historic Bungay and Earl Soham, riverside Dedham, Framlingham Castle, Heveningham Hall and a museum of rural life at Stowmarket. Yoxford village is famous for its cottage-gardens. Farming is done on a prairie-size scale, but villages are pretty.

The Broads are near (a steam train runs between Wroxham and Aylsham). At Tasburgh are the gardens of Elizabethan Rainthorpe Hall, with trees of botanical interest; at Badley Moor, a butterfly centre; in the direction of Diss, a monkey sanctuary; and near Fakenham one of the world's largest waterfowl collections. Several golf courses are within a few miles.

Readers' comments: Total peace, comfortable rooms, delicious food. Comfortable, and very good food. Excellent. Very warm welcome. Lovely people. Delicious supper. Nothing was too much trouble: very highly rated.

KNIPE GROUND   C(6) S
Coniston, Cumbria, LA21 8AE   Tel: 015394 41221
West of Windermere. Nearest main road: A593 from Ambleside towards
Broughton-in-Furness.

4 Bedrooms. £13–£17 (less for 2 nights). Tea/coffee facilities. Views of garden, country, lake. No smoking.
1 Sitting-room. With open fire. No smoking.
Small garden

When Mary Dutton and her late husband bought Knipe Ground, it was almost a ruin, with only one barely habitable room which had been occupied by a recluse, the roof leaking and the windows covered with cardboard where there were not bushes growing through them. They laboured for years to bring it to its present condition, farming and living almost self-sufficiently the while.

It sits in a pretty garden where there is still a rare old rose planted by the previous owner. Like most farmhouse cottages in the Lake District, it is stone-built and stone-roofed, tucked into the hillside above Coniston Water (the access is steep). Though built in the 16th century as a farmhouse, it was for a time a dame school (Ruskin knew it as such).

Inside, it is full of beams and old woodwork, with bedrooms (including two singles) reached by a staircase with open treads of slate. There are books and pictures all over the place. Breakfast (the only meal available, apart from packed lunches to order) is eaten in what was the dairy, with a good view. The bathroom is on the ground floor.

The farm was once the property of Furness Abbey, big landowners round here. When the dissolution of the monasteries was impending, the religious orders started to sell off their land, and each parcel took the name of its sitting tenant: hence the number of farms and houses round Coniston with a surname plus 'Ground' in their names ('Knipe' is a local surname).

This is the place for people to whom it is more important that a house should have character than that it should be spick and span. Character it has in abundance, as has its owner, who has been in her time physiotherapist, art teacher, farmer and carriage-driving enthusiast – she still rides, and keeps sheep (and dogs and cats).

Coniston Water, one of the largest lakes, is the setting for the *Swallows and Amazons* books. In its depths are the remains of *Bluebird*, there since Donald Campbell's last, fatal attempt on the world record. (The steam launch *Gondola* provides more sedate cruises.) It is also the habitat of a rare trout-like fish, the char. Overlooking it is Brantwood, the mansion that Ruskin had built for himself and lived in for the last part of his life. It is a pleasant house, with good craft gallery and restaurant in the outbuildings, and the gardens are being restored to Ruskin's original scheme.

Prices are per person in a double room at the beginning of the year.

167

LADY FARMHOUSE

Chelwood, (Avon), Bath & North-East Somerset, BS18 4NN
Tel: 01761 490770
South-east of Bristol. Off A368 from Bath to Weston-super-Mare.

3 Bedrooms. £17–£22. All have own bath/shower/toilet. Tea/coffee facilities. TV. Views of garden, country, lake, river. No smoking. Washing machine on request.
Dinner. £15 for 3 courses and coffee, at 7–7.30pm. Non-residents not admitted.
Light suppers if ordered.
1 Sitting-room. With open fire, central heating, TV, record-player. Piano. Bar.
Large garden
Closed from mid-December to mid-January.

More than 25 years ago, Judy and Malcolm Pearce visited the unreconstructed 300-year-old home of a farmer of their acquaintance who also dealt in horses. It transpired that bloodstock was not the only commodity in which he was prepared to deal. Before the Pearces went home, the two men had agreed to swap their houses and everything in them: lock, stock and barrel.

History does not record the reaction of the farmer's wife. Judy, however, seems to have confronted what others might consider a somewhat unnerving situation with unalloyed enthusiasm. The following spring, the only things that didn't change hands were the two families' cars, horses and children! The next day, Malcolm got up early to milk 200 cows before setting off for his business in Bath.

Later, realism prevailed and they made other arrangements for the cows (there is still a farm, elsewhere, which provides beef and lamb for the kitchen; also 'home-produced' are the Seville oranges from their house in Spain, from which Malcolm makes the marmalade), and began the long process of transforming a rather ramshackle property into a gracious Georgian-fronted house of great beauty, set in six acres of landscaped grounds including two small lakes, a tennis court, and a lovely garden which was recently accepted for the National Gardens Scheme.

Guests take breakfast in the conservatory, or in the big kitchen, homely with colourful fittings and old pine; dinner might be home-made soup, a casserole with vegetables from the garden, and fruit pie or home-made ice cream. The beamed dining-room is magnificent, with a vast open fireplace, impressive refectory table and fine paintings (the quarry-tiles in this room have been laid upside-down to produce a weathered effect). There is another huge open fire in the pale yellow sitting-room; and a grand piano in the hall. Bedrooms and bathrooms are lavish and lovely, furnished, like the rest of the house, with lots of antiques and richly decorative fabrics.

Located on the edge of the Chew Valley, the house is within easy reach of Glastonbury, Wells, Bath and Bristol; the Mendips too.

Reader's comment: A lovely farmhouse with beautiful gardens.

Book well ahead: many of these houses have few rooms. Do not expect dinner if you have not booked it or if you arrive late.

LAMB INN   **C D M**

Great Rissington, Gloucestershire, GL54 2LP   Tel: 01451 820388

East of Cheltenham. Nearest main road: A40 from Oxford to Cheltenham.

14 Bedrooms. £20 **(for 2 rooms to readers of this book, January to April)** –£37.50. Sunday nights free to over-60s. Less for 7 nights. Prices go up from April. Bargain breaks. All have own bath/shower/toilet. Tea/coffee facilities. Views of garden, country. No smoking. Washing machine on request.

Dinner. £18 for 3 courses, at 7pm. Less for 2 courses. Vegetarian or special diets if ordered. Wine available. No smoking. **Light suppers** if ordered.

1 Sitting-room. With open fire, central heating, TV. **Bar.**

Large garden

This is exactly what one asks of a typical old Cotswold inn! It is a place of little windows, zigzag corridors and stairs, quaint oak doors, thick stone walls; outside are magnificent views of the countryside, looking across to some of the highest Cotswolds. Kate and Richard Cleverly have furnished the bedrooms with care – restful colours, everything neat, a pretty tulip wallpaper in one room, and in the dining-room pine chairs at polished tables with candle-lamps lit at night. The menu includes such dishes as Stilton-topped fillet steaks, veal-and-sweetcorn pies, salmon-and-prawn mousse, lamb with apricots. Outside is a landscaped garden from which to enjoy the summer view with a glass of 'real ale' in hand; and a summer-house. In cold weather, there is a log fire in the bar, and in the attractive residents' sitting-room. There is a choice of suites – four-poster and king-size beds – including a luxurious honeymoon suite and two in the garden.

Richard is an imaginative as well as a skilled craftsman: the carving of a lamb over the sitting-room fire is his, and so are the conversions of old doors, pews and school desks to new uses. He has even made a four-poster with carved decorations. In former stables are two double bedrooms, with en suite showers.

Readers' comments: Excellent. Clean, friendly and comfortable. The food varied, well-cooked and plentiful. Superb accommodation, very friendly.

In the same village, in Rectory Lane, is **STEPPING STONE,** home of Jane and Allan Peates – a modern house yet blending beautifully with its surroundings. The Peates chose the plot for the breathtaking views it affords of the Windrush Valley. Bedrooms in the house are in celadon and pink chintzes, and outside are two stylish and well-equipped self-contained suites, both facing down the valley. One at first-floor level has its own balcony and the other is on the ground floor. Visit

the Lamb Inn close by for evening meals. £18–£21 (b & b). [Tel: 01451 821385; postcode GL54 2LL]

LANE END HOUSE
C D M PT

Green Lane, Tansley, Derbyshire, DE4 5FJ   Tel: 01629 583981
East of Matlock. Nearest main road: A615 from Matlock to Alfreton
(and M1, junction 28).

4 Bedrooms. £18–£23 (less for 3 nights). Prices go up from April. Bargain breaks. All have own bath or shower and toilet. Tea/coffee facilities. TV. Views of garden, country. No smoking. Washing machine on request.
Dinner. £14.50 **to readers of this book only** for 4 courses and coffee, at 7.30pm. Non-residents not admitted. Vegetarian or special diets if ordered. Wine available. No smoking.
1 Sitting-room. With central heating, TV. Bar. No smoking.
Small garden

Even the 18th-century pigsty is a 'listed' building here! But to the old house, opposite the Gate Inn, a new wing has been added, in which there is a big picture-window opening onto a stone terrace with lawn and flowers beyond. Antiques and ample sofas encourage one to linger indoors, but croquet awaits in the landscaped garden from which there is a spectacular view of gaunt Riber Castle looming over the horizon. Outside the dining-room's French windows is a watergarden.

One bedroom is on the ground floor, attractively furnished with silky mulberry quilts, while from the dining-room a staircase rises to others which have fine views of the wonderful scenery all around. One particularly pleasant room has a draped bedhead and figured walnut suite, with a rather splendid Victorian bathtub and cistern in its bathroom. The pink-and-green room enjoys windows on three sides – and houses part of Marion Smith's vast collection of pottery hedgehogs. Every detail has been thought out with much care, from Vanitory units neatly concealed behind louvred cupboard doors to the provision of towelling bathrobes, maps, videos of the Peak District and even tape-recorders with a selection of tapes.

Marion and her husband, who used to run a large Leicestershire hotel, apply professional standards to everything they do – particularly the meals (including a very varied breakfast). From a wide choice, one might possibly start with a chicken vol-au-vent or mushrooms à la grecque; to be followed by a sorbet and then trout with a honey, orange and raisin sauce or chicken with four garden vegetables and potatoes lyonnaise; and finally perhaps individual sticky-toffee puddings or a roulade. Vegetarian options are numerous and imaginative. Yogurt and muesli are home-made, stoneground flour is used for pastry, there is much emphasis on low-fat foods, low-sugar jams, and syrup-free compotes, for instance. There is a long wine list.

Readers' comments: Most comfortable. First-class, imaginative menus. Wines of excellent provenance. Most welcoming. Charming house and interesting garden. A gourmet's delight. Attentive and friendly proprietors. Delightful surroundings. Most peaceful, and so many personal touches. Meticulous care and attention. Home cooking at its very best. Exceptional in every way. Food beautifully cooked and served. Menus very imaginative; friendly.

LANGORF HOTEL   C M PT X

20 Frognal, Hampstead, London, NW3 6AG Tel: 0171-794 4483
(Toll-free from USA on: 1-800-925-4731)
Nearest main road: A41 (Finchley Road) from London to Aylesbury
(M1, junction 1, is near).

32 **Bedrooms.** £31 (with continental
breakfast) **to readers of this book only.**
Prices go up in April. All have own bath/
shower/toilet. Tea/coffee facilities. TV.
Washing/cleaning service.
Light snacks etc. (24 hours). **Bar.**

For readers visiting London, we have negotiated a very special price (just over half the usual cost – singles pay more) at a small but luxurious hotel.

Its quiet residential road, at the top of which Hampstead had its beginnings in Saxon times, has housed such famous residents as Stephen Spender (at no. 10), Kate Greenaway (no. 39), Charles de Gaulle (no. 99) and Ramsay MacDonald (no. 103); and walking up it – to Hampstead village, the church where Constable is buried and the famous Heath – you will pass many fine 18th-century houses.

Within yards is busy Finchley Road with its shops, buses into Central London, Underground station (Jubilee and Metropolitan lines) and British Rail (to the City in one direction, Richmond and Kew Gardens in the other). The hotel is particularly well placed for visiting the art treasures of Kenwood House, Regent's Park (with London Zoo), Keats's house, the shops of Baker Street and Oxford Street (Selfridges, etc.), the Wallace Collection, Madame Tussaud's, the Planetarium, West End theatres and cinemas, Lord's cricket ground and much else.

The bedrooms are elegant, and have every convenience that you might expect of a top hotel. Modern furniture is complemented by excellent soft furnishings such as coral fabrics on armchairs and padded bedheads, and silver-grey or floral quilts on beds. All bathroom and other fitments are of the highest quality: high-pressure showers, for example, and solid brass fittings on the white, panelled doors. There are remote-control satellite television sets in each room, direct-dial telephones, hair-dryers, etc. Some bedrooms are on the ground floor, others are served by a lift. Twenty-four-hour room service for snacks and drinks.

Downstairs, an attractive coral reception/sitting-area, with sofas of navy buttoned leather and prettily draped curtains, leads into the airy breakfast-room, which overlooks a leafy garden. Here one helps oneself from a buffet of some two dozen items that include melon and other fruits, ham, cheeses, croissants and much else. Throughout the rest of the day, light meals are available – such as sandwiches and soup – and a bar. Individual dietary requirements can be catered for, if the hotel is forewarned.

The manager is Caroline Bright.

Readers' comments: Very pleased. Very nice and helpful staff. Wonderful gem, everything superb. Each guest very special. The best value we have found in London. Excellent value for the city.

LANSCOMBE HOUSE

CDS

Cockington Lane, Cockington, Devon, TQ2 6XA   Tel: 01803 606938
West of Torquay. Nearest main road: A379 from Torquay to Paignton.

7 Bedrooms. £18–£22 (less for 5 nights). Prices go up from May. All have own bath/shower/toilet. Tea/coffee facilities. TV. Views of garden (some). No smoking in some.
1 Sitting-room. With open fire, central heating, record-player. No smoking. **Bar.**
Large garden
Closed in November.

An ideal spot for anyone who wants that 'off the beaten track' feel while being close to all the amenities of a major seaside resort. Picturesque and secluded, Cockington village has just survived being swallowed up by the spread of Torquay's palms and promenades.

The life of the thatched village, complete with its blacksmith's forge and ancient church, used to be dominated by a great house set in a park, Cockington Court (now a Rural Skills Centre, where you can watch traditional crafts being taught). Pink-walled Lanscombe was its dower house: when each lord of the manor died, his widow would move out of the Court to live here. It was built in the early 18th century and has the features of that very fine architectural period – for instance, the floor-to-ceiling sash windows in the tea-room, where the Perrymans serve an all-day snack menu including Devon cream teas during the summer season. This and other rooms overlook the secluded garden with pools fed by a stream that flows to the sea some 300 yards away.

Bedrooms are spacious, decorated in soft pastel colours and with flowery fabrics. Several of the beds have prettily draped coronas or pelmets, and one is a four-poster. Some rooms have armchairs.

Botanists are impressed by the huge magnolia (probably as old as the house) which usually flowers from July to the end of December – this coastline is well called 'the English Riviera'.

Those who want more than a snack supper in the tea-room can stroll to the thatched Drum Inn nearby, almost the only inn to have been designed by Lutyens.

Just north of Torquay is Maidencombe, a conservation village, and, perched on Steep Hill (where virtually no traffic goes), **THE BEEHIVE** – with stunning views across Lyme Bay which is at the foot of the hill. This modern house was designed by its owner Norman Sibthorp to handsome standards and is furnished immaculately. Comfort within is complemented by a beautifully tended garden, reached via a terrace of red sandstone outside the sliding glass doors of the dining-room. A few yards downhill is the Thatched Tavern for excellent meals at reasonable prices; just beyond this, a

sandy cove and the coastal footpath to Teignmouth. No smoking. £15–£16.
Readers' comments: Beautifully decorated. Never met hosts who were kinder and more anxious to please. Thoroughly enjoyed our stay. Superb quality, exceptional hospitality. [Tel: 01803 314647; postcode: TQ1 4TS]

LANSDOWNE HOUSE
C(5) M PT

Clarendon Street, Leamington Spa, Warwickshire, CV32 4PF
Tel: 01926 450505 or 421313
Nearest main road: A425 from Warwick to Southam (and M40, junctions 13/14).

15 Bedrooms. £19.95–£24.95. **To readers mentioning this book when reserving:** £35.95–£42.50 (2 nights), or £35.95–£39.95 (5 nights) for half board in a double or twin room. Prices go up from May. Bargain breaks. Some have own bath/shower/toilet. Tea/coffee facilities. TV. Laundry and dry-cleaning: 8-hour service.
Dinner. £16.95 for 3 courses (with choices) and coffee, at 6.30–8.30pm. Vegetarian or special diets if ordered. Wine available. No smoking. **Light suppers** if ordered.
2 Sitting-rooms. With open fire, central heating, TV. **Bar.**

A pretty creeper-covered house built in the 18th century, this small hotel cannot be described as truly 'off the beaten track' for it stands at a crossroads not far from the centre of Leamington. But bedroom windows are double-glazed to reduce any sound from traffic.

When David and Gillian Allen took it over they decided to furnish it to a very high standard and in keeping with its architecture. There is a particularly pretty sitting-room with tartan and strawberry Victorian sofas, for example; in the small dining-room, meals are served on fluted Rosenthal china and wine in elegant glasses; the bar has cherry-buttoned seats; and every bedroom is attractively decorated in soft colours with well-chosen fabrics, stripped-pine furniture and thick, moss-green carpet. (No. 2 is the quietest, with roof-light not windows.)

The same care goes into the food. David, who trained as a chef in Switzerland, is a perfectionist. He sends to Scotland for his steaks, to the Cotswolds for his trout, has coffee specially blended to his taste, and damson and other sorbets made for him on a fruit farm nearby. Connoisseurs will appreciate some little-known wines among his very good selection, and the range of malt whiskies.

There are always several choices of good English dishes at dinner. Starters include particularly imaginative soups (such as celery-and-walnut or cream of parsnip), while main courses are likely to be such things as roast pork with freshly chopped rosemary, or liver and bacon with fresh sage. Puddings might include walnut-and-chocolate fudge pudding or fruit cobbler.

Royal Leamington Spa is a health resort with a saline spring. It has fine Georgian terraces and lovely riverside gardens. A good base from which to visit not only Warwick and Kenilworth castles, but also Coventry (modern cathedral, some historic buildings), Southam (old market town), Stoneleigh (mediaeval village and the great National Agricultural Centre) and fine countryside towards Stratford-upon-Avon. Birmingham Airport is half an hour away.

For residents there are discounts at Warwick Castle (where Tussaud's 'royal house party' is a superb show) and many other sights. Free guided local walks.

Readers' comments: Excellent. Charming features, food excellent. The personal touch made such a difference.

LASKILL FARM

Hawnby, North Yorkshire, YO6 5NB   Tel: 01439 798268

North-west of Helmsley. Nearest main road: A170 from Thirsk to Helmsley.

CDMSX

rear view

7 **Bedrooms.** £18–£22.50 (less for 3 nights). Prices go up from Easter. Bargain breaks. Some have own bath/shower/toilet. Tea/coffee facilities. TV. Views of garden, country, river. Washing machine on request. **Dinner.** £11 for 4 courses and coffee, at 7pm (not Sundays or in winter). Vegetarian or special diets if ordered. Wine available. **Light suppers** if ordered.

1 **Sitting-room.** With open fire, central heating, TV.

Large garden

This stone farmhouse lies in a hilly, wooded area of great scenic splendour ('Herriot country'), and close to famous Rievaulx Abbey. Its courtyard is made pretty with stone troughs, flowers and rocks; and around lie 600 acres with cattle and sheep. A summer-house overlooks a duck-pond.

In the sitting/dining-room is oak furniture hand-carved by local craftsmen, each of whom 'signs' his work with his own particular symbol – an acorn, a beaver or a stag's head. Here Sue Smith serves home-made soup or pâté before a main course which is likely to comprise meat and vegetables from the farm, followed by (for instance) lemon meringue pie or a fruit fool, and then an interesting selection of cheeses. Television's 'Heart Beat' was filmed nearby.

Two bedrooms are in a beamy outbuilding and open onto the lawn. Two others, more recently converted, are in another farm building, stone-built and red-tiled, and face across the yard. These rooms have their own bathrooms.

The North York Moors are one of England's finest national parks: whether you walk or drive, the views are spectacular, particularly when the heather blooms.

Readers' comments: Excellent meals, complete relaxation. Charming and considerate hostess. Delightful; everything perfect. Mrs Smith was so welcoming and easy to get on with. Food excellent. Beautiful location. Comfort, good food and congenial company. Delightful room. Extremely comfortable. Food generous. A welcoming hostess. Delighted with all aspects. Food quite superb. Friendly welcome. Wonderful place, surrounding countryside cannot be bettered.

The addresses of houses are geographically correct but postal addresses sometimes differ (for correspondence, the only essential element is the postcode).

Information about the nearest town and 'A' road helps you to locate the whereabouts of any village on a map; but before setting off it is necessary to get precise instructions from your host as many houses are very much 'off the beaten track'.

LAUREL FARM   **C D P T S X**
Brafferton-Helperby, North Yorkshire, YO6 2NZ   Tel: 01423 360436
East of Ripon. Nearest main road: A1 from Wetherby to Catterick.

3 Bedrooms. £19 (less for 3 nights). All
have own bath/shower/toilet. Tea/coffee
facilities. TV. Views of garden, country,
river. Washing machine on request.
Dinner (if ordered). £16 for 4 courses
(with choices) and coffee, at 8pm. Less
for 2 courses. Non-residents not admitted.
Vegetarian or special diets if ordered. Wine
available.
1 Sitting-room. With open fire, central
heating.
Large garden

The Keys have been Yorkshire landowners for 300 years (though not at Laurel
Farm), so this house is rich with family portraits and antiques – including an out-
of-action square piano used as a side table in one bedroom. Less venerable are the
models and pictures of Spitfires and other aircraft, explained by Sam Key's many
years in the RAF.

Standing on a knoll, this tall, 18th-century house has fine views – of the village
church from two bedrooms and from the terrace, where coffee or drinks are
sometimes taken. It is surrounded by the Keys' 28 acres – a hobby farm but
enough land to provide lamb for the table and to support some rare breeds. There
is also enough for a tennis court and a croquet lawn. There is angling, too, in one
stretch of the River Swale, which bounds the holding on one side, reputedly the
best coarse fishing in the country. Even the river has a history: once navigable, it
was the scene of a mass baptism by the first Archbishop of York, St Paulinus, in
AD642.

Ann, who specialized in cookery at her finishing school, and Sam, who also
cooks sometimes, join visitors at the old oak dining-table for such candlelit meals
as prawns in garlic butter; roast lamb from the farm with home-grown vegetables;
and summer pudding.

Of appeal to families is the self-contained suite of double and single bedrooms
(with bathroom).

The twin villages of Brafferton and Helperby (it is hard to tell where one stops
and the other starts) make up a picturesque place where the wide street and cobbled verges show that they were once on a busy droving route – which may also
explain the plentiful pubs!

Readers' comments: Rooms are delightful; pleasant, attentive but relaxed hosts.

To find the right accommodation in the right area at the right
price, use an up-to-date edition of this book – revised every year.
For an order form for the next edition (published in November),
send a stamped addressed envelope with 'SOTBT 1998' in the top
left-hand corner, to Explore Britain, Alston, Cumbria, CA9 3SL.
You will receive a money-saving offer for 'Staying Off the Beaten
Track in Scotland' too.

LEWORTHY FARMHOUSE   C M S

Leworthy, Holsworthy, Devon, EX22 6SJ   Tel: 01409 253488
East of Bude. Nearest main road: A3072 from Holsworthy to Bude.

12 Bedrooms. £17–£18 (less for 3 nights). Prices go up from July. Some have own shower/toilet. Tea/coffee facilities. Views of garden, country. No smoking. Coin-operated laundry.
Dinner. £8.50 for 4 courses (with choices) and coffee, at 7pm. Vegetarian or special diets if ordered. Wine available. No smoking. **Light suppers** if ordered.
2 Sitting-rooms. With open fire, central heating, TV, video, piano, record-player. **Bar. Garden**
Closed in January and February.

Guests greatly appreciate genial Eric Cornish, and he goes to considerable lengths to give them a good time – young children in particular. Dozens of their drawings and letters to him are pinned up around the bar.

He has added to the rooms in the farmhouse to provide more accommodation in a bungalow close by, and sometimes has as many as 30 people staying – creating a friendly atmosphere by laying on all kinds of evening entertainments (games, dancing, conjuror, film) for which there is no extra charge. This is obviously appreciated by families tired of the spend-spend-spend involved in keeping youngsters entertained in most resorts. Eric also takes visitors on tractor-drawn hay-rides (dogs following) to see the crops, sheep, beef-cattle, lake, river and woods, while explaining to them what work is going on. It's a place where parents can leave their older children to go their own way – they find plenty to do, like organizing table tennis or badminton competitions. One of Eric's young guests landed an 18½-pound carp from the lake in 1995. There are deer, herons and even otters to be spotted; and lots of good picnic spots within the farm estate. Clay-pigeon shooting, pitch-and-putt, and riding can be arranged; tennis and pub skittle-matches are also available. And there is a wheelchair.

Something new is always afoot, so Eric and Marion keep in touch with past guests by means of a circular letter with news of what has been happening to the various pets and the family. Many guests become lifelong friends, and most get involved in one way or another (the gumboot rack was made by a group of dads).

Marion produces typical farmhouse meals such as soup, roast beef, fruit pie and cream, cheese, coffee. Visitors in the self-catering bungalow and newly converted granary may dine in the main house if they wish.

There is so much going on that many people hardly stir. However, within a short drive are the beaches of Bude and superb clifftop views, Hartland's dramatic reefs and lighthouse and quaint Clovelly. Holsworthy is only three miles away.

Readers' comments: Very much enjoyed the Cornishes' company; they make you feel welcome. A delightful couple who spared nothing to see that everyone had a good time. We had a high time! So genial and helpful; constant laughter. The very best type of English cooking. The atmosphere was more that of a party of friends than paying guests. Shall be back at the first opportunity! Wonderful holiday, a big house party. Holiday of a lifetime. Enjoyed our stay tremendously. As someone holidaying alone, made to feel welcome.

THE LIMES   C PT X
23 Stankelt Road, Silverdale, Lancashire, LA5 0TF   Tel: 01524 701454
North of Lancaster. Nearest main road: A6 from Carnforth to Kendal
(and M6, junction 35).

3 Bedrooms. £19.50 (less for 3 nights). Price may go up from April. All have own bath/shower/toilet. Tea/coffee facilities. TV. Views of country. No smoking. Washing machine on request.
Dinner. £12.50 for 5 courses, dessert wine and coffee, at 7 or 7.30pm. Vegetarian or special diets if ordered. No smoking.
Light suppers at 6pm.
1 Sitting-room (conservatory). No smoking.
Large garden

Near Carnforth (where railway enthusiasts will want to visit Steam Town) is an Area of Outstanding Natural Beauty, quite different from the Lake District National Park, whose boundary it meets. Almost at sea level, this is wooded countryside rich in wildlife, most of it protected in nature reserves. In nearby Warton, ancestral home of the Washingtons since the 13th century, the stars and stripes on their coat of arms in the church inspired the American flag.

The Limes is a Victorian house run by Noel and Andrée Livesey. From the tented conservatory with its basketwork chairs to the one attic bedroom, with its sunken bathroom, they have decorated the rooms with flair. The dining-room reflects their travels and their interest in art and antiques.

A typical dinner (of which guests in the self-catering accommodation may also partake) might be hot brandied grapefruit; chestnut and broad-bean soup; lamb blanquette; baked apple stuffed with vine fruits; and cheese.

Readers' comments: Candlelit meal impeccably served. No restaurant could have been better. Most friendly, helpful and attentive. Imaginative dinners, delicious and meticulously prepared. Warm welcome. Couldn't do enough for us. Comfortable, spotless, what a delight! Recommend it unreservedly. Hospitality unbeatable, meals out of this world.

A little inland is the small village of Yealand Conyers and **THE BOWER**, built as a farmhouse in 1745 and later gentrified. The cast-iron porch is handsome. There is a modern harpsichord in the entrance hall and hi-fi in both the sitting-room and the dining-room (as well as a piano in the former), for Michael Rothwell teaches music (also bridge). Sally-Ann serves for dinner such dishes as individual Stilton soufflés, chicken chasseur, pears in red wine, and cheese. The colours in the rooms are mostly muted greys and pinks, with elaborate floral curtains at the tall windows. These give views across a big garden, to the summit of

Ingleborough. No smoking. £19.95 **to readers of this book** –£28.
Readers' comments: Charming young couple, charming garden, comfortable dining-room, superb bedroom with every convenience. Most enjoyable in every respect. [Tel: 01524 734585; postcode: LA5 9SF]

177

14 Church Street, Ross-on-Wye, Herefordshire, HR9 5HN
Tel: 01989 565373
Nearest main road: A40 from Gloucester to Monmouth (and M50, junction 4).

6 Bedrooms. £20–£23. Some have own shower/toilet. All have tea/coffee facilities. TV. No smoking.
Light suppers available.
Small garden

Although close to the central market square of this historic town, the guest-house is in a quiet street opposite the church. It was built in 1680 but its façade was altered in the 18th century. At every sash window there is a window-box ablaze with geraniums during summer.

Indoors, Clare O'Reilly has stencilled fuchsias on bedroom walls. Some of the rooms are small (and there is no sitting-room) but all are pretty, and there are four with an attractive view of the old churchyard. Most rooms have brass beds.

Much is home-made, from the marmalades and jams at breakfast to the after-noon teas served at weekends and bank holidays from Easter to the end of September. A vegetarian cooked breakfast is available.

The old market town of Ross is ideally placed for touring some of the best parts of England and Wales, midway in a scenic corridor between Hereford and Chepstow. One could easily spend a fortnight here without exhausting all the possibilities.

For every visitor, a trip to Symonds Yat is a 'must': around the foot of this rock, 500 feet high, the great River Wye makes a loop that almost turns it into an island and in every direction are superb views of river, wooded slopes and fields. Also in this direction is Goodrich Castle, the red towers and walls of which seem almost part of the rock on which it stands, a moat deep-hewn around – and it, too, is perched high above a meander of the River Wye. (It was built in 1160 to mount guard over a crossing of what was then a strategically important waterway. It proved impregnable until, during the Civil Wars of the 17th century, the 200-lb cannon balls of 'Roaring Meg' battered it into submission: 'Meg' still exists, on Hereford's Castle Green.)

Visitors come to Ross not only for the surrounding scenery (the Black Mountains, Malvern Hills and Forest of Dean) but to go antique-hunting in the town itself and to see the 'lost streets' museum (old shops preserved and re-erected). There are also many fine gardens in the county – such as those of Westbury Court (the pavilion reflected in clear water and the formal beds in Dutch style have been restored exactly as they were in the 17th century); and 18th-century Berrington Hall with grounds designed by Capability Brown on a commanding site – the house itself, classical without, is elaborately decorated within.

LISLE COMBE C PT S
Undercliff Drive, St Lawrence, Isle of Wight, PO38 1UW
Tel: 01983 852582
West of Ventnor. Nearest main road: A3055 from Ventnor to Niton.

3 Bedrooms. £17.50 (less for 2 nights).
Price goes up from June. Tea/coffee facilities.
Views of garden, country, sea. No smoking.
Light suppers if ordered.
1 Sitting-room. With open fire, TV.
Large garden

'East of the garden, a wild glen glimmers with foxgloves,
And there, through the heat of the day,
In a fern-shadowed elf-ring of sand, with pine logs round it,
Three bird-voiced children play,
With a palm to shelter their golden heads from the sun,
When the noon-sun grows too strong . . . '

One of Alfred Noyes' 'bird-voiced children' about whom he wrote this poem in 1936 now owns that garden, glen and the family home. Hugh Noyes grew up to become *The Times* parliamentary correspondent until 1982, but is now occupied in dairy-farming and breeding rare species of waterfowl. He has also been High Sheriff of the Isle. Surrounding the house is his rare breeds and waterfowl park (in 30 acres of Outstanding Natural Beauty) to which guests have free access.

Visitors staying at Lisle Combe see not only the scenes which inspired so many poems but many of the poet's possessions, such as a series of watercolours by Frederick Weld (who became New Zealand's first Prime Minister); and all his papers are preserved in his still intact library.

The house itself is exceptional. It was built in the early 19th century – but in Elizabethan style, by the same Lord Yarborough whose monument dominates one of the island's hills (he was a considerable landowner on the island – Pelham Woods, opposite the house, carries his family's name).

It has barley-sugar chimneys and lozenge-paned bay windows, many overlooking the English Channel; and a paved verandah with grapevine where breakfast is sometimes served. Hugh's mother brought to the house some very exceptional furniture and paintings that were salvaged when, in the 'thirties, her former home – Lulworth Castle (in Dorset) – was burnt down. One of the most attractive rooms is a small, pale-blue sitting-room with sea views. Through the garden and among palm trees, pools and streams a path leads down to the sandy beach.

No dinners: Judy recommends such nearby inns as the Crown at Shorwell.

Lisle Combe is close to Ventnor's botanical gardens, full of subtropical flowers, and with an excellent museum of smuggling. This south-facing part of the coast is the warmest, and Ventnor itself looks rather Mediterranean because the houses are built on terraces zigzagging steeply down to the sea.

Readers' comments: Beautiful house and setting. Warm, welcoming feeling. Helpful and courteous; interesting and delightful; friendly welcome. Memorably happy. A haven of interest, beauty and peace.

179

LITTLE OREHAM FARM

off Horn Lane, Henfield, West Sussex, BN5 9SB Tel: 01273 492931
North-west of Brighton. Nearest main road: A281 from Horsham towards
Shoreham.

3 Bedrooms. £17.50–£19 (less for 7
nights). Prices go up from April. Bargain
breaks. All have own bath/shower/toilet.
Tea/coffee facilities. TV. Views of garden,
country. No smoking.
Dinner (only if ordered). £12 for 3 courses
and coffee, at about 6.30pm. Non-residents
not admitted. Vegetarian or special diets
if ordered. No smoking. **Light suppers** if
ordered.
2 Sitting-rooms. With open fire, central
heating, TV, video. No smoking.
Large garden

Inside this brick and timbered house, 300 years old, rooms have beams and oak-
mullioned or lattice-paned windows. There is a great inglenook fireplace with iron
fireback as old as the house itself (a collection of big copper vessels is housed on
its slate hearth), and red tiles cover the dining-room floor.

Some of the well-furnished bedrooms for visitors (pine furniture and sprigged
fabrics) are in the converted outbuildings, but meals are taken in the house itself:
typically Josie Forbes provides (if these are ordered in advance) such dinners as
lettuce soup, salmon with watercress sauce, and strawberry tartlets.

Readers' comments: Beautiful surroundings; most charming lady and a marvellous
cook; made me so welcome I am planning to return. Very friendly and warm.
Peaceful. My best ever stay, ambience of house remarkable.

At Wineham, also near Henfield, is
GREAT WAPSES, a farmhouse
which, having been extended in 1720
from a 16th-century building, has all
the elegance of that period – pine-
panelled walls and doors, for example,
and shuttered windows. One ground-
floor bedroom is lined with white and
apricot panelling to which Eleanor
Wilkin has matched the brocade bedspreads, contrasting with a moss-green
carpet and comfortable settee from
which to enjoy the view of the trees
and duck-pond. (There is also a tennis
court.) Another bedroom has a lacy
four-poster; while (for those nimble
enough to manage the twists and turns
up to the sloping attic floor) there is a
suite which includes a sitting-room
with homely furniture.

Eleanor provides simple but generous meals if ordered: often a roast
(as much as you want) and then
perhaps chocolate mousse. £18 (b & b).
[Tel: 01273 492544; postcode: BN5
9BJ]

For explanation of code letters (C, D, M, PT, S, X) see inside front cover.

LITTLE PARMOOR   **C S X**

Parmoor Lane, Frieth, Buckinghamshire, RG9 6NL   Tel: 01494 881447

North-east of Henley-on-Thames. Nearest main road: A40 from Oxford to
High Wycombe (also M40, junctions 4/5; and M4, junctions 8/9).

3 Bedrooms. £20–£25 (less for 4 nights).
One has own shower/toilet. Tea/coffee
facilities. TV. Views of garden, country. No
smoking. Washing machine on request.
Dinner (by arrangement). £14 for 3 courses
and coffee, at 7.30pm. Less for 2 courses.
Non-residents not admitted. Vegetarian or
special diets if ordered. No smoking. **Light
suppers** if ordered.
1 Sitting-room. With open fire, central
heating. No smoking.
Large garden

Within a mere half-hour of Heathrow (and little further to London) is a peaceful
spot among the lovely Chiltern Hills, and in it this attractive house built in 1724.
(It used to be the house of the estate manager who looked after the lands of Sir
Stafford Cripps's father, Lord Parmoor, when he occupied the nearby great house.)

Inside are green and white panelling, a log fire and watercolours painted by
Wynyard Wallace's grandfather. An elegant pine staircase leads to two large
panelled bedrooms and another, single, that is very good – unlike so many single
bedrooms. Julia Wallace provides breakfast (sometimes taken under the vine outside) and dinners which may include such dishes as home-made vegetable or fish
soup, Chiltern game pie with locally grown vegetables, and lemon mousse. Also,
within five miles are 10 inns, all of which serve good food.

Although so many busy roads skirt this area, it is very secluded and few
motorists explore its narrow lanes where boughs reach overhead, pheasants dart
from hedges or vanish into the glades, beech woods turn to fiery colours in
autumn, and one finds unknown villages tucked away, built in flint and brick.

Southward is one of the finest and most winding stretches of the River
Thames – from Sonning through Henley (of regatta fame) and Maidenhead to
Windsor, best explored by boat – arguably at its best in uncrowded autumn when
the hills descend to the river in a blaze of colour.

Readers' comments: Made us feel part of the family. Lovely. Most impressed by the
warmth of welcome, the comfort and the outstanding quality of the meals.
Excellent. Charming people. Thoughtful, caring hospitality. Kindness itself.

**Houses with short entries are just as good as ones with longer
descriptions; and they include some of the most popular houses in
the book. They may, however, have fewer rooms, a shorter season,
higher prices or fewer amenities (such as meals).**

LODGE FARM

Fersfield, Bressingham, Norfolk, IP22 2BQ   Tel: 01379 687629

C(8) **D S**

West of Diss. Nearest main road: A1066 from Thetford to Diss.

3 Bedrooms. £17–£18. Views of garden, country. Washing machine on request.
Light suppers if ordered.
2 Sitting-rooms. With open fire, central heating, record-player.
Large garden

Henry VIII had a 'palace' for hunting near here and at the boundaries of his great estate were lodges, of which this was one. Its windows and pink walls give little hint that the house goes back so far, for each subsequent century saw additions and alterations. But inside are chamfered beams, low ceilings, odd steps and angles.

David and Pat Bateson have furniture that is very much in keeping – for instance, a wedding-chest dated 1682; a big refectory table; and an iron fireback of 1582 which furnishes the great inglenook where logs blaze on chilly nights. Bedrooms are cottagey in style, one lime-and-white, one (with brass bed) pink-and-white. This is a marvellous place for a family holiday, with plenty of sightseeing outings likely to appeal to older children. Outside is a garden and the Batesons' smallholding (they keep sheep, ducks and horses). There is also accommodation in a converted coach house which can be booked on a b & b or self-catering basis.

Breakfast and light suppers only; for a full dinner, most visitors drive to the White Horse at South Lopham (two miles).

Bressingham is famous for its live steam museum, and acres of very lovely gardens. Among the hundreds of exhibits is the *Royal Scot*. Historic Diss hums with life on market day (Friday) but the lanes and meres remain peaceful.

Readers' comments: Made so welcome. Delightful weekend. Reasonable bill.

A few miles north of Diss, at Gissing, is the **OLD RECTORY**, a solidly handsome 19th-century building which is the home of Ian and Jill Gillam. Its rooms are well furnished with good colour schemes and fabrics, and decorated with Ian's unusual collection of architectural drawings. Outside is a very large garden with terrace and conservatory. There is also a heated indoor swimming-pool. Jill serves such meals as iced lettuce soup, cod-and-prawn pie, chocolate mousse

and cheeses. (No smoking in dining-room or bedrooms.) £18–£27. [Tel: 01379 677575; postcode: IP22 3XB]

Prices are per person in a double room at the beginning of the year.

182

LOW GREEN HOUSE

C D

Thoralby, Bishopdale, North Yorkshire, DL8 3SZ   Tel: 01969 663623

East of Hawes. Nearest main road: A684 from Leyburn to Hawes.

4 Bedrooms. £18–£20. All have own shower/toilet. Tea/coffee facilities. TV. Views of garden, country. No smoking.

Dinner. £13 for 4 courses and coffee, at 6.45pm (not Thursdays). Non-residents not admitted. Vegetarian or special diets if ordered. No smoking.

1 Sitting-room. With open fire, central heating. No smoking.

Garden

This stone house in a tiny hamlet is the home of Tony and Marilyn Philpott, who are founts of information on where to walk and what to see.

Within rugged walls are particularly comfortable and pretty rooms. (Two bedrooms are in a 17th-century cottage annexe.) There is a pink-and-white bedroom with deep brown carpet; and the bathroom is excellent. In the sitting/dining-room (which runs from front to back of the house, with a picture-window looking towards Wensleydale), soft colours, deep armchairs around a log fire and plentiful books provide a relaxed atmosphere. For dinner Marilyn may serve – with decorative flourishes – local smoked trout, pork cooked with cream and mushrooms, blue Wensleydale cheese, and raspberry torte. With the coffee comes a dish of chocolates. (All carefully prepared, and remarkably good value.)

The Yorkshire Dales have many peaks over 2000 feet high: wild and windy, with lonely farms on their foothills, and waterfalls rushing down the valleys. Wensleydale is only five minutes away. Bishopdale itself follows a stream south, the road rising high up at Kidstones Pass, to join Langstrothdale and much more tourist-ridden Wharfedale. Sights worth seeing include Aysgarth Falls, Malham Cove, Hardraw Falls, Jervaulx Abbey, Fountains Abbey (and gardens), the Settle–Carlisle railway, Newby Hall gardens, Thorpe Perrow arboretum, Bolton Castle. (Bicycles, including mountain bicycles, for hire locally.)

The ropeworks in Hawes is also well worth a visit, both to see ropes being made and to buy anything from a bellrope to a lead for the dog: once in danger of closing, it is now flourishing thanks to a combination of traditional craft methods and modern technology. From Hawes, a drive over the bleak spine of the Pennines takes one to Sedbergh, where there is a bookshop specializing in valuable collectors' items and works of local interest.

Readers' comments: Comfort, hospitality and value cannot be bettered. Lovely hosts. Food was a delight, breakfasts huge and dinners delicious. A Gundrey gem! A happy welcome. Friendly attention. Very comfortable, delicious meals. Very comfortable and friendly. Good value. Exceptional hosts. A divine cook. A most special place. An absolute delight. Very welcoming and comfortable.

Facts (prices, etc.) at the top of entries are supplied by the proprietors themselves. While every effort is made to ensure that these are correct at the time of going to press, they may alter thereafter: please check when you book.

LOW HALL   C(10) **S**
Brandlingill, Cumbria, CA13 0RE   Tel: 01900 826654
South of Cockermouth. Nearest main road: A66 from Keswick to Cockermouth.

5 Bedrooms. £20–£26 (less for 7 nights). Prices go up from Easter. All have own bath/shower/toilet. Tea/coffee facilities. Views of garden, country, river. No smoking.
Dinner. £18 for 5 courses (with choices) and coffee, at 7–7.30pm. Non-residents not admitted. Vegetarian dishes. Wine available. No smoking.
2 Sitting-rooms. With open fire, central heating, TV, piano. Bar. No smoking.
Large garden
Closed from November to February.

Low Hall is mostly of 17th-century origin but was enlarged to accommodate a big Victorian family. When the previous owners renovated it, they uncovered a huge fireplace in what was the dairy and is now the dining-room, where candlelit dinners are accompanied by classical music. Current owners are Hugh and Enid Davies, respectively an anaesthetist and an ex-teacher.

There is one big sitting-room with log fire and grand piano, and a second smaller one for television addicts.

The bedrooms, most of which are spacious, give views of the Lorton fells in the north-western corner of the Lake District or of the grounds of the house. This is an area of great beauty, wooded rather than rugged, where the Cumbrian mountains start their descent to sea level. It is never overrun by tourists, yet the well-known parts of the Lake District are only a short drive away. Guided walks available.

The menus always include a vegetarian or fish alternative to the meat course. A typical menu: avocado and prawn mousse; soup; pork celeste or baked trout, or courgette and carrot crumble; and a choice of puddings, followed by cheese. Breakfasts are interesting. Preserves, rolls and ice cream are home-made.

Readers' comments: A real winner. A happy house party. Perfect in every detail. Meals a delight. Food as good as in any top-class restaurant. Everything one could wish for. Made us so welcome. Food delicious. A memorable place to stay, excellent value. Very comfortable. Thoughtful attention to detail. Standards excellent.

A few miles away, on the edge of High Lorton, Ann Roberts provides dinner, bed-and-breakfast at **OWL BROOK**, Whinlatter Pass, all the year round. This architect-designed and attractive bungalow of green lakeland slate with pine ceilings was built a few years ago, and all the airy bedrooms have fine views. Dinner might comprise soup, risotto, and fresh fruit salad, using wholefood ingredients. £16.50–£17.50 (b & b).

Readers' comments: Beautiful views and utter tranquillity. Breakfasts were superb. Very friendly family atmosphere. [Tel: 01900 85333; postcode: CA13 9TX]

LOWER GREEN FARMHOUSE   C D

Haresfield, Gloucestershire, GL10 3DS   Tel: 01452 728264

South of Gloucester. Nearest main road: A38 from Gloucester to Bristol (and M5, junction 12).

3 Bedrooms. £16–£17 (less for 2 nights or continental breakfast). Prices go up from April. Bargain breaks. One has own bath/shower/toilet. Tea/coffee facilities. TV. Views of garden, country. No smoking. Washing machine on request.
Light suppers if ordered.
1 Sitting-room. With wood-burning stove, central heating, TV, record-player. No smoking.
Large garden

This attractive house of stone walls and mullioned windows sits at the foot of a National Trust hill (Haresfield Beacon) on the western edge of the Cotswolds; the light and airy family bedroom has views in the other direction across the Severn to the Forest of Dean (superb sunsets); yet with all this Lower Green Farmhouse is still within easy reach of the motorway carrying traffic between Birmingham and the west country. All the bedrooms are spacious, with board-and-latch doors and beamed ceilings; downstairs, the sitting-room has a stone fireplace with ogee arch, the dining-room a huge inglenook. In the garden is a stone barbecue, a pool with bulrushes and yellow flag irises, and a 40-foot well, and all around is lovely countryside with countless picturesque villages to explore.

Margaret Reed will provide light suppers by arrangement, but the local pub (within easy walking distance) does good food at very reasonable prices, and there is a wide variety of eating-places only slightly further afield.

The Rococo Garden at nearby Painswick is a popular draw for visitors as are the Roman villa at Witcombe and Prinknash Abbey, where you can buy the famous pottery as well as other monastic products (tonic wine from Buckfast, scent from Caldey Island).

Readers' comments: Can't recommend too highly. Excellent cook and hostess.

In Oxlynch Lane, Oxlynch, is 400-year-old **TILED HOUSE FARM**, the first house in the area to have the innovation of tiles to replace thatch on its roof. In the big sitting-room, with huge stone fireplace, the original bacon-hooks in the beams and gun-racks above the hearth still remain. Steep stairs go up from the dining-room (which overlooks the farmyard) to some of the bedrooms, the largest of which has timber-framed walls; there is also a self-contained ground-floor suite with good bathroom. (No smoking.)

For visitors not wanting to go out, Diane Jeffery will make an inexpensive

meal of, say, tuna mousse with salad, baked potato and garlic bread, or chicken casserole, followed by apricot gâteau with cream. £17–£18 (b & b).
Readers' comments: First-class accommodation and superb breakfast. Delightful. [Tel: 01453 822363; postcode: GL10 3DF]

LOXLEY FARMHOUSE   C D M

Stratford Road, Loxley, Warwickshire, CV35 9JN   Tel: 01789 840265
South-east of Stratford-upon-Avon. Nearest main road: A422 from Stratford
to Banbury (and M40, junction 15).

2–3 Bedrooms. £18–£21 (less for 7 nights
or continental breakfast). Prices go up from
Easter. Bargain breaks. All have own bath/
shower/toilet. Tea/coffee facilities. TV. Views
of garden, country.
Light suppers if ordered.
2 Sitting-rooms. With open fire (one),
central heating, TV.
Large garden

Loxley is a hilltop village with diminutive church. From a seat on its sloping
green, where crab-apple trees are bright in autumn, there are far views across
woodland and fields of red earth. Just downhill from here Loxley Farm is tucked
away: a picture-postcard house of half-timbering and thatch, parts dating back to
the 13th century. Perhaps Robin Hood ('Robin of Loxley') knew the house;
there's a worn stone in the churchyard on which, tradition has it, he and his
companions used to sharpen their arrow-tips. And certainly Charles I stayed here
after the nearby Battle of Edgehill.

Inside, everything is in keeping with the style of the ancient house: low
ceilings with pewter pots hanging from the beams, flagged floors, small-paned
windows, log fires, oak doors. You can see the cruck construction of the house –
at its heart, the unhewn trunks of two trees support the roof timbers. There
is not a single straight wall or floor. Anne Horton has furnished the rooms in
appropriate style. In the dining-room, leather chairs surround a large oak table;
here, breakfast – with home-made muesli and buns – is served.

Two of the bedrooms are in a separate, half-timbered, thatched barn conversion, together with a sitting-room and kitchen. Both have en suite bathrooms. In
the main house is a family suite (sometimes available for guests) which has its
own sitting-room furnished with deep armchairs, Staffordshire figures, copper
and brasses, lavender and dried flowers.

The broad River Avon gives character to the peaceful countryside: cattle grazing in green meadows where once Shakespeare's Forest of Arden spread for miles
around. It is easy to visit Stratford-upon-Avon from here, the Cotswolds and
Oxford. It is also worth travelling to Dudley to see the excellent new Black
Country Museum. Warwick Castle, Blenheim Palace, Charlecote, Hidcote (and
many other great gardens) make this area a tourist honeypot.

Readers' comments: Idyllic surroundings. Much care and attention. Most welcoming and comfortable. Not a jarring note. The most delightful of all. Have enjoyed
Mrs Horton's hospitality over the past ten years. Pleasant place and very pleasant
people.

**When writing to the authors, if you want a reply please enclose a
stamped addressed envelope.**

LYE GREEN HOUSE
Lye Green, East Sussex, TN6 1UU   Tel: 01892 652018
North of Crowborough. Nearest main road: A26 from Tunbridge Wells to Newhaven.

3 Bedrooms. £20–£27.50 (less for 4 nights or continental breakfast). Bargain breaks. All have own bath/toilet. Tea/coffee facilities. TV. Views of garden. No smoking.
Light suppers if ordered.
1 Sitting/dining-room. No smoking.
Large garden

Built in the tile-hung style that is a Sussex tradition and with wisteria on its red brick walls, the Edwardian house was dilapidated until the Hynes family restored it – and its grounds too. Part of these comprises formal gardens divided by yew hedges, part a chain of three ponds in woodland. There are a rose garden with pergola, a potager of vegetables and flowers, and an avenue of pollarded limes. Most rooms have views from big windows at each end, and sometimes breakfasts are served in the garden.

Soft blues, pinks and greens predominate in the rooms. In the dining-room, the long mahogany table is laid with good silver; there are prettily pleated curtains, big sofas, a marble fireplace with Britannia and tall ships, brass beds, flowery wallpapers, quilted patchwork spreads, cases of butterflies, antique mirrors and fans . . . every room is full of interest.

Although there is a choice of good inns locally, supper can be provided by special arrangement.

In the vicinity are Ashdown Forest (miles of footpaths) and also Penshurst, Hever and Chiddingstone Castle as well as a number of great gardens. Close by are high rocks on which climbers practise.

Readers' comments: Delightful house and gardens, in charming, restful location; sumptuous room.

Supper in bedroom at Toll Barn (see page 271)

MAELCOMBE HOUSE

East Prawle, Devon, TQ7 2DE Tel: 01548 511300

South-east of Kingsbridge. Nearest main road: A379 from Kingsbridge to Dartmouth.

8 Bedrooms. £20 (less for 7 nights). Price goes up from April. Some have own shower. Tea/coffee facilities. Views of garden, country, sea. Washing machine on request.

Dinner. £9.50 for 4 courses and coffee, at 7pm. Non-residents not admitted. Vegetarian or special diets if ordered. No smoking. **Light suppers** if ordered.

2 Sitting-rooms. With open fire, central heating, piano.

Large garden

Closed from November to March.

A mile-long track winds down to a big house that was built by the district coast-guard officer in 1908, close to the shore of Lannacombe Bay and with wooded cliffs behind it. Not surprisingly, there are stories of wrecks and raids associated with the house in the past, but today it is peaceful, comfortable and well kept.

The atmosphere is informal and easy-going. For instance, in the sun-room that opens onto the terrace are old armchairs and limitless help-yourself tea. Outside, one can stroll down to a little beach with rock pools and a sandy cove. Large bedrooms with sea-view windows on two sides are particularly popular, and there are ample bathrooms. Birdwatchers find much of interest (including some rarities), and butterflies abound too. There is a hard tennis court, and the coastal footpath for walkers. Some guests try milking the cow or helping Mark to haul in the lobster-pots – home-caught seafood is a speciality here.

Lucy Davies uses much garden produce for such meals as courgette soup, plaice with crab sauce, and Bakewell tart.

Readers' comments: Beautiful house, very tasty food, friendly and relaxing. Beautifully situated, food plentiful and good. They did everything to make our stay pleasant.

In East Prawle itself, **HINES HILL** is a luxuriously furnished modern house with big windows to make the most of spectacular sea views from the 400-foot promontory, and a terrace overlooking the tiny sandy beach below. Many oriental pieces are among the antiques, and the elegant soft furnishings were made by Sylvia Morris herself.

A typical dinner: ratatouille with feta cheese and smoked chicken as a starter, fillet of lamb with plum and ginger sauce, lemon sorbet layered with meringue and lime cream, and cheeses (an aperitif and wine ad lib are included in the price). When Sylvia ran a restaurant previously, she received Michelin's coveted commendation. Closed in winter. £18–£27 (b & b).

Readers' comments: Wonderful views, peaceful, furnished to a high standard, attentive and helpful. Imaginative and ample cooking. [Tel: 01548 511263; postcode: TQ7 2BZ]

MANOR FARMHOUSE   C(5) **D S X**
Wormington, Gloucestershire, WR12 7NL   Tel: 01386 584302
(Messages: 01386 584565)
South-east of Evesham. Nearest main road: A46 from Broadway to
Cheltenham (and M5, junction 9).

3 Bedrooms. £16–£20 (less for 4 nights or continental breakfast). Bargain breaks. All have own shower/toilet. Tea/coffee facilities. Views of garden, country. No smoking. Washing machine on request.
Light suppers if ordered.
1 Sitting-room. With open fire, central heating, TV.
Small garden

Once this house was known as Charity Farm because 'dole' was dispensed to wayfarers. The farm was connected with Hailes Abbey (in the 13th century, its phial of Christ's blood made it a centre of pilgrimage; now there are only ruins), hence some ecclesiastical touches like the pointed arch beside the log fire – possibly it was a leper window. There are leaded casements in the comfortable sitting-room, a stone inglenook in the hall, slabs of Welsh slate on the floor, steps and turns everywhere on one's way up to beamy all-white bedrooms well furnished with mahogany pieces. There's still a cheese room dating from the time when this was a dairy-farm.

What was once a cattle-yard is now a very attractive court with lawn, fountain and stone sinks planted with flowers. To one side is an old granary of brick and timber which dates, like the house itself, from the 15th century. From the stable door five small ponies watch visitors' comings and goings. On the farm are shooting and trout fishing.

Pauline Russell usually serves only breakfast, recommending for other meals Goblets wine bar in Broadway – that world-famous showplace, best known of all the picturesque villages hereabouts.

From here one can drive to the fruitful Vale of Evesham (loveliest in spring), high Bredon Hill ringed by pretty villages, Tewkesbury to see the abbey, historic Evesham for boat trips on the Avon, Pershore (abbey church and 18th-century houses), or little Ripple with old houses and quaint carvings in the church.

Readers' comments: Lovely farmhouse; looked after us so well.

A few miles away lies Little Comberton, (in Worcestershire), and in Wick Road is **WINDRUSH** where two thatched 17th-century cottages have been combined as one, with a particularly pretty garden created around them. Rooms are low-beamed, and the inexpensive little bedrooms furnished in appropriately cottagey style. Altogether, a really 'old world' effect. Bed-and-breakfast only, but there is good food to be had at the Mill (Elmley Castle) or the Fox & Hounds (Bredon). £13.

Readers' comments: Beautifully preserved; garden a joy. A gem of a find. Mrs Lewis is charming and friendly. Warm welcome and hospitality. [Tel: 01386 710284; postcode: WR10 3EG]

Wellow, (Avon), Bath & North-East Somerset, BA2 8QQ
Tel: 01225 832027
South of Bath. Nearest main road: A367 from Bath to Shepton Mallet.

3 Bedrooms. £17.50–£20 (less for 5 nights). Two have own bath/shower/toilet. Tea/coffee facilities. TV (in two). Views of garden, country. No smoking. Washing machine on request.
Light suppers if ordered. No smoking.
2 Sitting-rooms. With open fire, central heating, TV. No smoking.
Large garden

This lovely old house began life in 1634 as Hungerford Manor, built by the local landowning family of that name whose coat-of-arms can still be seen above the fireplace in the panelled music room. Oak panelling, stone fireplaces, wide floorboards and mullioned windows testify to a long and relatively untroubled history (though the Hungerford of the day was a Parliamentarian commander in the Civil War).

Sarah Danny makes her own bread and yogurt for breakfast – home-mixed muesli and stewed fruit too, as well as bacon and eggs; guests sit round a gateleg table in the panelled dining-room.

There are books everywhere, including the bedrooms: the double is huge, with a mullioned window in the en suite bathroom; the twin room next door is big enough to swallow a huge sofa and a desk without appearing crowded. There is a pretty single room.

Outside is a pleasing conglomeration of old outbuildings (cream teas in summer), courtyard and walled garden, and a paddock with tennis court, croquet and an ancient manorial dovecote.

Readers' comments: Very nice and good house. Good food.

Bedroom at Fairview Farmhouse (see page 246)

MANOR HOUSE FARM

C S

Prestwood, Denstone, Staffordshire, ST14 5DD   Tel: 01889 590415 and 01335 343669
North of Uttoxeter. Nearest main road: A5032 from Cheadle to Ashbourne.

3 Bedrooms. £17–£22 (less for 6 nights or continental breakfast). All have own bath/shower/toilet. Tea/coffee facilities. TV. Views of garden, country. No smoking. Washing machine on request.
Light suppers if ordered.
1 Sitting-room. With open fire, central heating, TV.
Large garden

Once his family farmed here, but now Christopher Ball has turned to dealing in antiques; a fact reflected in the handsome furnishings of the 17th-century house. It was built of sandstone from nearby Hollington quarry.

High-backed settles flank the log fire in the sitting-room, which has stone-mullioned bay windows in its thick walls – with fine hill views. On the oak-panelled walls of the dining-room hang oil paintings. The bedrooms (with beams and exposed stone walls) have four-posters. The latest to be acquired by the Balls is a fine antique example with its original drapes.

The terraced garden is particularly attractive: weeping ash, pinnacled summer-house (it was once the cupola on a hospital roof), steps ascending between clipped yews, a tennis court and croquet. You can barbecue your own meat if you wish.

Conductor Howard Snell and his musical family used to live at 16th-century Hollington House in Hollington – another moorland village. They have now moved 25 metres across the old farmyard into the **RED BARN**, which they have restored splendidly. Partly of stone and partly of red brick, their new home has a galleried sitting-room with exposed roof trusses, and a stone and tiled floor with a modern turquoise rug. This room has lovely views eastwards across open country towards the distant Pennine foothills. The patchwork cushions were made – like the bedspreads – by Angela Snell herself (a former Hallé violinist).

Outside the village is the quarry

from which came both pink and white stone for nearby Croxden Abbey, now a ruin, and for the modern cathedrals of Coventry and Liverpool. Light suppers only. £16.50 (b & b).
Readers' comments: Treated like royalty; a haven of peace; Mrs Snell extremely thoughtful in her attention to detail. [Tel: 01889 507221; postcode: ST10 4HH]

MAPLEHURST MILL

C(12) **M X**

Mill Lane, Frittenden, Kent, TN17 2DT   Tel: 01580 852203
North-east of Cranbrook. Nearest main road: A229 from Maidstone towards Hastings.

3 Bedrooms. £20–£28 (less for 4 nights). All have own bath/shower/toilet. Tea/coffee facilities. TV. Views of garden, country, river. No smoking.
Dinner. £18 for 4 courses and coffee, at times to suit guests. Less for 2 courses. Non-residents not admitted. Vegetarian or special diets if ordered. Wine available. No smoking.
1 Sitting-room. With woodstove, central heating, piano. No smoking.
Large garden

'It was like the Marie Celeste,' said Kenneth Parker, describing this 18th-century mill when they took it over. It had hardly been touched since the day it ceased to grind, and the tools of the miller's trade lay where he had left them: the governor for the millstones, the key to open the sluices, the sack-hoist, the flour chest beneath the chute, smutter and scourer, floury hoppers . . . On the grinding floor, the Parkers are now creating with the help of these finds a little museum of milling, and are researching the history of the mill, which dates back to 1309. (One grisly item: they discovered that in the religious persecutions of 1557, the miller and his wife were burnt at the stake.)

Their conversion of the mill has been faultless. It now has every up-to-date comfort, yet the ambience of the past has been vividly preserved. Through the entrance hall, which has baskets of dried flowers, one comes to a pleasant bedroom (being on the ground floor, it would suit anyone who finds stairs difficult). There is a window right by the waterwheel and the mill-race flows under its floor.

Everywhere are exposed beams, low doorways, white or pine-boarded walls, a tree-trunk that forms part of the structure, iron pillars or mechanisms and brick or cast-iron fireplaces. Each bedroom has different soft furnishings – lacy duvet covers and festoon blinds, a pine four-poster draped with a pink and blue honeysuckle fabric, or flowery Habitat linens. Bathrooms are excellent. From some windows are views of yellow waterlilies and dabchicks on the stream, or of cows and hayfields. You may even glimpse foxes or a heron. In the grounds are a small vineyard, a heated swimming-pool, and a nature trail with over 70 species of birds.

The mill would be worth going out of one's way to visit not only for all this but because Heather's meals are so imaginative. Here is an example: Sussex smokies (haddock) in a cheese and wine sauce followed by chicken breasts with a sauce made from avocados, sherry and cream (the accompanying vegetables are home-grown) and then a home-made chocolate, coffee and almond ice cream. Afterwards, one can relax either on the waterside terrace or in the huge sitting-room where Heather has a rare grand piano, perfectly semicircular. It is a gracious room in which the sofas are covered with cottage-garden fabrics and aquamarine curtains hang at the casements on opposite walls. Beauty, character, good food and peace: what more could one want? Maplehurst Mill is also well placed to visit such famous sights as Sissinghurst and Leeds Castle.

Reader's comment: Outstanding.

MARINA HOTEL

D PT X

The Esplanade, Fowey, Cornwall, PL23 1HY   Tel: 01726 833315
East of St Austell. Nearest main road: A390 from Lostwithiel to St Austell.

rear view

11 Bedrooms. Normally £26–£40 (less for 2 nights) **but for readers of this book only there are 2 rooms at a dinner-inclusive price of £72 for 2 days; also half-price b & b for 2 nights, November to mid-December and in March.** Prices go up in June. Bargain breaks. All have own bath/shower/toilet. Tea/coffee facilities. TV. Sea views, balcony (some).
Dinner. £16 for 5 courses (with choices) and coffee, at 7–8.30pm. Less for 3 courses. Vegetarian or special diets if ordered. Wine available. No smoking. **Light suppers.**
3 Sitting-rooms. With central heating, piano. **Bar.**
Small garden
Closed in January and February.

Built in 1830 as a seaside retreat for the Bishop of Truro, this fine house has been furnished with the elegance it deserves. The handsome mouldings, arches and panelling of the hall and octagonal landing are now decorated in green and cream; and each bedroom is different – a pale colour scheme in one; sprigged covers and pine in another (its rounded window overlooking the sea); four with covered verandahs of lacy ironwork facing the tiny walled garden and waterfront beyond it. The dining-room has Indian Tree china on pink tablecloths, with spectacular views from the big picture-windows; the bar, rosy armchairs and a thick pale carpet. Eight-foot marble pillars were uncovered in one bedroom.

Carol and John Roberts give equal attention to the standard of the food. At dinner, you might choose your main dish from a selection that includes (for instance) boned chicken in a sauce of mushrooms and cider, beef Wellington, rack of lamb and local fish in a variety of ways.

Fowey (pronounced Foy) is on that mild stretch of the coast known as the Cornish Riviera. It is an old and picturesque harbour of steep, narrow byways (parking is difficult; a minibus takes visitors to a carpark each morning), its waters busy with yachts and fishing boats. Some people arrive by car ferry. It is easy to find secluded coves and beaches nearby, or scenic walks along clifftops. The little town is full of antique, book and craft shops; historic buildings; restaurants and good food shops. Easily reached from here are Lanhydrock House and gardens, Restormel Castle, Charlestown and Wheal Martin China Clay Museum. Cornwall has a spring gardens festival – ask the Marina for a leaflet about the 55 gardens that participate. One very near here, famous for camellias in an 18th-century setting, is perched on the clifftop at Trewithen; another, with superb sea views, is Trelissick; and Polruan is a spectacular Headland Garden.

Go to Falmouth to visit Pendennis Castle, built by Henry VIII to guard the estuary, and for the maritime museum. There are rare breeds to be seen in the country park at Kea and, near the cathedral city of Truro (which also has Cornwall's county museum), is a cider farm with activities to view.

Book well ahead: many of these houses have few rooms. Do not expect dinner if you have not booked it or if you arrive late.

MARSHGATE COTTAGE HOTEL   C D M PT X
Marsh Lane, Hungerford, Berkshire, RG17 0QX   Tel: 01488 682307
West of Newbury. Nearest main road: A338 from Hungerford to Ludgershall
(and M4, junction 14).

6 Bedrooms. £19–£22.50 (less for 3 nights mid-week). Most have own shower/toilet. Tea/coffee facilities. TV. Views of garden, country, canal. Some no-smoking rooms.
Dinner (if ordered in advance). £15 for 3 courses and coffee, at 7.30–9pm (not Sundays). Less for 2 courses. Non-residents not admitted. Vegetarian diets. Wine available. **Light suppers** if ordered.
1 Sitting-room. With open fire, central heating. Bar.
Large garden

The marshes which give this cottage its name stretch down to the 18th-century Kennet & Avon Canal, a haven for birds and wildflowers. Marshgate (used as a pest-house during the plague of 1640) is even older than the canal, its thatched roof descending almost to ground level; but it is an extension which provides guest-rooms, in keeping with its original character. Most rooms overlook the marshes, which are a sheet of yellow in buttercup-time. Wild orchids grow there, frogs croak in spring and kingfishers can be spotted hunting.

Mike Walker, once a journalist, did most of the conversion himself, re-using old handmade bricks and laying floors of beautiful chestnut boards. The breakfast-room is in white and pine with brick walls. All bedrooms are on the ground floor, furnished with a pleasing simplicity – modern pine and various shades of pastel predominate. A patio with garden benches allows guests to enjoy the view of canal life including passing narrow-boats.

In the grounds are goats and ducks, also a 'dipping hole': that is, the point where an underground stream pops up – watercress grows in it.

Dinner (for parties of six or more) may comprise such dishes as mussels in garlic sauce, roast pork with sugar potatoes and red cabbage, followed by sorbet or cheese and biscuits.

In addition to many good eating-places, nearby Hungerford abounds with shops selling antiques and there is scenic downland in every direction. Newbury's Watermill Theatre is one of many interesting spots (the wheel is still to be seen). Walkers make for the high Ridgeway Path, which is of prehistoric origin. This is also a good cycling area: bicycles can be hired at the hotel. Barge trips available, drawn by horses.

A popular local sight are the oldest working beam-engines in the world, at Crofton.

Readers' comments: Agreeably cosy. Delightful river setting. Friendly atmosphere. One of the most delightful places. Accommodation first-rate, good hosts, smashing breakfast.

Ducks at Marshgate Cottage Hotel

MAYS FARMHOUSE

Longwood Dean, Hampshire, SO21 1JR   Tel: 01962 777486

South-east of Winchester. Nearest main road: A272 from Winchester to Petersfield (and M3, junction 9).

C(7) **D M S**

3 Bedrooms. £18 (less for 4 nights). Price goes up from April. Bargain breaks. All have own bath/shower/toilet. Tea/coffee facilities. TV. Views of garden, country. No smoking. Washing machine on request.
Dinner (only if ordered). £12.50 for 4 courses and coffee, at 7pm. Less for 2 courses. Non-residents not admitted. Vegetarian or special diets if ordered. No smoking. **Light suppers** if ordered.
1 Sitting-room. With open fire, central heating, TV, piano. No smoking.
Large garden

Twelve-foot trees grew in the kitchen and the 16th-century house had no roof. Undeterred, James Ashby (expert in renovations) bought and transformed it to the highest standards – unvarnished oak beams in the dining-room are now complemented by a woodblock floor, and a handsome log stove stands in the old inglenook, for instance.

Rosalie has painted bedroom furniture decoratively – she runs classes on how to do this (on Mondays). All the rooms have views of the Ashbys' white goats, and of a pretty garden and the woods beyond. One has a Jacuzzi. A stair-lift is available for those who need it. Dinner (with fresh garden produce) might include pheasant pâté, pork in orange and cider sauce, and a raspberry flan.

Nearby Winchester was England's capital in the days of King Alfred (indeed, it had been a considerable town long before that, during the long Roman occupation). The Norman cathedral dominates all, its most famous bishop – William of Wykeham – being the founder of one of England's great public schools, Winchester College (which can be visited). There are the remains of two castles here, the Bishop's Palace, and a 'Crusades Experience' with animated models, sounds and so forth. The byways in the heart of the city are full of ancient buildings, in one of which Jane Austen lived at the end of her life. Main streets are partly colonnaded, there is a statue of King Alfred, pleasant gardens, and at 8pm a bell sounds curfew every day.

At hives beyond the badminton court, a swarm of two dozen veiled bee-keepers were holding a 'meet' when we arrived at **MORESTEAD GROVE**, Morestead, a late Georgian rectory with handsome rooms. Katharine Sellon serves such dinners (if ordered in advance) as smoked haddock mousse, chicken in wine and mushroom sauce, and candied oranges, using her own vegetables and eggs (special diets possible). No smoking. £18 (b & b).

Readers' comments: Hospitable and helpful; house charming, comfortable and stylish. [Tel: 01962 777238; postcode: SO21 1LZ]

MEDBOURNE GRANGE

Medbourne, Leicestershire, LE16 8EF   Tel: 01858 565249

North-east of Market Harborough. Nearest main road: A427 from Market
Harborough to Corby.

3 Bedrooms. £16–£17. Prices go up from
April. Tea/coffee facilities. Views of garden,
country. Washing machine on request.
Light suppers if ordered.
1 Sitting-room. With central heating, TV.
No smoking.
Large garden

At Nevill Holt's great 17th-century Hall (now a school) Emerald Cunard held her
salons, attended by the leading political and literary lions of the Edwardian era.
Medbourne Grange was a principal farm on its large estate, a dignified house
standing at the heart of 500 acres of dairy pastures and arable fields.

Sally Beaty has furnished it attractively: the capacious, cut-velvet armchairs
are of the same soft blue as the sitting-room carpet; one rosy bedroom (with far
view) has a carved walnut suite, another (overlooking the dairy-yard) is paisley-
patterned – this, though a single bedroom, has a sofa-bed too.

Outside are stone troughs of flowers and, sheltered by old walls, a heated
swimming-pool; while beyond lies the valley of the River Welland which flows all
the way to The Wash.

Medbourne village has handsome buildings and a particularly pretty stream
frequented by kingfishers and herons. In East Carlton Park are not only woods
and ponds but a heritage centre that features the history of iron-making. Market
Harborough has a great many 18th-century houses and a school (1614) on
wooden pillars.

Reader's comment: An excellent stay, fully recommended.

In the main street of picturesque
Medbourne, the **OLD FORGE**, built
of reddish sandstone and with
panoramic views, is now the very
attractive home of Margaret Locke –
every room decorated in carefully
chosen colours and with good pictures.
One has a private bathroom. Her snack
suppers, well presented, comprise
home-made soup and hot rolls, cheeses
and fruit. Some visitors enjoy the
grand piano, others relax on the patio
in her sunny garden with tea and
home-made cakes. £17–£18.

Readers' comments: Lovely house, very
comfortable, have stayed three times,
strongly recommended. [Tel: 01858
565859; postcode: LE16 8DT]

MELLINGTON HOUSE   **C D PT S**
Broad Street, Weobley, Herefordshire, HR4 8SA   Tel: 01544 318537
North-west of Hereford. Nearest main road: A4112.

3 Bedrooms. £16.50–£19 (less for 7 nights). Bargain breaks. All have own bath/shower/toilet. Tea/coffee facilities. TV. No smoking.
Dinner. From £11 for 3 courses (with some choices) and coffee, at 7.30pm (not weekends). Non-residents not admitted. Vegetarian or special diets if ordered.
1 Sitting-room. With open fire, central heating, TV, piano, record-player.
Large garden

Once, mediaeval houses were considered old-fashioned and so householders often put new façades on them. That is why Mellington House has a front in Queen Anne style, but its real age is revealed at the back where the original half-timbering is still exposed – typical of most buildings in Weobley, which is a particularly fine mediaeval village set in the lovely Herefordshire countryside. Although the house is in the centre of the village, it is quiet because its walls are thick and the big sash windows double-glazed (not that Weobley gets heavy traffic). It was once the home of the notorious Baroness de Stempel.

Ann Saunders has furnished the house very pleasantly (for instance, brass beds and wildflower duvets), the sitting-room is large and comfortable, and there is a downstairs bedroom which Ann (a physiotherapist) provides for people who have mobility problems. The dining-room opens onto a large, old, walled garden where, on sunny mornings, she serves breakfast.

Ann prepares such meals as: melon, roast beef with garden vegetables, home-made cheesecake, and cheeses. These can be provided for guests in the self-catering 'hayloft' too. (Walking or bridge weekends can be arranged.)

From Weobley, there are plenty of sightseeing options. The picturesque black-and-white village of Eardisland is close. There are a dozen bookshops (most belonging to Richard Booth) in Hay-on-Wye, now nicknamed 'Book City'; Brecon, Offa's Dyke and numerous stately homes provide other destinations for a day out; and, as this is an area of orchards and nursery gardens, many people return home laden with pot-plants and pick-your-own soft fruits. The Malvern Hills and the Black Mountains are close, and several market towns are nearby. Add to these the Brecon Beacons, Radnor Forest, the 'Golden Valley', Welsh and Shropshire market towns, a motor museum, a lovely drive along Wenlock Edge, Ironbridge, the Wye Valley and innumerable garden centres.

Travel northward for Worcestershire, which has a tremendous amount to see. Fine scenery, historic buildings (including churches), hill walks, waterside dairy-farms, a magnificent cathedral in Worcester itself, hopfields and cider orchards, woods, and sights which include Elgar's birthplace (Broadheath).

Readers' comments: Could not praise more. Made most welcome. Extremely comfortable. Beautiful surroundings. I will return. Delicious dinners. Could not have been made more welcome. Spacious accommodation. Warm and friendly. Everything done to make us comfortable. Such good service.

MICHELMERSH HOUSE
Michelmersh, Hampshire, SO51 0NS   Tel: 01794 368644
North of Romsey. Nearest main road: A3057 from Romsey to Stockbridge.

2 Bedrooms. £17–£19 (less for 3 nights). Prices go up in April. Both have own bath. Tea/coffee facilities. TV. Views of garden, country. No smoking. Washing machine on request.
Dinner. £12 for 3 courses and coffee, at 8pm. Less for 2 courses. Non-residents not admitted. Vegetarian or special diets if ordered. No smoking. **Light suppers** if ordered.
1 Sitting-room. With open fire, central heating, TV, piano. No smoking.
Large garden
Closed from mid-December to mid-January.

Where this largely 18th-century house now stands, Henry V assembled his army before departing from Portsmouth for France and the Battle of Agincourt. The adjacent church goes back even further: its tower is Saxon.

All this contrasts with 20th-century comforts within the house, tennis court and heated swimming-pool without.

Through the high sash windows of the primrose sitting-room is a view over the valley of the River Test towards Salisbury (beyond banks of daffodils in spring). Ancestral portraits line the walls of the dining-room where Jennifer Lalonde serves such meals as fish pâté, roast beef, and Mississippi mud pie.

Bedrooms are attractive, and the pink one has a cushioned seat in its bow window from which to enjoy a view of the walled garden, a field of wildflowers and the swimming-pool. Many old features remain to give the house character, from the elegant staircase to bacon-racks and a coal stove for flat-irons in the former kitchen.

Readers' comments: Very tastefully decorated, most comfortable. Beautifully cooked meal. Made most welcome. Superb home, charming bedroom. Warm welcome. Faultless breakfast.

Mottisfont is famous for the rose gardens of its 13th-century abbey (NT), converted into a stately home in the 18th century and decorated in trompe l'oeil by Rex Whistler in the 20th. The village used also to have a lesser claim to fame: the 'sprat and winkle' railway line along which were once carried not only villagers but loads of chalk for export to Canada. The Victorian **OLD STATION** beside the disused track (now part of the River Test Way – a long and lovely walk from Andover to Totton) is today the home and crafts studio of Helen

Hall. Her visitors' bedrooms (and the sun-room) overlook the River Test, frequented by herons and swans. They are simply furnished, but the bathroom is quite splendid! £16.50–£17.50. [Tel: 01794 368609; postcode: SO51 0LN]

THE MILL   **C D S**

Mungrisdale, Cumbria, CA11 0XR   Tel: 017687 79659

West of Penrith. Nearest main road: A66 from Keswick to Penrith (and M6, junction 40).

9 Bedrooms. £38–£44 including dinner, to readers of this book only. Less for continental breakfast. Prices go up from Easter. Most have own bath/shower/toilet. Tea/coffee facilities. TV. Views of garden, country, river. Washing machine on request. **Dinner.** 5 courses (with choices) and coffee, at 7pm. Vegetarian or special diets if ordered. Wine available. No smoking. **Light suppers** if ordered.
2 Sitting-rooms. With open fire, central heating, TV. Snooker. Table tennis.
Large garden
Closed from November to February.

It is only a generation since the watermill in this Lake District valley stopped working. By the old stone building which used to house the saw which the mill powered is the sawyer's cottage, now a private hotel. It is a peaceful spot, with little more than the sound of the River Glenderamackin rushing down its rocky bed.

The Mill (which is next to, but not connected with, the Mill Inn) is a simple white house with moss on the slate roof. A small conservatory faces a stone terrace and a lawn with seats by the water's edge.

Eleanor and Richard Quinlan believe that dinner is the high point of a stay. One might start with a tartlet of wild mushrooms, followed by green bean and apple soup with freshly baked soda bread. The main course might be quail with orange, brandy and thyme, or baked fillet of sea bass with lemon and soy dressing – there always is a vegetarian option.

The main sitting-room is pretty (the stone surround to the log fire bears the date 1651), and there is a small TV room with well-filled bookshelves. In the dining-room each small oak table has burgundy napkins, willow-pattern china, candles and a nosegay. Bedrooms are trim and simple, with colourful bedspreads, and each has a bowl of fruit. All have views of fellside, trees, or garden. On the walls are pictures from Richard's collection of Victorian paintings. Early arrivals are greeted with tea and home-made fruit log.

Though not in the heart of the Lake District – and therefore quiet even in the tourist season – Mungrisdale is not far from Ullswater in one direction and Derwent Water in the other. Closer are the fells where John Peel hunted, now popular with walkers (Carrock Fell is known for the variety of minerals to be found there). There is a pub with its own brewery at Hesket New Market on the way to picturesque Caldbeck, where there is a thriving craft centre in Priest's Mill. Dalemain and Hutton-in-the-Forest are privately-owned mansions well worth visiting, as are Dacre church, with its carved stone bears in the graveyard, and the restored Friends' Meeting House at Mosedale, one of the oldest in the country.

Readers' comments: Beautiful, quiet, excellent food. Service attentive and friendly. Food is superb. Outstanding. Interesting dinner with Mozart background. Food good. Charming. Hospitality exceptional, food absolutely delicious.

MILL FARMHOUSE   C D S

Westbury, Buckinghamshire, NN13 5JS   Tel: 01280 704843

East of Brackley. Nearest main road: A422 from Brackley to Buckingham.

3 Bedrooms. £17–£20 (less for 3 nights or continental breakfast). Bargain breaks. Some have own bath/shower/toilet. TV. Views of garden, country, river. Washing machine available.

Dinner. From £10 for 3 courses and coffee, till 9pm. Non-residents not admitted. Vegetarian or special diets if ordered. **Light suppers.**

1 Sitting-room. With open fire, central heating, TV.

Large garden

The mill itself is now used as workshops, and the miller's stone house (built in the 18th century) is the heart of a 1000-acre farm with sheep, cattle and horses. The building has been immaculately restored and furnished by the Owens. Although the old, deep-set casements and shutters remain, as do panelled oak doors and other traditional features, Jacqueline has used pretty fabrics and colours to give a light and attractive look to the bedrooms – a wisteria frieze, figured cotton spreads and velvet bedheads in one, for instance; while another has a rosy frieze and bamboo furniture. These rooms are reached by a stair rising from the sitting/dining-room which has a big refectory table at one end, hunting-prints on cream walls and coral striped sofas at the other. Carved oak furniture recalls the past while sliding glass doors to the garden are wholly of today (as is the covered, heated swimming-pool).

For dinner, you may be treated to home-made pâté followed by plaice in mushroom and prawn sauce under a topping of courgettes and cheese, and the choice of hot chocolate pudding or banana cheesecake.

The garden has stone-walled terraces and shrubs with foliage and berries selected to be colourful even in winter. The village has many 17th-century thatched cottages and there are pleasant walks by the river. There is stabling for horses and ponies – this is good riding country.

By the manor house of George Washington's family in Sulgrave (Northamptonshire) is **RECTORY FARM**, thatched without and stone-flagged within. Generously proportioned rooms have wide, panelled doors and deep-set windows with white shutters behind velvet curtains that match rust-red rugs on the floor and the peonies on the capacious armchairs. Bedrooms are in pleasant country-house style; and Joanna Smyth-Osbourne, despite bringing up a young family, finds time to produce such beautifully cooked dinners as parsnip soup flavoured with ginger and orange,

pork-and-apple ragoût, and a delicious kiwi fruit ice cream. Outside are ponies, feathery-legged bantams and pheasants strutting the autumn fields. £17.50. [Tel: 01295 760261; postcode: OX17 2SG]

MILL HOUSE C D PT S X
Millgate, Bracondale, Norwich, Norfolk, NR1 2EQ Tel: 01603 621151
Nearest main road: A47 from Swaffham to Great Yarmouth.

2 Bedrooms. £17–£20 (less for 3 nights or continental breakfast). Both have own bath/shower/toilet. Tea/coffee facilities on request. Views of garden, country, river. No smoking. Washing machine on request.
Light suppers if ordered.
1 Sitting-room. With open fire, central heating, TV, piano, record-player. No smoking.
Large garden

It is a surprise to find this quiet backwater so near the city centre. Facing the placid River Yare, its waters a haven for coots and kingfishers, with other birds among the ivy-clad chestnuts and wild daffodils, stands a handsome 18th-century house built of flint and brick. It was originally the home of a prosperous miller (the mill – destroyed in a fire – used to grind mustard for Colman's). Behind the walled garden run the trains from Norwich to London, but all is silent at night. You can borrow Gillian Evans's rowing boat and take a picnic out onto the marshes; or the strenuous might even get as far as Norwich cathedral.

Inside the house is a higgledy-piggledy mixture of good antiques and old leather armchairs, interesting pictures (many by Gillian's husband) and pot-plants, log fire in the sitting-room, stone flags on the hall floor. There are handsome architectural details – classical archways and the plaster cornices, for example – and an elegant staircase to bedrooms that include a good family suite. (Light suppers only, which are from organic wholefood produce whenever possible.) Bicycles on loan; croquet.

Readers' comments: Lovely peaceful retreat; wonderful to row down the river in the family boat. Highly recommended.

A few miles southward is 17th-century **GREENACRES FARM** at Wood Green, Long Stratton, right on the edge of a 30-acre common with ponds and ancient woods. Bedrooms are spacious and comfortable, with own shower or bath. Children are welcome, and in the huge games room you can peer into the floodlit depths of a 60-foot well as old as the house itself. Joanna Douglas's dinners are homely two-course meals, such as meatballs in tomato sauce and cheesecake. (Bicycles on loan; tennis court.) £18–£20 (b & b).

Reader's comment: Very friendly, and quiet. [Tel: 01508 30261; postcode: NR15 2RR]

MILLER'S COTTAGE C D M S

Pig Lane, Bishop's Stortford, Hertfordshire, CM22 7PA Tel: 01279 503487

Nearest main road: A1184 from Bishop's Stortford to Ware.

4 Bedrooms. £17.50–£19 (less for 2 nights or continental breakfast). Prices go up from April. Two have own bath/shower/toilet. Tea/coffee facilities. TV. Views of garden, country. Washing machine on request.
Dinner (by arrangement). £12 for 3 courses and coffee, at times to suit guests. Less for 2 courses. Vegetarian meals if ordered. **Light suppers** if ordered.
1 Sitting-room. With open fire, central heating, TV, record-player.
Large garden

Just past a lock where colourful narrow-boats cluster and a once-active watermill still stands, a narrow track leads to this picturesque thatched cottage, 450 years old. Outside it are an old pump, a fig tree, and a paved terrace brimming with petunias and sweet peas around its sundial. Chickens wander the lawns, beyond which lie fields.

One room, in the cottage itself, is on the ground floor (it has a wall of exposed brick and timber) and has the use of the sitting-room of the cottage – furnished in homely country style, and with an inglenook fireplace. Others, simply furnished, are in an annexe (under the rafters there is a good family room).

Catherine Cook provides meals (such as soup, casserole, and home-made ice cream or pudding) only sometimes, but can recommend local inns and restaurants.

Bishop's Stortford, an old town of pargeted (decoratively plastered) and half-timbered houses, is on the River Stort, which is flanked by attractive gardens.

As with much that's good in Hertfordshire, myopic travellers miss all that can be seen around the old town if they hustle northward through the county en route to sometimes less attractive places up the A1. There are ancient villages if you wander off to the east or west, and – because in Tudor and Stuart times magnates built themselves palatial homes in hunting forests yet within easy reach of London – an exceptional number of mansions to visit.

To the attraction of historic (16th-century) **OLLIVER'S FARM-HOUSE,** Toppesfield (in Essex), is added that of a particularly interesting garden created only a few years ago, by Sue Blackie, a qualified landscape gardener. Her award-winning architect husband James makes wine from the small vineyard adjoining the garden: Domesday Book records a vineyard here.

In the huge sitting-room, with an equally huge brick fireplace, hang some of the modern paintings which James collects. His paintings also fill

the terracotta walls of the landing. Sue brings breakfast up to bedrooms furnished with antiques. £18.50–£25 **to readers of this book.** [Tel: 01787 237642; postcode: CO9 4LS]

MILTON FARM

CD

East Knoyle, Wiltshire, SP3 6BG Tel: 01747 830247
North of Shaftesbury. Nearest main road: A350 from Shaftesbury to
Warminster.

2 Bedrooms. £18–£22.50. Prices go up in
July and August. Both have own bath/
shower/toilet. Tea/coffee facilities. TV.
Views of garden, country.
Dinner. £13.50 for 3 courses (with choices)
and coffee, at 7pm. Less for 2 courses.
Vegetarian or special diets if ordered. Wine
available. **Light suppers** sometimes.
1 Sitting/dining-room. With open fire,
central heating.
Large garden
Closed in December and January.

This is a truly picturebook farmhouse – a stone-flagged floor in the entrance hall,
glimpse of a kitchen with pine table and a gun-case beside the gleaming Aga. In
the sitting-room, which has a boarded ceiling, logs hiss gently on the stone hearth.
There are old oak furniture, deep chairs, and flowers everywhere.

The Hydes removed a lot of later accretions to reveal the original beams in
this mainly Queen Anne house, and then added comfortable furniture and elegant
fabrics. Janice Hyde serves candlelit dinners – she is a superb cook – which
consist of interesting dishes using local produce. One example: onion quiche,
followed by a huge trout from the River Nadder (stuffed with almonds, mushrooms, lemon and I-know-not-what) and then the lightest of mousses. Clotted
cream, milk and butter are from the farm's cows; pheasant, hare and rabbits are
local. (Heated swimming-pool; hand-painted Portuguese pottery for sale.)

Readers' comments: Janice Hyde is a delight; countryside and house are beautiful.
Delicious cooking. Very welcoming; delicious dinner; very comfortable. Excellent
service. Splendid bedroom, most enjoyable dinners.

In a leafy valley at The Green, part of
East Knoyle, is sheltered **SWAINS-
COMBE**: a lovely thatched stone
house with an equally lovely garden.
Antiques and elegant fabrics furnish the
beamed rooms, and two staircases lead
to separate suites of bedrooms: in one,
two bedrooms with William Morris
fabrics, bathroom and sitting-area with
velvet wing chairs; in the other, three
bedrooms and two bathrooms – the
four-poster reproduces a mediaeval
design. Joy Orman is a skilled cook,
serving such candlelit dinners as
creamed aubergine, marinated and
stuffed chicken breasts, steamed orange
pudding, and cheese. No smoking.
£18–£19 (b & b).
Readers' comments: Delectable dinners.

Superb. Most helpful, warm and
welcoming. Very attractive, comfortable and cosy. Lovely garden. Well
looked after. Immaculate. The most
delightful place, nothing too much
trouble. Perfect hosts. Outstanding.
Delightful. [Tel: 01747 830224; postcode: SP3 6BN]

MILTON HOUSE BARN

Crooklands, Cumbria, LA7 7NL   Tel: 015395 67628
South of Kendal. Nearest main road: A65 from Kirkby Lonsdale towards
Kendal (and M6, junction 36).

2 Bedrooms. £18 (less for 3 nights). Price goes up from Easter. Both have own bath/toilet. Views of garden, country. No smoking. Washing machine on request.
Dinner. £11 for 3 courses and coffee, at 7pm. Non-residents not admitted. Vegetarian or special diets if ordered. No smoking. **Light suppers** if ordered.
1 Sitting-room. With central heating, TV. No smoking.
Small garden
Closed from December to February.

On what was once a busy coaching road but is now only a backwater close to the M6, Milton House Barn has been ingeniously converted to give lots of nooks and crannies. Guests use a characterful sitting-room at the top of the building, and they have their breakfast by a double-height window where the wide barn doors used to be.

The house was a 'bank barn' – typical of Westmorland – built into the hillside to house cattle below and hay above. The lowest storey is a self-catering flat sometimes available to b & b visitors.

Pauline Jones serves such dinners as home-made soup, beef cooked in ale with puff-pastry crust, and sticky-toffee pudding. Otherwise, many visitors eat at Crooklands or else at one of the numerous restaurants in the nearby town of Kirkby Lonsdale. The town also has a number of antique shops (and 3-day auctions), some near curiously named streets such as Salt Pie Lane and Jingling Lane or off the pleasant market square with its monument and cross. The church is Norman and some of the many inns are two or three hundred years old. Signs point to Ruskin's View (over the River Lune, which gave Lancashire its name), which he considered the finest in England. During the first weekend in September, there is an annual Victorian fair when the whole town dresses in period costume.

A few miles westward is Levens village. In Hutton Lane is another converted barn called **BIRSLACK GRANGE** where Jean Carrington-Birch offers comfortable accommodation overlooking the Lyth Valley, famous for damsons. Evening meals (such as home-made vegetable soup, beef in wine, and apple sponge and cream) can be provided. The house is close to two mansions: Levens Hall and Sizergh Castle, both of which have fine gardens. Kendal's attractions range

from bargain shoes to fine art. £15–£17.50.
Readers' comments: Good fortune to stay. Delicious breakfast. [Tel: 015395 60989; postcode: LA8 8PA]

THE MOHAIR FARM

York Road, Barmby Moor, (Humberside), East Riding of Yorkshire,
YO4 5HU   Tel: 01759 380308 or 0836 343215
East of York. On A1079 from York to Market Weighton.

3 Bedrooms. £14–£15 (less for 3 nights). Prices go up from April. All have own bath/shower/ toilet. Tea/coffee facilities. TV. Views of garden, country. Washing machine on request.
Large garden

This would be a good choice for anyone who wants to see the city of York but prefers to stay in the country (especially if they are approaching via the Humber Bridge). And they will stay on an intrinsically interesting farm as a bonus. For this is the only farm in the country where the main enterprise is angora goats, whose long silky hair provides mohair ('angora' yarn is made from rabbit fur). Originally from Turkey (the word angora is a corruption of Ankara), they are widely kept in other countries and, when Lesley Scott formed her flock about 12 years ago, she assembled breeding stock from as far away as New Zealand and Canada, travelling back with them. Visitors to the farm can get to know these friendly and intelligent animals, which now number about a hundred. They can also buy, at surprisingly low prices, garments made from their hair. Yarn and kits are on sale too, as are tops and fleeces for hand spinners.

In the farmhouse, which is decorated with some imagination, most rooms are rather small, and there is no sitting-room. However, the family room is spacious, with armchairs and a writing table. Ask to hear the story of Lesley's great-grand-father's will, which hangs on the breakfast-room wall.

The farm, which is well away from the road, is on the site of a Roman settlement with a pottery. A more recent installation is an outdoor spa bath.

Those who do not want to travel the 10 miles into York to dine have a fair choice in Pocklington, the nearest large village.

Readers' comments: Exactly as described; delightful.

In York, just outside the city walls, close to historic Clifford's Tower and the interesting Castle Museum, is **THE DAIRY** (3 Scarcroft Road), which was just that until only some years ago: to prove it, a milk churn now planted with flowers stands in the creeper-hung yard at the back. Rooms are cottagey in style, with original Victorian joinery, plasterwork and fire-places, furnished with sprigged fabrics and stripped pine. One of the best, off the yard, is the room where Yorkshire curd was made; another has the use of a big Victorian bath. Breakfasts can be

of wholefood. For dinner, there is an award-winning restaurant next door, or a big choice within walking distance. £16–£20. [Tel: 01904 639367; postcode: YO2 1ND]

MONAUGHTY POETH

C(7) D

Llanfair-Waterdine, Shropshire, LD7 1TT   Tel: 01547 528348
North-west of Knighton (Powys, Wales). Nearest main road: A488 from
Knighton to Shrewsbury.

2 Bedrooms. £18 (less for 2 nights). Price goes up from April. One has own toilet. Tea/coffee facilities. TV. Views of garden, country, river. Washing machine on request. **Light suppers** by arrangement. Vegetarian or special diets.
1 Sitting-room. With open fire, central heating, TV, piano.
Small garden
Closed in December and January.

Here, where the border between Wales and Shropshire runs, two sisters grew up in the 1940s: Brenda and Jocelyn. Later they wrote a nostalgic history of their parish, tiny though it is. The girls' great-grandfather built many of the farmhouses in the area and worked on the huge Knucklas viaduct nearby, the stones of which came from a demolished castle where Queen Guinevere is said to have lived. Now a scenic railway takes tourists over its 13 arches.

Monaughty Poeth itself has an 800-year-old history, for it once belonged to the Cistercians of Abbey Cwmhir: Monaughty means 'monastery grange' and Poeth 'burnt' – the house burnt down and was rebuilt in the 19th century. This is where Jocelyn, now married to farmer Jim Williams, lives and welcomes visitors. (Her sister is at **Bucknell House** – see elsewhere in this book.)

The accommodation at Monaughty is in traditional farmhouse style, with comfort the keynote, and in every room Jocelyn's pretty flower arrangements. For dinner, most visitors go to the picturesque old Red Lion nearby for steaks, duck, etc.

Readers' comments: Treated like royalty! Enjoyed every comfort. Warmest of welcomes. Large, pretty bedroom and lovely view. Wonderful concern for her guests. Attractive accommodation. Extremely friendly. Idyllic location. Charming and unassuming people.

WOODSIDE OLD FARMHOUSE,

Clun, shelters on the side of a valley outside the unspoilt little town that A. E. Housman called 'one of the quietest places under the sun'. There are fine views and much wildlife. The house is at the foot of a sloping lawn with a willow tree, its old stone walls made colourful by baskets of busy Lizzies. Thick walls and a wood-burning stove help to create a cosy sitting-room, off which is a sunny conservatory, and in the dining-room beams still carry old bacon-hooks. Cottage-style bedrooms are light and bright.

For dinner Margaret Wall may offer you leek and potato soup; chicken and broccoli; and a compote made from the garden's summer fruit, or perhaps Malvern pudding at other seasons. Closed in winter. £15–£17 (b & b).

Readers' comments: Accommodation and cuisine superb. Lovely house in beautiful surroundings. [Tel: 01588 640695; postcode: SY7 0JB]

MORNINGTON HOUSE
C D

Hambledon, Waterlooville, Hampshire, PO7 4RU   Tel: 01705 632704
North of Portsmouth. Nearest main road: A3 from Portsmouth to Petersfield.

2 Bedrooms. £15 (less for 4 nights). Tea/coffee facilities. Views of garden, country. Washing machine on request.
Light suppers if ordered.
1 Sitting-room. With open fire, central heating, TV.
Large garden

The form in which we know cricket dates from the 18th century – when Hambledon produced the first cricket club of all (still going strong) and laid down today's complicated rules (in 1760, the year when Mornington House was built). There is a cricket memorial here, and cricketing memorabilia in the inn.

Charles Lutyens, for many years chairman of the club, is a great-nephew of Sir Edwin Lutyens and may show his Delhi plans to interested visitors as they relax in the bay-windowed sitting-room or the adjoining conservatory with grapevine overhead. There are splendid views over brimming herbaceous flowerbeds, beech hedges, rooftops and church, and over Speltham Down – which the villagers collectively bought for the National Trust to save it from development. The Wayfarers' Walk passes by here on its long trail from the coast to Inkpen Beacon. In the garden is a swimming-pool (unheated).

Everywhere are interesting antiques – an inlaid escritoire from Holland, Edwardian chairs painted with garlands, a clock with windjammer pitching and tossing in time with its ticking and tocking. Open fires crackle in the sitting-room and in the hall. In the dining-room (overlooking a paved courtyard), 'spitting images' of Disraeli and Gladstone preside over the breakfast-table, and an unusual hide-covered rocking horse is a magnet to little children.

One bedroom, with lace spread and bamboo bedheads, leads to a bathroom with another bedroom, in blue and white, adjoining it.

You may have seen the house on TV: used for a Ruth Rendell mystery.

Readers' comments: Delightful. Lovely welcome and attention. Look forward to returning. Delightful house, charming hosts. Excellent supper. So comfortable. Shall return. My vote for the b & b of the year. Very pleasant, every kindness. A warm, inviting welcome.

On the other side of the village is **CAMS**: its 17th-century pine-panelled dining-room is impressive, with marble fireplace and shuttered glass doors opening onto the garden; beyond a haha sheep graze (beside a tennis court). Spindle-backed rush chairs surround a great circular table of polished yew, where Valerie Fawcett may serve such meals as pâté, chicken breasts in lemon and coriander, and apple pie. In the sitting-room, chinoiserie curtains and pink walls make a pleasing background to antique furniture. Up the impressive staircase are pretty bedrooms: the oldest, in pink and white, has beamy walls and leaded windows. £16–£18. [Tel: 01705 632865; postcode: PO7 4SP]

207

MULBERRY HALL

Burstall, Suffolk, IP8 3DP   Tel: 01473 652348

West of Ipswich. Nearest main road: A1071 from Ipswich towards Sudbury.

3 Bedrooms. £17.50 (less for 3 nights). Price goes up from May. Views of garden, country. No smoking. Washing machine on request.

Dinner. £14 for 4 courses (with choices) and coffee, at 7.45pm (except in August). Less for 2 courses. Non-residents not admitted. Vegetarian or special diets if ordered. No smoking. **Light suppers** if ordered.

1 Sitting-room. With open fire, central heating, TV, piano, record-player.

Large garden

Cardinal Wolsey owned this house in 1523. Son of an Ipswich butcher, he had had a meteoric rise under Henry VIII (a cardinal and Lord Chancellor of England while still in his thirties) and he used his consequent wealth to commission fine properties and works of art. But in 1529, having failed Henry in the matter of divorcing Catherine of Aragon, he was stripped of nearly all his honours.

It is Henry VIII's colourful coat-of-arms which embellishes the inglenook fireplace in the big sitting-room – pink, beamed and with a grand piano. From this a winding stair leads up to well-equipped bedrooms. There is a small dining-room with raspberry walls and wheelback chairs round an oak table, where Penny Debenham serves such meals – to be ordered in advance – as trout mousse with watercress purée; pork au poivre accompanied by dauphinoise potatoes, broccoli, courgettes and salad; fruit tartlets with elderflower cream; and cheeses. Breakfasts, too, are good, with such pleasant options as local apple juice, chilled melon, home-baked bread and smoked haddock in addition to the usual bacon and eggs.

Outside is an exceptional garden – or series of gardens, enclosed within walls of yew or beech. Beyond a brick-paved terrace is a lawn with long lavender border, and a pergola leads past a rose garden to the tennis court.

Nearby Ipswich, a port even in Saxon times, has a plethora of mediaeval churches with fine monuments. The traffic in the town is heavy, so exploring is best done on foot. Wolsey made it a twin to Oxford, such was its reputation for learning – but only the gateway of his uncompleted college remains, near the quays where old inns and a classical Custom House survive. The town museum includes replicas of two local Saxon treasures now in the British Museum, the Sutton Hoo and Mildenhall finds; Christchurch Mansion (in a park) is a Tudor house with a collection of furniture and toys, as well as paintings by Constable and Gainsborough. Stroll down the Buttermarket to find the Ancient House, its façade covered in elaborate 17th-century plasterwork representing the (then) four continents: it is now a bookshop.

The surrounding scenery is of open farmland, dotted with particularly pretty villages.

Readers' comments: Beautiful house, outstanding food and service; will visit again. A lot of loving care. Bedrooms light and airy, extremely comfortable; excellent food, breakfast a highlight. Warm welcome, lovely house, superb breakfast. Very relaxed.

MUNK'S FARMHOUSE
C(12)

Headcorn Road, Smarden, Kent, TN27 8PN   Tel: 01233 770265

West of Ashford. Nearest main road: A274 from Maidstone to Tenterden
(and M20, junction 8).

2 Bedrooms. £20–£23 (less for 7 nights). Both have own bath/shower/toilet. TV. Views of garden, country. No smoking.
Dinner (weekends only). £15 for 3 courses and coffee, at 7.15pm. Less for 2 courses. Non-residents not admitted. Vegetarian or special diets if ordered. **Light suppers** if ordered.
1 Sitting-room. With open fire, central heating.
Large garden

You had better behave yourself if you stay here, for in the garden is a prison-cell. The old wood lock-up (double-walled and with tiny barred window), now a 'listed building', was moved here in 1850 from the village for, once the railway had been built, there was no longer a stream of brawling railway navvies to fill it.

The house itself has an even longer history. Weatherboarded in typically Kentish style, it was built nearly three centuries ago. Inside are beams, inglenook fireplaces, iron-latched doors, the original built-in cupboard and a very wide oak staircase: clearly the yeoman-farmer who originally lived here was a man of substance. Even the quarry tiles he laid were so large and thick that they are still as good as new. These are in the dining-room (formerly the kitchen) where guests now eat at a big refectory table. Josephine Scott serves such dinners (if these are ordered in advance) as pâté, poached salmon, and home-made desserts or fresh fruit.

There is a sitting-room with log fire and William Morris sofa, and pretty twin-bedded rooms with sloping ceilings and country views. Outside is a heated swimming-pool. At nearby Pluckley, *The Darling Buds of May* was filmed.

Munk's Farmhouse is situated between Leeds and Sissinghurst castles and within reach of Canterbury, Rye and Ashford international station (for the Channel Tunnel).

Readers' comments: Really attractive and comfortable place, pretty garden, amiable hostess, excellent dinners.

MURCOTT MILL   C D PT S X

Long Buckby, Northamptonshire, NN6 7QR   Tel: 01327 842236
North-west of Northampton. Nearest main road: A428 from Northampton to
Rugby (and M1, junction 17).

3 Bedrooms. £15–£18 (less for 5 nights).
All have own bath/shower/toilet. Tea/coffee
facilities. TV. Views of garden, country.
Washing machine on request.
Dinner. £6.50 for 2 courses (with choices)
and coffee, at 7pm. Vegetarian or special
diets if ordered. Wine available. No smoking. **Light suppers** if ordered.
1 Sitting-room. With open fire, central
heating, TV, record-player.
Small garden

This 18th-century house is a mill no longer but a farm. Carrie, descendant of the
original owner, married Australian Brian Hart who (reversing the usual order of
things!) immigrated here to keep sheep and raise a young family. The house – no
ordinary mill – has big bay windows, marble fireplaces, handsome doors, alcoves
and pretty plasterwork, all of which Carrie has complemented with pretty colour
schemes such as coral and pale turquoise in the en suite bedrooms, with wisteria-
patterned chintz downstairs. She serves snacks or such traditional meals as chops
and apple pie.

The mill is well placed for seeking out not only the pretty and unspoilt villages
hidden in Northamptonshire's unappreciated lanes but also such masterpieces as
the stately homes of Boughton ('the English Versailles'), Canons Ashby and
Castle Ashby, Cottesbrooke (inspiration for Jane Austen's *Mansfield Park*), mediaeval Deene Park, Kirby and Lamport Halls, spectacular Rockingham Castle,
and Sulgrave Manor, which Henry VIII sold to an ancestor of George
Washington. The great public school of Oundle stands comparison with Oxford
colleges. There are magnificent churches at (for instance) Fotheringhay,
Higham Ferrers and Brixworth; many outstanding gardens and parks. The
Northamptonshire countryside which inspired John Clare, the 'ploughman's
poet', is very similar to the Cotswolds – but minus all the tourists.

Thatched **HOME FARM**, Spratton,
once belonged to the farm supplying
great Spratton Hall nearby (now a
school). Today its few acres support
only horses and a small number of
sheep. Rooms have beams, lattice-
paned windows, and doors with
wrought-iron latches. Sue Roberts has
furnished the house appropriately, with
Regency chairs around the mahogany
table in the breakfast-room. The larger
bedroom has windows on three sides, a
carved chest and rosy bedspread; the
other is particularly good for a single

room – unlike so many. No smoking.
£16. [Tel: 01604 847303; postcode:
NN6 8HW]

NALDERHILL HOUSE   C X

Nalderhill Road, Wickham Heath, Berkshire, RG20 8EU Tel: 01635 41783
West of Newbury. Nearest main road: A4 from Newbury to Hungerford
(and M4, junctions 13/14).

5 Bedrooms. £18–£20 (less for 3 night or continental breakfast). Some have own bath/shower/toilet. Tea/coffee facilities. TV. Views of garden, country. Washing machine on request.
Dinner (by arrangement). £11.50 for 3 courses with wine and coffee, at 7pm. Non-residents not admitted. No smoking. **Light suppers** if ordered.
1 Sitting-room. With open fire, central heating, TV. No smoking.
Large garden

In 1876, the heir to a vast estate – all the land you can see from Nalderhill, and a great deal more – was only four years old, so trustees were appointed, and their chairman built this fine house for himself high up above the Kennet Valley. The estate was cleverly landscaped to give an almost park-like view from the house, which is surrounded by impeccable lawns, a flagstone terrace and rosebeds.

One enters through a hall with pale beige carpet and sofas of cut velvet. There is a very big dining-room with a French window opening onto the terrace – the wily pheasants know when breakfast is served and tap on the glass for titbits. Everywhere the architectural details are handsome: the solid oak of the doors, staircase and woodblock floors came from trees felled when the house was built. There are plentiful bathrooms, and most bedrooms have big windows making the most of the fine views. In one is a 17th-century four-poster, while another has been furnished by the Mackeys with 'thirties furniture in palest walnut.

Visitors eat at a local pub or here by arrangement (perhaps pâté, lamb casserole, and plum pie – all fruit and vegetables are home-grown). A Jacuzzi and steam room are available.

Near the M4, huge **CHAMBER-HOUSE MILL**, Thatcham, dates from at least 1086. It has been skilfully converted into a number of modern houses. Betty de Wit, her husband and six cats live at no. 2, right over one of the two great wooden wheels – the sound of rushing water is always present.

The second-floor guest-room is neat as a ship's cabin but more spacious, with a room-divider of louvred fitments. Here and elsewhere are Betty's landscape photographs: she is a Fellow of the Royal Photographic Society. Both she and Gerry enjoy cooking the meals which they serve in their own dining-kitchen. Dinners have a Provençal influence. £19.50 (b & b).

Readers' comments: Felt very much at home. Cosy and comfortable. A real delight. Room was great, snug. Mrs de Wit extremely pleasant. Setting very beautiful, accommodation most comfortable. [Tel: 01635 865930; postcode: RG19 4NU]

NEWBARN

Wards Lane, Wadhurst, East Sussex, TN5 6HP Tel: 01892 782042
South-east of Tunbridge Wells. Nearest main road: A267 from Tunbridge
Wells to Heathfield.

3 Bedrooms. £18–£20 (less for 4 nights).
Prices go up from April. Tea/coffee facilities.
Views of garden, country, lake. No smoking.
Washing machine on request.
Light suppers if ordered.
2 Sitting-rooms. With open fire, central
heating, TV, record-player. No smoking.
Large garden
Closed in December and January.

Sitting on the brick terrace with the blue lake view below and hills beyond, one
could easily imagine one was in the Lake District.

In the 18th century this was a farmhouse, lattice-paned and tile-hung in traditional Sussex style. Indoors, knotty pine floorboards gleam with polish, there are
low beams, and the wood-latched doors were specially made by a local joiner for
Christopher and Pauline Willis, who took great care, when renovating the house,
to ensure that every detail was in harmony. Bedrooms are light and flowery,
predominantly yellow and green, or pink and blue. The sitting-room, which has
an inglenook, is decorated in apricot and cream. There is a games room in one of
the barns, and Shetland ponies in the fields.

Usually only breakfast is served (with Pauline's preserves to follow) because
the area is well supplied with good restaurants. Visitors are welcome, however, to
use the Aga cooker when it is convenient.

The landscaped garden descends right to the edge of Bewl Water reservoir.

Readers' comments: Views and peace superb. Outstanding. We will definitely
return. Absolutely beautiful. The best b & b ever. Beautiful location, tasteful
decoration. Exceptionally kind; a wonderful peaceful haven. Wonderfully well
appointed. The most accomplished host and hostess; a delightful stay. High
standard of comfort, very welcoming hostess, friendly atmosphere. Delightful.

West of Crowborough is the hamlet of
Chelwood Gate (once literally a gate
into Ashdown Forest) and **HOLLY
HOUSE** where former teacher Dee
Birchell welcomes guests to rooms
given character by her flair for spotting
'finds' such as iron balustrades salvaged from a great house and old furniture she re-upholstered herself. Some
bedrooms are on the ground floor,
each with its own good shower-room;
one upstairs has a balcony over the
garden with its azaleas and magnolias,
fish-pond and small, heated swimming-pool. Garden produce goes into
such meals as leek soup, chicken in

sherry and mushrooms, and gingernut
gâteau. £18–£20 (b & b).
Readers' comments: Comfortable, pretty
home; friendly service, well-equipped
room. [Tel: 01825 740484; postcode:
RH17 7LF]

NEWTON HALL

CDPTSX

Tattenhall, Cheshire, CH3 9AY Tel: 01829 770153

South-east of Chester. Nearest main road: A41 from Whitchurch to Chester.

3 Bedrooms. £17.50–£20. Prices go up from April. Some have own bath/shower/toilet. Tea/coffee facilities. Views of garden, country. No smoking.
1 Sitting-room. With central heating, TV. No smoking.
Large garden

The centre of a big dairy-farm, Newton Hall is a 300-year-old house surrounded by gardens and with fine views of both Beeston and Peckforton castles. Anne Arden's rooms have an air of solid comfort (the blue bedroom is particularly beautiful, with handsome Victorian mahogany furniture and an en suite bathroom). In the breakfast-room are wheelback chairs, oak table and dresser, the original quarry-tiles, a brick fireplace, huge beams and oak doors with great iron hinges. Like those in the sitting-room, its casements open onto sweeping lawns.

The walled city of Chester is famous for its cathedral, castle and 'rows', an outstanding zoo as well, and the River Dee for salmon. Except for the hills in this part of the county, Cheshire consists mostly of level pastureland which supports the cows whose milk has made Cheshire cheese into a classic variety.

Readers' comments: Exceptionally charming. Hostess of great care. Most warmly received. Outstanding. Very pleasant. Exceeded our expectations. Lovely room and gracious hostess.

Handy for north Wales as well as historic Chester, the pretty village of Tilston is surrounded by the Peckforton and Bickerton hills. **TILSTON LODGE** is now home to Kathy Ritchie and her collection of rare breeds. The original Victorian features include a handsomely tiled hall with pretty marble fireplace and galleried mahogany staircase. Kathy has made patchwork bedspreads; stencilled woodbines on walls; draped a four-poster with lace; and collected an array of Victorian jugs. In the raspberry-walled dining-room – with William-and-Mary style chairs, good linen and silver – she serves imaginative meals using home-grown produce,

free-range eggs, local lamb, Cheshire and other local cheeses. £19–£30 (b & b) **to readers of this book**.
Readers' comments: Excellent in every way. Fine bedroom and bathroom. Very good, quiet setting. [Tel: 01829 250223; postcode: SY14 7DR]

For explanation of code letters (C, D, M, PT, S, X) see inside front cover.

213

91 LANGTHORNE STREET   C(10) **M PT X**
Fulham, London, SW6 6JS   Tel: 0171-381 0198
Nearest main road: A219 from Hammersmith to Putney.

3 Bedrooms. £17.50–£20 (with continental breakfast). Bargain breaks. TV. Views of garden (from two). No smoking preferred. **Light suppers** if ordered. No smoking preferred.
1 Sitting-room. With open fireplace, central heating. TV. No smoking preferred.
Garden

Lining a quiet residential street between Fulham Palace Road and the River Thames is a terrace of turn-of-the-century houses apparently indistinguishable from the thousands which sprang up all over the country in the building explosion of that period: staircase leading up from narrow hallway, two rooms to the side, kitchen at the end, garden beyond. Within this basic framework, however, the scope for individual development is pretty well unlimited, and Brigid Richardson has coaxed her ground and first floors into the kind of bed-and-breakfast accommodation that visitors condemned to hotels never know.

The hall floor still boasts its original coloured tiles. The cork-floored kitchen is a haven of up-to-date comfort, modern appliances cheek-by-jowl with period furniture, an elegant Edwardian table at which guests take breakfast (juice, cereal, and a choice of excellent breads), and glass doors leading to the long, south-facing garden – ideal for relaxing in on summer evenings. Brigid does not offer dinner, but is happy to allow guests to use the kitchen (a nearby supermarket provides easy-to-prepare meals). A range of teas – including herbal ones – and coffee are always available.

On the ground floor is a charming blue-and-white bedroom (the bedhead is an intricately carved panel from a 15th-century chest) and the bathroom next door is a delight: huge, free-standing, old-fashioned bath as well as roomy shower. Upstairs are two more attractive bedrooms, both overlooking the garden, and another spacious bathroom. At the front of the house, over the downstairs bedroom, is a cosy sitting-room crammed with books and pictures – many of the latter watercolours, drawings or prints, for Brigid restores works of art on paper and thus tends to be more or less surrounded by them. Her work has included paper conservation at Burghley House in Lincolnshire and at the Bank of England.

Three minutes' walk away in Fulham Palace Road, frequent buses (or a stiffish walk) will take you to Hammersmith Broadway, where you can catch tube trains to Heathrow or central London; buses in all directions too.

Readers' comments: A very charming typical English house, very well equipped. Each room has its own character; beautiful old furniture; warm-hearted host. Have stayed 10 times. Very helpful and kind. Elegantly decorated.

Houses which accept the discount vouchers on page ii are marked with a V on the lists at the beginning of this book, see pages xi–xix and pages xxi–xxii.

NORTH COURT

Shorwell, Isle of Wight, PO30 3JG   Tel: 01983 740415
South-west of Newport. Nearest main road: A3055 from Totland to Ventnor.

3 Bedrooms. £19–£20 (less for 3 nights). All have own bath/toilet. Tea/coffee facilities. TV. Views of garden, country. No smoking. Washing machine on request. **Light suppers** if ordered.
Large garden

Swinburne and his girl cousin used to play the organ that stands in the hall of this 17th-century manor house – a big stone-flagged room with pale blue walls, logs piled high around the stove.

The house is now the home of John and Christine Harrison, portraits of whose ancestors hang on the walls of the large dining-room with mahogany tables and marble fireplace. The great staircase was reputedly designed by Grinling Gibbons, and nearly every room has handsome detailing from that period – arched or scallop-framed doorways, egg-and-dart mouldings, shuttered windows in thick stone walls. All bedrooms are large, with armchairs.

Impressive though the house is, the really outstanding feature is the large and undulating garden with many plants of botanical interest. You can wander through woodlands or down terraces to a stream with water-plants, try to tell the time from a sundial in the knot garden, look down into the ancient bath-house, wander through arches of wisteria or lilac, play croquet . . . As only snacks are served, dinner for most people always involves a stroll through this lovely garden (opened to the public occasionally) to reach the nearby Crown Inn.

The island's coastline, its inland scenery and pretty villages appealed to the Victorians' love of the picturesque, and it was they who established it as an ideal holiday destination. Some feel that this has now ruined parts of the coast but, in a village such as this, one is well away from the summer crowds and yet so central that every part is within easy reach, with many footpaths round about. Small though the island is, the scenery is extraordinarily varied – and at its best in spring or autumn, when visitors are few. You could stay a month and every day find a different 'sight' to visit, as varied as Carisbrooke Castle or Osborne House on the one hand and the ferny chines (ravines) or wildlife reserves, or a working smithy on the other. Some of the least famous places are the most attractive – unspoilt villages such as Calbourne or Mottistone for instance. One of the nicest, old-fashioned resorts on the south coast is Ventnor and to the east of it lies picturesque little Bonchurch, complete with duck-pond; while on the St Lawrence side there stretches a 6-mile walk or drive among myrtles and ilex – the Undercliff, created when towering cliffs broke and slid down to the sea, a disastrous spectacle until nature moved in abundantly with self-seeded plants and trees. At the end of the Undercliff is a headland, St Catherine's Point, with lighthouse and far sea views. The home of Julia Margaret Cameron, the Victorian pioneer of photography, is near Freshwater Bay.

215

NORTHLEIGH HOUSE   C D M

Fiveways Road, Hatton, Warwickshire, CV35 7HZ   Tel: 01926 484203
North-west of Warwick. Nearest main road: A4177 from Warwick to Solihull
(also M40, junction 15; and M42, junction 5).

7 Bedrooms. £19–£27.50. All have own bath/shower/toilet. Tea/coffee facilities. Refrigerators and remote-control TV. Views of garden, country. No smoking. Washing machine on request.
Dinner. £14.50 for 3 courses (with choices) and coffee, at times to suit guests. Vegetarian or special diets if ordered. No smoking. **Light suppers** if ordered.
1 Sitting-room. With central heating, woodstove, TV. No smoking.
Small garden
Closed from mid-December to end of January.

A former dress designer, Sylvia Fenwick – a vivacious personality – has turned her creative talents to decorating every bedroom with elegance – each is different, each memorable, and many verge on the luxurious (for instance, some double rooms have two washbasins). They are all very well equipped and heated.

The L-shaped blue suite (with kitchenette in cupboard) has a sofa, bamboo tables and a carved bed in a silk-curtained alcove. There's a huge poppy-room, with white furniture, in which the pale green leafy wallpaper is matched by the carpet. Another room, Victorian and frilly in style, has a mink-and-white colour scheme; while yet another is in Chinese style. On two sides of the big sitting-room are garden views; the room has comfortable furniture, pleasant colours and an ornate little wood-burner.

Sylvia serves supper trays, or dinners (by arrangement) at which you might get something like avocado salad, chicken provençale, and tropical fruit pavlova. But she also provides guests with a map showing a dozen local inns that do good food. She used to farm here, and she maintains her interest in rare breeds (of sheep in particular).

Rural quiet surrounds the house – and yet it is only a few miles from Birmingham's National Exhibition Centre and international airport; the National Agricultural Centre; Stratford-upon-Avon, Warwick and Coventry.

Readers of Edith Holden's *Country Diary of an Edwardian Lady* will be familiar with a number of place-names around here such as Knowle, a historic village on a hill, with half-timbered houses; and Packwood House (NT) which has a lovely garden containing conical yews representing Christ and the disciples (and fine furniture inside) – Edith did many sketches here.

Readers' comments: Very superior, one of the best I have found, bedrooms spacious and breakfasts excellent. First class! Immaculate. We loved this place so much we spent an extra night there. Sylvia Fenwick is a very warm and hospitable lady. Her scrambled eggs are heavenly! Warm welcome, comfortable stay. Sylvia is a real character. Well equipped and luxurious.

NORWOOD HOUSE   C(12)
Hiscott, Devon, EX31 3JS   Tel: 01271 858260
South of Barnstaple. Nearest main road: A361 from Barnstaple to Tiverton.

3 Bedrooms. £19. Price goes up from April. Bargain breaks. All have own shower/toilet. Tea/coffee facilities. TV. Views of garden, country. No smoking. Washing machine on request.
Dinner. £14 for 4 courses and coffee, at 7pm. No smoking.
2 Sitting-rooms. With open fire, central heating, TV, video. No smoking.
Large garden
Closed from December to February.

At the heart of a hundred acres of pastureland is a 17th-century farmhouse with beams, inglenook and log stove on a slate hearth, panelled doors of pine, and furnishings chosen well for this setting. There are sofas of buttoned brocade in the sitting-room, a brass bed prettily draped, Laura Ashley and other good fabrics, dried-flower arrangements and on the walls Linda Richard's own accomplished paintings of local scenes. Her husband was born in this house, where three generations of Richards have farmed.

For dinner, Linda serves (after a glass of sherry) such meals as timbale of smoked salmon, tarragon chicken, lemon meringue pie and clotted cream, and cheeses – after which (in what was once the dairy) guests relax in front of television (with video), with a book by the fire, in a Victorian conservatory, in chairs on the south-facing terrace, or strolling in Norwood's own woodlands. Those using the farm's self-catering accommodation are also welcome to dine in the house.

Norwood is only a few miles from ancient Barnstaple which, in addition to the centuries-old attractions of its Pannier Market on Tuesdays and Fridays, has plenty of modern shops, an antiques bazaar, and a very big swimming-pool in its leisure centre. Many 18th-century buildings and a colonnaded walk survive in the centre; there is a museum of local history in a 14th-century chapel; and the bridge of 16 arches dates from the 13th century. Tourist attractions include a farm park at Landkey, the Cobbaton collection of vehicles and other relics from the Second World War, RHS Rosemoor at Torrington, and Marwood Hill gardens (Marwood church has a magnificent carved screen).

Good beaches lie beyond Barnstaple, at Woolacombe, Saunton and Croyde which overlook Barnstaple Bay and have National Trust landscape behind them. In this direction, too, are the wildflowers of Braunton Burrows, a nature reserve with sand dunes; and another of Devon's few very fine churches, at Braunton (which also has an excellent gallery of crafts and paintings, with wholefood restaurant).

Readers' comments: Comfortably furnished; attractive dinner – generous and healthy food. Warm welcome. Made to feel at home. A well-adorned house. By far the best. Well-furnished and very comfortable. Meals plentiful and of highest quality. Exceptional by any standards. Meals delicious, service immaculate and unpretentious. Made extremely welcome; beautifully appointed home.

> **When writing to the authors, if you want a reply please enclose a stamped addressed envelope.**

217

NUMBER ONE　　　　　　　　　　　　　　　　　　**C D PT X**
1 Woodlands, Beverley, (Humberside), East Riding of Yorkshire,
HU17 8BT　Tel: 01482 862752
Nearest main road: A1079 from York to Beverley (and M62, junction 38).

3 Bedrooms. £16–£20 (less for 7 nights). Prices go up in May. One has own bath/shower/toilet. Tea/coffee facilities. Views of garden. No smoking. Washing machine on request.
Dinner. £12 for 4 courses (with choices) and coffee, at about 7pm. Less for 2 courses. Non-residents not admitted. Vegetarian or special diets if ordered. No smoking.
Light suppers.
1 Sitting-room. With open fire, central heating, TV. No smoking.
Garden

Like York but on a smaller scale, Beverley consists of a minster rising from a warren of small streets within what was once a moated town. Traffic is restricted in the centre, which means that streets such as Woodlands are relatively quiet. Number One is in a dignified late-Victorian terrace.

The Kings have furnished the house with some brio, using wallpapers and bright colours to good effect. There is an abundance of house-plants, books and pictures, the last ranging from original works, through reproductions, to old school photographs. And some quirky decorative touches: a pair of antlers hung with assorted hats, for example. There is a grandfather clock on the landing, which leads to well-windowed bedrooms. The dining-room doubles as Neil King's study: guests particularly appreciate finding the fire already burning here at breakfast time.

Sarah King provides for dinner a choice of several courses which might include grilled courgettes with walnuts and goat's cheese, a meat or fish main course (barbecued spare ribs or salmon in wine sauce, for example); and a choice of out-of-the-ordinary puddings, including locally made ices; and cheese. Over coffee, which comes with chocolates, the Kings like to talk to their guests in front of the sitting-room fire. There is croquet, and cycles can be hired.

Beverley is best known for the minster, but it would be an enjoyable town even without it. St Mary's church is almost as fine an example of Gothic architecture: a carving in it (one of many notable grotesques here and in the minster) is said to have put the idea of the White Rabbit into Lewis Carroll's head. St Mary's is minutes from Number One. It is also worth seeking out a restored arcade with dealers in such things as pot-pourri and oriental artefacts. In the opposite direction is the Westwood, a historic park-like common with the town's race-course. (Racing enthusiasts often use Beverley as a base for all Yorkshire's many meetings.)

The Museum of Army Transport is popular: the oldest exhibit here is the waggon used by Lord Roberts in the Boer War.

Should you tire of 'this place made for walking in', as John Betjeman called Beverley, where a Georgian frontage often conceals a much older building, there is plenty to visit within driving distance: York and Hull, and the North Sea coast, notable mansions, and more recently created attractions such as farm museums and model railways.

OAK TREE INN   C D M P T X

Tantobie, County Durham, DH9 9RF   Tel: 01207 235445

West of Stanley. Nearest main road: A692 from Gateshead to Consett.

8 Bedrooms. £15–£22 (less for 3 nights). **5% off to readers of this book.** Bargain breaks. All have own bath/shower/toilet. Tea/coffee facilities. TV. Some have views of garden.
Dinner. £9.50 for 3 courses (with choices), at 8–8.30pm. Vegetarian or special diets if ordered. Wine available. No smoking area in breakfast-room. **Light suppers** if ordered.
Bar. With open fire, central heating, TV, piano, pool table, etc.
Small garden

The inn was once a small manor house, the property of the local Member of Parliament. The rooms, some of which have four-poster or half-tester beds, still have original Victorian fireplaces, and the overall decor is Victorian in feel. Some rooms are in a converted coach house; others, less elaborate (and cheaper), in a cottage.

It is a surprising place to find in – it has to be said – an unattractive village: a combination of guest-house, gourmet restaurant and village pub, kept by a former college lecturer in fashion who describes herself as a lifelong devoted glutton!

In the dining-room, also Victorian in character, guests can have a table d'hôte meal, or they can choose from a very long à la carte menu, mostly French bourgeois in inspiration. The wine list is also long. On occasion, there are special continental evenings (Austrian, French, German, Alsace-Lorraine). And once a month there is live music – light classical, continental café-style, for example, or soloists. If this is not to your taste, there are games to play in the bar downstairs: Sylvia Hurst says the locals love to hear of 'foreign parts'. (Sunday lunch is available.)

The Oak Tree would be a good haven for those whose business takes them to the north-east, but the area has much to offer the tourist too, with the city of Durham on one side and unspoiled hilly country on the other.

In particular, there is the North of England Open-Air Museum at Beamish, only a few miles away. Awarded the accolade of European Museum of the Year some time ago, Beamish has as its object the preservation of the heritage of the north-east – urban, rural, and industrial – 'in the round' and, as far as possible, 'live'. The following are some of the things which have been assembled on the 200-acre site.

There is a recreated town of the early 1900s – houses (one with dentist's surgery), shops with authentic stocks, pub with beer on sale and dray horses in the stables, sweetshop and garage. A typical country station is complete with signal box, goods yard, locomotives and rolling stock. You can travel by tram or horse-drawn carriage to the colliery village. The farm is complete with local breeds of livestock and old implements. By the recreated coalmine buildings is the drift mine, into which one can go. A yeoman's farmstead illustrates life in the early 1800s. And there is much more: a day here would hardly be enough to make the most of the place.

OLD EGREMONT HOUSE   C(12) **PT**

31 Egremont Street, Ely, Cambridgeshire, CB6 1AE   Tel: 01353 663118

Nearest main road: A10 from Cambridge to King's Lynn.

rear view

2 Bedrooms. £18–£20.50 (less for 3 nights). Prices go up from April. Bargain breaks. One has own bath/toilet. Tea/coffee facilities. TV. Views of garden. No smoking. **Large garden**

The 300-year-old house has been filled by Sheila Friend-Smith with attractive furnishings, the garden is lovely and there is a cathedral view.

One bed/sitting-room has a cream carpet and beribboned duvet, sprigged wallpaper and stripped pine furniture. There are armchairs from which to enjoy a view of the winding flower garden and its herbaceous bed; from the other bedroom one sees the neat vegetable garden where Victorian hedges of box flank the symmetrical paths, and the tennis lawn. The house is full of interesting things to look at: Jeremy's collection of clocks (one is silent, being gravity-operated), pretty Portuguese tiles in bathrooms (and some depicting old military costumes), embroideries from Jordan and stone-rubbings from Thailand. Breakfast is served at a big mahogany table surrounded by Chippendale-style chairs, with antique china, numerous books and prints around.

Either Ely or Norwich could be the starting-point of a cathedrals' tour up the east side of England. More-or-less linked by what was once called the Great North Road (from London to Scotland), now known as the A1, are the exceptionally fine cathedrals of Peterborough (in Cambridgeshire), Lincoln, York and Durham. As to Ely itself, the city still has an 18th-century air. There is a particularly attractive riverside walk linking its quays, and a nature trail with not only birds to be seen but also a fine view of the cathedral. Ely is one of Europe's most glorious cathedrals, a multiplicity of pinnacles and spires outside, lofty vista within.

Reader's comments: Character, comfort and good food.

The original **SPINNEY ABBEY** near Wicken, Cambridgeshire, was closed by Henry VIII, and later pulled down. Its stones were used to build a new house in 1775. This is now the home of Valerie Fuller (and of her inherited collection of Victorian stuffed birds), who has three roomy and comfortable bedrooms with private bathrooms and, from the farm lands, views into ancient Wicken Fen, a National Trust nature reserve. (B & b only.) £19.

Readers' comments: Excellent hostess, capable and friendly. Very comfortable. Accommodation, service and food exceptionally good. Lovely hostess. [Tel: 01353 720971; postcode: CB7 5XQ]

OLD FARMHOUSE

CDS

Raskelf, North Yorkshire, YO6 3LF   Tel: 01347 821971
North of York. Nearest main road: A19 from York to Thirsk.

10 Bedrooms. £19–£23. Prices go up from March. Bargain breaks. All have own bath/toilet. TV.
Dinner. £16.50 for 4 courses (with choices) and coffee, at 7–7.45pm. Vegetarian or special diets if ordered. Wine available. No smoking. **Light suppers** if ordered.
2 Sitting-rooms. With open fire, central heating, TV.
Small garden
Closed in late December and January.

Bill and Jenny Frost's 18th-century guest-house has immaculate accommodation and decorative touches like a bouquet of silk flowers in the brick hearth whenever a log fire is not burning; and a particularly luxurious bathroom adjoining one bedroom. Chairs were made by an apprentice of Thompson, the 'mouse man'.

But it is the outstanding dinners which bring most visitors here. At every course there are several choices, from which one might select (for example) rabbit terrine, chicken breast en croûte, old English trifle; and finally the most interesting selection of a dozen English cheeses one could come across, ranging from yarg (mild and low-fat, wrapped in edible nettle-leaves) to potted Stilton (buttery and port-laden). There is a big choice of malt whiskies too. Bread and preserves at the 7-item breakfast are home-made, as are the 6 kinds of cheese-biscuit.

Readers' comments: Wholehearted recommendation. High standard. Excellent and varied food, very amiable and faultless service. Spotless and comfortable accommodation. Quite outstanding. Our favourite: so friendly, and food is first class. Excellent value in every way. Imaginative cooking, friendly host. Attention to detail amazing, beautifully presented food tasted wonderful. Superb food.

In a barn adjoining tiny **POND COTTAGE** (Brandsby Road, Stillington) is a treasure-trove of domestic bygones. For the Thurstans are antique dealers, specializing in 'kitchenalia' and pine furniture. The 18th-century house itself is furnished with antiques, and its shelves and nooks are filled with curios. There are collections of coronation mugs and Staffordshire dogs in the low-beamed sitting-room, where high-backed wing chairs are grouped around an inglenook fireplace. This is a house of twists and turns, unexpected steps and low windows. Its pleasant bedrooms overlook the pond.

Dianne serves only breakfast and

light suppers because the area is very well supplied with eating-places. £15–£16.
Readers' comments: A brilliant discovery. Fantastic treatment. Accommodation and catering excellent. Wonderful. Outstanding. Delightful and caring hostess. Nothing too much trouble. [Tel: 01347 810796; postcode: YO6 1NY]

OLD FORGE   C D M PT S X
Burgage Lane, Southwell, Nottinghamshire, NG25 0ER   Tel: 01636 812809
North-east of Nottingham. Nearest main road: A612 from Nottingham to
Southwell.

5 **Bedrooms.** £18–£22 (less for 4 nights).
All have own bath/shower/toilet. Tea/coffee
facilities. TV. Views of garden, country. No
smoking. Washing machine on request.
Light suppers if ordered.
1 **Sitting-room.** With open fire, central
heating, TV, record-player. No smoking.
Small garden

Flower-baskets hang on the pale pink house where once a blacksmith lived and
worked; yet it was only about twenty years ago that there ceased to be a forge
here. The forge itself, at the back, is now two bedrooms, clematis growing over its
roof; and the great stone rim round which iron for wheels was hammered now lies
idle by the lily-pool in the little garden. This is overlooked by a small quarry-tiled
conservatory from which there is a view of historic Southwell Minster nearby.

Hilary Marston has filled the 200-year-old rooms with treasures such as a very
old 'log cabin' quilt from Boston (now used as a wall-hanging), Staffordshire figures, a tapestry chair stitched by a great-aunt, and a brass bed with lace spread.

Each bedroom has its own character. One has a trellis-effect bedhead built in,
and tulip-bud wallpaper; another is pink and flowery; a third – with a good view
of the minster floodlit at night – has pale cottage-garden flowers.

Because there are 10 eating-places within 5 minutes' walk, full evening meals
are not provided.

At the heart of the peaceful old town, surrounded by fields of red earth
reminiscent of Devon's soil, is the minster, founded in Saxon times, with remarkably fine stone carvings (in its chapter house) of leaves from all the native trees of
England. Most visitors also want to see Newstead Abbey, founded in 1170 (it
later became Byron's home), Belvoir Castle on its lofty crag, Lincoln's cobbled
lanes and dominating cathedral high up, the National Water Sports Centre (at
Holme Pierrepont) and the Robin Hood Centre in Sherwood Forest.

Nottinghamshire is, like certain other counties, stupidly ignored by most
tourists – which means it is less crowded for those who do appreciate its many
attractions (not least, a multitude of things appealing to children: farm parks,
shows about Robin Hood, 'adventure' parks, exhibitions about cave men's lives –
at Cresswell Crags, the National Mining Museum, canal trips and so forth). The
River Trent winds northward, flowing through Nottingham and past Newark – a
town dominated by ruins of the castle where King John died in 1216, and centred
on a big market square with 14th-century inns. There are five antique fairs a year.
Near it is Hawton's church, worth a detour for its fine tower and 14th-century
Easter sepulchre. Eastwood is where D. H. Lawrence grew up, in a miner's
cottage now open to the public.

Readers' comments: Made to feel very welcome, nothing too much trouble. Well-
decorated, comfortably furnished, each room very individual. Warm welcome.
Well-appointed rooms. Outstanding breakfast. First class. Excellent rooms.
Superb breakfast, altogether a pleasant experience.

OLD GRANARY **C PT**
The Quay, Wareham, Dorset, BH20 4LP   Tel: 01929 552010
Nearest main road: A351 from Poole to Swanage.

5 **Bedrooms.** £19.50–£32. **20% discount in winter to readers of this book (2 days, excluding Fri and Sat).** All have own bath/toilet. Tea/coffee facilities. TV. Views of country, river. No smoking.
Dinner. £13.95 for 4 courses (with choices), at 6–9pm. Vegetarian dishes. Wine available.
Bar. With open fire, central heating.

Standing right on the quay (where cars park) by the River Frome, this 18th-century brick building was once a warehouse for grain that went by barge to Poole, and it still has much of its old character.

Derek and Rosemarie Sturton run a restaurant here, furnished with cane chairs and attractive colours. A typical dinner might comprise, for instance, fresh mussels, sea bass, and banoffee pie. There is a riverside conservatory for cream teas and drinks, and a bar with open fire. Upstairs are three floors with pretty, beamed bedrooms, their windows giving a view of the river, swans, and the Purbeck Hills beyond. The local landscapes on their walls are for sale.

Wareham is a most interesting old town, a great mixture of history and of architectural styles. It is encircled by high earth banks built by the Saxons to fortify their village against Viking raids. The roads within this were laid out, Roman-style, on a grid. St Martin's church is Saxon and contains, rather oddly, a monument to Lawrence of Arabia (whose home at Clouds Hill is open).

All around this area are marvellous places to visit – the following is merely a selection. Poole Harbour, the second largest and loveliest natural harbour in the world, the Blue Pool, Corfe Castle, Lulworth Cove, the Purbeck Hills; Arne – heathland nature reserve; Swanage, old-fashioned resort with sandy bay and architectural curiosities salvaged from London; Durlston Head – cliffs, birds, country park, lighthouse; Studland's beaches with Shell Bay beyond; Wool and Bere Regis (with Thomas Hardy associations); Bindon Abbey; the army Tank Museum at Bovington; Bournemouth, Compton Acres gardens, and any number of pretty villages down winding lanes.

Readers' comments: Superb in every respect; a real find; haven't words to describe food, room and attention to detail; absolutely professional but very personal; welcoming and friendly, spotlessly clean, excellent food. Lovely situation, a personal touch. Food superb. Pretty bedrooms, high quality food. Unique place, very comfortable. Wonderful! Exceptionally friendly and welcoming.

Houses with short entries are just as good as ones with longer descriptions; and they include some of the most popular houses in the book. They may, however, have fewer rooms, a shorter season, higher prices or fewer amenities (such as meals).

OLD HALL

Poolside, Madeley, Staffordshire, CW3 9DX   Tel: 01782 750209
(Messages: 01782 621728)
West of Newcastle-under-Lyme. On A525 from Newcastle-under-Lyme to
Whitchurch (and near M6, junction 15).

3 Bedrooms. £19–£27.50 (less for 3
nights). Prices go up in April. Some have
own bath/shower/toilet. Tea/coffee facilities.
TV. Views of garden, country. No smoking.
Washing machine on request.
Dinner (by arrangement). £12 for 3
courses (with choices) and coffee, at 7pm.
Less for 2 courses. Vegetarian or special
diets if ordered. No smoking. **Light
suppers** if ordered.
2 Sitting-rooms. With open fire, central
heating, piano. No smoking.
Large garden

Cheshire is famous for its black-and-white houses, and this – though just over
the county boundary – is a good example, with its beams and gables. Beams
and fine woodwork abound inside as well, and the house is full of old oak
furniture.

In one sitting-room there is an inglenook fireplace with glittering brassware
around it; in another, a grand piano by the wood stove, and sometimes music-
stands as well, for Mary Hugh is a professional musician. She teaches the violin,
but the viola is her principal instrument, and visitors may sometimes enjoy
chamber music or even join in impromptu. Through oak-boarded doors is the
dining-room, with an old Welsh dresser and small-paned mullioned windows.
Here guests (and sometimes small private parties) are served with, for example,
watercress soup, cheese soufflé, beef sirloin in mushroom and pepper sauce,
chocolate roulade, and cheeses – cooked by Ann O'Leary, a professional caterer.
Guests in the Hall's self-catering accommodation may dine in too.

Up the wooden staircase, past a coloured-glass panel for 'stolen light' to
another room, are the bedrooms with low beams, antiques and handsome brass
door-fittings. The tiled bathroom with its huge bath is almost unchanged since
the 1920s, when it was one of the first illustrated in *Ideal Home*.

Off the breakfast-room is a high-Victorian conservatory, made of cast iron at a
local foundry. The two-acre garden outside, with pond and pergola, is annually
opened to the public. In it are croquet and tennis lawns. At the front of the house
(adjacent to the village pond) are handsome yews and cedars.

As well as historical appeal (Chester, Shrewsbury and Little Moreton Hall are
not far), the area has much for anyone interested in our industrial past, or in
notable gardens such as that at Biddulph Grange.

Readers' comments: Very good and unusual. Wonderful house. Serene atmosphere.
First-class food.

Prices are per person in a double room at the beginning of the year.

OLD INN   **C D S**
Burford Road, Black Bourton, Oxfordshire, OX18 2PF   Tel: 01993 841828
West of Oxford. Nearest main road: A40 from Oxford to Burford.

2 Bedrooms. £16 (less for continental breakfast). Bargain breaks. Tea/coffee facilities. TV. Views of garden, country. Washing machine on request.
Dinner. £11 for 5 courses (with choices) and coffee, at 7.30pm. Non-residents not admitted. Vegetarian or special diets if ordered. **Light suppers** if ordered.
1 Sitting-room. With open fire, central heating, TV.
Small garden

No longer an inn, this 17th-century house is now the elegant home of Pat and John Baxter. It has thick stone walls, low beams in the sitting/dining-room and outside are views of the village, with the mediaeval church close by.

The bedrooms are very attractive: one is all-white (a crisp and light effect); another is a beamy room with nice old furniture. Even the bathroom has been furnished with style – soft green carpet and William Morris wallpaper. The breakfast-room has pine chairs, scarlet cloths and a garden view. Only one family (or group of friends) is taken at a time.

Mrs Baxter provides the best of typically English food, asking her guests beforehand what they would like. Melon with port might be followed by a joint or a steak-and-kidney pie, and then perhaps brandy-chocolate cake – all served on pretty Blue Baltic china. Afterwards, when guests relax on the sofas and armchairs in front of the log stove, the Baxters may join them for coffee. (Sunday lunch by special arrangement.) And only a minute or two away is the very pretty village of Clanfield where, as an alternative, the Tavern serves meals of gourmet standard.

Readers' comments: Comfort and service superb. Excellent food served with zest and style. Extremely comfortable and pleasant; delicious dinner. Extremely good value, very hospitable. Delightful, charming – just like staying with friends. Warm, welcoming, a very high standard. Lovely place, good meal, very helpful. Very convivial hosts, beaut rooms.

Close to Burford, on Westhall Hill, Fulbrook, is the **DOWER HOUSE**, another handsome house of golden stone, which Diana Westall has furnished with flair. You might sleep in a four-poster, or a brass bed with porcelain panels in a room with panoramic views on two sides and a bathroom which, like other rooms, has William Morris wallpaper. (Light suppers only: plenty of restaurants in Burford.) £17–£18.
Readers' comments: Highlight of our trip. Perfect hostess. Very welcoming.

[Tel: 0199382 2596; postcode: OX18 4BJ]

OLD MANSE C
Swingbridge Street, Foxton, Leicestershire, LE16 7RH   Tel: 01858 545456
North-west of Market Harborough. Nearest main road: A6 from Market
Harborough to Leicester.

3 Bedrooms. £19.50. All have own
bath/shower/toilet. Tea/coffee facilities. TV.
Views of garden, country. No smoking.
Washing machine on request.
Light suppers if ordered.
1 Sitting-room. With open fire, central
heating. No smoking.
Large garden

Ancient and tiny Foxton, its 13th-century church restored by John of Gaunt and
preached in by Wycliffe, is famous for its 'staircase' of 10 locks on the Grand
Union Canal, which raises boats 75 feet uphill (there are a canal museum and
horse-drawn barge trips). It played a part in the Civil Wars (Naseby is near); and
the little booklet called *The Foxton Story* is well worth reading.

The Old Manse was built in the 17th century, just beyond a swing-bridge over
the canal; and in it the Baptist minister later ran a school. Now it is home to the
Pickerings and their collection of classic cars.

Rooms are elegant and immaculate, and there is a fine garden – open to the
public at times – with an array of fuchsias. Some of the light and flowery bedrooms have a good view of this. Downstairs, an attractive sitting-room houses a
grand piano and pink velvet furnishings, alcoves are full of books, and there is a
big collection of saucy china fairings. Altogether, a characterful house in a little-
known spot of considerable interest; and surrounded by such sights as Boughton
House, Canons Ashby, Rockingham Castle, the gardens of Holdenby and Coton
Manor, and Rutland Water.

Between Market Harborough and
Dingley is Victorian **DINGLEY
LODGE,** overlooking the Welland
Valley, which two young teachers,
Bruce and Christine Kirkman have
converted into a hotel. Most of the en
suite bedrooms, spacious and with
their original little iron fireplaces, enjoy
the far view – as does the bay window
of the dining-room, which opens onto
a brick terrace where sometimes there
is a barbecue. Meals usually comprise
a menu such as local Brixworth pâté
with Cumberland sauce, coq au vin,
and bananas in brandy sauce. There

are two bars with Victorian-style wallpaper and pine seating. £19. [Tel:
01858 535365; postcode: LE16 8PJ]

**Book well ahead: many of these houses have few rooms. Do not
expect dinner if you have not booked it or if you arrive late.**

OLD MILL

D

Little Petherick, Cornwall, PL27 7QT   Tel: 01841 540388
South of Padstow. On A389 from Padstow to Bodmin.

6 Bedrooms. £18.65–£26.55 **to readers of this book** (less for continental breakfast). Prices go up from May. Some have own bath/shower/toilet. Tea/coffee facilities. Views of garden, country, river. Washing machine on request.
Dinner. £10 for 3 courses, at 7pm. Vegetarian or special diets if ordered. Wine available. No smoking.
3 Sitting-rooms. With central heating, TV. Bar.
Small garden
Closed from November to February.

This picturesque 16th-century watermill (with a working waterwheel) is beside a stream that winds its way into the Camel estuary – an Area of Outstanding Natural Beauty, along a coastline celebrated for its many beautiful beaches (a number are protected by the National Trust).

Michael and Pat Walker have furnished the Mill very attractively. The beamy sitting-room has white stone walls, one with a mural of ploughing. William Morris fabric and Berber carpet contrast with the green slate of the floor. All around are unusual 'finds': an ancient typewriter and sewing-machines, clocks, and old tools such as planes and picks. The paved terrace by the stream is enclosed by sun-trapping walls, and there is a waterside seating-area at the bottom of the garden. Bedrooms are homely (very nice bathrooms); quieter ones at the back. Evening meals consist of a three-course cold supper, with hot main dishes also available.

Little Petherick is a pretty village with (just across the road from the Mill) a beautiful church, close to Padstow which is still agreeably antiquated. Narrow, crooked lanes lead down to Padstow's harbour, a pretty group of houses encircles the quay, and there are several outstanding buildings including the Court House where Sir Walter Raleigh dealt out judgments when he was Warden of Cornwall. The world-famous Hobby Horse street dance takes place on 1 May here. There are idyllic, golden beaches around here (go to Treyarnon to see surfing). Near St Columb Major (impressive church) is an Iron Age fort called Castle an Dinas; St Mawgan is a pretty village in a woodland valley; by contrast, St Wenn is a wild and windy moorland spot; by the lighthouse on Trevose Head you can see the whole coast from St Ives to Lundy Island. At Wadebridge, there is an exhibition centre, housed in a converted railway station, dedicated to the life and work of Sir John Betjeman. He is buried at St Enodoc, just across the estuary.

On the whole, north Cornwall is far less touristy than the south, its greatest attractions being scenery (not only coastal but inland too) with fewer commercial entertainments, sights, etc.

Readers' comments: Beautifully furnished. Could not be more pleasant and helpful. Lovely setting. Very hospitable. We found the service and quality of meals excellent. Excellent in every way. Greatly enjoyed our stay.

OLD MILL

Mill Lane, Tallington, Lincolnshire, PE9 4RR   Tel: 01780 740815
East of Stamford. Nearest main road: A16 from Stamford to Market Deeping.

5 Bedrooms. £20 (less for 3 nights or continental breakfast). Price goes up from April. Bargain breaks. All have own bath/shower/toilet. Tea/coffee facilities. TV. Views of country, river. No smoking. Washing machine on request.
Light suppers if ordered.
1 Sitting-room. With open fire, central heating, TV. No smoking.
Garden

Tourists 'discovered' mediaeval Stamford when it was used for filming *Middlemarch* (though true George Eliot country is in Warwickshire). It is a jewel of a largely unspoilt stone town, rich in old inns and churches, on the River Welland.

As the river flows eastward, it passes by Tallington village and here stands the 18th-century watermill where the Olvers now welcome guests. Much of the conversion was done by John himself, a task that would daunt most men, but he is a PE teacher and once played rugby for England. Though the mill ceased to grind corn long ago, its gears, shafts, winches and millstones still survive; and he retained them all in their proper place. This means that the low, beamed breakfast-room and even bedrooms have such curious features incorporated in the decor. Some rooms look out over the river as it flows beneath.

Susan has chosen pretty fabrics (delphinium-patterned, or blue-and-white striped, for instance) to complement pine furniture that is in keeping with the old timbers of the mill. There are some particularly spacious bedrooms at the top, under the sloping rafters; and every room has its own neat and elegant bathroom, prettily tiled and with gilt taps.

The Mill is likely to be full every September when there are horse trials at great Burghley House nearby, or in spring when Spalding's bulb-fields are a big attraction; but at all seasons there is much to see – Lincoln's cathedral (and Peterborough's and Ely's), Boston for its Pilgrim Fathers associations, the mediaeval port of King's Lynn, and the Lincolnshire Wolds (Tennyson country).

Dining-room at Holmhead (see page 150)

OLD ORCHARD   **C S**
Stoney Lane, Thorpe, Derbyshire, DE6 2AW   Tel: 01335 350410
North-west of Ashbourne. Nearest main road: A515 from Ashbourne to
Buxton.

3 Bedrooms. £16.50 (less for 7 nights or
continental breakfast). Price goes up from
April. Two have own shower/toilet. Views of
garden, country.
1 Sitting-room. With open fire, central
heating, TV. No smoking.
Small garden
Closed from December to February.

Dovedale is one of the loveliest parts of the Peak District; and in this area there
are particularly fine views of it where the Manifold Valley runs down into the dale
(at the foot of Thorpe Cloud – one of several 1000-foot hills here).

On the edge of Thorpe village is a very prettily sited stone house in traditional
style, which stands where once an orchard of damson trees grew. This is the
comfortable home of Barbara Challinor and her husband; keen gardeners, as is
obvious from the herbaceous beds, stone terraces, rock garden and stream with
waterfalls in their sloping, landscaped grounds.

This part of the National Park is known as 'the White Peak' because the
underlying rock is limestone (further north, in 'the Dark Peak', the geology
changes). There is a network of paths around here by which to explore Milldale,
Wolfscote Dale and Beresford Dale – leading to other valleys further afield.

But scenery is not the only attraction of the area. There are the stately homes
of Chatsworth and Haddon Hall to visit, the old towns of Matlock and Bakewell,
and busy Ashbourne with a splendid church and antique salerooms.

It takes a long stay to do justice to the Peak District, a particularly scenic
National Park, but if you are pressed for time it would be possible to see some of
the finest parts by driving the following route. After walking in the beautiful park
of Ilam Hall (NT), continue to the head of Dovedale – a scenic route known as
Little Switzerland, with weird crags and pillars of rock, stone packhorse bridges
and a dramatic gorge – all familiar to Izaak Walton (who described them in his
Compleat Angler). Among the stone-walled fields and woodlands of Beresford
Dale is the pretty village of Hartington, its busy past as market and lead-mining
town now long gone. Arbor Low is a place of mystery – a circle of white stones
erected on a windswept site 4000 years ago and with burial mounds nearby.
Beyond it lies possibly the most perfect mediaeval stately home in this country
(parts built by a son of William the Conqueror): turreted Haddon Hall, with
terraced gardens descending to a sparkling river. Across high heather moors (with
another stone circle) lies Matlock – there is a mining museum worth visiting here.
This is where the River Derwent has cut a dramatic gorge through the hills.

Readers' comments: Ideal hostess. Excellent: went out of her way to make us
welcome. Excellent accommodation, homely and friendly people. Excellent. Most
satisfying accommodation with friendly atmosphere.

For explanation of code letters (C, D, M, PT, S, X) see inside front cover.

OLD PARSONAGE FARMHOUSE   **D**

Hanley Castle, Worcestershire, WR8 0BU   Tel: 01684 310124

South-east of Malvern. Nearest main road: A38 from Worcester to Tewkesbury
(also M5, junctions 7/8; and M50, junction 1).

rear view

Prices go up from May. All have own
bath/toilet. Tea/coffee on request. Views of
garden, country. No smoking. Washing
machine on request.
Dinner (by arrangement). £14.75 for 4
courses (with choices of dessert) and coffee,
from 7pm. Less for 2 courses. Non-residents not admitted. Vegetarian or special
diets if ordered. Wine available. No smoking. **Light suppers.**
2 Sitting-rooms. With open fire, central
heating, TV, record-player. Bar.

3 Bedrooms. £20–£22.50 (less 5% for 3
nights mid-week or 7 nights December to
January **to readers of this book only**).

Large garden
**Closed from mid-December to mid-
January.**

It is not just the surrounding views of the Malvern Hills or the handsome 18th-
century house of mellow brick which makes this worth seeking out: Ann Addison
has a flair for both cookery and interior decoration, while Tony is a wine expert.
He runs wine-tastings in the one-time cider mill adjoining the house.

You enter the house via a vaulted entrance hall (with Edwardian fireplace),
then through double doors into the sandalwood sitting-room with its small library
and television. On the right is the elegant, pale sea-green drawing-room with its
arched Georgian windows and marble Adam fireplace. To the left is the sunflower-
yellow dining-room which has the original brick hearth and bread oven.

Damask cloths and Rorstrand china from Sweden create an appropriate setting
for the kind of meals Ann serves, such as mushrooms and herbs in puff pastry,
chicken breasts with prawns in cream and brandy, bramble mousse, cheeses.

Upstairs are elegant bedrooms (for instance, one has fruit-and-flower fabrics
complemented by peach walls, another has a vast bathroom with oval chocolate
bath).

All around is superb countryside. Drive southward and you come to Upton-
upon-Severn where a 14th-century bell-tower still stands near the bridge: once it
was part of a church, was given a 'pepperpot' cupola in 1770, and is now a
heritage centre – the church itself was dismantled in the 'thirties. The town's
historic byways and riverbank inns are well worth exploring.

Westward lie the Malvern Hills, with stupendous views from the
Herefordshire Beacon (over 1100 feet high) and the remains of one of the greatest
Iron Age forts in Britain. Near here is the village of Eastnor which has two castles,
the moated one (15th-century) is real and ruined; the other (1812) is a romantic
mansion, turreted in Norman style, which was designed by Smirke – architect of
the British Museum – and has armour, tapestries, etc. inside. Worcester has its
cathedral, Charles II's headquarters in the Civil War (the Commandery), Royal
Worcester porcelain (museum, factory and shop) and various good shops.

Readers' comments: Very impressed. Warm and friendly welcome, helpful and
charming. Extremely comfortable. High standard of imaginative food. Superb
standards and unrivalled personal service. Lovely, large bedroom. Very friendly.
Most welcoming and comfortable.

OLD PUMP HOUSE

C D PT S

Holman Road, Aylsham, Norfolk, NR11 6BY   Tel: 01263 733789
North of Norwich. Nearest main road: A140 from Norwich to Cromer.

5 Bedrooms. £17–£21 (less for 7 nights). Prices go up from July. Bargain breaks. Some have own shower/toilet. Tea/coffee facilities. TV. Views of garden. No smoking. **Dinner** (by arrangement). £9.50 for 2 courses and coffee, at 7pm. Non-residents not admitted. Vegetarian or special diets if ordered. No smoking. **Light suppers** if ordered.
1 Sitting-room. With open fire, central heating, TV, record-player. No smoking.
Small garden

There is peace as well as beauty inside this house, which is a surprise as it is on a junction of roads. But the old walls are thick and the view from the back (originally it was the front) is of a secluded garden: ask for a bedroom that overlooks this. Those at the front look onto the quaint, thatch-roofed pump which gives the former farmhouse its name.

It is a house of twists and turns, extended many times since it was built about 1750, with innumerable steps. To this characterful background Hazel Stringer's decorative flair has contributed strong colours like raspberry and turquoise, complemented by bamboo or pine furniture and jungly-patterned duvets. The apricot walls of the staircase contrast with a traditional floor of terracotta slabs; and, in the dining-room, scarlet walls with a very dark board floor and pale pine shutters. There is a small sitting-area on the landing.

Very English dishes are served at dinner, such as home-made mushroom soup, salmon mayonnaise, and bread-and-butter pudding.

Within a short stroll are Aylsham's historic church and the market place.

Every year, James and Rosalind Snaith travel in Europe looking for new wines and recipes to add to their repertoire. At **GREY GABLES** (Norwich Road, near Cawston), a former rectory, dinner may include, after an hors d'oeuvre, creamed salmon or Italian bean soup, chicken Wellington, choux pastries, and cheese. There is a long wine list. Dinner is eaten at mahogany tables with velvet-upholstered chairs, an elegant occasion.

Embroidery has been a family tradition here for at least four generations; Rosalind continues it.

There is a grass tennis court. £20–£30.

Readers' comments: Excellent; marvellous food. Very friendly, good food. Very comfortable and friendly. Remarkable service. Very professional. Dinners delicious, with exotic choices. Friendly staff. [Tel: 01603 871259; postcode: NR10 4EY]

OLD RECTORY   C D PT

Byford, Herefordshire, HR4 7LD   Tel: 01981 590218
West of Hereford. Nearest main road: A438 from Hereford to Brecon.

3 Bedrooms. £18–£19 (less for 3 nights). All have own bath/shower/toilet. Tea/coffee facilities. TV. Views of garden, country. No smoking. Washing machine on request.
Dinner. £13 for 3 courses and coffee, at 7pm. Less for 2 courses. Vegetarian or special diets. No smoking. **Light suppers** if ordered.
1 Sitting-room. With central heating. No smoking.
Large garden
Closed from December to February.

An enormous cedar of Lebanon dominates the garden outside the Rectory, a handsome brick house which, though built in 1830, is Georgian in style – having big, well-proportioned rooms and great sash windows which make the most of the very fine views of hills and church. Audrey Mayson and her husband have put a great deal of loving care not only into the restoration of the big house (recently adding Victorian-style bathrooms) but also the landscaping of the formerly neglected garden. The house is run in an informal, caring way.

The sitting/dining-room has pale green walls, deep pine-shuttered windows, pine-panelled doors, and their collection of unusual Escher pictures.

For dinner Audrey serves such dishes as caesar salad, almond chicken, and hazelnut meringue. Local crafts are on display.

Byford is on the way to Wales, but there are many reasons to pause here for more than a stopover. Nearby are Hereford and its cathedral; Hay-on-Wye for second-hand bookshops; the lovely River Wye with footpaths alongside.

Readers' comments: Very friendly, relaxed and roomy. Good food. Outstanding.

Because Monica Barker previously lived in India, **APPLETREE COTTAGE** (at nearby Mansell Lacy), built of half-timbering and brick in the reign of Henry VI, is full of exotic touches such as Kashmiri crewel bedspreads and curtains. These nevertheless assort well with pretty fabrics, antique oak furniture, and chairs covered in traditional tapestry or velvet. Previously two cottages, then a cider-house, the building still has many of its original features, such as low beams and small, deep-set windows; and when Monica had to put in a new, twisting staircase, she had it woodpegged in the traditional way. (En

suite facilities available.) By arrangement, she will cook such meals as cucumber and yogurt soup, steak pie, and meringues – using wholefood ingredients. The cottage stands at the foot of a hill popular with walkers and birdwatchers alike. £15–£18. [Tel: 01981 590688; postcode: HR4 7HH]

OLD RECTORY   **C D S X**
Northleigh, Devon, EX13 6BS   Tel: 01404 871300
South-east of Honiton. Nearest main road: A35 from Axminster to Honiton.

2 Bedrooms. £18–£20 (less for 4 nights). Bargain breaks. Both have own bath/shower/toilet. Tea/coffee facilities. TV. Views of garden, country. Washing machine on request.
Light suppers if ordered.
1 Sitting-room. With open fire, central heating, TV.
Large garden

It is in a conservatory – furnished with pine, and heated when necessary – that Rosemary Cohen serves breakfasts in summer (in the library in winter), so that visitors can enjoy the view to the south, across lovely Farway Valley. The rectory, which was built in 1825 – an excellent period for domestic architecture – has nicely arched doorways and marble fireplaces. The house is surrounded by stables, coach house and a big walled garden for vegetables.

Rosemary has furnished the handsome sitting-room in white and yellow; while the green-and-white dining-room has a hand-printed William Morris wallpaper and a large bay window with arched panes. As Honiton has plenty of restaurants, only light-supper trays are served here, by arrangement, for those who want to eat in. Bedrooms, too, are very pleasant: a soft green one overlooks the stables; in a rose room are stencilled ribbon garlands. Rosemary, antique-dealer and designer, has filled the house with unusual and elegant furniture. Off-road riding is available locally.

Because farming is done by old-fashioned methods round here (no 'agribusiness'), wildflowers have not been sprayed out of existence and wildlife flourishes – buzzards and even rarer birds, for instance; rare moths, badgers and deer.

In the valley to which it gives its name nestles the little village of Farway, and close to it is pretty little **KEEPER'S COTTAGE,** built early in the last century for the gamekeeper who looked after the pheasants on the surrounding estate. Today, Gaby Ryrie lives there, having surrounded it with a lovely rose garden and filled it with antiques. The dining-room's big doors open onto a terrace and lawns from which there are far views – as there are, too, from the huge bathroom and many of the other rooms, all decorated in pretty colours. Gaby produces such meals as melon cocktail, roast chicken with a full complement of the tradi-

tional trimmings, and apple pie with Devonshire clotted cream – wine is included in the price. £19 (b & b).
Readers' comments: Charmingly decorated, warm welcome, stunning views. [Tel: 01404 871328; postcode: EX13 6DL]

OLD RECTORY

CSX

Thurloxton, Somerset, TA2 8RH Tel: 01823 412686
North-east of Taunton. Nearest main road: A38 from Taunton to Bristol (and M5, junctions 24/25).

4 Bedrooms. £15–£16 (less for 6 nights). One has own shower. Tea/coffee facilities. Views of garden, country. No smoking. Washing machine on request.
Light suppers if ordered.
1 Sitting-room. With open fire, central heating, TV.
Large garden
Closed from November to March.

At the end of the Quantocks is Thurloxton, the old Victorian rectory of which is an enticing sight in summer when flowerbeds, hanging-baskets on the white walls, and a conservatory of bougainvillaea and other subtropical flowers make a colourful scene beyond the smooth lawn. Ann Comer has put pretty sofas and chairs in the spacious blue sitting-room. The L-shaped family bedroom is excellent; and outside is a putting green, with views across the fen-like Somerset Levels towards Glastonbury.

Thurloxton is centrally placed to visit all parts of Somerset – the Quantock Hills in one direction, the Mendips in the other, the reedy Somerset Levels, the coast, and the county town of Taunton – its secret places best discovered on foot. Beyond the early mediaeval castle (housing a particularly good museum and with a Norman garden close by) are lovely lawns beside the River Tone. A waterside path leads to French Weir – or you can take a boat trip. Vivary Park, named for the monastic fishponds (*vivaria*) which used to be there, stretches a mile out into the countryside – parts of it with flowerbeds and fountain, the rest a natural area. Near great St Mary's church (angels in its roof, an outstanding Perpendicular tower) are a number of craft studios and speciality shops. All around are interesting places to visit – picturesque villages (Bishop's Lydeard, Crowcombe, Combe Florey, Wiveliscombe), Blagdon Hill for views, the Palladian mansion of Hatch Court, steam railway to Minehead, Hornsbury watermill, the gardens at Hestercombe House, handsome Dunster Castle and, wherever you go, exceptional scenery: in summer, wisteria against old stone walls, fields of buttercups, willow-fringed streams and thatched cottages, ponds of swans and ducks, pinnacled and crocketed church towers soaring high (often built of orangey Ham stone), buttercrosses in market squares, imposingly pillared town halls, wayside inns and sunlight flickering through trees meeting over narrow lanes.

Readers' comments: Lovely position, beautiful garden. Quite exceptional treatment in lovely surroundings. The most welcoming and accommodating hostess we ever met. Tasty meals. Delighted.

Some proprietors stipulate a minimum stay of two nights at weekends or peak seasons; or they will accept one-nighters only at short notice (that is, only if no lengthier booking has yet been made).

OLD RECTORY
Wetherden, Suffolk, IP14 3LS   Tel: 01359 240144
North-west of Stowmarket. Nearest main road: A14 from Stowmarket to Bury St Edmunds.

3 Bedrooms. £20–£25 (less for 2 nights). Two have own bath/shower/toilet. Tea/coffee facilities. TV. Views of garden, country. No smoking. Washing machine on request.
1 Sitting-room. With open fire, central heating. Piano.
Large garden
Closed from December to February.

Readers who used the first edition of this book may have stayed with Mrs Bowden when she lived near Hadleigh. Now she has an equally elegant house here, into the decoration of which she has put the same tremendous amount of care.

The house, which dates from the 18th century, stands in extensive grounds (where sheep, horses and donkeys wander in summer). There is also a croquet lawn. One steps into a hall with stone floor, a piano in one alcove and pot-plants.

Up the deep pink and white staircase are elegant bedrooms – a particularly nice one is decorated in apricot with an antique brass bed and comfortable armchairs. Fine paintings, interesting fabrics and graceful curtains are features of this imaginatively renovated house. In the drawing-room is a wallpaper patterned with classical medallions. Pamela, a member of the Embroiderers' Guild, has made many of the furnishings herself: cushions, curtains, bed-hanging and sheets with broderie anglaise, for example.

Bed-and-breakfast only. For other meals, Pamela Bowden recommends local inns, such as the King's Arms at Haughley.

Central Suffolk, once forested, is now an area of wide open fields with prairie-size farms. Villages cluster around greens, big mediaeval houses like that at Parham are often moated – less for defence than to drain the site and provide a water-supply for the inhabitants (rainfall being low in this part of England). The area has had a turbulent history, hence the presence of so many castles (the one at Framlingham is outstanding, and so are the monuments in the church).

The many attractive villages include Debenham, threaded by a pretty stream and with rush-weaving to be seen; Eye, for the fine roodscreen in its church and the Minstrels' Gallery at the White Lion; Hoxne, scene of St Edmund's martyrdom at the bridge. Earl Soham, unusually leafy, has a great variety of architectural styles from every period; Saxtead Green, a working windmill. Yoxford is called the 'garden of Suffolk' because of the abundance of spring flowers at every cottage. The pretty Victorian seaside town of Southwold is an hour's drive away. Ickworth House (NT) is on the other side of Bury St Edmunds.

From Wetherden, so centrally situated, it is easy to motor to the coast and Ipswich (beyond it the seaside resort of Felixstowe), and even to Cambridge, Norwich and Colchester in adjacent counties.

Readers' comments: The ambience was delightful, the house beautifully furnished, the breakfast excellent. Outstanding, beautifully maintained. Welcoming atmosphere. Excellent. Kind, hospitable, friendly. A top-class place.

OLD VICARAGE

Affpuddle, Dorset, DT2 7HH   Tel: 01305 848315

East of Dorchester. Nearest main road: A35 from Dorchester to Poole.

3 Bedrooms. £17.50–£20. All have own bath/toilet. TV. Views of garden, country. Tea/coffee facilities and washing machine on request.
Light suppers if ordered, in winter.
Large garden

Before Anthea and Michael Hipwell moved here, it was an ambassador's country home: a handsome Georgian house with fine doorways, windows and fireplaces – surrounded by smooth lawns (with croquet) and rosebeds within tall hedges of clipped yew, the old church alongside.

Anthea has a flair for interior decoration. Even the corridors are elegant, with portraits and flower-prints on walls of apple-blossom pink. In one bedroom, the curtains are of ivory moiré, the bedspread patterned with rosebuds.

Breakfast is served in the prettiest dining-room in this book. Taking as the starting-point her collection of aquamarine glass (housed in two alcoves) and a series of modern lithographs in vivid turquoise, Anthea decorated the walls to match, and chose a dramatic turquoise curtain fabric reproduced from a Regency design in Brighton's Royal Pavilion. Against this all-blue colour scheme, the pale furniture shows to advantage. As no evening meal is provided, many visitors go to the Brace of Pheasants at Plush or the Martyrs at Tolpuddle.

The Old Vicarage is well placed for a stopover on the long journey (by A35) to the west country. The Hipwells lend walkers Ordnance Survey maps, and will advise guests on sightseeing possibilities.

Readers' comments: Very pleasant. Excellent service. Delightful hosts. Our favourite b & b. Delightful decor. Tea on the porch especially nice. Delightful house, charming hostess. Excellent in every way. Elegant and beautiful rooms.

Sir Ernest Debenham's plans for a picturesque model village outside Briantspuddle were halted by war in 1914, so its wide grass-verged main avenue, called Bladen Valley, leads nowhere. Among the thatched houses flanking the avenue is Beverley Stirling's **GARDEN COTTAGE**. In the big garden (where chickens roam at the end, and goat Hebe too), visitors have their own private annexe, prettily decorated. In the comfortable sitting/dining-room, its dresser laden with old

china finds, Beverley serves breakfasts and snack suppers. £16.50. [Tel: 01929 471287; postcode: DT2 7HP]

OLD VICARAGE

PT

Avebury, Wiltshire, SN8 1RF   Tel: 01672 539362
West of Marlborough. Nearest main road: A4361 from Swindon to Devizes
(and A4 from Marlborough to Chippenham).

3 Bedrooms. £19–£20 (less for 3 nights). One has own shower/toilet. Tea/coffee facilities. TV. Views of garden, country. No smoking. Washing machine on request.
Dinner. £15 for 3 courses and coffee, at times to suit guests. Less for 2 courses. Non-residents not admitted. Vegetarian or special diets if ordered. No smoking. **Light suppers** if ordered.
1 Sitting-room. With open fire, central heating, piano, record-player. No smoking.
Small garden

The prehistoric stone circles which surround picturesque Avebury village are even older than Stonehenge. Almost opposite the Norman church is the Old Vicarage, parts of which date back to the 17th century.

Jane Fry has a flair for interior decoration, so each room has beautiful colour schemes – even the blue-and-salmon kitchen, with tiled alcove for the blue Aga, 'dragged' kitchen units and festoon blinds. The front door opens into the canary dining-room with Chippendale chairs, window-seat in a bay, and Indian curtains embroidered with birds of paradise. Jane's collection of unusual blue-and-white china adorns the mantelpiece, and the woodblock floor is covered with Wilton and oriental rugs. The terracotta sitting-room, where pride of place goes to a handsome Broadwood concert grand piano, has a selection of comfortable arm-chairs and working shutters of stripped pine; it looks onto the walled garden with its begonia tubs and roses.

There is a deep buttoned velvet sofa in a small sitting-area upstairs, too, next to a very pretty primrose bedroom. Another room has bedheads lifted out of the ordinary by a peony decoupage, and an unusual carved wooden chair from India; the third (en suite) is dramatically decorated in deep pink and white toile de jouy with toning beribboned headboards and olive-green carpet.

Jane is an accomplished cook, serving such dinners as double cheese Swiss soufflé, salmon steaks with dill sauce, and chocolate mousse; she is also happy to recommend a variety of nearby eating-places, from worthwhile pubs to French restaurants.

Apart from magical Avebury itself, the area is steeped in prehistory with long barrows at West and East Kennett, ancient Silbury Hill, and a Neolithic camp at Windmill Hill; the Ridgeway path starts at Overton Hill a mile from Avebury, and passes Wayland's Smithy and the Uffington White Horse on its way – eventually – to Beacon Hill in Buckinghamshire. Less demanding walks might be along the fully restored Kennet & Avon Canal, or through Savernake Forest.

Reader's comment: Everything splendid.

> **Houses which accept the discount vouchers on page ii are marked with a V on the lists at the beginning of this book, see pages xi–xix and pages xxi–xxii.**

237

OLD VICARAGE

Higham, Suffolk, CO7 6JY   Tel: 01206 337248

North of Colchester. Nearest main road: A12 from Colchester to Ipswich.

3 Bedrooms. £20–£27 (less for 3 nights). Some have own bath/shower/toilet. Tea/coffee facilities. TV. Views of garden, country, river. Washing machine on request.
Light suppers sometimes. No smoking.
2 Sitting-rooms. With open fire, central heating, TV. No smoking.
Large garden

One of the most elegant houses in this book, the Old Vicarage stands near a tranquil village and is surrounded by superb views, with the old church close by. Everything about it is exceptional, from the Tudor building itself (its walls colour-washed a warm apricot), and the lovely furnishings, to the pretty south-facing garden – which has unheated swimming-pool, tennis and river boats (it's surprising that few families with children have discovered the house, particularly since the coast is near; Felixstowe and Frinton have sandy beaches).

Colonel and Mrs Parker have lived here for many years, and their taste is evident in every room. Lovely colours, pretty wallpapers and chintzes, antiques, flowers and log fires all combine to create a background of great style. In the breakfast-room, eight bamboo chairs surround a huge circular table (of mock-marble), and the walls have a trellis wallpaper the colour of watermelon. Bedrooms are equally pretty: one green-and-white with rush flooring; another has mimosa on walls and ceiling (its tiny windows are lattice-paned); the family room is in lime and tangerine. There are lace bedspreads, Indian watercolours, baskets of begonias – individual touches everywhere.

Bed-and-breakfast only; most visitors dine at the Angel, Stoke-by-Nayland.

Lynne, from the village, comes in to help and (herself a lively source of information) is evidently as greatly impressed as the visitors themselves with all that the Parkers do to help people enjoy their stay – information on sightseeing and eating-places, where to watch local wildlife, and so on.

Higham is very well placed for a great variety of activities and outings. One could easily spend a fortnight doing something totally different each day. There are Roman Colchester (lovely gardens on the ramparts), Constable's Flatford Mill and Dedham, the seaside, racing at Newmarket, sailing, the mediaeval villages and great churches of central Suffolk, tide-mill at Woodbridge, market and Gainsborough's house at Sudbury, and lovely villages. Beth Chatto's garden, Ickworth and East Bergholt Lodge attract garden-lovers.

Readers' comments: A firm favourite; superb and beautiful; hospitality outstanding. Perfect! Delightful weekend; privileged to be there. Excellent in every way. Most beautiful house. Very friendly. Thoroughly enjoyed it, superb. Very helpful. Food of highest standard, attention to detail outstanding. Splendid home and hospitality. Very interesting, friendly hostess, comfortable room.

OLD VICARAGE

C D PT

Mentmore, Buckinghamshire, LU7 0QG   Tel: 01296 661227
South of Leighton Buzzard. Nearest main road: A418 from Leighton Buzzard
to Aylesbury (and M1, junction 11).

2 Bedrooms. £20 (less for 3 nights). Both
have own bath/shower/toilet. Tea/coffee
facilities. TV. Views of garden, country.
Washing machine on request.
Dinner. £15 for 3 courses, wine and coffee,
at times to suit guests. Vegetarian or special
diets if ordered. **Light suppers** if ordered.
2 Sitting-rooms. With open fire, central
heating, TV, record- and CD-player.
Large garden

In the 1850s, the Rothschilds dotted this part of England with stately homes of
which 'Jacobethan' Mentmore Towers is one (others open to the public are
Ascott and Waddesdon; and Tring's museum houses the exceptional Rothschild
wildlife collection). Not only is the mansion a spectacular building in a commanding position but the estate for miles around was laid out in style, too: hence
the great grassy verges to the lane connecting the Towers to the nearest railway
station (close to the scene of the 'Great Train Robbery' in 1963). At much the
same time, this handsome stone vicarage was built.

It is now the home of the young Kirchner family who have furnished it in style
and with good colours everywhere: for instance, the book-lined study (with
satellite TV and a log stove) has cherry walls and carpet set off by white panelling
at the deep-set windows. In the large formal dining-room, Susie serves outstanding meals such as roasted tomatoes 'à la Saint Delia' (she is devoted to Delia
Smith's cookbooks) with home-made olive bread, chicken accompanied by
garden vegetables, apple flan with Barbados cream, and cheeses.

There is a second, large sitting-room with big windows, coal fire and antique
walnut furniture; and in the landscaped garden is an oval, heated swimming-pool.

Just across the Bedfordshire border, at
the foot of Dunstable Downs is the
village of Totternhoe and **GOWER
COTTAGE** (5 Brightwell Avenue),
well built in the 1920s in vernacular
style. Views are of Ivinghoe Beacon in
one direction, Adele Mardell's exceptionally pretty garden in the other.
Everything is pristine inside, Adele is a
most kindly hostess, and you will enjoy
such meals as ham-and-lentil soup,
lamb cutlets, sherry trifle, and cheeses.
On Totternhoe Knolls wild orchids
grow. Nearby Doolittle Mill is almost
unique – wind and water combined.
There are numerous old inns, you can
have a balloon ride, pop into north

London to shop at Ikea or the excellent Brent Cross shopping centre, go
to old Ampthill for its antique shops.
£16. [Tel: 01582 601287; postcode:
LU6 1QT]

239

OLD VICARAGE   C S

Morwenstow, Cornwall, EX23 9SR   Tel: 01288 331369
North of Bude. Nearest main road: A39 from Bude to Bideford.

3 Bedrooms. £20. All have own bath/shower/toilet. Tea/coffee facilities. Views of garden, country, sea. No smoking. Washing machine on request.
Dinner. £15 for aperitif, 4 courses, wine and coffee, at 7–7.30pm. Less for 2 courses. Non-residents not admitted. Vegetarian or special diets if ordered. No smoking. **Light suppers** if ordered.
2 Sitting-rooms. With open fire, central heating, TV, record-player. No smoking (in one). **Bar.**
Large garden
Closed in December and January.

Find Morwenstow church and you are within calling distance of the Old Vicarage, although you might think you are never coming to it as you descend the winding, wooded drive. Then, below, you will see the extraordinary chimneys of this splendid Victorian pile, each reputedly modelled on the tower of a church with which its first incumbent had been associated - except the kitchen's, which is apparently of the exact shape and dimensions of his mother's tomb. This eccentric builder, parson and poet was R.S. Hawker, who became vicar of Morwenstow in 1834. He was the author of several volumes of verses, of which the best-known, 'And Shall Trelawny Die?', has been adopted as a popular Cornish rugby song. One wonders how the author might react . . .

Jill and Richard Wellby have collected much information on their endearing predecessor and are happy to encourage guests' interest, providing a folder of local information in the cosy study. Indeed, their whole aim is to create an elegant and comfortable ambience for their visitors, while retaining such original features as the handsome slate-and-tile hall floor and the marble fireplace in the dining-room. The sitting-room is pink and grey, with claret velvet curtains and a carved stone fireplace. There is an old wind-up gramophone, complete with a 'master's voice' trumpet and a stock of 78s, in the mushroom-and-cream dining-room. Up the shallow staircase, all the bedrooms have arched windows and an individual style: one with a high old wooden bed, the others (one a pretty, blue single) with brass bedsteads. There is a three-quarter-size billiard-room up here, too, with a bar and a row of cinema seats lending a clubby atmosphere.

A typical dinner might comprise crab bisque, chicken in herbs, and summer pudding with Cornish cream, followed by cheese and biscuits.

A footpath runs from the grounds to the South-West Coastal Path; Tintagel is near, and the ancient holy well of St John still supplies the Old Vicarage with its pure water.

Readers' comments: Delightful, a mouthwatering place, a gastronomic feast.

Facts (prices, etc.) at the top of entries are supplied by the proprietors themselves. While every effort is made to ensure that these are correct at the time of going to press, they may alter thereafter: please check when you book.

OLD VICARAGE   **C**(10) **PT**

66 Church Square, Rye, East Sussex, TN31 7HF   Tel: 01797 222119

Nearest main road: A259 from Folkestone to Hastings.

6 Bedrooms. £20–£28 for a suite (less for 7 nights). Some prices go up from April, but **5% less to readers of this book staying 3 nights from April to October, excluding bank holidays.** Bargain breaks. Most have own shower/toilet. Tea/coffee facilities. TV. Views of country. No smoking. Washing machine on request.
Light suppers if ordered. Vegetarian or special diets.
1 Sitting-room. With central heating.
Small garden

This pink-and-white, largely 18th-century house is virtually in the churchyard, a peaceful spot since it is traffic-free and the only sound is the melodious chime of the ancient church clock (its pendulum hangs right down into the nave of the church). One steps straight into a very pretty sitting-room, yellow sofas complemented by Laura Ashley fabrics and prints. Curved windows, antiques and pot-plants complete the scene. Beyond is the breakfast-room.

The bedrooms are prettily decorated, mostly with pine furniture and flowery fabrics. Two have elegant four-posters. Those at the front have views of the church and its surrounding trees; others, of Rye's mediaeval roofscape. Henry James wrote *The Spoils of Poynton* while living here in 1896 with his fat dog, servants and a canary, before moving to nearby Lamb House. He said in a letter '. . . the pears grow yellow in the sun and the peace of the Lord – or at least of the parson – seems to abide here' (no pears now, but the rest is still true).

As only breakfast is served (and cream teas in the garden on sunny weekends), for dinner Julia Lampon recommends – out of Rye's many restaurants – the Landgate bistro, Flushing Inn or Old Forge. Julia will also do snack suppers (if ordered); and all guests are invited to a complimentary sherry with the Lampons in the evening.

There is a weekly sheep market and a general market. The Rye Heritage Centre features a sound-and-light show and an authentic town model. Romney Marsh (famous for its autumn sunsets and its spring lambs) attracts painters and birdwatchers. Rye itself was the setting for E. F. Benson's *Mapp and Lucia* stories. Benson lived in Georgian Lamb House after Henry James (it is now a National Trust property).

The town deserves a lingering visit to explore its cobbled byways, antique and craft shops and historic fortifications, for there are few places where a mediaeval town plan and original houses have survived so little altered. In addition there are in the area 20 castles, historic houses such as Kipling's Batemans, Ellen Terry's Smallhythe and (with fine gardens) Great Dixter, Sissinghurst and Scotney.

Readers' comments: Charming house, pretty rooms, friendly welcome. Outstanding. Charm and helpfulness of the owners gave us a perfect weekend. Very beautifully furnished and comfortable rooms. Friendly hosts. Fantastic – best breakfast I've ever had. Very friendly. Beautiful garden room. Huge and delicious breakfast.

OLD VICARAGE

PT

Leighton Road, Wingrave, Buckinghamshire, HP22 4PA   Tel: 01296 681235
North-east of Aylesbury. Nearest main road: A418 from Aylesbury to Leighton
Buzzard.

2 Bedrooms. £19 (less for 3 nights). Both have own bath/shower/toilet. Tea/coffee facilities. No smoking. Washing machine on request.
Dinner. £10 for 3 courses and coffee, at times to suit guests. Less for 2 courses. Non-residents not admitted. Vegetarian or special diets if ordered. No smoking. **Light suppers** if ordered.
1 Sitting-room. With open fire, central heating, TV, piano, record-player. No smoking.
Garden

Mallards and moorhens nest on the village pond in front of this 1840s house, a view enjoyed by one of the pleasant bedrooms; other rooms overlook the old-fashioned garden of lupins and roses at the back. Throughout, there are such handsome features as arched doorways and tall bay windows, which language teacher Jean Keighley has complemented with strong plain colours for the walls.

One passes through a golden-yellow hall to the pink sitting-room with its marble fireplace and grand piano. On the other side of the hall is a dining-room that has handsome mahogany furniture in period with the house; and here Jean serves such meals as home-made pâté, French classics like coq au vin (she lived in France for many years), English puddings (crumbles, tarts, etc.) and then cheeses.

Quite near London yet truly rural, Wingrave is surrounded by places of interest such as high Dunstable Downs (NT), Whipsnade, the Chiltern Hills, canals with boat trips near Tring, Saxon or Norman churches (the one at Dunstable is of considerable splendour), the gardens at Stowe and at Wrest Park, impressive beech woods and vistas of the Ashridge estate, Woburn Abbey and Mentmore Towers.

Towards Milton Keynes is **RICH-MOND LODGE**, high up at Mursley, which was built as a hunting-lodge in Edwardian times. Sedate, solid comfort still prevails: even the garden is formal, with immaculate lawn, stately blue cedar, croquet, lawn tennis and far views. Chris Abbey, once a hotel manager, sets high standards in all her rooms (one, in jade and strawberry, overlooks a lily-pool) and in the preparation of such meals as salmon mousse, pork chops with a celery and pineapple sauce, and summer pudding. Breakfast may be served among the fuchsias and clematis of a sunny patio. (No smoking.) Waddesdon Manor,

recently refurbished by the National Trust, is close. £18–£21.
Readers' comments: Most luxurious and comfortable. Charming, perfect room. Warm hospitality and care. Wonderful dinners. Strongly recommended. [Tel: 01296 720275; postcode: MK17 0LE]

OLD VICARAGE

C(5) **D S**

Yedingham, North Yorkshire, YO17 8SL Tel: 01944 728426
North-east of Malton. Nearest main road: A170 from Pickering to
Scarborough.

3 **Bedrooms.** £13–£18 (less for 7 nights).
Some have own shower/toilet. Tea/coffee
facilities. Views of garden, country. No
smoking. Washing machine on request.
Dinner (by arrangement). £8.50 for 3
courses and coffee, at 7pm. Vegetarian or
special diets if ordered. No smoking.
1 **Sitting-room.** With central heating, TV.
No smoking.
Large garden

Queen Anne's Bounty (a charity which subsidised poor livings) helped to fund
the renovation of this 18th-century house a hundred years ago: Henry Rayment
found the details and the architect's drawings in the glebe terrier (record of
parish-owned property) in the York diocesan archives. Henry (a land agent for
the largest local estate) and Joy have not had to do much fundamental work on
the house but to furnish and decorate it rather pleasantly.

Those architectural drawings hang on the pale green walls of the dining-area
at the foot of the staircase (re-orientated during the renovation). Here Joy can
serve straightforward evening meals, but the village inn almost opposite the house
– or plenty of others in the vicinity – offers dinners.

Bedrooms – each with a draped bedhead – overlook the Vale of Pickering with
the North York Moors in the background; nearer is the paddock where the
Rayments keep bees and their sheep graze.

The tiny village by the River Derwent is near walking country – you can be
driven to the start of whatever route you want – and not far from plenty of tourist
attractions for those who prefer motoring in unspoiled countryside: Castle
Howard is the best known, but there are many castles and mansions in the area,
including Ebberston Hall (two miles), reputedly the smallest mansion in England.
Malton is an old town with Roman remains and its own museum.

On the other side of Malton
at **RYDERS CORNER**, Crambe,
Maureen Hewitt offers bed and
breakfast only in her modernized 18th-
century cottage, with a well-tended
garden and a little land (with sheep
and free-range hens). There are smartly furnished bedrooms but only a small
sitting-area (from which to admire the
hilly view). The fine grounds of Sheriff
Hutton and famous Castle Howard are

not far. No smoking. £17.   [Tel:
01653 618359; postcode: YO6 7JR]

**When writing to the authors, if you want a reply please enclose a
stamped addressed envelope.**

243

OLD VICARAGE HOTEL   C D PT

Parc-an-Creet, St Ives, Cornwall, TR26 2ET   Tel: 01736 796124

Nearest main road: A30 from Redruth to Penzance.

8 Bedrooms. £17–£23 (less for 3 nights). Prices go up from April. Some have own bath/shower/toilet. Tea/ coffee facilities. TV. Views of garden.
Light suppers.
1 Sitting-room. With central heating, TV, record-player. **Bar.** Piano, etc.
Large garden
Closed from November to March.

Built of silvery granite in the 1850s, this hotel (among houses on the outskirts of St Ives) is entered via a small conservatory and a great iron-hinged door of ecclesiastical shape, which opens into a hall with red-and-black tiled floor. Mr and Mrs Sykes have done their best to preserve this period ambience, furnishing the bar with crimson-and-gold flock wallpaper and all kinds of Victoriana. There's a piano here, which occasionally inspires visitors to join in singing some of the old songs of that period. In addition, there are a sitting-room and a blue-and-gold dining-room. Big windows and handsome fireplaces feature throughout; and the Sykeses have put in excellent carpets, along with good, solid furniture – a 'thirties walnut suite in one bedroom, and velvet-upholstered bedheads. The Anna French fabrics and wallpapers were designed by the Sykeses' talented daughter, and many of the paintings in the house are hers too. There is a refurbished Victorian loo, preserved in all its glory of blue lilies and rushes.

Readers' comments: Beautifully restored; excellent in all aspects. Pleasant, and good value. Excellent in every way. Attention to detail outstanding. Cannot praise highly enough. So good, beautifully kept, warm welcome. Thoroughly recommended. Atmosphere most civilized, attention to detail impeccable.

At nearby Zennor is **BOSWEDNACK MANOR**, overlooking a magnificent headland. It is run in slightly Bohemian style by Graham and Elizabeth Gynn, former wardens of Skokholm Island nature reserve. Inside are Turkish hangings, bamboo furniture, stuffed birds, dragons painted on the dining-room's blue ceiling (conservatory beyond). Outside are three acres of grounds, a studio, a games room, open-air chess and a meditation room for visitors' use. Organic produce goes into the vegetarian meals. Visitors in the self-catering cottage may eat in. The Gynns offer bird-watching and archaeology holidays,

and guided walks. No smoking. £15–£18.
Readers' comments: A truly wonderful spot, quiet and comfortable. [Tel: 01736 794183; postcode: TR26 3DD]

244

OLIVER'S   C(10) **PT S X**
Church Street, Scawby, (Humberside), North Lincolnshire, DN20 9AH
Tel: 01652 650446
South-east of Scunthorpe. Nearest main road: A15 from Lincoln to Brigg
(and M180, junction 4).

3 Bedrooms. £17.50–£20 (less for 5
nights). All have own bath/shower/toilet.
Tea/coffee facilities. TV. Views of country.
No smoking. Washing machine on request.
Dinner. £12.50 for 4 courses (with
choices) and coffee, at 7pm. Less for
2 courses. Non-residents not admitted.
Vegetarian or special diets if ordered. No
smoking. **Light suppers** if ordered.
1 Sitting-room. With central heating.
Large garden

This 17th-century house in the village centre was once the post office. Within is a
cosy guests' lounge leading to the dining-room, traditionally furnished. Here
Hazel Oliver serves such meals as spiced hot grapefruit, chicken in white wine,
and raspberry-and-apple crumble. Derek Oliver, who practised as a surveyor until
recently, is an able watercolourist, and his framed pictures of the area are on
sale.

Bedrooms are sizeable; the largest has lemon walls, a flowered border and
velvet bedheads; another pale green walls with white furniture. There is a large
and pleasant garden.

The nearest town is Brigg, whose fair, at which gypsy horse-dealers used to
gather, has been commemorated in music by Delius. Cleethorpes is a traditional
seaside resort, with sandy beaches and one of the few remaining piers. Near it is
Grimsby, with a reconstruction of an Iron Age village and the new National
Fishing Heritage Centre. Westward of Scawby is the 'Isle' of Axholme, where John
Wesley's Epworth birthplace is open to the public. Bog oak is often ploughed up in
fields round here. Look out for the area's many windmills, some almost vanished
or incorporated into other buildings, a few in working order. Down a long, straight
road – surely Roman – is historic Lincoln with its grand cathedral.

To go over the enormous, modern suspension bridge that soars across the
Humber is an experience in itself; and on the other side are not only Beverley
and York, but that much undervalued city, Hull. Once a great port – particularly
in the heyday of whaling – it has perhaps the finest maritime museum outside
London, a fascinating area of old wharves and warehouses where once the
docks were busy with more than today's pleasure-craft, a church of considerable
splendour (almost the biggest in England), a notable collection in the Ferens
art gallery, the 17th-century house where Wilberforce was born (with a
museum about slavery and its abolition), and much, much more. A very
memorable city.

Equally undervalued are the Wolds which – on this side of the Humber – run
down into Lincolnshire and Tennyson country ('calm and deep peace on this
high Wold' he wrote of his birthplace). The rich pastures of these gentle hills are
threaded by lanes where now you rarely encounter another car; but they bear
traces of extensive prehistoric habitation, of Viking settlement and of mediaeval
prosperity. Here is Gainsborough (its tidal bore described in George Eliot's *Mill
on the Floss*), with the Old Hall where Richard III once stayed.

ORCHARD COTTAGE
Back Lane, Upper Oddington, Gloucestershire, GL56 0XL

C(5) D S

Tel: 01451 830785

East of Stow-on-the-Wold. Nearest main road: A436 from Stow-on-the-Wold towards Chipping Norton.

rear view

2 Bedrooms. £17.50–£18.50 (less for 3 nights). Bargain breaks. Both have own bath/shower/toilet. Tea/coffee facilities. Views of garden, country. No smoking.
Dinner. £14.50 for 3 courses and coffee, at 7–8pm. Less for 2 courses. Vegetarian or special diets if ordered. No smoking. **Light suppers** if ordered.
1 Sitting-room. With open fire, central heating, TV, record-player. No smoking.
Small garden
Closed from December to mid-February.

A few ancient apple-trees are all that remain of the great orchard which gave this 18th-century cottage its name. Originally two tiny dwellings, the house has been repeatedly modernized over the last two hundred years, most recently by its present owner, Jane Beynon. She has used soft colours in the rooms – for instance, creams and pinks in a bedroom with lace bedspread; rush-seated and spindle-backed chairs in the small dining-hall. The garden is her pride and joy.

A typical dinner might comprise spicy avocado; chicken in a creamy piquant sauce; local fruits or tangy lemon Dutch flummery. As an alternative to a cooked breakfast, she can provide cold meats and cheeses in continental style.

The Cotswolds are not too well provided with bus services, so Jane is one of a team of volunteers who drives a community minibus around eight villages and the town of Chipping Norton once a week. She gladly takes visitors along, or will provide routes for their own car tours. Stow-on-the-Wold merits unhurried exploration: it's a little town of antique and craft shops, restaurants and byways.

Readers' comments: Hospitable, outgoing and kind. Every comfort. Cooking, comfort, hospitality all first class. Outstanding meal and cheerful warmth. Accommodation and facilities excellent. Superb cooking. Very pleased. Very high standard. Extremely satisfied with high standard. Imaginative cooking, well presented. Kind and helpful. Delightful. A lovely place. Perfect in every way.

About a mile distant, in Bledington Road, Upper Oddington, is **FAIRVIEW FARMHOUSE**, the home of Susan and Andrew Davis. Sue, a fitness instructor, is also an accomplished cook. An evening meal might comprise home-made soup, then chicken in mushroom and wine sauce, and a sunken chocolate soufflé with Amaretto prunes to finish. (Light suppers too.) Bedrooms, all with their own bathrooms, are decorated in burgundies and pinks with draped canopies above the beds. Fair views

indeed – of rolling countryside to Icomb Hill. No smoking. £19–£22.
Reader's comment: Wonderful hosts. [Tel: 01451 830279; postcode: GL54 1AN]

ORCHARD FARMHOUSE

C D PT S

Mordiford, Herefordshire, HR1 4EJ   Tel: 01432 870253
South-east of Hereford. Nearest main road: A438 from Hereford to Ledbury.

3 Bedrooms. £16.50. Price goes up from April. Tea/coffee facilities. Views of garden, country, river. No smoking. Washing machine on request.
Dinner. £11.50 for 3 courses and coffee, at 7pm. Non-residents not admitted. Vegetarian or special diets if ordered. Wine available. No smoking. **Light suppers** if ordered.
2 Sitting-rooms. With open fire, central heating, TV. No smoking in one. Bar.
Large garden

Country antiques and Victorian china decorate this 17th-century house of reddish stone walls, inglenooks, flagged floors and beams. An old Norwegian stove (decorated with reindeer) warms the sitting-room. Pink and pine bedrooms with wicker armchairs have high ceilings and nice bathrooms; the dining-room has rush chairs and a dresser with more china dishes. Beyond woods at the back, the Black Mountains rise high. You may spot deer, foxes and even badgers; kestrels and buzzards; cowslips and violets – for the house is in an Area of Special Scientific Interest within the Wye Valley, itself an Area of Outstanding Natural Beauty.

Fishing can be arranged on the Wye, the Lugg or the Frome (all within a mile); guided walking holidays (from one to seven days) are available, and Ken James also runs driving courses (both learners' and advanced).

Angela specializes in good farmhouse cooking. With dinner – which might comprise home-made leek and potato soup, lamb cooked in cider, honey and rosemary, and home-made apple pie, for example – she offers you Herefordshire wine, cider or perry. Bread rolls are home-made; most produce is local.

Dining-room at Orchard Farmhouse, Mordiford

247

ORCHARD HOUSE

SX

Marton, North Yorkshire, YO6 6RD   Tel: 01751 432904
West of Pickering. Nearest main road: A170 from Kirkby Moorside to
Pickering.

3 Bedrooms. £15–£18 (less for 3 nights or
continental breakfast). Bargain breaks. All
have own bath/toilet. Tea/coffee facilities.
Views of garden, country. No smoking.
Washing machine on request.
Dinner. £11.50 for 3 courses (with choices)
and coffee, at 7pm. Less for 2 courses.
Vegetarian or special diets if ordered. Wine
available. No smoking. **Light suppers**
available.
1 Sitting-room. With open fire, central
heating, TV, record-player. No smoking.
Bar.
Large garden

The village of Marton is so neat and tidy that there is hardly even a parked car to
be seen by the wide grass verges that line the street – the residents voluntarily
leave them in a hidden carpark. Orchard House is one of the stone houses that
face each other across the street, with some of the old fruit trees to which it owes
its name still at the back (where there is a small self-catering cottage). It was built
in 1784 as a farmhouse and extended in the next century, when part was briefly a
shop.

Immediately inside the front door is the dining-room, with open fireplace.
Walls are painted terracotta, except for one which consists of an expanse of
stripped panelling. Behind one panel is the wine 'cellar', for Paul Richardson –
ex-art student, ex-paratrooper and ex-telecommunications engineer – is a
connoisseur. He is also a keen cook – producing such meals as grilled peppers
with fennel; stuffed pork fillet; and spiced pears.

There is a large, light sitting-room with walls of pale yellow, carpeted like the
rest of the ground floor with handsome woven sisal, and with well-filled bookshelves. Throughout the house, the interior design is particularly pleasant, which
is not surprising since Alison Richardson is an architect (she works for English
Heritage on the conservation of historic buildings). One bedroom, reached from
the sitting-room, has windows on two sides, those on one overlooking the long
garden. This goes down to the River Seven, where fishing is possible, and
includes a pond, a vegetable patch and a poultry run. Sometimes breakfast is
served on the terrace. This may include scrambled eggs with smoked salmon,
home-made jam and home-produced honey, and a choice of four teas and three
coffees.

Readers' comments: Standard of accommodation very high; too good to be
hidden from a wider audience. Quite exceptional; decorated with taste and style;
excellent and enthusiastic hosts; cooking to a high standard.

**Houses with short entries are just as good as ones with longer
descriptions; and they include some of the most popular houses in
the book. They may, however, have fewer rooms, a shorter season,
higher prices or fewer amenities (such as meals).**

ORCHARD HOUSE C P T S

High Street, Rothbury, Northumberland, NE65 7TL   Tel: 01669 620684
South-west of Alnwick. Nearest main road: A697 from Morpeth to Wooler.

6 Bedrooms. £20–£23 (less for 7 nights). Most have own shower/toilet. Tea/coffee facilities. TV. Views of garden, country. Washing machine on request.
Dinner. £13.50 for 4 courses and coffee, at 7pm. Non-residents not admitted. Vegetarian or special diets if ordered. Wine available. No smoking.
1 Sitting-room. With central heating. Bar.
Small garden
Closed from December to February.

Rothbury, a pleasant little market town with some interesting shops, stands in the very centre of Northumberland, and so many of the pleasures of that large and underestimated county are within an easy drive: the Roman wall to the south, Holy Island to the north, and in between countryside which can change from open moorland to woods and arable fields within a few miles, with picturesque villages and historic monuments for punctuation. Castles and peel towers (fortified farmhouses) remind one of border raiders.

Orchard House is Georgian. It stands well aside from Rothbury's bustling main street. Jeff and Sheila Jefferson took it over several years ago when Jeff left the RAF after years as an engineer (some of them spent in Malaysia) and have turned it into a comfortable and unpretentious place to stay. Like many people who provide good accommodation in relatively unknown spots, they have found that guests who stayed a night or two while passing through have returned for a longer holiday.

Sheila's four-course menus are out of the ordinary and varied, the only fixture being roast beef every Sunday. Otherwise you might get (for instance) salmon tartlets in filo pastry; turkey with almond and tarragon sauce; summer pudding; and cheese (local produce is used whenever possible). There is a cabinet well stocked with miniatures of drinks for you to help yourself and enter in a book.

The sight closest to Rothbury is Cragside, the mansion which Norman Shaw (best known, perhaps, for his government buildings in London) designed for Lord Armstrong, the armaments king. It is one of the most complete late-Victorian houses there are. Among the oddities are a Turkish bath and a hydraulic lift, but its main distinction is that it was the first house in the world to be lit by electricity. The grounds are elaborately landscaped.

Brinkburn Priory, Alnwick Castle, Wallington Hall and gardens are all near. Strange stone beasts' heads glare from the lawn in front of the last.

Readers' comments: A delightful couple. Outstanding food; rooms sparkling clean and spacious. Excellent food – first-rate value. Comfortable, spotless; we thoroughly endorse all you say. Excellent in every way. Very good food, everything of the highest standard. Marvellous food and accommodation. Our all-time favourite. Quite outstanding. Exceptionally comfortable; good, unpretentious food and service.

249

OVERCOMBE HOTEL   **C D M PT S X**
Old Station Road, Horrabridge, Devon, PL20 7RA   Tel: 01822 853501
South-east of Tavistock. Off A386 from Plymouth to Tavistock.

11 Bedrooms. £20–£26 (less for 2 nights).
Prices go up from June **except to readers
of this book.** Bargain breaks. All have own
bath/shower/toilet. Tea/coffee facilities. TV.
Views of garden, country.
Dinner. A la carte or £12.50 for 4 courses
(with choices) and coffee, at 7.30pm.
Vegetarian or special diets if ordered. Wine
available. **Light suppers** if ordered.
2 Sitting-rooms. With open fire, central
heating, TV. **Bar.**
Small garden

Conveniently placed for one to explore Dartmoor and the coast, the Overcombe
Hotel (now run by Brenda and Maurice Durnell) consists of two houses joined in
one to make a very comfortable small hotel. You can relax in either of the sitting-
rooms, according to what you want – a bar in one, TV in another, log fires, pleasant views. From the bay window of the dining-room, one looks across to the
moors. Bedrooms are pretty (two on the ground floor) and one has a four-poster.

There is always a selection of dishes on the menu with such choices as pear
and parsnip soup, salmon in filo pastry, traditional puddings and cheeses.

Visitors come here for a variety of reasons (the least of which is that it's a good
staging-post if you are on that long slog to furthest Cornwall). The Dartmoor
National Park attracts people touring by car, anglers, riders, golfers and – above
all – walkers (for them, Maurice organizes special two- to seven-day bargain
breaks, with experienced guides accompanying visitors on walks of eight miles or
more, and illustrated after-dinner talks about the moors). Plymouth is near; and
among visitors' favourite outings are Cotehele, Buckland Abbey and Saltram
House (all National Trust), Morwellham Quay and the Shire Horse Centre.

Further east lie the delectable South Hams: flowery valleys, sands, mildest of
climates. To the west is the Cornish coast: dramatic cliffs, sandy coves and some
harbours so picturesque (Polperro, Looe, etc.) that popularity threatens to ruin
them. But go inland, and you will still find undisturbed villages and towns.

Plymouth was heavily bombed, which means that its shopping centre is very
modern. But the old quarter, the Barbican, which Drake and the Pilgrim Fathers
knew so well, survived, and it is to this that visitors throng. Here are the old warehouses and the harbours full of small boats, the narrow alleys with beguiling little
shops and restaurants, the mediaeval houses now turned into museums, the fish
market and 17th-century citadel. Plymouth has an outstanding aquarium,
Drake's Island out in the Sound (to be visited by boat), the naval dockyard and
the famous clifftop – the Hoe – with its unique seascape, memorials and flowers.

Other local sights: the 15th-century cottage where Drake's wife grew up (at
Saltash); and the Garden House (Buckland Monachorum).

Readers' comments: A wonderful stay. Made us very welcome and could not
have been more delightful hosts. Excellent food, fresh vegetables daily.
Comfortable and warm. We will go again. A relaxed, easy atmosphere; we could
recommend this hotel to any of our friends. Quite perfect in every way.
Wonderfully imaginative cooking. Most comfortable. Probably the best so far for
welcome, food, organization.

PARADISE HOUSE   **C M PT**
88 Holloway, Bath, (Avon), Bath & North-East Somerset, BA2 4PX
Tel: 01225 317723
Nearest main road: A367 from Bath to Radstock (and M4, junction 18).

10 Bedrooms. £20 **to readers of this book**–£35 (less for 3 nights mid-week). Prices go up from April. Bargain breaks. Most have own bath/shower/toilet. Tea/coffee facilities. TV. Views of garden, country, city.
1 Sitting-room. With open fire, central heating.
Large garden

It stands half way up a steep, curving road which was once indeed a 'hollow way': a lane worn low between high banks by centuries of weary feet or hooves entering Bath from the south: the last lap of the Romans' Fosse Way. It is now a quiet cul-de-sac in the lee of Beechen Cliff, with panoramic views over the city, the centre of which is only 7 minutes' walk away – downhill. (As to uphill – take a taxi! Or else a bus to the Bear Flat stop.) Look the opposite way and all is leafy woods.

The house itself was built about 1720, with all the elegance which that implies: a classical pediment above the front door and well-proportioned sash windows with rounded tops in a façade of honey-coloured Bath stone.

David and Janet Cutting took it over many years ago and restored it impeccably throughout, stripping off polystyrene to reveal pretty plasterwork ceilings, for instance, and gaudy tiles to expose a lovely marble fireplace in which logs now blaze. They stripped dingy paint off the panelled pine doors and put on handles of brass or china. They furnished to a very high standard indeed, with both antique and modern furniture, elegant fabrics, and well-chosen colours, predominantly soft greens and browns. The sitting-room is especially pretty, with Liberty fabrics and wallpaper, pictures in maple frames and a collection of Coalport cottages. There is also a Jacuzzi. The bedrooms, given as much care as the rest, vary in size and amenities.

At the back, beyond a verandah with ivy-leaf ironwork, is quite a large walled garden (a sun-trap in the afternoon), with lawns, fish-pool, a rose-covered pergola and marvellous views of the city and hills all around. This secluded setting extends behind the mediaeval Magdalen Chapel next door, which was once a hostel for lepers banned from the city.

In 1982 David and Janet acquired the adjoining Georgian house, which they then completely restored, furnished and decorated to the same elegant standards as the main house. (Lock-up garages for a small fee; croquet and boules available.)

As to Bath itself – which attracts more visitors than any other place in England except London – the attractions are so varied that they can hardly be compressed into one paragraph. Just wandering among the Georgian perfection of its streets and squares, which spread from the historic centre right up the sides of the surrounding hills, and in its award-winning gardens, is a pleasure in itself, and it would take many days to explore them all (the best method is to take a bus to each hilltop in turn and walk back downhill).

Readers' comments: Top class! Truly excellent. Ideal, with excellent facilities. Superbly equipped, very attractive. Outstanding hotel. Extremely comfortable. Beautiful home; made us very welcome. Lovely house and garden.

PARK FARM   C(12) **X**

Spring Road, Barnacle, Warwickshire, CV7 9LG   Tel: 01203 612628
North of Coventry. Nearest main roads: M69 and M6 (junction 2).

2 **Bedrooms.** £18 (less for 5 nights or continental breakfast). Tea/coffee facilities. TV. Views of garden, country. No smoking. Washing machine on request.
Dinner. £12.50 for 3 courses (with choices) and coffee, at 7pm. Non-residents not admitted. Vegetarian or special diets if ordered. No smoking. **Light suppers** by arrangement.
1 **Sitting-room.** With open fire, central heating.
Large garden

The Roundheads burnt down the original house: several great Civil War battles took place in this region. This one was built about 1670. Outside it stand fine yews and within are such handsome features as the balustered staircase. All around is the 200-acre farm.

The house is immaculate, furnished with antiques and decorated in restful colours. In the green and cream sitting-room are flowery cretonnes and a small fireplace of pink marble. The big dining-room has windows at each end, and here Linda Grindal serves such meals as home-made pâté, chicken and broccoli casserole with dauphinoise potatoes, and blackcurrant shortcake. She began taking visitors almost by chance: some Australian farmers visiting the Royal Show at Stoneleigh in 1979 were desperate for accommodation, so she put them up. Having enjoyed this experience, she decided to do it regularly.

Upstairs are pleasant bedrooms – fine walnut beds in the yellow one, a prettily draped one in the pink room; and a very good bathroom.

The house is well placed for visiting the cathedral at Coventry; Warwick Castle and Stratford-upon-Avon are only 25–35 minutes away; and there are plenty of fine houses to visit – such as Charlecote and other National Trust properties, and Arbury House near Nuneaton (George Eliot territory). Ryton Organic Garden Centre attracts some visitors.

Readers' comments: Just like being in your own home. Extremely well cared for. Wonderful dinner, wicked breakfasts. The Grindals are delightful. Pleasurable experience. Comfortable, food excellent. Family charming, accommodation first class. Pretty home, gracious host.

PARKFIELD HOUSE

C S

Hogben's Hill, Selling, Kent, ME13 9QU   Tel: 01227 752898
South of Faversham. Nearest main road: A251 from Faversham to Ashford
(and M2, junctions 6/7).

5 Bedrooms. £16–£17.50 (less for 2 nights). Views of garden, country. No smoking.
Light snacks.
1 Sitting-room. With open fire, central heating, TV. No smoking.
Large garden

There were Hogbens on this hill in 1086 (they are named in the Domesday Book) . . . and there still are!

It is Mr and Mrs Hogben who own Parkfield, a largely modern house with a pretty garden, as well as the small joinery works alongside – John Hogben's principal activity. It is worth staying at Parkfield House simply to listen to him talk about Kentish ways and history (especially his stories of past Hogbens, who were blacksmiths, farmers, wheelwrights and smugglers). Next door there used to be an inn called Ye Olde Century in memory of a John Hogben who lived there until he died when he was 101.

The house, built in 1820, had become run down until about 40 years ago when Mr Hogben renovated and extended it. Now it is immaculate and very comfortable. In the sitting-room are big, velvet armchairs in which to relax by a log fire. And if you want something special for breakfast Mrs Hogben will get it.

Selling is in a very beautiful and tranquil part of Kent, well situated for touring and the Channel ports. It is, of course, the cathedral which brings most visitors to nearby Canterbury: one of Britain's finest and most colourful.

Readers' comments: Excellent in all respects, exceptional hospitality. Excellent service, well cared for. Warm welcome. Spotless. Attractive bedroom.

Having taken early retirement, Alan Brightman, with his wife Annette, moved to **THE GRANARY**, a converted oasthouse in Plumford Lane, near Faversham, a quiet byway in the midst of apple-orchard country. A comfortable sitting-room, with exposed beams and richly coloured stripped pine floors, opens onto a large balcony running the length of the house, where guests can sit in warm weather. Rooms (all with own bathrooms) are boldly decorated in simple blues and whites. The family room has a particularly spacious bathroom. The Brightmans are keen golfers and can arrange for guests to play at the local Belmont

course. Supper trays by arrangement, but there is good local eating too. No smoking. £18–£19.50.
Readers' comments: A delightful home. Everything we could hope for. The warmest welcome. Superb, ideal hosts. [Tel: 01795 538416; postcode: ME13 0DS]

PEACOCK FARMHOUSE

C D M PT X

Redmile, Leicestershire, NG13 0GQ   Tel: 01949 842475

West of Grantham. Nearest main road: A52 from Nottingham to Grantham.

10 Bedrooms. £20–£22.50 (less for 7 nights). **Less 10-50% for Sundays to readers of this book.** Some have own shower/toilet. Tea/coffee facilities. Views of garden.
Dinner. A la carte or £13.50 for 3 courses (with choices) and coffee, at 7.15pm. Vegetarian or special diets. Wine available. No smoking. **Light suppers.**
1 Sitting-room. With central heating, TV, piano. **Bar.**
Large garden

This guest-house with restaurant (built as a farm in the 18th century and later a canal bargees' inn) is ideal for a break when doing a long north-south journey on the nearby A1, particularly with children – or as a base from which to explore the many little-known attractions of Nottinghamshire and adjacent counties.

It is in the outstandingly beautiful Vale of Belvoir, with the Duke of Rutland's Belvoir Castle (full of art treasures) rearing its battlemented walls high above a nearby hilltop: an unforgettable sight. The topiary yew peacock on the front lawn, started in 1812, was inspired by the peacock in the crest of the Duke.

The Needs have created a happy family atmosphere here. Four upstairs rooms have views of Belvoir Castle, while others on the ground floor (with en suite bathrooms) include a self-contained pine cabin and a coach house outside the main building. Children can safely play in the garden which has a large lawn, hammock, swings, small covered swimming-pool, playroom, pool-room, bicycles, barbecue, and farm pets. Indoors are snooker and table tennis.

Food is above average, with home-made bread and soups, herbs from the garden and much local produce. Starters may include trout and cream cheese terrine or herb and beansprout omelette; main courses, beef and venison carbonnade or salmon with sorrel sauce; puddings, fresh fruit pavlova and 'tipsy' bread-and-butter pudding.

There are many popular sights in this region: Belvoir Castle, Belton House, Stapleford Park, Rutland Water and Wollaton Hall in its park; also Holme Pierrepont Hall, Doddington Hall, and Newstead Abbey (Byron's home). Eastwood has D.H. Lawrence's birthplace. Lincoln (cathedral), Southwell (minster), Sherwood Forest (Robin Hood display) and Nottingham are also near – the last a much underrated city. There is an arts museum in the castle and others at its foot (the lace museum is fascinating), river trips and walks through the Georgian quarter. The historic market towns of Stamford (in particular) and Newark are of great interest. One can shop for local Stilton, crafts and Nottingham lace to take home – Melton Mowbray is famous for pies and other pork delicacies.

Readers' comments: Good food, delightful hosts. Helpful, very nice people. Comfortable.

PEACOCK HOUSE   **C D S X**

Peacock Lane, Old Beetley, Norfolk, NR20 4DG   Tel: 01362 860371
or 01760 24172

North of East Dereham. Nearest main road: A47 from East Dereham to
Norwich.

3 Bedrooms. £17–£18. All have own
bath/shower/toilet. Tea/coffee facilities. TV.
Views of garden, country. No smoking.
Light suppers if ordered.
1 Sitting-room. With open fire, central
heating, TV, piano, record-player. No
smoking.
Large garden

rear view

Once a farm, the tranquil house hides its Elizabethan beams behind a façade
added in Victorian times. On arrival, guests are taken by Jenny Bell into their own
little sitting-room with cretonne chairs facing a log stove and given home-made
flapjacks or scones with tea. In another, larger sitting-room an open fire blazes on
cold days – or when it is sunny you may prefer to wander out to the large lawn,
with old apple-trees and a pond, surrounded by fields with the Bells' sheep and
chickens (lambs among the daffodils in spring).

Upstairs are rooms with impressively handsome brass beds, sprigged wallpaper
matching the curtains, exposed timbers, and a really huge bathroom (carpeted,
with pine fitments and flowery wallpaper).

Breakfasts are both generous and varied (home-produced eggs and local
sausages are very popular with guests); and as to dinner, the Bells will either ferry
you to and from a local inn or, by arrangement, serve you a snack.

Readers' comments: Truly rural. Wonderful welcome. Spared no efforts in caring
for our comfort. Tastefully furnished; lovely room.

Bedroom at Edgehill Hotel (see page 92)

PEAR TREE COTTAGE

C(3) **M PT**

Church Road, Wilmcote, Warwickshire, CV37 9UX   Tel: 01789 205889
North-west of Stratford-upon-Avon. Nearest main road: A3400 from
Stratford to Birmingham (and M40, junction 15).

7 **Bedrooms.** £19–£22.50 (less for 7
nights). All have own bath/shower/toilet.
Tea/coffee facilities. TV. Views of garden,
country. Washing machine on request.
2 **Sitting-rooms.** With central heating,
TV.
Large garden

Mary Arden, Shakespeare's mother, grew up in the big half-timbered house which
overlooks this cottage of much the same date. It now holds a museum of rural
life.

Pear Tree Cottage, too, is half-timbered. From its flowery garden one steps
into a hall with stone-flagged floor, oak settle, other antiques and bunches of dried
flowers. The floor is of blue lias, once quarried at Wilmcote, and to be seen also in
Stratford's famous Clopton Bridge and the steps of St Paul's Cathedral in London.

In the beamed dining-room, country Hepplewhite chairs and colourful
Staffordshire pottery figures show well against rugged stone walls. There's a little
television room and a pretty reading-room opening onto the gardens. Bedrooms
(reached by steps and turns all the way) have very pleasant colour schemes. Some
are in a new extension.

Outside are two gardens, a stream, a pool with pink waterlilies, stone paths
and seats under old apple-trees. Although Margaret Mander does not serve
evening meals, there are kitchens in which guests can prepare their own snack
suppers, and two inns serving good food in the village.

Readers' comments: Ideal in all respects. Have always received most kind and courteous attention and a wonderful breakfast. Thoroughly enjoyed every stay. Very
friendly.

In Stratford-upon-Avon itself is
HARDWICK HOUSE, 1 Avenue
Road – a quiet residential part of the
town. Built in 1887, it is a guest-house
of high standard run by the Wootton
family. Bedrooms vary, but most are
spacious – particularly those on the
ground floor. In an airy dining-room,
substantial snacks are served. There
is only a small sitting-reception
room but, perhaps more important
in Stratford, there is a carpark.
Furnishings are conventional and comfortable, everything is spick-and-span,
and Drenagh is a hospitable hostess.

The house is only a few minutes'
walk from Shakespeare's birthplace,
the coach terminus, and the start of
round-Stratford guided tours by
open-top bus. £18–£28. [Tel: 01789
204307; postcode: CV37 6UY]

PETER BARN   C(5)
Cross Lane, Waddington, Lancashire, BB7 3JH   Tel: 01200 28585
(Messages: 01200 22381)
North-west of Clitheroe. Nearest main road: A59 from Preston to Clitheroe.

3 Bedrooms. £18–£22 (less for 3 nights). Bargain breaks. All have own bath/shower/toilet. Tea/coffee facilities. TV. Views of garden, country. No smoking. Washing machine on request.
Light suppers if ordered.
1 Sitting-room. With open fire, central heating, TV, balcony.
Large garden

Cross Lane – locally known as Rabbit Lane for obvious reasons – is a single-track road that runs through a tunnel of trees near the village of Waddington. Peter Barn was indeed a barn until the Smiths turned it into a family home; now they use the upper floor exclusively for guests. The large, airy sitting-room is reached by an open-tread staircase and has a roof made of old church rafters. By a stone fireplace are leather-covered settees and armchairs, near the head of the staircase is the breakfast-table, and off the other end of this well-proportioned space are the bedrooms and bathroom. (The arrangement is such that a large family would have the use of a virtually self-contained flat.) Much of the furniture consists of antiques, and there is some interesting bric-a-brac, as well as verdant houseplants.

Jean Smith has the greenest of fingers, for the one-acre garden is a remarkable achievement, having been a field when the house was converted 15 years ago. Now it is beautifully landscaped and lovingly tended.

There is no shortage of places for an evening meal, not least in Clitheroe, the lively market town a couple of miles away.

The Smiths also organize special weekend breaks to coincide with interesting local activities and 'hibernation' weekends from January to March.

Readers' comments: Beautiful conversion. Homely and friendly atmosphere. Hope to visit again – a wonderful experience. A superb stay. Highlight of our holiday. Like being entertained by good friends. A visit is pure pleasure; can't wait to return.

Sitting-room at Low Hall (see page 184)

PETHILLS BANK COTTAGE   C(5) **M**
Bottomhouse, Staffordshire, ST13 7PF   Tel: 01538 304277
(Messages: 01538 304555)
South-east of Leek. Nearest main road: A523 from Leek towards Ashbourne.

3 Bedrooms. £19–£20.50 (less for 3 nights or continental breakfast). All have own bath/shower/toilet. Tea/coffee facilities. TV. Views of garden, country. No smoking.
Dinner. £16.50 for 4 courses (with choices) and coffee, at 7.30pm. Non-residents not admitted. No smoking. **Light suppers** if ordered.
1 Sitting-room. With central heating. No smoking.
Small garden
Closed in January and February.

This 18th-century farmhouse, much modernized, stands in landscaped gardens on the crest of a hill, at the edge of the Peak District. The thick and rugged stone walls are exposed to view in a snug sitting-room which was once a cowshed – now soft lighting falls on pinky-beige chesterfields of buttoned velvet, and from the big window there is a view of the Martins' rock garden. In the dining-room are carved Dutch chairs upholstered in green velvet and a log stove on a tiled hearth.

One particularly pretty bedroom, on the ground floor, has its own verandah overlooking the hills, silky draperies and a private sitting-room. Up an open-tread stair are more bedrooms, one in a former hayloft. Each has its own style: for instance, bamboo sofa in a room of peach and green; louvred cupboards, onyx Vanitory and briar-rose patterns in the other.

Yvonne's dinners (available on only some evenings) include such dishes as pasta, trout en croûte, chocolate cheesecake, cheese with fruit.

Apart from visiting the Peak District, Dovedale and the Manifold Valley from here, you can explore lesser-known Derbyshire and the much underrated north of Staffordshire. In the south the scenery is pastoral, with calm rivers. Derby city has an 18th-century quarter and other historic buildings, many parks, and Kedleston Hall – an Adam mansion. Alton Towers – an exceptional leisure park – is near.

Six towns make up the 'Ceramic City' of Stoke-on-Trent containing Coalport, Spode, Wedgwood and other well known potteries. Closer are the many antique and mill shops of the interesting town of Leek, surrounded by moorlands. Lichfield has a cathedral and Denby pottery; Tutbury, Smedley knitwear mills (bargains!). The M6 will take you south to Dudley and one of the region's most popular attractions – the open-air Black Country Museum of bygone industries.

Readers' comments: Made most welcome, well looked after. Warm and cheerful hostess. Excellent cook. Nothing was too much trouble. Very attractive lounge, extremely attentive service. Warm and friendly, very helpful. Excellent in every way and very good value. Breakfast here surpasses all others.

Prices are per person in a double room at the beginning of the year.

PHEASANT INN   C D M PT S

Stannersburn, Northumberland, NE48 1DD   Tel: 01434 240382
North-west of Hexham. Nearest main road: A68 from Corbridge to Jedburgh
(Scotland).

8 Bedrooms. £20–£26 (less for 7 nights).
Prices go up from June. Bargain breaks. All
have own shower/toilet. Tea/coffee facilities.
TV. Views of garden, country. No smoking.
Washing machine on request.
Dinner. £15 for 4 courses (with choices)
and coffee, at 7–9pm. Less for 3 courses.
Vegetarian or special diets if ordered. Wine
available. No smoking. **Light suppers.**
2 Lounge bars. With open fires, central
heating.

Close to Kielder Water, this is everything one wants a country inn to be – nearly
four centuries old, stone-walled and low-beamed and in particularly lovely
countryside. The Kershaws are determined to keep it unspoilt. The bedrooms,
however, are modern, in a former hemel (farm implements store) and barn;
many of them are on the ground floor.

The main bar (where very good snacks are served) is big and beamy, with a
stone fireplace and some agricultural bygones, such as hay-knives and peat-
spades; and a stuffed pheasant appropriately sits on the window-sill.

The dining-room is light and airy, with raspberry-coloured walls and pine
furniture. Food is freshly prepared – one interesting starter is avocado with
grapefruit and Stilton; trout comes with a sauce of yogurt and herbs.

Stannersburn is in the southern part of the Border Forest Park – 200 square
miles of hills and moors that stretch from Hadrian's Wall to Scotland.

Readers' comments: It's super. A very good welcome. Delicious breakfast. Such
a wonderful start to our holiday. Delightful country inn. Mr Kershaw and
his family could not have been more friendly and courteous, our room was
delightful and spotlessly clean, and the food was truly delicious – we look forward
to a return. A real pub, very good food, friendly and helpful staff.

MANTLE HILL, Hesleyside, near
Bellingham, is a 17th-century farmhouse with well-proportioned rooms
and two acres of fine gardens. These
provide most of the fruit and vegetables which Charlotte Loyd uses for
the dinners she provides by arrangement; and the farm, run by her
husband, provides the lamb and beef.
As he is also in the wine business, the
short wine list is well chosen. Close by,
the River North Tyne (in which fishing
is often possible) runs through peaceful, well-wooded country – at its most
beautiful in May. In the nearby
mansion, a reiver family (bandits, now
reformed!) has lived for 650 years.
Views from all rooms are magnificent.
£18–£24.

Readers' comments: Jewel in the crown
of this area. A feeling of warmth
and friendship. Most attractive house,
wonderful setting. Never felt more at
home. Made very welcome, food
delicious. [Tel: 01434 220428; postcode: NE48 2LB]

PICKFORD HOUSE   C M PT S X
Bath Road, Beckington, Somerset, BA3 6SJ Tel: 01373 830329
South of Bath. Nearest main road: A36 from Bath to Warminster.

4 Bedrooms. £15–£17.50 (less for 4 nights). Bargain breaks. Some have own bath/shower/toilet. Tea/coffee facilities. TV. Views of garden, country. No smoking. Washing machine on request.
Dinner. £12 for 3 courses and coffee, from 7pm. Non-residents admitted by arrangement. Vegetarian or special diets if ordered. Wine available. **Light suppers** if ordered.
2 Sitting-rooms. With open fire, central heating, TV, piano, record-player. Bar.
Garden

Sometimes parties of friends take the whole of this hilltop house for a gourmet weekend together – for Angela Pritchard is a cordon bleu cook.

On such weekends, the guests are invited to enjoy a Somerset cream tea to be followed later by a candlelit dinner of 6 courses with appropriate wines. On the next day, they explore the area's attractions (on their own or with the Pritchards at the helm) before another gourmet meal. There is a heated swimming-pool in which to pass the time before a Sunday lunch.

Even on everyday occasions Pickford House food is exceptional. Angela offers the choice of a 4-course dinner or what she calls a 'pot-luck' one of 3 courses. Dishes might include: mushroom roulade, lamb en croûte, mulberry mousse (made from garden fruit) and cheeses.

The house is one of a pair that were built from honey-coloured Bath stone in 1804. The furnishings are comfortable with two modern bedrooms in the old school house (one with kitchen adjoining). In addition to the main sitting-room, there is a family room (TV and toys).

Readers' comments: Absolutely superb; food was excellent, hospitality outstanding. Delightful people, meals delicious. Excellent: accommodation and dinner beyond praise. Welcome relaxed, warm and personal. Great care to make us comfortable. First class. Beautifully decorated, very peaceful area. Excellent; remarkable value, especially the evening meal. B & b at its best. Sheer delight; meals superb.

In Charlton, nestling in the Somerset hills near Radstock, south of Bath, is **MELON COTTAGE VINEYARD** from the 200 vines of which come about a thousand bottles of dry white wine each year (go in October to see the harvest, and in spring for the bottling). It is known that the Romans, too, had vineyards in the area. The Pountneys are great linguists. Their cottage has 39-inch stone walls, parts dating from mediaeval times. There are small stone-mullioned windows; one large bedroom is under the exposed rafters of the roof. (Light suppers by

arrangement, or the Somerset Wagon in Chilcompton serves excellent meals.) £14–£16.
Readers' comments: Very comfortable. Excellent hospitality. Made very welcome. [Tel: 01761 435090; postcode: BA3 5TN]

PILLMEAD HOUSE
North Lane, Buriton, Hampshire, GU31 5RS   Tel: 01730 266795
South of Petersfield. Nearest main road: A3 from Petersfield to Portsmouth.

C D PT S

2 Bedrooms. £19–£20 (less for 3 nights). Tea/coffee facilities. TV. Views of garden, country. No smoking. Washing machine on request.
Dinner. £13 for 4 courses (with choices) and coffee, at 7pm (not Sundays). Less for 2 courses. Vegetarian or special diets if ordered. No smoking. **Light suppers** if ordered.
1 Sitting-room. With open fire, central heating. No smoking.
Large garden

The lozenge-paned windows and brick-and-flint walls are typical of many houses in this area, but the Tudor chimneys – very elaborate, and 8 feet high – came from a mansion. The house overlooks a valley, its lawn and rock garden descending steeply among terraced beds of roses and lavender. Visitors can enjoy a view of the Queen Elizabeth country park and Butser Hill while drinking their after-dinner coffee in the garden.

The dining-room's bow windows, too, make the most of the view. This is a pretty room, with pink wildflower curtains and Victorian mahogany furniture.

Upstairs, white walls contrast with moss-green carpets. One bedroom, cottage-style, has pink fabrics and patchwork cushions; in another primrose predominates, with a patchwork bedspread and cushions.

Sarah Moss serves such meals as soufflé, free-range chicken, and fresh fruit compote, using much produce from her large kitchen garden.

In Buriton, a picturesque downland village, are a Norman church and a pond. All around are pleasant walks; and, a few miles away, the historic towns of Portsmouth, Chichester and Winchester.

Readers' comments: Excellent: our second visit. Magnificent dinners, an inspired cook. A lovely cook, always makes us most welcome.

There really are toads at **TOAD'S ALLEY** in South Lane on the other side of Buriton, home of interior designer Patricia Bushall. They can sometimes be seen heading to the stream which lies between the garden and the crest along which walkers follow the South Downs Way. The secluded house comprises three tiny farmworkers' cottages built in the 15th century, with brick-floored hall and low-sloping ceilings upstairs. Both bedrooms have splendid views of sheep grazing on the hillside. A sitting-room for guests is attractively furnished, like the other rooms, with pale colours.

Meals are taken at a handsome, oval table of oak. A typical dinner menu might include stuffed tomatoes, lemon and lime pork, and pancakes. £16–£18 (b & b). [Tel: 01730 263880; post-code: GU31 5RU]

261

PINDARS

Lyminster, West Sussex, BN17 7QF   Tel: 01903 882628
South of Arundel. Nearest main road: A27 from Chichester to Brighton.

3 Bedrooms. £16–£20 (less for 3 nights). Bargain breaks. Some have own shower/toilet. Tea/coffee facilities. TV. Views of garden, country. No smoking. Washing machine on request.
Dinner. £11 for 3 courses (with choices) and coffee, at 7pm (not Sundays). Non-residents not admitted. Vegetarian or special diets if ordered. No smoking. **Light suppers** if ordered.
1 Sitting-room. With open fire, central heating, TV. No smoking.
Garden

The Newmans themselves designed this attractive house on the road between Littlehampton and historic Arundel, with its castle and cathedral.

Some of the light, bright bedrooms overlook the beautiful garden at the back, where stonework contrasts with beds that brim with flowers and shrubs (there is a swimming-pool too); and the sitting-room – furnished with antiques – opens onto it. Garden produce goes into such meals as mushroom-and-spinach soup, chicken in a pimento sauce, and apple crumble with home-made ice cream: Jocelyne loves cooking. Breakfast may include kedgeree or fishcakes; preserves and scones are home-made.

Sunny rooms are furnished with Paisley sofas, Victorian miniatures and other characterful touches, and the Newmans have a variety of paintings collected when they ran an art gallery in Arundel.

Readers' comments: Warm welcome, delightful room. Artistically decorated, very comfortable, much care and attention to detail. Superior ambience, facilities and service. Made very welcome. Immaculate. Delicious food.

Along Church Lane, Lyminster, is **ARUNDEL VINEYARDS** – one of 30 such now flourishing in the south-east. Its owner, genial John Rankin, takes b & b guests in his house where, behind a simple frontage, is found excellent accommodation. Sheep, goats, speckled hens, guinea-fowl and, of course, the vineyard (with tastings) add to the interest of staying in this peaceful spot; together with the Saxon church, the Knuckerhole (the 'bottom-less' pool where St George is said to

have slain a dragon), the coast and Arundel Castle, which are all near. £18–£19. [Tel: 01903 883393; post-code: BN17 7QG]

Book well ahead: many of these houses have few rooms. Do not expect dinner if you have not booked it or if you arrive late.

PIPPS FORD

C(5) D M PT S

Needham Market, Suffolk, IP6 8LJ Tel: 01449 760208

North of Ipswich. Nearest main road: A14 from Ipswich to Bury St Edmunds.

6 Bedrooms. £17–£32.50 (less for 4 nights). All have own bath/shower/toilet. Tea/coffee facilities. Views of garden, country, river. No smoking. Washing machine on request.
Dinner. £16 for 3 courses (with choices) and coffee, at 7.15pm (not Sundays). Less for 2 courses. Vegetarian or special diets if ordered. Wine available. **Light suppers** by arrangement.
3 Sitting-rooms. With open fire, central heating, TV, video, piano, record-player.
Large garden
Closed from mid-December to mid-January.

On a stretch of the River Gipping that has been designated an Area of Outstanding Natural Beauty stands a large Tudor farmhouse. Raewyn Hackett-Jones has made patchwork quilts or cushion-covers for every room and searched out attractive fabrics (Laura Ashley, French ones and so on) for curtains or upholstery. She puts flowers in each bedroom. Many of the beds are collectors' pieces: a four-poster, a French provincial one and several ornamental brass beds. Oriental rugs cover floors of wood or stone. Even the bathrooms attached to each bedroom are attractive. One is spectacular, with a huge oval bath. Some bedrooms are in converted stables, with sitting-room.

This is a house of inglenook fireplaces, sloping floors, low beams and historic associations, for it once belonged to Tudor chronicler Richard Hakluyt. There are three sitting-rooms and in one visitors can enjoy the family's huge collection of records. Meals may be served in a flowery conservatory, grapes overhead.

Breakfasts are exceptional. From an enormous choice, you could select exotic juices; home-made sausages or black pudding; home-made yogurt, croissants or cinnamon toast; waffles, crumpets, muffins; kidneys, mackerel, fishcakes.

Popular dinner dishes include avocado and smoked salmon baked with cheese; breast of duck with port; a roulade of salmon, turbot and spinach; fillet of beef; home-made ice creams; traditional puddings and tropical fruits.

Beyond the garden (with croquet and tennis), there is coarse fishing in the river, where cricket-bat willows grow, and a Roman site. Interesting places to visit by car are Constable country, Aldeburgh and Ipswich.

Readers' comments: Most impressed; made very welcome; food absolutely super; most hospitable place; relaxed and informal, thoroughly happy and comfortable; delightful house, beautifully furnished; food and service outstanding; one of the best holidays ever; friendly good humour. A fitting climax to our wonderful trip with your book. Charming and talented hostess, food beautifully garnished.

1997 has been designated Britain's 'Year of Opera and Musical Theatre'; and it is the East of England which has received the top accolade for its programme of events then (the runners-up were Devon & Cornwall and, in Yorkshire, Leeds). So music-lovers need to book early there!

PORCH FARMHOUSE

C(12) D PT S X

Grindon, Staffordshire, ST13 7TP Tel: 01538 304545
South-east of Leek. Nearest main road: A523 from Leek to Ashbourne.

3 Bedrooms. £18.50 **to readers of this book only** (less for 7 nights). Price goes up in March. Bargain breaks. All have own bath/shower/toilet. Tea/coffee facilities. TV. Views of garden, country. No smoking. Washing machine on request.
Dinner. £16 for 5 courses and coffee, at 7pm. Non-residents not admitted. No smoking. Vegetarian or special diets if ordered. **Light suppers** if ordered.
1 Sitting-room. With central heating. No smoking.
Garden

Known by locals as the 'village on the road to nowhere', Grindon lies 1000 feet high, above the Peak District's lovely Manifold Valley. Sally Hulme, previously a primary school teacher, and her husband Ron, an ex-Commando, came upon the village on a walking tour and moved to this large 500-year-old limestone cottage some 13 years ago.

Bought from the Burton Abbey estate in the 1600s by one John Port – the house name is a corrupted version of his – this beamed cottage is comfortable and smartly furnished. A complimentary pre-dinner sherry is served in the sitting-room which has well-sprung sofas, pink-patterned walls and small antiques. Meals are taken in the dining-room hung with Victorian 'lace' plates, and a lovely old oak dresser displaying a collection of glass and silver. A typical menu might comprise melon with smoked salmon followed by carrot and coriander soup, then marinated breast of chicken, a choice of local cheeses and finally apricot and apple tart with home-made ice cream. Traditional breakfasts are complemented by a good choice of fresh and dried fruits.

Bedrooms, all with modern facilities, are decorated in cottage style: one with peony and rose wallpaper and curtains and another with blue and pink sprigged paper and a locally made star-patterned bedspread. Another has a stylish writing-desk made to Sally's own design.

Despite the village's isolated position, it lies only three miles from a National Express bus stop (with a phone box nearby), and the Hulmes are able to collect visitors from there by prior arrangement.

Readers' comments: Full of character, warm welcome, cordon bleu food. Hospitality beyond compare. Food excellent. Very welcoming. Perfect meals; very comfortable. First-class accommodation, cooking excellent. Wonderful – can't speak too highly. Entertained most royally. Lovely home, friendly personality. Cannot fault it.

Some proprietors stipulate a minimum stay of two nights at weekends or peak seasons; or they will accept one-nighters only at short notice (that is, only if no lengthier booking has yet been made).

POSTLIP HALL FARM
Winchcombe, Cheltenham, Gloucestershire, GL54 5AQ
Tel: 01242 603351
North-east of Cheltenham. Nearest main road: A435 from Cheltenham to Evesham.

C D

3 Bedrooms. £20 (less for 3 nights). All have own bath/shower/toilet. Tea/coffee facilities. TV. Views of garden, country. No smoking. Washing machine on request.
Light suppers if ordered.
1 Sitting-room. With open fire, central heating, TV, record-player. No smoking.
Large garden

This livestock farm, situated at the end of a sweeping and tree-lined drive in the hamlet of Postlip, was at one time part of the local Broadway family estate. Fine views of 15th-century Postlip Hall, with its magnificent gabled frontage, are to be had from this modern farmhouse of Cotswold stone.

Valerie and Joe Albutt have created a comfortable atmosphere for their guests. The large sitting-room, with panoramic views, has brocade sofas and armchairs and two recliners gathered around a wood-burning stove. Bedrooms are of a good size. One in beige and peach has unusual antique headboards; another, with double aspect, has views of open farmland and the old Hall beyond.

The farm adjoins Cleeve Common, at 1800 acres the largest area of common land in the county, so there are attractive cross-country walks, one of which takes you to nearby Winchcombe, a picturesque village that was the capital of the ancient kingdom of Mercia. Sudeley Castle, too, is a short walk away: once the home of Catherine Parr, parts of the old building are included in Sir Gilbert Scott's 19th-century reconstruction.

Readers' comments: Immaculate. Breakfast the best ever.

In springtime a cherry tree in bloom marks **PARKVIEW**, at 4 Pittville Crescent, Cheltenham. Overlooking Pittville Park, this elegant Georgian house in a quiet residential area is a useful base for exploring the town, or for travelling further into the Cotswolds. The stairway of the house is lined with Sandra and John Sparrey's interesting finds from local auctions: old playbills, sepia-toned photographs and a land deed with George IV's royal seal. Bedrooms are pleasantly furnished; one has a lovely

art deco dressing-suite. Guests share a bathroom, but there are washbasins in all rooms. £17.50. [Tel: 01242 575567; postcode: GL52 2QZ]

Houses which accept the discount vouchers on page ii are marked with a V on the lists at the beginning of this book, see pages xi–xix and pages xxi–xxii.

PRESTON FARMHOUSE
C(4) S

Harberton, Devon, TQ9 7SW   Tel: 01803 862235
South of Totnes. Nearest main road: A381 from Totnes to Kingsbridge.

3 Bedrooms. £18–£19. All have own bath/shower/toilet. Tea/coffee facilities. TV. Views of garden, country. No smoking. Washing machine on request.
Dinner. £12 for 4 courses and coffee, at 6.45pm. Non-residents not admitted. Vegetarian or special diets if ordered. No smoking.
2 Sitting-rooms. With woodstove, central heating, TV, record-player, video. No smoking.
Small garden

The Steers' house, built in 1680, has been in the same farming family for generations: Isabelle was born in it. All the rooms are comfortable, and bedrooms have pretty co-ordinated fabrics. Next to the farmhouse kitchen is the dining-room, with beams and inglenook.

At the back is a sunny courtyard for guests to use, and an unimaginably ancient iron-studded door.

There is good home cooking at dinner, with dishes as varied as fresh salmon from the River Dart, chicken Marengo, roasts, pies, baked Alaska, treacle pudding. The ingredients are mostly home-grown or local. Breakfast comes on 'help-yourself' platters – conventional bacon and eggs or more unusual things like hog's pudding or smoked haddock.

Harberton is a picturesque cluster of old cottages with colourful gardens, set in a valley. Its 13th-century church has a magnificent painted screen and pulpit, and stained-glass windows. The local inn is of equal antiquity. Preston Farm was once a manor house, which is why rooms are spacious.

Readers' comments: Quite the best place we have ever stayed. A perfect week. Excellent meals, beautifully served. Excellent in every way. Enjoyed our stay immensely. Warm welcome, excellent accommodation, delicious meals. Quiet, comfortable, charming hostess, amazing food. Will certainly go back. Quite simply the best b & b. One of the best. Of the best we have encountered. Most comfortable and delightful four days. Very good value.

THANK YOU . . . to those who send details of their own finds, for possible future inclusion in the book. Do not be disappointed if your candidate does not appear in the very next edition. We never publish recommendations from unknown members of the public without verification, and it takes time to get round each part of England and Wales in turn. Please, however, do not send details of houses already featured in many other guides, nor any that are more expensive than those in this book (see page xxiv).

PRIORY COTTAGE   C(5)

Low Corner, Butley, Suffolk, IP12 3QD   Tel: 01394 450382
East of Woodbridge. Nearest main road: A12 from Ipswich to Lowestoft.

3 Bedrooms. £18–£25 (minimum 2 nights). All have own bath/shower/toilet. Views of garden, country, river. No smoking. Washing machine on request.
1 Sitting-room. With open fire, central heating, TV, video, record-player. No smoking.
Large garden

On arrival, visitors are greeted by Megan, the Newnhams' slightly daffy dog; all around is a prettily landscaped garden.

The entrance hall has an unusual floor of polished 'pamment' tiles, sofas and arrangements of dried flowers. There are velvet chairs in the L-shaped sitting-room. For dinner, there are several inns and restaurants in the area: at one inn, Suffolk folk songs can be heard on Sundays.

Upstairs, rooms with clear bright colours, flowery wallpaper friezes, pine doors and beds, and louvred built-ins are neat and cheerful: some have views of Butley Creek and the bird reserve on Havergate Island. The blue-and-white one has a prettily draped bed.

The cottage is in a designated Area of Outstanding Natural Beauty, and completely unspoilt. It is virtually on the Suffolk Coast Path (50 miles of footpath and bridleway) which wanders through forests where deer roam and along a shore much frequented by migrant wildfowl and by small yachts. There is a ferry across Butley Creek for a 3½-hour circular walk. Beyond the elaborately carved gatehouse of Butley Priory lies Orford – celebrated for its oysterage and for its huge polygonal castle (early Norman). Further up the coast is the old-fashioned resort of Aldeburgh (made famous by Britten's opera, 'Peter Grimes'), with an internationally famous music festival centred on the Maltings at nearby Snape and with events in numerous churches too. Inland lies Framlingham and another outstanding castle. South of the sailing centre of Woodbridge is the only big resort, Felixstowe: sedate and orderly, with well-tended flowerbeds along the seafront.

The sunny, breezy coast here has been much eroded (entire towns have vanished into the sea after floods or storms) and so the principal road lies some way inland (through heaths and across estuaries), with only lanes penetrating to the shore, which means the area is undisturbed by traffic or crowds. There are any number of outings: horse-drawn wagon rides, walks with a naturalist, a cruise in a motor launch, a cordon bleu picnic with champagne and much else.

Readers' comments: Beautiful location. Exceptionally well furnished. Friendly, hospitable and attentive. Food was superb. Wonderful, convivial evenings. Could not have had better accommodation, food and friendliness. Amusing hostess.

For explanation of code letters (C, D, M, PT, S, X) see inside front cover.

QUINTON GREEN FARM

Quinton Green, Northamptonshire, NN7 2EG   Tel: 01604 863685
South-east of Northampton. Nearest main road: A508 from Northampton to
Roade (and M1, junction 15).

4 Bedrooms. £18 (less for 3 nights or
continental breakfast). Price goes up from
April. Bargain breaks. Some have own
shower/toilet. Tea/coffee facilities. TV. Views
of country. Washing machine on request.
Light suppers by arrangement.
1 Sitting-room. With open fire, central
heating, TV.
Garden

Steadily extended from the 17th century onwards, the house is at the peaceful
heart of a big farm (400 cows, as well as arable fields), beyond which lies Salcey
Forest – its 1500 acres threaded by waymarked footpaths.

Margaret Turney accommodates visitors in a wing that is separate from her
large family, in rooms she has decorated very attractively – for example, with
wildflower spreads and curtains, armchairs from which to enjoy the rural views,
and particularly good shower-rooms. On the window-seats and coral sofas of the
sitting-room are Berlin-work cushions she made herself.

Within a very short distance there is much to see, such as the fine gardens of
Castle Ashby and Holderby (Elizabethan); exceptional churches (in Northampton
itself is a rare, circular 'Crusader' church); museums (the footwear and leather
ones are unusual, the latter with Egyptian and Roman exhibits; another is devoted
to mechanical music instruments; and there's a very good museum about the
canals for which the county is famous); Pitsford has an 800-acre reservoir with
watersports; and walkers will enjoy the long and scenic Nene Way.

Built right across the bubbling River
Nene, **UPTON MILL,** Upton (just
west of Northampton), is the focal
point of many lovely footpaths: they
were first trodden by farmers carrying
grain to the mill. From the rather
higgledy-piggledy dining-room (with
fine Jacobean-style chairs, carved with
mermaids) and a sun-room, one steps
into a wildlife garden on the river
bank, with pond for moorhens beyond
and over 1000 acres for sheep and
cows. Jane Spokes cooks such meals as
apple and curry soup, chicken, and
lemon soufflé. £17.50–£20 (b & b).

[Tel: 01604 753277; postcode: NN5
4UY]

> Houses with short entries are just as good as ones with longer
> descriptions; and they include some of the most popular houses in
> the book. They may, however, have fewer rooms, a shorter season,
> higher prices or fewer amenities (such as meals).

RECTORY FARM
Northmoor, Oxfordshire, OX8 1SX   Tel: 01865 300207
(Messages: 01865 300689)
South-west of Oxford. Nearest main road: A415 from Witney to Abingdon.

2 Bedrooms. £19–£20 (less for 3 nights). Both have own shower/toilet. Tea/coffee facilities. Views of garden, country. No smoking. Washing machine on request.
1 Sitting-room. With wood stove, central heating, TV, piano. No smoking.
Large garden
Closed from mid-December to January.

Until a generation ago, this ancient stone farmhouse (the ogee arches of its fireplaces have been dated to the 15th century) was owned by St John's College, Oxford: college priests used to stay here when preaching at the adjacent church – which explains why one bedroom has such a finely decorated ceiling.

The deep-set windows are stone-mullioned, with views of fields and a great slate-roofed, timber dovecote that was built in the 18th century – like the house itself and the granary perched on its staddlestones, a listed building. The Floreys' 400 acres are used for sheep, pedigree cattle and crops. In the house are Mary Anne's beautiful arrangements of dried flowers, which used to be grown on the farm.

Having a growing family to look after, she provides breakfasts only, but there are many restaurants nearby. The breakfast/sitting-room has chamfered beams overhead, red Turkey rugs on the floor, tapestry armchairs, and a sideboard laden with Victorian silver-plate.

The bedrooms are particularly spacious, light and attractively decorated, their shower-rooms immaculate (outsize bath-towels much appreciated!); and their windows have farm or garden views. On the farm are Thames-side walks (fishing too). A series of lakes which were once gravel pits attract wildfowl.

Old brewhouse sitting-room at Severn Trow (see page 290)

RED HOUSE

Sidmouth Road, Lyme Regis, Dorset, DT7 3ES   Tel: 01297 442055
Nearest main road: A3052 from Lyme Regis to Exeter.

3 Bedrooms. £20 **(or £18 to readers of this book)** – £24 (less for 4 nights). Prices go up from Easter. All have own bath/toilet. Tea/coffee facilities. TV. Views of garden, sea. No smoking.
Light suppers if ordered.
Garden
Closed from December to February.

Delightful old Lyme has many claims to fame – Jane Austen; fossils (including dinosaur bones) found along its beaches; the landing of the Duke of Monmouth in 1685 to start his abortive rebellion; and, in more recent times, *The French Lieutenant's Woman*, the author of which, John Fowles, lives locally.

This dignified 'twenties house was built for Aldis (inventor of the famous signal-lamps which bear his name) on a superb site with a 40-mile sea view southeast as far as Portland Bill. It is a house with handsome features – iron-studded oak doors, leaded casements and window-seats, for example. On sunny mornings (occasionally even in late autumn), you can take breakfast on the wide verandah and enjoy sea breezes while you eat; at your feet, sloping lawns with colourful rhododendrons, camellias, fuchsias and wisteria. On chilly mornings, breakfast is served in an attractive room with a fire.

Each bedroom is equipped with armchairs, TV, a refrigerator, flowers and books – the aim being to provide individual bedsitters for guests, as there is no communal sitting-room, only a large landing which has seats and a supply of leaflets, maps and local menus.

The house is full of pictures and objects from the Normans' overseas postings (Anthony was in the Navy) and in the garden is a timber cabin where Vicky makes exceptionally pretty cloth dolls: she also teaches this skill.

Readers' comments: Splendid views and pleasant gardens. Rooms perfectly equipped. Top rate.

In a flowery hollow down Lyme's pretty Ware Lane is **WILLOW COTTAGE** where now the Griffins (formerly of Red House) welcome guests, who not only have their own bedsitting-room (with balcony overlooking the sea, which is reached by footpath) plus single room if required, but also a private breakfast-room below: here Liz also serves snack suppers out of season by arrangement. Closed from December to February. From £18 **to readers of this book.**

Readers' comments: Kindness itself, so caring. Gracious hosts. Griffins delightful. [Tel: 01297 443199; postcode: DT7 3EL]

REGENCY HOUSE

CDPTSX

Neatishead, Norfolk, NR12 8AD   Tel: 01692 630233

North-east of Norwich. Nearest main road: A1151 from Norwich to Stalham.

3 Bedrooms. £18–£22 (less for 2 nights and **for en suite rooms to readers of this book**). Prices go up from July. Bargain breaks. Two have own bath/toilet. Tea/coffee facilities. TV. Views of garden, country. **Light suppers** if ordered.
1 Sitting-room. With cassette-player.
Small garden

Former Manchester bank-manager Alan Wrigley was so touched by the friendliness of Neatishead people towards a newcomer that, after a few years here, he began planting wayside trees as a 'thank you': the total has already passed 4000. He and his wife Sue, formerly a *Daily Express* reporter, run this 18th-century guest-house to an immaculate standard.

The breakfasts are outstanding: standard issue is 2 sausages, 4 rashers of bacon, 6 mushrooms, 2 whole tomatoes, 2 slices of fried bread and as many eggs as you request! But if you prefer it, Sue will produce a vegetarian breakfast instead. This is served in an oak-panelled room with willow-pattern crockery on tables that were specially made by a local craftsman. Bedrooms have Laura Ashley fabrics (two have king-size beds). The sitting-room has red leather armchairs and a beamed ceiling.

Pretty little Neatishead – in the heart of the Norfolk Broads – fortunately does not attract the crowds which sometimes ruin Horning and Wroxham. For dinner, there is a choice of eating-places within yards of the guest-house. Self-catering visitors can breakfast in the house.

Readers' comments: Welcoming, friendly. Large rooms, lovely furnishings. Amazing breakfasts, generous hospitality. The best b & b we've stayed in. Very neat, well-appointed rooms. Excellent in every way. Highly recommended.

Off the Norwich Road, North Walsham, is the huge, 18th-century **TOLL BARN**, now immaculately converted and handsomely furnished. Beyond two courtyard gardens with fountains are six spacious, ground-floor bedrooms. All have en suite facilities and pretty colour schemes; and are very well equipped, including fridges. Annette Tofts provides good suppers which guests have in their rooms. Breakfast is served in bedrooms or the large, brick-and-beamed dining-room in the main house. £19.
Readers' comments: Delightful home, superb conversion. Spacious, comfortable. Ideal hosts, professional but

warm and relaxed – and a half-melon for breakfast! Could have stayed for ever! Food outstanding. Owners absolutely charming, rooms and facilities first class. [Tel: 01692 403063; postcode: NR28 0JB]

271

RIDGE COTTAGE
C PT X

164 Burley Road, Bransgore, Hampshire, BH23 8DE   Tel: 01425 672504
North of Christchurch. Nearest main road: A35 from Christchurch to
Southampton.

3 Bedrooms. £15 (less for 4 nights or continental breakfast). Bargain breaks. Tea/coffee facilities. Views of garden, country. Balcony. No smoking. Washing machine on request.
Dinner. £8.50 for 2 courses (with choices) and coffee, at 7–8pm. Non-residents not admitted. Vegetarian or special diets if ordered. No smoking. **Light suppers** if ordered.
1 Sitting-room. With open fire, central heating, TV, piano, record-player. No smoking.
Large garden

From a gardener's cottage in 1913, this has gradually been extended to become a quite large house in the New Forest, handsomely modernized and with an attractively landscaped and walled garden all round it – sloping upwards to a polygonal, glass-walled summer-house. Big windows give clear views of this and of the terrace where barbecues are sometimes organized. The sitting-room, dark green and white, is full of small antiques and other finds the Blythes have collected over the years. There are excellent carpets, a piano and open fire, hanging pot-plants and a rocking-chair. The dining-hall is furnished with oak chairs made for them by a Cornish craftsman, with seats of needlepoint stitched by Janet – who is also a good cook, serving such meals as roast lamb or Dover sole followed by profiteroles or traditional puddings.

One bedroom has a balcony, with a pretty bathroom (with bidet) adjacent. There's a family suite; and a games room for table tennis and darts. Books galore – rag dolls, too.

Within a few miles are Bournemouth, historic Christchurch, the popular forest village of Burley, and beaches.

Old Christchurch is particularly worth a visit: its spectacular priory, built in stages from Saxon to Renaissance times, is on a site where two rivers flow out to sea. The choir stalls and a monument to Shelley are of particular interest. There are castle remains and a good museum of local geology and wildlife. The walk to Hengistbury Head leads to a point where birdwatchers gather to watch migrations.

Bournemouth is a bustling city, celebrated for its miles of sands below the cliffs (there are lifts), two piers, fragrant pines and gardens that flourish in the mild climate (one-sixth of Bournemouth comprises parks, etc.), and its internationally acclaimed symphony orchestra.

It is, however, the 90,000 acres of the New Forest that are the main reason to stay at Ridge Cottage: varied woods and heaths, thatched cottages and old inns, deer and ponies roaming free, walks and wagon-rides – there is so much to do and see here.

Readers' comments: Made very welcome, delicious meals, convivial company.

RIGGS COTTAGE   C(5) **D PT X**
Routenbeck, Bassenthwaite Lake, Cumbria, CA13 9YN   Tel: 017687 76580
East of Cockermouth. Nearest main road: A66 from Keswick to Cockermouth.

3 Bedrooms. £19–£25. Some have own bath/shower/toilet. Tea/coffee facilities. TV. Views of garden, country. No smoking.
Dinner. £12.50 for 3 courses and coffee, at 6.30pm. Non-residents not admitted. Vegetarian or special diets if ordered. No smoking.
1 Sitting-room. With open fire, central heating, TV. No smoking.
Large garden

Hidden at the foot of a (rather steep) private lane is a little group of dwellings of which 17th-century Riggs Cottage is one. It is a low-beamed place, literally with roses round the door, where a big L-shaped settee faces a dog-grate under an iron canopy.

Hazel and Fred Wilkinson share the cooking, offering unusual choices for breakfast: a variety of sausages, wild mushrooms in season, or kedgeree. Bread is home-made, herbs and many vegetables are home-grown, going into a dinner menu such as lettuce and coriander soup, gravadlax (using local wild salmon), and a traditional pudding - hot or cold according to season – and local cheese. If you feel like a change (or a drink), the excellent Pheasant Inn is close.

Hazel's watercolours of owls and hawks decorate the staircase; elsewhere there are examples of her china-painting (which, as well as decoupage, she teaches). In one bedroom is a collection of the drawings of Arthur Wainwright, the famous author of hand-written Lake District walkers' guides.

Nearby Bassenthwaite Lake is the most northerly of the lakes and the only one with the word 'lake' in its name (the others being 'meres' or 'waters'). On one side is the great peak of Skiddaw and on the other Thornthwaite Forest, with a visitor centre provided by the Forestry Commission. Westward is Cockermouth, Wordsworth's birthplace.

Near Bassenthwaite Lake, Victorian **LINK HOUSE** has, as well as a sitting-room with a log fire, a conservatory bar with tiled floor and cane seats. Tables are laid with fine linen, Wedgwood china and Cumbria Crystal glassware. The pleasant bedrooms also include single rooms of a high standard.

Guests can use the leisure club at the nearby Castle Inn Hotel (swimming-pool, solarium, sauna, tennis court, etc.).

The house is run by Michael and Marilyn Tuppen, previously owners of **Hill Top**, Morland. £20–£26.

Readers' comments: Lovely setting. Comfort super. Food and accommodation remain very good. [Tel: 017687 76291; postcode: CA13 9YD]

RIVER PARK FARM   C S

Lodsworth, Petworth, West Sussex, GU28 9DS   Tel: 01798 861362
East of Midhurst. Nearest main road: A272 from Petworth to Midhurst.

3 **Bedrooms.** £18 (less for 5 nights).
Tea/coffee facilities. Views of garden, country. No smoking.
Dinner. £6–£7 for 2 courses (with choices) and coffee, at 7pm (not Wednesdays and Fridays). Non-residents not admitted. No smoking.
1 **Sitting-room.** With central heating, TV.
Large garden
Closed from December to Easter.

The farm (of 340 acres of corn, bullocks, sheep and poultry) is in a secluded position among woods where, if you are up early enough, you may encounter deer. There is a 4½-acre lake with plentiful carp and ducks, and in front a pretty garden. The house itself, built in 1600, is old and beamy with comfortable bedrooms along twisting passageways. In the dining-room Pat Moss has a strikingly colourful collection of green leaf plates and wooden ducks. Outside are golden roses and wisteria clambering around the door. Altogether it is a tranquil spot.

Pat does not do full-scale dinners (available elsewhere locally) but has a list of homely dishes like shepherd's pie or macaroni cheese, and for puddings like banana split she uses rich Jersey cream from the farm's own cows. Bread is home-baked and eggs free-range. There are flowers in every room. Pat also makes and sells marmalade, dried flowers and decorative herbal hangings. Coarse fishing available.

Many people come for the local walks and birdwatching. Pat has pinned up bird-identification charts and gives visitors field notes on the crops and wildlife in each season, with map, and her own daily nature notes.

Readers' comments: Warm hospitality, generous home cooking. Enjoyed ourselves so much that we have twice visited for a week. Marvellous setting and house, kind hosts, good food. Outstanding. Very relaxed atmosphere. Comfortable, quiet. Warm, relaxed, friendly atmosphere and lovely farm. House charming, surroundings idyllic, rooms comfortable.

In pretty Billingshurst (in East Street), right by the mediaeval church, is a beamy 17th-century house, **CHURCHGATE,** which Sheila Butcher has furnished in traditional country-house style. Views from its windows (double-glazed in case light sleepers are disturbed by bell-ringing or passing cars) are of a flowery little garden and the church. Dinner (to be ordered in advance) might typically be pâté, coq au vin, home-made desserts and cheeses. Light suppers too. £17.50 (b & b).
Readers' comments: Excellent, personal service. Most delightful place. Superb atmosphere, excellent food. Very comfortable, dinner superb, value for money. [Tel: 01403 782733; postcode: RH14 9PY]

ROCK HOUSE

PT S X

Alport, Derbyshire, DE45 1LG   Tel: 01629 636736
South of Bakewell. Nearest main road: A6 from Bakewell to Matlock.

3 Bedrooms. £20. All have own bath/shower/toilet. Tea/coffee facilities. TV. Views of garden, country. No smoking. Washing machine on request.
Light suppers if ordered.
1 Sitting-room. With gas fire, central heating, TV. No smoking.
Small garden

The rock for which this house is named is a great crag of tufa (a type of volcanic stone, perforated like Gruyère cheese, which was formed 300 million years ago) rearing up alongside it. Only a few yards from the 18th-century house two rivers join, splashing over weirs constructed long ago to contain trout downstream – you can watch these drifting in water so transparent that the locals call it 'gin-clear'. Lathkill Dale is a National Nature Reserve: Tony and Jan Statham are first-rate sources of information about the history of this most beautiful of valleys. They will lend maps, tell you the best riverside walks, and where to find river pools (created for washing sheep).

The front door opens straight into the stone-flagged sitting-room, its walls now painted mushroom, with buttoned velvet armchairs, where you will be served tea on arrival. Glass doors lead through to the breakfast-room.

By pre-arrangement, Jan may serve supper platters, beautifully presented (but most visitors go to the nearby Druid Inn or other pubs). Breakfast possibilities include muffins, poached fruit, home-made jams and some vegetarian dishes. All bedrooms are well furnished.

Readers' comments: Breakfast excellent, rooms large and comfortable. Beautiful house, much pampering, what breakfasts! One of our favourites, lovely house; thoughtful and friendly people. A charming house with lovely walks all round, and delicious breakfasts. Very friendly, couldn't do enough for us. One of the best. Nothing too much trouble.

Truly remote, **WOLFSCOTE GRANGE** near Hartington is an isolated beef and sheep farm, parts of the ancient building dating back to the 13th century. Just outside, the land drops down 200 feet to the River Dove. Jane Gibbs keeps her rooms as traditional as is compatible with modern comfort: in keeping with the narrow, mullioned windows and low rafters, her armchairs are cretonne-covered and antique sporting-guns hang on the walls. Frequently, television companies seek out this

authentic setting for costume dramas. Twists and steps lead you to bed: for the best view, ask for the pink room. (Snack suppers only). Closed in winter. £16.50–£17. [Tel: 01298 84342; postcode: SK17 0AX]

ROGAN'S   **C**

Satron, Gunnerside, North Yorkshire, DL11 6JW   Tel: 01748 886414
West of Richmond. Nearest main road: A684 from Leyburn to Sedbergh.

3 Bedrooms. £17–£20 (less for 7 nights).
All have own bath/shower/toilet. Tea/coffee
facilities. TV. Views of garden, country. No
smoking.
1 Sitting-room. With open fire, central
heating, cassette-player. No smoking.
Large garden
Closed in December.

When Maureen and Bill Trafford renovated Stable Cottage, they decided to call
it after Rogan's Seat, the highest point in the hills that line Swaledale – though
nobody seems to know who Rogan was. Visitors to this early 19th-century house
have their own entrance to their sitting-room, where white-painted walls, bamboo
furniture, and a colour scheme based on pink and green, together with vigorous
house-plants, give a conservatory-like atmosphere. There is a large garden, from
which footpaths lead directly into the countryside.

The bedrooms, also with white-painted textured walls, are fitted out in
mahogany or pine; outlooks are leafy.

The house lies by the road which snakes through the series of villages and
hamlets along Swaledale in the Yorkshire Dales National Park. The next village,
Muker, is the largest and almost the last settlement before the watershed of the
Pennines, where the River Swale rises. Here there is a shop for woollens hand-
knitted by a team of farmers' wives and daughters, mostly from the wool of
Swaledale sheep, the breed to which the valley has given its name. From near
here, the Buttertubs Pass leads past Hardraw Force, one of the highest waterfalls
in England. This is a way into Wensleydale, perhaps for a particularly good pub
meal at the King's Arms in Askrigg. Simpler pub meals are closer at hand.

The attractions of Swaledale, or within easy reach of it, include Richmond
(with its Georgian theatre), castles, relics of past lead-mining, strange rock
formations, and craft workshops of many kinds.

Maureen and Bill's enthusiasm for the dale is infectious. They have a fund
of knowledge and are such good raconteurs that the history of the dales people
is vividly brought to life by their stories: of the building of the Settle Railway, of
the 'corpse path', of the 'crinoline path', and of the bridge haunted by a headless
dog.

Readers' comments: Thoroughly enjoyed our stay. They take a lot of trouble to
ensure one's comfort.

Facts (prices, etc.) at the top of entries are supplied by the
proprietors themselves. While every effort is made to ensure
that these are correct at the time of going to press, they may alter
thereafter: please check when you book.

ROOKS ORCHARD   C D

Little Wittenham, Oxfordshire, OX14 4QY   Tel: 01865 407765
South-east of Abingdon. Nearest main road: A423 from Oxford to Wallingford
(and M40, junction 7).

2 Bedrooms. £17.50–£19 (less for 3
nights). Tea/coffee facilities. TV. Views of
garden, country. No smoking. Washing
machine on request.
Dinner. £10.50 for 3 courses and coffee, at
7pm (not Sundays). Less for 2 courses.
Vegetarian or special diets if ordered. **Light
suppers** if ordered.
1 Sitting-room. With open fire, central
heating, TV, piano.
Large garden

'Mother Dunch's buttocks', they rudely called the twin hills dominating the
nature reserve that surrounds Rooks Orchard – the lady in question, who once
owned this village, was Cromwell's aunt, now buried in the church. In snowy
winters skiers speed down the slopes, while summer brings out wild orchids.
Waterfowl frequent the ponds below, and at twilight you may spot badgers at
play.

The 17th-century house has not only the beams and inglenooks you might
expect but a fascinating collection of family heirlooms – from a rocking-horse
used by generations of young Welfares to a portrait of the Duke of Burgundy,
antique fishing-rods to embroideries done by Jonathan's great-grandfather to
while away long hours aboard HMS *Challenger* on her four-year voyage charting
the oceans for the British government.

Deborah Welfare has complemented antique furniture with restful colours,
chinoiserie or beribboned fabrics, and pretty flower arrangements. From the old-
fashioned garden comes produce for such meals as chilled lettuce-and-mint soup,
salads to accompany chicken with avocado and cashew nuts, and gooseberry fool
served with almond meringues.

In an ancient side street of old
Abingdon itself, Susie Howard
welcomes visitors to her early 18th-
century house: **22 EAST ST HELEN
STREET** (St Helen's is the town's
handsome church, five aisles wide).
Once the home of an estate bailiff, it is
notable for the pine panelling of many
rooms and of pilastered doorways – up
the narrow and twisty staircase, too.
From the attic room is a river view;
second-floor rooms overlook an old
roofscape; others have views of a very
pretty garden. Antiques, attractive
fabrics and a stone-flagged breakfast-
room all add to the character of the
building. Close by is a house where
William III stayed during 'the glorious

revolution' of 1688, one of the town's
many historic houses; and round the
corner you can board a pleasure-boat
to go to Oxford. £17–£20. [Tel:
01235 533278; postcode: OX14 5EB]

ROOSTERS   **C D S**

Todenham, Gloucestershire, GL56 9PA   Tel: 01608 650645
North-east of Moreton-in-Marsh. Nearest main road: A429 from Moreton-in-Marsh to Warwick.

3 Bedrooms. £18–£20. All have own bath/shower/toilet. Tea/coffee facilities. TV. Views of garden, country. No smoking. Washing machine on request.
Dinner. £13 for 3 courses and coffee, at 7.30pm. Less for 2 courses. Non-residents not admitted. Vegetarian or special diets if ordered. No smoking. **Light suppers** if ordered.
1 Sitting-room. With open fire, central heating. No smoking.
Large garden

Situated near the old 'four shires' stone, this 17th-century cottage provides an ideal base for touring not only the Cotswold villages but also Stratford-upon-Avon (only 20 minutes away) and, further afield, Cheltenham to the west or Warwick and Leamington Spa to the north.

Returning after a busy day sightseeing, and having been greeted by Rory the golden retriever, you can relax by the inglenook fireplace with its gleaming copper cowl and admire Chris Longmore's eclectic collection of china, before she serves dinner. Chris and her husband Paul, a former golf professional, lived for some time in Sweden, so after perhaps broccoli-and-cheese soup you might be served Scandinavian pork, followed by a more traditional summer pudding or strawberry cheesecake.

Bedrooms are all individual, comfortable and furnished with imagination. One in yellow and blue has unusual pale pine and leather scrolled headboards, and a striking golden pine and green bathroom. Another has pretty rose-stencilled walls and white lace bedspreads. Some of Paul's grandfather's watercolour landscapes adorn the walls in the low-beamed hallways.

Nearby Moreton-in-Marsh on the Fosse Way is well worth a morning's exploration. There are lots of old inns and antique shops, with a busy general market on Tuesdays and a collectors' fair later in the week.

Walking or motoring in the Cotswolds is a pleasure in itself, but there are many other things to do too – the Roman villa at Chedworth, Sudeley Castle, the Cotswold Wildlife Park, horseracing, shopping for antiques or country clothes, visiting gardens such as those at Hidcote, Kiftsgate or Batsford (it has a Japanese-style arboretum) or the many stately homes and even statelier churches for which this county is famous.

The addresses of houses are geographically correct but postal addresses sometimes differ (for correspondence, the only essential element is the postcode).

Information about the nearest town and 'A' road helps you to locate the whereabouts of any village on a map; but before setting off it is necessary to get precise instructions from your host as many houses are very much 'off the beaten track'.

278

ROUGHLOW FARMHOUSE

C(6) **S X**

Chapel Lane, Willington, Cheshire, CW6 0PG   Tel: 01829 751199
East of Chester. Nearest main road: A54 from Congleton towards Chester (and M6, junction 18).

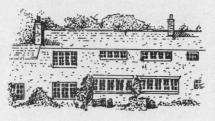

3 Bedrooms. £20–£30 (less for 3 nights). All have own bath/shower/toilet. Tea/coffee facilities. Views of garden, country. No smoking. Washing machine on request.
Dinner. £17.50 for 4 courses and coffee, at 7.30pm. Less for 3 courses. Vegetarian or special diets if ordered. No smoking. **Light suppers** if ordered.
2 Sitting-rooms. With open fire, central heating, TV, piano, record-player. No smoking.
Large garden

Warm sandstone was used to build this 200-year-old farmhouse, well sited 450 feet up for superb views towards Shropshire in one direction and Wales in the other – but these were obscured by a silage pit, earthworks and piggeries until the Sutcliffes came here and cleared all away. They created the garden (with haha instead of any obtruding fence or hedge), pretty cobbled courtyard and tennis court. All so peaceful, and yet the historic city of Chester is only 15 minutes away and Manchester Airport just over half an hour.

From a graceful sitting-room in shades of pink and grey (a curvaceous sofa faces the cast-iron fireplace, and doors are of stripped pine), stairs wind up to the bedrooms. There is an enormous suite above the barn with big, beamed sitting-room in lemon and exceptionally pretty quilts contrasting with bedheads of white bamboo; beyond it is a luxurious, outsize shower (glass and gilt). Sally used to be an interior decorator and this shows in her choice of colours, antiques, and pictures by a local artist. The terracotta single room is well up to standard; another has a prettily draped bamboo bedhead.

A typical dinner (provided there are at least four people dining) might be soup made from freshly picked field mushrooms; chicken in a sauce of cream, lemon and tarragon; local strawberries with shortbread; and cheeses.

Readers' comments: Most excellent. Superb bedrooms. Meals delightfully served and overwhelming in abundance. Very friendly and attentive. Quite enchanting. Beautifully appointed, peaceful, elegant. Absolutely delighted with the reception we received. Delightfully secluded. Very comfortable. Thoroughly enjoyed my stay. Breathtaking views. Delicious dinner.

To find the right accommodation in the right area at the right price, use an up-to-date edition of this book – revised every year. For an order form for the next edition (published in November), send a stamped addressed envelope with 'SOTBT 1998' in the top left-hand corner, to Explore Britain, Alston, Cumbria, CA9 3SL. You will receive a money-saving offer for 'Staying Off the Beaten Track in Scotland' too.

RUDSTONE WALK FARM   C D M X
South Cave, (Humberside), East Riding of Yorkshire, HU15 2AH
Tel: 01430 422230
West of Kingston-upon-Hull. Nearest main road: A1034 from Market
Weighton towards Hull (and M62, junction 38).

14 Bedrooms. £20–£35 (less for 2 nights). All have own bath/shower/toilet. Tea/coffee facilities. TV. Views of garden, country, river. Balcony (some). No smoking (some). Washing machine on request.
Dinner. £15.50 for 3 courses and coffee, at 7–7.30pm. Less for 2 courses. Vegetarian or special diets if ordered. Wine available. No smoking. **Light suppers** if ordered.
2 Sitting-rooms. With open fire, central heating, TV, video, piano, record-player. No smoking (in one). **Bar.**
Large garden

Always painted white to serve as a landmark for sailors on the Humber estuary, this farmhouse stands on the highest point of a plain bounded by the river to the south and the sea to the east. It goes without saying that the views are wide: as far as 50 miles on a clear day, when York can be seen across the lawn. The farm, built on a site occupied since Roman times, is mentioned in Domesday Book (the name comes from that of a vanished Saxon hamlet), and its oldest buildings date back about 900 years.

The main sitting-room is in the 18th-century part: a large space recently created from two rooms, it has a big inglenook fireplace built of stone and ornamented with copper kettles. There are chintz-covered settees and a grand piano, and the windows have been enlarged to take advantage of the view. A smaller, stone-walled room has been modernized and fitted with a bar and French windows opening onto the garden.

The dining-room was once the hired hands' quarters. Here, under a boarded ceiling from which corn dollies hang, guests dine round one enormous table on, for instance, soup, roast pork, oranges in Grand Marnier, and cheese. There are lots of family antiques around.

Along a covered flagged path are rooms suitable for families or guests requiring ground-floor accommodation. These are available either on a self-catering or b & b basis. Each 'cottage', in a row converted from a farm building to an architect's design, has the use of a sitting-room and a small kitchen. French windows in most of these rooms open onto a terrace overlooking the fields of the farm, entirely arable now except for pet shire horses. The farm is run by Pauline Greenwood's two sons while she looks after not only visitors but also participants in the small conferences for which there are facilities. (Sunday lunch is also available.)

Beverley and York and half a dozen mansions are easily reached by car, and there are plenty of footpaths for walking in the Wolds. The nearest city is Hull – still a busy port after many centuries, though the original docks, by the historic Old Town, have been filled in to create open space or have been converted into a marina. You can visit the Jacobean birthplace of William Wilberforce, with relics of the slave trade he helped to abolish.

Readers' comments: Great hospitality and warmth, food most delicious.

RUTLAND COTTAGES CMSX
5 Cedar Street, Braunston-in-Rutland, Leicestershire, LE15 8QS
Tel: 01572 722049
South-west of Oakham. Nearest main road: A6003 from Oakham to Kettering.

5 Bedrooms. £16–£18 (less for 5 nights). Prices go up from April. Some have own bath/shower/toilet. Tea/coffee facilities. TV. Views of garden, country. No smoking.
Light suppers if ordered. Vegetarian or special diets. No smoking.
2 Sitting-rooms. With open fire, central heating, TV, piano. No smoking.
Small garden

A 17th-century bakehouse is the home of John and Connie Beadman (she taught music); and in addition they own nearby cottages let on a bed-and-breakfast basis. All guests take breakfast together in the beamed dining-room of the house (on Sundays, cooked breakfasts are available only between 7.30 and 8.30am). Visitors can eat at two inns in this pretty conservation village of golden stone, or Connie will provide sandwich suppers.

Guests have the use of the Beadmans' huge and beautifully furnished sitting-room (it has a see-through stone fireplace in the middle, and a 'curfew window' through which the village watchman could check that the baker's fires had been properly extinguished for the night). Its windows open onto a heather garden.

John and his sons are keen bell-ringers, willing to take visitors on guided tours up into the bell-towers of local churches. This is a good area for walks or cycling (maps on loan) and other country pursuits, and for sightseeing too: the historic schools at Uppingham and Oundle, the mediaeval town of Stamford, castles at Rockingham and Belvoir as well as the stately homes of Burghley and Belton – at the former, horse trials take place each September. Connie often helps visitors trace their family history locally.

Man-made reservoirs when naturalized can be as beautiful as any lake, and Rutland Water, one of the greatest in northern Europe, is particularly fine.

Readers' comments: Most friendly. Cottage excellent. B & b at its best. Nothing is too much trouble. The accommodation is first class. Very pleasant welcome, excellent. Good breakfast. Warm welcome. Most helpful and friendly. B & b at its very best in every way.

Humphrey Repton, famous as a landscape gardener, designed the whole village of Laxton, Northamptonshire, in 1804; which is why its **OLD VICARAGE** is so attractive, in 'gothick' style. Susan Hill-Brookes and her husband have filled every room with Victorian landscapes and still-lifes, portraits of dogs and other treasures. A twisting stair at the back leads to old-fashioned bedrooms furnished with antiques. There is a swimming-pool. (Snack suppers only.) £15.50.

[Tel: 01780 450248 or 450259; postcode: NN17 3AT]

ST CHRISTOPHER'S   C(12) **D PT S**
High Street, Boscastle, Cornwall, PL35 0BD   Tel: 01840 250412
South of Bude. Nearest main road: A39 from Bude to Wadebridge.

9 Bedrooms. £18–£19 (less for 3 nights or continental breakfast). Prices go up from June. Bargain breaks. All have own shower/toilet. Tea/coffee facilities. Views of country, sea.
Dinner. £9 for 3 courses (with some choices) and coffee, at 7pm. Non-residents not admitted. Vegetarian or special diets if ordered. Wine available. No smoking. **Light suppers** if ordered.
1 Sitting-room. With log burner, central heating, TV.
Small garden
Closed from November to February.

This 18th-century guest-house in an unspoilt harbour village (a conservation area) belongs to Brenda and Brian Thompson, who used to run a local restaurant.

One enters it through a slate-floored hall with roughcast walls. There is a large sitting-room, well furnished with damask wallpaper and a big velvet sofa. It is heated by a log burner and adjoined by a cottage-style dining-room. Bedrooms have well-chosen colour schemes.

A typical dinner might comprise a mushroom-and-wine savoury, then tenderloin of pork in a cream sauce, syllabub, and cheeses. There is an extensive wine list.

This is a splendid area for scenery, birdwatching and wildflowers, and secluded beaches as at Trebarwith Strand and Bossiney Cove.

All along this coast are picturesque fishing villages such as Boscastle, Tintagel and Port Isaac, but the scenery inland deserves to be explored too. An interesting day's drive might start at Tintagel with a visit to the seashore castle.

Readers' comments: Very good. Pleasant welcome and good food. Excellent hospitality, very relaxing. Very good value. Excellent food with plenty of variety. Very comfortable. Excellent fare. A friendly and attractive b & b in a lovely area. Excellent hosts. Warm welcome. Varied meals. A lovely old house.

1683 is carved on one wall of **OLD BOROUGH HOUSE,** Bossiney Road, Tintagel, built of slate that came from England's largest quarry (at Delabole, near Camelford), a spectacular sight.

Once the house was the residence of the mayors of Bossiney (later, of J.B. Priestley). It has small windows set in thick walls, low beams, steps up and down, twisting corridors, a log stove in the sitting-room which has crimson velvet armchairs, and a bar in the roomy entrance hall. From the garden there is a sea view.

Christina Rayner serves such meals as tomato soup with cream, carbon-nade of beef, crème brûlée, and cheeses. £16.50–£18.50 (b & b).
Readers' comments: Charming and friendly. Lovely old house. Food of consistently high standard – sweets delectable! Could not fault the house. [Tel: 01840 770475; postcode: PL34 0AY]

ST ELISABETH'S COTTAGE   D S X
Woodman Lane, Clent, West Midlands, DY9 9PX   Tel: 01562 883883
South-east of Stourbridge. Nearest main road: A456 from Kidderminster to
Birmingham (and M5, junctions 3/4).

2 Bedrooms. £18–£20 (less for 3 nights). Both have own bath/toilet. Tea/coffee facilities. TV. Views of garden, country. No smoking. Washing machine on request.
Dinner (by arrangement). £12 for 3 courses (with choices) and coffee, at variable times. Non-residents not admitted. No smoking. **Light suppers** if ordered.
3 Sitting-rooms. With open fire, central heating, TV, piano, record-player. No smoking in two.
Large garden

The 18th-century cottage – once laundry to the big mansion nearby – has been much extended over the years and is now quite a large house, surrounded by a particularly beautiful garden. There is a willow-fringed pool which attracts herons, rosebeds, a big sloping lawn, summer-house and swimming-pool.

Sheila Blankstone has furnished her home elegantly with, for instance, deep-pile carpets of pale moss-green in a bedroom that has a bathroom with pheasant-patterned wallpaper; pink chintz and a fine inlaid walnut table and cabinet in another. Huge picture-windows make the most of garden views. In addition to the large sitting-room there is a sun-room and a small 'snug'. Some visitors will appreciate having their own entrance to their bedroom (with child's room adjacent), and the choice of continental breakfast (in their room) or a cooked breakfast in the dining-room. Everywhere are Sheila's lovely flower arrangements. She will sometimes do dinners, such as melon, roast lamb, cheese and fruit – or visitors may use her kitchen. Vegetables are grown in the garden.

The village is in the Clent Hills (a lovely area even though the busy M5 and Birmingham are so near). Symphony Hall, the convention centre and the Hippodrome – home of the Royal Ballet – are close. Stourbridge has since Tudor times been famous for glassmaking: visits to glass works can be arranged. A few miles to the south of it is Hagley Hall, Palladian outside and ornately decorated with plasterwork inside. In its grounds are mock ruins and temples.

On the other side, head for Kinver – not just for its historic houses and church, but to walk to the dramatic summit of Kinver Edge, looming overhead: a 200-acre beauty-spot belonging to the National Trust, from which there are far views of the Cotswolds, the Malvern Hills and other heights. People used to live in the sandstone caves up here.

This is the edge of the Black Country – one great iron-furnace during the Industrial Revolution of the 19th century. Now, proud of its past, local people are conserving historic industrial buildings and creating museums which have turned Dudley, in particular, into a tourist centre. Its Black Country Museum recreates life and work in Victorian times. You can go to the Geochron for a primaeval forest experience, or view underground caverns from a canal boat. Dudley also has a Norman castle, priory and particularly good zoo.

Readers' comments: Bedroom was the largest and most elegant we have ever stayed in. Made most welcome.

ST JAMES'S HOUSE   C M PT

The Green, Thirsk, North Yorkshire, YO7 1AQ   Tel: 01845 524120
Nearest main road: A19 from Middlesbrough to York.

4 Bedrooms. £16–£20 (less for 7 nights). Some have own shower/toilet. Tea/coffee facilities. TV. No smoking.
1 Sitting-room. With central heating. No smoking.
Small garden
Closed from mid-November to February.

Barry Ogleby being an antique dealer, it is not surprising that every part of his 18th-century house is well endowed with period pieces. You may sleep in a room with a bedstead of prettily turned spindles, for example, and in corridors as well as rooms there are such interesting pieces as inlaid blanket-boxes or unusual chairs. On the ground floor is a particularly convenient family room, looking onto flowerbeds, winding paths and lily-pool.

Only two minutes' walk from the quiet green, a conservation area, is Thirsk's busy market place and many restaurants – only breakfast is served by Liz Ogleby. This is where the world's most famous vet, writing under the name of James Herriot, had his surgery, which is now a museum. There are local guides who will accompany you on car tours, pointing out sites associated with Herriot, his books or the films.

In the immediate vicinity are the stupendous view from Sutton Bank, Castle Howard (famous even before television's 'Brideshead Revisited'), thriving Ampleforth Abbey and its school, the pretty villages of Coxwold and Kilburn – the latter associated with 'the mouse-man' and his furniture, the former with Shandy Hall (home of Laurence Sterne). A few miles away is Northallerton, a town of fine houses, with characterful villages all around. Fountains Abbey, Newburgh Priory, the white horse of the Hambleton Hills, Byland Abbey, Helmsley (old market town), the arboretum at Bedale and Harlow Car gardens are other attractions.

There are landscaped gardens at Duncombe Park, Helmsley – a town dominated by great castle ruins on a huge earthwork. Seventeenth-century Nunnington Hall not only has fine rooms but a display of miniature rooms too. Sion Hill Hall, at Kirby Wiske, is not historic – except in style – but is notable for its displays of period furniture. What was once the home of Thomas Lord – of cricketing fame – is now Thirsk's museum of local history and of cricket. In an area of spectacular abbeys, do not overlook some of the smaller gems such as Mount Grace Priory (with 23 monastic cells) or Saxon St Gregory's Minster at Nawton.

Readers' comments: A warm welcome. Comfortable, quiet room; good breakfast. Friendly hostess, very good house, beautifully furnished. Breakfasts are something special. One of the best b & bs we have encountered. Superb hospitality. Very warm welcome. Beautiful bedroom. Wonderful breakfasts in generous quantities. Every detail perfect. We were made comfortable and welcome.

ST MARY'S HOUSE   C D M PT X

Church Street, Kintbury, Berkshire, RG17 9TR   Tel: 01488 658551
West of Newbury. Nearest main road: A4 from Marlborough to Newbury
(and M4, junctions 13/14).

3 Bedrooms. £16.50–£21 (less for 4 nights). All have own bath/shower/toilet. TV. Views of garden, country. Clothes-washing on request.
Light suppers if ordered.
2 Sitting-rooms. With woodstove, central heating, TV. Bar.
Small garden

Old-fashioned roses and a grapevine up the walls add to the picturesque look of the Barrs' unusual house. Its pointed windows are lozenge-paned, and little dormers punctuate the roof: it was a school from 1856 until 1963.

All bedrooms are on the ground floor, one of them (with particularly hand-some bathroom, chaise longue and flowery chintzes) opening onto a paved terrace with lavender hedge. The sitting-room is furnished with antiques, and the dining-room with a great, 17th-century refectory table surrounded by leather chairs. Alcoves of books, pointed arches, three outsize sofas around a lacquer table in front of the handsome fireplace, and great copper vats of logs all add to an interior of outstanding distinction.

The lovely Kennet & Avon Canal is only a hundred yards away, for Kintbury lies midway between Hungerford and Newbury – towns described elsewhere in this book. Only a few miles south are the Hampshire Downs; and, westward, Wiltshire's Vale of Pewsey, both of which are scenic areas which take days to explore. Northward is a region rich in prehistoric remains – hill forts, barrows, etc. The valley itself is quite different: woodland, commons and meadows as the backdrop to villages of flint, brick and thatch with narrow lanes and some richly decorated churches. Birdwatchers and walkers love the whole area. Favourite out-ings include Avebury (prehistoric ring), Marlborough, Newbury (racecourse), and the recently opened Legoland, on the site of the former Windsor safari park, is a major attraction for families.

Picturesque Hungerford has scores of antique shops (many open on Sundays). And, of course, most visitors go to Windsor for its famous castle and neighbour-ing Eton College.

Readers' comments: Lovely atmosphere, lovely place. High standard of furnishing; so welcome.

Sitting-room at Welam House (see page 88)

SAMPSONS FARM RESTAURANT   C D PT S X
Preston, Devon, TQ12 3PP   Tel: 01626 54913
North of Newton Abbot. Nearest main road: A380 from Newton Abbot
towards Exeter (and M5, junction 31).

5 Bedrooms. £16–£22 (less for 3 nights or continental breakfast). Prices go up from June to September. Some have own shower/toilet. Tea/coffee facilities. TV. Views of garden, country. Washing machine on request.
Dinner. £14.95 for 3 courses (with choices) and coffee, or à la carte, from 7pm. Less for 2 courses. Vegetarian or special diets if ordered. Wine available.
1 Sitting-room. With open fire, central heating. **Bar.**
Large garden

To this traditional Devon house, all whitewash and thatch, came a Cornish farming family who gave it a new way of life – as a renowned restaurant. Hazel Bell runs the bed and breakfast, and her son Nigel the restaurant. Kristin the chef, who has been at Sampsons for nine years, cooks the gourmet-class lunches and dinners.

After scallops with garlic, one might have the house speciality – a half-duckling in orange sauce with vegetables cooked to perfection, and then a lemon ice cream with biscuity topping. (There is a good wine list too.) Dinner is served in a low, cosy dining-room, with candle-lamps and flowers brightening the plum tablecloths and a warm glow coming from the stone hearth. Beyond the small bar is a snug, timbered sitting-room with log fire in an inglenook.

The way to the bedrooms is all steps and twists (one of the rooms has a four-poster), for the house has grown in a higgledy-piggledy way since its probable beginnings in the 15th century: no one is quite sure of its age. It started as a long-house: family at one end and cattle at the other, with a cross-passage between – the passage, with screen walls of hefty oak planks, still survives.

Readers' comments: Most welcoming, food excellent. Restaurant fabulous; very helpful. Hospitality outstanding, food exceptional.

A few miles south-west, between Ashburton and Totnes, is **GREEN-COTT**, Sue Townsend's immaculate tile-hung 1970s house in Landscove. You can see Haytor Rocks from one of the two attractive en suite bedrooms; from the quarry-tiled kitchen (with Aga) one steps through glass patio doors straight into the colourful garden. Rooms are compact and restfully furnished. The nationally renowned Hillside garden centre is close, and for steam enthusiasts the South Devon Railway in the Dart Valley. After a starter such as melon or pâté, dinner will probably include a roast, or steak pie, perhaps followed by fruit pie with

Devonshire cream, then cheese and coffee. £17 (b & b).
Readers' comments: Sue is one of the best cooks; food beautifully presented. Warm welcome, good food. Sensational cook. Caring hostess. Superb food. [Tel: 01803 762649; postcode: TQ13 7LZ]

SAXELBYE MANOR HOUSE   C D PT
Church Lane, Saxelbye, Leicestershire, LE14 3PA   Tel: 01664 812269
North-west of Melton Mowbray. Nearest main road: A6006 from Melton
Mowbray towards Derby.

3 Bedrooms. £18–£20. One has own shower/toilet. Tea/coffee facilities. TV. Views of garden, country. Washing machine on request.
Dinner. £10.50 for 4 courses and coffee, at 7pm. Less for 2 courses. Non-residents not admitted. Vegetarian or special diets if ordered. Wine available. **Light suppers** if ordered.
1 Sitting-room. With open fire, central heating, TV, piano.
Large garden
Closed from December to February.

In this little hamlet is an especially attractive farmhouse, tucked within a garden where willows and fuchsias flourish. Parts of it are 800 years old. Margaret Morris has furnished it with a fascinating collection of Victoriana (even in the cloakroom): little velvet chairs and chaises longues, old prints and pot-plants in abundance. Narrow passages lead to a grand staircase constructed four centuries ago in the old stone stairwell. There's even a big Victorian bath in the huge bathroom. She provides traditional 4-course dinners: for instance, prawn cocktail, the farm's own lamb with four vegetables, sherry trifle, then Stilton and other local cheeses.

On the farm are cows and sheep. It provides not only free-range eggs for breakfast but very good, tested milk.

Melton Mowbray is a pleasant market town (from which you can go home laden with its famous pork pies and other products of the pig), and is well placed for visiting other historic Leicestershire towns such as Loughborough and Oakham (as well as Grantham and Stamford in Lincolnshire, and Nottingham for its castle and other historic buildings). Belvoir Castle and Rutland Water are well worth a visit.

Readers' comments: Have stayed repeatedly. Another wonderful Gundrey house! Meals and lovely bedroom were first class. Nothing was too much trouble. Lovely room, wonderful meal. Good cook, charming hostess. Friendly welcome.

The conservation village of Holwell has a particularly ancient church (1200) alongside which is 18th-century **CHURCH COTTAGE**, full of steps and turns inside. Here Brenda Bailey gives visitors not only a beamed bedroom with brass bed and a spacious bathroom but their own small sitting-room too, and their own front door. Breakfasts and light snacks are served in her dining-room, which overlooks the sloping, landscaped garden. £17.
Readers' comments: Delightful, beautiful. Superb hospitality. Amazing breakfast on silver salver, with newspaper. A delightful weekend; impressed by attention to detail. [Tel: 01664 444255; postcode: LE14 4SZ]

SAYWELL FARMHOUSE

C(12) S

Bedmonton, Kent, ME9 0EH Tel: 01622 884444
South-west of Sittingbourne. Nearest main road: A249 from Sittingbourne to
Maidstone (also M20, junction 8; and M2, junction 5).

3 Bedrooms. £20–£25 (less for 4 nights). Some have own bath/shower/toilet. Tea/coffee facilities. TV. Views of garden, country. No smoking. Washing machine on request.
Dinner (by arrangement). £16.50 for 3 courses and coffee, at 6–8pm. Less for 2 courses. Vegetarian or special diets if ordered. No smoking. **Light suppers** if ordered.
1 Sitting-room. With open fire, central heating, TV. No smoking.
Large garden

High up in the North Downs, mossy lanes thread their way between orchards sheltered from the wind by long lines of poplars. When autumn leaves are drifting down and traveller's joy tops the hedges with its shadowy foam, the golden apples are gathered and loaded for London's markets.

Here – far from the busy world – is found a white farmhouse, approached by a long brick path across its trim lawn, roses clinging to the flint walls of the garden. The oldest part – the kitchen – is 13th-century, its low beams hung with copper pans. The dining-room is four centuries younger: '1611' and the then owner's initials are carved on a beam.

Yvonne Carter has used pale colours for walls with exposed timbers, a good foil to the oak furniture which admirably complements this background and the big brick inglenooks. Some bedrooms have floors sloping with age, and windows that enjoy views of the dovecote and the Downs beyond.

Yvonne is an accomplished cook who sometimes does dinners for private parties; while for her resident visitors she ordinarily prepares such meals as avocado and kiwi fruit in a sour cream dressing; chicken with lemon sauce (and home-grown vegetables); profiteroles.

The tiny hamlet of Bedmonton, although it feels so remote, is well placed for visiting most of Kent's great sights, including Canterbury itself. Particularly near are the famous moated castle of Leeds, the county town of Maidstone (a celebrated museum of historic carriages near its ancient episcopal palace and mediaeval church), Rochester – cathedral, castle and considerable Dickens' associations, and Chatham – where the opening of the great dockyard to visitors is now proving a major attraction.

The hamlet is also close to picturesque Hollingbourne: right on the ancient Pilgrims' Way to Canterbury, this village has half-timbered inns and a church which is worth a visit to see the fine tomb of Elizabeth Culpeper (1638).

And all around are the North Downs: 'turfy mountains where live nibbling sheep' is a Shakespearean definition of the Downs.

This house may prove a handy stopover for Sheerness port or Dover or when going through the Channel Tunnel by train.

Readers' comments: Wonderful food. Hosts most kind. Very peaceful and cosy. Delightful hosts. Meals were wonderful. Courteous owners, very welcoming. Food very good. Beautiful place, everything for our comfort. History and charm. Exceptionally warm and friendly.

SCHOOL HOUSE
Newnham, Hertfordshire, SG7 5LA   Tel: 01462 742815
North-east of Letchworth. Nearest main road: A1 from Baldock to Biggleswade.

2 Bedrooms. £20. Both have own bath/shower/toilet. Tea/coffee facilities. Views of garden, country. No smoking. Washing machine on request.
Light suppers if ordered. Vegetarian or special diets if ordered. Wine available. No smoking.
1 Sitting-room. With open fire, central heating, TV. No smoking.
Large garden

Farrs have farmed here for generations; but this house had different beginnings, being first a village school – hence the bell high up on the peach-coloured façade, above a porch now covered in roses – and then a shooting-lodge. All around are fields and deep peace.

Trish Farr has an eye for striking colours, and every room seems to sing – with walls of brilliant viridian or coral, raspberry or mint. There are such distinctive touches as butterfly tiles in a fireplace, a budgerigar-patterned bedspread, and unusual antiques or junk-shop finds.

As she has four young children, she serves only simple meals (like chicken Kiev and fruit fool) and breakfast, sometimes eaten on the terrace; but there are lots of inns with good food, particularly in nearby Ashwell – famous for its church, music festivals (every Christmas) and old houses. (The high-towered church has mediaeval graffiti – old sayings, a record of the Black Death in 1350, and even an important picture of St Paul's Cathedral before the Great Fire.) Newnham's own church is 10th-century, with frescoes of St Christopher and a moat alongside, where trout are caught.

A talented lady lives at Wrestlingworth, over the Bedfordshire border. At thatched **ORCHARD COTTAGE**, once the village bakery and now a tearoom, Joan Strong makes delicate bobbin-lace – an old craft for which the area was once famous – while some of the furniture in the house was made by her husband, Owen. The pleasant rooms have views of fields, or of the garden enclosed by high cupressus hedges. From the large sitting-room (with log fire) glass doors open onto a paved terrace. For dinner, sample the many inns in this area. (No smoking.) £17–£19.

Readers' comments: Very good value; spotless and comfortable. [Tel: 01767 631355; postcode: SG19 2EW]

Prices are per person in a double room at the beginning of the year.

SEVERN TROW   **M**
Church Road, Jackfield, Ironbridge, Shropshire, TF8 7ND Tel: 01952 883551
South of Telford. Nearest main road: A442 from Telford to Bridgnorth
(and M54, junctions 4/5).

4 **Bedrooms.** £18–£22 (less for 3 nights).
Prices go up from March. All have own
bath/shower/toilet. Tea/coffee facilities. Views
of garden, country, river. No smoking.
2 **Sitting-rooms.** With open fire, central
heating, TV, record-player. Bar. No
smoking.
Small garden
Closed in November and December.

Through the Ironbridge gorge, scenic birthplace of the Industrial Revolution, sailing-barges called trows bore goods downriver to Bristol. The Severn Trow provided
the men with beer, dormitory lodgings and brothel. Then it became a church hall.

There are carpets on floors of red and black quarry-tiles, an old pine dresser
serves as a bar, and an outstanding and very colourful mosaic floor. The brewhouse is now another sitting-room.

Upstairs are excellent bedrooms with light colour schemes such as yellow and
white, and interesting furnishings – a net-draped brass bed, for example. One bedroom, with good bathroom and small kitchen area, is accessible from street level.

Very substantial breakfasts are provided by Jim and Pauline Hannigan but no
evening meal. However, there are over two dozen eating-places within a mile
radius. In winter (for parties of 6 or 8 guests) the inglenook, now re-equipped with
iron trivets, spit and cauldron, is used for cooking dinners and mulling wine.

Readers' comments: Most comfortable, wonderful welcome. Has to be seen to be
believed. Friendly couple, superb breakfasts, extremely helpful. The best we have
visited. Breakfast fruits a work of art! Friendly hosts. Enormous breakfast. Four-
poster a delight. Excellent.

ALBYNES, Nordley, is the house
where Frances Pitt lived and wrote
nature books. It was built in 1823 for
the Burgher of Bridgnorth, who named
it after his son Albinius. The dining-
room was designed to accommodate
fine carved panelling removed from a
nearby Tudor house, and there is an
elegant oak staircase that spirals its
way up to the bedrooms. Several of
these overlook the lake (or far hills), as
does the sitting-room – furnished with
antiques and gold brocade chairs.
Twisting passages and steps, unusual
doors and alcoves add character.

Cynthia Woolley's husband farms
the adjoining land – a mixture of
arable fields and pastures. A typical

dinner may comprise curried parsnip
soup, grilled lamb chops with fresh
herbs, and lemon-cream pudding.
£18–£18.50 (b & b).
Readers' comments: Wonderful cook;
generous and friendly hostess.
Wonderful hosts, lovely home. [Tel:
01746 762261; postcode: WV16 4SX]

SHIELDHALL

C(10) **D M S**

Cambo, Northumberland, NE61 4AQ   Tel: 01830 540387

West of Morpeth. Nearest main road: A696 from Newcastle to Otterburn.

6 Bedrooms. £17–£20 (less for 3 nights). All have own bath/shower/toilet. Tea/coffee facilities. Views of garden, country. Washing machine on request.
Dinner. £13.75 for 4 courses and coffee, at 7pm. Vegetarian or special diets if ordered. Wine available. **Light suppers** sometimes.
2 Sitting-rooms. With open fire, central heating, TV. No smoking. Bar.
Large garden
Closed from November to February.

Eighteenth-century stone buildings enclose a courtyard where white fantails strut, the former barns to left and right providing very well-equipped ground-floor bedrooms for visitors – each with its own entrance. Meals are taken in a beamed dining-room in the centre, furnished with antiques and an inglenook fireplace (a typical dinner might be home-made soup, a roast or coq au vin, blackcurrant tart, and local cheeses – with produce from the garden and orchard); and to one side are two sitting-rooms (one with library) for visitors.

Stephen Robinson-Gay is an accomplished cabinet-maker, happy to show visitors the workshop where he makes or restores furniture. Most of the work in all the rooms is his. For instance, beyond the arched doorway of the mahogany room is a colonial-style bed with very fine inlay, and in the oak room a four-poster with carved canopy, copied from a Flemish bed in Lindisfarne Castle (on Holy Island), complete with a secret cupboard to hold a shotgun.

Celia is a fount of information on local history and what to see. Close by is one of the National Trust's biggest houses, Wallington Hall.

Readers' comments: Super place. Fantastic holiday; everything you said and much more; lovely couple, food delicious.

Comfortable armchairs face a log fire in the big sitting-room of Christine Rodger's Victorian house, **OLD POST OFFICE COTTAGE**, at Little Bavington. Scots-born Christine serves such dishes as garbure paysanne and carbonnade of beef, followed by a choice of puddings. John Rodger can be relied on to produce trout and game in season. This is a quiet spot, with open views from the bedrooms, and all rooms are decorated in a refreshingly plain style. As well as the notable mansions open to the public, Bobby Shaftoe's family home is nearby. Hadrian's Wall and the city of Newcastle are other draws. £14–£15.
Readers' comments: Stayed for a week,

such being the welcome, homeliness and comfort, plus good home cooking . . . Very clean, well appointed, good food. Well furnished; lovely lounge and bathroom excellent. Meals superb. Nothing too much trouble to make us at home. We'll return. [Tel: 01830 530331; postcode: NE19 2BB]

SHOTTLE HALL   C D M PT S
Shottle, Derbyshire, DE56 2EB   Tel: 01773 550 276
North-west of Belper. Nearest main road: A517 from Ashbourne to Belper
(and M1, junction 28).

9 Bedrooms. £20–£29.50 (less for 7 nights and for senior citizens). Some have own bath/shower/toilet. Tea/coffee facilities. TV. Views of garden, country. No smoking.
Dinner. £12.50 for 4 courses and coffee, at 7.30pm (not Sundays). Less for 2 courses. Vegetarian or special diets if ordered. Wine available. **Light suppers** if ordered.
2 Sitting-rooms. With central heating, TV. Bar.
Large garden
Closed in November.

The guest-house is over a century old and has all the solid Victorian quality of that period: big rooms, fine ceilings and doors, dignity in every detail. Not only the bedrooms but even the bathrooms are large and close-carpeted, with paint-work and everything else in pristine condition. As well as a sizeable sitting-room, there are two dining-rooms – one is used for breakfasts because it gets the morning sun. From both, the huge windows have views of hills and of the fertile valley stretching below the house. There are a rose garden and lawns – and not another house in sight. Two bedrooms are on the ground floor; and there is a self-contained suite, which is suitable for partially disabled people.

Guests enjoy Phyllis Matthews's straightforward home cooking. As well as traditional roasts, a typical dinner menu might include: mushrooms in cream and garlic, chicken with brandy and cream sauce, hazelnut meringue, English cheeses, and coffee with cream. Phyllis collects antique cheese dishes; and has other antiques for sale.

Shottle is in the middle of a rural area of fine landscapes. Close by are the Derbyshire Dales and the Peak District. The Matlocks are a hilly area with pretty villages to be found. The old spa of Matlock Bath has interesting places to visit (stately gardens, wildlife park, model village, a museum of mining, and the tower, terraces and caverns of Abraham's Heights). Cromford is both attractive and historic, with Arkwright's first mill. There are six stately homes – including Chatsworth House – and innumerable good walks.

Around Derby, magnates built themselves great houses such as Wingfield Manor where Mary Queen of Scots was imprisoned, the very splendid Sudbury Hall which now houses a museum of childhood, Melbourne Hall where Lord Melbourne lived (the formal gardens are particularly fine and the Norman village church is outstanding), Kedleston Hall – a magnificent Adam house, and Calke Abbey (1701), the contents of which remained scarcely disturbed over the last century. In the Matlock direction is mediaeval Carnfield Hall. The traffic of Derby is worth braving to visit the cathedral and museums.

Readers' comments: Lovely room, excellent dinner: a winner. Wonderful! Delightfully warm and friendly couple. Superb cook. Thoroughly enjoyed our stay, charming and friendly people. Very impressed; could not have been more helpful. Very good hosts. An idyllic country house. The best! Spacious, comfortable bed-room. Friendly and helpful. Warm welcome, delicious food, comfortable room.

SISSINGHURST CASTLE FARM C(5)
Sissinghurst, Kent, TN17 2AB   Tel: 01580 712885
East of Tunbridge Wells. Nearest main road: A262 from High Halden towards Tunbridge Wells.

5 Bedrooms. £19–£25 (less for 4 nights). Prices go up from Easter. **Bargain breaks in winter to readers of this book.** Two have own bath/shower/toilet. Tea/coffee facilities. Views of garden, country. No smoking. **Light suppers** by arrangement. Vegetarian or special diets if ordered. No smoking.
1 Sitting-room. With open fire, central heating, TV.
Large garden

'Hydrangea petiolaris will grow under trees and ramble over an old stump', wrote Vita Sackville-West to her tenant at the Castle Farm. 'I asked the Director of Kew and he specially advised this.' In the same note she said: 'I can give you a lot of columbines – ask Vass [her gardener] for them.' James Stearns (grandson of that tenant, who still farms here) treasures this note from one of England's most famous gardening ladies, creator of the adjacent gardens at Sissinghurst Castle (now NT). It was in fact James's great-uncle, an estate agent, who first introduced the Elizabethan castle to Vita.

The farmhouse, which dates from 1855, was once a mansion inhabited by a substantial family – hence the row of servants' bells which still survives, along with such period features as panelled sash windows, fretted woodwork and the galleried staircase. Here hang two fine paintings lent by Nigel Nicolson (son of Vita and Harold Nicolson) who still lives in a wing of the castle. Furniture is a homely, pleasant mixture of old pieces; and one bedroom, with windows on two sides, has a good view of the castle. (B & B only, but Pat Stearns will provide light suppers if specially requested.)

It is worth climbing to the top of the tower at the splendid brick castle to look across the Weald towards the North Downs: below are woods, lakes, oast houses, Castle Farm's fields of cereals and sheep – and, of course, the world-famous gardens, with outbuildings and remnants of a moat. The castle was virtually a ruin when Vita and her husband, Harold Nicolson, rescued it in 1930. The gardens were planned as a series of 'rooms' and so although they extend to six acres the overall effect is intimate: a major part of their charm. Vistas open up unexpectedly; in every month there is something different in flower – from cottage-garden to rare species. One of the most popular of the gardens contains nothing but old-fashioned roses. Inside the castle you can see rooms where the two pursued their profession as writers.

Near here is the picturesque market town of Cranbrook (with cathedral-like church), and beyond its steep main street the biggest working windmill in the country, built before the Battle of Waterloo.

Reader's comment: We enjoy the very homely atmosphere and friendliness.

When writing to the authors, if you want a reply please enclose a stamped addressed envelope.

293

SLOOP INN   C D
Bantham, Devon, TQ7 3AJ   Tel: 01548 560489
West of Kingsbridge. Nearest main road: A379 from Kingsbridge to Plymouth.

5 Bedrooms. £20 **(to readers of this book only)**–£26. Less for 7 nights. Prices go up from Easter. Bargain breaks. All have own bath/shower/toilet. Tea/coffee facilities. TV. Views of country, sea, river. Washing machine on request.
Dinner. From £10.50 for 3 courses à la carte, at 7–10pm. Vegetarian or special diets if ordered. Wine available. **Light suppers. Bars.**
Closed in January.

It goes without saying that this 400-year-old inn by the sea has a history of smuggling.

One of its owners was in fact a notorious wrecker, luring ships (by means of false lights) onto rocks in order to plunder them. Since the law was that 'if any man escape to shore alive, the ship is no wreck' – and so plundering it would be theft, wreckers were murderous wretches too. Neil Girling can tell you many stories of the smugglers and point out places in the village where they hid their kegs of French brandy. Once, the Sloop minted its own coins (some are now in the interesting museum at Kingsbridge) with which to pay for goods and services – the coins were usable only to buy drinks at the Sloop: good business!

The inn is unspoilt: everything one hopes that a village inn will be but rarely is, low-beamed, stone-flagged and snug. Some walls are of stone, some panelled.

One of its several bars is made from old boat-timbers. Here you can take on the locals at a game of darts or table-skittles after enjoying an excellent bar meal; or stroll down to the sandy dunes to watch the sun set over the sea. Bathing, building sandcastles and exploring rock pools delight children; and there is surfing. Many of the plainly furnished bedrooms have a view of the sea or River Avon. (Sometimes the traffic noise is noticeable.) There is a yard and well at the back with seats.

Soups are home-made and ham home-cooked; smoked salmon, crabs and steaks are all local produce; granary bread is served. Fish is, of course, particularly good and fresh. All portions are generous.

Bantham is one of Devon's most ancient villages (the remains of prehistoric dwellings were laid bare in an 18th-century storm, and there was a Roman camp here later). Once, its main livelihood was pilchard-fishing – but no longer.

The whole area is remote, peaceful and unspoilt with good walks through beautiful countryside or along the coastal footpath; and yet the cities of Plymouth and Exeter are within reach, and the great resort of Torquay. In early spring, wildflowers are everywhere and the blue waves are beginning to be dotted with boating enthusiasts. This is a rich farming area ('the fruitfullest part of Devonshire'), with villages of colourwashed cottages thickly thatched.

On the other side of the Avon is Bigbury where a strange, long-legged 'tram' takes people across the sea to Burgh Island.

Readers' comments: Food very good. A most enjoyable stay. Quiet, peaceful, idyllic scenery. Excellently furnished. Food the best I've eaten lately. Really comfortable.

294

SNOWFORD HALL FARM C

Hunningham, Warwickshire, CV33 9ES   Tel: 01926 632297

East of Leamington Spa. Nearest main road: A423 from Coventry to Banbury (and M40, junction 12).

3 Bedrooms. £18–£19. Some have own shower/toilet. Tea/coffee facilities. Views of garden, country. No smoking.
1 Sitting-room. With central heating, TV, piano. No smoking preferred.
Large garden

A very long drive through fields leads to this spacious 18th-century house at the heart of a 200-acre farm (cattle and crops) with fine views around it. One enters through an interesting hall with a big, china-laden dresser and polished wood floor. The huge sitting-room is very attractively furnished. Here and there around the house are many things made by Rudi Hancock herself, a skilled craftswoman – samplers, for example, and corn dollies; and furniture which she has restored.

The most interesting of the bedrooms has a very unusual and decorative Dutch bed of solid mahogany, handsomely carved.

Snowford Hall is near Leamington Spa and its environs, and such sights as Kenilworth Castle, Coventry Cathedral and Draycote Water country park. Packwood House has an exceptional garden, and the National Centre for Organic Gardening is nearby. Southam is an old market town; Stoneleigh a mediaeval village (with the great National Agricultural Centre outside it). The National Exhibition Centre is within easy reach, so are Warwick University and Rugby School. And all around are some of England's finest landscapes.

Hunningham is close to the ruler-straight Fosse Way, which goes all the way from Devon to Lincolnshire, built by the Romans to link their most important forts. It still survives the centuries, so well was it engineered, on the line of a prehistoric trail which was an important trade route linking the mines of the south-west to ports that traded with Scandinavia.

Leamington gained the prefix 'Royal' when the young Queen Victoria stayed there only a year after coming to the throne. Fine 18th- and 19th-century squares and terraces give the town a discreet charm. There are some outstanding gardens in the area – including the public Jephson Gardens in Leamington and those of the Mill House by the river at the foot of Warwick Castle.

Readers' comments: Lovely rooms; gorgeous, silent countryside. Wonderful reception, beautiful house, plenty of very good food, wholly pleasurable. Very comfortable. A very warm welcome and excellent breakfast.

Houses which accept the discount vouchers on page ii are marked with a V on the lists at the beginning of this book, see pages xi–xix and pages xxi–xxii.

SOMERSET HOUSE C D M PT S X
35 Bathwick Hill, Bath, (Avon), Bath & North-East Somerset, BA2 6LD
Tel: 01225 466451
Nearest main road: A36 from Bath to Bristol.

10 Bedrooms. £20–£32 (less for 3 nights). Prices go up from September. Bargain breaks mid-week. All have own bath/shower/toilet. Tea/coffee facilities. Views of garden or city. No smoking. Laundry facilities.
Dinner. £19 for 4 courses (with choices) and coffee, at 7pm (not Sundays). Less for 2 courses. Vegetarian or special diets if ordered. Wine available. No smoking. **Light suppers** on Sundays.
2 Sitting-rooms. With open fire, central heating, TV, piano. Bar. No smoking.
Large garden

Above the Doric-columned portico of this handsome Georgian mansion, only a 12-minute walk from the city centre, is a decorative iron verandah; wisteria and roses climb up the walls of honey-coloured stone.

The entrance hall (with a Greek key border round the ceiling) leads to a sitting-room, with conservatory opening onto lawn. There are two bedrooms on the ground floor. The dining-room is below stairs (it has an open fire and pine dresser).

On the first floor is another sitting-room with a particularly pretty plasterwork ceiling and very old Venetian glass chandelier. The original panelled shutters flank the high sash windows; outside is the long verandah, with fine city views.

Bedrooms are large and pleasantly furnished, many with antique fireplaces (one has an antique loo) and attractive views. Some have Laura Ashley fabrics.

Malcolm Seymour (once a tourist board director) is a mine of information on what to see in the neighbourhood. Throughout the year he arranges weekends with special themes: Georgian Bath, canals, opera, Brunel. (Ask for programme.) Jean, formerly a teacher, enjoys cooking recipes appropriate to each of these occasions, assisted by other members of the family.

At breakfast, few people opt for the full cooked version because there is such an array of home-baked breads (nutty, spicy or fruity), preserves, muesli, freshly squeezed fruit juice and so forth; often haddock, kidneys, Cumberland sausage or muffins are offered. As to dinner, when nothing more exotic is afoot, daughter Anna-Clare or son Jonathan may produce something like game soup, their own 'rolypoly, gammon and spinach' recipe with home-grown vegetables, and apples in cider served with home-made ice cream. On Saturdays, special gourmet dinners (at 7.30pm) are offered; Sunday lunch is also available except in summer.

Perhaps the greatest glory is the garden. Every tree flowers at a different season, and the centrepiece is a great 300-year-old Judas tree – at its purple best in May. All around, between beds of peonies and columbines, is a 7¼-inch rail track installed by a former owner.

Readers' comments: The best establishment I've stayed at, where people count; the cooking reinvigorates the taste buds. Superb comfort and food. Excellent accommodation; nicest food we have ever experienced. Particularly delighted. A favourite. The Seymours make guests welcome. Delightful.

SOUTH FARM
East Meon, Hampshire, GU32 1EZ   Tel: 01730 823261
West of Petersfield. Nearest main road: A272 from Winchester to Petersfield.

3 Bedrooms. £19–£21 (less for 3 nights). Some have own bath/toilet. Tea/coffee facilities. Views of garden, country, river. No smoking. Washing machine on request. **Light suppers** if ordered.
1 Sitting-room. With open fire, central heating, TV.
Large garden

The approach to the farm is delightful. There are specimen trees on a lawn (ash, chestnut), an old granary and a grapevine under glass. In the 500-year-old house is a brick-floored dining-room with huge inglenook, rush ladderback chairs and a big oak table. The very large sitting-room has antique furniture and chinoiserie curtains in gold and blue. Bedrooms have been very agreeably furnished by Jane Atkinson: one with poppy fabrics, for instance; in another are exposed beams and a lace bedspread. An oak-panelled room has peony fabric. All are outstanding.

The house is full of flowers because Jane, an accomplished flower-arranger, regularly has large deliveries from Covent Garden market. You can dine at the George or Izaak Walton inns in East Meon if you want more than a light supper.

The Meon Valley amid the South Downs has churches that go back to Saxon times, flint-walled houses, and prehistoric burial mounds. To the south are woodlands, remnants of the once-great Forest of Bere, and then comes Portsmouth Harbour. Despite heavy traffic on roads into the port, this is well worth a visit – to see Nelson's *Victory*, Henry VIII's *Mary Rose* and his Southsea Castle, Victorian forts up on the hills and Norman Portchester Castle down by the waterfront. There are boat trips and ferries to the Isle of Wight; excellent museums (don't miss the Royal Marines one); Dickens's birthplace; much ceremonial on Navy Days; and waterfowl on the wilder shores of the two natural harbours here. Queen Elizabeth Forest contrasts with all this (drive to Georgian Buriton, go up Butser Hill, or visit the recreated Iron Age village).

The clear chalk streams, with occasional watermills, have made this lovely area well known for its watercress and its trout: the River Itchen is famous among anglers, and its valley is outstandingly beautiful – to drive or walk along it from Itchen Stoke is an unforgettable experience, pausing at Ovington's mediaeval inn on the way. Old and New Alresford are on opposite banks of the River Alre: in the latter, colourful Broad Street, with 18th-century houses, is well worth visiting (and in its churchyard are the graves of French prisoners from the Napoleonic wars). At the north end of Broad Street are a millstream and dam built in the 12th century; and also a lovely footpath through watercress beds and past a black-and-white thatched mill spanning the river. Other villages worth seeking out include Tichborne – famous for a *cause célèbre* in 1871 when an Australian imposter laid claim to the estate here; and for the Tichborne Dole, flour given to villagers since 1150.

SPION KOP

C(5) **S X**

Spring Lane, Ufford, Suffolk, IP13 6EF   Tel: 01394 460277
North of Woodbridge. Nearest main road: A12 from Ipswich to Lowestoft.

3 Bedrooms. £16–£20 (less for 7 nights). Some have own bath/shower/toilet. Tea/coffee facilities. TV. Views of garden, country. Washing machine on request.
Dinner. £15 for 3 courses and coffee, at 7pm. Non-residents not admitted. Vegetarian or special diets if ordered. **Light suppers** if ordered.
1 Sitting-room. With open fire, central heating, record-player.
Large garden

When Colonel Walters returned from the Boer Wars he built himself a house reminiscent of his years on the veldt, with an almost conical roof of thatch and a wide-eaved verandah. Its site must have reminded him of the hill on which 300 British died at the hands of the Boers, for he named it after this.

The Fergusons have added their own distinctive touches to what was already a very unusual house. Along the verandah (hung with brimming baskets of lobelias and begonias) are life-size marble nymphs – the Four Seasons – with more among the flowerbeds. Indoors, along with much other Victoriana which surely would have delighted the colonel, are bronzes and paintings of turn-of-the-century beauties well displayed against the pale pink walls of sitting- and dining-rooms, through the lattice windows of which (or from the glass sun-room) there are wooded valley views more typical of Devon than of Suffolk. There is a meadow brilliant with kingcups and wild orchids in spring.

Bedrooms are spacious and elegantly furnished; and Susan's meals are delicious. One example – a herby soup with croûtons was followed by pork in a sauce of mushrooms, cream and wine (with vegetables cooked to perfection); raspberry meringues; and a glass of wine included.

The house overlooks pastoral countryside. Woodbridge, a few miles away, has a restored tide mill and much else of interest. Snape Maltings and Sutton Hoo (where the Anglo-Saxon treasure was found) are not far.

Readers' comments: First-class stay. Most welcoming, excellent cook. Accommodation better than 3-star hotels. Food is of cordon bleu standard. Bedrooms very comfortably and stylishly furnished. What a glorious surprise! Idyllic house and garden, warm and genuine welcome, delightful room. Excellent, made very welcome. Beautiful setting, friendly attitude, marvellous food. Probably the most interesting house we have stayed in.

About 40 houses, mostly in Suffolk, but some in Hampshire, are in a scheme under which one-third of whatever you pay is given to Oxfam. Between them over £95,000 has been raised. The scheme was originated by Rosemary and Robin Schlee, at whose own very lovely home – with equally lovely garden – visitors are also welcomed. All charge similar prices to Spion Kop (simpler houses in the scheme charge less); and all have been inspected. On departure, every visitor is given a special receipt for the one-third that goes to Oxfam. Phone Mrs Schlee: 01394 382740.

SPLATT HAYES

CMS

Buckerell, Devon, EX14 0ER   Tel: 01404 850464
West of Honiton. Nearest main road: A30 from Honiton to Exeter (and M5, junction 28).

5 Bedrooms. £17.50–£19 (less for 4 nights). Prices may go up from April. Some have own shower/toilet. Tea/coffee facilities. TV. Views of garden, country. No smoking.
Dinner. £15 for 4 courses (with choices) and coffee, at 7pm. Less for 3 courses. Vegetarian or special diets if ordered. No smoking. **Light suppers** if ordered.
1 Sitting-room. With open fire, piano, record-player.
Large garden

This is what everyone thinks a Devon cottage should be: thatched roof and white cob walls; flagged floors, beams and brick hearth inside. It is 400 years old. In the pretty garden are 30 eucalyptus trees, a ginkgo and a sequoia (with fields of sheep beyond), a view you can enjoy from an L-shaped, ground-floor bedroom which has its own sitting-area.

It is Douglas Cowan who cooks the dinners, to a very high standard. A typical menu might include (among several choices) cannelloni filled with smoked mackerel and spinach as a starter, pork fillet with cherry sauce, blackberry and apple filo, then cheeses. He uses much home-grown and organic produce, makes his own bread and preserves, and has a repertoire of imaginative vegetarian dishes. Mandy has trained in aromatherapy and electro-crystal therapy - treatments are available while you stay.

Honiton, celebrated for lace-making, is full of antique shops and has twice-weekly markets too. Historic Exeter is only 15 miles away. The Blackdown Hills are an Area of Outstanding Natural Beauty, and in the opposite direction is a lovely coastline dotted with such old-fashioned resorts as Sidmouth, Branscombe and Beer. Visitors also enjoy the nearby donkey sanctuary, Bicton Park and the old Seaton–Colyton tramway.

Readers' comments: Delicious meal; nothing too much trouble.

Equally old and picturesque is **GOLDCOMBE FARMHOUSE** (near pretty Gittisham), where renovations revealed a rare feature – a screen wall of oak planks dividing rooms downstairs. The house has beautiful views across the Otter Valley and towards far Dartmoor. A sun-room and one ground-floor bedroom open onto the garden with its lavender bushes and old apple-trees. There are a grass tennis court and a games barn. One breakfasts in the hall, with a view into the kitchen where Ann Stansell, a trained cook, also produces cordon

bleu meals (but only by arrangement), such as eggs dijonnaise, trout with hollandaise sauce and spinach timbales, and lemon soufflé. £17.50 (b & b). [Tel: 01404 42559; postcode: EX14 0AB]

299

SPRINGFIELD
C PT S X

16 Horn Lane, Linton, Cambridgeshire, CB1 6HT   Tel: 01223 891383
South-east of Cambridge. Nearest main road: A1307 from Cambridge to
Haverhill (and M11, junctions 9/10).

2 Bedrooms. £16–£20 (less for 4 nights). Prices go up from April. One has own bath/toilet. Tea/coffee facilities. TV. Views of garden, country, river. No smoking. Washing machine on request.
Light suppers if ordered.
1 Sitting-room. With open fire, central heating, TV. No smoking.
Large garden

Unexpected in the peaceful countryside is the distant roar of lions as dusk falls!
But Springfield is quite near Linton Zoo.

The spring which gives the 19th-century house its name rises in a carp pond
at the far end of the garden – or, rather, gardens; for there is a succession of
hedge-enclosed areas, each with its own character. One of these (almost islanded
by a twist of the River Granta) is equipped for children.

The house is of gracious design, its gables decorated with fretted bargeboards
and at its side a spacious conservatory where breakfast is often served (or you can eat
in your bedroom, provided with table and chairs for the purpose). Judith Rossiter
has filled the conservatory with white flowering plants. Adjoining it is a comfortable
sitting-room with paintings of sailing ships on the walls.

Bedrooms are on the second floor, furnished with antiques including old maps
of America and other Americana (Fred is descended from George Washington's
aide-de-camp). The obvious reason for staying in this pretty conservation village
is to visit nearby Cambridge (there is a bus).

Readers' comments: Very comfortable, and a really splendid breakfast. Charming
and very comfortable. Warm welcome. Strongly recommended.

In picturesque Hadstock, just across
the Essex border, is a flowery close
called Orchard Pightle ('pightle' is an
old word for an enclosure) within
which is Gillian Ludgate's home,
YARDLEYS. Above one of the
sitting-rooms are well-equipped bedrooms in pale colours, neat and airy,
with private bathrooms; and at the
back a conservatory brimming with
flowers, where meals are sometimes
served. Gillian is a keen cook, serving
suppers or such meals as salmon
mousse, pork fillet with apricots, and
pavlova. Breakfast may include garden
fruit, local sausages, her own jam,
and dry-cured bacon. £18–£18.50
(b & b).

Readers' comments: You really feel
welcome. Like home from home, one
of the nicest. Vegetarian breakfasts substantial and imaginative. All sorts of
generous little extras, excellent evening
meals. A lovely place; the most pleasant
of hosts; food second to none. Friendly
and helpful hostess, lovely house. [Tel:
01223 891822; postcode: CB1 6PQ]

SPROXTON HALL
Sproxton, North Yorkshire, YO6 5EQ   Tel: 01439 770225
South of Helmsley. Nearest main road: A170 from Thirsk to Helmsley.

3 Bedrooms. £19.50–£22.50 (less for 3 nights). Some have own bath/shower/toilet. Tea/coffee facilities. TV. Views of garden, country. No smoking. Washing machine on request.
1 Sitting-room. With open fire, central heating, TV. No smoking.
Large garden

Under a high-beamed ceiling, deep chintz-covered armchairs and a settee face a stone wall with an open fireplace in the large sitting-room, with plentiful antiques around. The bedrooms in this 17th-century house are just as prettily furnished, with flowery fabrics and sprigged wallpaper, and the double rooms have brass half-tester beds with crisp draperies. (The bathrooms too, whether private or shared, are pretty – Margaret Wainwright is understandably house-proud!) Views are of a trim garden with a bed of dwarf conifers, beyond which are the fields of this large mixed farm; or of a farmyard, with hills in the background.

Margaret Wainwright does not serve evening meals, for the area has excellent pub restaurants. It is also rich in 'sights' – castles, mansions, gardens, and the famous ruined abbeys of the Cistercian monks. One imposing castle is at nearby Helmsley, a picturesque market town with superior shops and galleries. Many of the villages in the area are very attractive, with their carefully conserved houses of honey-coloured stone and red pantiled roofs. Coxwold is an example: here is Laurence Sterne's house, Shandy Hall, and one of those good pubs.

Readers' comments: Excellent value, a beautiful house, genuine Yorkshire hospitality.

Tucked away behind Ampleforth village street, the **OLD SUMMER-HOUSE** in East End contains not only a twin bedroom (and shower-room) but a sitting-room, where Linda Chambers serves breakfast. This she brings across from her cottage, built on the site of the orchard which the summer-house once overlooked (it belonged to the old house just behind). She is a keen and able gardener, and guests can enjoy her work from a small crazy-paved patio by the stone and pantile summer-house. Ampleforth, best known for its Catholic public school, has the North York Moors

to the north and York to the south. No smoking. Closed in winter. £17 (minimum 2 nights).
Readers' comments: Our second delightful stay. Highly recommended. [Tel: 01439 788722; postcode: YO6 4DA]

For explanation of code letters (C, D, M, PT, S, X) see inside front cover.

SPURSHOLT HOUSE   **C D S X**
Salisbury Road, Romsey, Hampshire, SO51 6DJ   Tel: 01794 512229
(Messages: 01794 522670)
Nearest main road: A27 from Romsey to Salisbury.

3 Bedrooms. £18–£20 (less for 4 nights). Prices go up from April. Bargain breaks. All have own bath/shower/toilet. Tea/coffee facilities. Views of garden, country, river. No smoking. Washing machine on request.
Dinner. £12.50 for 4 courses and coffee, at 7.30–8.30pm (not weekends). Less for 2 courses. Non-residents not admitted. **Light suppers** if ordered.
1 Sitting-room. With open fire, central heating, TV. No smoking.
Large garden

In the 1830s this was the home of Lady Cowper, one of Lord Palmerston's many mistresses (he was nicknamed Cupid!).

There are paved terraces with urns of geraniums, overlooking a lawn, impressive topiary, and a view of Romsey Abbey. Beyond flowerbeds, yew hedges enclose a succession of further pleasures – one garden leading into another, a parterre with lily-pool, followed by apple-trees, and a dovecote with fantails.

Rooms have been furnished by Anthea Hughes in keeping with the character of the house. The spectacular sitting-room has stained glass originally in the Palace of Westminster. One bedroom is oak-panelled, and all contain antiques and extra-large beds. Two have open fireplaces, elegant sofas and garden views.

Dinner, served in a dining-room handsomely furnished in Victorian style, may consist of such dishes as potted shrimps, marinated lamb kebabs, lemon meringue pie, and cheeses. There is also self-catering accommodation, with the option of dining in.

Readers' comments: Thoroughly enjoyed staying. Made most welcome. Lovely house with beautiful gardens. Most comfortable. Couldn't have been kinder. A joy to stay in, keynote seems to be quality; atmosphere most welcoming.

On Tote Hill near Sherfield English is **LITTLE FOSTERS**, Barbara Boby's fully modernized 18th-century cottage on her mixed smallholding – very much off the beaten track. Bedrooms, neat and trim, overlook fields and a lawn with weeping birch. Using local produce (much of it organically grown), Barbara provides two- or four-course meals which might include stuffed mushrooms or fresh asparagus; trout or pheasant in red wine; gooseberry crumble or pears and apple with crystallized ginger, yogurt and cream; or sandwiches. The house is surrounded by a large garden and rolling countryside threaded with footpaths for walkers. £16–£16.50.

Readers' comments: Most kind. Small but comfortable room. Absolutely wonderful food and very good value. Charming cottage, peaceful setting. Most delightful place, most interesting people. [Tel: 01794 340309; messages: 01794 340558; postcode: SO51 0JS]

STANSHOPE HALL

Stanshope, Staffordshire, DE6 2AD   Tel: 01335 310278
North-west of Ashbourne. Nearest main road: A515 from Ashbourne to
Buxton.

3 Bedrooms. £20–£30 (less for 3 nights).
Prices go up from April. All have own
bath/shower/toilet. Tea/coffee facilities. TV.
Views of garden, country.
Dinner. £17.50 for 3 courses (with choices)
and coffee, at 7.30pm. Vegetarian or special
diets if ordered. Wine available. No smoking. **Light suppers.**
1 Sitting-room. With open fire, central
heating, piano, record-player.
Large garden

Built in 1670 by Cromwell's quartermaster, Jackson, the Hall has seen many
changes. It was greatly extended in the 1780s and when, at nearby Ilam, a great
mansion burnt down in the 19th century, salvaged fireplaces were re-installed
here. Later a theatrical designer made it his home, embellishing it with all sorts of
trompe l'oeil effects. The murals with peacocks and trees in the sitting-room are
in the manner of Rex Whistler, while in the entrance hall a stairway and arches of
Hopton stone contrast with painted marbling.

Recently, local artists have repainted bedrooms with decorative murals (bathrooms too), each with its own theme – Moorish, Egyptian or piscine.

Not only the ambience but also the food provided by Naomi Chambers and
Nick Lourie is out of the ordinary. A typical menu: carrot and ginger soup or
pancakes stuffed with leeks and cream cheese, followed by lamb in red wine and
honey, then either gooseberry ice cream or Bakewell tart.

Readers' comments: A real home from home. Food excellent. Very relaxing and
enjoyable break. Warm and comfortable with excellent views. Faultless; food
exceptionally good. Charmed with the history and decor.

BEECHENHILL FARM, just outside Ilam, is a long low house built
from limestone two centuries ago.
Perched on a south-facing hillside, it
overlooks grazing sheep and cows. Sue
Prince has stencilled flowers and stars
on the walls. Her breakfasts have won
an award (there is always plenty of
fruit and, in winter, porridge); self-
catering guests sometimes partake. No
dinners, but there are local inns.
There's a pretty garden and a goat
wanders in the paddock. One of the
two pleasant bedrooms (own showers
and toilet) is a light and spacious
family room. Author William Horwood
stays here; and you'll find the farm

described as 'the best place in the
world' by one of the moles in
his *Duncton Quest*. £17.50–£19.50.
[Tel: 01335 310274; postcode: DE6
2BD]

STODY HALL

Stody, Norfolk, NR24 2ED Tel: 01263 860549

North-east of Fakenham. Nearest main road: A148 from Cromer to Fakenham.

3 Bedrooms. £18–£25 (less for 7 nights). Some have own bath/toilet. Tea/coffee facilities on request. Views of garden, country, river.
Dinner. £16 for 3 courses and coffee, at approx. 7.30pm (not Sundays). Less for 2 courses. Non-residents not admitted. **Light suppers** if ordered.
1 Sitting-room. With open fire, central heating, TV, piano.
Large garden

This handsome, 400-year-old house has the flint walls typical of the area. Inside, there are comfortable sofas in a sitting-room with silky coral walls and marble fireplace, log fire, watercolours of local scenes on the walls. There are mementoes of Khartoum (where a family forebear served with General Gordon); and 'Spy' cartoons on the green and white panelled walls of another sitting-room. In the garden are a hard tennis court and a croquet lawn. (Carriage drives available.)

The dining-room is particularly dramatic, the colour of its Turkey carpet repeated in the scarlet walls that are the background to a great Regency table and chairs. Miriam Rawlinson serves such dinners as haddock mousse, beef Stroganoff (with garden vegetables), and crème brûlée.

Upstairs are attractive bedrooms with, for example, a tufted white spread contrasting with the rosy satin of bedhead and curtains, lacy cushions (made by Miriam), a fine wardrobe of figured mahogany, and draped dressing-tables.

The house overlooks rolling pastures and all around are quiet lanes for walks. Nearby is Holt, a picturesque market town; and the very beautiful heritage coastline is only five miles away. The bird sanctuary and seal colony at Blakeney are worth a visit.

Readers' comments: Wonderful food, ambience and hosts. Elegant house in charming village; cooking imaginative and excellent.

BURGH PARVA HALL (at Melton Constable) was a farm in the 16th century; in the 1840s an imposing wing was added. It is the only house left at Burgh (pronounced 'borough') Parva, for the village was destroyed after the Great Plague of 1665.

One enters through the dining-hall where logs crackle under the ogee arch of the fireplace. Furniture is old in style, rooms huge; your bedroom will have a sofa or armchairs from which to enjoy the view through sash windows – fine sunsets, and even a distant glimpse of the sea. William Heal will either give you a lift to and from a local inn for dinner, or by arrangement you may dine at the house. £16–£17.

Readers' comments: Impressive house, excellent breakfasts. Very helpful. [Tel: 01263 860797; postcode: NR24 2PU]

STOTSFOLD HALL   C S
Steel, Northumberland, NE47 0HP   Tel: 01434 673270
South of Hexham. Nearest main road: A695 from Hexham to Corbridge.

4 Bedrooms. £18.50–£19.50. Prices go up from May. Some have own bath/toilet. Views of garden, country.
Light suppers if ordered.
1 Sitting-room. With central heating, TV.
Bar.
Large garden

Hexhamshire – the area of south Northumberland around the town of Hexham – is little known to visitors. Much of it is well-wooded countryside of steeply rolling hills. Off a quiet road which leads to nowhere in particular is Stotsfold Hall.

Once the heart of a big estate now broken up, the present house stands at the end of a long drive in a 15-acre park. There are big lawns, flowerbeds, a rose garden, and a large greenhouse. Even though the house is at 800 feet, the lie of the land is such that everything seems to flourish. Particularly impressive are the trees which are a feature of the grounds: copper beeches, lodgepole pines, larches and cedars, to name only a few.

The house was built in 1900 and is full of the monumental joinery characteristic of the time. The scale is large, ceilings high, windows big. Furnishings are conventional and comfortable. On the walls hang old deeds and mortgages.

The Woottons do not usually provide an evening meal, and guests go to Hexham or Slaley to eat, or more often to the nearby Fox & Hounds – generally known as the 'Click 'Em In' from the cry of the waggoners who used to change horses here. On their return, visitors can make use of the house bar.

Readers' comments: The greatest feature for us was the way the Woottons welcomed us. Difficult to conceive of a better place to stay. Brilliant! Very warm welcome, thoughtful touches. Idyllic. A splendid country house. What a delight to walk in the garden and woodland. So many comforts and extras. Incredible value. Absolutely everything supplied. Excellent hosts. In a class of its own.

Only 10 minutes' walk from the centre of characterful Hexham, **WEST CLOSE HOUSE** is in a quiet, cul-de-sac (Hextol Terrace). Designed by an architect for himself about 70 years ago, it is a redbrick villa comfortably furnished in an uncluttered style. The gardens, enclosed by tall, clipped beech hedges, are beautifully tended, with a revolving summer-house at the back. Patricia Graham-Tomlinson provides varied breakfasts; also simple snacks (restaurants nearby). £17.50.

Readers' comments: The best so far: a winner. Made to feel at home. Breakfast and accommodation excellent. [Tel: 01434 603307; postcode: NE46 2AD]

STOURCASTLE LODGE   C PT X

Gough's Close, Sturminster Newton, Dorset, DT10 1BU   Tel: 01258 472320
South-west of Shaftesbury. Nearest main road: A357 from Blandford Forum
to Wincanton.

5 Bedrooms. £20–£33 **(less 10% for 2 nights half board to readers showing the current edition of this book on arrival).** Prices go up from April. All have own bath/shower/toilet. TV (some). Views of garden. No smoking.
Dinner. £16 for 4 courses (with choices) and coffee, at 7.30pm. Vegetarian or special diets if ordered. No smoking.
1 Sitting-room. With open fire, central heating, TV.
Garden

Gourmets seek out this secluded town house, for peace as well as good food. Although just off the market place, Gough's Close is traffic-free and quiet: a narrow lane opening out into a green and pleasant place, with the River Stour beyond. The 17th-century Lodge has been agreeably furnished by Jill Hookham-Bassett, with soft greens and pinks predominating. Everything is very spick-and-span, the bedrooms cottagey in style, and all rooms have views of the secluded garden where one can take tea.

Ken and Jill, who achieved a gold star for cooking when she trained at Ealing Technical College, provide food well above average. A typical dinner might be: kedgeree, chicken cooked in tarragon and mushroom sauce, and charlotte Malakoff (made with cream and almonds). An unassuming house with a lot to offer in the way of hospitality.

From the Lodge, it is easily possible to explore not only Dorset but parts of Wiltshire and Somerset as well. Mediaeval Sherborne's superb 15th-century abbey of golden stone deserves a lingering visit.

Readers' comments: Friendly; eager to help and please. Tastefully furnished house and spotlessly clean. Jill's cooking was superb. Delightful. Made to feel welcome and at home. Room charming. Enjoyed our visit so much. Delicious food. Evening meal was highlight of my stay; breakfast faultless with vast array of choice.

Nearer Shaftesbury, and by lovely Cranborne Chase, a watermill at Melbury Abbas was mentioned in Domesday Book. On its Saxon foundations the present **MELBURY MILL** was built in the 18th century (its historic wheel still turns). Architect Richard Bradley-Watson has done a beautiful conversion of beamed out-buildings to provide two exceptionally good bedrooms with en suite facilities overlooking the millpond. In the house itself there is a third, large bedroom, sitting-room with woodstove, and a stone-flagged dining-room where Tavy (cordon bleu trained) serves such meals as marinated mushrooms, pheasant, and meringue gâteau. £19–£20 (b & b). [Tel: 01747 852163; postcode: SP7 0DB]

STOWFORD HOUSE

C

Stowford Lane, Stowford, Devon, EX20 4BZ Tel: 01566 783415
South-west of Okehampton. Nearest main road: A30 from Okehampton to
Launceston.

6 Bedrooms. £19.50–£22 (less for 2 nights;
**further reductions for 3 nights mid-week
to readers of this book only**). Most have
own bath/shower/toilet. Tea/coffee facilities.
TV (in some). Views of garden, country.
Dinner. £15.50 (or £19 to non-residents)
for 4 courses (with choices) and coffee,
at 7–8.30pm. Vegetarian or special diets if
ordered. Wine available. **Light suppers** if
ordered.
1 Sitting-room. With open fire, central
heating, TV. **Bar.**
Large garden
**Closed from mid-December to mid-
March.**

This former country rectory is now a comfortable hotel, dignified by its 18th-
century features such as the fine windows, handsome front door, a graceful
archway inside and impressive staircase. The large garden is at its best in May.

The hotel has a reputation for good food. With over 25 years' experience of running first a catering service for businessmen and then a restaurant in Winchester,
Jenny Irwin has accumulated a wide repertoire of recipes. Typical dishes she may
serve – in a dining-room with a particularly fine Victorian fireplace – include Stilton
and apricot mille-feuilles, casserole of venison, and pecan and date tart.

Bedrooms are large, light and airy. Everywhere is a profusion of pot-plants;
and on some walls are delicate watercolours by David's father, Sydney Irwin.

Nearby is Lydford which, a thousand years ago and more, was a place of note
(its tin was exported to the Mediterranean). In Saxon times it even had its own
mint; and seven coins from the time of Ethelred the Unready are displayed at the
Castle Inn. The neat, square castle was built in 1195 for use as a 'stannary' prison
(the tin-miners had their own stannary laws and courts – *stannum* is Latin for tin),
with a pretty little church beside it. Lydford is also famous for its gorge – one can
walk by foaming waters with oak woods hanging overhead to the roaring 200-foot
waterfall known as the White Lady. Lichens, mosses and ferns give the scene a
subtropical look as the waters hurtle around smooth black boulders.

Within about 30 miles are Princetown (high and bleak, famous for Dartmoor
Prison, which was built by Napoleonic prisoners, and for prehistoric stones nearby), Plymouth, the sandy resort of Bude with rocky Tintagel beyond, Exeter,
lovely Salcombe, Looe and Clovelly, and a new steam museum.

From here one can explore the 400 square miles of Dartmoor's wild hills, its
forest and woodlands, granite tors, archaeological sites and moorland villages. As
well as the famous Dartmoor ponies roaming free, there is a great deal of wildlife.
Granite quarries, stone slab bridges, waterfalls, ruins of tin mines, thatched
cottages – all contribute to the variety of the scene. There are guided walks with
experts to explain what one sees, or National Park leaflets to consult.

Readers' comments: Delightful accommodation, wonderful meals. Excellent. Very
impressed with the ambience and the owners. Really beautiful house. Exceptional
food. Very quiet. Warmest welcome. Food excellent. Wonderful experience.
Exceptionally warm and welcoming; devoted to making guests comfortable. The
place we'd most like to visit again. Wonderful; food quite superb. Welcomed
most heartily; standard of meals cannot be too highly commended.

STRATFORD LODGE   C(8) M PT
4 Park Lane, Castle Road, Salisbury, Wiltshire, SP1 3NP
Tel: 01722 325177

8 Bedrooms. £20–£27 (less for 2 nights). Prices go up from Easter. Bargain breaks. All have own bath/shower/toilet. Tea/coffee facilities. TV. Views of garden. Balcony (one). No smoking. Washing machine on request.

Dinner. £18 for 4 courses, or fewer *pro rata,* (with choices), sherry and coffee, at 7–8pm. Special diets if ordered. Wine available. No smoking. **Light suppers** if ordered.

2 Sitting-rooms. With open fire, central heating, piano, record-player.

Garden

In a quiet byway overlooking a park stands a fine Victorian house, now a handsomely furnished guest-house. Jill Bayly has taken a lot of trouble to find good furniture in keeping with the style of the house. The sitting-room has much Victoriana and a large array of flowering plants; the pale green dining-room, mahogany tables laid with pretty rosy china (napkins to match) and rose curtains at the windows. Bedrooms are attractive, particularly one with a cane and carved bedhead on a bed with cover to complement the apricot walls. In another room, pale pink, brass beds have lace spreads. After dark one can go on sitting by candle-lamp in the garden, which is enclosed by flowering shrubs.

Jill's varied repertoire of dishes for dinner always includes some choice for vegetarians, and she cooks to a high standard. A typical meal: home-made soup, avocado with a Roquefort and walnut dressing; duckling with a sauce of port and redcurrant jelly; and a help-yourself dessert table. Breakfasts, too, are generous, with options such as kedgeree.

Salisbury is also known as New Sarum (new in 1220!) because the first town was elsewhere, on the hill now known as Old Sarum, which began as an Iron Age fort – you can still see traces of a Norman cathedral up there.

Readers' comments: Dinner superb, a meal to remember. Friendly and helpful. The very best place we've found. Enchanting rooms. Delightful and amusing hostess. Food subtle, interesting and delicious – even the light suppers. Lovely old house, delightfully furnished, charming hostess, superb dinners and breakfasts. Wonderful food, fantastic facilities, tremendous hostess.

FARTHINGS, at 9 Swaynes Close, Salisbury, is very central (there's a view of the cathedral spire over rooftops) yet very quiet, and it has a garden with brimming flowerbeds. All rooms are immaculate, and pleasantly furnished. Gill Rodwell's breakfast choices include croissants and much else. No smoking. £18.

Readers' comments: Clean, quiet and excellent value for money. Very charming lady. Gleamingly clean. Delighted. A treasure. Charming lady; accommodation and breakfast first rate. [Tel: 01722 330749; postcode: SP1 3AE]

STREET FARMHOUSE

C P T S X

Alton Road, South Warnborough, Hampshire, RG29 1RS
Tel: 01256 862225

South-east of Basingstoke. Nearest main road: A287 from Odiham to
Farnham (and M3, junction 5).

3 Bedrooms. £15–£19 (less for 3 nights).
Some have own bath/shower/toilet. Tea/coffee facilities. TV. Views of garden, country.
No smoking. Washing machine on request.
Dinner (if ordered). £15 for 4 courses
(with choices) and coffee, at 7.30pm.
Non-residents not admitted. Vegetarian or
special diets if ordered. No smoking. **Light suppers.**
1 Sitting-room. With open fire, central
heating, TV, record-player.
Large garden

Two 16th-century cottages were combined into one to make this attractive house,
beamed and with inglenook fireplace, in an ancient village through which a
stream runs. Wendy Turner's choice of furnishings admirably complements the
old house. There are prettily carved chairs in the pale green dining-room; pine
doors have been stripped and brick walls exposed; buttoned chairs in rust-colour
covers are gathered around a log stove in the sitting-room. Bedrooms are very
pleasant – for instance, furnished with chest-of-drawers of woven cane, with very
good armchairs and colour schemes. One bathroom has an oval bath in peach,
and a bidet. Standards throughout are high and in the garden there is a heated
swimming-pool. Dinner might include pork in cider with apricots, and raspberry
pavlova.

North Hampshire (quickly accessible along the M3) is an ideal base from
which to explore southern England: within an hour are Winchester, Southampton
and the New Forest. But anyone who lingers here will find plenty of interest, not
least because this is Jane Austen country (her house is at Chawton, and scenes
from the area feature in her books). Farnham still has streets much as she knew
them, and a hilltop castle. Not far away is Selborne where Gilbert White wrote his
natural history (1789) and one can still see countryside that he saw. Both his and
Jane Austen's homes are open to the public – his has a museum about Captain
Oates and Scott's Antarctic expedition and it is surrounded by National Trust
woodlands. Nearby Odiham, too, retains the appearance of an 18th-century
market town, with ruined castle nearby; and there are pretty villages – Greywell,
Upton Grey (houses encircling a pond), Sherborne St John (with a Tudor NT
mansion, the Vyne, and moated Beaurepaire), Basing (castle ruins). Silchester
was once a great Roman fort.

Westward lie Litchfield, a flowery village in an area of prehistoric remains;
Wherwell, a real showpiece – all timber and thatch, with fine views of the famous
River Test; streamside Hurstbourne Tarrant; and Highclere – castle and hilltop
grave of Lord Carnarvon (who discovered Tutankhamun's tomb in 1922). In
marked contrast to all these quiet pleasures are Farnborough's air show and
Aldershot's military tattoo.

Readers' comments: An outstanding experience. A place of great character; seldom
have we met such friendly people. Excellent in all respects. Our third visit, excellent value. Beautifully kept. Made most welcome; warm and comfortable.

SUGARSWELL FARM X
Shenington, Warwickshire, OX15 6HW   Tel: 01295 680512
South of Stratford-upon-Avon. Nearest main road: A422 from Stratford to Banbury.

3 Bedrooms. £18–£20. Prices go up from May. All have own bath/toilet. Tea/coffee facilities. Views of country. No smoking. Laundry facilities on request.
Dinner. £18 for 4 courses and coffee, at 6.30pm. Less for 3 courses. Non-residents not admitted. No smoking. **Light suppers** if ordered.
1 Sitting-room. With open fire, central heating, TV. No smoking.
Large garden

Rosemary Nunnely is a cook of cordon bleu calibre – her greatest delight is preparing meals. Visitors who stay with her are likely to get something very different from ordinary 'farmhouse fare': for instance, seafood gratin followed by fillet steak (home-produced) in a sauce of port, cream and garlic, with crème brûlée to finish. Rosemary uses wine and cream in many of her dishes, rum in such specialities as Jamaican torte.

The house is modern but made from old stones taken from a demolished cottage. It has big picture-windows, and a striking staircase with 18th-century portraits. Sofas are grouped round a huge stone fireplace in the sage green sitting-room. The hall, like the dining-room, has terracotta walls. Guests sit on Chippendale chairs to dine; and one side of the dining-room consists of a glass wall filled with Rosemary's collection of Crown Derby.

Upstairs are elegant bedrooms – one with a sofa from which to enjoy woodland views beyond the fields where cows graze, and a very large bathroom decorated in bright mulberry.

Included in the price is the gift of a touring map of the region, showing how to get to (for instance) Warwick, Stratford, the Cotswold towns, Woodstock (Blenheim Palace), Oxford, Silverstone (car races) and Sulgrave (the Washington ancestral home) or such stately homes as Upton House (horse trials in autumn) and Farnborough Hall. In Shenington itself is an outstanding garden, at Brook Cottage.

As to the curious name Sugarswell: shuggers (mediaeval slang for robbers) made a settlement here, which their more respectable neighbours destroyed. Vestiges can still be seen from the air.

Readers' comments: Time capsule of the good life! Charming hostess, comfortable and delightful accommodation, delicious food. Very pleasant rooms and good views. Superb welcome, superb cooking. A lovely place to stay. An outstanding cook. Accommodation excellent. First class; food excellent; nicely furnished. Very pleasant room. *And from the former manager of a 5-star hotel:* We have been back nine times. A truly beautiful house and excellent food.

Book well ahead: many of these houses have few rooms. Do not expect dinner if you have not booked it or if you arrive late.

SULNEY FIELDS

Colonel's Lane, Upper Broughton, Nottinghamshire, LE14 3BD
Tel: 01664 822204
North-west of Melton Mowbray. Nearest main road: A606 from Melton
Mowbray to Nottingham.

5 **Bedrooms.** £17.50–£20 (less for 3 nights or continental breakfast). Some have own bath/shower/toilet. Tea/coffee facilities. Views of garden. Washing machine on request.
Dinner (by arrangement). £12.50 for 3 courses and coffee, at times to suit guests. Less for 2 courses. Vegetarian or special diets if ordered. **Light suppers** if ordered.
1 **Sitting-room.** With open fire, central heating, TV.
Large garden

Panoramic views over the Vale of Belvoir stretch in front of this handsome 18th-century house, entered through a pretty 'gothick' porch filled with flowering plants. A big sitting-room has a wall of tall windows making the most of this scene. Its silky coral walls are matched by the armchairs.

Hilary Dowson's bedrooms are equally handsome. A big blue one, with fine mahogany furniture and good paintings, has a pretty bathroom and an adjoining room, which makes it ideal for families; the pink room, a bay window for enjoying those views. Outside is a sheltered swimming-pool.

Melton Mowbray is famous for pies (visit Ye Olde Pork Pie Shoppe) and Stilton cheese, made in Colston Bassett village where you can buy it direct; there are riverside parks and an ancient church. Other churches (and villages) well worth a visit include those of Waltham-on-the-Wolds (carved monks), Denton (gatehouses; manor with lakes) and Bottesford (monuments, and witchcraft associations). Go to Loughborough for its carillon of 47 bells.

What remains of great Sherwood Forest lies to the north of Nottingham, and here (in Ricket Lane, Blidworth) is a Victorian hunting-lodge, **HOLLY LODGE**. It is near the estate of ancient Newstead Abbey which became Byron's home: it and its grounds are open to the public. Most of the visitors' bedrooms at the Lodge are in converted stables opening onto a grassy court with chairs. A Laura Ashley suite with mahogany-fitted bathroom is particularly attractive. Dinners are eaten in the house, sometimes in the big kitchen with its dresser and copper pans: by arrangement, Ann Shipside produces such meals as stuffed tomatoes, salmon, apple-and-sultana custard crumble. Afterwards, one can sit under the grapevine and fuchsias of the conservatory to enjoy a

view of old roses and woodland, or by a log fire in the William Morris sitting-room. £20–£21.

Readers' comments: The most congenial accommodation we have found. Everything was done with a smile. Superb meal. Rooms beautifully appointed. [Tel: 01623 793853; postcode: NG21 0NQ]

311

SUNDAY SCHOOL

CMSX

Copthorne, North Petherwin, Cornwall, PL15 8NB   Tel: 01566 785723 or 781552

North-west of Launceston. Nearest main road: A30 from Launceston to Bodmin.

3 Bedrooms. £16–£18. All have own bath/shower/toilet. Tea/coffee facilities. TV. Views of garden, country. No smoking. Washing machine on request.
Dinner. £12.95 for 3 courses (with choices) and coffee, from 7pm. Less for 2 courses. Vegetarian or special diets if ordered. No smoking. **Light suppers** if ordered.
1 Sitting-room. With central heating, record-player. No smoking.
Large garden

A tiny hamlet deep in the Cornish countryside is not perhaps the most obvious site for a top-class restaurant, but Sharon Seal has succeeded in creating something quite out of the ordinary in quiet Copthorne. A hundred years ago, farming folk from miles around stabled their horses in what is now a comfortable sitting-room, with its original roughcast stone walls and an arched window in place of the old doorway, while their children trooped up the wide, shallow stairs to the huge room above to learn their Bible stories and sing about sunbeams, pilgrims and Christian soldiers. That space has now been beautifully converted into two immaculate, unfussy bedrooms bright with fresh flowers, patchwork and pine furniture, and pretty stencils enhancing cream paintwork; in one, a ladder leads to a gallery bed above. Shower-rooms are neat and spacious, and there is a separate bathroom for those who wish to soak out the day's exertions before going down to one of Sharon's dinners, an occasion of no mean order. On Thursdays to Saturdays, the pretty blue-and-green dining-room is open to non-residents and the choice of dishes is wide; on other nights, the choice is more limited but the quality just as good – for Sharon is a professional cook whose last position was head chef in Esso's European headquarters. After a starter of smoked mackerel and horseradish pâté served with oatcakes, or pork saté, for instance, one might tuck into beef cooked in stout with herb and cheese dumplings, or a magical stuffed pepper which leaves one wondering why everyone isn't vegetarian. Puddings are equally delicious, and everything is served on gaily patterned china. (Guests bring in their own wine.) Round the walls are several photographs of the Sunday School as it used to be, though it is doubtful whether any of those sober farmers in their Sunday best would recognise the house now.

A cosy third bedroom, on the ground floor, is attractive to those who find stairs difficult (it has grab-rails in its bathroom, too). The house is within easy reach of spectacular walking country as well as less demanding attractions such as the Tamar Otter Sanctuary or the famous garden at Lanhydrock.

Reader's comment: Renovated in a most attractive way.

Prices are per person in a double room at the beginning of the year.

SUNSHINE COTTAGE   **C M PT S X**
The Green, Shepherdswell, Kent, CT15 7LQ   Tel: 01304 831359 or 831218
North-west of Dover. Nearest main road: A2 from Dover towards Canterbury
(also M2, junction 7; and M20, junction 13).

5 Bedrooms. £18–£21 (less for 7 nights). Prices go up from April. Some have own shower/toilet. Tea/coffee facilities. Views of garden, country. No smoking. Washing machine on request.
Dinner. £14 for 3 courses (with choices) and coffee, at 6.30–8.30pm. Less for 2 courses. Vegetarian or special diets if ordered. No smoking. **Light suppers** if ordered.
2 Sitting-rooms. With open fire, central heating, TV, record-player. No smoking.
Small garden

Neither shepherd nor well gave this pretty village its name: the Saxons knew it as Sibert's Wold. Sunshine Cottage, built in 1635, is now the home of Barry and Lyn Popple.

One steps into a cosy sitting-room with shaggy, cocoa-coloured carpet and low beams, a velvet sofa facing a brick inglenook that has logs piled high and hop bines draped across it. In a kitchen that is open to view, Lyn cooks such meals as home-made soups, chops or chicken, fruit salad or spotted dick. These are served in a dining-room where antique pine is complemented by coir matting, dressers display antique plates, old pews and stickback chairs surround tables laid with pretty china.

There is one ground-floor bedroom (with shower), decorated with Liberty fabrics. Those upstairs vary in size and style; several have antique iron bedsteads and views of village rooftops. Barry is an artist and some of his pictures are on the walls.

Readers' comments: Full of treasures. A relaxed cottage atmosphere. Made us very welcome. Quite delightful.

Distinctive Kentish oast house

TAILRACE
Crowdy Mill, Bow Road, Harbertonford, Devon, TQ9 7HU
Tel: 01803 732340
South of Totnes. Nearest main road: A381 from Totnes to Kingsbridge.

4 Bedrooms. £18.50–£23.50 (less for 5 nights). Three have own bath/shower/toilet. Tea/coffee facilities. Balcony (in two). Views of river, country. Washing machine on request.
Dinner (by arrangement). £14.50 for 4 courses and coffee, at 7.30pm. Non-residents not admitted. No smoking.
2 Sitting-rooms. With open log stove (in one), TV, video.
Large garden

Don and Ann Barnes used to run the working watermill here, but they now live in one of two well-converted cottages. This cottage, called Tailrace, has two comfortable en suite double bedrooms. Guests have the use of the living-room with antique furniture, paintings, books, and sculpture by Ann's father, William Reid Dick. One window looks out directly onto the river where, in season, trout can be seen swimming upstream, wild ducks can be fed, kingfishers flash past and wagtails and the occasional dipper can be watched. The other large window opens onto a terrace where, in warm weather, breakfast can be enjoyed with a lovely view of the surrounding hills.

The other bedroom is on the ground floor of the second cottage, just across the garden (which is also available for self-catering), where guests have the use of the whole cottage, including a single room for family or friend. Upstairs, there is a sitting-room with a south-west facing balcony, a kitchenette and dining-area. Breakfast and dinner are served in Tailrace.

Don Barnes is responsible for the free-range eggs and organic vegetables; Ann makes all the breads, jams, marmalades and chutneys. There is a wide choice of meals all made from local produce (mostly organic) and fish fresh from Brixham market, plus the famous local cheeses.

The surrounding countryside is superb, with marvellous walks along the coast and over the moors. Dartington with its gardens, sculpture and craft shops is only a few miles away, and the newly opened High Cross House, (a mini St Ives Tate) is also there. The trip down the River Dart from Totnes to Dartmouth should not be missed.

Being perched on a high bank, 18th-century **WOODSIDE COTTAGE**, at Blackawton, has superb valley views. A steep little garden of slabs, ferns and flowers brings you to the front door, inside which is a beamed breakfast-room, which Val and John Clark have furnished with antiques, a conservatory with bamboo chairs, and stone fireplaces. Bedrooms are very pretty (pine and delicate fabrics predominate) and en suite bath/shower-rooms too. Once a gamekeeper lived here, and the woods are still full of pheasants (in the

stream, herons pursue the trout). This is a great area for wildflowers. For meals, village pubs are close. £16–£18. *Readers' comments:* Peaceful and pretty. Hospitable. [Tel: 01803 712375; postcode: TQ9 7BL]

TANHOUSE FARM

Rusper Road, Newdigate, Surrey, RH5 5BX   Tel: 01306 631334
South of Dorking. Nearest main road: A24 from Dorking to Horsham
(and M25, junction 9).

2 Bedrooms. £16–£18.50. Prices go up
from Easter. Tea/coffee facilities. Views of
garden. No smoking. Washing machine on
request.
Light suppers if ordered.
1 Sitting-room. With open fire, central
heating, TV. No smoking.
Large garden

A dozen shoes, at least two centuries old, are displayed in the kitchen of this
16th-century, half-timbered farmhouse. They were discovered at the back of
chimneys when alterations were being done – inside several children's shoes were
ears of corn (fertility symbols). The shoes came as no great surprise because,
throughout this area, these are often found: putting them up chimneys was
believed to bring good luck. This was once the house of tanners and cobblers,
who could doubtless afford to be liberal with their shoe charms.

One can see through into the kitchen from the breakfast-room (low-beamed
and with latched doors), which opens onto a terrace overlooking a small brook
and a pond with an island frequented by 40 ducks, geese and coots. There's a
76-foot well and a lily-pool too, with fields of sheep and cows beyond.

All rooms have character. In a brick inglenook is an iron fireback dated 1644;
around it are greeny-blue velvet armchairs and low oak tables, solid and heavy,
which began life as wood-chopping or pig-slaughtering benches. A carved sideboard is loaded with old china. On the landing is revealed the cruck construction
of the house (that is, massive curving tree-timbers used in their natural shape
to support the roof). Pastel walls and fabrics (complementing pale green or pink
carpets) give the bedrooms a fresh, light look.

For dinner, Nina Fries recommends several of the many local inns.

There's a hidden corner in Dorking:
an oval green, high up, where horses
graze (within minutes of the High
Street). Around this conservation area
pretty villas were built in 1830, one
of which, **THE WALTONS**, 5 Rose
Hill, is now the home of Margaret
Walton. She has chosen lovely fabrics
and wallpapers while retaining such
features as graceful cast-iron fireplaces
and even rather splendid Victorian
baths. The bedroom with the best view
is on the second floor: beyond
Dorking's mellow rooftops you can
see Ranmore Common (NT) and
Denbies' huge vineyard (open to visitors for tastings). In the handsome din-

ing-room, she provides candlelit dinners (such as smoked salmon, chicken
fricassée, pavlova), Sunday lunches
and snacks. Breakfast is sometimes
served on the sunny terrace overlooking a secluded garden. (Baby-sitting
available.) £15–£17.50. [Tel: 01306
883127; postcode: RH4 2EG]

EXPLANATION OF CODE LETTERS

(These appear, where applicable, in alphabetical
order after the names of houses)

C   Suitable for families with children. Sometimes a minimum age is stipulated, in which case this is indicated by a numeral; thus **C**(5) means children over 5 years old are accepted. In most cases, houses that accept children offer reduced rates and special meals. They may provide cots and high chairs; or games and sports for older children. Please enquire when booking. And do not expect young children to be lodged free, as babies are. Many houses have playing-cards, board games, irons, hair-dryers, maps, wellingtons, bicycles, and so forth to lend – just ask. Families which pick establishments with plenty of games, swimming-pool, animals, etc., or that are near free museums, parks and walks, can save a lot on keeping youngsters entertained. (Readers wanting total quiet may wish to avoid houses coded **C**.)

D   Dogs permitted. A charge is rarely made, but it is often a stipulation that you must ask before bringing one; the dog may have to sleep in your car, or be banned from public rooms.

M   Suitable for those with mobility problems. Needs vary: whenever we have used the code letter **M**, this indicates that not only is there a ground-floor bedroom and bathroom, but these, and doorways, have sufficient width for a wheelchair, and steps are few. For precise details, ask when booking.

PT   Accessible by public transport. It is not necessary to have a car in order to get off the beaten track because public transport is widely available; houses indicated by the code **PT** have a railway station or coach stop within a reasonable distance, from which you can walk or take a taxi (quite a number of hosts will even pick you up, free, in their own car). The symbol **PT** further indicates that there are also some buses for sightseeing, but these may be few. Ask when booking.

S   Indicates those houses which charge single people no more, or only 10% more, than half the price of a double room (except, possibly, at peak periods).

X   Visitors are accepted at Christmas, though Christmas meals are not necessarily provided. Some hotels and farms offer special Christmas holidays; but, unless otherwise indicated (by the code letter **X** at top of entry), those in this book will then be closed.

THORN MILL FARM   C(8) **PT S**
Frogmore Road, East Budleigh, Devon, EX9 7BB   Tel: 01395 444088
North-east of Exmouth. Nearest main road: A3052 from Exeter to Lyme Regis
(and M5, junction 30).

4 Bedrooms. £18–£20 (less for 7 nights).
Prices go up from May. Some have own
bath/shower/toilet. Tea/coffee facilities. TV.
Views of garden, country. No smoking.
Light suppers if ordered.
1 Sitting-room. With open fire, central
heating, TV, piano, record-player. No
smoking.
Large garden

Sir Walter Raleigh was born in the picturesque village of East Budleigh, where the
Budleigh brook winds through the main street, past thatched cottages and cobbled paths. At the edge of the village, on the site of a former old mill, lies this
16th-century converted Devon long-house. The mill was demolished and the
watercourse diverted in 1904, when it became a dairy farm. Now, no longer a
working farm, it has been carefully restored by David and Jennie Capel-Jones and
retains many period features.

The guests' sitting-room still has its original oak beams and inglenook fireplace where on colder evenings you will find a log fire. Here you can relax in comfortable armchairs or sofas. David, a former concert promoter, has a keen interest
in boats and amateur dramatics: maritime paintings hang on the walls, and the
room is decked with personal memorabilia and books. Off the sitting-room is a
pleasant dining-room where breakfast is served.

Upstairs, along a narrow corridor, are pretty cottage-style bedrooms, well
equipped, with matching floral bed coverings, curtains and lampshades all made
by Jennie, and views over the Otter Valley.

By prior arrangement you can sup with the family; or you can eat in one of the
two excellent village inns.

David and Jennie can recommend many splendid coastal walks in the area and
will even drive you to a spot and drop you off. The beach at Budleigh Salterton is
a 5-minute drive away, or a 40-minute walk along the river to the red sandstone
cliffs. There is also trout fishing available on the River Otter.

16th-century, thatched **JUBILEE
COTTAGE** at Sidbury overlooks the
lovely Sid Valley. All bedrooms are
neat and pleasant – two spacious back
rooms have a good view of Buckley
Hill. Front rooms, overlooking Chapel
Street, are double-glazed. There is a
snug sitting-room, and all walls are of
very thick white-painted cob (solid
clay, built up lump by lump). German-
born Marianne Coles is an adventurous cook, and dinner might include
such German and Italian specialities as
chicken, vegetable and noodle soup; a
schnitzel in a creamy mushroom sauce;

and apfelstrudel or tiramisu. No smoking. £16–£18 (b & b).
Readers' comments: Enjoyable time,
good accommodation. Meals carefully
prepared. [Tel: 01395 597295; postcode: EX10 0RQ]

317

THORNLEY HOUSE C(9) D S X
Allendale, Northumberland, NE47 9NH Tel: 01434 683255
South-west of Hexham. Nearest main road: A69 from Newcastle to Hexham.

3 Bedrooms. £17.50 (less for 4 nights). All have own bath/shower/toilet. Tea/coffee facilities. TV. Views of garden, country. Washing machine on request.
Dinner. £10 for 3 courses and coffee, at about 7pm. Non-residents not admitted. Vegetarian or special diets if ordered.
2 Sitting-rooms. With central heating, TV, piano, record-player.
Large garden
Closed in November.

Allendale Town is a large village in a sheltered valley amid some of the most open scenery in England – deserted grouse moors and breezy sheep pastures which stretch for uninterrupted miles, punctuated only by isolated farmhouses and the occasional relic of the lead mining which once made this area important. On the outskirts of the village is Thornley House, a large and solid inter-war house in a big garden with woods and fields around it. Rooms are spacious and light, with views of the wooded roads into the village and of the Pennines.

Eileen Finn is a keen cook, and though guests are offered conventional fare (vichyssoise soup, breaded chicken, salad, and chocolate mousse, for example, served on Wedgwood china), she needs only a little encouragement to cook a dish from Mexico, where she lived for eight years, or from another of the many countries to which she has paid long visits. Bread, yogurt and muesli are home-made, orange juice freshly squeezed. Mementoes of her journeys abound in the house: batik pictures from Kenya, onyx figures and chess sets from Mexico, Chinese paintings (one on cork), rugs from Turkey and elsewhere (and others she has made herself). As well as being a linguist and chess-player (she enjoys playing with guests), she is an able pianist, and there is a Steinway grand in one of the two sitting-rooms. Visitors may be taken on guided walks on occasion. Otherwise, they can make their way through woodland to the village. At Christmas, there is a full-board house party.

Allendale is Catherine Cookson's country. She lives nearby and many of her Mallen stories are set here. It is one of the loveliest parts of the north country, wild and rocky, in parts comparable with some Swiss scenery. Allen Banks, where two rivers converge, is a beauty-spot. Not far off is the Killhope Pass (nearly 2000 feet high) with a great wheel once used for crushing ore when these hills were mined for lead. A long process of restoration (by Durham County Council) is approaching completion: the result will be one of the most interesting 'working museums' in the country. In Allendale Town, on every New Year's Eve costumed 'guizers' parade with blazing tar-barrels on their heads – vestige of a half-forgotten pagan fire rite. At Allenheads a few miles away, an award-winning heritage centre houses a small display about the history of the area, shops and a café. At Hexham is a great Norman abbey, well worth visiting.

Readers' comments: Very welcome. Delightful venue. Very comfortable. Friendly. Nice house, excellent room. Superbly quiet and comfortable. Wonderful food. Outstanding. Most welcoming. Piano duets a real bonus.

318

THORNTON MANOR

C(5)

Ettington, Warwickshire, CV37 7PN   Tel: 01789 740210
South-east of Stratford-upon-Avon. Nearest main road: A429 from Warwick
to Stow-on-the-Wold (and M40, junction 15).

3 Bedrooms. £17.50–£19 (less for 3 nights
or continental breakfast). All have own
bath/shower/toilet. Tea/coffee facilities in
kitchen. Views of garden, country. No
smoking. Washing machine on request.
Light suppers sometimes.
1 Sitting-room. With log stove, central
heating, TV, piano.
Large garden
Closed from December to February.

A stately home in miniature, this stone manor house, E-shaped in plan, declares
its date, 1658, on a doorpost. Through an iron-studded oak door with decorative
hinges, heavy bolts and locks, one enters a great hall dominated by a large stone
fireplace with log stove. Overhead are massive chamfered beams.

Through the leaded panes of deep-set, mullioned windows in the breakfast-
room (and in a bedroom above it) there are views of the garden, woods and the
fields of this farm, which is well tucked away at the end of a long drive. Little
humps in the grass show where there was once a village in view until, in the 13th
century, the Black Death killed off all its 60 inhabitants. Ancient outbuildings
include an old pigeon-house from the days when the birds were farmed.

Gill Hutsby (who occasionally sings at the Royal Shakespeare Theatre) has
used old-fashioned furniture and rosy cretonnes in the bedrooms. There is a
kitchen for guests' use, and also a tennis court. Visitors can fish for trout in the
Hutsbys' lake or enjoy coarse fishing in the River Dean. Stratford-upon-Avon is
best visited out of season.

Readers' comments: The place to get away from it all. Full of character.

Also at Ettington is **GROVE FARM**,
a house found at the end of a brick
path, with grapevine beside it and an
old pump. It is full of character, with
unusual furniture and trifles Meg and
Bob Morton have collected: from a
spectacular carved sideboard to an old
imp's head built into one wall, an elm
manger to a collection of knobkerries.
The chased silver pheasant-gun
belonged to Bob's grandfather and the
old dough-chest to Meg's (he was a
baker). Bedrooms, under the sloping
eaves, have own bathrooms, pretty fabrics, good carpets and old-fashioned
furniture. Meg serves only light suppers. (The bar food at the Houndshill
Inn is very good.) Meg cares for elderly
horses; they are to be seen grazing in

the fields beyond which are deer woods
and a panoramic view of the
Cotswolds. Closed in December and
January. £17–£18.50.
Readers' comments: Warm, friendly welcome. Most impressed. The most
friendly we encountered, welcome
fabulous. [Tel: 01789 740228; postcode: CV37 7NX]

TIBBITS FARM   **C D X**
Nethercote, Flecknoe, Warwickshire, CV23 8AS   Tel: 01788 890239
South of Rugby. Nearest main road: A425 from Leamington to Daventry (and
M45/M1, junction 17).

3 **Bedrooms.** £19–£22.50 (less for 4
nights). Prices go up from Easter. All have
own bath/shower/toilet. Tea/coffee facilities.
TV. Views of garden, country. No smoking.
Washing machine on request.
Light suppers if ordered.
1 **Sitting-room.** With open fire, central
heating, TV, piano, record-player. No
smoking.
Large garden

Very well tucked away near the banks of the River Leam (which gives Leamington
its name) is a 17th-century farmhouse that once belonged to Baron Tibbits: in the
nearby church you can see 13th-century monuments to his forebears. Since his
time, the house has been modernized – for instance, French doors now open onto
the garden from a beamed sitting-room, where the huge, stone-hooded fireplace
in an inglenook still survives. Alison Mills has decorated this room in pale green
and pink to match the Chinese carpet; and has chosen a similar colour scheme for
her bow-windowed dining-room where roses on the fabrics complement
mahogany furniture. There are far views over fields of crops and across the humps
which are telltale traces of a village that had to be deserted in the 18th century,
after the Enclosure Acts. These legalized the confiscation of what had previously
been common lands, farmed by villagers, for the advantage of big landlords – the
devastating effect of which inspired many poems of John Clare, the 'peasant poet'
who lived in the adjacent county of Northamptonshire.

Out in the garden there survives a curiosity – a three-seater loo used by
parents and child even as late as this century.

Bedrooms are large and airy. One has a silky quilt with bedhead painted to
match; another (with lots of furry toys), white furniture painted with roses; the
smallest, sprigged bedlinen and wallpaper to match.

Alison does not provide dinners but gladly takes visitors to and from the
nearby Olive Bush, where there is a cordon bleu cook.

TIMBER HALL   C(8) **D S**
Cold Christmas, Wadesmill, Hertfordshire, SG12 7SN   Tel: 01920 466086
North of Ware. Nearest main road: A10 from Ware to Cambridge.

4 Bedrooms. £17.50–£20. Some have own bath/toilet. Tea/coffee facilities. TV. Views of garden, country. No smoking. Washing machine on request.
Dinner. £13.50 for 4 courses and coffee, at 8pm. Less for 2 courses. Non-residents not admitted. Vegetarian or special diets if ordered. **Light suppers** by arrangement.
1 Sitting-room. With open fire, central heating.
Large garden

One steps straight into the raftered, mediaeval hall which gives this house its name. Beyond is a gracious sitting-room added much later, its many windows and French doors opening onto an attractive garden. The carpet and walls of soft green are a good background to interesting pictures and to the huge, oak court cupboard which has been in Angela Shand's family since it was made in 1604 (she is distantly related to the earls of Verulam, whose stately home nearby – Gorhambury House – is occasionally open to the public). All around the house are wide fields and complete tranquillity (even though London is half an hour away), a scene that can be enjoyed from any of the pleasant bedrooms.

Angela is a good cook of such candlelit meals as leek and prawn gratin, roast chicken (with a sauce of pine nuts and raisins), summer pudding and cheeses; fruit and vegetables come from the garden.

From here one can visit historic Stansted Mountfichet, the old market towns of Ware and Hertford (the latter at a confluence of five rivers), the Lea Valley (country park, boat trips), Hatfield House, St Albans and Cambridge. Golf courses abound, and Stansted Airport is handy.

Ware is a good spot from which to take a boat trip on the River Lea (the town is where John Gilpin started his headlong ride, where hapless Jane Grey was proclaimed queen in 1553, and where 'the great bed of Ware' was made – over 10 feet square, it rests now in the Victoria & Albert Museum: it is mentioned in *Twelfth Night*). Hertford still retains fine buildings and castle ruins. In fact, the whole area has a lot of historic mansions (including Knebworth) and lesser houses in villages worth a detour – such as hilly Essendon, picturesque Much Hadham, Bramfield encircled by woods (Thomas Becket was rector here in the 12th century), old Braughing where a little river passes the green, the Pelhams, and Westmill for Charles Lamb's delightfully named cottage, Button Snap. There are quiet byways still, because major traffic keeps to the motorways.

The addresses of houses are geographically correct but postal addresses sometimes differ (for correspondence, the only essential element is the postcode).

Information about the nearest town and 'A' road helps you to locate the whereabouts of any village on a map; but before setting off it is necessary to get precise instructions from your host as many houses are very much 'off the beaten track'.

TREGADDRA FARM   C X
near Cury, Cornwall, TR12 7BB   Tel: 01326 240235
South of Helston. Nearest main road: A3083 from Helston to Lizard.

4 Bedrooms. £18–£19.50. Most have own bath/shower/toilet. Tea/coffee facilities. Views of garden, country, sea. Balcony (two). No smoking.
Dinner. £9 for 3 courses and coffee, at 6.30pm. Non-residents not admitted. Vegetarian or special diets if ordered. No smoking. **Light suppers** if ordered.
2 Sitting-rooms. With open fire (in one), TV. No smoking.
Garden

A beautifully kept garden of winding flowerbeds and spacious swimming-pool (heated) is the setting for this immaculate house, built in the 18th century but much modernized since. Two upstairs bedrooms have balconies. All around are distant views, especially fine when the sun is setting over the sea – in the other direction, Goonhilly's satellite station on the moors is quite spectacular too.

Rooms are well furnished in conventional style, with plenty of space and comfort. When evenings are chilly, logs blaze in a granite inglenook, and there is a glass sun-room to make the most of the mild climate in this very southerly part of England.

For dinners, June Lugg uses the produce of the farm (vegetables, beef) whenever she can. With the beef comes something different from the usual Yorkshire pudding: Cornish cobblers. This might be followed by blackberry and apple crumble – one for each family – with clotted cream.

The Lizard peninsula is a particularly beautiful area. There are sandy beaches and coves, fishing villages, old inns, coastal walks and all the creeks of the River Helford to explore.

Swimming-pool at Coombe Farmhouse (see page 67)

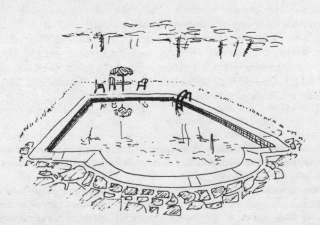

TREGONY HOUSE   C(7) PT S
Tregony, Cornwall, TR2 5RN   Tel: 01872 530671
East of Truro. Nearest main road: A3078 from St Mawes towards St Austell.

rear view

6 Bedrooms. £18.75–£21.75 (less for 7 nights). Prices may go up from Easter. Some have own bath/shower/toilet. Tea/coffee facilities. Views of garden, country. Washing machine on request.
Dinner. £11 for 4 courses (with some choices) and coffee, at 7pm. Less for 2 courses. Vegetarian or special diets if ordered. Wine available. **Light suppers** if ordered.
1 Sitting-room. With open fire, central heating, TV, record-player. Bar.
Garden
Closed in December and January.

Behind a cream façade is a house partly dating from the 17th century; later, additions were made – so the slate-flagged dining-room, for instance, is low-beamed and thick-walled while the hall and sitting-room have great elegance, particularly since the addition of a honeysuckle wallpaper in the hall, and rounded alcoves crammed with books. All the bedrooms have their own individual character and comfortable style.

In the dining-room (furnished with oriental rugs, oak tables and Windsor chairs) Cathy and Andy Webb serve such meals as home-made soup, Spanish pork (cooked with olives and tomatoes), and lemon pudding (plus local cheeses). Herbs, etc. come from the cottage-garden, where you can have tea.

From Tregony you can quickly reach the warm south coast of Cornwall, with all its coves, beaches, harbours and scenic drives.

Readers' comments: Warm and friendly welcome. Extremely comfortable. Dinners excellent and varied. A very happy stay. Well looked after, kindness itself. Friendly and obliging hosts, dinners particularly enjoyable. Exceptional value, comfort and attention to detail.

Further east and along the coast is Gorran Haven with, at Trewollock, **WOODLANDS,** a homely 1930s house on a lovely site with sea views and a 10-minute path leading down to the sands and rocks. In the garden is a pair of wild ponds – the top one has fish and waterlilies, and by the secluded bottom one are seats from which to enjoy the sight of the sea below. There's a verandah to sit on, too, and a barbecue for visitors' use. Four bedrooms have sea views; one is on the ground floor.

Lynn Shelton makes all her own scones, cakes and jams and cooks such evening meals as celery chowder, roast beef with organic local vegetables, and apple strudel – served in a sun-trapping dining-room. £18.50–£19.50 (b & b).
Readers' comments: Impressed with the decor of the bedrooms and the wonderful views. Entertained us with imagination and generosity. [Tel: 01726 843821; postcode: PL26 6NS]

323

TREMEARNE   C D PT S

Bone Valley, Heamoor, Cornwall, TR20 8UG   Tel: 01736 64576
West of Penzance. Nearest main road: A30 from Penzance to Land's End.

5 Bedrooms. £17.50–£25 (less for 7 nights). All have own bath/shower/toilet. Tea/coffee facilities. Views of garden, country. No smoking. Washing machine on request.
Dinner. £12.50 for 2 courses and coffee, at 7pm. Non-residents not admitted. Vegetarian or special diets if ordered. No smoking. **Light suppers.**
1 Sitting-room. With open fire, central heating, TV, video.
Large garden
Closed from November to February.

The granite house was neglected and the walled grounds completely overgrown with brambles, a Sleeping Beauty scene, when Sally Adams and her family came here. They restored the 'Jubilee' rose garden (planted in the year of Queen Victoria's diamond jubilee), and found many old-fashioned varieties still surviving – such as the lovely Albertine rambler rose, the scent of which greets you as you arrive.

One enters through a tiled conservatory, decorated with garlands of dried flowers. This is where Sally serves such dinners as beef cooked in Guinness, and plum crumble, using garden produce.

In the Victorian-style sitting-room, there are carpets and armchairs of deep turquoise contrasting with cream walls, and an open fire. Bedrooms have artistic touches and features such as a crochet bedspread in one, old toys in another. Two family suites are in a converted stable block.

Readers' comments: Thoroughly recommended. It was home from home and with very friendly attention when needed. Warm welcome, delicious meals.

East of Penzance is the village of St Hilary where, in Trewhella Lane, is a mine-owner's house of silvery granite, ideal for gourmets in particular: 17th-century **ENNYS FARM**. Sue White is a dedicated cook, who prepares such candlelit meals as avocado mousseline with smoked salmon, chicken in green peppercorn sauce, and iced nut-cake with Kirsch (even more elaborate menus in winter). Bread is home-baked. There are a barbecue, a grass tennis court, a patio for breakfast and a swimming-pool. Indoors one finds alcoves, deep-set sash windows, pretty plasterwork and a shapely staircase. Rooms have handsome beds (two are four-posters), lacy pillows, leather and velvet armchairs and flower pictures by a local artist. Family suites and a laun-

dry-room have been created in the stables. £19–£25.
Readers' comments: Wonderful hostess. Beautifully situated. Super food. Happy, caring atmosphere. Food exquisite. Highest commendation. The perfect place to unwind. Total peace and quiet. Made very welcome. Very welcoming, comfortable. [Tel: 01736 740262; postcode: TR20 9BZ]

TREROSEWILL FARM C M PT S

Paradise, Boscastle, Cornwall, PL35 0DL   Tel: 01840 250545
South-west of Bude. Nearest main road: A39 from Wadebridge to Bude.

7 Bedrooms. £15–£21 (less for 3 nights or continental breakfast). Bargain breaks. All have own bath/shower/toilet. Tea/coffee facilities. TV. Views of garden, country, sea. No smoking. Washing machine on request. **Dinner.** £15 for 4 courses and coffee, at 6.30pm. Less for 2 courses. Non-residents not admitted. Vegetarian or special diets if ordered. Wine available. No smoking. **Light suppers** if ordered.
1 Sitting-room. With log-burning stove, central heating, TV. Piano. No smoking.
Large garden

Perched high above the picturesque fishing village of Boscastle is this modern farmhouse built by Steve and Cheryl Nicholls, whose families have farmed and fished in this area for generations. In each bedroom is a copy of an old newspaper photograph of Steve's great-grandfather, who was rescued and brought home by a Welsh fishing vessel after his own boat had foundered and he had been given up for lost. In the photograph, he is wearing a Guernsey sweater knitted in the traditional Boscastle style: each fishing village had its own distinctive pattern so that bodies salvaged after accidents at sea could be brought home to their own communities for identification and burial.

Bedrooms – named after areas of Boscastle – are delightful, varying considerably in size but all prettily decorated in pastel shades and flowered fabrics; several have sea views. One has a brass bed, another a four-poster. Downstairs in the cheerful peppermint-green dining-room, Cheryl serves such farmhouse fare as home-made soup, a roast (the farm produces its own pork and lamb) or a dish like steak-and-kidney pudding, and apple pie. Breakfast options often include croissants and cheese, or naturally smoked haddock; marmalade is home-made.

This is grand walking country, and the Nicholls are happy to drive you out to a starting-point of your choice to give you a one-way hike back to the farm; there are also several circular walks to be had round attractive Boscastle, one of Britain's oldest harbours. There are Hardy connections, the author having stayed many times in Boscastle; Beeny Cliff to the north-east is mentioned in *A Pair of Blue Eyes* (its 'castle Boterel' is Boscastle). More recently, John Betjeman too admired Boscastle; the poet is buried on St Enodoc's golf course at Daymer Bay on the Camel estuary.

TREVIADES BARTON   C D
High Cross, near Constantine, Cornwall, TR11 5RG   Tel: 01326 340524
South-west of Falmouth. Nearest main road: A39 from Truro to Falmouth.

3 Bedrooms. £19–£25. Two have own bath/shower/toilet. Tea/coffee facilities. Views of garden, country, river. Washing machine on request.
Dinner (by arrangement). £16.50 for 4 courses, wine and coffee, at 8pm. Vegetarian or special diets if ordered.
1 Sitting-room. With open fire, central heating, record-player. Piano, TV room.
Large garden

This most unusual, U-shaped, 16th-century house is approached through a narrow and picturesque courtyard (paved with slate and full of daisies). Some parts of the present building may be as old as the 13th century, and successive owners have discovered old wells, fish tanks, disused fireplaces and windows, ancient steps and alcoves.

The long sitting-room is 18th-century. It is lined with cream-and-white panelling and has an Adam fireplace at one end, flanked by alcoves of china. Elegant tapestry and patchwork cushions (Judy's skilled work) are on the armchairs and sofas, marine watercolours on the walls. From here one can step out to a succession of individual walled gardens where camellias (and roses) flourish, with a croquet lawn and kitchen garden. The camellias are at their best in February or March.

Judy Ford runs courses on needlework, and cookery. As to the latter, here is an example of her dinners: pâté with green mayonnaise, salmon trout, French apple flan with elderflower sorbet, and cheeses (wine included).

Such meals are served in a granite-walled dining-room, Regency chairs surrounding the big mahogany table, Royal Chelsea china on the table, scarlet candles in the silver candelabra. There is a pretty French stove on the hearth, and in one corner is – surprise! – one of the earliest vacuum cleaners, bellows-operated.

Readers' comments: A unique experience. Charming and welcoming hosts. Exceptionally attractive gardens. Excellent dinner, comfortable room. Best place we have stayed in. Helpful, pleasant and friendly. Wonderful food. Sheer delight.

Bedroom with Flemish-style four-poster at Shieldhall (see page 291)

TREWORGIE BARTON

C(10) S

Crackington Haven, Cornwall, EX23 0NL   Tel: 01840 230233
South-west of Bude. Nearest main road: A39 from Bude to Camelford.

4 Bedrooms. £18–£23 (less for 7 nights). Bargain breaks. All have own bath/shower/toilet. Tea/coffee facilities. TV. Views of garden, country, sea. No smoking.
Dinner. £14 for 4 courses and coffee, at 7pm. Non-residents not admitted. Vegetarian or special diets if ordered. No smoking.
1 Sitting-room. With open fire, fixed heating. No smoking.
Large garden
Closed from October to January.

Although the name of this 16th-century house means 'homestead above the water, capable of growing corn', the farmland is now confined to grazing for sheep and cattle, with 30 acres of ancient woodland (there are marked trails for walkers). Annexed to the Duchy of Cornwall by Henry VIII, illegally sold by Elizabeth I and then repossessed by James I, the manor was previously held by the Prior of Launceston; and the ancient inglenook in the dining-room (with original 'cloam' – or bread – oven) has been dated back to the period. Its recent history, however, has been less turbulent; before Pam and Tony Mount came here, the house had been in the same family for 120 years.

Stairs lead up from the slate-floored hall to a small landing sitting-area and two attractive bedrooms (one with far sea view), with pine furniture and pretty floral fabrics. Some guests prefer the privacy of the family suite, immaculately converted, in a former tractor shed, where board-and-latch doors and a pine four-poster complement walls of primrose yellow and a moss-green carpet.

Pam, an accomplished cook, serves such dinners as leek and bacon soup with freshly baked rolls, Treworgie lamb cooked with fresh rosemary, and whisky-and-coffee pudding with hazelnut macaroons and Cornish clotted cream.

In such an idyllic spot, there is little temptation to go elsewhere. However, the resort of Bude is very near and the border of Devon. Bude is more sedate than many west country resorts, in a setting of grassy downs and golden sandy beaches on which the Atlantic thunders in.

Inglenook at Brookside (see page 37)

TRIGGER POND COTTAGE   C S

33 Bicester Road, Bucknell, Oxfordshire, OX6 9LP   Tel: 01869 245560
North-west of Bicester. Nearest main road: A41 from Oxford to Bicester
(and M40, junction 10).

2 **Bedrooms.** £18–£19 **to readers of this
book.** Tea/coffee facilities. TV. Views of
garden, country. No smoking.
Garden

Each side of the sign outside the Trigger Pond Inn (notable for its food) tells a
different story as to the pond's name: its trigger shape is on one side; the 'twig-
gers' who collected basket-making twigs from its banks on the other. The cottage
itself, nearly four centuries old, once belonged to the local thatcher (though today
its roof is tiled). Roses clamber up its thick walls of golden stone.

The low, beamed rooms have been attractively decorated by Joan Hemsley. A
fresh and pretty bedroom has sprigged white fabrics that go well with the cane
furniture, for instance; a cocoa-coloured bathroom is full of pot-plants. As there is
no sitting-room for guests, they are welcome to relax in the small conservatory
where breakfast is served; wisteria climbs overhead and there is a view of a little
waterfall and fields beyond.

In an outbuilding, a surprise awaits – an array of hand-made dolls' houses,
correct in every period detail. These are the work of Jim Hemsley, who started
doing them as a second career in mid-life.

Only an hour from London (and even less from Birmingham), peaceful little
Bucknell is well placed to visit world-famous tourist honeypots all round Oxford –
Stratford, Warwick, the Cotswolds. There is plenty of interest in the immediate
vicinity too, such as the market at Bicester and Stoke Lyne bluebell woods.

UPPER BUCKTON   C S X
Leintwardine, Herefordshire, SY7 0JU   Tel: 01547 540634
West of Ludlow. Nearest main road: A4113 from Knighton towards Ludlow.

3 Bedrooms. £18–£20 **to readers of this book** (less for 5 nights or continental breakfast). Bargain breaks. All have own bath/shower/toilet. Views of garden, country, river. No smoking. Washing machine on request.
Dinner. £16 for 4 courses (with choices) and coffee, at 7pm. Special diets if ordered. No smoking. **Light suppers** if ordered (for late arrivals).
1 Sitting-room. With open fire, central heating, TV. No smoking.
Large garden

Yvonne Lloyd is an accomplished cook, serving such starters as bananas and bacon with curry sauce or stuffed mushrooms; then roasts, salmon, or chicken with orange and almonds; vacherins or chocolate roulade. Such meals are presented on Doulton's Old Colonial china with Harrods silver. It is largely her reputation for good food which brings visitors here – that, and the peace and quiet of this 18th-century house (at the centre of a 300-acre sheep and cereal farm) in which antiques furnish the comfortable rooms.

All bedrooms are named after local sites (one is Coxall, with a view of Coxall Knoll, where there was an Iron Age fort). Yvonne has a decorative touch, with a taste for ribbon-and-posy fabrics in one room (used even on the scalloped and quilted bedhead), poppies in another, for instance. All the frilled or pleated valances are made by her.

Outside is a verandah on which to sit with pre-dinner drink or after-dinner coffee to enjoy the view towards the high ridge of the Wigmore Rolls. A lawn slopes down to a clear millstream fringed by hostas, to one side a tall and graceful birch and to the other a high, feathery ash and the mound where once a Norman fort stood. A granary has been equipped with table tennis, darts and snooker; there are also a croquet lawn and other games.

This is very good country for walking and birdwatching, or for leisurely drives, and only a little further afield are the Shropshire hills, Radnor Forest, Elan Valley and Offa's Dyke. There are many picturesque black-and-white villages (typical of this area), and castles (relics of the centuries of border warfare with Wales): Ludlow, Stokesay, Croft, Powis, Montgomery. Museums cover all manner of special interests from cider-making to industrial archaeology, farming to local history. The Severn Valley steam railway is popular with children and adults.

Visitors might enjoy an evening drive high up where the buzzards fly, the still higher hills a distant blue, to see the sun going down on the glorious colours of gorse and rosebay willowherb which adorn the ever-varied shapes of hills and valleys. One might drive along lanes flanked by the blowsy hedges and golden fields of a hot summer's day.

Readers' comments: Outstanding location, imaginative and generous cooking, most comfortable. Marvellous hosts, lovely house, food excellent. Warm, attractive rooms, delicious meal, we felt completely at home. Gracious country living. First-class hosts. Welcoming and comfortable. Could not have been more warmly and sensitively welcomed. Every course was a treat. Wonderful weekend. Super retreat for jaded townies. Highly pleasurable; meals outstanding.

UPPER GREEN FARM
M

Manor Road, Towersey, Oxfordshire, OX9 3QR   Tel: 01844 212496

East of Thame. Nearest main road: A4129 from Thame to Princes Risborough (and M40, junctions 6/8).

10 Bedrooms. £19–£27.50. All have own bath/shower/toilet. Tea/coffee facilities. TV. Views of garden, country. No smoking.
2 Sitting-rooms. With central heating, TV. No smoking.
Large garden

A building of whitewash and thatch overlooking a duck-pond at the front, Marjorie and Euan Aitken's house is one of the prettiest in this book. They uncovered 15th-century beams with the original carpenters' identification marks; came across Elizabethan coins; restored the wood shutters which (window-glass having yet to be invented) were all that kept out wintry blasts five centuries ago; found a secret priest-hole where, in the days of religious persecution, a Catholic priest might have to hide for days when the search was on. In one huge chimney, there were still the iron rungs up which small boys were forced to clamber to clear the soot. An old kitchen-range and adjoining copper boiler have been preserved, together with the rack on which spits for roasting whole sheep were kept, and the special hooks used for drying the farmer's smocks by the fire. In the hall is a pump (still working). Across the lawned farmyard is Paradise Barn, dated 1790, with six en suite bedrooms. Breakfast is served in the barn which has the original hayrack (now filled with dried flowers), a beamed ceiling and brick floors.

Marjorie, who used to be an antique dealer, has filled every room with fascinating trifles – shelves of old bottles (found discarded in the garden), bead-work pincushions and watch-cases, huge marble washstands, naive Staffordshire figures, old brass scales (which she uses) and tin toys.

The Aitkens not only tell visitors about the well-known sights nearby (which include Claydon House, Waddesdon Manor, West Wycombe's 'hellfire' caves, the horses' home of rest, etc.) but introduce them to other sides of local life. For instance, you may go and see the sorting and grading of sheep fleeces, join in bell-ringing, pick up bargains at local markets or auctions, chat to balloonists as they glide by only a few yards above the farm. And, of course, their ducks, chickens and geese are an entertainment in themselves.

Bed-and-breakfast only; there is excellent pub food within a short walking distance. Guests who bring their own snacks will be provided with plates, tea, etc.

Readers' comments: Charming home, warm hospitality: we arrived as guests and left as friends. Much impressed by warm welcome, delightful house and excellent breakfast. Wonderful couple – it always feels like going home! Charming people, absolutely delightful house. Superb breakfast. Absolutely excellent.

For explanation of code letters (C, D, M, PT, S, X) see inside front cover.

UPPER HOUSE FARM   C D

Hopton Castle, Shropshire, SY7 0QF   Tel: 01547 530319
West of Ludlow. Nearest main road: A4113 from Knighton towards Ludlow.

3 Bedrooms. £18–£19.50. All have own bath/shower/toilet. Tea/coffee facilities. TV. Views of garden, country. No smoking. Washing machine on request.
Dinner. £10.50 for 4 courses and coffee, at 7pm. Non-residents not admitted. Vegetarian or special diets if ordered. Wine available. No smoking.
1 Sitting-room. With open fire, central heating. No smoking.
Large garden
Closed in December.

A very beautiful garden surrounds this 18th-century house, and indoors everything is of an equally high standard: from the good carpets and the velvet armchairs grouped around the fireplace to the cut-glass and silver on the dining-table, the antiques and the excellent bathrooms. You can enjoy a huge and sunny bedroom, a game at the pool table, or a stroll on the farm to look at cattle or Clun forest sheep. There's trout fishing to be had, free, in the river.

But above all it is Sue Williams's rich and imaginative cooking that brings visitors back repeatedly. (Typically, after a vol-au-vent she may serve pheasant casseroled in red wine, followed by blueberry tart and cream, then cheeses.)

The picturesque ruins of Hopton Castle are on the farm's grounds (it was built by the Normans; and in 1642 thirty Roundheads held it against 300 Royalists for three weeks before being brutally massacred). Set in the lovely Clun Valley, high among wooded hills, there are fine views and walks all around it. Offa's Dyke and the Long Mynd are near.

If you approach Ludlow from the Wigmore side, you will see it all spread out before you – a panorama of Norman towers, soaring church pinnacles, crowded mediaeval and 18th-century houses, a hilly backdrop. Stones of varied colours went into the construction of the castle, now an impressive ruin, originally built as the central stronghold to control the turbulent Welsh border. The 15th-century church is equally magnificent in scale: look up to the roof for gilded angels and under the choir stalls (misericords) for mermaids. The Feathers Hotel is famous for its carved façade and balconies; Dinham House is a centre for craftsmen.

Taking the road from Ludlow to Craven Arms, you pass through Bromfield with priory ruins in its watermeadows and, in the impressive church, an unusual ceiling of cherubs' heads and painted scrolls. Onward lies Stokesay Castle, a little gem, with fruit trees in its moat now but old features retained within (the carved gatehouse is still inhabited); and, at Aston-on-Clun, a historic poplar annually redecorated with flags in celebration of a landowner's wedding long ago: a popular background for wedding photographs today.

Readers' comments: Cannot praise highly enough. Glorious countryside. Meals an absolute delight. Most charming and a wonderful cook. Friendly, warm and welcoming. An excellent few days, utterly peaceful. Lovely old house, splendid meals. Most friendly and cheerful service. Courteous owners. Food very good. Made most welcome. Truly rural retreat. Food with flair and imagination. Perfect in every way. Outstanding.

UPPER VINEY FARMHOUSE C D

Viney Hill, Lydney, Gloucestershire, GL15 4LT   Tel: 01594 516672
South-west of Gloucester. Nearest main road: A48 from Gloucester to
Chepstow (and M4, junction 22).

3 Bedrooms. £18–£20 (less for 3 nights).
Bargain breaks. All have own bath/shower/
toilet. Tea/coffee facilities. TV. Views of
country. No smoking. Washing machine on
request.
Dinner. £15 for 4 courses (with choices)
and coffee, at 7pm. Less for 2 courses. Non-
residents not admitted. Vegetarian or
special diets if ordered. **Light suppers** if
ordered.
1 Sitting-room. With open fire, central
heating, TV.
Small garden

Occasionally the Littens lay on two-day breaks of forest walks with an expert guide.
Often, participants are shown such things as salmon-net making, or a cider-press in
a private house: not typical tourist 'sights'. The house is on the southern edge of
the historic Forest of Dean, a royal hunting forest since before the Norman
Conquest. An area of great beauty and wildlife interest, it also has coal mines
owned privately by 'free-miners' under traditional forest laws. There are remains of
Roman iron mines, strange rock formations, caves, rivers, gardens . . .

Upper Viney is a 16th-century house of stone walls and floors, exposed timbers
and ancient, twisting staircase. The sitting/dining-room has an inglenook with
bread oven, and in an alcove are finds that have turned up in the garden (clay
pipes, hand-forged nails), as well as a small child's boot which has been dated at
1835: an expert said the iron studding shows the child worked in a coal mine.

There is a particularly big family room and very nice shower/bathrooms.

Mary Litten cooks straightforward meals like sardines on toast, chicken
chasseur, and apple charlotte (always with two choices of starter and pudding).

Reader's comment: Very welcoming and friendly.

Parkend is in the middle of the Forest
of Dean and here, facing the cricket
green, is **EDALE HOUSE**, in Folly
Road. The five en suite bedrooms are
luxurious – decorated in soft blues
and cream, with pretty fabrics and
furniture of polished pine. Village
cricket can be watched from the
rooms, two of which are on the ground
floor. There is a lobby designed for
walkers' wet shoes and coats.

In the comfy sitting-room is Sheila
Reid's growing collection of unusual
honeypots. The dining-room overlooks the garden, with its numerous
feathered visitors from the Nagshead
RSPB reserve at the rear of the house.
Ex-restaurateurs James and Sheila
serve such meals as seafood chowder,
suprême of chicken with Madeira
and green peppercorns, and chocolate
brandy mousse. Closed in January.
£18–£24 (b & b) **to readers of this
book only.** [Tel: 01594 562835; postcode: GL15 4JF]

UPTON FARMHOUSE   C D PT S X
Upper Brighton Road, Sompting, West Sussex, BN14 9JU
Tel: 01903 233706
East of Worthing. Nearest main road: A27 from Brighton to Worthing.

3 Bedrooms. £17.50 (less for 3 nights). Bargain breaks. Two have own bath/shower/toilet. Tea/coffee facilities. TV. Views of garden, country. No smoking. Washing machine on request.
Light suppers if ordered.
1 Sitting-room. With open fire, central heating. No smoking.
Large garden

Close to Worthing is the old village of Sompting, with a Rhenish-style Saxon church. Behind the handsome 18th-century façade of this house are parts built in the 15th century. The bedrooms – which have soft colours, deep, velvety carpets, private bathrooms, and views over farmland – are all spacious, immaculate and well equipped. Breakfast is served on lace tablecloths, with locally smoked kippers offered as an option. The massive sitting/dining-room is very comfortably furnished – its walls lined with prints of old sailing ships. Penny Hall is a particularly caring hostess.

The area round here is not only scenic but full of gardens, stately homes, Roman remains and castles to visit. Walkers enjoy wending their way up to Cissbury Ring, a prehistoric hill fort. South coast resorts within easy reach include not only sedate Worthing (a considerable number of retirement homes are here) but also Brighton, celebrated for its oriental-style Pavilion and sophisticated pleasures. Arundel (castle, Catholic cathedral and wildfowl reserve) is nearby. Gatwick is 50 minutes away by car.

Readers' comments: Warm welcome, excellent food.

The previous owner of **RACE-HORSE COTTAGE**, Nepcote, chose a position where he could watch strings of horses and their jockeys go by on their way to the surrounding South Downs for daily exercise. He built in traditional Sussex style: its upper storey weatherboarded, the doors panelled. Trim bedrooms have velvet bedheads and views of the Downs. There is a small garden and glasshouse from which come the fresh vegetables and fruit that Jean Lloyd uses for such meals (if ordered in advance) as ramekins of eggs with Stilton and cream or melon with kiwi fruit; gammon with Cumberland sauce; and loganberry flan. Bread,

muesli and jams are home-made. The Lloyds dine with their guests. £16 (b & b).
Readers' comments: Everything necessary for comfort. Evening meal delicious. [Tel: 01903 873783; postcode: BN14 0SN]

VARTREES HOUSE

Moreton, Dorset, DT2 8BE Tel: 01305 852704
East of Dorchester. Nearest main road: A35 from Dorchester to Poole.

3 **Bedrooms.** £18–£23. Some have own
bath/shower/toilet.   Tea/coffee   facilities.
Views of garden. No smoking. Washing
machine on request.
1 **Sitting-room.** With central heating, TV,
piano.
Large garden

When Thomas Hardy's most trusted friend, the inspired eccentric Hermann Lea
(whose interests ranged from humane rabbit-traps to Goethe), built himself this
handsome house, Hardy helped to name it Vartrees, after the nearby River Frome
– once Var. It is in Arts and Crafts style, with much use of Japanese oak, maple,
exposed brickwork, iron-latched doors, and big windows overlooking grounds
brilliant with colour at azalea time.

Lea photographed and wrote about Hardy, 30 years his senior, and the sites in
Dorset which figure in his books: Doris Haggett can show you Lea's publications.
A small, bearded countryman, he cared passionately about animals (not only was
he a vegetarian but he refused to wear leather shoes). He kept 20 dogs, did water-
divining and was a pioneer motorist, often driving Hardy to the high viewpoints
that he loved. The secretive Hardy confided many private matters to Lea rather
than to more highbrow friends, and his trust was never betrayed.

This is the valley ('green trough of sappiness') where Tess was a dairymaid;
the sea is only 10 minutes away. Moreton's unique church is full of Laurence
Whistler windows. Lawrence of Arabia is buried in the graveyard. Doris can
show you a video of Hardy's Dorset as you sit where once he sat in this unusual
house.

Dining-room at Tregony House (see page 323)

VAULD FARMHOUSE

C(12) PT X

Vauld, Herefordshire, HR1 3HA   Tel: 01568 797898

North of Hereford. Nearest main road: A49 from Hereford to Leominster.

5 Bedrooms. £17.50–£25 (less for 3 nights). Some have own bath/shower/toilet. Tea/coffee facilities. TV. Views of garden, country.

Dinner. £15 for 4 courses and coffee, at 7.30pm (not Sundays). Non-residents not admitted. **Light suppers** if ordered.

Sitting-rooms: see text.

Large garden

'Sleepy hollow', the locals call this area where the ancient farmhouse lies hidden, its creamy, black-timbered walls lopsided with age (it was built in 1510). One steps through the front door into a great room with stone-slabbed floor, half-timbered walls, log fire and colossal beams overhead. (Farming is no longer carried on here.)

Those who book the granary suite (which has its own stone staircase from outside) have a private sitting-room, with deep velvet armchairs, bathroom and a choice of bedrooms (one a gallery); and, through windows with unusual crisscross glazing bars, a view of the pond. Other visitors may prefer the ground-floor oak room with a very impressive four-poster (this, too, has its own entrance and shower-room). Additional accommodation is also available in the converted, 17th-century timber-frame barn which is situated directly opposite the farmhouse. Here is also a guests' sitting-room with tea/coffee-making facilities and a television, a cloakroom and a patio.

Jean Bengry will prepare a meal using much local produce, for this is an area of fruit-farms. A typical menu: stuffed mushrooms, duck breasts, apple and hazelnut tart, and local cheeses. Some meals are served in the old bakery with its original ovens.

Ancient Hereford, its turbulent military history behind it, is still a market town with a mediaeval network of streets. The cathedral is full of treasures and, having been built in stages, has examples of almost every architectural style. The Norman nave is exceptionally impressive, some bishops' tombs particularly ornate, the cloisters tranquil. Hereford is the home of Bulmers, whose cider museum is well worth a visit – though those with other drinking habits may make for Broadfield Manor to taste wine from the vineyard there.

Many visitors, with 'The Black-and-White Village Trail' in hand, motor from one picturesque village to the next, along the route discovering an amazing number of really huge mediaeval churches tucked away in the countryside. Others go from one stately garden to another: Hergest Croft, Burford, Dinmore Manor, Queen's Wood (arboretum) and innumerable others. Hay-on-Wye ('book city') is near and there are interesting walks in all directions.

Readers' comments: Excellent accommodation, fine food, friendly folk. None of us wanted to leave. Nothing was too much trouble. Made us completely at home. A superb break. What a wonderful place! The food was a treat. Enchanting. Very comfortable. Our fourth visit, always excellent (food and rooms). Made very welcome, generously fed.

VINE FARM   C(12) **M**

Waterman Quarter, Headcorn, Kent, TN27 9JJ   Tel: 01622 890203

North-west of Tenterden. Nearest main road: A274 from Maidstone towards Tenterden (and M20, junctions 8/9).

3 Bedrooms. £19–£25 (less for 7 nights or continental breakfast). Bargain breaks. All have own bath. Tea/coffee facilities. Views of garden, country. No smoking. Washing machine on request.
Dinner (if ordered). £16 for 4 courses and coffee, at 7pm. Less for 2 courses. Non-residents not admitted. Vegetarian or special diets if ordered. No smoking. **Light suppers** if ordered.
1 Sitting-room. With woodstove, central heating, TV. No smoking.
Large garden

Nothing could be more typical of Kent than this white weatherboarded farmhouse, originally the home of a Tudor yeoman. It is surrounded by flowerbeds, lawns, landscaped ponds, paved courtyard, well, pots of flowers, a 16th-century barn and 50 acres of meadows where sheep are bred. (Coarse fishing in the grounds.)

One enters through what was the big brick-floored kitchen, its ceiling low and beamed. This is now the guests' sitting-room, with Victorian armchairs of buttoned velvet and book-lined walls. Next door is the dining-room which has a huge inglenook with log stove and is similarly furnished with fine antiques and pretty chintz curtains. Here Jane Harman serves dinners such as pancakes stuffed with shrimps in a cream sauce, fillet of lamb with home-grown vegetables, chocolate roulade, and cheeses.

Bedrooms have antiques, chintz fabrics, and bedheads of brass curlicues or ladderback mahogany. There is one ground-floor room (with en suite bathroom).

Vine Farm's ponds are 'sites of nature conservation interest' with many native species, including wild orchids, herons, nightingales and kingfishers.

Readers' comments: Absolutely delighted. Lovely house, super food, most charming hostess. Can't wait to go again.

Just outside Biddenden village, in Hareplain Road, is the 500-year-old **BETTMAN'S OAST**, a converted black-and-white timbered oast house and barn where Janet and Roy Pickup live. Exposed beams and modern pine furniture characterize this clever conversion. The guests' sitting-room where breakfast is taken has a large inglenook fireplace. There are log fires in winter, when evening meals may be ordered (such as soup, beef chasseur, and fresh fruit salad); also a large selection of videos. Off the sitting-room, the family room, with cottage-style furnishings and domed ceiling, has an en suite shower-room. Other

rooms are decorated in pastel shades – one has a picture-window with views overlooking the lane and fields beyond. £17.50–£20.
Readers' comments: Well-cooked and plentiful breakfast. Best ever shower. [Tel: 01580 291463; postcode: TN27 8LJ]

THE VINES   **C D PT S X**
High Street, Marlborough, Wiltshire, SN8 1HJ   Tel: 01672 515333
On A4 from Newbury to Bath (and near M4, junction 15).

6 Bedrooms. £20 (to readers of this book carrying the current edition)–£27.50. Also bargain breaks, available even at bank holidays. All have own bath/shower/toilet. Tea/coffee facilities. TV and much else (see text).
Dining- and sitting-rooms (see text).

From a modest guest-house, David Ball and Josephine Scott completely transformed the Ivy House Hotel at Marlborough into a large and elegant hotel with a restaurant that has won numerous accolades. They now also run a guest-house opposite.

This is the Vines, an 18th-century terrace house converted and decorated to the same high standards as the hotel itself. Bedrooms are furnished in style, and equipped with every possible facility (remote-control TV, good armchairs, hair-dryers, mini-bars in refrigerators and – for the businessmen who comprise most of the mid-week guests – trouser-presses and radio-alarms). Those overlooking the High Street are double-glazed.

What is more, two nights' accommodation and dinner are offered to readers of this book at a preferential rate, *provided that* the book is mentioned when making a reservation and the current edition is shown on arrival. Breakfast can be taken in the hotel, or will be brought to your room in the Vines. Other hotel amenities open to Vines visitors include a sitting-room, bar and sun-terrace. Clay-pigeon shooting can be arranged; and for walkers there is a drying-room and laundry for a nominal charge (the Ridgeway is near).

Dinner is always a memorable occasion. You can choose from a three-course menu which may include such dishes as smoked fish terrine encased in smoked salmon with dill sauce; breast of duck, stuffed with sage and almonds, in orange sauce; and warm sticky-toffee pudding served with walnut-and-caramel sauce. The wine list features a good selection of New World wines, as well as some lower-price alternatives to the château-bottled French wines. There is also a wholefood and fish restaurant, 'Options', where the style suits those who prefer to dine more simply.

Marlborough is a handsome and historic town, with one of the widest high streets in the country. Many of the houses are mediaeval, though this is not immediately apparent until you explore the byways and alleys because so many frontages were rebuilt in the 18th century. It was a stage-coach centre, which accounts for the number of old inns and hotels. At each end of the broad street is a church in Perpendicular style. Its famous public school, Marlborough College, is well worth a visit when open to visitors. Every August the college runs adult summer schools (subjects range from wine appreciation to word processors, golf to country-house history) and participants can stay at the Vines.

Readers' comments: Delighted with the welcome and concern. Wonderful! The high point of our tour. Accommodation excellent, food exquisite.

WALLTREE HOUSE FARM   C M
Steane, Northamptonshire, NN13 5NS   Tel: 01295 811235
North-west of Brackley. Nearest main road: A422 from Banbury to Brackley
(and M40, junctions 10/11).

6 Bedrooms. £20–£25 (less for 3 nights).
All have own bath/shower/toilet. Tea/coffee
facilities. TV. Views of garden, country.
Coin-operated laundry.
Dinner (by arrangement). £12–£15 for 4
courses and coffee, at 7pm. Less for 2 or 3
courses. Vegetarian or special diets if
ordered. Wine available. **Light suppers** if
ordered.
1 Sitting-room. With open fire, central
heating, TV.
Large garden

Quite a surprise to find, at the end of a long farm lane, a park-like setting in
which this handsome Victorian farmhouse stands.

Pauline and Richard Harrison have transformed the house and its outbuildings. Bedrooms in the adjacent courtyard, which look out onto specimen trees,
are modern in style: Stag furniture in some, rosy fabrics, much pine, very good
bathrooms. You can be sure of ample warmth at any time of the year, for Richard
installed a special straw-burner which means all his central heating costs him
nothing but the labour of gathering straw from his fields after each harvest. There
is a lovely sitting-room with adjoining conservatory.

Dinner (ordered in advance) may be anything from a farm supper to a
gourmet menu.

It was at Brackley that the barons negotiated Magna Carta before its sealing at
Runnymede later in 1215. Today the attractive town lies around a particularly
wide, mile-long main street flanked by trees and little lanes, and adorned by a
very fine 18th-century town hall, historic school, old inns and quaint almshouses.
The church is worth a visit, for its windows and monuments are of particular
interest.

The whole county is full of good things and quiet beauty, yet so many visitors
merely pass through it on the way to more celebrated places of interest. Its central
position makes it an excellent touring base, and Blenheim, Stowe, Oxford,
Warwick Castle, Silverstone and the Cotswolds are all within easy reach.

Reader's comment: Delighted by the facilities and the great welcome.

**Houses with short entries are just as good as ones with longer
descriptions; and they include some of the most popular houses in
the book. They may, however, have fewer rooms, a shorter season,
higher prices or fewer amenities (such as meals).**

WALNUT TREE FARMHOUSE   C(5)
Lynsore Bottom, Upper Hardres, Kent, CT4 6EG   Tel: 01227 709375
South of Canterbury. Nearest main road: A2 from Dover towards Canterbury.

3 Bedrooms. £20–£22 (less for 4 nights). Prices go up from May. All have own bath/shower/toilet. Tea/coffee facilities. Views of garden, country. No smoking. Washing machine on request.
Light suppers by arrangement.
Large garden

With its thatched roof, this house has one of the prettiest exteriors in Kent. Inside, too, it is full of charm. Gerald Wilton makes furniture, very decorative carved signboards, colourful decoy ducks and much else – including the long oak table which looks as if it, like the house itself, dates from the 14th century.

Guests' bedrooms in the house are reached by steep stairs. (Others are in a converted barn usually used as a self-catering cottage.) Every wall and floor slopes a little. Crisp white fabrics, flower-sprigged, and pine fitments combine to give rooms an airy, cottagey feel. An attic room with low windows has the ancient king-post that supports the whole structure. In the garden is a swimming-pool. (For evening meals, Sheila Wilton recommends the nearby Duck Inn.)

Readers' comments: Have returned may times, most exceptional. A lot of thought and care; made most welcome. Beautifully furnished. Made to feel like guests of the family.

At Stelling Minnis is **BOWER FARMHOUSE**, in Bossingham Road, the home of Nick Hunt, a secondary school head, his wife Anne, a part-time teacher in a special-needs school, and their teenage daughters. This 300-year-old house with exposed oak beams and central staircase was in Victorian times a small school. There is a cosy sitting-room with old and modern watercolours, wing chairs and a chesterfield in warm reds, and a piano. The double bedroom has pastel striped and sprigged wallpaper and pretty patchwork bedspreads; the other twin room (also with its own bathroom) has peach curtains, fine walnut veneered furniture and headboards, and a gently sloping floor encouraging one bedwards! Home-made bread and

eggs from the Hunts' own chickens are served at breakfast. The Minnis or common land of 125 acres lies opposite the house and two nature reserves are close by. Canterbury, the Shuttle terminal, Dover and Folkestone are short drives away. £18.50.
Readers' comments: Delightful house, charming hosts. [Tel: 01227 709430; postcode: CT4 6BB]

WATER MEADOWS FARMHOUSE C D X
Billington Road East, Elmesthorpe, Leicestershire, LE9 7SB
Tel: 01455 843417
North-east of Hinckley. Nearest main road: A47 from Hinckley to Leicester
(also M69, junction 1; and M1, junction 21).

3 Bedrooms. £14.50 (less for 3 nights). Bargain breaks. Two have own toilet. Tea/coffee facilities. TV. Views of garden, country. No smoking. Washing machine on request.
Dinner. £8 for 3 courses and coffee, at about 7pm. Less for 2 courses. Vegetarian or special diets if ordered.
1 Sitting-room. With open fire, central heating, TV, record-player.
Large garden

In the depression of the 1930s, smallholdings with houses were provided through the Land Settlement Association, a 'self-sufficiency' scheme eventually abandoned. Peter Robinson bought two of these plots (which are on the site of a lost mediaeval village and Roman remains) and has gradually turned them into his own private conservation area.

Bedrooms are good: for instance, a huge family room with sofa and large TV (concealed in a fitment) has fine inlaid Edwardian furniture and windows on three sides from which to enjoy the garden – floodlit at night.

June is an accomplished cook. You might be offered a Chinese or Mexican meal, or something less exotic like lettuce soup, fish Wellington, and home-made ice cream served with chocolate-fudge sauce. Most vegetables come from the garden. And every day breakfast is different, with such unusual choices as kidneys or cheese-and-potato pancakes. Preserves and pickles are home-made.

The Robinsons enjoy people and will help them to explore the neighbourhood (beginning with the local inn, designed by Voysey, who lived nearby). Too often their visitors use the house merely as a stopover en route to Scotland, but within an hour are many stately homes, the Battle of Bosworth site (excellent re-enactments and exhibition), Castle Donington races, and George Eliot country.

Just inside Warwickshire, between Caldecote and Mancetter, a rough track leads to 18th-century **HILL HOUSE** – brimming with antiques and bric-a-brac collected by Jane Cox, from rococo mirrors to a naive portrait of the Queen. All contribute to the distinctive character of the house (where once Edward VII kept a mistress, it is said). Several bedrooms overlook arches where coaches used to be housed. There are a games room, canalside walks, panoramic views across the River Anker, and three goats and a donkey to divert visitors. Dinner comprises such traditional dishes as

vegetable soup, cottage pie, and lemon meringue tart (vegetarian dishes a speciality). £16.50–£17.50 (b & b). [Tel: 01203 396685; postcode: CV10 0RS]

WATERCOMBE HOUSE
Huish Champflower, Wiveliscombe, Somerset, TA4 2EE
Tel: 01984 623725

C(10) S X

North-west of Taunton. Nearest main road: B3227 from Taunton towards Barnstaple (and M5, junction 25).

3 Bedrooms. £18.50–£21.50 (less for 3 nights half board). One has own shower/toilet. Tea/coffee facilities. Views of garden, river. No smoking.
Dinner (by arrangement). £14.50 for 4 courses and coffee, at 7.30–8pm. Less for 3 courses. Non-residents not admitted. Vegetarian or special diets if ordered. Wine available. No smoking. **Light suppers** if ordered.
1 Sitting-room. With open fire, central heating, TV. No smoking.
Garden

It is the River Tone which gives this 18th-century house its name, for it flows through the valley garden – in and out of a trout pool. A glass sun-room (used for breakfast) overlooks the shrubs, paths and nooks of the garden.

Moira Garner-Richards is a cordon bleu trained cook, and serves such dinners as pears with Roquefort, beef cooked in Somerset cider, baked cheesecake, and cheese; or two courses.

The Garner-Richardses have prepared a leaflet about the house, which originally dates from 1723 but has been extended since. For most of the 19th century it was a school, the children using water from the river to wash in, and only in 1984 did electricity come to the house.

Within reach are Hatch Court, Montacute House and Dunster Castle; the coast both north and south; and the county town of Taunton itself, only a few miles away (close to the M5): the Vivary Park and Hestercombe gardens here are well worth a visit, and also the castle (with exceptionally good museum).

Readers' comments: A place to unwind in. Simply furnished but with individual touches. Delicious breakfast (with fresh-picked raspberries!). Everything done for our comfort. Friendly and most helpful.

The excellence of the accommodation and Claire Mitchem's delightful personality make for an exceptional farmhouse holiday at **WHITTLES FARM**, Beercrocombe. At the end of a lane leading nowhere, part of the house dates back to the 16th century (hence the beams and inglenook). Every bedroom is attractively decorated.

A typical menu: boeuf bourguignonne accompanied by four vegetables and a salad; 'queen of puddings' with clotted cream; fresh fruit.

There are excellent woodland walks, and drives along lanes which

vary at every turn. Closed in winter. £18–£20.
Readers' comments: We liked it very much. Most pleasing. Cannot speak too highly of the care and attention. [Tel: 01823 480301; postcode: TA3 6AH]

341

Compass, Dartmouth, Devon, TQ6 0JN   Tel: 01803 833979
Nearest main road: A379 from Dartmouth to Kingsbridge.

3 **Bedrooms.** £19–£21 (less for 7 nights).
Prices go up from May. Views of garden,
country, sea. No smoking.
1 **Sitting-room.** With woodstove, central
heating, TV, record-player. No smoking.
Large garden

So beautiful is the coastal scenery beyond Dartmouth (owned by the National
Trust) that today no-one is allowed to build on it: Wavenden is the only house
there to enjoy the superb view of the River Dart's wide estuary.

When Ken (an award-winning journalist) and Lily Gardner moved here, it
was a rather ugly 'twenties bungalow which they rebuilt so sensitively that even
environmentalists have congratulated them on enhancing the previous scene. And
the garden too has been improved by them. Guests have easy access to the shore
where they can bathe or fish.

There is a large two-level dining- and sitting-room, with huge glass doors
through which to enjoy the views. Through these doors one steps onto a paved
sundeck with reclining chairs from which to watch every kind of craft go by.

From every bedroom, furnished in Laura Ashley style, are glimpses of the sea.

This is a good choice for walkers because the Devon Coastal Path and a
network of National Trust footpaths lie just beyond the gate.

For dinner the Gardners recommend The Dolphin and its seafood specialities.
It's kept by their son, Guy, who offers a 10% discount to holders of the current
edition of this book.

Readers' comments: The location, the welcome, the comfort, the decor – everything was superb value. Lovely views, and atmosphere generated by the Gardners.
Friendly and relaxed. Very well looked after. One of the most beautiful locations.

Along the scenic coast road lies the
steep, stone village of Slapton where
Roberta and Tim Price's 400-year-old
VALE HOUSE is tucked away within
a walled garden. All around is an Area
of Outstanding Natural Beauty.
There's a white-panelled dining-room
with a long mahogany table; a cream-
and-blue sitting-room with log fire and
big sash windows; marine paintings
everywhere; and, up a pretty galleried
staircase, very attractive bedrooms.
From Slapton it is easy to reach the
Dart (boat trips, and steam rail alongside) and Dartmoor. £18.

Readers' comments: Delightful house,
most enjoyable, lovely furnishings and
beautiful china. Made most welcome.
[Tel: 01548 580669; postcode: TQ7
2QT]

WEIR COTTAGE

C (5)

Bickton, Hampshire, SP6 2HA   Tel: 01425 655813
South of Salisbury. Nearest main road: A338 from Ringwood to Salisbury.

2 Bedrooms. £18–£22 (less for continental breakfast). Prices go up from Easter. Both have own bath/shower/toilet. Tea/coffee facilities. TV. Views of garden, river. No smoking. Washing machine on request.
Dinner. £12.50 for 3 courses and coffee, at 8pm. Less for 2 courses. Non-residents not admitted. Vegetarian or special diets if ordered. Wine available. No smoking. **Light suppers** if ordered.
2 Sitting-rooms. With open fire or central heating, TV, piano. No smoking.
Large garden

Near Fordingbridge, Weir Cottage was once the flour store for the nearby water-mill (now converted). Seated on the sofa in a turquoise and white ground-floor bedroom, one has a view of the tranquil watermeadows. On the sunny upper floor is another bedroom, and a vast room with rafters above a long chestnut table and armchairs grouped around the open log fire. A breakfast-table is placed to make the most of the mill-race view. From another sash window one can see the garden – winding herbaceous beds and a paved terrace with swing-seat.

Philippa Duckworth serves such meals as cucumber mousse, local pheasant with vegetables from the garden, and rhubarb fool.

There are two pianos in the house, played not only by Geoffrey but by guests too. A retired brigadier, he also catches the trout which often appear on the dinner-table. His grandfather, and the Duckworths' daughter, painted the water-colours seen on the walls.

To the north lies Salisbury and its cathedral, but most people stay here to enjoy the New Forest – William the Conqueror's hunting reserve nearly a thousand years ago. Now forest is interspersed with heaths of gorse or heather, bogs and ponds, pastures and thatched cottages. Deer, ponies, pigs and donkeys roam wild among the beeches, oaks and birches. In its 'capital', Lyndhurst, the church was ornamented by Leighton, Burne-Jones and Millais. 'Alice in Wonderland' (really Alice Hargreaves) is buried outside it. Particularly picturesque villages include Breamore (with 16th-century Breamore House open to the public, and a mediaeval maze on a nearby hill), Rockbourne (Roman villa close to it), the hamlets of Moyles Court, Swan Green and Burley. Not only are there innumerable footpaths but this is a good area for riding, cycling or wagon-rides.

Facts (prices, etc.) at the top of entries are supplied by the proprietors themselves. While every effort is made to ensure that these are correct at the time of going to press, they may alter thereafter: please check when you book.

WELLPRITTON FARM
Holne, Ashburton, Devon, TQ13 7RX   Tel: 01364 631273
West of Ashburton. Nearest main road: A38 from Exeter to Plymouth.

C D M S X

4 Bedrooms. £17 (less for 7 nights). Only weekly bookings in high season. All have own bath/shower/toilet. Tea/coffee facilities. TV (in family suites). Views of garden, country. Washing machine on request.
Dinner. £8 for 3 courses and coffee, at times to suit guests. Vegetarian or special diets if ordered.
1 Sitting-room. With central heating, TV. Games room (snooker, table tennis).
Small garden

Tucked away in a fold of the gentle hills south of Dartmoor is this small farm where sheep and hens are kept; horses, goats and rabbits too. Children's riding by arrangement.

Sue and Colin Gifford have furnished the bedrooms prettily, and supply them with fruit-squash and biscuits as well as tea. There are two family units of two rooms and a shower, and a ground-floor suite. A comfortable sitting-room is available to guests.

After a starter such as melon or pâté, dinner will probably include a roast, poultry or steak pie, perhaps followed by fruit pie or flan, always accompanied by Devonshire cream, then cheese and coffee. Bread is home-baked. There is no charge for washing and ironing facilities, mealtimes are flexible, the welcome warm, and many extra services provided (loan of maps, hair-dryer, packed lunches, free tea on arrival). From the farm, which has a small swimming-pool, there are views of the moors.

One of the local beauty-spots is 60-foot Becky Falls in oak woodlands threaded by nature trails. At Bovey Tracey are exhibited local crafts of high quality in a granite watermill. There is a vineyard and a rare breeds farm, and the National Trust has 200 acres of riverside park.

Other local NT properties include mediaeval Bradley Manor with its own chapel, and the 16th-century Church House at Widecombe. Ugbrooke House by Adam contains a collection of armour and uniforms, Trago Mills the largest model railway in the county. Yarner Wood is a national nature reserve with a trail.

Chudleigh has something for everyone: Victorian rock gardens with an 80-foot cliff and a cave, and, in a mill with working waterwheel, 17 craft workshops.

Readers' comments: Excellent in every way. Made welcome and comfortable. Extremely good food. A delightful break. Welcome, helpfulness and food are memorable.

Livestock at Wellpritton Farm

WENTWORTH HOUSE

C(5) M PT

**106 Bloomfield Road, Bath, (Avon), Bath & North-East Somerset,
BA2 2AP**   Tel: 01225 339193

18 Bedrooms. £20–£26 **(but to readers of this book only, 5% less for 2 nights, 10% less for 3 nights).** Prices go up from April. Some have own bath/shower/toilet. Tea/coffee facilities. TV. Views of garden, city.
Dinner. £15 for 4 courses (with choices), wine and coffee, at 7pm (not Sundays). Non-residents not admitted. Vegetarian or special diets if ordered. No smoking. **Light suppers** if ordered.
1 Sitting-room. With central heating. **Bar. Small garden**

The big, four-storey house was built for a coal merchant a century ago – those were the days when smoke from millions of hearths brought wealth to a few. It is a fine building of creamy stone, now furnished and equipped to very good standards. The dining-room has a glass extension overlooking the swimming-pool and a lawn. Some of the nicest rooms are below this: they not only open onto the garden but in some cases are suites, each consisting of a small sun-room with armchairs and glass walls beyond the bedroom. At the other extreme, top-floor rooms have the finest views over the city far below.

The hotel has three other attractions for visitors. There is an ample carpark (a rarity in Bath). A six-minute bus halts just outside, saving you the steep walk up from the city after a day's sightseeing. And close by is a rural walk.

Avril Kitching cooks the meals herself – straightforward menus such as melon, haddock in cheese sauce, and fresh fruit salad (there is always a fish and a meat dish to choose from). With breakfast cereals come bowls of various seeds.

Bath itself deserves at least a week-long stay and the surrounding countryside is full of interest.

Readers' comments: A delightful stay. Owners kind and helpful. Charming, relaxing and home-like. Service excellent. The best to date. Exceptional breakfast choices. Lots of character and very comfortable. Beautifully appointed. The room was lovely. A wonderful stay. Food very good; very comfortable. Rooms of high standard, menu first class. Could not have been more satisfactory.

Just off a steep main road out of Bath is **OLDFIELDS** (102 Wells Road), a late Victorian house (or, rather, two) of honey-coloured stone. The big sitting-room, with marble fireplace, is decorated in soft browns and mossy greens and has lace curtains at the high windows with their fine views of the city. The owners, Anthony and Nicole O'Flaherty, are charming; breakfasts are generous (with herbal teas, if you like) and there is much emphasis on wholefoods and local produce. Care is taken over every detail. £20.

Readers' comments: Wonderful! Exceptionally nice people. Spacious comfort. [Tel: 01225 317984; postcode: BA2 3AL]

WESTERN HOUSE

High Street, Cavendish, Suffolk, CO10 8AR Tel: 01787 280550

North-west of Sudbury. On A1092 between Long Melford and Clare.

C(5) **S X**

3 Bedrooms. £15. Tea/coffee facilities. Views of garden. Only one has basin. **Large garden**

Twice made redundant, Peter Marshall decided he had had enough of industry and – his children now being grown up – would instead make a living from his best asset: his attractive 400-year-old house in the historic village of Cavendish.

He and his wife Jean (who teaches singing) are vegetarians, so at one end they started a wholefood shop, full of the smells of dried fruit and fresh herbs, and refurnished several bedrooms to take bed-and-breakfast guests. Options include all kinds of good things (such as their own muesli, eggs, mushrooms, tomatoes and home-made bread) but no bacon. They will recommend good restaurants of all kinds in the village, at Long Melford or in Sudbury.

Each beamed bedroom, reached via zigzag corridors, is very pretty, and spacious – well equipped with chairs, table, etc. One at the front (double-glazed, because it looks onto the main road through the village) has a fresh white-and-green colour scheme extending even to the sheets.

One of the nicest features is the large and informal garden where paved paths wander between old-fashioned flowers, elderly fruit trees, and plant troughs.

Cavendish is one of a string of mediaeval villages. Clare is close, so is Sudbury town and Long Melford. The greatest jewel is Lavenham: lanes of half-timbered and lopsided weavers' cottages still intact, great Guildhall housing a museum of wool history, resplendent church.

Readers' comments: Excellent, with very good breakfasts. Much enjoyed it; and the shop is excellent. Extremely comfortable; warm welcome. Absolutely excellent, high standard. Charming and interesting people. Extremely attractive.

In nearby Clare is the **SHIP STORES**, in Callis Street. Miles from the sea, this one-time inn was originally called the Sheep, not the Ship. Now it is a small shop run by Colin and Debra Bowles, with a few en suite bedrooms and an upstairs sitting-room for guests. It is a place of low beams, creaking floors, undulating roof and pink-plastered front: full of character. In the dining-room there is solid elm furniture locally made. There are two en suite rooms in a flint-walled annexe. For dinner, Debra serves such meals as vegetable soup, lamb chops, then fruit or a cream cake. Bread and croissants

are home-baked. £17.50–£25 (b & b). *Readers' comments:* A beautiful, charming and superbly run establishment. [Tel: 01787 277834; postcode: CO10 8PX]

WESTERN HOUSE

PT

Winchelsea Road, Rye, East Sussex, TN31 7EL Tel: 01797 223419
On A259 from Hastings to Folkestone.

3 Bedrooms. £18–£22.50. Prices go up from May. All have own bath/shower/toilet. Tea/coffee facilities. TV. No smoking. Views of garden, country.
Dinner. From £12 for 3 courses (with choices) and coffee, at 7pm. Non-residents not admitted. Vegetarian or special diets if ordered.
Large garden

The mediaeval port of Rye was perched high on a thumb of land (almost an island) projecting into the sea. But centuries ago the sea receded, leaving behind dry land which became ideal pasturage for sheep. It is here, at the foot of Rye town, that tile-hung Western House was built in the 18th century, commanding far views – you can even see Hastings in clear weather – from its paved terrace (with working pump) where tea may be taken, or from the huge lawn surrounded by brilliant flowerbeds set against mellow stone walls. On summer evenings, the terrace is lit by an old Victorian street-lamp.

Artist Ron Dellar is the present owner of Western House, and his paintings fill the dining-room walls. Up the staircase, and in the bedrooms, are all manner of finds he has amassed over the years: African masks, a parrot in a glass dome, an 1820 box of paints ('Constable was alive then', he comments), Rupert Bear books, antique toys. Melanie, his wife, sells Victorian lace, linen and baby-gowns which are laid out in the big entrance hall. Ron's own prints of Rye are on sale.

This is a house of character, as befits its long history. A boat-builder lived here and, later on, Members of Parliament. Among its visitors (in 1913) was the Impressionist artist Pissarro; and Ron has incorporated him in a mural featuring Rye church which he painted for one of the bedrooms. All these rooms are attractively decorated, with interesting wallpapers and fresh flowers, and some have good views of the marshes across which you can walk to Winchelsea. There's a moated Martello tower out there, giant marsh-frogs croak throatily, you may see herons or marsh harriers flying overhead. (Although the house is on the road to Winchelsea one can sleep undisturbed.)

As to dinner, a typical meal may include home-made soup, baked trout with honey and almonds, and a whimwham, an 18th-century trifle. Otherwise, visitors can try one of Rye's many good inns and restaurants, such as the Old Forge nearby.

The Cinque Ports (seven, in spite of the name) stretch along the south-east coast, and in the centuries before the Navy existed their seamen would serve the king in time of war. In return, they were given trading privileges which made them rich – hence the number of fine old houses and churches still to be found in most of them, from Sandwich in Kent to Hastings in Sussex (and Rye is the jewel of them all). Their history is told in Hastings museum.

Readers' comments: We were particularly delighted. View magnificent. Fabulous: great people, great room, great food. Comfortable. Very helpful.

347

WESTLEA C D M PT S
29 Riverside Road, Alnmouth, Northumberland, NE66 2SD
Tel: 01665 830730
South-east of Alnwick. Nearest main road: A1068 from Newcastle to Alnwick.

7 Bedrooms. £18–£21. Prices go up from Easter. Bargain breaks. All have own shower/toilet. Tea/coffee facilities. TV. Views of garden, country, estuary. Balcony. Laundry facilities.
Dinner. From £12 for 4 courses (with some choices) and coffee, at 6.30–7pm. Non-residents not admitted. No smoking.
1 Sitting-room. With central heating, TV, video.
Small garden

This is a very comfortable modern guest-house facing the Aln estuary, immaculately kept by Janice Edwards. One attractive bedroom (wildflower fabrics and cane bedheads) opens onto the sunny front garden; others vary in size and style but all, even if small, are well equipped. The upstairs sitting-room has a balcony from which to enjoy the river view. Just a few yards from the house are good, sandy beaches.

Breakfasts are imaginative; and for dinner there may be such dishes as beef, salmon, Cheviot lamb (with Northumbrian baked suet-puddings) or game pie. For the way she runs Westlea, Janice has received three local Hospitality Awards. (The Edwardses are willing to collect guests without their own transport from the nearby railway station.) As many visitors come repeatedly for long holidays, booking well ahead is essential.

This area is a good place in which to follow riverside walks; to explore the dramatic coastline and its many castles; or to visit Craster for its succulent kippers.

Readers' comments: A most enjoyable week. Nothing was too much trouble for Janice Edwards. Excellent food and an amazing choice for breakfast. Excellent value for money. We shall certainly go back. Very impressed with warmth of welcome and unrivalled concern for their guests. Immense trouble taken to make guests feel comfortable and at home. All sorts of kindnesses. Very kind and helpful; hearty meals.

Over at Bilton on a 400-acre mixed farm is **BILTON BARNS**, an early 18th-century house with very spacious rooms, which – like the sun lounge – all overlook the sweep of Alnmouth Bay across a croquet lawn. For dinner, Dorothy Jackson offers for instance, smoked trout from Craster, a roast, and sticky-toffee pudding, or something more elaborate on occasion. A farm walk can be arranged. Closed in winter. £18 (b & b).
Readers' comments: Most hospitable

and helpful. Spacious and comfortable. Dinner delicious. I would heartily recommend it. [Tel: 01665 830427; postcode: NE66 2TB]

348

WHASHTON SPRINGS FARM
C(5) S

Whashton, North Yorkshire, DL11 7JS   Tel: 01748 822884

North-west of Richmond. Nearest main road: A1 from Catterick to Scotch Corner.

8 Bedrooms. £18–£20 (less for 3 nights). Bargain breaks. All have own bath/shower/toilet. Tea/coffee facilities. TV. Views of garden, country, stream. No smoking in some.
1 Sitting-room. With open fire, central heating. Bar.
Small garden
Closed in mid-December and January.

Far more handsome than the average farmhouse, 18th-century Whashton Springs has great bow windows and other detailing typical of this fine period in English architecture. Around it is a large, mixed farm run by two generations of Turnbulls. It is high among wooded hills, with superb views of the Dales and of a stream with mediaeval bridge below.

Fairlie Turnbull has decorated each bedroom differently. One, for instance, has flowery fabrics, broderie anglaise on the bedlinen, pretty Victorian antiques and a bow window; another, a four-poster with William Morris drapery and buttoned velvet chairs. Others in a converted stable-block are more modern in style (velvet bedheads, flowery duvets and pine furniture); most of these overlook a courtyard where tubs and stone troughs brim with pansies and petunias; one has a garden view.

The many gardens of this region are at their best in spring, and the famous 'sights' (York, Durham, Richmond and the Dales) less crowded. One can even drive across to the Lake District from here. It's an area not only of spectacular scenery but of dramatic or romantic ruins (great abbeys and castles). Walkers seek out waterfalls and caves, fells and crags, for which the Dales are famous.

Whashton's nearness to the A1 means many people use it as a one-night stopover on their London–Edinburgh journey, but it deserves better than this because there are so many good reasons to linger. Swaledale alone takes days to explore, and so does Teesdale. It is a region of contrasts. Lonely moors rise to 2000 feet (this is where to listen for curlews and plovers, and to wonder at lives passed in such few isolated farms as there are), while every dale differs – Wensleydale is wide and either pastoral or wooded; Swaledale winds between steep hills; some others are like deep clefts – Arkengarthdale, Coverdale, Bishopdale, for instance. Heather moors, houses of 18th-century dignity, the distinctive curly-horned sheep: all contribute to the individuality of this area.

Readers' comments: Very comfortable. Made very welcome. High praise. Lovely surroundings and easy access to many places. Very comfortable. Lovely place, hope to return. Wonderful welcome, very good food. Charming proprietors, food and accommodation excellent. Exceptional value for comfort, amenities, atmosphere, food and personal welcome.

Prices are per person in a double room at the beginning of the year.

WHEATHILL FARM   C S
Church Lane, Shearsby, Leicestershire, LE17 6PG   Tel: 0116 247 8663
North-west of Market Harborough. Nearest main road: A50 from Leicester to
Northampton (also M6, junction 1; and M1, junction 20).

4 Bedrooms. £16–£17 (less for 3 nights).
Prices go up from June One has own
shower. Tea/coffee facilities. Views of
garden, country. No smoking. Washing
machine on request.
Light suppers if ordered.
1 Sitting-room. With open fire, central
heating, TV, record-player. No smoking.
Large garden

In 1823, the owners of this cottage (part Saxon, part mediaeval) put a new façade
on the front: brick, with trim white paintwork. But behind this the old beamed
rooms remained unchanged, with a huge inglenook housing a log stove, and a
twisting stair.

Sue Timms has a decorative touch, and uses pretty fabrics or beribboned net
in cottage-style bedrooms, one downstairs (and even in one of the bathrooms
too). The house is full of unusual heirlooms, including a 100-year-old pot-plant
which originally belonged to a lighthouse-keeper (her great-uncle) on the wild
Farne Islands off the Northumberland coast. Outside is an attractive garden with
lily-pool and lake (you can feed the carp), croquet and boules; and fields of
Wheathill's cows.

Shearsby is, like many others around here, a particularly pretty village, not far
from Georgian Market Harborough (its lively markets date from 1200) and at the
centre of rich grazing country – a tranquil region threaded by waterways with, at
Foxton, 10 locks stacked in a tier to raise boats up a 75-foot incline.

Further north is the scenic Charnwood Forest area – a mixture of heath, crags,
ridges and remnants of oak forest with fine views from its hilltops. Within a short
distance are Anstey's mediaeval packhorse bridge, the pretty little spa town of
Ashby de la Zouch, a particularly interesting church at Breedon-on-the-Hill, and
Loughborough which has a carillon of 47 bells in a high tower in the park. Other
sights include Birdland, Twycross Zoo and Stanford Hall.

Sitting-room at Wheathill Farm

WHEATLEY FARM   **C**
Maxworthy, Cornwall, PL15 8LY   Tel: 01566 781232
North-west of Launceston. Nearest main road: A39 from Wadebridge to Bude.

4 Bedrooms. £18–£20 (less for 4 nights). Bargain breaks. All have own bath/shower/toilet. Tea/coffee facilities. TV. Views of garden, country. No smoking. Washing machine on request.
Dinner. From £12 for 4 courses (with choice of puddings) and coffee, at about 7pm. Less for 2 courses. Non-residents not admitted. Vegetarian or special diets if ordered. No smoking. **Light suppers** if ordered.
1 Sitting-room. With wood-burning stove, central heating, TV, record-player. No smoking.
Garden
Closed from November to February.

Wheatley has been in the same family for generations; Raymond and Valerie Griffin's son will be the fifth in succession to work this substantial dairy and sheep farm deep in the rolling Cornish countryside. The handsome farmhouse was built in 1871 by the Duke of Bedford; when the Griffins repaired an ageing window, they discovered the ducal seal stamped in the original oaken lintel.

One enters the house through the imposing hall, large enough for a snooker table (not for children's use, this - there is a popular games room in the cellar for them) and Parker Knoll chairs. It is beautifully decorated in shades of green, with floral curtains and frieze. The sitting-room, too, is sumptuous and welcoming, and there is a granite inglenook with cloam (bread) oven in the dining-room, which also has a magnificent antique mahogany table and matching sideboard.

Upstairs, the bedrooms are attractively furnished with country-style pine; one has a four-poster and en suite corner bath, and there is a very good family suite with bunk beds for children.

A typical dinner might be home-made soup or pâté, home-produced or local beef or lamb, rhubarb-and-blackcurrant crumble topped with Cornish clotted cream, and English cheeses.

A few miles to the south-west, at Treneglos, is the idyllically situated 18th-century **OLD VICARAGE**, where Maggie Fancourt grows old-fashioned, fragrant sweetpeas and shrub roses for her guests, as well as organically produced fruit and vegetables. Dinners, such as goat's cheese soufflé, Normandy pork (local meat with apples and cream), and home-made ice cream or orange and lemon mousse, are served in the elegant blue and cream dining-room with its lovely Chinese-style curtains. Cream teas with home-made jam are irresistible. In the bedrooms, Maggie's attention to

detail extends even to the coathangers, which are covered in fabric to match the pretty flowered wallpaper. No smoking. Closed in winter. £19.50–£21. [Tel: 01566 781351; postcode: PL15 8UQ]

WHICHAM OLD RECTORY

C S

Silecroft, Cumbria, LA18 5LS   Tel: 01229 772954
West of Ulverston. Nearest main road: A595 from Broughton-in-Furness to
Whitehaven.

3 Bedrooms. £17–£19 (less for 3 nights or
continental breakfast). One has own bath/
shower/toilet. Tea/coffee facilities. Views of
garden, country, sea.
Dinner. £10 for 3 courses (with some
choices) and coffee, at a time to suit guests.
Non-residents not admitted. Vegetarian or
special diets if ordered. **Light suppers** if
ordered.
1 Sitting-room. With open fire, central
heating, TV, piano.
Large garden
Closed in December.

So many people head for the heart of the Lake District that the outlying areas of
the National Park remain uncrowded and uncommercialized. The south-west
corner in particular, around Millom, is often overlooked, even though it is within
an easy drive of famous beauty-spots and has its own particular attractions –
uncrowded beaches, for example, and a mild maritime climate. The last accounts
for the peaches and other fruit that flourish in the garden of the Old Rectory –
some appearing on the dinner-table, or going into the wine which guests usually
sample.

The house is typical of those Victorian rectories built for Trollope-size clerical
families with domestic staff in proportion. David Kitchener, an ex-RAF supply
officer and an accomplished woodworker, has put a lot of work into the spacious
house, some of it to display intriguing family possessions – Victorian dish-covers,
an ancient cast-iron pressure cooker and other interesting bric-a-brac: a big
model of a dhow he bought when in the Middle East, a fairground flare, woodwork from a Warwickshire church, a collection of kukris and other weapons.

He and Judy Kitchener also find time to grow most of the vegetables which
she uses in her enthusiastic cooking. There is always a home-made soup, with
alternative first courses, then perhaps coq au vin (which may be half a chicken per
head) with at least three vegetables, to which guests help themselves, and a sweet
such as raspberry mousse, to which the garden is likely to have contributed too.
The freshly baked bread is David's speciality.

All the bedrooms overlook the lawn, next to which is a small semicircular conservatory which David has built onto the end of the stable, so that guests can
enjoy the garden even when a sea breeze is blowing. The energetic can take a
footpath to the top of Black Combe (2000 feet) for views of Scotland and Wales.
The less energetic can explore the beach at Silecroft, with its sands and rock
pools. Up the coast are mansions and gardens, a narrow-gauge railway and old
seaports. Eastward are pleasant market towns.

For – almost literally – a cross section of Lake District scenery, one could
drive up the Duddon Valley (or Dunnerdale), which was a favourite of
Wordsworth's. From Duddon Sands at sea level, the road follows the river
upstream through increasingly rugged scenery. At the top, Hardknott Pass takes
one westward to the coast, Wrynose Pass into the central Lake District.

Readers' comments: Lovely people. Felt really welcome and at home. Good food.

WHITE HALL

C

Carbrooke, Norfolk, IP25 6SG   Tel: 01953 885950

North-east of Thetford. Nearest main road: A1075 from Thetford to East Dereham.

3 Bedrooms. £18–£22 (less for 4 nights). Some have own bath/toilet. Views of garden, country. No smoking. Washing machine on request.
Light suppers if ordered.
1 Sitting-room. With open fire, central heating, TV, piano, record-player.
Large garden

The hamlet was already an ancient settlement when the Romans came here. In the mediaeval church, the hammerbeam roof and rood-screen are particularly fine. White Hall is, by contrast, quite a recent addition to the scene – little more than two centuries old. An elegant Georgian house, it is surrounded by grounds where you may encounter guinea-fowl and bantams.

Inside, Shirley Carr has furnished the sitting-room with peony sofas facing the marble fireplace, and the light bedrooms with pink roses or green-sprigged fabrics complementing white or shell-pink walls. The dining-room has a big log stove and, like other rooms, large sash windows through which to enjoy tranquil views.

For active visitors, there are available croquet, bicycles, badminton. For others, Carbrooke is well placed for motoring to Norwich, King's Lynn, Sandringham, the Broads, Bury St Edmunds and the coast, with innumerable stately homes, wildlife parks, country auctions, markets and steam railways to visit.

Readers' comments: I felt like a very privileged guest. Delightful couple, easy-going attitude. Staying there was a real pleasure. Nothing too much trouble. Beautifully decorated. Friendly and welcoming. Excellent decor.

Southward lies Thompson where priests used to live in **COLLEGE FARMHOUSE** until Henry VIII disbanded them. Later owners added oak panelling, a coat-of-arms and other features. There are Gothic windows; walls (some three feet thick) have odd curves. Lavender Garnier has collected interesting furniture, family portraits (it was an ancestor who selected dark blue as Oxford's boat-race colour), and attractive fabrics for bedrooms that have armchairs and TV (no sitting-room). A lovely garden slopes down to eel-ponds. Inn food one mile away. £18.
Readers' comments: Warm hospitality.

Magical peace in a beautiful house. Very comfortable, warm and friendly. Breakfasts a joy. Excellent. As near perfect as makes no difference; excellent value. Quite wonderful. [Tel: 01953 483318; postcode: IP24 1QG]

WHITES' FARMHOUSE   D S
Town End Road, Radnage, Buckinghamshire, HP14 4DY
Tel: 01494 482333
North-west of High Wycombe. Nearest main road: A40 from High Wycombe
to Oxford (and M40, junction 5).

1 **Bedroom.** £20 **to readers of this book**
(less for 3 nights). With own bath/toilet.
Tea/coffee facilities. Views of garden,
country. No smoking. Washing machine on
request.
Light suppers if ordered.
1 **Sitting-room.** With open fire, central
heating, TV, piano.
Large garden

Claudia Wilcox's husband having been chairman of the Contemporary Applied
Arts gallery, it is hardly surprising that their home, all mellow brick and rambling
roses outside, is filled with the best in modern, craftsman-made furniture
(designed by Makepeace, La Trobe Bateman and others), ceramics and textiles –
to all of which the 17th-century house has proved an admirable background.
Even the two baby-chairs are craftsman-made, to the same design as Prince
William's; and the weather-vane on the roof is a modern sun-sculpture in steel.

Guests have a bedroom with views over the Radnage valley to beech woods
and a Saxon church, a private sitting-room and their own entrance.

Claudia can provide light suppers (such as soup and sandwiches), after which
guests are welcome to enjoy a stroll in the garden with its collection of rare flowering shrubs and trees, or just sit with a drink and watch the tame white doves fly
across the unspoilt valley. The more energetic walk the many well-signed paths,
or even the long-distance Ridgeway footpath.

At West Wycombe there is much to see, including an underground cave system
and the 18th-century church with so immense a golden ball on top of its tower that
parties were held in it by Sir Francis Dashwood – leader of the 'Hell Fire Club'.

Readers' comments: Couldn't praise more highly; really peaceful; thoughtful and
caring hostess.

A few miles eastward is **WHITE
HOUSE** (Widmer End, High
Wycombe) which actually comprises
three 18th-century farmworkers' cottages. Visitors sleep in a self-contained
suite in a rear extension. From the
bedroom, with its view of grazing
animals, one descends via a staircase of
exposed beams and brickwork to the
breakfast-room in the old part of the
cottage. No dinners (the Vaughans will
provide light snacks if ordered in
advance) but there are good inns nearby and plenty of restaurants in the old
quarter of Amersham. £17–£18.

Readers' comments: Very comfortable,
warm and friendly. Every comfort
thought of. Really nice, big bedroom.
Friendly and good value. [Tel: 01494
712221; postcode: HP15 6ND]

WHITEWEBBS

26 Lower Road, Chalfont St Peter, Buckinghamshire, SL9 9AQ
Tel: 01753 884105
South-east of High Wycombe. Nearest main road: A413 from Amersham to
Denham (also M40, junction 1; and M25, junction 16).

2 Bedrooms. £18–£19 (less for 4 nights).
Both have own bath/shower/toilet. TV.
Views of garden. No smoking.
Dinner (by arrangement). £10 for 2 courses
and coffee, at 7pm. Non-residents not
admitted. Vegetarian or special diets if
ordered. No smoking. **Light suppers.**
Small garden

This house, secluded by tall oaks and pines, was built in 1928 on ground belonging to the nearby Grange, once the home of William Penn's father-in-law (who
sailed with him on the *Mayflower*). Now it is the home of artist Maureen Marsh,
who specializes in portraits of houses and country views: visitors are welcome to
enter her studio and to see the little printing-press on which she and her husband
produce Christmas cards and so forth.

Often tea (with home-produced raspberry jam and cakes) is served in the
garden, pretty with flower baskets and rose bushes – or visitors can use the
kitchen to make their own at any hour. Maureen enjoys cooking and gives her
guests such meals as a courgette and cheese gratin with a salad, followed by pecan
pie into which go sherry-soaked raisins. These are served in a cream and pine
dining-room with lattice-paned windows.

Upstairs are trim, cottagey bedrooms with pretty flowery wallpaper and
matching bedspreads and everywhere her delightful watercolours.

This is a tranquil spot for a break from London or to recover from a flight to
Heathrow. For walkers, the South Bucks Way passes close by; for sightseeing
there are Milton's cottage, the ever-growing Chiltern Open-air Museum, beautiful walks and drives in the Chiltern Hills (famous for their autumn colours), the
Bekonscot miniature village – 1½ acres recreating life in the 'twenties complete
with a 20-locomotive railway – the Quaker centre of Jordans, and the historic
streets of, for instance, Beaconsfield and Marlow. Some of the Thames's
loveliest reaches are in the vicinity, as are the Italianate mansion and grounds of
Cliveden and Tudor Chenies Manor, Stanley Spencer's paintings in pretty
Cookham, the 'hell-fire' caves at Medmenham, the historic chair museum of
High Wycombe, Gray's monument at Stoke Poges and Disraeli's house
(Hughenden Manor). Pevsner described Denham as 'one of the most attractive
villages in any direction near London'.

Readers' comments: Warm hospitality. Large, airy and comfortable rooms. Have
stayed several times. One feels like a family guest. Delicious breakfasts. Extremely
pretty. Warm and welcoming. Surrounding countryside beautiful. Food and
ambience perfect. Comfortable and charming. Welcoming, caring; lovely room,
excellent breakfast.

WHYKE HOUSE   C PT S X

13 Whyke Lane, Chichester, West Sussex, PO19 2JR   Tel: 01243 788767

Nearest main road: A27 from Worthing to Portsmouth.

rear view

4 Bedrooms. £18 (less for 3 nights). Price goes up in April. All have own bath/shower/toilet. Tea/coffee facilities. TV. Views of garden. No smoking.

1 Sitting-room. With central heating, TV. No smoking.

Small garden

In a peaceful suburban cul-de-sac, very close to the historic centre of Chichester (and overlooking a grassy Roman site at the back, where children now play) is an unusual bed-and-breakfast house, ideal for families, with private parking.

Here Tony and Lydia Hollis provide continental breakfasts (and service rooms), give advice on sightseeing, then depart to their own home next door. There is a fully equipped kitchen which guests are then welcome to use to prepare other meals, if they do not wish to go to Chichester's many restaurants and cafés. Guests can also use the sitting-room and back garden (with croquet), glimpsed in the drawing. It is almost like being in a home of your own, with complete freedom.

The furnishings throughout have great individuality. Family antiques mingle with Russian folk art, local paintings (you may meet the artist) with soft furnishings made by Lydia. She also has a flair for decorative painting, evident both in the bedrooms and in the light, colourful dining-room. Here the baby's highchair is a century-old heirloom, so is the grandmother clock. For some older guests, the ground-floor bedroom and shower are particularly convenient.

Readers' comments: What good value. Comfortable, quiet, convenient; most welcoming. Pleasant weekend; a real treat to stay. Pleasant and warm. Most kind. Most convenient. Home was an inspiration, welcome was heart-warming.

East of Chichester, the accommodation at **ST HUGH'S**, Boxgrove, is in a separate annexe in the garden. It comprises a spacious, well-furnished bedsitting-room which opens onto a private patio. There is an excellent shower-room; and cooking facilities are hidden away in pine fitments. For breakfast, guests enter the main house and its dining-room (lined with ancestral portraits of Cornish farmers). B & b only: for other meals, Edwina Tremaine recommends restaurants in nearby Chichester. Boxgrove itself deserves a visit because the Norman nave of its parish church is quite outstanding. £17–£18.

Readers' comments: Wholly recom-

rear view

mended, beautifully furnished. Absolutely ideal. Very comfortable. Made very welcome. Helpful hosts. Extremely comfortable. Most enjoyable. [Tel: 01243 773173; postcode: PO18 0DY]

WIGBOROUGH FARM

C D PT S

Lower Stratton, Somerset, TA13 5LP   Tel: 01460 240490
West of Yeovil. Nearest main road: A303 from Ilminster to Wincanton.

3 Bedrooms. £18–£20. TV. Views of garden, country. No smoking. Washing machine on request.
Dinner. £12.50 for 3 courses (with choices) and coffee, at 8.30pm. Less for 2 courses. Non-residents not admitted. Vegetarian or special diets if ordered. No smoking. **Light suppers** if ordered.
1 Sitting-room. With open fire, central heating, TV, piano, record-player.
Large garden
Closed in December and January.

But for a fire in 1585, this mansion would doubtless have been one of England's oldest. Only one wing was rebuilt: even so, it remains among the most impressive of the houses in this book.

Outside are pinnacled gables, Tudor roses carved in the spandrels above the arched doorway, handsome dripstones above the narrow-paned mullioned windows – all in tawny Ham limestone which lichen has enriched over the centuries: the same local stone from which the National Trust's great Montacute House was built about the same time as this house.

Inside are ogee arches, stone floors and iron-studded doors; there are still spit-racks above one of the huge fireplaces. The ground-floor rooms are high-ceilinged: one has a minstrels' gallery overlooking the great refectory table and its leather chairs (this gallery is now a bedroom). The sitting-room has a quite exceptional plaster ceiling with bas-reliefs of foxes, stags, pheasants and even a unicorn (made by Italian plasterers in Elizabeth I's reign); and over its fireplace is the great coat-of-arms of a local family.

Guests' bedrooms (varying in size and style) are on the second floor: the most outstanding has oak walls, its panels decoratively carved with arches and pilasters, and a four-poster bed.

From many windows are views of lawns with specimen trees, tubs of busy Lizzies, old stables and the walled vegetable garden.

Where meals are concerned, Joan Vaux and one of her daughters prepare such dishes as mushroom soup, beef cooked in wine, and fruit mousse.

Yeovil (a glove-making centre) has nine springs flowing into a very lovely lake: the walk to it, along a wooded riverside path, is well worth seeking out. All around the town are historic villages, such as Milborne Port with its old guildhall, Tintinhull which still has punishment stocks, Hinton St George with fine stone houses among its tangle of lanes, picturesque Compton Pauncefoot named after a Norman landowner of big belly ('paunch-fat') and South Cadbury, whose high and massive earthworks were reputedly King Arthur's stronghold, Camelot. Langport is a hilly market town with a chapel on top of a mediaeval arch.

There are important National Trust houses in the area, the Fleet Air Arm Museum at Yeovilton, and some wonderful gardens within 10 miles.

Readers' comments: As if out of a dream! Historic but comfortable, lovely gardens. Wonderful people. The best! Very loath to leave this most beautiful place and the relaxed generosity and the warmth of these charming people.

357

WILLOW COTTAGE

C(10) **PT S**

Bassenthwaite, Cumbria, CA12 4QP   Tel: 017687 76440
East of Cockermouth. Nearest main road: A591 from Keswick towards Carlisle.

2 Bedrooms. £17.50 (less for 2 nights). Both have own bath/toilet. Tea/coffee facilities. Views of garden, country. No smoking. Washing machine on request.
Light suppers on Sundays. No smoking.
1 Sitting-room. With open fire, central heating, record-player. No smoking.
Small garden

You will sleep under gnarled rafters at Willow Cottage, which Chris Beaty and her husband have carefully converted from an ancient barn (together with self-catering accommodation next door). One bedroom has views of Skiddaw, the other the use of a big cast-iron bath. At the foot of the staircase (on which hangs Chris's collection of antique baby-linen) is a beamed sitting-cum-breakfast room, with comfortable seats facing an iron stove in a nook. A smaller room has French windows opening onto a paved area by the vegetable and herb garden, where guests often sit to enjoy the sunset behind the mountains. The cottage is attractively decorated, with unobtrusive stencilling and furniture-painting by Chris. She offers some choice at breakfast, and she sometimes provides snack suppers, though most guests eat well at the Sun Inn a few hundred yards away in the village. Otherwise there is plenty of choice in Keswick and Cockermouth.

Bassenthwaite Lake, to which the village has given its name, is popular with small-boat sailors, but this, the most northerly part of the Lake District National Park, is never as crowded as the more popular centre, and Cockermouth is one of the least spoiled of the towns. For good pub lunches, Ireby and Caldbeck are not far, and Isel Hall and the nearby Norman church are well worth visiting.

In the tiny, remote hamlet of High Ireby, **FELL EDGE**, which was built in the 18th century as a chapel, is the home of the highly musical Allison family. This is a place for people who appreciate quietness and views – of the northern fells in one direction and, across the garden which Arthur Allison is landscaping, as far as Dumfries in the other. The garden contributes to such dinner menus as tomato and basil soup, pork in raisin sauce, and meringue glacé. The Allisons have produced a leaflet of walks of various standards. Apart from the northern Lake District, the area is worth exploring for the rather fen-like Solway Plain (an Area of Outstanding Natural

Beauty) and the deserted coast. No smoking. £15.
Readers' comments: Stayed there twice and been very satisfied. Wonderful hospitality. Very interesting people. Each meal well cooked and well presented. [Tel: 016973 71397; postcode: CA5 1HF]

WINDRUSH HOUSE   S
Hazleton, Gloucestershire, GL54 4EB   Tel: 01451 860364
South-east of Cheltenham. Nearest main road: A40 from Cheltenham to
Oxford.

4 Bedrooms. £18.75–£22. Bargain breaks. Some have own shower/toilet. Tea/coffee facilities. Views of garden, country. Washing machine on request.
Dinner (by arrangement). £18.75 for 4 courses and coffee, at 7.30pm. Wine available. **Light suppers** if ordered.
2 Sitting-rooms. With open fire, central heating, TV, video, piano, record-player.
Large garden
Closed from mid-December to January.

The greatest attraction of this small guest-house built of Cotswold stone is Sydney Harrison's outstanding cooking. Not only is everything impeccably prepared – vegetables delicately sliced and lightly cooked, bread home-baked, breakfast orange juice freshly squeezed – but she has a repertoire of imaginative dishes that puts many an expensive restaurant in the shade.

Sydney's friendly welcome is manifest the moment you arrive, and a free glass of sherry awaits you in your room.

As to the house itself, this is furnished with much attention to comfort, and in tranquil colours. All the rooms are immaculate, the furnishings traditional.

The house stands in a quiet spot some 800 feet up in the Cotswold hills, where the air is bracing and the views are of far fields and grazing sheep. It is on the outskirts of a rambling village of old stone farmhouses – under two hours from London – and close to beautiful Northleach, which has a mediaeval church of great splendour and an excellent museum of country life.

Readers' comments: Absolute calm. First-rate; inventive menu; highly recommended. Excellent food and genial hosts. Food outstanding; what a find! Superb cooking. The best meal we'd had – highly recommended. Excellent in every way, especially food and wine. The best cook we've found in England. Excellent food; very comfortable; welcoming. Our third visit. Excellent cook and hostess; very comfortable. Nothing but praise, excellent cook, very pleasant hostess. World-class cook.

In the central square of Northleach is **MARKET HOUSE** – so called because fleeces were marketed here in the time of Elizabeth I. Next to an old inn, it still retains ancient beams and rugged stone walls (even in the cottage-style bedrooms at the top of a steep stair) as a background to the immaculate modern comforts provided by Theresa Eastman. There is a walled garden at the back. In the breakfast/sitting-room, logs blaze in an inglenook when the weather is chilly.

£17–£20. [Tel: 01451 860557; postcode: GL54 3EJ]

WINDYRIDGE C D M P T S X
Wraik Hill, Whitstable, Kent, CT5 3BY Tel: 01227 263506
North of Canterbury. Nearest main road: A299 from Faversham towards
Ramsgate (and M2, junction 7).

8 Bedrooms. £18–£20. Bargain breaks.
Some have own shower/toilet. Tea/coffee
facilities. TV. Views of garden, country, sea.
Dinner. £12 for 3 courses and coffee, at
6.30pm. Less for 2 courses. Vegetarian or
special diets if ordered. Wine available.
Light suppers if ordered.
2 Sitting-rooms. With wood-burner,
central heating, TV, record-player, piano.
No smoking in one.
Large garden

The architectural eccentricities of this house are due to the fact that a demolition
contractor once lived here, and in the course of expanding what was originally a
small cottage he built in all kinds of curios – even gargoyles from a chapel, and
rare Norman panes of purple glass. Some iron-framed windows came from a
prison. Two-foot-thick walls have a mixture of granite slabs, bricks and low stone
archways combined in an odd assortment.

Elizabeth and Colin Dyke run this pleasant guest-house. At one end of the
very big sitting-room, sofas and cretonne wing chairs face a great stone fireplace
with log stove (there is another sitting-room elsewhere) while at the other end a
steep, open-tread staircase rises to the bedrooms – and there is a telescope from
which to enjoy the panoramic sea views. Even without its aid, one can often see
from this high vantage-point the distant shores of Essex and, at night, the twin-
kling lights of its liveliest resort, Southend-on-Sea. All the bedrooms are fresh and
trim; there is a particularly good family room with curtained annexe for children,
and a ground-floor room for disabled people.

Elizabeth serves such dinners as Whitstable oysters in garlic butter, fish pie,
and meringues filled with fresh fruit and cream. Rolls are home-baked, vegetables
come from the garden.

Beyond the conservatory, where one eats while enjoying the wide views, is a
rambling garden. Along the coast (15 minutes' walk away), sandy beaches are separated by the Swale from the Isle of Sheppey – this waterway is a haven for wildfowl.

Of all counties, Kent – fertile and wealthy – has played a greater part in
English history than any other because its coast is only 20 miles from Europe (to
which it was once joined) and because of its proximity to London.

Once, Whitstable enjoyed an important role in all this and was busy with
travellers who came by coach from Canterbury to embark there for a sea journey
to London (which says much about the sad state of road transport to the capital
at that time). Then in 1830 the world's first passenger train took over this route:
you can see its locomotive (Robert Stephenson's *Invicta*) in Canterbury.

But it was only in this century that Whitstable really prospered as a seaside
resort. It still has rows of black-and-white weatherboarded fishermen's cottages to
give it character, and seafood restaurants where you can eat well. Eastward lie
Herne Bay, an old-fashioned Victorian resort, and Reculver's twin towers –
Norman, but within the remains of a great Roman fort.

Readers' comments: Food superb, welcome warm and genuine. Wonderful family
atmosphere, location ideal.

WOLD FARM   C D M PT S X
Old, Northamptonshire, NN6 9RJ   Tel: 01604 781258
(Messages: 01604 781122)
North of Northampton. Nearest main road: A508 from Northampton to
Market Harborough (also M1, junction 15; and M1–A1 link).

6 Bedrooms. £18–£20 (less for 3 nights).
All have own bath/shower. Tea/coffee facilities. Views of garden. Washing machine on
request.
Dinner. £13.50 for 4 courses, wine and
coffee, at 7pm. Less for 2 courses.
Vegetarian or special diets if ordered. **Light
suppers** if ordered.
2 Sitting-rooms. With open fire, central
heating, TV, record-player. Billiards.
Garden

This 18th-century house has particularly attractive and spacious rooms, and two
delightful gardens with rose pergola, golden pheasants and swing-seat. A garden-
cottage has been converted to provide more bedrooms (en suite), one of which is
on the ground floor. Throughout the house are attractive fabrics and wallpapers;
one room, for example, with Country Manor pattern on walls, bed and curtains.
In the sitting-room are alcoves of Hummel figures, in the dining-room a carved
17th-century sideboard, and in the breakfast-room a dresser with the exhortation:
'Nourish thyself with lively vivacity'. Window-seats, antiques and white-panelled
doors add further character to the rooms. Throughout, standards are of the
highest. The house is at the heart of a beef and arable farm.

For dinner, Anne Engler serves – in an oak-beamed dining-room with
inglenook fireplace – such meals as home-made soup followed by a roast and then
perhaps fruit salad or Bakewell tart, and cheeses – with a sherry, wine or beer
included. (Occasional barbecues; and Sunday lunch also available.) Anne, once a
'Tiller girl', is a most warm and welcoming hostess.

A feature of the rolling agricultural landscape round here is the network of
18th- and 19th-century canals, and the reservoirs (now naturalized) that were
built to top up the water in these. At Stoke Bruerne a waterways museum tells the
whole story of the canals. The many stately homes of this prosperous county
include Althorp (childhood home of the Princess of Wales) and Boughton House
(modelled on Versailles). There are Saxon churches at Brixworth and Earls
Barton. The county is famous for its high-spired churches and for its many
historical associations: it has two 'Eleanor crosses' erected in the 13th century
by Edward I wherever his wife's coffin rested on its journey to burial in
Westminster Abbey; Fotheringhay is where Mary Queen of Scots was executed;
Cromwell defeated Charles I's army at Naseby in 1645 (good bar food at the
Fitzgerald Arms, and a museum of the battle). In the Nene Valley is a scenic
steam railway.

Staying here would be a very good all-weather alternative to a traditional
seaside holiday for the family.

Readers' comments: Cooking outstanding. Very thoughtful attention. Harmony and
friendliness. Exactingly high standard. Kind and generous. It excels. Outstanding
success. Warmest of welcomes. Attractive garden. Pretty and very comfortable
room. Food a delight; table-settings superb. Friendly, attentive and patient. All of
us enjoyed our stay very much. Very comfortable.

THE WOOD
De Courcy Road, Salcombe, Devon, TQ8 8LQ   Tel: 01548 842778
South of Kingsbridge. Nearest main road: A381 from Salcombe to Totnes.

6 Bedrooms. £20–£37 (less for 4 nights). Prices go up from June. All have own bath/shower/toilet. Tea/coffee facilities. TV. Views of garden, country, sea. Balcony (some). No smoking. Washing machine on request.
Dinner. £16 for 4 courses (with some choices) and coffee, at 7.30pm. Vegetarian or special diets if ordered. Wine available.
Light suppers if ordered.
1 Sitting-room. With open fire, central heating, piano, CD-player.
Terraced garden
Closed from December to February.

rear view

One of the most spectacular sites in this book is occupied by a turn-of-the-century house which seems almost to hang in the air, so steep is the wooded cliff below it. One looks straight down onto the pale golden beach of South Sands (a small cove) and the blue waters of Salcombe estuary with the English Channel beyond. Rocky headlands stretch into the distance. To make the most of this exceptional view, some bedrooms have balconies, and the elegant, split-level sitting-room has huge windows that open onto a paved terrace, where breakfast is sometimes served. One can walk through the garden to a steep woodland footpath which goes down to the sands – but what a climb up again! – and from there take the ferry to Salcombe. Moorings are available for boat owners.

Bedrooms, on two floors, have different styles. No. 1 is sunny yellow. No. 2 has a sensational bay window framing a view of the estuary; it has a canopied bed, balcony, a power-shower and a whirlpool bath. A small single is very pretty: Victorian-style cream and deep pink fabrics. No. 4, with jade, peach and cream fabrics, has a balcony; as does no. 5, with four-poster and outsize bathroom. No. 6 is a twin-bedded room level with the lounge and dining-room.

In the dining-room (handsomely furnished with pink velvet chairs, white-gold Minton china and linen napkins), Pat Vaissière serves candlelit dinners that use much local produce – such as cheese-filled eggs, lamb with apricot-and-almond stuffing, chocolate rum trifle, and cheeses. Rolls are home-baked.

Salcombe is Devon's southernmost resort, and arguably its most beautiful one. Even orange and lemon trees grow here which, together with palms, remind one of parts of the Mediterranean. The estuary is very popular for sailing, garden-lovers come to see Sharpitor (NT), walkers make for the viewpoints of Bolbery Down and Bolt Head. All along the coast from here to Plymouth are picturesque waterfront villages, such as Bantham and Newton Ferrers.

In the opposite direction are Kingsbridge (old market town), Slapton Sands (nature reserve, with lagoons), picturesque Dartmouth (of outstanding historical interest – two castles, quaint quays, the Royal Naval College).

Readers' comments: Outstanding standards. They go out of their way to provide that little bit extra at every turn. Made to feel so much at home. Worth coming for the food alone! Lovely site; delighted. Superb comfort, food and hospitality. Food excellent. Setting and personal service superb.

WOODGATE

Birling Road, Leybourne, West Malling, Kent, ME19 5HT
Tel: 01732 843201
West of Maidstone. Nearest main road: A228 from West Malling to Rochester
(also M20, junction 4).

3 Bedrooms. £18–£20 (less for 7 nights).
Some have own bath/shower/toilet. Tea/
coffee facilities. TV. Views of garden,
country. No smoking. Washing machine on
request.
Dinner. £15 for 4 courses and coffee, up
to 9pm. Non-residents not admitted.
Vegetarian or special diets if ordered. No
smoking. **Light suppers** if ordered.
2 Sitting-rooms. With open fire, TV. No
smoking.
Large garden

This old brick and tile-hung cottage – originally two woodcutters' houses – is now
the unusual home of Judy and Ken Ludlow. They moved to it from Beirut in
1976, and the unusual artefacts about the house testify to their many years of
travel in Egypt and the Middle East. Ken still travels as a journalist.

Guest bedrooms are small but well decorated in a bold style - one has old iron
bedsteads (with modern mattresses), peony curtains and Impressionist-style wallpapers; another has duck-egg blue walls, pine bed and a table made from old
Indian blue- and silver-coloured window shutters.

One small sitting-room has a good selection of classical CDs for guests to
listen to; the main sitting-room in gold has scroll-ended and Knole sofas,
Egyptian and Chinese *objets d'art*, and on one wall an intricately carved dark
wood shutter from Bosnia. The large conservatory, heated in winter, where guests
dine, has brightly coloured ornaments, Haitian paintings and a big, beautifully
polished table made from South African railway sleepers.

Judy's cooking is eclectic and inventive in style: sometimes with Middle-
Eastern influences, at others traditionally English, with some Delia Smith recipes.
The result might be roasted red peppers, Thai chicken, and bread-and-butter
pudding.

The Ludlows are justifiably proud of their four-acre landscaped garden, much
of it their own design and making. There are unusual trees such as Sapporo new
elms, Indian bean trees and sequoias. Also a small pond, an aviary, chickens, and
a fox who visits nightly to feed - usually not on the chickens.

Readers' comments: Never stayed in a more interesting house. Magnificent dining.
More than value for money.

To help those en route to the continent, via tunnel or ferry, Kent County
Council has produced an excellent booklet with map, called *Off the
Motorway,* which will tempt you to tack on a day or so (going or coming)
to explore any of 139 attractive places to visit in this beautiful and historic
county.

WOODMANS GREEN FARM   C D S

Linch, West Sussex, GU30 7NF   Tel: 01428 741250
North of Midhurst. Nearest main road: A3 from Guildford to Petersfield.

3 Bedrooms. £18.50–£25 (less for 3 nights). Tea/coffee facilities. Views of garden, country. No smoking. Washing machine on request.
Dinner. £12 for 3 courses and coffee, at 7.30pm. Less for 2 courses. Non-residents not admitted. Vegetarian or special diets if ordered. No smoking. **Light suppers** if ordered.
2 Sitting-rooms. With open fire, central heating, TV, record-player. Piano.
Large garden
Closed in January and February.

This Tudor house has interesting features of the period, which include a particularly grand staircase, stone-mullioned windows in the gable, low doorways (on which Mary Spreckley drapes swags of dried flowers) and, in the farmyard, an unusual roofed and brick-walled midden. (There is a heated swimming-pool.)

Bedrooms are spacious and peaceful; under the beamed roof is a large and attractive family room. Adjoining the sitting-room is a bright garden-room.

By arrangement, Mary – who is a very good cook – will prepare either a full dinner (such as chilled lettuce, pea and mint soup; rosemary and honey roast lamb; and tarte tatin) or a light supper (such as pasta with broccoli, mushrooms and ham).

This very attractive area around Haslemere, Petersfield and Petworth is a good base from which to visit Chichester, Fishbourne Roman palace, Petworth House, and the open-air Weald and Downland Museum of ancient buildings. There are good walks and country inns (mountain bicycles, wellies and maps on loan). Polo is played at Midhurst – a town with many antique shops and restaurants.

Readers' comments: Friendly atmosphere, cooking imaginative and attractively served; very pleasant indeed. Delicious breakfast. Delightful hosts.

Sitting-room at Street Farmhouse (see page 309)

WOODPECKER COTTAGE
C(8) M S

Star Lane, Warren Row, Berkshire, RG10 8QS   Tel: 01628 822772
West of Maidenhead. Nearest main road: A4 from Maidenhead to Reading
(also M4, junction 8/9; and M40, junction 4).

rear view

3 Bedrooms. £18–£25 (less for 4 nights). Prices go up from April. All have own bath/shower/toilet. Tea/coffee facilities. TV. Views of garden, country. No smoking. Washing machine on request.
Dinner (by arrangement). £12 for 3 courses and coffee, at 8pm. Less for 2 courses. Non-residents not admitted. Vegetarian or special diets if ordered. No smoking. **Light suppers** if ordered.
1 Sitting-room. With open fire, central heating, TV. No smoking.
Large garden

There really are woodpeckers here – three kinds – for the cottage is deep in blue-bell woods, their many old tracks frequented by birdwatchers. A pretty garden (with breakfast on the terrace a possibility) and croquet lawn add to the attractions, while further afield are tranquil reaches of the Thames and several golf courses. All this within a half-hour of Heathrow Airport and Windsor, Oxford and Henley.

Flint-walled cowsheds were converted and extensions added to create this attractive home. One ground-floor bedroom overlooks fish-pools, sundial and rock garden; another (with leather sofa and television) has a woodland view. There's an en suite single room, a small 'snug' for visitors to sit in after dinner, and a dining-room where Chippendale-style chairs surround a Paisley-clothed table. Here, by arrangement, Joanna Power serves such meals as onion tart, chicken breasts on spinach with tarragon sauce, and gooseberry fool. Much produce is from the garden, and even bread and pasta are home-made.

For a quick 'away-from-it-all' break out of London, this could be an ideal choice. From Maidenhead you can explore that reach of the Thames where fashionable Edwardian celebrities built homes, boarding a steamer or hiring a boat (August brings out straw boaters and striped blazers for the Regatta): Boulter's Lock is the high spot of any trip. Go to picturesque little Bray for black-and-white cottages, fine river views and the old church of that most celebrated of turncoats, the Vicar of Bray.

On the way to Windsor and Eton is 16th-century Dorney Court; and past Windsor you come to Runnymede, with the Magna Carta and John Kennedy memorials. Plant-lovers head for the Savill Gardens (400 acres of rarities), and to Valley Gardens (200 species of heather) by one of the largest ornamental lakes in Britain, Virginia Water, which is flanked by Roman columns, a 100-foot totem pole and an 18th-century waterfall.

Readers' comments: Excellent. Attentive and very welcoming. Fantastic breakfast. Will stay again. Totally uncontrived atmosphere.

Book well ahead: many of these houses have few rooms. Do not expect dinner if you have not booked it or if you arrive late.

WYCK HILL LODGE   **M**
Wyck Hill, Stow-on-the-Wold, Gloucestershire, GL54 1HT
Tel: 01451 830141
On A424 from Stow to Burford.

3 Bedrooms. £18–£22 (less for 5 nights and at mid-week). Prices go up from April. All have own bath/shower/toilet. Tea/coffee facilities. TV. Views of garden, country. No smoking. Washing machine on request.
Light suppers if ordered.
1 Sitting-room. With open fire, central heating. No smoking.
Garden

This picturesque house was built around 1800 as the lodge to a nearby mansion. Now it is surrounded by very lovely gardens, from which come the abundant flowers in every room. There are far views across Bourton Vale and good walks straight from the door.

In the L-shaped sitting-room are big leather armchairs and, in winter, a crackling fire. A small reading-room is particularly attractive: like some other rooms, it has windows set in pointed arches with stained-glass panes at the top. There is a view of the terraced garden (with pond) and far hills.

Two of the bedrooms (one opening onto the garden) are on the ground floor, and there is another upstairs – this is a big, two-level room with a cane sofa.

As this edition went to press, we learned that Wyck Hill Lodge had changed hands. The new owners, Gloria and Eddie Holbrook, plan to maintain the standard set by the previous proprietor, Jackie Alderton. Evening meals or light suppers may be available by special arrangement in advance.

Nearby Bourton-on-the-Water is too picturesque for its own good (it is thronged in summer) but **THE RIDGE** guest-house, at Whiteshoots, off the Bourton–Cirencester road, is well away from all that. A gabled Edwardian house, it is surrounded by lawns and fine trees, with hill views. Breakfast-tables are in a new conservatory overlooking a sunken garden; Pamela Minchin has several comfortable bedrooms, two on the ground floor (one with its own entrance). No smoking. Good pubs are close for meals. £16.50–£19.

Readers' comments: Superb. Delightfully furnished, hospitable hostess. Have stayed three times. [Tel: 01451 820660; postcode: GL54 2LE]

Some proprietors stipulate a minimum stay of two nights at weekends or peak seasons; or they will accept one-nighters only at short notice (that is, only if no lengthier booking has yet been made).

YEW TREES

Silver Street, Misterton, Somerset, TA18 8NB   Tel: 01460 77192
South of Crewkerne. Nearest main road: A356 from Crewkerne to Dorchester.

3 Bedrooms. £16 (less for 3 nights or continental breakfast). Price goes up from April. All have tea/coffee facilities. Views of garden. No smoking. Washing machine on request.
Light suppers if ordered. No smoking.
2 Sitting-rooms. With central heating, TV. No smoking.
Small garden

Two 17th-century cottages – beamed and stone-walled – have been turned into one house, providing an unusually large sitting/dining-room, furnished with antiques. Bedrooms have pale colours and pine furniture, with low windows tucked under the eaves of the house.

Ann and Geoffrey Clifton sometimes teach English here to individual overseas visitors, whom many English guests enjoy meeting – often sitting in the garden where flagstoned steps curve down towards the lily-pool.

One of Anne's light suppers might be soup, quiche and salad, and orange Boodle.

Misterton is a quiet and friendly village with lovely countryside around, and is an excellent centre for visits to famous old buildings such as Sherborne Abbey, Montacute House, Forde Abbey and Parnham House, a beautiful Renaissance manor house where John Makepeace has a world-famous school for craftsmanship in wood. Or you can explore a host of picturesque hamstone villages with their thatched cottages and fine mediaeval churches. Visit, too, some of the beautiful gardens – East Lambrook Manor (designed by Margery Fish), Tintinhull House, Hadspen House (once the home of Penelope Hobhouse), and the tropical gardens and famous swannery at Abbotsbury. At Hornsbury Mill you can have cream teas in a 300-year-old mill with large waterwheel.

There are lovely walks in the surrounding countryside, or along the spectacular Dorset coast a short drive away (maps can be borrowed), while towns such as Crewkerne, Lyme Regis and Honiton provide happy hunting-grounds for collectors of antiques or crafts.

Readers' comments: Most delightful house of great character, beautifully furnished, food and hospitality exceptional. Most friendly welcome, good and ample food. Have booked again. Very comfortable, food excellent, service first class. What a find – enjoyed every minute. Super hosts. Most impressed.

Houses which accept the discount vouchers on page ii are marked with a V on the lists at the beginning of this book, see pages xi–xix and pages xxi–xxii.

YOAH COTTAGE

West Knighton, Dorset, DT2 8PE   Tel: 01305 852087

South-east of Dorchester. Nearest main road: A352 from Dorchester to Wareham.

C(8) **D S**

2 **Bedrooms.** £15.50–£17.50 (less for 7 nights). Prices go up from May. Tea/coffee facilities. Views of garden, country. No smoking. Washing machine on request.
Dinner. £12.50 for 3 courses and coffee, at 7.30pm. Vegetarian or special diets if ordered. No smoking. **Light suppers** if ordered.
1 **Sitting-room.** With open fire, TV. No smoking.
Large garden
Closed from mid-December to early January.

In every room of this picturesque cottage, all whitewash and thatch, are ceramic sheep, pigs, Noah's Arks or Gardens of Eden – which both Furse and Rosemary Swann make in their studio at the back. (There is a garden-house with a display of them for sale.) 'Becoming redundant was one of the best things that happened to me', says Furse, who changed career in mid-life (he previously taught English).

The great beam over one of the inglenook fireplaces carries the date 1622. Rooms are low and white-walled, the staircases narrow and steep, floors stone-flagged, windows small and deep-set.

The Swanns have filled the house with an immensely varied collection of treasures, from a 19th-century glass painting of a bull to modern abstracts, pictures of Borzoi dogs by Weschke and prints by Munch to a portrait of 'Mrs Darling' (in *Peter Pan*) by a great-uncle. There is a collection of green Bristol glass and another of Breton plates, a splendid samovar of Polish brass, odd-shaped pebbles from the nearby beach at Ringstead, oriental rugs and Victorian raised-cotton bedspreads, metal animals by an award-winning sculptor whose work they spotted in India . . . in every room there is a visual feast. Bedrooms are equally attractive (the pretty bathrooms are on the ground floor).

The large garden is a romantic spot, with flagged paths wandering among cottage flowers, hedges separating one secret spot from another.

Rosemary produces not only imaginative dishes of her own (for instance, pork tenderloin with mushrooms in a green pepper and cream sauce) but also specialities from Sweden, where she lived for many years. Furse prepares breakfasts, which can include such unusual options as scrambled eggs on anchovy toast or kedgeree; and he makes all the jams.

Next door is the friendly 18th-century New Inn. Thomas Hardy is said to have owned the cottage opposite and, when writing his last major novel, *Jude the Obscure*, he also undertook the restoration of West Knighton's church. In this western part of Dorset, a lovely area, you will find Hardy's birthplace, 'Egdon Heath', an exciting coastline, the market town of Dorchester, Iron Age hill forts, and a great many literary associations.

Readers' comments: Most beautiful and characterful. Warm and welcoming, most interesting people. Comfortable and extremely well fed. A most enjoyable week, super experience. Delightful atmosphere. Idyllic. A memorable place to stay. Truly outstanding. A stimulating visit.

ALPHABETICAL DIRECTORY OF
HOUSES AND HOTELS IN
WALES

For map and list of houses and hotels,
see pages xx and xxi–xxii

Prices are per person sharing a double room, at the
beginning of the year. You may be quoted more later
or for single occupancy.

Prices and other facts quoted at the head of each entry
are as supplied by the proprietors.

Where county names were replaced on 1st April 1996,
they have been given in brackets in the first line of main
entry addresses.

Sitting-room at Upper Trewalkin Farm (see page 401)

ABERCELYN   C D PT
Llanycil, (Gwynedd), Caernarfonshire & Merionethshire, LL23 7YF
Tel: 01678 521109
South-west of Bala. Nearest main road: A494 from Bala to Dolgellau.

3 Bedrooms. £18–£20.50 (less for 4 nights). Prices go up from April. Bargain breaks. All have own bath/shower/toilet. Tea/coffee facilities. Views of garden, country, lake. No smoking.
Dinner. £12.50 for 3 courses and coffee, at 7.30pm. Less for 2 courses. Vegetarian or special diets if ordered. No smoking. **Light suppers** if ordered.
1 Sitting-room. With open fire, central heating, TV. No smoking.
Large garden

The Cunninghams were themselves regular users of *Staying Off the Beaten Track* (as are many proprietors with houses in the book) before they took to offering b & b in their 18th-century house close to the shore of Lake Bala (on some maps named Llyn Tegid). Once the home of a reclusive shipping magnate, it stands in landscaped grounds with a stream, a stone house with deep-set shuttered windows, log fires and its own mountain-spring water. There is a cottage, too, in the garden, mainly let on a self-catering basis but sometimes available for b & b.

Judy has chosen attractive colour schemes: for instance, restful greys and greens in the sitting-room or, in one of the bedrooms, a particularly brilliant poppy wallpaper contrasting with all-white in the rest of the room. There are nice touches like embroidered pillowcases, antiques and interesting pictures.

She is a very good cook, providing full dinners (such as a pâté with home-made bread, lamb, and chocolate pots de crème) only outside high season. However, her light suppers (quiches, etc.) are at least as good as many people's dinners.

Readers' comments: Thoroughly recommended. Comfortable, lovely home. Most attentive without being intrusive. Nothing was too much trouble. Wonderful; friendly and hospitable.

Above the opposite (less frequented) side of Lake Bala is another 18th-century house, which has very fine views across lily-pond and lake to the mountains of Snowdonia: **PLAS GOWER**, Llangower. One enters past a cascade of begonias in the verandah to rooms furnished with good antiques, Victorian watercolours of Wales and such interesting features as an old spinet converted into a desk. There is a particularly elegant bathroom. A previous owner was the Welsh poet Euros Bowen who lived here until 1973, but the site has been inhabited since 1312 and Olwen Foreman has a sampler which lists all owners from then until

now. She enjoys telling visitors about lesser-known routes to follow and cooking for them traditional meals such as leek soup, Welsh lamb, and blackberry-and-apple crumble. Her sister, too, takes b & b guests – at **Plas Penucha** in Flintshire. £17.50–£18. [Tel: 01678 520431; postcode: LL23 7BY]

ABERYSCIR OLD RECTORY

C S

Aberyscir, Brecon, Powys, LD3 9NP Tel: 01874 623457

West of Brecon. Nearest main road: A40 from Brecon to Sennybridge.

3 Bedrooms. £18 (less for 7 nights). Price goes up from April. All have own bath/shower/toilet. Tea/coffee facilities. TV. Views of garden, country, river. Washing machine on request.

Dinner. £10 for 3 courses (with some choices) and coffee, at 7pm. Vegetarian or special diets if ordered.

1 Sitting-room. With central heating, record-player. Piano.

Large garden

Well tucked away in the hills, this Victorian stone house, standing in large grounds, has been furnished by Elizabeth Gould to high standards of comfort and solid quality. Bedrooms are particularly attractive, two with windows on two sides and very lovely views. Dinners include generous quantities of such dishes as smoked haddock ramekins, beef Stroganoff and Elizabeth's Malibu dessert – coconut liqueur combined with tropical fruits and whipped cream. Afterwards, there are velvet chairs and a chaise longue in the green sitting-room from which to enjoy the views or occasionally watch Elizabeth use her New Zealand spinning wheel.

The Brecon Beacons are the highest mountains in South Wales, with several peaks over 2000 feet. Ice Age glaciers scored deep valleys in the red sandstone; to the south, the underlying rock is limestone or millstone grit, producing different scenery and a multitude of cave systems, gorges and waterfalls.

The Eppynt Hills to the north are softer (at their feet runs the lovely River Wye) but even here you can enjoy panoramic views all the way to Carmarthen.

Scenery is the main but not the only attraction of the area. There are plenty of castles to visit: for instance, Y Gaer (very close to the Old Rectory) was the Romans' largest inland fort, and mediaeval castles are at Builth Bronllys and Crickhowell among other places. Brecon has a Norman cathedral, and in many villages are churches with fine rood-screens. Zulu War relics can be seen in the museum of the South Wales Borderers regiment, which fought at Rorke's Drift; and everywhere are craft workshops (excellent tweeds and flannels).

However, it is outdoor activities which bring most people here. There is superb walking country, even if you do not want to tackle the mountain paths. Forest trails are well waymarked; and there are guided walks, too. Vast areas around Builth are relatively unexplored. For the intrepid, caving, climbing, hang-gliding and watersports await. Golf and private fishing can be arranged.

Good day trips by car along scenic routes include the Usk reservoir (visiting the Black Mountain bird park on the way), and also the Llyn Brianne reservoirs (perhaps picnicking in the Gwenffrwyd bird reserve, or following a riverside nature trail to the cave of outlaw Twm Catti, before arriving at the dam viewpoint).

The Elan Valley has a chain of lakes and five dams extending over nine miles; a short detour brings you to yet another stupendous dam at the Claerwen reservoirs.

Readers' comments: Outstanding value, lovely scenery, food and people. Wonderful accommodation and food. Exceptionally generous portions. Excellent. Most restful. Absolutely spotless, food delicious and attractively presented, warm welcome.

ARGOED FAWR

Llanwrthwl, Powys, LD1 6PD   Tel: 01597 860451
(Messages: 01597 860367)

C(14) S

South of Rhayader. Nearest main road: A470 from Rhayader to Builth Wells.

4 Bedrooms. £16–£17 (less for 4 nights).
Views of garden, country. No smoking.
Washing machine on request.
Light suppers if ordered.
1 Sitting-room. With central heating, TV.
No smoking.
Large garden
Closed in November and February.

In the 18th century this house was owned by James Watt of steam-engine fame. Overlooking the River Wye, it is now the home of Maureen Maltby; and although old features have been retained – such as a ham-rack, slab floors and slate hearths – every room is comfortable and immaculate; the bathroom is excellent. Breakfast choices may include kidneys, black pudding or Ayr haddock. Supper is a help-yourself buffet of such things as chicken, salmon, quiches and pâtés. Water comes from a pure spring and there is an exceptional garden.

The region south of Rhayader has some spectacular areas. Take, for instance, a little road north of Llanwrthwl, high over the mountains. This began when Cistercian monks making their way from the distant abbey of Strata Florida to that of Cwmhir established a long footpath which became known as the Monks' Trod – a delight to walkers today because, ascending to open moorland at 1600 feet, it passes through an area of true wilderness with superb views as you go. Rare birds nest here (there is an RSPB sanctuary) and the wind blows free where once there were oak forests – felled by the monks to provide grazing for black-faced sheep.

Then head for the Elan Valley, so spectacularly beautiful that one wonders why it is not world-famous in the way that the Lake District is. Long may it stay so: there is not a trace of commercialization and traffic. The miles of wooded valley hold a chain of enormous man-made lakes, each more lovely than the last, and each with its dramatic dam towering high – best seen in October or November, for instance, when there usually has been enough rain to send the overflowing waters from the reservoirs cascading down the dams.

The whole area belongs to the Water Board, who allow no buildings other than their own. They have a village of silvery granite cottages for workers, on the pretty banks of the downstream Elan (there is a good interpretative centre here).

Readers' comments: Delightful. Nicest ever visited. Breakfast fit for a king. Beautiful surroundings, many personal touches, nothing too much trouble.

Facts (prices, etc.) at the top of entries are supplied by the proprietors themselves. While every effort is made to ensure that these are correct at the time of going to press, they may alter thereafter: please check when you book.

BRON HEULOG

C PT S X

Waterfall Road, Llanrhaeadr-ym-Mochnant, (Clwyd), Powys, SY10 0JX
Tel: 01691 780521
North of Welshpool. Nearest main road: A483 from Welshpool to Oswestry.

3 Bedrooms. £18 (less for 3 nights). Bargain breaks. All have own shower/toilet. Tea/coffee facilities. TV. Views of garden, country. No smoking.
Dinner (by arrangement). £10 for 3 courses and coffee, at 6–8pm. Less for 2 courses. Non-residents not admitted. Vegetarian or special diets if ordered. No smoking. **Light suppers** if ordered.
1 Sitting-room. With open fire, central heating, TV. No smoking.
Large garden

There is a very lovely drive through hills, moors and woods from Bala to the Tanat Valley. Here, on the way to the country's highest waterfall, is this handsome stone house of 1861 which, as its name (*bron*) suggests, is on a hillside.

Karon and Ken Raines have decorated the house to an immaculate standard. Period furniture, pine shutters and a fine Chinese carpet complement Ken's collection of militaria in the rosy sitting-room; original prints line the elegant curving staircase. Bedrooms are named after the flowers suggested by their colour schemes: the sunflower room looks out onto an unusual weeping ash; another has a four-poster. The shower-rooms are excellent. Karon's dinners (served by arrangement only) include such dishes as Stilton soup, French lamb casserole (with garlic and tomato), and flambé bananas.

Llanrhaeadr, surrounded by the Berwyn Mountains, is very near the English border, Offa's Dyke and the Shropshire towns of Shrewsbury and Oswestry. In the opposite direction lie lakes Vyrnwy and Bala and Llangollen (on the way to it, call at Llanarmon's curious church with two pulpits), home every July to the world-famous *eisteddfod*. Salmon leap beneath its 14th-century bridge over the Dee (one of the 'seven wonders of Wales'), castles crown the surrounding peaks.

Readers' comments: Food delicious, room delightful, hosts friendly yet discreet. House beautiful, wonderful view, standard of decor the highest, meals excellent value. Superb food; lovely hosts, generous with their time.

South-westward in the beautiful and little-known Tanat Valley is Pen-y-Bont-Fawr. Enid Henderson and her niece live at 17th-century **GLYNDWR**. Behind is a pretty riverside garden. Beams, low doorways and open fires give the house character. There is good home cooking, and bedrooms have their own bathrooms. £15.50–£17.50 (the latter, an adjoining cottage).
Readers' comments: Superb meals, cosy

and warm. Everything possible was done to make us feel at home. [Tel: 01691 860430; postcode: SY10 0NT]

WALES

BRYNARTH
C(10) **M S**

Lledrod, (Dyfed), Cardiganshire, SY23 4HX   Tel: 01974 261367
South-east of Aberystwyth. Nearest main road: A485 from Tregaron to
Aberystwyth.

7 Bedrooms. £17–£19 (less for 3 nights).
Most have own bath/shower/toilet. Tea/
coffee facilities. Views of garden, country.
Dinner. £9.50 for 3 courses and coffee, at
7–7.30pm. Less for 2 courses. Vegetarian or
special diets if ordered. Wine available.
Light suppers.
1 Sitting-room. With open fire, central
heating, record-player. **Bar.**
Large garden

A very pretty group of white stone buildings, three centuries old, encloses a big
courtyard with lily-pool, flowering shrubs and benches of stone and timber –
inviting one to linger.

Inside the guest-house is a sitting/dining-area where the slate-tiled floor and
stone walls are complemented by old pews and a chunky pine table. There is a
small bar adjoining this; and an inglenook with a large, open log stove.

Brenda Ball serves such meals as ratatouille, lamb fricassée (with egg and
lemon sauce), and plum or apple pies, often using organically home-grown
produce.

Attractive bedrooms have king-size double, or twin, beds with panelled bedheads and wardrobes, flowers painted on their doors, and stone walls. There is
also a games room with pool, darts and table tennis. Water comes direct from a
pure spring. Painting courses are run throughout the year.

The seafront at Aberystwyth still has a sedate, Victorian air along the
promenade. But it is much more than a resort – near the pier is the main building
of its university and on a headland, its ruined castle. Fishing boats come and go.
The university has an outstanding arts centre (with gallery, theatre and cinema)
high above the town and with views across the bay. The town also houses the
distinguished National Library of Wales, a museum of rural and maritime history
in what was once an ornate music-hall, and the biggest *camera obscura* in the
world (over 400 feet up a hill and reached by a near-vertical railway) which gives
you a view of over two dozen distant mountain peaks. Or you can take a steam
train which goes from the town up to its mountainous destination, Devil's Bridge:
a 12-mile valley ride. Waterfalls plummet 300 feet down a wooded ravine, and
three bridges span a dizzying gorge. By car, you can get as high as 1200 feet.

This area is the principal breeding ground in Britain of the rare red kite.

Readers' comments: We give them the highest marks. Could not have been happier
with food and accommodation. A delightful setting. Delightful. Glorious and
remote setting.

> **Houses with short entries are just as good as ones with longer
> descriptions; and they include some of the most popular houses in
> the book. They may, however, have fewer rooms, a shorter season,
> higher prices or fewer amenities (such as meals).**

BUCK FARMHOUSE
Hanmer, (Clwyd), Wrexham, SY14 7LX   Tel: 01948 830339
South-east of Wrexham. On A525 from Wrexham to Whitchurch.

3 Bedrooms. £17 (less for 3 nights or continental breakfast). Price goes up from April. Bargain breaks. Views of garden, country. No smoking. Washing machine on request. (Bathrooms are downstairs.)
Dinner. £11.50 for 3 courses and coffee, at 7.30pm. Less for 2 courses. Vegetarian or special diets if ordered. No smoking. **Light suppers** if ordered.
2 Sitting-rooms. With woodstove, central heating. TV. No smoking.
Small garden, and woodland.

In this 16th-century house a surprise awaits. For both Frances Williams-Lee and Cedric Sumner were much travelled before they decided to settle here among the pastoral scenes of Clwyd – and this is reflected in the wide range of dishes you may be offered, with much emphasis on organic produce freshly and simply cooked.

Frances, though of Chinese ancestry, comes from Trinidad – a meeting-place for a variety of cuisines – and worked under an accomplished French chef in Normandy. Cedric lived in Canada, another country where a mingling of cultures has influenced cookery. The result is a series of very varied and imaginative menus. Just one example: celery and almond soup; a pie of sweetcorn, leeks and red peppers (the range of vegetarian and vegan dishes is particularly wide) or perhaps pork with onions, tomatoes and garlic; and Nova Scotia bread-custard. Breakfast options include home-made muesli or granola, fruit compotes, omelettes and much else.

Such meals are eaten in a low-beamed dining-room and prepared in a kitchen lined with jars of spices and other ingredients, through which visitors walk to reach the pretty little garden of herbs, rock plants, shrubs and lawn (unless they prefer to sit after dinner in the snug sitting-room, well stocked with books).

Steep stairs lead to neat bedrooms furnished in cottage style: necessarily double-glazed as the house is, despite its rural surroundings, on a main road.

Cedric produces, with the help of his computer, very clear and detailed half-day car tours for visitors to follow. Chester, Shrewsbury and all of north Wales are within comfortable driving distance, through scenic areas. Nearby Llangollen is not only a walking centre but home of the international *eisteddfod* every July. National Trust properties include Chirk Castle (best visited in May, for the rhododendron display) and Erddig Hall. The abbey of Valle Crucis, horse-drawn boat trips on the historic canal and Telford's spectacular aqueduct are other local attractions. Walkers can choose between Offa's Dyke, mountain paths further afield, or less demanding country lanes; there is one of the last great peat bogs at Whixall Moss, which is of great interest to naturalists. The cross-country Maelor Way, close by, links Offa's Dyke with 'the Sandstone Trail'.

But this is also one of the houses in this book at which visitors are welcome to linger all day, when sightseeing palls, and to make full use of the music and books that are available; and even to lie late in bed, knowing that breakfast is a movable feast in this easy-going house. (Antiques and bric-a-brac for sale.)

Readers' comments: Have returned 3 times. Fascinating house, interesting meals.

CAE DU   PT X
Manod, (Gwynedd), Caernarfonshire & Merionethshire, LL41 4BB
Tel: 01766 830847
South-west of Betws-y-Coed. Nearest main road: A470 from Betws-y-Coed to
Dolgellau.

7 Bedrooms. £18–£19. All have own
bath/shower/toilet. Views of garden, country, sea, stream. No smoking. Washing
machine on request.
Dinner. £12 for 4 courses (with choices)
and coffee, at 7.30pm. Vegetarian or special
diets if ordered. No smoking.
2 Sitting-rooms. With open fire, central
heating. No smoking.
Large garden

One crosses the track of a mountain railway and climbs to a breezy height where a
small stream chatters down through a pretty garden. Inside the 16th-century
farmhouse, where narrow passages twist and turn, are pretty rooms brimming
with the Lethbridges' finds, collected from as far afield as West Africa (where they
were relief workers) to local antique shops. Colours and patterns (in bathrooms as
well as bedrooms) are imaginative, books and pictures abound, and each bedroom is named after a Welsh worthy – with biographical details supplied.
Decorative friezes adorn the walls. The needlepoint is Keith's as well as Liz's. Liz
cooks such meals as cream cheese and broccoli soup, local salmon or beef, and
bread-and-butter pudding.

Cae Du (pronounced *ky dee* and meaning 'dark meadows') is on a site inhabited for a thousand years; and all around this area are historic remains such as
castles, mines (some of which go back for centuries), stately houses and gardens.
There are mountain walks straight from the garden, nature trails, pony-trek paths,
waterfalls and lakes.

In the hamlet of Llanfrothen towards
Porthmadog, alder trees gave their
name to **Y WERN** when it was built as
a farm in the 17th century. It is a
beamy house with homely furniture,
deep-set windows, slate floors and
stone inglenooks; the best hill views are
to be had from the cottagey second-
floor bedroom under the rafters. Paddy
Bayley can tell you tales of the 18th-
century *eisteddfod* bard Richard Jones,
to whom there is a plaque over the
front door, and of a local legal case
which first made the reputation of a
very young solicitor here – Lloyd
George. Dinner is usually cooked by
Tony (for instance, barbecued peppers, chicken in cider, and French
pâtisserie) and is sometimes served on

the terrace but usually in the dining-
kitchen. Sheep, ducks and a rocky
stream make a very special holiday for
children. £17–£20.
Readers' comments: Memorable meals.
Very peaceful and friendly. Shall certainly return. [Tel: 01766 770556;
postcode: LL48 6LX]

CAERLYR HALL HOTEL   C D M S X
Conwy Old Road, Dwygyfylchi, (Gwynedd), Aberconwy & Colwyn, LL34 6SW Tel: 01492 623518
West of Conwy. Nearest main road: A55 from Conwy towards Bangor.

9 Bedrooms. £20–£25. All have own bath/shower/toilet. Tea/coffee facilities. TV. Views of garden, country, sea. No smoking. Washing machine on request.
Dinner. £14.95 for 4 courses (with choices) and coffee, from 7.30pm. Vegetarian or special diets if ordered. Wine available. No smoking. **Light suppers.**
1 Sitting-room. With open fire, central heating, record-player. No smoking. **Bar. Large garden**
Closed from November to February.

In 1891, Leicester's MP, James Pickton, chose this superb position for his summer home (*Caerlyr* is Welsh for Leicestershire), perched high up for a view over what is now a golf course to the sea at Conwy Bay (this is one of 16 golf courses in the area). The best outlook is from the first floor where, as well as bedrooms, there is a characterful bar. It has the original stained glass and swallow-patterned fireplace, an old billiard table, golfing mementoes, tapestry chairs and lattice-paned skylights: all much as it was when Gladstone regularly visited his friend Pickton here. Not only the dining-room but some bedrooms (big and comfortable) open onto verandahs. Ground-floor rooms are available for visitors who find stairs difficult, but you have to go up if you want the one which still has a really splendid Victorian bathtub.

Michele Harpur and her partners run the hotel on thoroughly traditional lines – old-fashioned, in the best sense of the word. Meals, too, are traditional with such classics as mackerel with peppercorn vinaigrette; lamb cooked with honey, cider, rosemary and mead; treacle pudding.

Readers' comments: Heartily recommended. Pretty rooms, good cooking, excellent hospitality. Beautifully situated.

SOME WELSH PLACE NAMES			
Aber	River mouth	**Hafod**	Summer dwelling
Afon	River	**Hen**	Old
Bach/Fach	Little	**Hendre**	Winter dwelling
Bryn/Fryn	Hill	**Llan**	Parish
Cae/Gae	Field	**Llwyn**	Copse
Caer/Gaer	Fort	**Llyn**	Lake
Coed	Woods	**Mawr**	Big
Cwm/Gwm	Valley	**Mynydd**	Mountain
Dol	Bend	**Nant**	Valley
Dref/Tref	Town	**Pentre**	Village
Du	Black	**Plas**	Mansion
Dy/Ty	House	**Rhaeadr**	Waterfall
Eglwys	Church	**Rhos**	Moor
Gwyn/Wyn	White	**Ynys**	Island

CAERNEWYDD FARM   C M PT
Pembrey Road, Kidwelly, (Dyfed), Carmarthenshire, SA17 4TF
Tel: 01554 890729
North-west of Llanelli. On A484 from Llanelli to Carmarthen.

6 Bedrooms. £15–£16 (less for 3 nights).
All have own shower/toilet. Tea/coffee
facilities. TV. No smoking. Washing
machine on request.
Light suppers if ordered. No smoking.
1 Sitting-room. With open fire, central
heating, TV, piano. No smoking.
Large garden
Closed in December.

rear view

Despite its position on the road, all is peace once you are inside the house for
rooms are at the back. The huge sitting-room is where the stables used to be:
its sliding glass doors open onto a sheltered, heated swimming-pool and it is
furnished with handsome and ample modern sofas. There is much polished pine,
bedspreads are of Paisley-patterned fabric (all are ground-floor rooms), and
everything is neat as a new pin.

Margaret Beynon is willing to provide light suppers.

This would be a good choice for families wanting to enjoy the miles of clean,
golden beaches along this coast, for walkers (who can follow footpaths on the
sheep-farm's own land) or for birdwatchers who want to visit the nearby wildfowl
reserve.

All the area around Carmarthen Bay has a serene beauty (unlike the rugged
coast further west). You can still see salmon fishermen in coracles – small,
bowl-shaped boats, just as were used in pre-Roman times.

There are legends of Merlin; and innumerable ruined castles as well as the site
of a huge Iron Age fort, 1½ miles across (Carn Goch). Splendid though
Kidwelly's own moated castle is, it is not the most impressive – that is Carreg-
Cennen, near Llandeilo, perched above a 300-foot precipice. Built in the 14th
century, it has a long underground passage to a spring.

Nearby Pembrey is famous for its miles of sand dunes by the sea, a particularly
ancient church with barrel-roof of timber, and the landing place of Amelia Earhart
on her record-making Atlantic flight in 1928. Pembrey Country Park and the
Motorsports Centre are also worth a visit, and the Ashburnham golf course is
close. In the opposite direction is Laugharne, where Dylan Thomas's boathouse
home can be visited. It is a delightful little harbour, with fine estuary views and a
castle. Yet another coastal village with castle is at Llanstephan, to which you can
cross by boat. In a cave along here fossilized mammoths were found; and at the
resort of Amroth a prehistoric forest reappears as petrified stumps whenever tides
are very low; the long Pembrokeshire Coastal Path starts here.

Readers' comments: Excellent. Made very welcome. Very good value. Enjoyed all
and much more than promised in your book. Could not fault the accommodation
and generous attention. Exceptionally high standard. Spacious. Everything
exceeded our expectations. A totally satisfying choice.

CWMTWRCH   **C D M X**
Nantgaredig, (Dyfed), Carmarthenshire, SA32 7NY   Tel: 01267 290238
North-east of Carmarthen. Nearest main road: A40 from Carmarthen to
Llandeilo (and M4, junction 49).

6 Bedrooms. £20–£25 (less for continental breakfast). Prices go up from April. Bargain breaks. All have own bath/shower/toilet. Tea/coffee facilities. TV (some). Views of garden, country. Washing machine on request.
Dinner. £18.50 for 4 courses (with choices including vegetarian) and coffee, from 7.30pm. Less for 2 courses. Special diets if ordered. Wine available. **Light suppers** if ordered.
2 Sitting-rooms. With open fire, TV, record-player. Restricted smoking. **Bar.**
Large garden

The name of this farmhouse-turned-hotel means 'valley of the wild boar'. Nothing so wild now disturbs the peace of this civilized spot where Jenny Willmott and her husband have transformed a group of old farm buildings with great sensitivity. The restaurant, run by two of the Willmotts' daughters and a son-in-law, has stone walls painted white, slate floor and boarded roof above. At one side, the kitchen is open to view; on the other is a conservatory overlooking the courtyard, pots of flowers, and sheep-fields beyond. The food is exceptional, with such dishes as individual quiches as a starter, followed by fresh salmon or boned Barbary duck, and a flan of grapes among the choices. Bread is baked daily. All rooms have interesting and lovely objects, paintings and pottery (for sale). Bedrooms (full of character) are in the house or in former stables. There is a 9-hole golf course and heated swimming-pool with Jacuzzi and exercise machine.

Readers' comments: Excellent. Charming owners. Superb cooking. Marvellous. Most comfortable, made to feel at home. Food excellent. Really good. Helpfulness and friendliness had to be seen to be believed. First class. Good food, friendly hosts, comfort and quiet. Delicious dinner. Professionally run; cosy and tastefully decorated. One of the very best.

Also in this area is Llanpumsaint and **FFERM-Y-FELIN** or 'mill farm', the 18th-century home of Anne Ryder-Owen: a place of particular interest to birdwatchers. You can be told where to spot pied flycatchers, buzzards and even the rare red kite. Beyond the dining-room is a sitting-room so large that it has a fireplace at each end; pink, buttoned velvet sofas and a walnut piano contrast with rugged stone walls. Anne serves snacks or such meals as corn-on-the-cob, wild trout, and apple crumble; breakfast options include laverbread and cockles.

    This would be a good place for a family holiday: the farmhouse stands in

15 acres of countryside, with a large lake and interesting waterfowl; there is a pet donkey as well as other livestock. Self-catering accommodation too, with meals provided in the main house if wanted. No smoking. £16–£19.
Readers' comments: Wonderfully looked after. Food excellent and plentiful. Kind, considerate, welcoming. [Tel: 01267 253498; postcode: SA33 6DA]

DOLFFANOG FAWR PT
Tal-y-llyn, (Gwynedd), Caernarfonshire & Merionethshire, LL36 9AJ
Tel: 01654 761247
South of Dolgellau. Nearest main road: A487 from Dolgellau to Machynlleth.

4 Bedrooms. £20 **to readers of this book only.** All have own shower/toilet. Tea/coffee facilities. TV. Views of garden, country, lake. No smoking. Washing machine on request.
Dinner. £13.50 for 3 courses and coffee, at 7pm. Non-residents not admitted. Vegetarian or special diets if ordered. Wine available. No smoking. **Light suppers.**
1 Sitting-room. With open fire, central heating, record-player. No smoking. Honesty bar.
Large garden (use all day)
Closed in December and January.

Rooms and food alike are exceptional in Pam Coulter's house, in a beauty-spot at the head of Lake Tal-y-llyn, over which looms great Cader Idris. (*Dolffanog* means a meadow of springs and *Fawr* a big house.)

There is a wall of rugged stone in the dining-room, appropriately furnished with oak sideboard and ladderback chairs, and another in the pretty pink and blue sitting-room with its log fire. Bedrooms are most attractively furnished (flowery duvets and well-chosen wallpapers, with much stripped pine); all have good lake or other views and particularly good showers.

Pam's meals are outstanding. On 'ordinary' occasions you might be served (after a complimentary sherry) parsnip and apple soup, pork in peach chutney, and cherry cobbler. (Vegetables too are imaginatively prepared – for instance, cabbage cooked with bacon and onion.) But if you stay several days, she produces at no extra cost a veritable banquet of 7–8 dishes, usually Chinese or Indian, presented with a flourish of flower decorations too.

It was not surprising to learn that one couple have a fixed monthly booking for two days. Fortunately, there are plenty of scenic walks in the Snowdonia National Park all around to help burn up some of the calories!

Entrance hall at Bron Heulog (see page 373)

DYSSERTH HALL

by **Powis Castle, Welshpool, Powys, SY21 8RQ**   Tel: 01938 552153

South of Welshpool. Nearest main road: A483 from Welshpool to Newtown.

rear view

4 Bedrooms. £18–£19 (less for 3 nights). Some have own bath/shower/toilet. Tea/coffee facilities. Views of garden, country. No smoking. Washing machine on request. **Dinner.** £15 for 3 courses (with some choices) and coffee, at 7.30–8pm. Less for 2 courses. Non-residents not admitted. Vegetarian or special diets if ordered. Wine available. No smoking. **Light suppers** if ordered.
1 Sitting-room. With open fire, central heating, TV, record-player. Piano.
Large garden
Closed from December to February.

A crag of red rock and a moat provided strong defences for 13th-century Powis Castle, from which the princes of Powis ruled much of Wales. The management of their descendants' estates was in the hands of Paul Marriott until he retired. His 18th-century manor house is close to the castle (now NT).

Paul and Maureen's elegant home is furnished with fine antiques, well-chosen wallpapers and fabrics – delicate clematis paper in one bedroom, blue brocade on the walls of the dining-room, for instance. There are good paintings everywhere. From a paved terrace with rosebeds one can enjoy the view across the Severn Valley to Long Mountain. (Tennis court in the grounds.)

Dinner (by arrangement) may be a candlelit meal of avocado and prawns, Welsh lamb or pheasant, meringues or, possibly, local cheeses. Vegetables come from the Victorian kitchen garden.

Readers' comments: Warm and welcoming, dinner very good. Wonderful comfort.

On the other side of Welshpool, at Trelydan, is mediaeval **BURNT HOUSE**. Above a big, open-plan sitting/dining-room with ample sofas are two attractive bedrooms. One – in the oldest part of the house – has exposed timbers and pretty walnut beds. The other has a view of the Berwyn Mountains; its bathroom is outstanding – textured tiles around the built-in bath. Summer visitors see the garden at its best: Tricia Wykes won the 'Wales in Bloom' award for hotels, pubs and guest-houses throughout North Wales in 1994 and 1993 (runner-up in 1992). Tricia used to cook cakes professionally and so, after perhaps home-made pâté and pork fillet in a sauce of cream and sherry, one may be offered a gâteau or a

tempting meringue confection. £16 –£17 (b & b).
Readers' comments: Lovely views, welcoming hostess, excellent cook. Delightful, cooking admirable. Lovely old house. Hospitality and cuisine excellent. Truly marvellous. Enjoyed every minute. Excellent value for money. Delightful place, peaceful and so comfortable. Cottage warm, welcome equally so; dinners delicious. [Tel: 01938 552827; postcode: SY21 9HU]

ERW HEN CDSX
Pumpsaint, (Dyfed), Carmarthenshire, SA19 8YP Tel: 01558 650495
South-east of Lampeter. Nearest main road: A482 from Lampeter towards Llandovery.

3 Bedrooms. £15–£17. Some have own shower/toilet. Tea/coffee facilities. Views of garden, country. No smoking. Washing machine on request.
Dinner. £13 for 6 courses (with choices) and coffee, at 7–8pm. Less for 5 courses. Vegetarian or special diets if ordered. Wine available. No smoking. **Light suppers** if ordered.
2 Sitting-rooms. With open fire, central heating, TV.
Large garden

From Pumpsaint, a long and devious track leads up into the forested hills, past the Roman gold mine, to this remote house, whose name means 'old acre'. This valley is an Area of Special Scientific Interest for its wildlife (especially birds of prey), and Roman remains abound.

The 400-year-old house has been furnished by David and Brenda Vockings with individuality: plum-coloured tiles and wallpaper, a carved Burmese table, prints of hawks, salvaged black and red quarry-tiles.

Dinners comprise such things as peppered mackerel, chicken chasseur (with four vegetables), mandarin flan, and cheeses. Riding holidays (week-long or shorter) can be arranged with an established stable.

This area is one of vast moorlands – sweeping up some 2000 feet or descending into marshes. There are wonderful views to be had from the heights where the meadow pipits and the larks sing and rare red kites soar high. Birds are far more numerous than humans here. Wooded valleys stretch towards a coast of fine beaches, cliffs and coves. In the other direction lies the Brecon Beacons National Park – dotted with cascades and caves, lakes and gorges, historic ruins.

About 1830, a great 14th-century mansion was torn down and its stones used to build this elegant house, extended in recent times to make a spacious hotel – the **GLANRAN-NELL PARK**, Crugybar.

The least expensive bedrooms – in converted stables – are simply furnished but have the advantage for some visitors of being on the ground floor and with space to park immediately outside. Those in the house vary in size and outlook. Glanrannell stands in 23 acres of grounds (with a lake), and there are plenty of footpaths in the rest of the lovely Cothi Valley too. The hotel's name comes from the Annell trout stream which runs along its boundary.

Dinner always includes much local produce (such as rack of Welsh lamb served on a coarse tomato sauce) or sewin (sea trout) from the local rivers. Closed in winter. £15–£31.
Reader's comment: A delightful holiday. [Tel: 01558 685230; postcode: SA19 8SA]

FAIRFIELD COTTAGE

C(5) D PT S

Knelston, Gower Peninsula, (West Glamorgan), Swansea, SA3 1AR
Tel: 01792 391013
West of Swansea. On A4118 from Swansea to Port Eynon
(and M4, junction 47).

3 Bedrooms. £17 (less for 2 nights). TV (in one). Tea/coffee facilities. Views of garden, country. No smoking.
Dinner. £11 for 4 courses and coffee, at 7pm. Non-residents not admitted. No smoking. **Light suppers** if ordered.
1 Sitting-room. With open fire, central heating, TV. No smoking.
Small garden

The Gower peninsula (especially its cliffs, bays and sandy beaches) is so scenic that there are few more attractive places.

Knelston is roughly equidistant from north, west and south coasts – a tranquil hamlet within what was the very first region to be officially designated an Area of Outstanding Natural Beauty. One reaches it across Cefn Bryn ('the brown ridge'), a stretch of moorland where ponies roam free and yellow waterlilies brighten the pools. It is an area dotted with castle ruins, prehistoric burial chambers and other traces of a far distant history.

Caryl Ashton's 18th-century home is a little white cottage made colourful by window-boxes, tubs and hanging-baskets of flowers. One steps straight into the sitting/dining-room from which a staircase rises between the joists to small but pretty, cottagey bedrooms in which she has used sprigged or tulip-patterned fabrics to complement simple bamboo furniture and white walls. There is a very good bathroom.

One can take a complimentary aperitif by the inglenook fire or in the garden (it has a summer-house) before enjoying such a meal as gratin of haddock, roast beef accompanied by creamed parsnips with almonds and baked potatoes in cheese sauce, home-made lemon meringue pie, and a selection of cheeses. Fruit and vegetables come from local farms, and yogurt, Welsh cakes and scones are home-made. Caryl is a dedicated cook.

Readers' comments: Kind and well organized. Very well kept and comfortable. Treated with particular care and love. Superb cook, wonderful hosts. All meals delicious; a most memorable experience. Friendly, helpful and very thoughtful.

THE FFALDAU　　　　　　　　　　　　　　　　C(10) **D PT S X**
Llandegley, Powys, LD1 5UD　Tel: 01597 851421
East of Llandrindod Wells. Nearest main road: A44 from Kington to Rhayader.

4 Bedrooms. £20-£22.50 (less for 3 nights). All have own bath/shower/toilet. Tea/coffee facilities. TV (some). Views of garden, country. Washing machine on request.
Dinner. £15-£18 for 4 courses (with alternatives) and coffee, at 7.30pm. Less for fewer courses. Vegetarian or special diets if ordered. Wine available. **Light suppers** if ordered.
2 Sitting-rooms. With log fires, central heating, TV. **Bar.**
Large garden

Set back from the road is one of the prettiest mediaeval houses in this book: roses climb up stone walls, rustic seats overlook colourful beds of heather. Beyond the lawns are grazing sheep and distant hills.

Ffaldau ('sheepfold') began life around 1500 as a long-house: people lived at one end, livestock at the other. When the Knotts took over, the ceilings leaked, floors had rotted, and all around was a litter of railway wagons and hen-houses. Not only have they transformed the house and garden but – with no previous experience – they run a house which has an ever-widening reputation for fine food (even bar meals are exceptional). They serve one, two, three or four courses of the dinner menu, or light suppers.

Old features have been retained and restored, from a wig-cupboard built into one thick wall to a characterful old iron grate with Prince of Wales feathers in its decoration. Upstairs one can see the cruck construction of the house: the great tree-trunks used to support the roof. Mullioned windows are set into the stone walls, slabs of slate floor the hall, a log stove stands on an old inglenook hearth.

In the 'Victorian' dining-room the tables might be spread with white lace, or linen cloths exquisitely embroidered and edged with crochetwork by Sylvia's grandmother, whose photograph is one of many family portraits on the walls. Slate flags glow in the candlelight, and crannies are bright with flowers. On the landing is a sitting-area well stocked with books and games.

There is a simple 'country' menu and, once a month, a more expensive 'gourmet' menu from which to choose such imaginative dishes as langoustine packets with cucumber sauce, glazed poussins with pine kernels and grapes, and lemon and vodka meringue cake. There is a wide list of wines.

Nearby Llandrindod Wells has the faded charm of a one-time spa (indeed, you can still 'take the waters' there) and stands in an area of great beauty, little troubled by traffic or tourists. One can drive almost without sight of another car among hills like dusty velvet, with mountain sheep occasionally silhouetted on the skyline.

Readers' comments: Extremely hospitable. Best steak and breakfast that we can remember. Exceptional food, wonderful hosts. Perfectly situated. One of the happiest and most comfortable stays anywhere. Family most welcoming and helpful. Food excellent and imaginative. Perfect hosts, food outstanding. A real jewel. One of the very best. Beautiful surroundings, meal superb. Epitomized our idea of a very well run, delightful country hotel.

HAFOTY   C
Rhostryfan, (Gwynedd), Caernarfonshire & Merionethshire, LL54 7PH
Tel: 01286 830144
South of Caernarfon. Nearest main road: A487 from Caernarfon to Porthmadog.

5 Bedrooms. £18–£20. Prices go up from April. Bargain breaks. Most have own bath/shower/toilet. Tea/coffee facilities. TV. Views of garden, country, sea. Washing machine on request.
Dinner. £10.95 for 3 courses and coffee, at 7pm. Non-residents not admitted. Wine available.
1 Sitting-room. With open fire, central heating, TV.
Large garden
Closed in December and January.

The name means 'summer house', referring to the season when farmers would tend their livestock on the upper pastures of Snowdonia before bringing them down to their winter quarters. Perched up here, you get a view beyond Caernarfon Castle of the Menai Strait and the Isle of Anglesey, and towards the lovely Lleyn Peninsula: in every direction, tempting sights to explore. And many footpaths lead out from here, too.

In the 18th century, Hafoty comprised not only farmhouse and courtyard but an old mill and barns (since converted). Now there are attractively furnished rooms of high standard: some bedrooms, for instance, have lace draperies and soft colours to complement pine or bamboo furniture. The beamed dining-room has a large patio window to make the most of the spectacular castle view; and the sitting-room a big inglenook fireplace where logs crackle on chilly evenings.

Mari Davies serves straightforward meals such as egg mayonnaise, local trout, and fruit salad in ample quantity; and at breakfast you can even have Welsh rarebit if you choose.

At the top of the Lleyn Peninsula (looking over the Menai Strait to Anglesey) is **BRONANT**, a handsome Victorian house in Bontnewydd, kept in immaculate order by Megan Williams and her nieces, who run a tea-room here. Their traditional Welsh teas are really authentic: the ginger-bread, *bara brith* (speckled bread) and Welsh cakes regularly take first prizes at county shows.

Most rooms are spacious, with Welsh tapestry bedspreads in rich colours and views of sheep, pine trees and mountains. Some windows have stained glass depicting apples and pears, appropriate to a house where good, natural food excels. The light suppers are quite substantial. £16–£18 (b & b).

Readers' comments: Tasty, well-cooked meals. Spacious, comfortable bedroom. A great place with spectacular views. Very good value. Marvellous cakes. Beautiful and comfortable house; Megan Williams and her nieces charming. [Tel: 01286 830451; postcode: LL54 7YF]

HEN FICERDY C(10)
Abererch, (Gwynedd), Caernarfonshire & Merionethshire, LL53 5YH
Tel: 01758 612162
East of Pwllheli. Nearest main road: A497 from Pwllheli to Porthmadog.

3 **Bedrooms.** £17–£19 (less for 7 nights). All have own bath/toilet. Tea/coffee facilities. TV. Views of garden, country, sea. No smoking. Washing machine on request. **Light suppers** if ordered.
1 **Sitting-room.** With open fire, central heating, TV. No smoking.
Large garden
Closed from November to March.

A Victorian vicarage with spacious grounds was built high enough up to provide outstanding views over Cardigan Bay in one direction and Snowdonia in the other: tall windows make the most of these, and one can step straight out into a garden with terrace, lawns and palms (for the Lleyn Peninsula has an exceptionally mild climate all year round).

Medi Lloyd Hughes has created a welcoming atmosphere with warm pinks and reds in a sitting-room of flowery sofas, shining brass and marble fireplace, and gently ticking grandfather clock. A Welsh dresser is laden with willow-pattern plates that contrast with coral walls in the dining-room. Bedrooms, too, are attractive: a green-and-white gingham room has pine and bamboo furniture, for instance; and one of the bathrooms is as luxurious as it is large.

The peninsula is one of the most Welsh parts of Wales, with the native language still very much alive. It has wild and dramatic scenery inland, sandy beaches along its shores – many secluded. Past Trefor (near where a 1700-foot mountain looms above the sea, with deserted quarries in its sides) are the secret valley of Nant Gwrtheyrn, a shadowy place of old legends, and the Lleyn's highest peak – Yr Eifl. Porth Nefyn is a particularly long and lovely bay with a safe, sandy beach and clifftop walks; and still further west you can find the 'whistling sands' of Porth Oer (at times, the grains of sand squeak when you walk on them). Right at the end of the Lleyn is Mynydd Mawr, a National Trust headland with coastal views comparable to those of Cornwall's Land's End. Over two miles of choppy waters lies Bardsey Island (known to pilgrims as the isle of 20,000 saints).

Along the south coast, in a wilderness of subtropical flowers, are the little manor house (part mediaeval) of Plas-yn-Rhiw; another great bay – Porth Neigwl, otherwise known as Hell's Mouth because of the treacherous rocks on which so many ships foundered; and Abersoch, a busy little harbour, near which is the showpiece village of Llangian. Seek out the old part of Pwllheli to find a Georgian arcade and canopied Victorian shops in sharp contrast to the popular modern attractions of this resort. Penarth Fawr is a rare survival, a stone hall house – basically one great room in which family and servants all dwelt together in the 15th century. A mossy stone path leads to the clear waters of St Cybi's well, behind Llangybi village.

The Lleyn's most famous village is, of course, Portmeirion, an Italianate waterside fantasy designed by Sir Clough Williams-Ellis in 1925. Every architectural style, and every colour of the rainbow, seems to be represented here.

LAKESIDE

Llanrug, (Gwynedd), Caernarfonshire & Merionethshire, LL55 4ED
Tel: 01286 870065
East of Caernarfon. Nearest main road: A487 from Caernarfon to Porthmadog.

3 Bedrooms. £18 (less for 7 nights). Some have own shower/toilet. Tea/coffee facilities. TV. Views of garden, country. Washing machine on request.
Dinner. £13 for 4 courses and coffee, at any agreed time. Less for 2 courses. Non-residents not admitted. Vegetarian or special diets if ordered. **Light suppers.**
1 Sitting-room. With open fire, central heating, TV, record-player.
Large garden

In the foothills of Snowdonia, an early Victorian magnate built himself a turreted mock-castle, Bryn-Bras, surrounding it with spectacular gardens (now open to the public). A huge artificial lake was dug, beside which stood a lattice-paned gamekeeper's cottage – now the home of the young Kanes, who also own half the lake.

They have transformed the house and created its own flowery garden with little statues, which is frequented by peacocks and pheasants; there is also a hide from which to watch barn owls.

The rooms are most attractive, with pretty colours and unusual finds from antique shops, oriental treasures, good carpets on tiled floors and modern leather chairs. In places there are walls of exposed granite, a log fire blazes in winter, and less mobile visitors will appreciate the elegant ground-floor bedroom with quite luxurious bathroom. The suite in a former barn has a bed with barley-sugar posts and an unusual Dutch chair (also a well-designed kitchen area, as it can be rented on a self-catering basis if preferred).

For dinner, Lyn may serve home-made vegetable soup with hot rolls, chicken cooked with pineapple and ginger, chocolate and pear mousses, and then cheeses – together with home-brewed cider or fruit juice.

Readers' comments: Felt so much at home. Tasty, varied and plentiful meals. Beautiful surroundings. Most comfortable, excellent cook. Have had several pleasant weekends here.

Close by is Llanddeiniolen and 18th-century **TY MAWR** ('big house') on a farm where once-rare 'badger-faced' sheep are bred, now often bought as pets. Superb views of Snowdonia are one of the attractions of staying here; another is young Jane Pierce's cooking of such meals as prawns in puff pastry, lamb with baked leeks and other vegetables, and trifle. In two beamy sitting-rooms and elsewhere are a mixture of antiques and family possessions, pretty fabrics and colours, flow-

rear view

ery armchairs grouped around a log stove. £14–£18. [Tel: 01248 670147; postcode: LL55 3AD]

387

LLWYNDÛ FARMHOUSE
C D PT X

Llanaber, Barmouth, (Gwynedd), Caernarfonshire & Merionethshire, LL42 1RR Tel: 01341 280144
West of Dolgellau. Nearest main road: A496 from Barmouth to Harlech.

7 Bedrooms. £20–£28 (less for 2 nights). Prices go up from April. Bargain breaks. All have own bath/shower/toilet. Tea/coffee facilities. TV. Views of garden, country, sea. No smoking. Washing machine on request.
Dinner. £16.45 for 3 courses (with choices) and coffee, at 7–7.30pm. Less for 2 courses. Vegetarian or special diets if ordered. Wine available. **Light suppers** if ordered.
1 Sitting-room. With open fire, central heating, TV.
Large garden

In the year that the youthful Shakespeare wrote *The Taming of the Shrew*, an even younger man made his way from remote Llwyndû to London, to study law in the Inner Temple. It was 1597, and this house had already seen generations of his family grow up. Peter Thompson, whose home it now is, researched the history of the house and its inhabitants for a university dissertation: he even has some of their very early wills.

This, therefore, was a house of considerable consequence in the neighbourhood, and handsomely built. The walls are immensely thick, and the living-room huge; one ceiling-beam is over two feet thick, and great blocks of granite form the fireplace. New discoveries continue to come to light – for instance, a 16th-century oak-mullioned window which had long been blocked up.

Most bedrooms have views (and sounds) of the sea waves, and two have four-poster beds – also excellent bathrooms (one with oval bath and bidet, for example). One room has a dressing-room, another its own stone stair to the garden; some are in a converted granary. Everywhere are attractive furnishings, and great pieces of driftwood from the beaches stand here and there like sculpture.

Peter and Paula are very keen cooks, preparing such meals as parsnip-and-apple soup, lamb in a mushroom and cinnamon sauce, rhubarb-and-banana pie.

Readers' comments: House has tremendous character. Lovely food, great value. Delightful situation, friendly welcome. Food superb. Excellent hostess and cook. Stunning views.

On the water's edge of Mawddach estuary is **HERONGATE**, at Arthog, the simple and inexpensive but pleasant home of Pat Mallatratt whose late husband's paintings line the walls of the small sitting-room. Herons, oyster-catchers and tame sheep seeking titbits can be seen from the bay windows. The house is in a small, isolated crescent built by a Victorian entrepreneur as part of a grander plan that never materialized, in an excellent area for walks. (Light suppers

only.) £15. [Tel: 01341 250349; postcode: LL39 1BJ]

MANOR HOUSE HOTEL C D PT S
Main Street, Fishguard, (Dyfed), Pembrokeshire, SA65 9HG
Tel: 01348 873260
Nearest main road: A40 from Haverfordwest to Fishguard.

6 Bedrooms. £20–£24 (less for 3 nights). Prices go up from April. Some have own bath/shower/toilet. Tea/coffee facilities. TV. Views of sea.
Dinner. £15 for 3 courses (with choices) and coffee, at 7–8.30pm. Less for 2 courses. Vegetarian or special diets if ordered. Wine available. **Light suppers** if ordered.
1 Sitting-room. With open fire, central heating. **Bar.**
Small garden

In the main street of Fishguard (but with quiet rooms overlooking the sea at the back) is Manor House Hotel, built in the 18th century. Most rooms are spacious, with a good deal of 'thirties furniture and interesting objects around. In a room on the ground floor, antiques are for sale.

Austrian-born Beatrix Davies has given the small hotel a reputation for its food. There is always a wide à la carte choice that includes such dishes as mussel pâté; chicken cooked in a purée of plums, garlic and parsley; a syllabub of black-currants and sherry. From the garden (where you can take breakfast) there are fine views across the sea to Dinas Head.

Fishguard, a picturesque port, is on a coastline so spectacular that it has been designated a national park: windswept and dramatic cliffs alternate with sunny, sheltered coves, some accessible only by footpath. Islands (to which boats make trips) are home to rare grey seals and all kinds of seabirds. Inland the hills are deeply cleft by streams and around them are rich farmlands. The harbour for ferries to Ireland is actually at Goodwick, a little further along the bay.

Tucked away behind Goodwick's small square is Elizabeth Maxwell-Jones's **COACH HOUSE COTTAGE**, where there is a multitude of pictures, books and interesting objects.

One reaches it up 20 steps beside a rushing mountain brook and enters through a stable-type door, straight into the dining-kitchen. From the little bedroom are hill views and a glimpse of the sea; the long-distance Pembrokeshire Coastal Path runs close by.

Elizabeth is an accomplished cook who serves, for example, cauliflower soup, excellent chicken Marengo, and summer pudding – all made with

organic ingredients. She also teaches lace-making. (No smoking.) £13.
Reader's comment: Extraordinarily kind and considerate. [Tel: 01348 873660; postcode: SA64 0DH]

389

MELIN MELOCH

C D M PT S

Llanfor, Bala, (Gwynedd), Caernarfonshire & Merionethshire, LL23 7DP
Tel: 01678 520101
East of Bala. Nearest main road: A494 from Corwen to Bala.

4 Bedrooms. £18–£19.50 (less for 6 nights). Some have own shower/toilet. Tea/coffee facilities. TV (some). Views of garden, country, river. No smoking. Washing machine on request.
Dinner. £12 for 3 courses (with some choices) and coffee, at 7pm. Non-residents not admitted. Vegetarian or special diets if ordered. No smoking.
2 Sitting-rooms. With open fire, central heating, TV, record-player. No smoking.
Large garden
Closed in December and January.

This 13th-century watermill is a galleried house with pretty bedrooms. Through an arch by the big stone fireplace in the beamed sitting-room is a great table flanked by pews, where Beryl Fullard serves (by arrangement) such meals as melon with raspberry coulis, lamb, brandy-cake and cream.

The miller's cottage has a ground-floor bedroom and spacious family suite; other rooms are in a granary. Everywhere are lovely arrangements of dried flowers and 'finds' such as a milkchurn and mangle. Richard has landscaped the large gardens, making the most of the stream, the waterfall and the ponds, and has annually received an award for his work.

The River Meloch (*melin* means mill) feeds the mill-race, which drives a Pelton wheel, a Victorian form of waterwheel which Richard has restored.

Readers' comments: Spectacular. Food and location excellent. Lovely house. Perfection. Spoilt me with excellent cooking. The house is a beauty. Absolutely wonderful time. Never-to-be-forgotten, unique house. Garden is the heart and soul of this place. Eminently satisfactory.

'Meeting of drovers' roads' is a rough translation of the name **CWM HWYLFORD**: a remote inn-turned-farm in the hills at Cefn-ddwysarn, still retaining its 400-year-old character. The Bests (civil engineer and teacher) bought it on impulse when holidaying in this spectacular area above the Dee Valley, falling in love with its odd-shaped walls, beams, deep-set windows, log fires, and screen wall of old timbers which once separated people from cows and hayloft. They keep 300 sheep as well as other livestock: children love the streams, sheepdogs, collecting eggs and exploring footpaths. Bedrooms are simple, and

Joan's food is good: a typical meal might be lettuce soup, a joint of lamb (one per family), and raspberry mousse. £14–£16 (b & b).
Readers' comments: Received most warmly. Children in seventh heaven! Will certainly return. [Tel: 01678 530310; postcode: LL23 7LN]

THE MOUNT C(12) **D PT X**
Higher Kinnerton, (Clwyd), Flintshire, CH4 9BQ Tel: 01244 660275
South-west of Chester (England). Nearest main road: A55 from Chester to
Conwy (and M56, junction 16).

3 Bedrooms. £18–£22 (less for 3 nights).
All have own bath/shower/toilet. Tea/coffee
facilities. TV. Views of garden, country. No
smoking. Washing machine on request.
Dinner. £12 for 4 courses and coffee,
at any agreed time. Non-residents not
admitted. Vegetarian or special diets if
ordered. No smoking. **Light suppers** if
ordered.
1 Sitting-room. With open fire, central
heating, TV, piano, record-player. No
smoking.
Large garden

Because of Rachel Major's enthusiasm for gardening, among the attractions of
staying here are the fine grounds (sometimes open under the National Gardens
Scheme) with herbaceous beds, flowering shrubs and cedar and other trees as
mature as the early Victorian house itself. The garden also supplies fresh produce
for the table.

Rooms are spacious, with (for instance) yellow panelling as the background to
a Sheraton sideboard and ancestral portraits; and a prettily carved fireplace as the
focal point in a very long, coral-walled sitting-room. Guest often relax among the
plumbago in the conservatory or (more energetically) on the croquet lawn or tennis court, with views of the Peckforton Hills beyond.

For dinner, Rachel (a cordon bleu cook) often serves game, but her repertoire
is large. Her other accomplishment is canvaswork, of which there are examples
around the house.

Just south of Ruthin, a disused railway
station is now an unusual – and unusually excellent – guest-house. **EYARTH
STATION**, at Llanfair-Dyffryn-Clwyd
in Denbighshire, has been imaginatively converted and furnished by Jen
Spencer. Outside, all is white paint and
flowers. Ground-floor bedrooms have
such touches as festoon blinds and
canopied bedheads; some (more simply furnished) are in what were the
porters' rooms. Excellent bathrooms
(even a bidet). What was once the
waiting-room is now a very large sitting-room (one of two) with a balcony
just above the fields: big sofas, log
stove and thick carpet make this particularly comfortable. The conservatory/
dining-room – once the platform –
overlooks a small, well-heated swimming-pool which gets the afternoon

sun. Jen offers suppers of such dishes
as chicken and leek pie followed by
chocolate fudge cake; also snacks. £20
(b & b).
Readers' comments: Excellent accommodation, and welcoming. Delightful
lounge and grounds. Meals superb.
One of the best places. Exceptional
food, wonderful hosts. [Tel: 01824
703643; postcode: LL15 2EE]

WALES

OLD VICARAGE C S

Moylegrove, (Dyfed), Pembrokeshire, SA43 3BN   Tel: 01239 881231
West of Cardigan. Nearest main road: A487 from Cardigan to Fishguard.

3 Bedrooms. £20–£22.50 (less for 7 nights). All have own bath/shower/toilet. Tea/coffee facilities. TV. Views of garden, country, sea. No smoking. Washing machine on request.
Dinner. £13.50 for 3 courses (with choices) and coffee, at times to suit guests. Less for 2 courses. Non-residents not admitted. Vegetarian or special diets if ordered. Wine available. **Light suppers** if ordered.
2 Sitting-rooms. With open fire, central heating, TV, piano, record-player. No smoking in one.
Large garden
Closed in December and January.

An air of quality and comfort pervades every room in this substantial Edwardian house, set on a sweeping lawn with glimpses of Cardigan Bay not far away. The unusual slate and turf wall of the garden is traditional to the area. High up in the countryside, the house has superb views for it is in the middle of the Pembrokeshire Coast National Park.

Peach, brown and green predominate in the restful colour schemes of the rooms, many of which have bay windows. Crystal glasses and fluted white china on blue cloths help to create a particularly attractive effect in the dining-room. Here Peggy Govey serves imaginative meals such as smoked salmon quenelles, chicken breasts cooked with apricots and brandy, praline mousse or treacle tart, and cheeses.

The large bedrooms have flowery duvets and good bathrooms.

Within a mile, the long Pembrokeshire Coastal Path passes on its way, following the dramatic cliffs, beaches and steep valleys that make this coast so outstanding. Ceibwr Bay, under a mile away, and Newport Sands, 5 miles, are particularly beautiful. Further afield the Preseli Mountains rise high. It was from here that the Ice Age swept immense blueish stones over 200 miles, from which Stonehenge was built; and the deep river valleys in this area are full of prehistoric remains.

On the other side of Cardigan, in Cardiganshire, and within easy reach of National Trust beaches, on a rocky hillside (*bron*) stands an ivy-clad, grey stone house, **BRONIWAN**, Rhydlewis, built in 1867, with much use of pitch-pine.

Carole and Allen Jacobs combine organic farming with teaching English and running courses in painting. They have Aberdeen Angus beef-cattle, sheep, hens and a vegetable garden. The rooms are very attractive with, for instance, striped wallpaper, Welsh tapestry bedspreads, watercolours, books and old Staffordshire pottery figures.

A typical dinner: watercress soufflé, home-raised beef (with garden vegetables), pears in white wine. Vegetarian meals are also served. No smoking. £17–£18 (b & b). [Tel: 01239 851261; postcode: SA44 5PF]

PENTRE BACH   **PT S**(outside high season)
Llwyngwril, (Gwynedd), Caernarfonshire & Merionethshire, LL37 2JU
Tel: 01341 250294
South-west of Dolgellau. Nearest main road: A493 from Dolgellau to
Machynlleth.

3 Bedrooms. £19–£24 (less for 4 nights).
All have own shower/toilet. Tea/coffee
facilities. TV. Views of garden, country, sea.
No smoking. Washing machine on request.
Dinner. £14.45 for 3 courses (with choices) and coffee, at 6–8pm. Less for 2 courses.
Vegetarian or special diets if ordered. No
smoking. **Light suppers** if ordered.
Large garden

Close by the sea and with a backdrop of mountains, a tree-lined drive leads to 'little village' (as its name translates), a serene old farmhouse together with cottages now used for self-catering or b & b. It is near the pretty and scarcely bigger hamlet of Llwyngwril, and the lovely estuary of the River Mawddach as it flows into Cardigan Bay. But, best of all, it is in the middle of one of the most attractive yet least crowded stretches of breezy coastline in Snowdonia.

The Smyths have made really sensitive use of this treasure, converting and furnishing to high standards without compromising the original character of the old stone buildings. Each bedroom enjoys a different view: panoramic seascape with spectacular sunsets, a vista of hills over which dawn rises, or looking to the picturesque village church.

Colours are tranquil, old fireplaces and window-shutters have been retained, and pictures are well chosen. (Alas, no sitting-room.)

Margaret Smyth, to her own great astonishment (but not her guests') won the title 'Mid-Wales Cook of the Year' in 1994. She has a range of Welsh specialities, using a lot of Pentre Bach's own organic produce for her candlelit dinners, and you are invited to order in advance from a wide choice of such sophisticated dishes as mushroom pâté, venison escalopes with wine sauce, and mocha parfait with raspberry sauce.

A little way inland, **TY MAWR** ('big house') is perched among the hills at Llanegryn: stone-walled, slate-floored and oak-beamed but with a modern conservatory where you can sit to enjoy the view towards Aberystwyth 40 miles away. At your feet is the Dysynni Valley, world-famous for 'bird rock' where (uniquely) cormorants nest inland. What was once a milking-shed is now a sitting-room with coral walls and flowery frieze. Through its big glass doors you can step straight onto the terrace (ground-floor bedrooms, too, open onto this). Elizabeth Tregarthen is an accomplished cook of

such meals as apple and parsnip soup, chicken and mushroom pie with a filo pastry crust, and baked peaches; and a hostess able to arrange for you to seafish, golf, ramble, or whatever takes your fancy. £18.
Readers' comments: Made us so welcome. Lovely home. [Tel: 01654 710507; postcode: LL36 9SY]

PLAS PENUCHA   C S X
Caerwys, (Clwyd), Flintshire, CH7 5BH   Tel: 01352 720210
North-west of Mold. Nearest main road: A55 from Chester to Conwy.

4 Bedrooms. £17.50 (less for 4 nights). Bargain breaks. Some have own shower/ toilet. Tea/coffee facilities. TV. Views of garden, country. No smoking. Washing machine on request.
Dinner. £10.50 for 4 courses (with choices) and coffee, at 7pm. Less for 2 courses. Vegetarian or special diets if ordered. No smoking. **Light suppers** if ordered.
2 Sitting-rooms. With open fire, central heating, TV, piano, record-player. No smoking.
Large garden

Nêst Price (her forename is that of a mediaeval Welsh princess) is a harpist and violinist who used also to run the North Wales Music Festival; and this is her ancestral home. Ever since she took it over, ancestral 'finds' keep coming to light, for it has a long history. Spanish gold financed the original building (sited on top of a spring), home of one of Elizabeth I's buccaneers, but it has been much added to and altered by successive generations.

In the main room, there is a genial greeting, *Aelwyd a Gymhell*, carved on the oak beam across the fireplace: it means 'A welcoming hearth beckons'. Very appropriate in this hospitable house! There is another sitting-room (with built-in log stove), the blue in its oriental rugs on the polished wood-block floor matched by the blue damask sofas; books line one wall and Elizabethan panelling another.

Bedrooms are attractive and comfortable; and Nêst is an excellent cook of such meals as soup; rack of Welsh lamb; syllabub; Welsh cheeses. Outside is a large garden, very colourful at rhododendron-time, with a view towards the Clwydian Hills.

Readers' comments: First-class atmosphere, facilities, food and comfort.

Towards St Asaph, at Bodfari, stands **FRON HAUL** ('breast of the sun') guest-house and tea gardens, perched high on the edge of the lovely Vale of Clwyd. Originally the home of a Victorian surgeon, it has balconies from which to enjoy the wonderful view – or you can relax in sitting-rooms, conservatory or garden. Bedrooms are comfortable but homely, and the house is much used by long-distance walkers – it is on the Offa's Dyke path.

Gwladys Edwards provides an à la carte choice for dinner, with such dishes as salmon, steak, lamb from Fron Haul's farm or local trout. (Lunches

too. Bread and cakes are home-made.) £16.50 (b & b).
Readers' comments: Excellent food (super sweet trolley!). Made very welcome and nothing too much trouble. Stayed on numerous occasions. Unfailingly helpful. Comfort and food memorable. [Tel: 01745 710301; postcode: LL16 4DY]

PLAS TREFARTHEN
Brynsiencyn, Isle of Anglesey, (Gwynedd), Anglesey, LL61 6SZ
Tel: 01248 430379

C

South-west of Menai Bridge. Nearest main road: A4080 from Rhosneigr to
Menai Bridge.

8 Bedrooms. £18–£20. Prices go up from
Easter. Most have own bath/shower/toilet.
Tea/coffee facilities. TV. Views of garden,
mountains, sea.
Dinner. From £10.50 for 2 courses and
coffee, at 6.30pm. Non-residents not
admitted. Vegetarian or special diets if
ordered. No smoking.
1 Sitting-room. With open fire, central
heating, piano, record-player. No smoking.
Large garden

It had seemed an ordinary day. True, the house is a handsome 18th-century
mansion at the heart of a 200-acre farm, and its waterfront site is outstanding
(there are superb views across the Menai Strait to Snowdon). But suddenly the
experience became exceptional . . . Standing by her piano in the dining-room,
Marian Roberts began to sing impromptu; her voice soared effortlessly, true and
clear, to the highest notes. Rarely does one hear such a lovely and unaffected
sound from any singer.

Marian, after repeatedly winning the highest accolades at the international
eisteddfod each year and spending much time on concert tours in America,
Australia and elsewhere, is now a 'bed-and-breakfast lady', welcoming visitors to
Plas Trefarthen.

In the sitting-room, a big picture-window makes the most of the view across
the water to Caernarfon Castle. The green brocade walls and a big Welsh dresser
display souvenirs of Marian's travels; musical mementoes are gathered in the
dining-room. Bedrooms are roomy – the pink one has an outsize bathroom and
windows on two sides; the pine-fitted one has the best views of Snowdon. There
are also attic rooms with large skylights.

Marian serves such dinners as soup, Welsh lamb, and apple tart.

The house stands in an Area of Outstanding Natural Beauty. Unlike the rest
of Wales, Anglesey's 300 square miles are rocky but not mountainous: they have
other charms.

The island, connected by bridges to the mainland and only a short drive from
Snowdonia, is still a centre of Celtic culture. There is a great deal to see: a huge
nature reserve of dunes at Newborough (wildfowl and wading birds); Holy Island
reached by a causeway from which there are views to the Isle of Man and Ireland,
glimpses of seals or seabirds on South Stack, and vast caves on North Stack;
Cemaes Bay for good bathing and clifftop walks; Amlwch, a resort surrounded by
fine coastal scenery; the picturesque fishing village of Moelfre; Penmon with
mediaeval remains and trips to Puffin Island; and heritage museum and weekly
markets at Llangefni. One of Anglesey's claims to fame is the village with
the longest name in Britain: Llanfairpwllgwyngyllgogerychwyrndrobwillantysilio-
gogogoch.

Readers' comments: Warm welcome, good advice. Spectacular and excellent value.

TALBONTDRAIN

C D PT(limited) S

Uwychygarreg, Powys, SY20 8RR Tel: 01654 702192
South of Machynlleth. Nearest main road: A489 from Machynlleth towards Newtown.

6 Bedrooms. £12.50–£20 (less for 6 nights or continental breakfast). Some have own bath/shower/toilet. Views of garden, country. No smoking. Washing machine on request.
Dinner. £11 for 2 courses and coffee, at 7.30pm. Non-residents not admitted. Vegetarian or special diets if ordered. No smoking. **Light suppers** if ordered.
1 Sitting-room. With open fire, central heating, pianola. No smoking.
Large garden

Hilary Matthews used to live in London before restoring this remote, slate-floored house, high in the hills, furnishing it very simply – for people who travel light – but with attractive colours and textures. No car is needed here: Hilary will book a taxi at Machynlleth station to drive you up her long, twisting lane; and she provides particularly well for children. She serves such two-course meals as bacon-and-leek flan with vegetables, followed by nectarines in a creamy sauce. Occasionally she does fungus identifying (and cooking) weekends or others on map-reading, singing, story-telling, etc. Her breakfasts feature Welsh specialities: for example, 'Glamorgan sausage', a type of cheese croquette. Some guests enjoy her excellent pianola as an after-dinner treat. Talbontdrain (its name means 'thorn tree at the end of the bridge') is in a varied area of woodland, waterfalls, moors and sheep pastures; utterly peaceful. Around the house are goats, bees, big tubs of petunias, wagtails and chickens; inside are warmth and comfort.

The market town of Machynlleth, at the head of the Dyfi estuary, did not grow up in the higgledy-piggledy way of many mediaeval towns but was laid out systematically in the 13th century, with its main streets forming a 'T'. The Welsh patriot Owaîn Glyndwr gathered his supporters (in 1404) where the 16th-century Parliament House now stands; other historic buildings include the Mayor's House, Royal House – Glyndwr's home, and the five-arched bridge over the river. The town is particularly well provided with craft shops, and has on its outskirts the exceptionally interesting Centre for Alternative Technology in a disused quarry – where you can see everything from aerogenerators to organic vegetable gardens, solar cells to fish-farming.

A great many scenic roads converge here, and all around are interesting villages and other sights. Derwenlas has attractive cottages on the estuary; Ffwrnais (meaning 'furnace'), a watermill which once powered iron-making and a very beautiful waterfall; in the Dyfi National Nature Reserve is a mile-long nature trail, at Corris a railway museum, in Tre'r-ddol a chapel with a museum of religion in Wales; Clywedog reservoir has the highest dam in Britain.

Readers' comments: Friendly; good food and company; extremely comfortable. Beautifully situated. Very friendly and interesting. Enriching atmosphere, beautiful environment.

Prices are per person in a double room at the beginning of the year.

TAN-Y-CYTIAU   C S
South Stack, (Gwynedd), Anglesey, LL65 1YH   Tel: 01407 762763
West of Holyhead. Nearest main road: A5 from Holyhead to Bangor.

7 Bedrooms. £18 (less for 2 nights or continental breakfast). Tea/coffee facilities. Views of garden, country, sea. No smoking. Washing machine on request.
Light suppers if ordered.
1 Sitting-room. With central heating, TV.
Large garden
Closed from October to February.

On Holy Island (now linked by causeway to the Isle of Anglesey), St Cybi founded a monastery in the 6th century: hence the island's name. But the name of this house is even older, taken from that of the nearby prehistoric hut circles now being excavated. It is spectacularly placed, looking across the sea towards Ireland (there are day trips to Dublin to be had, by catamaran).

South Stack is a craggy promontory with lighthouse (1806, open to the public) presiding over a heritage coastline and some very nice beaches. It is a great place for birdwatching in early summer, sailing and golf; and on the island there are a permanent exhibition of Tunnicliffe's celebrated bird paintings, a sea zoo, and a big RSPB reserve in which one can walk.

The house itself was built in 1915 as a holiday home for Lady Antonia Williams of Bodelwyddan Castle, which you may well have passed on the way to Anglesey (a statue of her as a child is in the nearby 'marble' church, itself worth a detour). Now it is a guest-house run by the Keatings, who welcome visitors to share this unique site with them. Huge picture-windows make the most of the wonderful views (Snowdon is visible in one direction), or you can sit in the big garden: there are plenty of loungers on the terrace.

Readers' comments: Lovely setting. Nicely appointed rooms. Lovely place.

Sitting-room at Tregynon (see page 398)

TREGYNON

Gwaun Valley, Pontfaen, (Dyfed), Pembrokeshire, SA65 9TU

Tel: 01239 820531

South-east of Fishguard. Nearest main road: B4313 from Fishguard to Narbeth.

CMX

8 Bedrooms. £20 (to readers of this book only to end of March)–£33.50. Less for 6 nights. Prices go up from April. Bargain breaks. All have own bath/shower/toilet. Tea/coffee facilities. TV. Views of country. No smoking.
Dinner. £15.95 for 3 courses (with choices including vegetarian) and coffee, at 7.30–8.30pm. Wine available. No smoking.
Light suppers if ordered.
2 Sitting-rooms. With open fire, central heating, piano. **Bar.** Smoking discouraged.
Large grounds

In the heart of the Pembrokeshire Coast National Park is something quite exceptional. Of all the places one could stay in Wales, this remote, 16th-century country farmhouse hotel, restored by Peter Heard, has some of the most spectacular scenery around it, including an Ice Age ravine with waterfall, ancient oak woods, countryside where badgers and polecats or buzzards and red kites are sometimes spotted, wild moorland and a prehistoric fort. From nearby peaks of the Preseli Mountains, one can sometimes see Ireland and Snowdon. Not far away are some of the sunniest sandy beaches in the country, renowned for their pure air.

Jane Heard's meals are imaginative and additive-free, with vegetarian options a speciality; and the wine list is outstanding. Speciality breads, sausages, traditionally smoked ham, cheeses and Tregynon's own spring water and naturalized ponds contribute to the experience of eating here. You can relax afterwards by a log fire in the beamed sitting-room which has a massive stone inglenook and button-backed chesterfields, with a snug stone-walled bar adjoining it. Some bedrooms are in the house, others in converted stone outbuildings – spacious, pretty and well equipped.

The National Park extends round almost the entire coast from Cardigan Bay to Carmarthen Bay and inland to mountains.

Readers' comments: Excellent host. Varied and original menus of excellent quality (best ice cream we have tasted). Nothing too much trouble. Very comfortable. Comfortable accommodation and superb food. The hosts went out of their way to make us feel welcome. Excellent value.

For anyone tracing their family history, a stay at inexpensive **MOUNT PLEASANT FARM** at Penffordd, a few miles north of Narberth, is recommended because Pauline Bowen is an expert on the subject. A warm, hospitable person, her small, beamed farmhouse of rugged stone is immaculate and comfortable. Good home cooking, and then relaxation in big armchairs of pink velvet. Fine views of the Preseli Mountains. (No smoking.) £16.

Readers' comments: Exceptional value. Very hospitable. Charming holiday, very helpful. [Tel: 01437 563447; postcode: SA66 7HY]

TY CROESO HOTEL CD PT S X
The Dardy, Crickhowell, Powys, NP8 1PU   Tel: 01873 810573
North-west of Abergavenny. Nearest main road: A40 from Abergavenny to
Brecon.

8 Bedrooms. £19–£29.50 (less for 2 nights). Prices go up from June. Bargain breaks. All have own bath/shower/toilet. Tea/coffee facilities. TV. Views of garden, country, river. Washing machine on request. **Dinner.** £14.95 for 4 courses (with choices) and coffee, from 7–9pm. Less for fewer courses. Vegetarian or special diets if ordered. Wine available.
1 Sitting-room. With open fire, central heating, record-player. **Bar.**
Large garden

The name means 'house of welcome', a far cry from its early Victorian origins as a workhouse. It was used as such up to the Second World War. Now it is run very professionally by Mandy and Ian Moore as a small hotel of character.

Bedrooms vary in size. The majority have magnificent panoramic views, for the hotel is perched on a hillside above the River Usk. Rooms have much pine furniture, and sometimes draped effects. Bath- and shower-rooms are very good, and single rooms as attractive as doubles. One huge and particularly elegant bedroom has a sitting-area.

The restaurant has a similar colour scheme, stencilled decorations on some walls (one is of rugged stone) and pretty arrangements of dried flowers. Here are served such meals as avocado and grapefruit with coriander dressing, chicken breast in a plum and brandy sauce, and a syllabub of honey and ginger (there are several choices at each course). A 'Taste of Wales' dinner is available: you may be offered such things as a salad of goat's cheese and samphire; loin of pork with Caerphilly cheese, cider and apple; honey, lemon and yogurt ice cream; and Welsh cheeses.

The little town of Crickhowell, right in the Brecon Beacons National Park, has many quiet attractions: old coaching inns, castle ruins, cobbled lanes.

Northward is an interesting drive to ancient Llanvihangel (sited where a river cleaves its way through the Black Mountains), pausing at the historic Skirrid Inn which, dating from 1110, is where Owaîn Glyndwr gathered his troops. Flagstone floors and ancient beams are still as he knew them; upstairs was a courtroom and from the great oak staircase at least 200 sheep-stealers were hanged. Near it is Tre-Wyn, an imposing 17th-century mansion with very splendid woodwork inside and outstanding mountain views from grounds that include terraces, arboretum and walled gardens. At hilly Grosmart, the skyline is pierced by the 13th-century church spire and by romantic castle ruins – it was here that Prince Hal (later Henry V) defeated Owaîn Glyndwr. The sinuous river below borders England.

Another scenic drive leads to an even more impressive 12th-century castle, with moat, where Rudolph Hess was held: the White Castle, Llanvetherine.

Readers' comments: Fresh home cooking. Cuisine almost as good as French. Ideal hosts; service, food and accommodation could not be better. Excellent menus and wine lists. Very pleasant, considerate hosts; above average food.

TY GWYN HOTEL

C D M PT S X

Betws-y-Coed, (Gwynedd), Aberconwy & Colwyn, LL24 0SG
Tel: 01690 710383 or 710787
On A5 from Betws-y-Coed to Llangollen.

13 Bedrooms. £17–£40. Most have own bath/shower/toilet. Tea/coffee facilities. TV. Views of garden, country, river. Balcony (one).
Dinner. £17.95 for 3 courses (with choices) and coffee, at 7–9.30pm. Vegetarian or special diets if ordered. Wine available.
Light suppers.
1 Sitting-room. With central heating, TV.
Bar with open fire.
Small garden

A former coaching inn, Ty Gwyn ('white house'), although on a road, has quiet bedrooms at the back. Sheila Ratcliffe has a flair for interior decoration, and every bedroom – small or large – is beautiful, many with en suite bathrooms (prices vary accordingly). The most impressive is an attic suite with four-poster and sitting-room; the most convenient for anyone with mobility problems, a pretty ground-floor room. A mountain rises up sheer at the back, where one tiny room has stone walls contrasting with a cane bedhead. Even in the ancient, beamed bar (fire glowing in the old black range, copper pots, carved oak settle) Sheila's colourful patchwork cushions are everywhere. There is also a very comfortable sitting-room and another where she sells antiques and old prints.

Cooking is done by chef Martin, the Ratcliffes' son, whose specialities include exotic dishes like pigeon with oyster mushrooms in Madeira, or Thai-style king prawns. These meals are served in a picturesque dining-room: antique furniture, crochet, crystal and silver on the tables. Even the bar snacks include such options as parrotfish in lemon sauce.

Young children may stay free.

Four wooded valleys meet at this village, with a high plateau looming above it. Walkers use it as a centre to explore in every direction, the serious ones making for Snowdon but most for the riverside paths, Gwydyr Forest or several lakes.

Readers' comments: Lovely setting, wonderful room. Good food. Very good, and a really beautiful attic suite. The highlight of the tour; have put real thought into vegetarian menu.

Also in Betws is a small, partly 13th-century watermill: **ROYAL OAK FARMHOUSE**. Although so central, the mill is hidden in a little valley with a deep salmon pool close by. The lattice-paned windows, great stone fireplace, carved oak settle and very pretty bedrooms (one en suite) give this guest-house great character. Elsie Houghton serves only breakfast, but there are good eating-places in Betws. £15–£17. [Tel: 01690 710427]

Equally attractive (and with en

suite bathrooms) is **ROYAL OAK FARM COTTAGE**, run by Elsie's daughter-in-law Kathleen. £15–£17. [Tel: 01690 710760; postcode for both: LL24 0AH]

UPPER TREWALKIN FARM   C(5) S
Pengenffordd, Powys, LD3 0HA   Tel: 01874 711349
East of Brecon. Nearest main road: A479 from Talgarth towards Crickhowell.

3 Bedrooms. £19 (less for 2 nights) Price goes up from April. Bargain breaks. Two have own bath/toilet. All have tea/coffee facilities. Views of garden, country. No smoking. Washing machine on request.
Dinner. £11.50 for 3 courses (with choices) and coffee, at 7pm (not Thursdays). Non-residents not admitted. No smoking. **Light suppers** if ordered.
2 Sitting-rooms. One with log-burner, central heating, TV. No smoking.
Small garden
Closed from December to March.

The reputation of hospitable Meudwen Stephens has spread far and wide: she is often invited to do overseas tours promoting Wales and its food. So one thing of which you can be sure is a good dinner – such as courgette and tomato soup, lamb chops cooked in white wine and mushrooms (accompanied by garden vegetables), bread-and-butter pudding or spotted dick.

But there is more to Upper Trewalkin than this. In the 16th century it was a long-house (animals at one end, family at the other), built on a site previously owned by a Norman knight. It was updated in the 18th century, although many original features were retained.

From many rooms there are superb views of the Black Mountains. Some walls are of exposed stone, some attractively papered. At every turn are paintings by local artists. Patchwork cushions decorate all beds.

The farm is in the Brecon Beacons National Park, an area of great interest to birdwatchers and walkers alike. Llangorse Lake is near and here, at the quieter end, grebes nest. Most visitors enjoy the immense variety of this area, in which can be found Tretower Court, little steam trains, craft workshops, waterfalls and the Big Pit museum of mining. Hay-on-Wye (for second-hand books) is not far. On the farm itself you will see sheep and cattle.

Readers' comments: Excellent home cooking, delightful hostess, comfortable accommodation. A gem.

Just outside Llangorse is Victorian **TREWALTER HOUSE**, the stone-built home of Jean Abbott (some readers of earlier editions enjoyed staying at her former home, Peterstone Court) who has renovated and decorated it to very high standards: everywhere is immaculate. You can wake to a panoramic view of the Brecon Beacons from some rooms, and of the Black Mountains (across the neighbouring farmyard) from others. Jean's ornamental 'bits and pieces' decorate every room. For dinner (by candlelight) she

serves such straightforward meals as melon, roast lamb, raspberry charlotte russe, and Welsh cheeses. £18 (b & b). [Tel: 01874 658442; postcode: LD3 0PS]

401

WENALLT FARM   **C D M PT S X**

Gilwern, (Gwent), Monmouthshire, NP7 0HP   Tel: 01873 830694

West of Abergavenny. Nearest main road: A465 from Abergavenny to Merthyr
Tydfil.

8 Bedrooms. £15–£18 (less for 7 nights or
continental breakfast). Bargain breaks.
Some have own bath/shower/toilet. Tea/
coffee facilities. Views of garden, country.
Washing machine on request.

Dinner. £10 for 4 courses (with choices)
and coffee, at 7.30pm. Non-residents not
admitted. Vegetarian or special diets if
ordered. Wine available. **Light suppers** if
ordered.

2 Sitting-rooms. With open fire, central
heating, TV. **Bar.**

Large garden

The name, 'wooded hill', was given to this remote stone house when it was first
built as a long-house: though most of it dates from about 1600, some parts are a
good deal older. Oak beams and mullioned windows are still the same as when
Oliver Cromwell reputedly stayed here on his march to Monmouth. What is now
a bar once housed cattle, and the bedroom above, hay to feed them; the sitting-
room was a dairy. And from many windows in this hilltop house you can see for
miles. Farmer Brian Harris made many improvements when he came here and in
the new dining-room installed a stone fireplace from Tredegar House (ancestral
home of buccaneer Henry Morgan, who became governor of Jamaica). He
converted a stone cow-byre to make more bedrooms.

There are scores of cups won at horse shows (Brian is now a judge at these),
and other touches that give the house individuality – from a stuffed pheasant on a
hearth to the beribboned fabrics in one of the bedrooms.

Meals are well above average – for example: stuffed courgette flowers followed
by turkey in walnut sauce, and the lightest of apple strudels. The table is laid with
distinctive Black Mountain pottery.

Although it is the scenery that brings most people here, there is much else to
enjoy, for this is a historic area. Henry V was born in the castle at Monmouth, a
town with other royal connections. Nelson stayed in Monmouth – hence the
naval temple on Kymin Hill, commanding far views. There are two Norman
churches in the vicinity (the one at Over Monnow has a wonderful doorway and,
near it, a mediaeval bridge with fortified gate). Then there is Raglan, with few old
houses left by its church but with spectacular castle remains nearby: each of its
two 15th-century courts has its own gatehouse and they are linked by a bridge to
a massive, polygonal tower with a moat round it.

There are fine drives and walks in the Wye and Llantony valleys as well
as along the Usk; and up into the Brecon Beacons and Black Mountains – the
former can be explored on a steam railway too. Llangorse Lake is used for sailing.
A very popular outing now is the Big Pit (coal mine) at Blaenavon.

Readers' comments: Friendly and helpful. Food excellent. Our spacious room was
furnished with lovely antiques. Enjoyed so much that I extended my stay. Food
and service excellent. Welcoming and friendly.

For explanation of code letters (C, D, M, PT, S, X) see inside front cover.

WEST USK LIGHTHOUSE   C X
Lighthouse Road, St Brides Wentlooge, (Gwent), Newport, NP1 9SF
Tel: 01633 810126 or 815860
South-west of Newport. Nearest main road: A48 from Newport to Cardiff
(and M4, junction 28).

5 Bedrooms. £18–£32 (less for 4 nights or continental breakfast). Some have own shower/toilet. Tea/coffee facilities. TV. Views of garden, country, sea, river. No smoking.
Dinner. £15 for 3 courses (with choices) and coffee, at 7pm. Non-residents not admitted. Vegetarian or special diets if ordered. No smoking. **Light suppers** if ordered.
1 Sitting-room. With open fire, central heating, TV, video. No smoking.
Large garden

Perhaps the strangest house in this book, the ex-lighthouse – found at the end of a very long, stony track – is an unusual example of its kind, built to a unique design: not tall as most lighthouses are, and considerably bigger in circumference. In 1821, it was on an island where the Severn and Usk run into the sea, with views far out into the Bristol Channel. Since then, land has been reclaimed and although on one side the loudest sound is of the sea when the tide (second fastest in the world) comes racing in to the foot of the building, on the other only the occasional mooing cow can be heard. The walls are over two feet thick, with rooms on both floors wedge-shaped. From the slate-paved hall a spiral stair rises to the bedrooms, above which is a flat roof with seats from which to watch ships go by and the spectacular sunsets – or, facing the other way, sunrises. Occasional barbecues are held up here. Old features have been retained, such as the indoor well for collecting rainwater, but everything else is comfortable and immaculate.

Bedrooms have been pleasantly but simply furnished with, for example, rattan bedheads and pretty fabrics, and in the sitting-room are unusual rococo armchairs from Italy. Modern sculptures stand here and there, and on many walls are framed record-sleeves: Frank Sheahan used to work for a major record company before turning his hand to restoring the derelict lighthouse, four years of hard slog.

The house is run in an informal, sometimes slightly scatty way, and often with an assortment of other enterprises on the go – from relaxation classes to aromatherapy sessions. An unusual and very popular facility is the flotation tank: an hour lying in warm and buoyant brine, lights dimmed or off, all sound silenced, is calculated to ease away every kind of stress.

You can sit by a log fire, go birdwatching or wander along the reedy dykes, looking for the plants that botanists find of particular interest. Rabbits scamper beneath the willows, butterflies flit among the blackberry bushes.

Meals are chosen from a short list of conventional choices, from pizza to steaks.

Quite close to the lighthouse are palatial Tredegar House (lake and craft shops in its grounds) and romantic little Castell Coch ('the red castle'). Also well worth visiting are the Roman city of Caerleon, and the castles of Cardiff, Caerphilly and Penhow. Both the Usk Valley and the Brecon Beacons are scenic.

Readers' comments: Charmingly and artistically furnished and very unusual; peaceful. An inspired conversion. Unusual and interesting. Friendly and open-minded host. Large and well-cooked breakfasts. Will return. Location excellent; an endearingly quirky experience.

WYE BARN   PT(limited) **S**
The Quay, Tintern, (Gwent), Monmouthshire, NP6 6SZ
Tel: 01291 689456
North of Chepstow. Nearest main road: A466 from Chepstow to Monmouth.

3 Bedrooms. £20–£21 (less for 7 nights). One has own shower/toilet. Tea/coffee facilities. TV. Views of country, river. No smoking. Washing machine on request.
Dinner. £12.50 for 4 courses and coffee, at 7pm. Non-residents not admitted. Vegetarian or special diets if ordered. No smoking.
1 Sitting-room. With open fire, central heating, TV. No smoking.
Small garden

Perched right on the river bank, the house is occasionally islanded when the Wye's spring tides rise 20 feet (which is why the house itself is built up, with steps to the door). Four centuries ago, the monks of Tintern Abbey built it as a bark house – oak bark, needed for tanning hides, used to be stored here.

From an exceptionally pretty garden, one steps through French doors into a pleasant sitting-room of soft blues and greys which complement the fireplace of grey stone quarried in the Forest of Dean.

Because Judith Russill used to work for Britain's most celebrated furniture designer, John Makepeace (she was responsible for his students' welfare), she has a number of very lovely and unusual pieces of furniture made by his students – to which she has added other finds of her own, such as Welsh cottage chairs with acorn or spindle backs, and an art nouveau one inlaid with mother-of-pearl.

Bedrooms are just as attractive – for instance, one has lotus-patterned spreads that match the pinkish carpet and Chinese silk pictures; in another, blue and pink, is her collection of teddy bears. From their windows are views of the River Wye.

Judith specializes in traditional Welsh cookery and you may be offered, for example, Anglesey eggs (they are cooked with leeks and cream en cocotte), Wye salmon with a herb sauce, and – the Welsh answer to cheesecake – a sour-cream and sultana tart. These may be followed by various Welsh cheeses.

Out in the garden (with a sun-trapping, glazed summer-house) you get a good view of Tintern Abbey's particularly beautiful ruins. The whole of the Wye Valley is famous for its beauty, with the nearby Usk Valley giving it some serious competition too. Tintern itself is an excellent holiday centre.

Sedbury, not marked on all maps, is tucked between Chepstow and the Severn estuary – quite close to the Severn Bridge. In rural Sedbury Lane stands an old farm, **UPPER SEDBURY HOUSE**, with cottagey bedrooms; and also an attic flat, usually let for self-catering but Christine Potts is happy to do meals for those guests too. (A typical dinner, using garden produce: pears in tarragon mayonnaise, casserole of beef, fruit crumble.) There is a swimming-pool, unheated;

badminton, etc.; and the Offa's Dyke footpath runs near the house. £16.50–£18.50. [Tel: 01291 627173; postcode: NP6 7HN]

WYNN HALL

C(12) **PT S**

Penycae, (Clwyd), Wrexham, LL14 1TW   Tel: 01978 822106
South-west of Wrexham. Nearest main road: A483 from Wrexham to Chirk.

3 Bedrooms. £16–£19 (less for 2 nights or continental breakfast). Tea/coffee facilities. TV. Views of garden, country. No smoking. Washing machine on request.
Light suppers if ordered.
2 Sitting-rooms. With open fire and other heating, TV, video, record-player. No smoking.
Large garden

Construction of this historic house was completed – by a Roundhead officer – in the year that Charles I was beheaded (the date, 1649, is on the façade). The gables have decorative timbering, the front door great wrought-iron hinges.

The Wynns were Nonconformists who, during the years of persecution, held secret religious meetings at the Hall: the head of the family was imprisoned for his faith. Some of them sailed with the Quakers to America.

The Hall remained in the same family's hands until Elian and Ian Forster came here in 1970 – by which time the ancient house was almost falling apart. Gradually they restored it, adding oak furniture to rooms that have exposed wall-timbers, stone inglenooks and low ceilings. Up the oak stair with its original finials are beamed bedrooms, one with a locally made patchwork duvet, some with pretty curtains that match the paper on walls and ceilings. The bathroom is excellent.

From the dining-room one can step straight into the garden with its winding lawn, badminton and croquet. Some guests enjoy the company of the dogs, others Ian's classic cars. Small antiques on sale.

Readers' comments: All rooms delightful – large, beautifully decorated and furnished. Owners very friendly and go to great lengths. It really is something special.

Just beyond Llangollen, perched high in the hamlet of Rhewl (Denbighshire), is **DEE FARMHOUSE** – so named because the River Dee lies just below its garden. Once this was a slate-miners' inn (hence the slate floor downstairs). From the garden come artichokes, spinach, herbs, etc. for the soups which form part of Mary Harman's light suppers (served in a huge dining-kitchen), as well as roses and lavender for her rooms. In the small and pretty sitting-room are antiques; cases of butterflies are in a beamy sitting/bedroom suite upstairs

which used to be a hayloft. Closed from November to January. £17–£18.
Readers' comments: Peaceful. Fine old furniture, extremely comfortable. Concerned for one's comfort. Lovely view. [Tel: 01978 861598; postcode: LL20 7YT]

EXPLANATION OF CODE LETTERS

*(These appear, where applicable, in alphabetical
order after the names of houses)*

C Suitable for families with children. Sometimes a minimum age is stipulated, in which case this is indicated by a numeral; thus C(5) means children over 5 years old are accepted. In most cases, houses that accept children offer reduced rates and special meals. They may provide cots and high chairs; or games and sports for older children. Please enquire when booking. And do not expect young children to be lodged free, as babies are. Many houses have playing-cards, board games, irons, hair-dryers, maps, wellingtons, bicycles, and so forth to lend – just ask. Families which pick establishments with plenty of games, swimming-pool, animals, etc., or that are near free museums, parks and walks, can save a lot on keeping youngsters entertained. (Readers wanting total quiet may wish to avoid houses coded **C**.)

D Dogs permitted. A charge is rarely made, but it is often a stipulation that you must ask before bringing one; the dog may have to sleep in your car, or be banned from public rooms.

M Suitable for those with mobility problems. Needs vary: whenever we have used the code letter **M**, this indicates that not only is there a ground-floor bedroom and bathroom, but these, and doorways, have sufficient width for a wheelchair, and steps are few. For precise details, ask when booking.

PT Accessible by public transport. It is not necessary to have a car in order to get off the beaten track because public transport is widely available; houses indicated by the code **PT** have a railway station or coach stop within a reasonable distance, from which you can walk or take a taxi (quite a number of hosts will even pick you up, free, in their own car). The symbol **PT** further indicates that there are also some buses for sightseeing, but these may be few. Ask when booking.

S Indicates those houses which charge single people no more, or only 10% more, than half the price of a double room (except, possibly, at peak periods).

X Visitors are accepted at Christmas, though Christmas meals are not necessarily provided. Some hotels and farms offer special Christmas holidays; but, unless otherwise indicated (by the code letter **X** at top of entry), those in this book will then be closed.

406